Madame de Sévigné

MADAME DE SÉVIGNÉ
A Life and Letters

FRANCES MOSSIKER

Alfred A. Knopf

NEW YORK

1983

Copyright © 1983 by Frances Mossiker

All rights reserved under International and Pan-American Copyright
Conventions. Published in the United States by Alfred A. Knopf, Inc.,
New York, and simultaneously in Canada by Random House of Canada
Limited, Toronto. Distributed by Random House, Inc., New York.

Library of Congress Cataloging in Publication Data

Mossiker, Frances.   Madame de Sévigné: a life and letters.

Bibliography: p.
Includes index.
1. Sévigné, Marie de Rabutin-Chantal, marquise de, 1626–1696—
Biography. 2. Sévigné, Marie de Rabutin-Chantal, marquise de, 1626–
1696—Correspondence. 3. Authors, French—17th century—
Biography. 4. France—Social life and customs—17th–18th
centuries.   I. Title.
PQ1925.M64   1983   846'.4 [B]   83-47781
ISBN 0-394-41472-1

Manufactured in the United States of America

FIRST EDITION

In memory of my mother,
Evelyn Warrene Beekman Sanger—
exquisite, elegant, charming, an ornament of society
in the tradition of Mme de Sévigné

This great lady, this robust and fertile letter writer, who in our age would probably have been one of the great novelists, takes up presumably as much space in the consciousness of living readers as any figure of her vanished age.

—*Virginia Woolf,* The Death of the Moth

Contents

Chronology

1663   Mlle de Sévigné presented at Court

1664   Trial of Fouquet

1665   Count de Bussy-Rabutin ordered to Bastille

1666   Count de Bussy-Rabutin exiled to his Burgundian estates

1669   JANUARY: Marriage of Mlle de Sévigné to Count de Grignan
       NOVEMBER: Countess de Grignan suffers first miscarriage

1670   APRIL: Departure of Count de Grignan for Provence
       NOVEMBER: Birth of Marie-Blanche de Grignan

1671   FEBRUARY: Departure of Mme de Grignan for Provence
       MAY: Departure of Mme de Sévigné and her son, Charles, for Brittany
       NOVEMBER: Birth of Louis-Provence, Marquis de Grignan
       DECEMBER: Return of Mme de Sévigné to Paris

1672   Death of Mme de La Trousse, aunt of Mme de Sévigné
       JULY: Mme de Sévigné joins her daughter in Provence

1673   Mme de Grignan suffers second miscarriage
       OCTOBER: Return of Mme de Sévigné to Paris

1674   Mme de Grignan joins Mme de Sévigné in Paris
       SEPTEMBER: Birth of Pauline de Grignan

1675   MAY: Departure of Mme de Grignan for Provence
       SEPTEMBER: Departure of Mme de Sévigné for Brittany

1676   Mme de Sévigné suffers attack of rheumatism
       Birth of Jean-Baptiste de Grignan, premature and malformed
       Marie-Blanche de Grignan sent to convent at Aix-en-Provence
       AUGUST: Sojourn of Mme de Sévigné at Vichy
       SEPTEMBER: Return of Mme de Sévigné to Paris
       DECEMBER: Mme de Grignan joins Mme de Sévigné in Paris

1677   Death of Jean-Baptiste de Grignan (aged sixteen months)
       JUNE: Departure of Mme de Grignan for Provence
       AUGUST: Departure of Mme de Sévigné for Vichy via Burgundy
       OCTOBER: Return of Mme de Sévigné to Paris
       Hôtel Carnavalet leased by Mme de Sévigné
       NOVEMBER: Mme de Grignan joins Mme de Sévigné at Hôtel Carnavalet

1679   Disgrace of Marquis de Pomponne
SEPTEMBER: Departure of Mme de Grignan for Provence

1680   Death of Duke de La Rochefoucauld
Death of Nicolas Fouquet
MAY: Departure of Mme de Sévigné for Brittany
OCTOBER: Return of Mme de Sévigné to Paris
DECEMBER: Mme de Grignan joins Mme de Sévigné in Paris

1684   FEBRUARY: Marriage of Charles de Sévigné to Marguerite de Mauron, at Rennes
SEPTEMBER: Departure of Mme de Sévigné for Brittany

1685   SEPTEMBER: Return of Mme de Sévigné to Paris to rejoin her daughter

1686   Mme de Grignan suffers another miscarriage

1687   AUGUST: Death of the Abbé de Coulanges, Mme de Sévigné's uncle
SEPTEMBER: Departure of Mme de Sévigné for Bourbon l'Archambault
OCTOBER: Return of Mme de Sévigné to Paris

1688   OCTOBER: Return of Mme de Grignan to Provence

1689   APRIL: Departure of Mme de Sévigné for Brittany

1690   OCTOBER: Departure of Mme de Sévigné for Provence to join her daughter

1691   DECEMBER: Return of Mme de Sévigné to Paris accompanied by her daughter, son-in-law, and granddaughter, Pauline de Grignan

1693   Death of Count de Bussy-Rabutin
Death of the Countess de La Fayette

1694   MARCH: Departure of Mme de Grignan for Provence
MAY: Departure of Mme de Sévigné for Provence to rejoin her daughter
Death of Mme de Sévigné's good friend, the Marquis de Lavardin

1695   JANUARY: Marriage of Mme de Sévigné's grandson, the Marquis de Grignan, to Anne-Marguerite de Saint-Amans
JULY: Critical illness of Mme de Grignan
NOVEMBER: Marriage of Pauline de Grignan to Louis, Marquis de Simiane

1696   APRIL 17: Death of Mme de Sévigné

1704   Death of Marquis de Grignan

1705   Death of Mme de Grignan

1713   Death of Charles de Sévigné

1714   Death of Count de Grignan

1715   Death of Louis XIV

1725   First edition of *Letters of Mme de Sévigné*

1737   Death of Pauline de Simiane

Preface

Bilingual as I was from childhood on, reading as readily in French as in English, it was inevitable that I should early encounter Mme de Sévigné, if only in anthological extract—as, unfortunately, most schoolchildren do; "unfortunately," that is, for the reason that anthologies offer only scattered bits and pieces plucked, here and there, out of context, to serve as random samples of the writer's syntactical pyrotechnics or anecdotal virtuosity. Such nuggets, however gilt and glittering, can only hint at the richness of the mother lode. It is continuity (by the thesis of Jean Cordelier in his superb study, *Mme de Sévigné in Her Own Words*) which is "the essential dimension" of the *Letters*. It is the correspondence in its entirety which yields the story of Mme de Sévigné's life and adventures and the metamorphosis wrought upon her character and spirit by the passage of time—the passage of time as important an element in the *Letters* as it would prove to be in a play by Chekhov. It is the sum and total of the *Letters*, their full and regular flow—day in, day out; week in, week out; month in, month out; across a span of twenty-five years—which furnishes the open sesame to the heart and mind and soul of the brilliant, passionate and gifted woman who wrote them.

The ideal, then, it seemed to me, would be to reconcile the writer and the *oeuvre*, to arrive at a blend of biography and autobiography, to turn over the story of her life—insofar as possible—to Mme de Sévigné herself; to allow her to tell it in her own glowing words, a technique available to a biographer in the rarest of instances.

It may be that, originally, Mme de Sévigné appeared to me as a mother figure: I had grown up, as had Mme de Grignan, in the shadow of a dazzling and glamorous mother, and felt a diffidence similar to that of Mme de Sévigné's daughter. In the 1960's when I wrote *The Affair of the Poisons*, I came to a fresh appreciation of Mme de Sévigné's talents. Her reportage on that scandal which had rocked the Court of Louis XIV proved a treasure trove for me: I had only to do a creditable translation of any account of hers to enhance any page of mine on which it appeared. Recently, in the course of my intensive research for this biography of Mme de Sévigné, I have felt a new and poignant rapport with her. By a curious happenstance, I found myself rereading and translating that portion of the *Letters* she had written in her declining years—just as I was approaching mine. I shared her apprehensions and dismay at the process of aging. I found myself echoing her words—whose better to echo?—when she expressed her yearning for some spark of faith to illuminate her store of religious theory. And I could appreciate the mental hygiene implicit in the determination with which she almost invariably broke off such somber reflections: "But enough of that!" or "Now, let's talk of other things."

Mme de Sévigné may be seen to represent the beau ideal, the *ne plus ultra*, of biographical subjects: her place in history as in literature assured, a figure of enchantment, a fascinating and complex human being; at once erudite, ardent, earthy; at once a *grande dame*, a bluestocking, a coquette, a woman of "infinite variety," a woman "for all seasons." What more could a biographer ask?

This biographer acknowledges her debt to the generations of Sévigné scholars who have built up the vast bibliography which enshrines her: the manifold editions of her *Letters*; the full-scale biographies, the profiles, studies and critiques by the dozens. There is no aspect of her life that has not been explored in depth: scholarly monographs abound on the subject of her genealogy, her library, her religious practice and principles, her travels, her cuisine, her wardrobe, her pharmacopoeia, her business affairs, her suitors, her bestiary.

But Sainte-Beuve, that arbiter of French literature, was mistaken when he declared, in the mid-nineteenth century, that all that could be said about Mme de Sévigné had, by then, been said. The impact of Mme de Sévigné's *Letters*, as is so often the case with works of genius, varies from century to century. With the dawn of the Freudian era, the mother-daughter relation came under new scrutiny. To feminists of the twentieth century, Mme de Sévigné appears a member of the avant-garde: she made voluble protest against the inferior education that was the lot of most women of her age, as she did against the legal system that robbed those women of their rights and delivered them over to the mercy of fathers, brothers, husbands.

All the letters and all the excerpts of letters of Mme de Sévigné's which appear in this volume are the products of my translation. When one is dealing with the prose of a Mme de Sévigné—remarkable for the grace and the wit which are her hallmark—one approaches the task of translation with due humility. The casual, the insouciant, the free and easy style on which Mme de Sévigné prided herself as a lady of quality is not easy to reproduce in another language. Since I find her sense of humor so delicious, I can only hope that I have captured it in translation. There were some letters, some passages so enchanting that I could not resist translating them even though I realized I could never find room for them all within these covers. Translation is not only a labor of love; it brings about an understanding of the text in a profundity impossible to achieve by any other method of study, no matter how diligent.

Certainly I could discover no English translation of the Sévigné *Letters* of which I would have availed myself in the preparation of this biography. Mme de Sévigné has remained little known in the United States because of the dearth of English translations, and because those few that do exist are lackluster, literal, stilted. Translations such as these constitute a grave injustice to France's First Lady of Letters. Should justice, one day, be done her in translation, she should become as well known here as she is in England, where a large part of the reading public has a facility for French. Somewhere in the back of my mind, as I approached this work, there must have lurked the thought that it might, somehow, someway, contribute to hastening that day.

Acknowledgments

I welcome this opportunity to convey formally my thanks to the Count de Ternay for the cordiality of his welcome to me at Les Rochers, his château in Brittany, and for the generosity with which he shared with me his knowledge of the history of that property since its acquisition by a member of his family in the early eighteenth century. The Count acted not only as *cicérone* but as chauffeur, driving me in his jeep when rains prevented our strolling through those stately treelined allées and avenues laid out and planted under the supervision of Mme de Sévigné herself, and excellently maintained ever since by the forebears of my host and by my host himself. This page likewise gives me the opportunity to express my gratitude to the Count Jean de Guitaut, who came to the Château d'Époisses expressly to receive me there and guide me to "Mme de Sévigné's Chamber" (in which she was lodged when she was a guest of the Guitauts on her various sojourns in Burgundy) and to the Archives Room, which is the repository of the largest collection of Sévigné holographs extant. To Professor Roger Duchêne, the premier Sévigniste of this generation, I here repeat in print the thanks I have already expressed to him for his courtesy in arranging an appointment for me to meet with him in Aix-en-Provence in 1978 and in giving me the benefit of his expert opinion on certain aspects of the research.

I wish also to express my appreciation to the staff of the Musée Carnavalet for the assistance given me not only in my study of the Hôtel Carnavalet itself but also in locating and viewing the several houses leased earlier by Mme de Sévigńe in the Marais district. I owe a debt of gratitude to a number of other people in France and in the United States for their assistance to me in the course of the research done over the past five or six years on this biography. Mme M. Odier-Lesourd, formerly *documentaliste* at *l'Office Français des Relations Publiques*, combed the catalogues of the *Bibliothèque Nationale* for certain magazine and newspaper articles about Mme de Sévigné which I needed to consult and then arranged for photocopies to be forwarded to me in Texas. Mme Jocelyne Cutright of Paris undertook the commission of assisting me in assembling the illustrations for this volume, locating those subjects I had requested and sending me the glossy prints for reproduction here. At the Fondren Library of Southern Methodist University in Dallas, Miss Anne Bailey, periodicals librarian, has been enormously helpful to me in research projects of various kinds. And, at the Dallas Public Library, the Inter-Library Loan office has performed its customary wonders in searching out obscure titles across the United States. I have Dr. Harold W. Kimmerling of Dallas to thank once again for his valiant efforts in reviewing the case histories of patients long since dust, and of bringing twentieth-century diagnostic techniques to bear on the symptoms of the ailments which brought them to their grave. I was privileged, too, to consult with Dr. Jerry Lewis who, out of his psychiatric expertise, gave me valuable insights into the complex and often troubled relationship between Mme de Sévigné and her daughter.

The last lines of this Acknowledgment page are a repetition of those which appeared on the Acknowledgments page of *The Queen's Necklace*, published in 1961. Those lines, as valid now as then, read: "My warmest thanks . . . above all, to my editor, Mr. Robert Gottlieb, for invaluable directives and ineffable understanding."

Madame de Sévigné

I

On the sword side, Madame de Sévigné could trace her Burgundian fore-bears—and did so, proudly—back into the eleventh and twelfth centuries, into what the official Court genealogists referred to as "The Mists of Time" (without which certificate of ancientness, a nobleman was unacceptable in the inner circles of the Court of France). The Rabutins had distinguished themselves in the Crusades, in the service of the Dukes of Burgundy—in the service of the French monarchy, once the Duchy of Burgundy had become part of France, as it had in the fifteenth century. The Rabutins belonged to the old nobility, the true *noblesse d'épée* or nobility of the sword, the warrior caste upon which country and countryside depended for defense. Throughout five centuries of chivalric record, the Rabutins of Burgundy had proven themselves an audacious, a bellicose lot, laughing at danger, literally as well as figuratively: Amé de Rabutin, a fifteenth-century family hero, was said to have rushed into the thick of battle, his hand on his scabbard, his voice raised in banter so blithe that not only his friends but his foes burst out laughing. It may have been he who established the Rabutin reputation for wit and humor, for a brand of raillery—a repartee as dazzling as his sword-play—that came to be known, according to one seventeenth-century dictionary,* as *rabutinage.* Generation after generation, Rabutin tongues and pens flickered as sharp and quick as Rabutin rapiers—men of learning as well as men of valor, an unusual combination for that day and time (for any day and time).

On the sword side, Mme de Sévigné could claim a grandmother who was a saint, or, rather, a grandmother who was to become a saint—Saint Jeanne de Chantal—in the Catholic Church's own good time, beatified in 1751, canonized in 1767.

The Baroness Jeanne de Chantal, left a widow with several young children in 1600, ten years later recognized and acknowledged her vocation

---

*Emile Littré's *Dictionnaire de la langue française* (*Dictionary of the French Language*), a remarkable reference book, was published between 1863 and 1872.

3

in the Church, and took the veil, abandoning her two daughters and adolescent son to devote her life to the foundation of the Visitandine Order. Her fifteen-year-old son, Celse-Bénigne de Rabutin-Chantal—future Baron de Chantal, future father of Mme de Sévigné—flung himself, in tears and hysteria, across the threshold of the door by which his mother was about to depart the château. If she loved her only son, as she would steadfastly claim she did, she loved God's work to which she had been called even more and, impervious to his pleas, stepped over the youth's prostrate form on her way to the beautiful lake town of Annecy, seat of the Order, site of the first of the hundred-odd Convents of the Visitation she was to establish across the length and breadth of France.

Her one unmarried daughter was later brought to the cloister to be brought up under her supervision. Her son, the Baron de Chantal, was placed under the supervision of a maternal uncle, Bénigne Fremyot, president of the Burgundian Parlement, and later sent to complete his education at the Jesuit College of Dijon.

In 1617, at age twenty-one, the Baron de Chantal, titular head of the senior branch of the Rabutins, set off for Paris and the Court of young Louis XIII where he could expect the offer of an honorable Court "charge" or post. Had not his father rendered outstanding service to Henri IV, first of the Bourbon Kings, father of the present monarch? And was not the young Baron de Chantal, himself, an ornament to any Court?: tall, handsome, valorous, a superb horseman, swordsman, dancer, talker, cutting as fine a figure in the salon and in the ballroom as on the field of battle! He was also a gay young blade, mettlesome, intractable, hell-bent on bettering his father's record of eighteen duels. Reports of his Paris escapades, his brushes with death on the duelling ground, and his mounting debts were enough to try the patience of even a saint like his mother, who made mild comment to the effect that "He was basically a good lad, with good impulses; it was his youth that burned too hot in him and accounted for his excesses." She prayed for maturity and for marriage—marriage, that is, to an heiress. For such a blessing his mother did more than pray; she made arrangements for him for a very good match in Grenoble. This prospect went glimmering, but a still greater heiress, Marie de Coulanges, appeared on the Paris horizon in 1623. For a Rabutin to marry a Coulanges was to marry beneath himself, but beggars could not be choosers, and the Rabutins had beggared themselves, had sorely depleted the family fortunes in the religious wars of the previous century, the wars of the Holy League, waged by French Catholics against French Protestants, the Huguenots.

On the distaff side, Mme de Sévigné's ancestors, the Coulanges, were far less distinguished, less flamboyant than the Rabutins; of bourgeois rather than noble origin, and *nouveau riche,* at that. Philippe de Coulanges—father of Marie de Coulanges, grandfather of Mme de Sévigné—was the founder of the family fortunes, having amassed his great wealth as tax collector for a large part of France. In Old Régime France, with its huge bureaucracy, the collection of taxes was farmed out to individuals. (The system of taxation must be considered one of the chief causes of the French Revolution of 1789: with the Church enjoying a tax-free status, then as now; with the nobility paying its tax in blood—in defense of the nation, in accordance with the feudal contract; with the bourgeoisie largely exempt from the general tax, the main burden fell upon the class least able to sustain it—the peasantry. Had the Devil himself—as a contemporary remarked—been given a free hand to plan the downfall of Old Régime France, he could not have devised a scheme more likely to achieve that object than the system of taxation.)

The upward mobility possible to the newly rich in seventeenth-century France could not be better exemplified than in the instance of Philippe de Coulanges: his first step up the Paris social ladder was the acquisition of one of the thirty-seven magnificent new town houses on the Place Royale (renamed Place des Vosges after the French Revolution; still one of the beauty spots of twentieth-century Paris), the first Place in the French capital to be developed in conformity with a prescribed, overall architectural design, all thirty-seven rosy-white façades identical. The stately Place Royale, in the opening years of the seventeenth century, was an address affordable to only a great nobleman or a powerful financier . . . such as Philippe de Coulanges.

The second step up the social ladder consisted of marrying into the nobility: Philippe de Coulanges's sweet, simple, pretty, young Marie was affianced in 1623 to Celse-Bénigne de Rabutin, the Baron de Chantal, that dashing cavalier, that hotheaded, superciliously smiling aristocrat. In the eyes of the Rabutins, it was a mésalliance, a derogation; not a member of the family would agree to sign—as was the custom—the marriage contract, but the wedding day was saved when the Archbishop of Bourges—brother of Saint Jeanne de Chantal and uncle of the groom—performed the wedding ceremony in the Coulanges's lovely country house at Sucy, in the Paris suburbs. The Archbishop had paid off his nephew's debts and guaranteed a modest allowance, and the newlyweds were installed in a luxurious apartment on the second floor of the Coulanges's Place Royale mansion, although the Baron proved even more of an extravagance than the Coulanges had bargained for.

As alarming to the thrifty, cautious, sobersided Coulanges as was the Baron's profligacy—his gambling and his spendthrift ways—even more so were the Baron's bellicosity, his repeated duelling sprees, in defiance of recent royal edicts banning the duel. Duelling had become a mania among seventeenth-century noblemen, who considered themselves a law unto themselves: they could still remember holding sway over their own feudal territories, they were jealous of their privilege, defiant of the encroachment of royal authority. They harked back to the days when knighthood was in flower and to the glory of single combat: a fearless and irreproachable knight (like Bayard) versus another fearless and irreproachable knight, resolving the issues of war without benefit of army. Touchy, fractious—raising a point of honor at the slightest pretext—they rushed to the field of honor like lemmings to the sea. Cardinal Richelieu, Louis XIII's all-powerful chief minister, came to see the practice as a national disaster and proscribed it, on pain of death.

Even the penalty of death could not deter the Baron de Chantal on Easter Sunday, 1624, when a summons reached him as he sat in church beside his wife and family for Easter services—a summons from his friend, the Count de Bouteville, to come immediately to the Gate St. Antoine to serve as "second" in a duel with the Count de Pontgibault. Without taking time even to change his black velvet slippers, the Baron de Chantal rushed from the church to keep the bloody rendezvous. To defile the holy day with a duel proscribed by royal edict was a case of *lèse majesté* against God and King. The case was brought before the Parlement of Paris for judgment: the four participants in the duel—the two principals and their "seconds"—were to be stripped of their rank and title, their properties confiscated by the Crown, their châteaux razed and moats filled up and, thus, having been declared "ignoble," the quartet of culprits were sentenced to death by hanging on a public gibbet, a method of execution to which a nobleman could not be subjected. It was a harsh sentence, but all four escaped—or were allowed to escape—from Paris, to go into hiding, in the provinces, there to hope and wait for royal pardon.

The royal favor in which Chantal had hitherto basked, the holy work upon which his mother was embarked, the intercession of his uncle, the Archbishop of Bourges, may have mitigated the royal displeasure. At any rate, after only a few months of retreat on the Burgundian estates of his sister, the Countess de Toulongeon, the Baron de Chantal apparently found it safe to return to Paris and to resume his marital obligations.

The first child, a son, born in 1624, the year of the duelling scandal, did not survive the year of his birth. A girl, born in 1625, did not survive the day of her birth. On February 5, 1626, a third child was born to the Rabutin-Chantal ménage; this one, a girl; this one, a survivor, blessed with a robust constitution, with a happy nature, with a touch of genius. On February 6, she was christened Marie de Rabutin-Chantal, the future Marquise de Sévigné, the ultimate flower—though none of the family's chauvinistic males would have recognized the fact—of the always flamboyant and often gifted race of Rabutins.

Her birth appears to have had a sobering effect on her father. In the spring of that year he zealously paid court to his monarch at Fontainebleau, as his uncle, the Archbishop, noted: "Here he is, a head of family . . . It is high time to remember his responsibilities." His mother was encouraged by the signs of change and wrote, in reply to the Archbishop, "May God confirm my son in this resolve of his to stability and salvation."

But her son was not so easily to escape the consequences of his madcap years. His hotheaded friend, the Count de Bouteville, challenged the Count de Beuvron to a duel in the Place Royale, at high noon on a May day in 1627. This time, the duellists were not allowed to escape: de Bouteville and his "second" were seized, sentenced to death and lost their heads to the executioner in Paris's Place de Grève in June. Although the Baron de Chantal had not been actively involved in the fracas, de Bouteville had hidden in the Coulanges's house, from which he attempted to make his escape, later that night, under cover of darkness. The Baron de Chantal found he could no longer count on the King's favor. Cardinal Richelieu had persuaded Louis XIII that Chantal was a troublemaker, a danger to the regime, a friend not only of the incorrigible de Bouteville but also of the subversive Prince de Chalais, who had died under the headsman's axe, the preceding year, for his role in a plot against the Cardinal. Richelieu further played on the young King's suspicious nature, reminding him of Chantal's inclination to mockery and sarcasm, and implying that not even the sovereign was exempt from that caustic tongue.

With two of his closest friends in their graves, with his own favor at Court seriously diminished, the Baron de Chantal concluded that the air of Paris was less than salubrious, and set off for the Île de Ré to offer his sword and services to his friend the Marquis de Toiras, commandant of that small fortified isle in the Bay of Biscay. King Charles I of England had threatened to intervene in behalf of the Huguenots, under siege in their stronghold of La Rochelle. To relieve that siege the English fleet would have to capture the Île de Ré, which guarded the approaches to La Rochelle, and—two thousand strong—ventured the attack on July 22, 1627. The Baron de Chantal, in command of one of the island's four squadrons of noble volunteers, contributed mightily to the repulse of the English, performing prodigies of valor during six hours of combat—three horses killed under him—before he finally succumbed to forces of superior strength, his body pierced by twenty-seven spear-wounds (the last—the mortal blow—struck, as legend has it, by the hand of Oliver Cromwell). In accordance with the chivalric code of honor, the English commandant returned the body of the gallant Baron to the French commandant for burial in the island church—but not until the valiant heart had been removed, to be returned to the weeping widow, for deposit in the Church of the Minimes, on the Place Royale in Paris.

The daughter, Marie de Rabutin-Chantal, at eighteen months of age, was too young to weep—too young to realize—the loss of a father. If ever she did. In all the fifteen-hundred-odd letters of hers remaining to us, there are to be found only four or five brief references to him. Once, casually, in 1671— on the forty-fourth anniversary of his death—she added to the dateline of her letter this airy, offhand reference: "Wednesday, July 22, Feast Day of St. Mary Magdalen, day of the death, some years ago, of a Father I once had" . . . as if in resentment of his having so recklessly deprived her of a child's right to a father's love and care. There is a widespread theory to the effect that a child often reacts with anger toward a parent whose death is felt as a desertion. In Mme de Sévigné's lack of deference in this reference to her father's death, there is the implication that had he been less of a hero, he might have been more of a parent to her. (Not that she did not appreciate his flamboyance: elsewhere in her correspondence, quoting and commenting on a witty, highly original letter of his—a form of clever verbal short-hand—she refers to him with pride: "He had style, my Father!")

When some among the multitude of her biographers across the centuries suggest that the fatherless Marie de Rabutin-Chantal suffered from the lack of a strong male influence in her life, they lose track of all the men in her young life: first and foremost, her grandfather Philippe de Coulanges, the patriarch of the family and household head, who played an active paternal role, living under the same roof with his granddaughter and concerning himself in every aspect of her life. He would serve as surrogate father and, later, after the death of the child's mother, as legal guardian. Philippe II, the Coulanges's eldest son, would succeed his father as Marie's legal guardian, and the second eldest Coulanges son, Christopher, Abbot of Livry, would establish a hold on the heart and a place in the life of his niece such as few uncles—in fact or fiction—have ever enjoyed. The Place Royale household was predominantly male: there was only one aunt (Henriette, Marquise de la Trousse) but a regiment of doting uncles: the three youngest Coulanges boys were, at that time, still adolescents, not too much on their dignity to play with and tease a seven-year-old niece.

If Marie de Rabutin-Chantal had been too young to feel the impact of her father's death, she was not—in 1633, at age seven—young enough to escape the traumatic consequences of her young mother's sudden death. No mention of that loss is to be found in all her voluminous correspondence, but the frantic desperation with which she would cling to her daughter, in later years, was probably a delayed reaction to the devastating sense of loss that racked her in her youth.

Fortunately, in the face of such misfortune as befell the child, two of the mainstays of her world remained intact: her maternal grandfather and grandmother on the Coulanges side. They and their large close-knit family enfolded the "poor little orphan"—her saintly maternal grandmother's term of reference—in a warm embrace. She was fortunate to grow up in that loving, lively, luxurious household on the Place Royale. She was fortunate to see about her not only familiar faces but familiar places: she was subject to no change of scene, but went on living in the same place, under the same roof, in the same handsome second-floor apartment she had shared with her mother, tended by much the same domestic staff (including Anne Gohory, her mother's faithful maid, who would devote the rest of her days to the child of her former mistress).

If anything could have taken the little girl's mind off the death of her mother it was—on the very day of her mother's funeral—the birth of her first cousin, Philippe-Emmanuel de Coulanges, first child of Philippe II de Coulanges and his wife, Marie d'Ormesson. The seven-year-old girl hovered over her cousin's cradle—a real live baby more exciting than any doll!—and appropriated him as her very *own*! Theirs was to prove a lifelong devotion. "To love me was the very first thing you did upon opening your eyes," she wrote him, years later: "A habit formed far too early for you ever to be able to break! Just as it was *I* who made it fashionable to love *you*!" He would call her "my adorable governess." She would call him her "little Coulanges," "the most adorable little man in the world," and they would correspond, all their lives, without fail, whenever they were apart (all too many of those letters, sad to say, somehow lost).

Before Marie had had time to recover properly from the last loss, she had sustained another: the death of her Grandmother de Coulanges in 1634, followed by that of her grandfather, two years later. In 1636, by the time she was ten, she had lost all four—father, mother, grandmother, grandfather— of those closest to her. One after the other, all those she had most loved had abandoned her—in death.* She may well have been haunted all her life by

---

*The mortality rate in seventeenth-century France owed some of its rise to duelling deaths, but it was already high from natural causes, such as smallpox.

the threat of loss of loved ones. If the intensity of her love for her daughter proved to be excruciating, abnormal, obsessive, morbid, it may have been because of her sad experience of loss in infancy and childhood: to be separated from her daughter—even temporarily—took on the aspect of a kind of death.

The death of the patriarch of the Coulanges family necessitated the convocation of a family council to designate a new guardianship and custody for the quadruply orphaned girl. A dozen or more representatives of the maternal and paternal sides of the family met in January, 1637, at the Châtelet Court in Paris, under the jurisdiction of a magistrate of that court, and promptly found themselves in heated contest for control of the orphan's person and her fortune. Her cousin Léonor de Rabutin (head of the family's junior branch, Lieutenant-General of the King in the Nivernais Region of Burgundy) was thinking more of the heiress than the orphan, was thinking of the ten-year-old heiress as a bride for his eighteen-year-old son and heir, Roger de Rabutin—her tender age no deterrent to matchmaking in that day and time—when he urged that supervision of the orphan's estate and custody of the orphan herself be confided to her father's sister, the Countess de Toulongeon, under whose auspices the match should not be difficult to arrange. Although the Countess de Toulongeon may have had ideas of her own in making a strong case for her stewardship: what more appropriate, she argued, than to entrust an aunt with the upbringing of an orphaned niece? Or could it have been that her ulterior motive was to cloister that niece and appropriate her fortune to augment the Toulongeon daughters' dowries?

However it was, the Rabutin faction might well have prevailed—the paternal side of the family exercising a claim superior to that of the maternal side—had not the Archbishop of Bourges thrown the weight of his influence behind the Coulanges, favoring Philippe II de Coulanges to succeed his father as guardian and his wife to act as mother to the orphan—as, indeed, she had already been doing so well for a year or more. The Archbishop gave it as his opinion that the child could not be in better hands than those in which she had found herself since birth. Apparently, the child's Grandmother de Chantal agreed, for the Archbishop had written to consult his sister (as the letter attests) and would never have acted against her wishes in the matter. "I find her being so well cared for and so perfectly brought up," his letter reads, "that I would be reluctant to see a change."

The magistrate presiding over the family council evidently agreed and awarded guardianship and custody of the minor to the distaff side of the family, to Philippe II de Coulanges and to his wife Marie—by birth a d'Ormesson, one of the most distinguished of Paris's Parliamentary families. The little orphan would live on happily in the bosom of her mother's family in their Place Royale mansion, in their fine country house and broad estates at Sucy-en-Brie, surrounded by fond uncles and aunts, by little cousins and playmates such as her beloved Philippe-Emmanuel de Coulanges and his two sisters, such as the three children of Aunt Henriette de Coulanges (who had also married into nobility, becoming the Marquise de la Trousse). "My happy youth," Marie de Rabutin-Chantal would years later characterize it. And again, reflecting on this period of her life: "Never a youth so halcyon as mine!" . . . and this despite the grievous loss of both parents, both grandparents by the age of ten. She apparently enjoyed a liberty few girls of her day and time had known: "Allowed to do whatever she pleases," as her Grandmother de Chantal had been alarmed to hear. Perhaps her adoring grandfather felt so sorry for the fatherless child that he spared her the usual disciplinary measures: if, however, "he exercised his authority mildly, still he could do anything with the child," as the Archbishop de Bourges assured his sister in Annecy. The Mother Superior of the Paris Convent of the Visitation confirmed the opinion of the Archbishop: Saint Chantal could later write, "Thank God my grandchild could not be better cared for and educated!" Saint Chantal could not have failed to appreciate the solid bourgeois virtues of the Coulanges. The child would have inherited—with her father's Rabutin blood—enough of his extravagant aristocratic tastes, his élitist prejudices and foibles. It might have been construed as a blessing that there would be inculcated in her—from youth—a sound bourgeois sense of balance, if not of thrift: that she would be inoculated with large doses of common sense; would be witness to the fact that the Coulanges lived sober, decent, moral lives; lived exceedingly well, and yet did not exceed their incomes—an example she was never to forget. The immorality of the Court and Age of Louis XIV—in which she would spend much of her adult life— would be notorious: the memory of the solid domestic virtues which had prevailed in her mother's house would stand Madame de Sévigné in good stead.

One wonders if she realized how narrowly she escaped the cloister in 1637. Had Saint Chantal, at that moment, claimed her granddaughter for the conventual life, it is unlikely that her claim would have been denied by the family council meeting at the Châtelet Court. Again, it must have been Marie de Rabutin-Chantal's paternal great-uncle, the Archbishop of Bourges, who saved her from that fate: he must have warned his sister that the independent, lively, high-spirited and highly intelligent little girl showed no disposition whatsoever for the religious life. If she was serious-minded, capable of profound study, she was also frankly frivolous, eager for diversion. Had she been immolated, immured—willy-nilly—in the Annecy Convent of the Visitation, she would have had to accept her destiny; there would have been a Sister Someone or Other, but no Marquise de Sévigné, with no beloved daughter to whom to write voluminously, no treasure trove of letters to delight the world, delight the centuries—no great gift to posterity.

Marie de Rabutin-Chantal was to have the education of a lady of quality—and far more than most: singing lessons, dancing lessons, riding lessons, declamation lessons, Latin, Spanish and Italian lessons . . . Italian being the language *à la mode* in France, in that century, just as French would be the language *à la mode* in England, Russia, most of Europe and the United States in centuries to come. Marie de Rabutin-Chantal could and did read the Latin classics in either the original Latin (with, perhaps, some slight assistance) or in Italian translation; the great works of Italian and Spanish literature she read in the original. Her foundation in French literature—sacred as well as profane—was solid; the emphasis, in that pre-Cartesian day, was on literature rather than on science. Her lifelong love of books was stimulated not only by her excellent instructors but by her bibliophile of an uncle, the Archbishop de Bourges, to whose extensive library she had access as a girl, in his house close by the Coulanges's, on the Place Royale. She was to be, with few exceptions, more highly educated than most women of her day and time; among those few exceptions were three of her friends: the brainy Countess de La Fayette; Mademoiselle de Scudéry, the popular novelist; and Madame de Maintenon, King Louis XIV's last mistress and morganatic wife. Mme de Sévigné was still grateful, decades later, for "the great masters" who had formed her mind: these, by some accounts, were Jean Chapelain and Gilles Ménage, Paris savants of repute; Chapelain was Cardinal Richelieu's literary arbiter, most influential member of the prestigious *Académie Française* at the very hour of its formation by Cardinal Richelieu in 1635. As for the Abbé Ménage, he was a darling of the Paris literary salons of the times, a critic and a grammarian and etymologist of note. Whether they were actually (as some biographers insist) her teachers or whether they served as educational advisers, selecting tutorial staff and suggesting curriculum (as other biographers contend), they did come to consider themselves—when she made her debut in Paris society at age sixteen or seventeen—as her friends. Such letters of hers to them as are extant are the letters of a friend and a disciple, but beyond that are not revelatory. (Precise information is scant as concerns the early years of her life, all the years preceding the beginning of the famous correspondence with her daughter which is the source of most of our biographical data. For the early period of her life, for such scraps and bits and pieces as have been forthcoming, her biographers have had to depend on vital statistics records, have had to dig deep into the archives of Church and Court and city for birth and death certificates, marriage contracts, wills and testaments and other various and sundry legal documents, and into the family archives, letters, journals, and such odds and ends as Marie de Coulanges's two neatly kept account books; Saint Chantal's correspondence, personal and official; Philippe-Emmanuel de Coulanges's reams of poetry.)

Some biographers see the young Abbé (Abbot) Ménage as enamored of his pretty, witty pupil. But, then, some of her biographers see her as irresistible to every male in her vicinity, see not merely two or three of her youngest uncles enamored of their teen-age niece, but even her eldest, her guardian-uncle, likewise smitten by her charms. Was she not—according to one perfervidly ardent biographical admirer—the woman for whom "the word 'charm' would have had to be invented, had it not already had its place in the dictionary"?*

"Was I ever really as pretty as that?" she once inquired by letter of her daughter, in response to a letter in which the beauty of her granddaughter, Pauline de Grignan, was compared to that of Grandmother de Sévigné. Having posed the rhetorical question, she answered it with the words: "It was said that I was very pretty, indeed!" One of those who said so, in print, was Madame de La Guette, a summer neighbor of the Coulanges's at Sucy, writing in her *Mémoires* that: "Mademoiselle de Chantal was possessed of a beauty to appeal to every heart. She was later to become the Marquise de Sévigné, known to all the world for her wit and delicious humor."† In the *Journal* of a family friend, Olivier d'Ormesson (brother of the wife of Philippe II de Coulanges), we catch one other glimpse of Marie de Rabutin-Chantal in her teens—at eighteen, in 1644, looking "more beautiful than an

*Emile Faguet, *Dix-septième siècle: études littéraires* (Paris, 1903).

†*Journal d'Olivier Lefèvre d'Ormesson et extraits des mémoires d'André Lefèvre d'Ormesson* (volumes IX and IX Collection de documents inédits sur l'Histoire de France).

angel"—as she takes up the collection of alms at the Church of the Minim Fathers, in the presence of the Queen-Mother, Anne of Austria, widow of Louis XIII and acting Regent during the minority of her six-year-old son, Louis XIV.

After that one glimpse, we lose track of Marie de Rabutin-Chantal, and the next thing we know, her hand is being sought in marriage. Not surprising for a beauty, for an heiress, who had attained the ripe old age of sixteen, seventeen or eighteen. Marriages were consummated between brides and grooms far younger than that in seventeenth-century France. (Had not Saint Chantal's daughter been wed at age eleven to the brother of Saint Francis de Sales?) Marie de Rabutin-Chantal's patrilinear surname had a noble ring to it, but the Coulanges had not yet achieved any real social standing, despite the ever increasing family fortune, despite the series of marriages into circles loftier than their own. Even so, Marie de Rabutin-Chantal's dowry was considerable, and several eligible suitors presented themselves, but were for one reason or another rejected. One of the suitors may have been the girl's cousin, Roger de Rabutin, eight years her senior and already making a name for himself in military circles, who would later claim (in his scandalous, surreptitiously published *Amorous History of the Gauls*) that his father favored a marriage with this well-dowered cousin, but that he had shied away for the reason that he found her a shade too skittish to suit his taste, concluding with the malicious comment that he thought she "would make the prettiest wife in the world—for someone else, but not for me."* Of course, it must be remembered that when Roger de Rabutin wrote those spiteful lines, he and his cousin were temporarily on bad terms—temporarily only, for they could never long remain estranged, affiliated too solidly by the bond of their mutually esteemed Rabutin blood. Roger would be wed in 1643—if not to one cousin, then to another: to Gabrielle de Toulongeon, another granddaughter of Saint Chantal's.

Marie would be wed the following year, in 1644: the groom chosen for her, a Breton nobleman, Henri, Marquis de Sévigné. The fact that both parties were physically attractive young people—she, at eighteen years of age; he, at twenty-one—had no bearing whatsoever on the decision of the matchmakers; the personal preferences of the pair being rarely consulted in Old Régime France. The matchmakers, consisting of predominantly male members of the families of the interested parties, took into consideration only the financial, social—and, in some instances, the political—advantages of the marital alliance. In this instance, both the fiancé and the fiancée were

*Roger de Rabutin, Comte de Bussy, *L'Histoire amoureuse des Gaules* (Liège, 1665), volume 1, page 197.

highborn: the Sévignés of Brittany as ancient and illustrious a line as the Rabutins of Burgundy. Where the bride was richly dowered, the groom could point to broad feudal acres scattered across the length and breadth of that eastern maritime province. Admittedly, these château-embellished estates were often debt-encumbered, having proven insufficient to maintain the lavish life-style of the proprietors. Not that the Sévignés were an exception: theirs, rather, was a plight common among the seventeenth- and eighteenth-century French feudal magnates. Young Sévigné held no army commission, no post or position at the Court of Louis XIII, but he might have been said to have promising connections in the Church and the Court—in that the Sévignés were related to the prominent and powerful Gondi-Retz families.

All in all, this undistinguished provincial nobleman could not have been termed a brilliant match for an important Paris heiress. Not that she had any say whatsoever in the matter, but Marie de Rabutin-Chantal may have found the man—if not the match—desirable. That good family friend and legal counsel, Olivier d'Ormesson, who had a hand in drawing up the complicated marital contract, made note in his *Journal* that young Sévigné was "a handsome man, a fine figure of a cavalier, and seems to be intelligent."

He seems also to have been a hothead, a hand always on his scabbard: the original date set for the nuptials in late May had to be postponed when, on the very eve of the wedding day, the groom-to-be fell wounded in a duel and was several months invalided. The wedding finally took place on August 3, 1644, in the early hours of the morning—curiously enough, a customary hour for such ceremonies among the social élite of Paris in the mid-seventeenth century. The d'Ormesson *Journal* gives us our only glimpse of the bride on the day following the ceremony: no blushing bride with downcast eyes, this Marquise de Sévigné, in elegant attire, ensconced on a formally draped day-bed (as was also the custom), blithely receiving the stream of visitors who came to offer their congratulations. "I went after dinner," writes d'Ormesson, "to see Madame de Sévigné who was very gay; she had been married at two hours after midnight at the Church of St. Gervais, with Monseigneur the Bishop of Chalons performing the ceremony." (If it was the uncle of the bride who officiated, it was the uncle of the groom, the Archbishop of Corinth, coadjutor to the Archbishop of Paris, the future Cardinal de Retz, who gave the benediction.) The honeymoon was spent in Brittany, at the groom's many-turreted gray rock château, Les Rochers (The Rocks), principal residence of the Sévigné family since 1485, situated on one of the heavily forested Sévigné estates, one and one-half leagues* from

*Jean Loret, *La Muse historique; ou Recueil des lettres en vers contenant les nouvelles du temps, écrites à son altesse Mlle de Longueville, depuis duchesse de Nemours (1660–1665)*, 4 vols. (Paris, 1870–91).

Vitré. To a Parisienne, born and bred, that walled medieval town must have seemed miniature, grim and gray, outlandish.

Commuting as they did, during the next several years, between Brittany and Paris, the couple's first child was born in 1646 in the capital: a daughter, Françoise-Marguerite de Sévigné; shortly, if not yet, to be the apple of her mother's eye; later, if not yet, the torment and the delight of her mother's existence—a mother-daughter relation of infinite complexity, fraught with Freudian overtones, a challenge to analysis. It is from the d'Ormesson *Journal*, not from Mme de Sévigné's *Letters*, that we owe any detail of that childbirth: "a fortunately easy delivery," d'Ormesson wrote on October 10, 1646, "with no one in attendance except my Mother and my wife"—no one, it would seem, ever properly to sever that umbilical cord.

The second child of the union was born, two years later: a son, Charles de Sévigné, who might have been expected, on every account, to be his Mother's favorite. Not all his lifelong devotion, however, not all his fond, assiduous attentions could distract her from her obsession with her daughter. Charles, a faithful and delightful companion to his mother all her life, could never make real inroads into her heart, which was totally preoccupied by his sister.

Charles was born at the Château Les Rochers, whither his father had repaired in 1648 not only to oversee his landed interests in Brittany but to live off the land for a while without expense—live off the produce of his vassal farmers—to effect a recuperation of his finances which had been strained by the profligate expenditures of his latest Paris sojourn.

Neither marriage nor fatherhood, it developed, could deter the Marquis de Sévigné from going his merry, spendthrift way, compromising his wife's estate as well as his own, as he went. In reaction to his ruinous disorders, his wife's uncles, Philippe II de Coulanges and Christopher, the Abbé de Coulanges, insisted on a legal partition of the couple's properties, as a means of preventing the husband from making further invasion of his wife's estate.

Mme de Sévigné should not have been too surprised to discover that her husband was a gay blade, a fiery one at that—such was the way of life of the young French nobleman in the 1600's—but she may well have suffered disillusion at the discovery that he was a rake, a roué, as well, flagrant in his infidelities. With his wife and newborn son abandoned in the fogs and forests of Brittany, his affair with the famous courtesan Ninon de l'Enclos became an open scandal in Paris.

Ninon not only became a legend in her own time, she had attained that status early, by the time she was thirty, as famous for her intellectual capacity as for her amatory skills. (Legend has it that Cardinal Richelieu offered her a staggeringly large sum—in the neighborhood of some half-million or more dollars in comparative value—to become his mistress, and that Ninon declined on the grounds that had he pleased her, the sum would have been exorbitant; and had he displeased her, the sum would have been insufficient.) Daughter of a petty nobleman from the Touraine, a sensual woman endowed with a beautiful body and a strong mind, a free thinker in matters of religion and of sex, a rebel against the tyranny of seventeenth-century marriage and the double standard, this *avant-garde* French feminist barely escaped confinement in a convent by royal edict. (Throughout his reign, Louis XIV never relaxed surveillance of this daring advocate of women's rights, inquiring regularly of his Paris informants, "And what is Ninon up to now?") Her salon became one of the most distinguished in France, frequented by eminent literary men, by high-ranking noblemen and Court dignitaries. (Mme de Sévigné might have found Ninon entertaining too, had not Ninon poached—more than once—on Mme de Sévigné's preserves.) Ninon's decades-long succession of lovers was taken strictly on her terms, taken and cast off at her sweet pleasure.

To be enjoying the lady's favors was a major matter of pride with the Marquis de Sévigné, and he boasted openly of his good fortune to his own wife's cousin, Roger de Rabutin (by then the Count de Bussy-Rabutin, the title and the estate having devolved upon him at the death of his father in 1644).

Describing a rapturous night of love, Henri de Sévigné declared that it was not his wife with whom he had spent it, but Ninon! To which Bussy replied (if we are to trust his scurrilous *Amorous History of the Gauls*): "So much the worse for you. My cousin is far more attractive than Ninon. Were she not your wife, she's the one whom you would seek as your mistress!"

Whereupon Bussy promptly related the entire conversation to Mme de Sévigné, who had by then followed her errant husband to the city. Recently a widower, Bussy was dancing attendance on his cousin of whom he was, by then, frankly amorous. Reminding her that jealousy was a potent aphrodisiac, this most dangerous of advisers advised his cousin to give her husband cause for jealousy by taking a lover of her own, and proposed himself to serve in that capacity.

"If he returns to the fold," Bussy said, "I love you so well that I am willing to sacrifice myself for the sake of your happiness, but, should this maneuver fail to bring him back, love me instead, dear cousin, and I will help you avenge yourself on him by loving you all my life."

The fact that she rejected his gallant offer, that she replied quite coolly that he "was jumping to conclusions," that she was "not so perturbed as all that," Bussy attributed, in a striking example of male egotism, to "the frigidity of her nature."

From Bussy's dialogue, when taken *in extenso*, it would seem clear that the Marquise de Sévigné had, by then, become a sophisticate, a woman of the world—that elegantly mannered, morally debased *haut-monde* of mid-seventeenth-century Paris. She appears to have acquired a reputation for frivolity, a reputation for an excessive, somewhat frenzied gaiety, a reputation for indiscretion. Her conversation, according to her cousin, the Count de Bussy, showed an inclination toward the bold, the racy. "For a lady of quality," Bussy criticized (though it must be remembered that he wrote in a temper tantrum), "her humor is a bit too broad, her manner a bit too free," while scandalmonger Tallemant des Réaux deplored a tendency of hers to say "whatever came into her head—no matter how daring—just so long as it was amusing." Emotionally volatile—perhaps even unstable—as Bussy saw her, "carried away" by the excitement of the verbal thrust and parry, "she will condone and even encourage the most risqué topics of conversation, so long as they are veiled in innuendo." If Bussy—with his designation of "frigidity"—implied that she was slow to respond to sexual stimuli, he likewise implied that she was prompt to indulge in intellectual—or verbal—foreplay.

If there was talk about her at the time, it may have been that, embarrassed by her husband's flagrant infidelities, she was guilty of some indiscretion in encouraging the advances of the gallants who flocked to pay her court, although it may have seemed to her the sole means of proving to the world—and to herself—that, despite her husband's gross neglect, she did not lack in feminine attractions.

When the Marquis de Sévigné was condemned in print for not being *"un honnête homme"*—an honest man—for lacking, that is, the attributes of a gentleman, the indictment was that of Tallemant des Réaux, whose *Historiettes* or *Short Stories* are comparable to a collection of gossip columns, each featuring a different Paris personality. An *"honnête homme,"* in seventeenth-century parlance, denoted an honest man in the sense of a man of integrity, to be sure, but far more than that—a man of honor, a cultivated gentleman, the ideal gentleman, example of all that was best in French culture. When one spoke of *"une femme honnête,"* an honest woman, one meant a woman who was chaste, virtuous, her honor intact—*honnête*, the very adjective that gossip-monger Tallemant used in his description of the wife of the Marquis de Sévigné.

Loret's gazette—a popular newsletter couched in execrably bad verse—devoted its July 18, 1650 issue to a report on a riotous, candle-lit dinner party hosted by the Marquis (and, presumably, the Marquise) de Sévigné at a Paris cabaret: the poetaster–society reporter carried away an impression of low-cut gowns and "fair bosoms," of "flowing wine and drinking songs," of rowdyism . . . of "spilled soup and broken crockery."*

Madame de Sévigné's reputation could not but have been impugned, if only by association with her husband's dissolute companions and by frequent public notice. She and the Countess de Fiesque and Mme de Montglas, two friends of dubious reputation, were suddenly forbidden the door of his home by the stern Prince d'Harcourt. "All three young and sparkling," according to Loret's versifying, "all three high-spirited and flirtatious," were suspected by the Prince of being "too frisky," and thus improper companions for his giddy wife (whom he would later order to be shut away in the Château of Montreuil to insulate her totally from further corruption). To be denied access to the Hôtel d'Harcourt, the Prince's Paris mansion, constituted a rebuff that Mme de Sévigné could not have taken lightly, shrug it off though she might.

Nor could she have relished being relegated by her husband to the provinces, in the dreary autumnal months of that same year of 1650. The Marquis de Sévigné deposited his wife and two young children (as was his custom, according to one Paris gossip) in his château, Les Rochers, in all its misty solitude, and then rushed back to Paris, alone. Business affairs—a lawsuit pending between the Marquis and his stepmother—may have been the pretext for his visit to Brittany, but it was an affair of the heart that prompted his speedy return to the capital. Ninon de l'Enclos had either given him his congé or been eclipsed by a new star, a disreputable hussy named Mme de Gondran, popularly known as "La Belle Lolo," for whose favors Sévigné triumphantly vied against all the gallants of Court and Capital.

If one wonders that a woman of independent spirit and independent means such as his wife sat meekly by, and submitted to this new affront, these fresh disorders on the part of her husband, one must remember that she simply had no choice, that the marital code of seventeenth-century France prescribed a wife's submission to her husband as her master, as head of the family—as her father or brother had stood in relation to her prior to her marriage. A husband, father or brother could, upon due provocation, request a *Lettre de Cachet* from the monarch—an arbitrary royal order of imprisonment, of cloistration or of exile—to be used against a recalcitrant or unruly wife, daughter or sister. Or a husband could simply order his wife shut away in some remote château, out of harm's way, as was the case with the Prince d'Harcourt and the Princess whom he sequestered at Montreuil.

Journal d'Olivier Lefèvre d'Ormesson.

The liaison with "La Belle Lolo" would cost the Marquis de Sévigné not only a fortune but his life. In Feburary of 1651, the Chevalier d'Albret ("a handsome fellow with a high score in duelling deaths") disputed Sévigné's claims to exclusivity over the favors of the lady, carrying the dispute to the field of honor (although the word "honor" was scarcely appropriate in connection with the courtesan over whom they were quarrelling). Pierced through the heart, the Marquis de Sévigné—at age twenty-eight—died the following morning, February 5, 1651, the day of his wife's twenty-fifth birthday.

In all the thousand and more letters of Mme de Sévigné which have been spared to us—neither lost nor misplaced, neither destroyed by accident nor by grim purpose—only one reference is to be found to her husband's numerous amorous involvements, and that one reference concerns not "La Belle Lolo" but Ninon de l'Enclos. The Marquis de Sévigné may have gotten himself killed over Mme de Gondran, but it was Ninon—her social and intellectual equal—whom Mme de Sévigné identified as a serious rival, Ninon whom she blamed for the disastrous effect on her husband's life— although, interestingly enough, she sedulously avoided use of the word "husband." It is in reference to her son Charles's involvement with that same lady, in 1671—exactly twenty years later—that she brings up Ninon's name, writing that Charles "was in the toils of Ninon," who had "blighted"— not her husband's—but rather "his father's life."

Word of the Marquis de Sévigné's death could not have reached his widow and children in far-off Brittany for several days—only two couriers a week galloping with the mail across the two hundred-odd miles between Paris and Vitré. Unless it was her widowed aunt, the Marquise de La Trousse, or her uncle, the Abbé de Coulanges, who undertook the five- or six-day carriage journey to break the news in person to their widowed niece.

Madame de Sévigné stayed on in Brittany for months, perhaps to mourn, perhaps merely to wait for the scandal associated with her husband's death to die down in Paris, perhaps to oversee his widespread properties in Brittany, to resolve legal problems pending prior to his death, to try to bring order out of the disorder wrought in his estate by his excesses, to salvage the children's father's estate for the sake of those children.

To find an expert financial adviser, she had not, fortunately, far to look: within the family circle itself, there stood her Rock of Gibraltar, her uncle, the Abbé de Coulanges, a churchman interested in economic rather than ecclesiastical affairs, more intent on his account book than on his breviary.

He was her "*Bien Bon*," a totally untranslatable pet name by which she always referred to him: *Bon*, meaning kind or good; *Bien*, a repetitively emphatic adjective modifying *Bon* . . . her very, very, very good and kind and dear, her Guardian Angel of an Uncle! "He rescued me," she would write years later, "from the abysmal depth into which Monsieur de Sévigné's death had plunged me . . . He was my father and my benefactor to whom I owed all the serenity and peace of mind that made my life so sweet." It was to the *Bien Bon* that she would owe her financial security—a security which left her free to follow her bent as a social creature and an intellectual. "He gave me the opportunity," she would say to Bussy, "to become the person you love today." It was to him her friends were beholden, she pointed out, for the blithe spirit, that effervescent, contagious humor they said they so prized in her. If the Marquis de Sévigné "wrought havoc in his wife's estate," as Tallemant charged, the Abbé de Coulanges restored it to good order. By the time Mme de Sévigné, in company with her five-year-old daughter and her three-year-old son, returned to Paris late in the winter of 1651, she had struggled up, at least partially, out of "the abysmal depths" into which she had, in her own words, been plunged by the shock of her husband's sudden, melodramatic, scandal-tinged death in the early spring.

How deeply could she have mourned this husband who had insulted her by remarking openly (as Valentin Conrart attests in his posthumously published *Mémoires*) that "she might have appeal for other men but none for him"?* How deeply could she have mourned a man who had humiliated her publicly and deliberately, who had flaunted his infidelities, who had wasted his substance and hers? ("I have been unfortunate when it comes to husbands," she would write in 1671.)

She mourned deeply, indeed, according to Loret, in his widely distributed, versified gazette, *La Muse historique:* Loret hymned Mme de Sévigné as "That beautiful young widow/ With her broken heart/ Her voice raised in song/ Like a chaste turtledove/ In lament for her late husband." The turtledove's cousin, on the other hand, the dapper and gallant Count de Bussy—once again in the vanguard of her admirers—disagrees, writing (in his *Amorous History of the Gauls*) that while the widow "appeared inconsolable over the death of her husband, she had so much cause to detest him, as everyone knows, that her mourning is suspected of being no more than a gesture of compliance with convention."

The widow's emotional state sparked debate among the couple's friends and acquaintances. Valentin Conrart calls attention to the fact that she loved her husband despite the fact that she could not respect him—while, on his

---

*Valentin de Conrart, "Mémoires," *Nouvelle collection des mémoires relatifs à l'histoire de France depuis le XIIIe siècle jusqu'à la fin du XVIIIe siècle,* volume XXVIII (Paris, 1854).

side, the sentiment held good stated vice versa. Tallemant des Réaux insists that the widow's grief was genuine and profound, recounting—to prove his point—the tale of her dramatic encounter, at a ball, in 1653, with the Chevalier d'Albret, who had impaled her husband on his sword two years earlier: she came close to fainting, according to Tallemant, at sight of this sinister figure (who would himself perish by the sword in 1671).

To read in her own words how she reacted to the trauma of her husband's death, one must turn to an oblique but revealing reference made by her to her widowhood, some thirty years later: in an exchange of letters with Bussy in 1687, she allowed herself, inadvertently, to be drawn into a discussion concerning the most memorable years of her life; only one or two seemed worthy of retention in her memory:

On first thought [she wrote], only two dates stand out in my mind: the date of the year of my birth and the date of the year of my marriage. But on second thought, I prefer to forget the year of my birth ... the thought of my age depresses and dismays me. In its place, I am substituting the year of my widowhood which was calm and happy enough, a blessedly uneventful year, free of notoriety, out of the public eye.

The calm after the storm, she seemed to say, for which she seemed highly grateful; a quiet time, after the debacle of her married life, a time in which to turn for comfort to her immediate family, to her two small children, her devoted Aunt Henriette de la Trousse, her adoring uncle, the Abbé de Coulanges ... a time in which to regain her equanimity, to rediscover herself and to regain her confidence in herself as an attractive female ... no longer the butt of her husband's derision, no longer the victim of his scandals, no longer at his command, but in full possession of herself and her future, her own woman, body and soul, heart and mind, free!—a rare privilege for a seventeenth-century woman—free to assert her own authority over her life.

III

Paris welcomed her back with open arms, with a fanfare of madrigals. Emerging from the chrysalis of mourning, this social butterfly had spread her shining wings and taken flight for the capital, sometime in the autumn of 1651.

We have the poets to thank for much of the little that is known concerning the life of Madame de Sévigné in the years immediately following the death of her husband. It is the poets who, in print or in manuscript, announce her return from the provinces, the poets who herald her reentry into the Parisian social whirl, who sing of her grace and beauty, her infinite charm and fascination.

It is certain that she was back in Paris by November 12, 1651: Loret's gazette (*La Muse historique*) published on that date hails her arrival with the lines, "Her radiance untarnished by her somber attire/ She has returned to swell the ranks of our Paris belles." And, lo and behold, here comes Mme de Sévigné, "Beautiful as an angel/ In her widow's weeds/ Rejoicing my eyes," to quote the verse of Paul Scarron (that second-rate poet with the first-rate wife who, as Mme de Maintenon, would later make it to the pinnacle of power, to share the bed—if not the throne—of the greatest of the Bourbon monarchs).

Renowned for her verve and beauty, the young widow of the Marquis de Sévigné soon achieved prominence in the Parisian pleasure-round, shining as one of the brightest stars of the capital's social firmament—sought after, paid court to, made much over.

The poets vied with one another to pay her honor, to lavish her with compliments: the Abbé Ménage, dedicating a book of verse (the *Miscellanea*), in 1652, to his cherished disciple, addressed her as the "Adorable Sévigné/ Most perfect of all the Works of Heaven/ Ornament of the Court/ Marvel of our Age!" She was on the way to becoming a cult figure, a Goddess of Love, apostrophized by poets, courted by noblemen of exalted rank—dukes, princes, maréchals of France. The Abbé Ménage, in another work published in 1668, genuflected to her as "Worthy object of universal worship/ To whom all mortals/ Following my example/ Erect their altars." In a collection of poetry edited by Sercy in 1653, homage was paid Mme de

Sévigné by Michel Montreuil, who likened her to Venus, and by Marigny, who celebrated the "Adorable and beautiful Marquise, her skin fairer a thousand times than the whitest of white satin." A quatrain by Beauchâteau in 1657 pled with her to veil her charms and to suspend the lightning flashes of her wit, "Your beauty alone suffices to bring us to our knees." Saint-Gabriel called her "An Angel on Earth, the Glory of the World," while Jean Segrais, in his *Variety of Verse* published in 1657, included three of the adulatory rhymed letters he had penned to her.

All signs point to the fact that by the mid 1650's Mme de Sévigné had taken her position at center stage on the Parisian social scene. Twenty-odd years later, people (like Mme de La Guette in her *Mémoires*) were still talking about Mme de Sévigné, "who was known to all the world for the brilliance of her mind and the piquancy of her humor." By 1664, the echoes of her fame, her reputation as a dazzling personality, had reached even the cloisters of the Convent of the Visitation of Paris's Rue Saint-Antoine. Mother Agnes Arnauld, who had gone into seclusion there, denied herself the pleasure of a visit from Mme de Sévigné, lest, she wrote, "I lose the hard-earned fruits of my solitude": Mother Agnes well knew that "to sit opposite the Marquise, alone, was more exciting than to mingle with a large company."

Not only the poets but the prose writers saluted Mme de Sévigné: she was the subject of numerous "pen-portraits," a literary fad of the mid-seventeenth century, originated by Madeleine de Scudéry, the most popular novelist of the period. The Marquise de Sévigné is featured in a leading role in Volume III of Mademoiselle de Scudéry's bestselling, ten-volume histor-ical romance entitled *Clélie*, published between 1654 and 1660—a *roman à clef*, a "keyed" romance wherein prominent contemporaries were portrayed in historical disguise, readily identifiable by those familiar with the social register.* Mme de Sévigné appeared under the fictitious name of Princess Clarinte, "a heroine with an air so open, a step so graceful, a bearing so noble that one recognizes at first glance how distinguished must be her lineage." Her physical attributes are described and eulogized, in detail, ad infinitum: "her blonde beauty ... her fair complexion ... her sparkling blue eyes ... her cherry-red lips ... her grace on the dance floor." In short, "To see her is to love her!" But, of all the attributes for which Mme de Sévigné was renowned among her contemporaries, none gave rise to so much comment as her talents as a conversationalist. Her conversation, according to Mlle de Scudéry, "is highly diverting, natural. She speaks well, she speaks clearly"

*Volume III was published in 1657, under the name of the author's brother, Georges de Scudéry.

(her command of the French language magical, as can be divined from her writing: her choice of words exquisite, precise, inspired, far more than could be said of the majority of the great ladies of that kingdom). Since Mme de Sévigné was widely read, in several languages, "a booklover"—if not a bookworm—by Mlle de Scudéry's definition, no great leap of the imagination is required to assume that she could hold her own conversationally with the most scholarly—as well as the most frivolous—habitués of the fashionable Paris salons. Having paid tribute to Mme de Sévigné's singing voice ("especially fine in impassioned Italian love songs"), Mlle de Scudéry takes special note of her speaking voice, that it was "sweet, well-modulated, pleasant to the ear." Last but not least, the prolific novelist makes the point that Mme de Sévigné "writes like she talks ... that is to say, in the most delightful, most scintillating manner possible to imagine!" (Mme de Sévigné's admirers—known as Sévignistes—knowing her only through her written word, would paraphrase Mlle de Scudéry to the effect that Mme de Sévigné must have *talked* as she *wrote*—divinely!—that her conversation must have been as enchanting as her letters.)

Of all the pen-portraits of the charming Marquise, that from the astringent, the sharply analytical pen of the Countess de La Fayette carries the most weight: the insight with which it is informed stems from a close, a lifelong, a cloudless friendship. In addition to the mutuality of their tastes—their involvement in the world of the intellect, their roles as arbiters of elegance in the capital—the two young women were drawn even closer by a family connection, tenuous though it may have been: the second husband of Countess de La Fayette's widowed mother was Rénaud de Sévigné, uncle of the Marquise's husband. In her portrait of Mme de Sévigné, the Countess de La Fayette, writing under the *nom de plume* of "An Unknown," protests her disdain for the panegyric tone common to the portraitist:

> *I positively refuse to smother you with praise or inundate you with encomiums or indulge myself by reporting that your figure is superb, that your complexion has a radiance and bloom typical of a twenty-year-old; that your mouth, your teeth and your hair are incomparable. I need not tell you all these things: you already know them from your mirror. But since you probably do not converse with your reflection, what your mirror cannot tell you is how utterly entrancing you are when you are engaged in conversation, and it is that which I have to tell you. Be advised, Madame, if by chance you are unaware of it, that your wit so greatly adorns and embellishes your person that there is none other on earth so delightful as you when you are carried away in*

*animated conversation from which restraint has been banished. Every-
thing you say has such charm, so well becomes you that your words
evoke spontaneous laughter, bring smiles to the lips of those who
surround you, and the brilliance of your mind brings such a glow to
your face and such a sparkle to your eyes that—although it would
seem that wit should strike only the ear—it is certain that yours dazzles
the eye as well, and that when one listens to you talk, one is oblivious
to your imperfections; one loses sight of the fact that your features are
not entirely regular; one credits you with a flawless beauty . . . Your
presence enhances every occasion, and every occasion enhances your
beauty.**

Mme de La Fayette makes clear that society was—at least, at that
moment in her life—Mme de Sévigné's element, that she thrived on social
contact. She tossed off epigrams and *bons mots* in such profusion that those
about her came in for some of the credit, flattering themselves that they had
somehow contributed to the verbal pyrotechnics. Her witticisms were widely
quoted, reproduced in print in such collections as Ménage's *Ménagiana* and
Tallemant's *Historiettes*. "Impossible to be bored in her company!" according to Bussy in a mellow mood. No wonder she was so popular! No wonder
she was so sought after as a guest! Sweden's Queen Christina, on a visit to
Paris in 1657, subsequent to her abdication, requested that the famous Marquise
de Sévigné be included among the ladies presented at the Château de Fontainebleau and declared that she "had succumbed, like everyone else, to the
Marquise's cultivated mind and personal charm."†

In addition to the famous "portrait" by the Countess de La Fayette,
there is another equally famous by the Count de Bussy; the first by Mme de
Sévigné's closest friend, the second by her blood relative. To see her through
the eyes of intimates like these—both skilled writers, although Bussy would
have professed aristocratic disdain for writing as a profession—is the next
best thing to seeing her in the flesh.

For his portrait of his cousin, the Count de Bussy had undoubtedly
dipped his pen in acid (for reasons to be shortly clarified); even so, his

---

*For full text of Mme de La Fayette's pen-portrait of Mme de Sévigné—of which above is an
excerpt—see page 521.

†From the *Lettres de Costar* (Archdeacon to the Bishop of Mans), a letter to Mme de Sévigné in
the summer of 1685: "Several months ago, Mme the Marquise de Lavardin showed me a wonderful
letter of Queen Christina's in which Her Majesty made clear that she had been as dazzled as the rest by
the brilliance of your wit, and enchanted by your personal charms." Mme de Sévigné went to see the
Queen of Sweden at Fontainebleau, according to a letter of Mme de La Fayette's dated November 9,
1657, "who was delighted by her wit and charm." (La Fayette *Correspondance*, Paris, 1942)

portrayal may be truer to life than the conventional, the cloying panegyrics. With malice aforethought, he calls attention to the blemishes: "the eyes that did not match in color" (one, blue; the other, green!); "the square-tipped nose," "the squarish jaw." He does concede her "shapely legs" (more shapely, in his view, than her arms, neck, hands) and "a beautiful figure."*

This select, this distinguished, aristocratic Parisian society of which Mme de Sévigné was so prominent a member, danced and banqueted at the magnificent private hôtels or palaces of such notables as the Prince de Condé (First Prince of the Blood) and Mademoiselle de Montpensier, first cousin of the young King Louis XIV, known simply and grandly as the Grande Mademoiselle, who made her residence at the Luxembourg Palace. But it is the Hôtel de Rambouillet, Paris mansion of the Marquise de Rambouillet, of which one invariably thinks as the principal rendezvous, the locus and focus of that social-intellectual élite which would give French society its tone, its style, its worldwide renown, for generations to come. Thanks to this noble, glittering, elegant and cultivated circle, the French code of courtesy, French manners, Gallic "urbanity" (one of the most useful of the many words coined on the premises of the Hôtel de Rambouillet), the social amenities of France were taken as models by the world.

Thanks to this same Hôtel de Rambouillet set, French would become the international language, the language of diplomacy. Poets, dramatists, grammarians and etymologists frequented Mme de Rambouillet's salon, but it was the hostess herself—seconded by Mme de Sévigné, Mme de La Fayette and Mlle de Scudéry—who must be credited, to a great extent, with the purification, the refinement and the polish given the language in that period. Language—like manners—had been crude, slipshod, awkward in the barracks-room court of King Henri IV, first of the Bourbons. It was in direct reaction, in revulsion to that dirty, smelly Court of the Louvre that Mme de Rambouillet, in 1618, opened her salon, the first and the most famous in French history: a salon, she made clear, not an Academy, offering divertissement as well as enlightenment—bright and beautiful young women interspersed with savants and scholars; last but not least, great seigneurs— some of the most exalted peers of the realm—deigning to mingle, perhaps for the first time in French history, with the literati, the men of learning. No matter how weighty the topic under discussion—philosophy, religion, history, dramatic theory—Mme de Rambouillet made sure that the treatment of the

---

*Mlle de Scudéry had defined Mme de Sévigné's height as "slightly above average," which is not so very tall by twentieth-century standards: Louis XIV, high red heels and all, exceeded the five-foot mark by only a fraction of an inch.

subject was not heavy-handed. Communication was not by lecture but by conversation—always sprightly, however scholarly. In that society, conversation ranked as one of the lively arts ... with Mme de Sévigné as its most brilliant exponent.

It was no accident that when, at last, in 1671, she picked up her pen to practice the craft of writing, she was capable of linguistic virtuosity. She, like the other regulars of the Hôtel de Rambouillet, had long been involved in a love affair with language. She and they played with words as others played with darts, cards or dice; debate on the definition or derivation of a word constituted a major pastime. She and they set out deliberately to cull the crass, the crude and the obsolete from the vocabulary, to simplify spelling, to eliminate vulgarisms, to reshape phraseology, to regularize grammar. Beyond the shadow of a doubt, the Hôtel de Rambouillet made a significant contribution to the excellence, the precision, the beauty of the French language; brought it to its ultimate perfection so that it might serve—the *summum bonum*—as the ideal instrument of conversation.

The Hôtel de Rambouillet inevitably came in for blasts of ridicule for its preciosity, for its pretentiousness, its excesses of speech and sentiment, its affectations of speech and manner, its hypersensibility. It was Molière, that dramatic genius of the Age of Louis XIV, who satirized the leading ladies of the salon in his "hit" comedy entitled *Les Précieuses ridicules* (which translates, roughly, as *The Ridiculous Female Pedants*).

Les Précieuses ridicules may still play well today, as do most of Molière's comedies of manners, but the twentieth-century perspective suggests that the playwright's point of view is presently outmoded. Jean Cordelier, whose inspired volume *Mme de Sévigné par elle-même* (*Mme de Sévigné in Her Own Words*) was published in the 1970's, considered that

> *Preciosity was in no sense an excess but, rather, a reaction, a form of self-defense, on the part of the women, against the crudeness and rudeness of morals as well as of language; and, in a sense still more profound, a reaction against the servitude imposed on them by law, by rule, by usage, by custom; a servitude which made of their lives a more or less gilded slavery ... Preciosity, one might say, is the revolt of women who, dissatisfied, for one reason or another, with their conjugal lives, seek to escape those bonds ... to run away, in whatever direction their impulses or their velleities may take them. Mme de Sévigné— married, if not against her will, yet still unhappily—could not but applaud these Précieuses in their demands for women's liberation, in their censure of men's boorishness and grossness.*

IV

Madame de Sévigné—with no desire to reenter matrimonial bonds of subservience and humiliation such as she had known—went blithely on her way in Paris, much courted, much fêted. "She had a positive penchant for pleasure," according to Cousin Bussy, was a very charming and very merry widow, with a stream of suitors, would-be lovers in her wake. The soul of discretion, she invited her widowed aunt, the Marquise de La Trousse, to act as duenna.

It was fortunate that Mme de La Trousse was on hand the day the Duke de Rohan-Chabot and the Marquis de Tonquedec came close to open combat in Mme de Sévigné's *ruelle* (the alcove accommodating the daybed upon which a fashionable Parisienne received her guests). It was a matter of precedence that brought the two noblemen close to blows: the Marquis stubbornly refusing to relinquish his chair at the lady's bedside to the Duke, who outranked him. It was a matter of jealousy: "They were both in love with the Marquise de Sévigné," according to Valentin Conrart and his *Mémoires* in which a page or more is devoted to the scuffle, all the more scandalous in that it occurred little more than a year after the death of the Marquis de Sévigné. Mme de Sévigné promised to forbid Tonquedec her door, but the Duke de Rohan returned the following week to find the insolent fellow there again. This time, voices were raised, curses uttered, swords unsheathed; Mme de La Trousse shrieked; "Mme de Sévigné cried out for Tonquedec to take his leave, and the Duke de Rohan showed him to the street." Each threatened to send a challenge to the other. The Duke d'Orléans, the King's brother, intervened to prevent bloodshed. "Every-one—especially the ladies—" Conrart wrote, "blamed the Duke de Rohan for such behavior in the presence of the Marquise de Sévigné." Even so, Loret's *Muse historique* (issue of June 23, 1652) carried the story of the scuffle in the *ruelle* and Paris buzzed with gossip, undoubtedly unpleasant for a lady who professed concern about her reputation in her recent widowhood.

Gallants with great names, great fortunes and great reputations all beat a path to her door. The memory of one romantic interlude would haunt her gently all her life, the one in which she was involved with the Count du

Lude (the future Duke du Lude and Grand Master of Artillery). Whether or not his intentions were honorable, he seemed to the Count de Bussy to have been the lady's "one great weakness," "the man toward whom she felt the strongest inclination . . . all her pleasantries on the subject not withstanding." Bussy attributed du Lude's success with the ladies to "his discretion . . . and his great talent as a lover." Unfortunately, "his attachments were not of long duration . . . Mme de Sévigné was one of those ladies with whom he fell in love . . . and, then, out again . . . just as she was beginning to respond to his wooing! It was this contretemps which saved her" (again, in Bussy's opinion). "Bad timing kept them apart." However it was between them in the mid-1650's, in 1680 she would go three times to the Palace of Saint-Germain, where he lay gravely ill, to inquire after him . . . an admission made somewhat sheepishly to her daughter, who always teased her mother about the Duke. And in 1690, she went miles out of her way, by litter, en route from Brittany to Provence, to the Château du Lude— a sentimental journey to stand and mourn beside his tomb.

As if the *ruelle* of Mme de Sévigné had not been crowded enough with two bumptious rivals vying for her favor, the gossip sheets pointed to a more mildly mannered third, young Jacques de Marigny, whose advances were confined to versifying. In 1653, he would indite a madrigal to her—addressing her as "Philis"—in which he described himself as "Ceaselessly sighing for your charms/ Being anxious, being jealous/ Shedding tears from time to time/ Restless, sleepless, night and day/ Is it love or is it friendship, Philis?"

The amorously inclined Abbé Ménage penned no madrigals to "Philis," but the exchange of letters between him and Mme de Sévigné, during this period, indicate that he danced attendance, mooned over her and sulked at her condescensions, at the thought of being slighted. ("Thou, tigress, with a heart of steel," he railed at her once in verse.) The discrepancy in their ages—he eight years older—was not so great as the discrepancy in their social position: she, a lady of quality, of substantial fortune; he, in his dingy clerical robes, struggling to carve a niche for himself in the literary pantheon. He divided his gallantries between his two bluestocking disciples, claiming "to have adored Mme de La Fayette in verse, and Mme de Sévigné in prose."

Bussy himself had entered the competition for his cousin's favors when he returned, in 1654, from the Catalonian campaign in which he had distinguished himself in his regiment, at the side of the Prince de Conti (younger brother of the Prince de Condé, who was the head of that collateral branch of the Bourbon family). Bussy, widowed, had remarried in 1649, but he was not the type to chafe under the marital bond. He claims, in his *Mémoires*, that— "as Mme de Sévigné's closest kin on the most distinguished branch of her family tree"—he had been the very first to pay court to the young widow on her return to Paris in 1651, and that he had tacitly agreed to play along with her game of "wait and see." Seeing her every day, delighting in her company, he "had not been loath to remain on that footing." Mme de Sévigné seemed likewise satisfied, he said, "so long as I did not love elsewhere." When his liaison with Mme de Montglas became public knowledge, things would change. Mme de Sévigné wanted to have her cake (to maintain her reputation intact) and to eat it, too (to keep Bussy dangling). For some years, he accepted her terms, writing to her in July of 1654:

My God, how witty you are, my cousin! How well you write! How adorable you are! You must admit, that prudish as you are, you owe me a debt of gratitude for not making love to you in a more ardent fashion [when his letters became too ardent, she warned him that her aunt, Mme de La Trousse, read all her mail] ... On my faith, the restraint costs me dear! Sometimes, I condemn your insensibility; at other times, I excuse it, but there is no time when I do not hold you in high esteem ... How to understand you? You flatter me, my cousin, you speak sweetly to me, but you deny me the right to feel the ultimate tenderness. Very well, then, I'll forego it: one must want only what you want, one must love you on your terms ...

So, he did, writing again in October:

You are the delight of the human race. In ancient days, they would have raised altars to you; you would surely have been the Goddess of Something or Other. In our century, incense is lit less prodigally and, above all, as concerns a living creature, one contents oneself by saying that there is no woman in all the world more delightful and more virtuous than you ... I know Princes of the Blood, princes from foreign lands, great seigneurs as powerful as princes, great captains, Ministers of State, gentlemen, magistrates, philosophers who would all line up at your door, at the slightest sign of encouragement ...

The "magistrates" and "foreign princes" have never been identified, despite centuries of research; Ménage might be categorized as "philosopher"; Fouquet, as "Minister of State"; Maréchal de Turenne, as "great captain." The "Prince of the Blood" was none other than Armand de Bourbon, Prince de Conti, Bussy's commander in Catalonia; an intellectual, a man of learning, like Bussy; like Bussy, a wit, cynical, satirical, inclined to raillery; like Bussy, signally valorous. The two could not but have found one another congenial. "He honored me with his friendship, with a genuine affection," Bussy wrote gratefully. Could Bussy's gratitude have been so great that he agreed to act as the Prince's advocate to press the Prince's suit with Mme de Sévigné? So it would seem, to judge from a letter written to her from Montpellier in June—an example of Bussy at his most cynical:

Do you remember a conversation you had with the Prince de Conti at Mme de Montausier's, last winter? He tells me that he spoke sweet nothings in your ear, that he found you much to his liking, as he would make clear to you next time he saw you. Give it some thought, my fair cousin: even if a woman has no mercenary interest, she may have ambitions of another kind, and even though she finds it best to resist the King's Minister of Finance [as Mme de Sévigné is said to have resisted Fouquet], she might not be able to resist the King's own cousin. From the manner in which the Prince spoke to me of his intentions, I can see that I have been chosen as his confidant in this affair . . . As for me, I am thrilled at the idea of your succession . . . Is my meaning clear, my dearest cousin? If Fortune lays such a gift at your feet and I fail to profit by it, the blame lies on your head . . .

Did Bussy, with an eye on his military career, also seek to play the role of confidant to the Maréchal de Turenne in his amours with Mme de Sévigné? The answer is yes, if we are to judge by the letter he wrote to his cousin on the subject of the Maréchal in 1655:

Your name came up in the course of a conversation with Monsieur de Turenne, several days ago: he asked whether I saw you often. I replied that being cousins-german, and of the same house, there was no one closer to me. He told me that he knew you, and that he had stopped twenty or thirty times at your door without finding you at home, that he holds you in high esteem . . . the truth of which you may judge by the fact that he pays visits to no other women. I told him that you were aware of the honor he had done you, and that you had given me to know how greatly you appreciated his attentions.

There were no amours, no love affair, so far as can be determined, between Turenne and Mme de Sévigné. The great military tactician may have preferred to raise the siege rather than to acknowledge himself defeated. Her letters on the occasion of his death in battle in 1675—expressive of her esteem of both the hero and the man—are superb examples of the epistolary art. No history of the reign describes the event so stirringly.

Nicolas Fouquet showed himself stubborner than Turenne, slower to concede defeat in the lists of love. Perhaps he took Boileau at his word, to the effect that, when it came to Fouquet, there could be "No cruel ladies in all of France"; none so cruel, that is to say, as to say him nay, to resist the irresistible Superintendent of Finance. The emblematic design on Fouquet's coat of arms was a squirrel on a field of argent, the motto reading, "*Quo Non Ascendam?*"—"To what height shall I not aspire?" His aspirations took the form of hubris: his Vaux-le-Vicomte, an unprecedented splendor, was the model for Versailles, a more beautiful creation, to some eyes, because homogeneous in design. With his connoisseur's eye, Fouquet had discovered the most gifted architects, landscape architects, sculptors and painters of the generation—Le Vau, Le Brun, Lenôtre—to design his chef d'oeuvre of a château, thirty miles from Paris. At sight of it, the King was envious, suspicious, resentful of his Minister. Fouquet had come highly recommended—by Cardinal Mazarin, on his deathbed—to the service of the monarch, and fully expected to succeed Mazarin as Chief Minister. He misjudged the twenty-two-year-old sovereign, never dreaming that Louis intended to govern as well as to reign, to act as his own Chief Minister. Fouquet saw himself as a Maecenas ... a role Louis XIV would choose to play himself, determined to extend the hegemony of France over Europe, artistically as well as politically. No wonder that Fouquet and the infinitely ambitious monarch—who took the Sun as his personal emblem and *Gloire*, glory, as his motto—moved on a collision course.

With almost all the resources of the kingdom at the disposal of the Superintendent of Finance, the temptations to which he could subject any woman he lusted after were considerable. In the case of Mme de Sévigné, if she stood proof against jewels, estates, treasures for herself—as she would claim she did—what about the subtler temptations? Was she equally adamant against the exercise of power in behalf of others—the grant of a pension to a necessitous playwright or poet, a prestigious government post or an army commission for a deserving friend or a favor for a relative? (One small favor, at most, she would insist on, later, to accommodate a first cousin, son of her duenna-aunt, the Marquise de La Trousse.) Fouquet's attentions to Mme de Sévigné set tongues to wagging, raised eyebrows, at the time. Her friends and acquaintances pondered the question, even then: "What's Hecuba to him, or he to Hecuba?"; her admirers have been mulling it over ever since.

Enough to turn the head of any woman to be wooed by the master of Vaux-le-Vicomte, where Fouquet held court before Louis XIV held court at Versailles, and on a scale almost as grandiose: the fifty fountains played as did the orchestras, the two hundred water-jets spouted, gala followed gala, fête succeeded fête. It was flattering to be asked by Fouquet to draw up the list of aspiring young literati deemed worthy of his patronage—no less a genius than La Fontaine, later famous for his *Fables*, is said to have been pensioned by Fouquet on Mme de Sévigné's recommendation. Did she manage to keep her head in the face of Fouquet's manifold blandishments? There are letters of hers extant to prove that he exercised a strong attraction for her, aroused profound emotions in her breast.

Also extant are letters written by the Count de Bussy to prove that Mme de Sévigné did not succumb to the aphrodisiac of power, to Fouquet's manifold techniques of seduction—not, that is, in Bussy's estimation. A friend of the Superintendent's and a confidant of his cousin, Bussy may be said to have been in a position to know better than most. "I am glad to know that you are pleased with the Superintendent," Bussy wrote Mme de Sévigné in 1654:

> *That's a sign that he is being reasonable, and that he does not take things to heart, as he was wont to do, previously. When you do not want what the other person wants, the other person would be wise to come around to wanting what you want. Everyone is still only too happy to stay on friendly terms. Except for you, I doubt that there's another woman in the kingdom who can transform her would-be lover into friend ... I am convinced that it takes a woman of extraordinary merit to prevent a frustrated lover from breaking off the relation in a huff.*

And, again, that same year, Bussy wrote to his cousin to ask "what was new with the Superintendent and his passion for you?" Most obligingly, Mme de Sévigné brought the Count de Bussy up to date on her romance with Fouquet: "I still observe the same precautions with him, still harbor the same fears ... which necessarily hampers any progress he might hope to make. I feel sure he will eventually weary of making the same futile efforts, over and over again."

Eventually, it would seem, he did—his passion giving way to respect for a virtue hitherto unknown to him in his wide experience with women. Bussy, with his overweening ego, would have been inclined to accept Mme de Sévigné's word for it that she had resisted Fouquet's advances. If Bussy could not overcome her scruples, no more—in his opinion—could Fouquet: she was "daft on the subject of virtue and honor," as Bussy had told her to her face or, rather, written her in a letter dated June of 1654.

V

The friendship, the intimacy so long enjoyed by Mme de Sévigné and the Count de Bussy came suddenly to an end, in 1658; the family bond which had held them so close was brusquely severed. It was a business affair, not a love affair, that brought about the rupture. In May, Spanish forces invested Dunkirk; Maréchal Turenne assembled his troops around Amiens. Bussy, as a Colonel of Light Cavalry, was expected to join his commander immediately, but found himself in a financial dilemma: horses, uniforms and arms to ready his regiment for the campaign required a large outlay of cash, and he could lay his hands on none, at the moment. He would eventually be reimbursed by the Royal Treasury, but the battle was about to be joined, at that hour, along the English Channel, and honor demanded that he set off immediately for Flanders. The thought of his wealthy cousin came to mind: if his military exploits brought glory to the House of Rabutin, it would redound on her and on her children. Furthermore, as he showed her, it was a service she could render a dear friend, a dear cousin, at no risk whatsoever: the death of their uncle, the Bishop of Châlon, had left them joint heirs of a sizeable legacy; he proposed that she collect the sum he was borrowing presently from his portion of the estate at the time of its division.

She agreed, she promised, and then reneged on the promise. Bussy blamed her uncle, the Abbé, for her turnabout: "Had you consulted only your heart," he wrote his cousin, two years later, "instead of those who love me less than you do," meaning the *Bien Bon* whom he suspected, and rightly, too, of being critical of the aristocracy's profligate life-style. Since it was the *Bien Bon* to whom Mme de Sévigné owed her financial security in the wake of her husband's depredations, it would have been difficult, indeed, for her to have spurned his advice, had he opposed her loan to Bussy.

Bussy fell into a rage, seethed with resentment at what he termed her betrayal of his trust. (Almost one can hear his volley of oaths, hear him revile the vile, the bourgeois Coulanges blood that debased the noble Rabutin blood coursing in her veins!) The idea of vengeance, after long ferment in his mind, would take the form of the popular literary portrait, this time satirical—vengeance via a pen as sharp as a sword.

Bussy's mistress, Mme de Montglas, more generous if less affluent than Mme de Sévigné, came to his rescue, pawning her jewels to raise the funds he needed. Thanks to her, Bussy reached Flanders on the eve of battle, in time to take command of one of the three wings of Turenne's army, in time to fight valiantly, brilliantly alongside the Maréchal, to make a signal contribution, according to numerous reports, to the victory of French arms over Spanish in the Battle of the Dunes. Cardinal Mazarin wrote to express his own gratitude and that of the King.

If a Field-Marshal's bâton seemed within Bussy's grasp on the morrow of that battle, it slipped through his fingers, eluded his grasp forever as a consequence of scandal.

Bussy, at age forty-two, athirst for military fame and honors, should have been more circumspect, should have avoided such a folly as to join the Easter weekend party at the country estate of the Duke de Vivonne. The small, select company that gathered at Roissy was composed of libertines and debauchees, deliberately choosing the holiest day of the year to profane it. An Easter orgy! Sexual license, including a variety of perversions! Rumors probably exceeded the excesses: talk of sacrilege at the altar, of frogs and suckling pigs carried from the baptismal font to the dinner table, hints of murder, even of cannibalism—a forerunner, a preview of the Affair of the Poisons, with all its poisonings, abortions, murders, and Black Masses, which would rock the Court of Louis XIV in the next decade.

Part of the entertainment at Roissy consisted of readings by Bussy from the erotic pages of his pen-portraits, the subjects of which were, for the most part, ladies of tarnished reputation: it was an insult for him to have included Mme de Sévigné in such company. It was an insult, a case of *lèse majesté*, when the drunken company—to the tune of "Hallelujah"—sang all the verses of a poem accredited to Bussy and full of disrespectful references to "Dieu-Donné" (Louis, the God-Given), and to his current mistress, Louise de La Vallière.*

Even in that licentious society, the reaction to the goings-on at Roissy was one of shock and outrage. Not even peers of the realm could expect to perpetrate such affronts to Church and State, with impunity—ten years earlier, perhaps, but not in 1659, as the central authority ever more strongly asserted itself, and the nobility buckled under. Not even the mighty Duke de Vivonne totally escaped the royal wrath.† Bussy was banished, too, to

---

*"He forfeited The Splendid Century," Sainte-Beuve, the eminent French literary critic, said of Bussy, "for the sake of a few lines of paltry verse."

†The Duke de Vivonne was First Gentleman of the King's Bedchamber; his sister, Mme de Montespan, was slated to succeed Louise de La Vallière, in the not-too-distant future, as the King's official mistress.

his several fine estates in Burgundy, his first—though not his last—taste of exile.

To relieve the tedium of exile in the provinces, Bussy devoted himself to developing the pen-portraits (which had so amused his audience at Roissy) into a full-length novel laid in ancient Gaul. Although he protested all his life that publication had been the last thing on his mind, a manuscript somehow found its way to Holland, to the press, to publication, in 1665, under the title *An Amorous History of the Gauls.* For anyone familiar with Court and Capital, it was child's play to tell who was who: King Theodosius of Gaul was none other than Louis XIV; Mme de Cheneville was none other than Mme de Sévigné, as she discovered to her dismay.

Cartoon though it was, still, the portrait of Mme de Sévigné retained just enough similarity to the original to be devastating. The somewhat disparaging references to her physical attributes—the mismatched eyes, the square-tipped nose, the less than perfectly shaped arms and hands—were less calculated to wound her vanity than the derogatory assessment of her character. Bussy painted her as pleasure-mad, intoxicated with flattery, inviting male advances:

> *The most convincing proof one can give her of one's intelligence is to sing her praises. She loves incense, loves to be loved; bestows praise in order to receive it. She likes men, all men, men in general, no matter what their age, their lineage, their merit or their profession. One and all appeal to her ... whether clad in a royal cloak or in a cassock, whether wielding a scepter or a pen! Among men, she prefers a lover to a friend; and among lovers, the frivolous rather than the serious-minded ... Temperamentally, she is cold ... at least if one can believe her husband, although it was—as he said—to her frigidity that he owed her virtuousness. Such fire as she had in her flamed in her wit, as if in compensation for her natural frigidity. To judge her by her actions, I am under the impression that she never violated the conjugal faith, but if one judges by intent rather than by action, that's another story. Frankly speaking, it is my belief that while her husband may not have appeared a cuckold in the sight of man, it may have been otherwise in the sight of God.*

"Madame de Cheneville is inconsistent to the very eyeballs!" the wicked sketch went on: "She has eyes of different colors, and the eyes being the mirror of the soul, this disparity serves as Nature's warning to those who approach her not to depend on her friendship."

Bussy did not spare her, to be sure, for what he considered her bad faith in the matter of the loan.

There are people who limit the bounds of their friendship on religious grounds, who would go to any length for their friends, so long as they do not offend God, in the process. People like that call themselves "friends up to the altar." There are other limits to the friendship of Mme de Cheneville: her friendship is constricted by her purse strings. She seems to put a higher value on financial security than on honor. Those who seek to justify her action attribute it to the fact that she takes counsel of people who can still remember the pangs of hunger, the pinch of poverty. [A jibe at the Bien Bon, *the parsimonious, the ignoble, the bourgeois Coulanges uncle.]*

His cousin's ignoble, bourgeois instincts were likewise discernible, Bussy pointed out in his malicious portrait, in the manner in which she fawned upon royalty:

For a woman of intelligence, a lady of quality, she allows herself to be somewhat overwhelmed by the grandeurs of the Court. When the Queen addresses her—if only, perhaps, to inquire with whom she came to Court—she is carried away with joy, and will find a way to bring up the subject long afterward, telling everyone whom she wishes to impress of how the Queen distinguished her. One night, after the King had danced with her, she came back to her seat near me, and said: "No one can deny that the King has qualities of greatness. I believe that his glory will overshadow that of all of his predecessors." I could not keep myself from laughing in her face, seeing on what she had based her judgment, and replied: "Who could doubt it, Madame, after what he has just done for you?" She was so pleased with His Majesty that I could see that she was on the verge of expressing her gratitude by crying, "Long Live the King!"

The King reacted even more vehemently than Mme de Sévigné to the publication of *The Amorous History of the Gauls.* The unfavorable light in which his Court and courtiers were depicted angered the monarch, jealous of his glory at home as well as abroad: a dread *Lettre de Cachet* was issued over Louis's signature, a royal order for incarceration; it was the Bastille for Bussy . . . there to languish thirteen months.

Not only to languish but to sicken. In May of 1666, obviously in dire need of medical attention, Bussy was removed from the grim Paris fortress on a litter, by special permission of the King, to the home of a surgeon-doctor. Three months of treatment restored Bussy to health to the point that he could travel home to Burgundy, whither he was exiled by the King, as it would prove, for life.

Mme de Sévigné, though not yet fully recovered from the blow to her pride and reputation, was moved to pity by Bussy's grievous plight, and was the first to reach his bedside when he was released from the Bastille. Rabutin blood called to Rabutin blood; the bond of consanguinity reasserted itself. (She felt it, she once wrote, "to the marrow of my bones": "We are close, we are of the same blood, we please each other, we love each other, we care about each other's well-being," she would later say to him, by letter.) The cousins, pride still rankling, each still convinced of the other's guilt, reached what was to prove an uneasy peace, and resumed their correspondence, at first haltingly, desultorily.

She could forgive, but not forget. He could beat his breast, cry *mea culpa*, and, in the same breath, seek to justify his actions. They returned endlessly to pick over the bones of the quarrel. She would grant him pardon but not until she had recounted, in detail, the anguish she had suffered because of what she called "that bitch of a book." She had heard rumors, she wrote him, of his poison-pen portrait when it had been privately circulated, passed from hand to hand, but had refused to believe that her friend, her cousin would ever allow her to be pilloried in print.

"But finally," she wrote, "came the unhappy day [the day of publication], when I could see—with my own mismatched eyes—what I had refused to believe possible. Had horns suddenly sprouted on my head, I could not have been more astonished. I read it, reread it, that cruel portrait, and would have found it very clever had the subject been anyone else but me, had the author been anyone else but you. To find oneself in print, in the hands of the whole wide world [elsewhere, in another letter, she added, "even translated into other languages"], to be a laughingstock throughout the provinces, where such things work irreparable damage to one's reputation, to find oneself in every library, to be dealt such a blow . . . and by whom!" It cost her, she wrote, "sleepless night after sleepless night."

Only an abject apology could satisfy her—a formal and humiliating acknowledgment of defeat: she used the metaphor of the code of the duello: the defeated duellist had to kneel before her and deliver up his sword, throwing himself on her mercy—death or pardon dependent on the victor. "Rise, Count, I do not wish to dispatch you on your knees—or take up your sword and resume combat. But it's better that I should grant you your life, and that we should live in peace. Admit to things as they happened, that's all I ask."

Bussy admitted: "I stand condemned for that portrait," he wrote in a letter, and made even handsomer apology, decades later, in the Preface of his *Letters* (published in 1697): "I can never sufficiently condemn myself, can never sufficiently regret having offended the prettiest woman in France, my close relative whom I have always loved, whose friendship for me I could never doubt. It is a stain on my life."

For Madame de Sévigné, the decade of the 1660's seemed ill-omened; was the comet that streaked the night skies in 1664 a portent of evil? So a superstitious seventeenth century interpreted it: Mme de Sévigné wrote a friend that she "would stay up all that night to see it."* That decade of the 1660's would see her name involved in not one but two ugly scandals, the Fouquet affair causing even more of a sensation than the publication of Bussy's salacious profiles.

It was effrontery on the part of the Finance Minister to outdo his royal master in magnificence, in splendor; to honor him with a fête more lavish than anything hitherto seen in the Île de France. At Vaux-le-Vicomte, on a night in May in 1661, the two hundred water-jets spouted heavenward, the fifty fountains played as did the twenty-four strolling violinists; nymphs danced their way—to Lully's music—through green groves and parterres of tulips; Molière's first comedy had its première under the stars that gala night; fireworks illuminated the heavens; Vatel, the premier chef of France (perhaps of all French culinary history), paraded his gastronomical triumphs before the royal party and hundreds of other distinguished guests.

The monarch construed this ostentatious entertainment as an affront to majesty; could scarcely restrain himself from arresting his host—in all his splendor—on the spot. It took his every ounce of self-control to bide his time, to wait until September to order D'Artagnan (Captain of the Muske-teers, one of the famous "Three") to seize the Superintendent of Finance and convey him to the Bastille. The official charges would be treason (a Crime of State) and malversation (misuse of office by fraudulent practice), but actually Fouquet's crime had been to take Richelieu and Mazarin as role-

*The night of December 17, 1664.

models: where Louis XIII was content to be dominated by his all-powerful ministers, Louis XIV was not. ("Not a passport is to be issued except at my command," he instructed his High Council.) It was Fouquet's fatal error that he failed to recognize the difference between the two kings, father and son, that he failed to comprehend that this young monarch intended to reverse the political practice of half a century.

Another fatal error of Fouquet's—fatal, that is, to his friends—was to have preserved intact his personal correspondence along with his official papers. The authorities, confiscating all his effects, came upon one coffer filled with love letters, some in the hand of ladies notorious for their amours, others signed by *grandes dames* hitherto above suspicion.

As rumor ran riot in Paris, the shocking news reached Mme de Sévigné in Brittany (where she travelled regularly to supervise the extensive Sévigné family properties). There, she learned to her dismay that the soon-to-be-famous coffer of Fouquet's was said to contain letters in her hand.

She panicked at the thought, writing letter after letter to her Paris friends to ask not only that the latest news be sent her by every courier but, more important still, to entreat them all to rise promptly to her defense in the scandal attaching itself to her name.

To the Abbé Ménage, her literary mentor, she wrote on October 9, 1661:

> *I am sure that you know how distressed I was to have found myself among the Superintendent's correspondents. It is true that it was neither a romantic impulse nor a matter of personal interest that prompted me to write to him. It should be clear that it was in the interest of Monsieur de La Trousse. But that does not mean that I do not bitterly regret that my letters were filed away among his [Fouquet's] love letters, nor is it pleasant to find myself named along with others whose motives were not so innocent as mine. In such an emergency, I need my friends to straighten out those who are less friendly toward me. I believe you are generous enough to want to disseminate such evidence as Mme de La Fayette will have for you.*

When she shortly wrote to thank him for his prompt good offices in her behalf, she would ask him "to thank Mlle de Scudéry for hers, as well."

Her former preceptor, Chapelain, wrote immediately to Mme de La Trousse, the aunt of Mme de Sévigné, to assure her that he had needed "no solicitation to serve as her [Mme de Sévigné's] champion" on what he termed "this abominable occasion where her name was included with many persons less virtuous than she." And he wrote, in the same mail, to assure Mme de Sévigné herself that "There is not one among your friends

41

who has not done combat in your cause. You can live and sleep in peace."

There is extant an interesting exchange of letters between Mme de Sévigné and Simon Arnauld, Marquis de Pomponne, a longtime friend, a distinguished statesman and diplomat, a member of the Fouquet faction. They wrote to commiserate with one another on the sad plight in which their good friend Fouquet found himself: "But what in the world are we to think," Mme de Sévigné inquired in a letter to Pomponne, dated October 11, 1661,

about the contents of those coffers? Would you ever have believed it possible that my poor little letters—confined to the subject of Monsieur de La Trousse's marriage and La Trousse family affairs—could have so inexplicably been filed away? Whatever small comfort I can derive from those who do me the justice of believing that I had no other correspondence with him save that, I am still greatly disconcerted to be obliged to defend my actions and vainly, perhaps, vis-à-vis a thousand people who will not be convinced of the truth. I know that you readily understand the anguish to a heart like mine. I conjure you to speak out on what you know about all this. I cannot have too many friends on this occasion . . .

The friend who rushed most effectively to her defense did so unsolicited, did so unexpectedly. It was none other than her cousin, the Count de Bussy, who—after a three-year estrangement—raised his voice in Court and Capital to proclaim her innocence; and loud enough to drown out skeptic titters. Bussy was genuinely convinced that Mme de Sévigné was not to be numbered among Fouquet's mistresses. So vehemently did Bussy espouse her cause that he and his brother-in-law, de Rouville, came close to blows: "It is amusing to see you of all people defend Mme de Sévigné after having drawn so malicious a sketch of her," de Rouville commented. To which Bussy objected: "In all my angry tirade against her, I never cast aspersions on her reputation." "In any event," de Rouville persisted, "it ill becomes you to champion her after the scandal you caused with her portrait." "Let me remind you, sir," Bussy countered with Gallic logic, "that I condone only such scandals as I have myself occasioned." Mme de Sévigné took steps to let Bussy know how deeply moved she was by his championship of her cause. Bussy joyously seized the olive branch she proffered. Their intimacy and their correspondence were resumed.

The question that troubled her friends in 1661, the question that has haunted her biographers, her admirers and her critics to this day, is whether the Pandora's Box of Fouquet's letter collection contained only letters written by her on the matter of her cousin's marriage—as she insists—or whether the La Trousse letter served as an alibi for other letters of a more incriminating nature.

Chapelain was elated to be able to write, on November 7, that no less an authority than the Marquise de Montausier, Lady of Honor to the Queen, had assured him that there had been no letters at all from Mme de Sévigné in Fouquet's "shameless collection." Mme de Montausier had had it from the Queen who had had it from the King! But that is a direct contradiction of what Secretary of State Le Tellier told the Count de Bussy, as Bussy related it in his *Mémoires*, intending it as a vindication of his cousin's honor:

I implored Le Tellier to tell me whether among the love letters found in the Superintendent's coffers there were any from Mme de Sévigné, as rumor had it. He tells me that such letters of hers as had been found there were of a totally innocent nature, nondescript letters, letters about this and that, letters of no significance whatsoever.

Which was it—a letter relating to La Trousse's marriage, as was claimed by Mme de Sévigné herself, or harmless little notes such as pass between friends in the course of social contact throughout the years, according to Le Tellier, or no letters whatsoever of any sort or description, as in the words of the Queen via Mme de Montausier? Of the three versions, which one has the ring of truth to it? The truth could be established only if the contents of the famous coffers had come to light. They never have.

Chapelain railed against Fouquet for his crimes: "Was it not enough," he inquired rhetorically of Mme de Sévigné, by letter, "to have brought about the ruin of the State, of the King," etcetera, etcetera: "Was it necessary for him, as well, to treat confidential letters as trophies of the chase, to compile a shameful record of his amorous conquests?" Mme de Sévigné could wish with all her heart that Fouquet had burned that whole accursed letter collection of his, could wish that he had not so damaged her reputation, but nothing, no one could turn her against her "poor dear unfortunate friend" whose misfortune had taken the form of three years of imprisonment and interrogation in the Bastille.

By the time Fouquet finally came to trial on November 17, 1664, the Marquis de Pomponne—in disgrace as a "creature of Fouquet's"—had been banished to his estates at Pomponne, on the Marne, some forty kilometers from Paris. So that it was upon the daily letters of Mme de Sévigné that

Pomponne depended for news of the trial of their mutual friend—forty letters in all, constituting a precious document on the legal process of Old Régime France—all forty fortunately preserved by Pomponne. A special tribunal had been set up by royal order to sit in judgment, in the Chamber of the Arsenal, on the former Superintendent of Finance—with Mme de Sévigné's good friend, Olivier d'Ormesson, appointed one of the two Court Recorders, one of her principal sources of information on the daily court proceedings.

Not just the account of Mme de Sévigné—clearly prejudiced in Fouquet's favor—but all accounts agreed that Fouquet's defense was magnificent, that he handled himself brilliantly throughout long weeks of interrogation and accusation, that he effectively withstood the attack of all the mighty legal battery assigned by the King to prosecute him. The evidence against him was not conclusive, the charges of treason and dishonesty were not substantiated, but there is little doubt that it was Fouquet's head the King had demanded of the judges.

As the weeks dragged by, the strain began to tell on Mme de Sévigné: she complained that she "was no longer recognizable." "I don't think I can endure much more!" she cried in her letter of December 5: "Monsieur d'Ormesson has requested me not to see him again until after the judgment is rendered. He is a member of the conclave, and wants to have no further contact with the world. He affects a great reserve and makes no comment on what I say, but he listens, and I had the satisfaction, as I bade him goodbye, of telling him what I think." "Goodbye, my dear Monsieur," she ended her letter to Pomponne, "I am so sad, so overwhelmed with grief that I cannot write another line ..." On December 19 she wrote: "These days pass slowly. The uncertainty is harrowing ... It will be a true miracle if things go as we hope ... still, in the bottom of my heart, I somehow find a ray of hope. I do not know whence it came or how long it will persist. It is too faint to permit me to sleep in peace ... Should the verdict be as we hope, it would be my pleasure instantly to dispatch a messenger at full gallop to bring you that joyous news ..." (Were it otherwise, she wrote on December 11, "I just do not know whether I could bear it . . . .")

Once, and only once, she managed to catch a glimpse of the prisoner's pallid face: "I must tell you what I have done," she wrote to Pomponne, the night of November 28:

Just imagine—some ladies proposed to me that we go and station ourselves at a house directly across from the Arsenal to see our poor friend as he came out. I wore a mask. I caught sight of him as he approached from a fairly long way off. Monsieur D'Artagnan was with him, while fifty Musketeers [in their blue velvet surtouts marked with a silver cross] followed thirty or forty paces to the rear. He seemed preoccupied, caught up in a revery. As for me, when I beheld him, my legs began to tremble, my heart to beat so fast that I could hardly stand. As they came close to us, D'Artagnan—who was walking just behind him—gave him a signal to call his attention to our presence. Where- upon, he doffed his hat and bowed, while that dazzling smile so famil- iar to us both adorned his lips. I do not think he recognized me, but I confess that I was strangely affected when I saw him disappear through that low doorway. If only you knew how miserable one is when one is born with a heart like mine, you would, I know, take pity on me . . .

By mid-December, as the summations droned on, rumors flew: some among the twenty-two judges loosened their tongues; there was talk of the direst punishment: the headman's axe, the stake, the wheel. In the beginning it had been easy for the man in the street to hate Fouquet as the functionary responsible for the evils of taxation, but, as the trial progressed, it was he who had somehow won the sympathy of the crowds.

Everyone is concerned about this important affair [Mme de Sévigné wrote Pomponne on December 17]. One talks of nothing else. One gives one's reasons, one draws one's conclusions, one counts on one's fingers, one grows emotional, one hopes, one fears, one curses, one wishes this or wishes that, one hates, one admires, one is sad, one is overwhelmed—in fine, my poor Monsieur, it is an extraordinary state in which we find ourselves, at this hour.

By December 19 ("a very hopeful day for us") she had the count on the judges: six in favor of the death penalty; seven, against. On the twentieth she could write: "Praise God, Monsieur, and thank Him. Our poor dear friend is saved!" On the final count, the vote had been nine in favor of the death penalty; thirteen (including Monsieur d'Ormesson, who would pay with a blighted legal career for his integrity), against.

On Sunday, December 21, she wrote:

I almost died of fear that someone else would have the pleasure of being the first to reach you with the good news! My courier was in no great hurry, planning to spend the night en route at Livry. Fortunately, he arrived ahead of all the others, according to his report. My God, I can imagine how sweet, how profoundly moving that news was to you! How rare such moments are in life—when heart and soul are suddenly relieved of stress and anguish! It will take me a long time to recover from the joy I experienced yesterday. Indeed, it was almost too much for me. I could scarcely bear it . . .

She had heard from reliable sources, she added, "that the King was changing the sentence of lifelong exile to one of lifelong imprisonment." (A not unusual precaution, although Mme de Sévigné bemoaned it: there was cause to fear that a man as familiar as Fouquet with French affairs of state might constitute a threat to French national interests abroad.)

Mme de Sévigné's "reliable source" had been reliable, indeed: "This morning at eleven o'clock," she reported to Pomponne on Monday, December 22, "a carriage was ready [at the Bastille] for Monsieur Fouquet, who stepped in, accompanied by four men. Monsieur D'Artagnan with forty or fifty Musketeers will escort him to Pignerol"—a dread French prison-fortress in the Piedmontese Alps.

It seemed to her a cruel and unusual punishment, contrary to the custom of the times, to deprive Fouquet of the company of his wife. Borrowing a verse from the *Aeneid*—and quoting it in the original—Mme de Sévigné demanded to know, as had Virgil, "Whether the hearts of the Gods could harbor such a violent anger?" "But, no!" she exclaimed in answer to her own question. "It is not from on high that vengeance so low and cruel as this originates . . . not from the heart of the master. Vengeance is being done in his name, profaning it . . ." It was not Louis XIV, she seems to say, but Jean Baptiste Colbert—the cold and vengeful Minister of Commerce and Internal Affairs, former rival and archenemy of Fouquet—who was responsible for the severity of Fouquet's sentence. She had reason to be discreet: Pomponne's mail had, in all probability, been placed under surveillance; her letters, probably unsealed. It would have been the height of folly to criticize an absolute monarch, holding the power of life and death over his subjects.

In addition to which, she had a purely feminine reason to watch her step: she had her beautiful, twenty-year-old daughter to think of—Mademoiselle de Sévigné, who had made her Court debut in 1663, who was, even then, in December of 1664, rehearsing in a ballet to be danced before the King in January of 1665.

VII

During his years of exile on St. Helena, Napoleon read Madame de Sévigné's letters to Pomponne and pronounced himself of the opinion that the Marquise had been in love with Fouquet. "In reading the reports of the Fouquet trial in *The Letters of Mme de Sévigné*" (according to Volume II of the *Memorial from St. Helena*), "he [Napoleon] remarked that her interest was too warm, too keen, too fond for simple friendship." Ironically, it was in Mme de Sévigné's letters to Pomponne on the subject of Fouquet's trial that the once-powerful Minister might have found the expression of tenderness and affection that he had been unable to elicit from her in palmier days: the very letters he would have cherished for his collection of *billets-doux* were addressed not to him but to Pomponne.

Whether it was a matter of "simple friendship" or an amorous liaison remains a matter of speculation. There is the possibility that Mme de Sévigné did not herself realize how strong an attraction Fouquet exercised over her until he fell victim to misfortune, and was lost to her. The Count de Bussy point-blank refused to credit the rumor that she had been Fouquet's mistress, but he was apparently, at that time, in the minority, as his alter-cation with his brother-in-law proves. Tallemant des Réaux, quick as he was to indict a lady's honor, never did so in the case of Mme de Sévigné, calling her "*une honnête femme*," a woman of good repute, of honor, of moral integrity.*

Her reputation has been the subject of endless debate, debate *ad nauseam*, ever since the day of her death, since the publication of her *Letters* which assured her an international reputation, literarily speaking. The long procession of worshipful biographers who have insisted on her virtuousness reflect a moral concern or preoccupation characteristic of other centuries, particularly the nineteenth and early twentieth. To this generation, the debate appears a tempest in a teapot, the subject, irrelevant—save only as Mme de Sévigné's sexual license or sexual abstinence affected her emotional stability, and, thereby, her relation with her daughter.

*Tallemant's *Historiettes*, it must be remembered, were completed circa 1657, prior to the Fouquet scandal.

If Mme de Sévigné loved Fouquet—or the Count du Lude or the Chevalier de Meré or the Duke de Rohan or any of the other aspirants to her favor—and chose to enter into a liaison with him, certainly she needed fear no censure from her peer-group, wherein an almost total sexual license prevailed: the King, with his succession of official and unofficial mistresses (some of the most exalted ladies in the land on the list), with his eight legitimized bastard sons and daughters, set no lofty moral standards for his Court.

Whether or not Mme de Sévigné was Fouquet's mistress, she was indubitably her own, subject to no man's dictate, financially independent, and free—unless those bourgeois moral scruples with which she had been imbued in the Coulanges's household served to restrict her. She was young, in her mid-twenties at the time of her husband's death; an attractive, healthy woman, and a vigorous one, walking many miles a day, horseback riding, hunting. She was highly emotional, romantic, responsive to love and affection. Would it not have been unnatural had she never again, from the day of her husband's death, assumed an intimate relation—a sexual relation—with another man? If she was frigid, as Bussy claimed her husband had claimed, might it not have been a frigidity for which her husband was unwilling to accept the responsibility? If he failed to arouse her passion, it may have been that—roué that he was—his own libido was less responsive to a virginal, innocent young bride than to a sexual sophisticate, a wanton like La Belle Lolo, for the sake of whose favors he perished.

Sainte-Beuve, the doyen of French literary critics, categorized Mme de Sévigné as "utterly lacking in sensuality." (Sainte-Beuve's arbitrary judgment calls to mind that of the Marquis de Lassay, who declared that Madame de Maintenon's life had been chaste from the day she was widowed by the death of the poet Scarron. "How in the world," the Marquise de Lassay demanded, "can you speak with such authority on such a matter as that?") Sainte-Beuve notwithstanding, one gathers from her letters that Mme de Sévigné faced life with all her senses open: she was enraptured by the autumnal splendor of the Livry woods, by the quality of moonlight filtering through the treetops at Les Rochers. Her descriptions of the rich, the golden butter of the Pré Valé, of the gamy ortolans and the luscious figs of Provence are mouth-watering, connotative of a supremely sensuous woman.

If Mme de Sévigné did draw the line at intimacy in her relations with men, there is evidence on every side that she was in love with love, that she enjoyed and encouraged men's attentions, men's advances, that she seemed to put off as long as possible saying an outright "No," and then made it sound much like "Yes." Tallemant as well as Bussy commented that her conversation was often provocative. She was a flirt, a tease, what the French call an "*allumeuse*," a lighter of fires. Having lit them, could she always put them out? Young, pretty, avid for pleasure and admiration, she had—by more than one report—a giddiness about her, a high-pitched gaiety suggestive of a nervous—perhaps, a sexual—tension. She seems to have played a dangerous game; did it ever get out of hand? ("A dangerous lady!" the poet Scarron called her.)

Would her position have been so precarious, her reputation so vulnerable at the time the Fouquet scandal broke, if she had not been already widely known as bold, daring, gallant, sportive in her manner and in her conversation, if her name had not already appeared too often in the rhymed gazettes, in amorous madrigals, in widely distributed pen-portraits?

The question of whether she did or did not have illicit relations with Fouquet or any other of the many men who sought her favors is not as interesting as the question of why she did not remarry. In her day and time and social milieu, most widows of her age did remarry, at the very first opportunity. Young, attractive, of good family, endowed with a considerable amount of worldly goods, she must have received numerous proposals of marriage. And rejected them. The argument that she eschewed marriage because of her two children is not convincing: it was precisely for her children's sake that she might have been expected to take a second husband—if for no other reason than because the children needed a father. She herself could, this time, make the choice—the suitor best suited to her own and her children's needs. Indeed, it might have been construed as her duty to provide her fatherless son and daughter with a *paterfamilias*.

On the other hand, she could not have failed to take into consideration the fact that, under the laws of Old Régime France, to take a husband was to give him absolute authority over her life. For a woman with a strong will and a mind of her own, freedom such as she enjoyed was not easily relinquished. Her own conjugal life had been a disaster; her experience of that licentious world in which she lived had confirmed her in her cynicism about marriage: no matter how fond and tender the suitor showed himself while he pressed his suit, he might prove, with the years, an unkind and unfaithful husband. Her views on the matter are known; she speaks for herself, in a letter dated July 12, 1690. Apropos of heavy battle casualties in the King's victorious armies, she expresses her sympathy with the mothers who lost sons—not with the young wives who lost husbands: "A young widow is not greatly to be pitied," she wrote, "she will enjoy being her own mistress—or changing masters."

Whether or not she was ever tempted to remarry constitutes another mystery: whether she ever hesitated on the brink, whether any man so attracted her as to make her waver in her decision not to remarry—if, actually, it was a decision at which she had consciously arrived or merely a state of uncertainty never to be resolved in the affirmative. The only proposal of marriage of which she makes mention in her *Letters* came when she was fifty-nine years old from the Duke de Luynes, whom she refused, *tabouret* and all. (Snob that she has been accused of being, the title of duchess and the *tabouret* or folding stool to which only peers and peeresses of the realm were entitled in the presence of the King and Queen must have been sorely tempting.) She would write, once, years later, that if it had been the intensity of her love for her daughter which had preserved her from temptation—the temptation of licit or illicit amorous involvement—then she was grateful for it. At that time, when her daughter was in her twenties and thirties, her maternal love had not reached that fever pitch to which it mounted later. If it is true that she abstained, subsequent to her husband's death, from any close, any intimate, any sexual relation with a man, then the imperative of love in her life may well have taken the form of that excessive, obsessive, abnormal—if not incestuous—love for her daughter which was to compli- cate their relation. It was not, properly speaking, a maternal love but, rather, a maternal passion—"a passion that was twisted and morbid," by Virginia Woolf's analysis.

There is no indication—no comment by friends or acquaintances—that leads one to believe that there was anything exceptional about Mme de Sévigné's maternal love during her children's youth. Had she been a more zealous mother than most, more attentive than most to her young children, that characteristic would almost certainly have been brought out in one of the three pen-portraits of which she was the subject in the late 1650's. In that era, in Mme de Sévigné's economic stratum, children were never allowed to be a nuisance to adults, were handed along from wet nurse to nursemaid, from nursemaid to governess, from governess to tutor. There is no reason to think it was otherwise with Mme de Sévigné. It would appear that, at that period, her life was oriented toward the salon, not the nursery. Her name appears repeatedly in the "society columns," the gazettes: she is a social butterfly, missing never a fête, never a gala. The only allusion to her in a maternal role, at that stage of her life, is to be found in the *Mémoires* of the Abbé Arnauld, brother of the Marquis de Pomponne. "I seem to see her still," he wrote of that day in 1657, "as she appeared to me for the first time, riding in the back of an open carriage, sitting between Monsieur, her son, and Mademoiselle, her daughter—just such a trio as the poets sing when they describe Latona with her young son, Apollo, and her young daughter, Diana . . . Mother and child, a vision of grace and beauty!"

We are vouchsafed that one glimpse of Charles de Sévigné at age nine, in 1657, the young Apollo—and then, no more. That is the last we hear of him until he springs full-fledged, from a letter of his mother's dated August 28, 1668, at which date he is sailing off to the island of Crete to defend the town of Candie (Heraklion) from the Infidel. France, under the banner of the Church, was mounting an expeditionary force, in 1668, to assist the Venetians in repulsing the Turks, and Charles de Sévigné, age twenty, decided on a quixotic impulse to volunteer. "My son has departed for Candie," Mme de Sévigné wrote to the Count de Bussy:

> *This is a fantasy that has captured his imagination. He discussed it with such dignitaries as Monsieur de Turenne [his mother's onetime admirer], with the Cardinal de Retz [a relative on the Sévigné side], with Monsieur de La Rochefoucauld [the Duke, a close family friend]. All of these august personages so heartily approved the project that the decision was made without even consulting me. At last, he has gone. I have wept bitter tears. I am sorely afflicted, and will not have a moment's peace of mind until the voyage is over. I envision all the attendant perils, and the prospect is killing me, but, still, mothers have little choice, little voice on such occasions.*

Absolutely nothing is known of Charles de Sévigné's education, except that it was evidently the very best available; he was a man of erudition. One can only conclude that excellent tutors had been selected for him in his boyhood, and that he had been sent to a good college for his higher education, the college at Clermont,* in all probability, where the emphasis was on the classics. Charles, when we meet him in his twenties, is an intellectual. And a voluptuary. And a spendthrift. And eminently loveable, winning, charming and gracious, like his mother—so many of the things his sister was not. Charles was endowed with a warmth, a quality of mildness and sweetness entirely lacking in his sister. There was far greater similarity between his tastes, his moods and those of his mother than between his mother's and his sister's. In actual fact, he and his mother were far more congenial than his mother and his sister. The harmony of the mother-son relation was unmarred by the dissonances present in the mother-daughter relation.

Charles's sister, Françoise-Marguerite de Sévigné, was also an intellectual, and had probably enjoyed some of the same educational facilities afforded

*Today, the Lycée de Louis-le-Grand.

her brother. We have, however, only fragmentary information concerning her early life and schooling. It was customary for girls to be sent to a convent for instruction at an early age, and Mme de Sévigné did not break with custom in this respect. She makes occasional, oblique references in her *Letters* to her daughter's convent days—or months or years, however long it may have been. We know of at least two convents at which Mademoiselle de Sévigné spent some time as a child, as a girl: the Convent of Sainte-Marie in Paris and the Visitandine Convent at Nantes, where she was placed during at least one of her mother's frequent sojourns in Brittany. "You were ten years old when you were at Sainte-Marie in Paris," Mme de Sévigné would reminisce almost twenty years later, in 1675: "Just the other day, I came across a letter of yours written from there, in which you called me your *'Bonne Maman'*." In another letter, written in 1676, she makes a point of the fact that she considered it barbaric to ship girls off to convents— though she did it just the same: "I wonder how I had the courage to do it; only the thought of seeing you often and of bringing you home shortly made me resolve upon that barbaric custom . . ."

In the seventeenth-century French convent, the curriculum was notoriously skimpy, few nuns being qualified to instruct in anything beyond the Catechism. A young lady of quality would be taught how to scrawl a letter of condolence or of congratulation; how to sew a fine seam; how to raise her voice in song, preferably religious; how to make a graceful entry into and exit from a salon; how to make a distinction in the mode of addressing a Princess of the Blood or a Duchess, as compared to a mere Marquise or Countess.

Mademoiselle de Sévigné's erudition could only have been the product of the excellent tutors and preceptors provided by her mother, who had enjoyed similar advantages. Mme de Sévigné probably did not actually instruct her daughter, but she supervised her education and worked closely with her: Mme de Sévigné later refers to their having read Italian poetry aloud together, in her daughter's youth. In 1639, with the publication of Descartes's *Discours de la Méthode*—a cornerstone of modern philosophy—scientific thought took on a new dimension, a new importance in the curriculum, as was evidenced by Mlle de Sévigné's turn of mind, as compared to her mother's (Mme de Sévigné made much of her daughter's capacity for abstract thought, her own inability to cope with abstractions).*

The faculty assembled by Mme de Sévigné for her daughter's instruction undoubtedly included a dancing master, undoubtedly the best in Paris,

---

*It was the Abbé de La Mousse to whom Mlle de Sévigné would owe her self-acknowledged competence in Cartesian philosophy.

who trained her so well that she would be invited to dance leading roles in the ballets popular at the Court of Louis XIV (as they had been at the Court of his father, Louis XIII).

With the ballet, in that century in France, regarded as a manly—even a kingly—exercise, Louis XIV starred in the lavish palace productions for which splendorous costumes and stage sets were designed by the leading artists of the realm, for which the foremost composers of the day were commissioned to write the score, and the foremost poets to write the lyrics for the songs which accompanied the dancing. Louis XIV, in his salad days, was known in Paris as the King of Ballet. (It was to this ballet mania of the seventeenth-century French Court that modern ballet owes its origin.)

In 1663, Mademoiselle de Sévigné, at age seventeen, made her Court debut in the Royal Ballet des Arts, assigned an important part as one of four Shepherdesses, dancing with the King, himself, in the role of Shepherd. On that stage, she had joined an illustrious company: one of the other three Shepherdesses was Madame (Henrietta Stuart, daughter of Charles I of England*), wife of Monsieur, the Duke d'Orléans (brother of the King); Louise de La Vallière, the King's Favorite, was another Shepherdess; the fourth, last but not least, was Athénaïs de Mortemart-Rochechuart, the future Marquise de Montespan, who had designs on La Vallière's place.

Mlle de Sévigné evidently held her own in even a quartet so distinguished as that. The librettist Benserade referred to her as, "That beauty/ Who had reached the age/ Where she can distinguish between Wolf and Shepherd." Loret, the gazetteer, reporting in rhyme on the gala performance of the Royal Ballet des Arts, sang her praises as, "A dazzling young beauty/ Daughter of a ravishingly beautiful Mother." And the Marquis de Tréville, a connoisseur of female flesh, predicted that "Hers was a beauty to set the world afire."

Mme de Sévigné must have beamed to see the sensation her daughter caused on her first appearance at the Palace of the Louvre. (Mme de Sévigné could never—not as long as she lived—behold a well-danced minuet without comparing the grace and skill of the dancer to that of her daughter, invariably in her daughter's favor.)

In 1664, Monsieur, the King's brother, invited Mlle de Sévigné to take part in a ballet to be produced under his auspices at his Palais Royal—he, dancing the role of a Marine God; she, that of a Water Nymph, evoking another paean of praise from Benserade for her grace and beauty.

Success followed upon success. The season of 1665 saw the production

---

*Who had recently lost his head to Cromwell.

of a ballet entitled *The Birth of Venus*, in which Louis XIV danced the role of Alexander, and Mlle de Sévigné that of Omphale.

In July of 1668, the radiant and handsome young King was host at a midsummer's night dream of a fête in the torch-lit gardens of Versailles. At the exclusive supper party which followed the première of a Molière comedy, Mme de Sévigné and her daughter were seated at the King's own table—a distinction that aroused comment. It was a moment at which the King was, so to speak, between love affairs: he was clearly tiring of the perhaps too sweet, too modest, too long-suffering La Vallière; he was eyeing the beauties of his Court, and the Court was waiting with bated breath to discover upon which one his favor would be bestowed. His devout, dumpy Queen, Maria Theresa of Spain, had by then learned to control her violent jealousy, learned the necessity of total submission to her adored husband's will: he came nightly to her bed to perform his dynastic duties; the Queen had trained herself to be content with that—and with his meticulous courtesy.

In 1668, the Court buzzed with gossip: Mlle de Sévigné was seen by the monarch's inner circle as "*un morceau royal*," a tidbit for the King. The name of the Marquis de Villeroy (nicknamed the "Charming" and one of the King's favorite companions) was mentioned in a popular street song in the list of Mlle de Sévigné's admirers. But was there another name —more exalted still—linked with hers, that season? So rumor had it: a rumor Mme de Montmorency wrote to report to the Count de Bussy, in exile on one or another of his Burgundian estates: "Madame [the King's sister-in-law]," she wrote, "is doing what she can to promote Mme de Soubise with the King. On the other side, La Feuillade* does what he can to interest the King in Mlle de Sévigné . . . not that that interest is, as yet, very marked."

Bussy's reply scarcely does him credit: "I would be very pleased, indeed, were the King to take a fancy to Mlle de Sévigné, for that young lady is very close to me, and His Majesty could not do better in his choice of a mistress." Bussy, of course, had visions of the King's new Favorite securing her cousin's pardon, his recall to the Court and to royal favor. It must be said in his defense that, in that day and time, there was scarcely a father, a brother or a husband in all France—no matter how lofty his title—who would not have rejoiced to see his daughter, sister or wife become the King's concubine. No less a nobleman than the Duke de Rohan sought to pique the monarch's interest in the Princess de Soubise, the Duke's own sister†:

---

*The Duke de la Feuillade.

†The Princess never became an "official mistress," made only random surreptitious visits to the royal couch, but those sporadic assignations proved the foundation of the Soubise family fortunes.

"Every woman was born with the ambition to become the King's Favorite," according to Primi Visconti, the Italian mystagogue at the Court of the Sun King. The French nobility had become totally dependent on the King's favor, the King's bounty: the King was the fountainhead of fortune and honor; from his hand, all blessings flowed.

The royal adulterer was encouraged to envision himself as an Olympian above all mortal men as above their laws. France's greatest poet condoned the pagan ethic in immortal verse: "To share with Jupiter," Molière wrote in *Amphitryon*, "can carry no dishonor."

The boon of royal favor was destined to be bestowed not upon Mlle de Sévigné but upon Athénaïs, Marquise de Montespan, as proud, brazen, beautiful and intelligent a creature as was to be found in the Sun King's kingdom, no modest violet like her predecessor. ("He had turned to her," she said, "only because he considered that he owed it to his public to have the most beautiful woman in the kingdom as his mistress."*) She could soar to meet the monarch on his Olympian heights; she was a match for him in his superbity, she could queen it at Versailles more effectively than could the Queen herself.†

There was a diamantine quality about the Marquise de Montespan—a brilliance, sharpness, hardness—lacking in Mlle de Sévigné. An introvert like Mlle de Sévigné—an essentially private person, reserved, inhibited, aloof, hypersensitive—may have known herself well enough to know that the role of official mistress was not for her, may have deliberately taken herself out of the running—if she was ever really in it.

La Fontaine, in dedicating his fable *The Amorous Lion* to Mlle de Sévigné, describes her as "A model for the Graces/ Born entirely beautiful/ Born indifferent." La Fontaine's adjective "indifferent" may have been a euphemism for haughty, arrogant. Benserade's lyrics for the *Birth of Venus* ballet show her as cold, reserved, remote, unbending:

> *She could stand by and watch*
> *Her most devoted lover perish*
> *Not deigning to assist him*
> *By so much as a glance*

---

*Mme de Montespan is quoted in the *Mémoires* of Mme de Caylus.

†Curiously enough, the Marquis de Montespan was the only husband in the Age of Louis XIV to make a scene about his wife's liaison with the monarch. He dared to object to sharing with Jupiter, declared himself in mourning for his wife, and drove up to the Château of Saint-Germain in a coach draped in black and decorated with antlers' horns, the classic symbol of the cuckold. He reaped prison and exile for his folly and intransigence.

A trait the maiden inherited from her Mother
That good lady with her superhuman courage
As beautiful and resolutely chaste as ever.

Mlle de Sévigné presents an enigma: was she cold and virtuous, as by the poets' lament? Or was she gallant, amorously inclined, as contemporary gossip has it? Street songs in 1665, hinted at a liaison between Mlle de Sévigné and the charming Villeroy; the *Mémoires* of Primi Visconti perpetuate in print the Italian Ambassador's claim to have enjoyed the favors of young Mlle de Sévigné. Her reputation, like her mother's before her, suffered some slight tarnish. Thanks to her beauty and excellence in the dance, she had been taken up by the fast set, the inner circle of Louis XIV's young Court. Would it have been more discreet on the part of Mme de Sévigné to have discouraged her daughter's intimacy with the King's coterie, already famous for its disregard of moral scruples? Had she wished to, could she have done so gracefully? Perhaps a move from Paris to the Château of Les Rochers, on a plea of business in Brittany? Remembering the Count de Bussy's lampoon of her obsequiousness in the shadow of the throne, it is more likely that Mme de Sévigné was carried away by the compliment paid her daughter at the Louvre. The flattering reception accorded Mlle de Sévigné at the Court of France could not but have raised her mother's hopes sky-high. She may well have abandoned herself to dreams of a splendid destiny for the girl, a brilliant matrimonial match which would assure Mlle de Sévigné the lofty position, the resounding title, the fortune and the honor for which that paragon seemed to have been created. But Mlle de Sévigné's hour of glory was soon over: her course had been that of a shooting star, flashing bright across the skies only to disappear into the darkness.

VIII

If Mademoiselle de Sévigné was, as the Count de Bussy called her, "the prettiest girl in all France," why then was she not yet wed, not yet affianced, in 1667, at the age of twenty? Not yet in 1668, at the age of twenty-one? It was most unusual, in that era, for a girl not to be married in her early 'teens.

Mlle de Sévigné had shown no inclination toward the religious life. Was it possible that such a paragon of beauty and intelligence would turn out to be an old maid? Were there no suitors for a young lady with a handsome dowry and a noble name, a famous beauty, celebrated by gazetteers and poets? Was she, perhaps, too famous, too highly publicized, too much in the limelight to suit the more conservative noble families with eligible sons and heirs? On the other hand, it may have been her family's lack of influence in royal circles that proved a handicap: her widowed mother had no husband to curry favor with the King; on the Rabutin side, the Count de Bussy was in disgrace; and, as for the Sévignés, having chosen the wrong side in the civil wars of the Fronde, they had no credit, no Court standing.

Or was it Françoise-Marguerite de Sévigné herself who put off prospective suitors? It would seem that exquisite as she was of face and form, as clever and well-educated, she lacked warmth and grace and charm, failed to win or hold the men who were originally attracted to her by her wit and beauty. She and her mother may have thought no one on earth good enough for her, as Saint-Pavin's verses indicate:

> *And so the world is just too small*
> *To find in it anyone at all*
> *Who could be deemed worthy of her.*
> *And the belle, knowing it well,*
> *Disdains all, finds none acceptable.*

The madrigal, intended as a lavish compliment, yet carries a hint of arrogance, of a sense of superiority, a narcissism encouraged by her mother as well as by the poets.

The criticism levelled at her, all her life and after her death, would focus on this hauteur, this overbearing and disagreeable manner of hers. Her features may have been flawless, as her mother and the portraitists agreed, but her expression was forbidding, supercilious, chilling; observers thought frequently to detect a sneer. The Count de Bussy's judgment on his cousin was not flattering: "She is intelligent, but hers is an intelligence tinged with bitterness. Her superbity is beyond bearing, and will lead her into many follies. She will make as many enemies for herself as her mother has made friends."

One after another, a number of matrimonial prospects presented themselves and were considered; negotiations were undertaken, eventually abandoned. In 1666, Mlle de Sévigné seemed on the brink of marrying Charles des Montiers de Mérinville: a match was in the making, foundered on financial clauses in the marriage contract, and was broken off (according to Mérinville family archives). Another proposal of marriage came from the Duke de Caderousse, and was rejected. Mlle de Sévigné apparently was not drawn to the Duke—tall and well-built, intelligent and well-educated though he was. Not even the prestigious title of Duchess could bring her to accept him. Nor would she accept the Count d'Étauges, rich as he was ("rich but stupid," according to a letter from the Countess de Fiesque to Bussy). It was a surprise to Mme de Sévigné herself to judge by the last lines of a letter of hers to Bussy, dated June 6, 1668: "My daughter was thinking about marrying, but negotiations have been broken off. Just why, I am not certain . . ."

On July 17, in reply to a letter from Bussy sending greetings to "the prettiest girl in all France," the girl's mother closed on a somewhat querulous note: "The prettiest girl in all France returns your greetings. The title is flattering, to be sure, but I must confess that I am growing slightly weary of doing the honors." To which Bussy replied on July 29: "The prettiest girl in all France knows very well how I feel about her, but it seems to me high time—as it does to you—for someone other than you to do the honors for her. Thinking of her, I must say I wonder at the bizarreness of destiny . . ." In reply to which, Mme de Sévigné would write on August 28: "The prettiest girl in all France is more than ever worthy of your esteem and friendship. She sends you her compliments. Her destiny is so unclear that I am baffled."

On December 4, 1668, Mlle de Sévigné's destiny was finally clarified: "I write to give you news to please you," Mme de Sévigné wrote to her cousin:

At long last, the prettiest girl in all France is marrying—not the prettiest boy—but one of the most distinguished men in the kingdom: he is Monsieur de Grignan, whom you have known [as had Mme de Sévigné] for many years. All his wives have been considerate enough to have died to make way for your cousin, and his father and son have likewise obliged, so that richer than he has ever been—and furthermore, by his lofty lineage, by his connections as well as his good qualities, he is just such a husband as we could wish for, and, therefore, we are not haggling over terms, as is customary, but instead are taking the word of the two illustrious families into which he married earlier. He seems highly pleased at the alliance, and as soon as we have word from his uncle, the Archbishop of Arles . . . the arrangements will proceed, and should be concluded before the end of the year. Respectful as I am of tradition,

I did not want to fail to ask your advice and approbation [as head of the male branch of the Rabutin family]. Everyone here seems to approve of the match, which is important since people are silly enough to be influenced by public opinion . . .

Upon word from Bussy that he, too, approved the match, she wrote delightedly, "I am very pleased to know that you approve the Grignan marriage. It is true that he is a good and distinguished man who has resources, a great name, a government post, a splendid character, the esteem and respect of all the world."

Bussy already knew François Adhémar de Monteil de Grignan, Count de Grignan. There was no need for Mme de Sévigné to identify the family to Bussy. The name of Grignan was well known to all of France—a prestigious name which Mme de Sévigné delighted in rolling on her tongue. The Grignans were a very ancient, very illustrious noble family of Provence, the Dauphiné and the Comtat Venaissin. Honoré Bouche, a seventeenth-century historian, traced the history of the Adhémars back to the seventh century to a Lambert Adhémar de Monteil.* As leaders in the Crusades, the Adhémars were commemorated in history and in the verse of Tasso; in the eleventh century they paid homage to Germanic emperors, later declared themselves sovereign lords in their own territories. The Grignans were related to another prestigious noble house, that of the Castellanes. The family tree included a Duke of Genoa. The Count de Grignan's two uncles ranked high in the hierarchy of the Church: one was Archbishop of Arles and the other Bishop of Uzès. Two of his brothers served the Church; two other brothers bore arms in the service of their nation—two for God, two for the King.

The Count de Grignan could no longer claim—as had his ancestors in the eleventh century—twenty-one leagues (fifty-odd miles)† along the fertile left bank of the River Rhône, but his holdings were still vast: family archives showed that the Count's properties throughout Provence and the Dauphiné were valued at 1,500,000 livres (roughly 15 million francs); the revenues from these properties were estimated at 50,000 livres a year (roughly, a half million francs).

What Mme de Sévigné may or may not have known was that these properties were debt-encumbered, that three-fourths of his annual revenues were hypothecated, pledged to pay off outstanding debts. What Mme de Sévigné may or may not have known was that the Count's extravagance

---

*The French town of Montélimar takes its name from the Monteil family.
†The league measured approximately two and a half miles.

was legendary, his life-style regal (or, as she would later term it, "Gothic"). She could not have been unaware of his financial difficulties for the reason that the marriage contract stipulated that of the original 200,000 livres cash payment on the dowry due on the eve of the nuptials, 180,000 were to be used in paying off the Count's creditors. (A *bon mot* of Mme de Sévigné's went the rounds at the time the marriage settlement was being concluded: she simply could not understand, she is said to have said, why she should be paying the Count de Grignan 200,000 livres to sleep with the prettiest girl in France!) The question is whether she did or did not fully realize the extent of the financial involvements of her future son-in-law. She had due warning from the Cardinal de Retz, a devoted friend and a relative on the Sévigné side: a letter of his is extant in which he expressed himself as very uneasy at the thought that she had neither requested nor been given a financial accounting by the Count de Grignan, at the thought that she had simply accepted the match as her daughter's destiny. Cardinal de Retz wrote that he found it difficult to understand her hurry to conclude the matter without further investigation. What is still more difficult to understand is that the Abbé de Coulanges, Mme de Sévigné's uncle and financial adviser— a stickler for figures and for fiscal accuracy—ever allowed his great-niece to enter into so slipshod a marital contract.

Why the sense of urgency, one wonders along with the Cardinal, in consummating that far from perfect match: one wonders if it was the matter of "public opinion" to which Mme de Sévigné had referred earlier in a letter to Bussy, whether the family was ill at ease about the gossip about Mlle de Sévigné and the King—and other gallants. One wonders if Mlle de Sévigné was simply too difficult to please, whether her mother was—as she had confessed to Bussy—"weary of doing the honors." In any event, to have still another betrothal end in a fiasco would have been embarrassing to both mother and daughter. There is, of course, the possibility that it was Mlle de Sévigné who put pressure on her mother to consummate the marriage contract. Every sign points to the fact that she had fallen in love with the Count de Grignan: a letter from Mme de Sévigné to the Count written several months later makes clear that Mlle de Sévigné had been attracted to the Count as to no other of her suitors.

The Count may have been homely, ugly—his ugliness a family joke, as both his wife and mother-in-law fondly admit—but he was an eminently attractive, seductive male—with emphasis on the male: of noble carriage, tall and graceful, an excellent athlete (an equestrian, swordsman, hunts-man)—in fine, a fine figure of a man, very dark, with hair and beard black as the raven's wing, and a hawk-like nose, all Grignan characteristics. A man of the world, a shining example of France's most polished, most elegant society, a fine musician with a fine baritone voice, a fine officer (Colonel of the renowned Regiment of Champagne, Captain of the Queen's Cavalry)— no wonder women found him fascinating. In 1668, Grignan held office as one of the Lieutenant-Governors of Languedoc (a region of Southern France of which the capital city was Toulouse).

His first wife had been Angélique-Clarice d'Angennes, daughter of the renowned Marquise de Rambouillet, whose salon exercised so great an influence on French society and French culture in the seventeenth century. At her death in 1664, after six years of marriage, the Count found himself a widower with two young daughters: the necessity of delivering to these two girls the money due them from their mother's estate constituted one of the Count's most pressing financial problems. In 1666, he married Angélique du Puy du Fou,* who died the following year in childbirth—an infant son surviving his mother by only a few months.

The Count de Bussy, in a humorous letter written before the wedding, in December, 1668, to Grignan's future mother-in-law, hinted that her future son-in-law was remarkable for his sexual proclivities: "Grignan, who is not old [he was thirty-seven], is already on his third wife! He uses up wives as fast as he does doublets or carriages! Except for that, I would say that my cousin has made a very good choice. From his point of view, it is a case of unadulterated good fortune."

Grignan's third wife's mother, undismayed by Bussy's warning, affixed her signature—along with those of seventy-three friends and relatives—to the marriage contract on January 27, 1669. The wedding was celebrated two days later, presumably in high style. Bussy, still in exile, could not attend the function, and Mme de Sévigné wrote to tell him how greatly he would be missed: "By my standards, you would be the premier gentleman at the festivities. Good Lord, how perfectly you would take your place in such a distinguished company! Since you have departed the scene, I find no wit to spark mine so satisfactorily, and I say to myself a thousand times, good heavens, what a difference!"

In April, a few months after the wedding, the newlyweds joined Mme de Sévigné in leasing—at a rather substantial figure—what Mme de Sévigné would refer to as a "pretty house" on the Rue de Thorigny, in the fashionable old Marais district where Mme de Sévigné felt most at home, close by the Place Royale where she had been born and raised—a new, handsome, spacious residence set back from the street with a large courtyard and

*Whose mother was a good friend of Mme de Sévigné's.

garden, with ample room for both households. Mme de Sévigné had no fear that her daughter's marriage would mean a separation; she and the Grignans would make their home together—a happy ménage, it would seem; the Count's mother-in-law as well as his wife apparently enchanted with him.

Mme de Sévigné wrote to the Count de Bussy in June of 1669, six months after the wedding, to try to resolve a sticky problem of etiquette in which the two Counts had become ensnarled, each insisting that it was up to the other to initiate the correspondence in the wake of the marital alliance between the Grignan and Rabutin families: "Mme de Grignan writes to you on the part of her husband," Mme de Sévigné began diplomatically:

> *He swears that he will not subscribe to the silly custom whereby the groom writes to all the relatives of the bride. He insists that it should be you who writes to congratulate him on the inconceivable happiness which is his lot in having won Mlle de Sévigné. He claims that, on such a point, there can be no fixed rule. And since he says all this so pleasantly and in so humorous a manner, and since he has so long admired and esteemed you, I beg you, Count, to write him a witty letter, as you know so well how to do. You will be giving great pleasure to me, whom you love, as well as to him who—between us—is the most desirable husband and—from a social point of view, the most divine man in the world.*

Mme de Sévigné could well congratulate herself on the marriage she had arranged for her daughter. Not only was her daughter happy with her choice of a husband, Mme de Sévigné herself—as she had written Bussy—could not have found a son-in-law more to her taste than the Count de Grignan. There was every reason to hope that the Count, with his great name, with his great personal charm, with his fine military record, with his experience in government administration in Languedoc, would be appointed by a grateful monarch to a Court position of distinction, and that the Grignans and Mme de Sévigné would live on happily together in the Rue de Thorigny house or some other residence appropriate to their rank and station.

IX

The family circle was complete in March of 1669, when young Charles de Sévigné returned to Paris from his bloody Cretan adventure. The Christian expeditionary force had failed to turn back the pagan horde which snatched the town of Candie from the Venetians after a four-hundred-year tenure. The casualties had been high, but Charles had come through unscathed, and showing some slight inclination to continue to bear arms. It was decided that he should follow a military career (only two careers being open, in that time, to young noblemen: the army and the Church); his mother purchasing for him, at great expense,* an ensign's commission in an élite corps, the Gendarmes-Dauphin.

The Countess de Grignan was pregnant, and the family spent much of the summer at Livry. Mme de Sévigné's uncle, the *Bien Bon*, the Abbé de Coulanges, was titular head or Abbot of the Abbey of Livry with its complement of four black-robed monks; its green groves and gardens, its fertile fields and grazing cattle, its limpid streams and ponds and bridges, all within horse-and-carriage commuting distance of Paris, a rustic retreat forever dear to Mme de Sévigné and her daughter—one of the few tastes they had in common.

There was a sudden uproar in those Elysian fields in early November when Mme de Grignan suffered a miscarriage—said to have been brought on by her fright at seeing her brother-in-law, the handsome Chevalier de Grignan, thrown from his horse on a path at Livry. (Gossiping tongues again lashed at Mme de Grignan, implying that it was her romantic interest in her handsome brother-in-law which caused her to miscarry.)

Madame de Sévigné, anxiously hovering over her daughter, as she recovered from her miscarriage, was about to suffer another shock, this one emanating from the throne: like a bolt from the blue came the news that the Count de Grignan had been named by Letters Patent issued November 29, 1669, to serve Louis XIV as Lieutenant-Governor of Provence, to represent His Majesty in that ancient province of meridional France.† The fifteen-

---

*At a cost of 75,000 livres.
†A region bounded on the south by the Mediterranean, on the west by the Rhône River, by Italy on the east and by Dauphiné on the north.

year-old Duke de Vendôme (great-grandson of that first Bourbon King, Henri IV) was the Governor of Provence, but he would govern in name only—never once setting foot in the region—although it would be he who would collect the lion's share of the emoluments and perquisites of the office.

It was a very flattering appointment for Grignan, to be sure, to serve as Viceroy in a large and important province—his natal province—but it was unlike his appointment in Languedoc where, as one of several Lieutenants-General, he could usually serve without actually being there. To Madame de Sévigné, the first shock came with the news that the Count would be expected to spend a great deal of time—and the Countess, presumably, with him—in the capital city of Aix-en-Provence, seat of the provincial Parlement, and in Lambesc where the Assembly of the Communities of Provence gathered annually (to vote the subsidies necessary for the administration of the province, and to ratify the taxes imposed on the province by the royal exchequer).

At the thought of a separation from her daughter, Mme de Sévigné must have known a sudden sense of panic. Such an idea had obviously never occurred to her at the time of her daughter's marriage to the Count de Grignan.

She was to have a reprieve: the Count de Grignan was not due to take up his new duties in Provence until the spring and, by then, the Countess was pregnant again—a condition precluding, at least in her mother's opinion, any possibility of her accompanying her husband on that long and difficult journey to the south.

In April of 1670, Mme de Sévigné—with her daughter safely at her side, and the moment of parting indefinitely postponed—could write blithely to the Count de Bussy: "You do not want me to talk about Mme de Grignan" (one of Bussy's favorite jokes was to claim that he was in love with Mme de Grignan and jealous of her husband), "but I want to talk about her: she is pregnant, and will stay here for her lying-in. Her husband is in Provence or, to be exact, he will be leaving for there in three days." In May, in reply to a letter from Bussy, she wrote: "Mme de Grignan is so unworthy of your affection, she is so in love with her husband, she is so enormous, that I dare not tell you that she thinks very often of you!" And a little later, "I am not accustomed to seeing her pregnant, and am as scandalized as you are!" (Since their quarrel, Mme de Sévigné's correspondence with her cousin Bussy had gone on by fits and starts, both of them quick to take offense, both quick to make up their differences. In recent months, Bussy had taken offense at the Count de Grignan's failure to send him formal notification of the impending nuptials; Mme de Sévigné had taken offense at Bussy's refusal to yield and write first to Grignan and, as she did whenever she was angry, she reminded him of his act of supreme treachery in the pen-portrait—a thing she had promised a dozen times never to bring up again! She was ready, by July of 1670, to make up, once again, writing to assure him that, "We never really abandon one another; our family bonds might occasionally be strained, but are never actually broken!")

By June, the Count de Grignan was in Provence. On June 25, Mme de Sévigné wrote her first letter to him, one of a series which might well serve as models for mothers-in-law:

> *Your letter is the most pleasant in the world. I would have answered sooner had I not known that you were off on a trip across your Pro-vence.* Besides, I wanted to send you the motets† you asked me for. I have not yet been able to find them, but while I am waiting, I want to tell you that I still love you tenderly, and that if that thought gives you pleasure, as you tell me it does, then, you should be the happiest man alive! You must be that already, thanks to the exchange of letters going on between you and my daughter; it seems brisk, indeed, to judge by her side of the correspondence. I do not believe it possible for anyone to love more wholeheartedly than she loves you. For my part, I hope to turn her back over to you, all in one piece, in perfect health, with a child in her arms, to boot . . .*

Mme de Sévigné's next letter to her son-in-law was dated August 6:

> *In all truth, did I not give you the prettiest wife in the world? Could anyone be more perfect, more trustworthy? Could anyone love you more tenderly? Could anyone manifest more Christian sentiments? Could anyone long so passionately to be with you? And could anyone show more devotion to her duties? It might seem ridiculous for me to speak so well of my own daughter, but it is because I—like all the rest—stand in admiration of her conduct. And I even more than all the rest, for the reason that—being so close to her—I have the opportunity more closely to observe her. . . . I assure you that everyone gives her her due, and that she merits every word of praise lavished on her. . . . You cannot*

---

*The Count had gone to make his first official visits to Marseille, Arles, Nîmes and Toulouse, the principal cities of the province under his jurisdiction.

†Choral compositions on a sacred text.

imagine how she anguished over your recent indisposition. I rejoice that you are well again, for love of her as well as for love of you. I beg that should your bile threaten to act up again, you will find a way to put it off until after this child is born. She still complains every day about being kept here, and says quite seriously that it is indeed cruel to have separated her from you. As if it were for our benefit to keep the two of you two hundred leagues apart! On that score, I beg you to relieve her mind by expressing to her your joy in the hope that she will bring her pregnancy to term safely here. It would have been totally impossible to have taken her with you, in the state she was in; and nothing could be better for her health—or even for her reputation, in view of her exemplary conduct—than for her child to be born here where the most expert assistance is available to her at her accouchement. Should she decide—after that—to indulge in folly and flirtation, she would have to do so for a year or more before anyone would believe her capable of it, so high an opinion of her virtue has she assured herself by her conduct. I call in all the Grignans here as witnesses! The pleasure I take in these circumstances relates, to great extent, to you, for I love you with all my heart, and am thrilled that your predilection for my daughter has been justified by developments. I write you no news; that would be to trespass on my daughter's preserves. I conjure you only to believe that no one could take a more tender interest in all that concerns you than do I.

The appeal to the Grignan family to witness Mme de Grignan's circumspect deportment heightens the impression that the gossip about her had been damaging and that it persisted. There is significance, as well, in Mme de Sévigné's plea to the Count to assure his wife that the separation was really necessary, that it was his wish as well as her mother's that she stay in Paris.

On August 15, from Paris, Mme de Sévigné's letter began:

I observe a correspondence so brisk between you and a certain lady that it would be ridiculous for me to try to tell you any news, or even being able to inform you that she loves you: all her actions, all her conduct, all her concern, all her sadness loudly bespeak the fact. I am a somewhat discriminating judge of love, and fancy myself knowledgeable on the subject. I admit to you that I am very pleased to see her love for you, and could have hoped for nothing better. Enjoy that blessing, and never show yourself ungrateful. If there is some small *corner of your heart left open, I would be very happy to have it, for you occupy much space in mine. I need not tell you whether I am taking good care of your better half, whether I keep watch over her health, whether I pray this bark comes safely to port. If you know how to love, you will easily understand my sentiments. Would to God your poor wife were as fortunate as the little Deville.* She has just given birth to a boy so husky he could be three months old. My daughter exclaimed, "Ah, how angry that makes me for the little Deville to have a boy. It's too much to hope for that there should be two boys in the same household at the same time!" I gave her—my daughter, I mean—a book for you; you will find it extremely beautiful. It's by an intimate friend of Pascal's.† Read it attentively. Here, too, are some good songs—while waiting for the motets. Don't give up your singing; don't give up your fine figure and, last but not least, don't give up being loveable, since you are so well loved.*

It was on November 15 that the Grignans' first child was born, though not the son and heir so eagerly hoped for: the first lines of the letter giving the news to the Count de Grignan are in the Countess's hand:

If my safety can console you for having a daughter I will not ask your pardon for not having given you a son. I am out of all danger, and think only of going to join you. My Mother will tell you the rest.

Mother told it pertly:

Madame de Pusieux says that if you want a son, it's up to you to sire one—a comment I find most apt. You have given us a little girl; we turn her over to you. Never was there a childbirth so easy. I must tell you that my daughter and I went, last Saturday, to stroll in the gardens of the Arsenal where she felt a few mild pains. On our return home, I wanted to send for Mme de Robinet [the midwife], but she would not hear of it. We had supper; she ate heartily. Monsieur the Coadjutor [the Count's brother, who was Coadjutor to the Archbishop of Arles] and I wanted to give the room a few delivery-room touches: this too, she opposed with an air that implied that the whole thing was no more than a maiden's colic. At long last, despite her protests, just as I was

---

*Mme Deville was the wife of the Grignans' maître d'hôtel, who served as *dame de compagnie*—companion—to the Countess.

†It was Nicole's just-published second volume of *Essays on Morality*, so dear to Mme de Sévigné.

about to send for La Robinette, sharp pains began, so severe, so close together, so constant, and so loud and piercing her cries that we were sure that she was about to give birth. The difficulty was we had no midwife. We did not know what we were about; I was frantic. She begged for help and for a midwife. At that point, she really wanted one, and she was right, for within a quarter of an hour, the child was delivered by the midwife of Deville for whom we had sent a carriage . . . At first glance, Hélène [one of Mme de Sévigné's two personal maids] said to me, "Madame, it's a little boy!" and so I passed on the good news to the Coadjutor, but when we looked closely, we found that it was a little girl . . . We can find no consolation save in my daughter's good health. Her daughter has been baptized and named Marie-Blanche . . . The malicious say that she will never surprise us by turning out a beauty, but it's these same people who add that she looks like you, and if that is the case, you can be sure that I shall love her dearly . . .

In reply to Bussy's letter of congratulations on her first grandchild, Mme de Sévigné wrote rather tartly, "I thank you for your good wishes on my daughter's accouchement. One wonders whether a third Grignan daughter deserves such lavish compliments."

Rejoice though Mme de Sévigné might to see her daughter's prompt recovery after childbirth, it was that resurgence of health and strength which affrighted her, for the reason that it presaged Mme de Grignan's departure. Mme de Sévigné was in an acute state of anxiety at the thought of their separation. On December 10, in a letter to the Count, she wrote:

I will soon again be in the same state in which you saw me last year [when his assignment in Provence had first been announced]. I must love you very much to send my daughter off to you in such bad weather. What folly on her part to leave so good a Mother to go gallivanting off after a man to the far ends of France! That kind of behavior is nothing short of shocking . . .

If the letter was written on a tone of banter, Mme de Sévigné's mood was deadly serious. She was panic-struck at sight of her daughter's preparations for departure. "Love me always, my dear Count," she said in closing, "I spare you the necessity of paying honor to my grandmotherhood, but you must love me and must know that you are loved nowhere in the world more deeply than here." (Of his three mothers-in-law, she once told him, she "undoubtedly loved him the best.")

X

On December 15, Mme de Sévigné—with her daughter and granddaughter both thriving—could catch up with her correspondence, writing to another member of the family, one closer and dearer to her heart than even her cousin Bussy. This was her cousin Philippe-Emmanuel de Coulanges, born on the day of her mother's funeral as if in compensation for that loss, her "little Coulanges," as she always fondly called him—never a cross word to pass between them, from the first day to the last. A witty, jolly, roly poly little man, he had somehow not succeeded at the Parliamentary care r his father had planned and facilitated for him. His only profession would be that of houseguest or, rather, château-guest, the most popular man in France, the pleasure of his company universally besought. His life's work consisted of delighting and entertaining his friends and family. A charmer, leading a charmed life, he was a man for whom the word "playboy" seems especially designed, though it was wine and song—not women—on which he doted (the songs his own, a volume of his poems to be published in 1694). "A very small man, plump, with a beaming face" (as the renowned *Mémoires* of the Duke de Saint-Simon described him), "a wit that was facile, pleasant, productive of only pretty trifles . . . but in a steady stream, and at a moment's notice; an entirely natural, a lighthearted and frivolous man whom nothing daunted save constraint and study." (Despite all his frivolity, his devotion to Mme de Sévigné was steadfast, lifelong.) "He could not take even his worries seriously," according to Mme de Sévigné—not even his wife's flirtations and/or affairs, despite which the couple got on together marvelously well, perhaps because so often apart. His wife, Angélique de Coulanges, the daughter of the Intendant of Lyon, could claim connections with the Court of France, making it strange indeed that grace and favor were not shown her husband; though Monsieur de Coulanges had hoped to share the Intendance of Lyon with his father-in-law—and later to succeed him—the appointment was never forthcoming. Perhaps Mme de Coulanges never really pressed the appointment; perhaps—like every good Parisienne—she shuddered at the idea of living in the provinces. As witty as she was charming and pretty, Mme de Coulanges was widely quoted in the capital and at Court, famous for her repartee, for her *bons mots* and her letters, even more famous—

during their lifetimes—than Mme de Sévigné, whom she adored as much as did her husband. The priest who served her as father-confessor relished the experience, commenting, "That lady's every sin comes out as an epigram!"

In December of 1670, Monsieur and Madame de Coulanges were visiting her parents at Lyon, and on the fifteenth, Mme de Sévigné hastened to write, determined to be the first to reach them with a news item so sensational as to set all Paris agog: "I am about to tell you," she began, little knowing that this letter would prove to be the most anthologized of all the eleven-hundred-odd letters of her composition to come down to us:

> the most astonishing thing, the most surprising, the most marvelous, the most miraculous, the most triumphant, the most bewildering, the most unheard-of, the most singular, the most extraordinary, the most incredible, the most unforeseen, the greatest, the smallest, the most rare, the most common, the most dazzling, the most secret until today, the most brilliant, the most enviable; in short, a thing whose parallel is only to be found in bygone centuries; and even this comparison is not exact; a thing which we cannot believe in Paris (so how could it be believed in Lyon?); a thing which makes everyone exclaim Merciful Heavens! ... a thing, finally, which will take place on Sunday, when those who witness it will think their eyes have tricked them; a thing which will take place on Sunday and which will perhaps not have taken place on Monday. I cannot bring myself to give it away. Guess. I give you three guesses. Has the cat got your tongue? Do you give up? Well, then, I must tell you: Monsieur de Lauzun is going to marry, on Sunday, at the Louvre—guess who! I give you four guesses; I give you ten; I give you a hundred. Mme de Coulanges says, "That's easy; it is Mme de La Vallière." No, absolutely not, Madame.—Then it is Mlle de Retz?— No, not so; how provincial you are!—"Ah!" you say, how silly we are; it is Mlle Colbert!—Even less likely.—Then, it must assuredly be Mlle de Créqui?—No, wrong again. So, finally, I shall have to tell you: Monsieur de Lauzun is marrying on Sunday, at the Louvre, with the King's consent, Mademoiselle, Mademoiselle de ... Mademoiselle ... guess the name! He is marrying Mademoiselle, my faith, by my faith, my sworn faith! Mademoiselle, the Grande Mademoiselle, Mademoiselle daughter of the late Monsieur, granddaughter of Henri IV, Mlle d'Eu, Mlle de Dombes, Mlle de Montpensier, Mlle d'Orléans, Mademoiselle, first cousin of the King, Mademoiselle destined to a throne, Mademoiselle the only match in France really worthy of Monsieur ... Now, there's a fine topic for discussion. If you cry out, if you are beside

yourselves, if you accuse us of having fabricated this story, of having made it up, if you call it a lie, if you feel you are being made fools of, if you conclude that it's all a big joke, impossible to imagine; if, at last, you insult us, we will feel that you have reason to; we had the same reaction when it was told to us.

For a Princess of the Blood to marry a mere Duke such as Lauzun was to stir up a hornet's nest: the royal family, the Queen and Monsieur, the King's brother, above all, deplored the mésalliance, and could see far better uses for the Grande Mademoiselle's great fortune, could she but be persuaded to die an old maid. Under such pressure, the King withdrew his consent. The Grande Mademoiselle ended up in tears; the Duke de Lauzun, a year later, ended up in prison, at the fortress of Pignerol with Fouquet, paying with ten years of his life for the impertinence of having aspired to the hand of the King's first cousin.

Mme de Sévigné paid a condolence call on her friend, the Grande Mademoiselle. "I found her in bed," she wrote to Coulanges, on December 31, 1670:

She wept afresh on seeing me, called me to her, embraced me, and drenched me in her tears. "Alas, do you remember what you said to me yesterday?" [What Mme de Sévigné had said was that if the Grande Mademoiselle were wise, she would hurry through the marriage cere- mony before the King had time to change his mind.] "Ah, what prudent advice you gave me!" The sight of her weeping set me to weeping, too. I have been back twice; she is sorely afflicted, and has always treated me as a person who sympathized with her; in which, she is not mistaken. On this occasion, I have been aware of feelings one does not usually entertain for persons of that rank . . .

It is a wonder that, in December of 1670, Mme de Sévigné could be even momentarily distracted by the romantic fiasco in the Louvre. With the new year, Mme de Sévigné's world would come to an end. Mme de Grignan had set a date for her departure. "Alas, I still have her here," Mme de Sévigné wrote on January 16, 1671, to her son-in-law in Provence:

Poor child, her efforts notwithstanding, it was not in her power to leave on the tenth of this month, as she had planned. The rains have been, and still are so heavy that it would have been madness to risk the roads.

*All the rivers are overflowing their banks, all the high roads are inun-
dated, the wheel tracks under water; there's great danger in fording
rivers. This has been a dreadful winter. There have been no freezes,
but it rains in rainstorms every day. The river is so high that the water
is up to the arches of the Pont Neuf. It is surely a strange season. I
admit that this spell of dreadful weather has led me to oppose her
departure, these last several days. I cannot hope to see her avoid the
cold, the mud, the fatigue of a winter journey, but I do not want to see
her drowned. This reason, cogent as it is, would not now hold her
back, were it not for the fact that the Coadjutor, who is supposed to
travel with her, has promised to perform the wedding ceremony of his
d'Harcourt cousin . . . The wedding has been put off from one day to
the next, and won't perhaps take place for another week. However, I
see my daughter so impatient to be on her way that it cannot be called
living, the way things are going here, at this time. And if the Coadjutor
does not give up the marriage ceremony, I see her about to commit a
folly, to set out—that is, without him. It would be a very strange thing
for her to go on alone, and such a fortunate thing for her to be able to
travel with her brother-in-law, that I am doing all I can to see to it that
they do not travel separately. In the meanwhile, the water may recede
a little.*

*I must tell you, furthermore, that I find no pleasure in having her
here with me, at this time. I know that she must leave. All she is doing
here now is to attend to her duties and to business matters. We have
no social life; we have no pleasures; our hearts are heavy; all we talk
about is the condition of the roads, the rains, the accidents of those
who venture out. In a word, although I love her you well know how
dearly, the state we are in is burdensome, unhappy. There is nothing
agreeable about these last days.*

*I am most grateful, my dear Count, for all the manifestations of
your affection, for your pity of my plight. You, better than any other,
can understand how I am suffering, how I will go on suffering. I am
sorry, however, that your joy in seeing her will be diminished by that
thought of me. But such are the changes, such the sorrows with which
this life is fraught. Adieu, my very dear Count, I am killing you with
these long letters, and only hope that you will understand the fond
heart which prompts them.*

Those long letters for which she apologized were many pages long—
one printed page roughly the equivalent of three pages in her own hand.

The sheets of letter-paper which she used were large; her handwriting, expansive. Some of her letters to her daughter ran as many as twenty-six, even twenty-seven pages in manuscript. (The French script of the seventeenth century was beautiful: it was the script of the goose-quill pen, the script of Kings, of ladies and gentlemen of quality.)

On February 4, Mme de Grignan drove away from Paris, and for Mme de Sévigné, the anguish of separation began. "My sorrow would be mild if I could compress it into words," she wrote to her daughter on Friday, the sixth, not two days after the departure:

Nor would I attempt to do so. I look in vain for my dear daughter; I no longer see her, and every step she takes increases the distance between us. Still weeping, still swooning with grief, I went over to Sainte-Marie [the Visitandine Convent attended by Mme de Grignan in her youth]. I felt as if my heart and soul were being torn out of me . . . oh! what a cruel separation it is! I asked to be left alone. I spent five hours there, sobbing incessantly; my thoughts were mortal wounds. I wrote to Monsieur de Grignan, you can imagine in what tones! Then I went to Mme de La Fayette's, who only intensified my grief by sharing in it. She was alone, and ill, saddened by the loss of a sister who had died in a convent; she was in a mood perfectly suited to my own. Monsieur de La Rochefoucauld came in.* We talked only of you, of the good reason I had to be overcome with sorrow . . . I came back home at eight o'clock from Mme de La Fayette's. But on entering this house, Good God! can you understand how I felt as I came up the staircase? That room into which I always went—alas! the doors all open, but the furniture all gone, all in disorder, and only your poor little girl in place of my own!† Can you imagine how I suffered? My awakenings during the night were dismal, and in the morning I was no closer to peace of mind. After dinner, I went to visit Mme de La Troche at the Arsenal. In the evening, I received your letter which only started up the same waves of emotion that I had suffered at our parting. Tonight I will finish this letter at Monsieur de Coulanges's house, where I will hear all the news . . .

---

*The Duke de La Rochefoucauld, author of the *Maxims*, one of the greatest noblemen in France, whose fifteen-year liaison with Mme de La Fayette has baffled succeeding generations as it had their own.

†Since it was out of the question to take a two-and-a-half-month infant on so arduous a journey, little Marie-Blanche de Grignan had been left in Paris with her grandmother.

By "all the news" Mme de Sévigné meant all the news and gossip of Court and Capital so dear to every Parisian away from Paris—to whom, to be away from Paris was to be in a kind of limbo. Paris was the capital not merely of France but of the world: the Court of Louis XIV, the navel of power. From the first day of the correspondence, Mme de Sévigné would undertake to keep the Grignans posted, to keep them informed on national affairs as well as on the latest scandal, to keep them diverted—in short, to keep them reading! These news and gossip columns were to be a regular feature of her Paris letters: some of it, stale seventeenth-century chitchat, of interest solely to Mme de Grignan or her contemporaries (eliminated, therefore, by this editor, from these excerpts); some of it, concerning Louis XIV and his inamoratas, gossip for the ages—a flashback into another age, another world, causing the historians to jump for joy. Flourishing her pen like a magician's wand, Mme de Sévigné invites her readers to join her as bystanders in the Sun King's Court. She, in her letters, and the Duke de Saint-Simon, in his *Mémoires*, offer us insights, glimpses of another age, vignettes of seventeenth-century life, character studies to illuminate the past not to be found in the chronicles of history.

"All the news," that day of February 6, included:

> The marriage of Mlle d'Houdancourt and of Monsieur de Ventadour has been signed this morning. The Abbé de Chambonnas has today been named Bishop of Lodève. Madame the Princess will leave Cendres on Wednesday for Châteauroux where Monsieur the Prince wants her to spend some time. Monsieur de La Marguerie takes the place on the King's Council left vacant by the death of Monsieur d'Étampes. Mme de Mazarin arrives in Paris tonight; the King has declared himself her protector, and has sent a splendid carriage, an exempt and eight guardsmen to bring her back from Lys . . .

And so on, and so on for another lengthy page or so. "I implore you, my dearest daughter," that first letter of the sixth continues:

> to take care of your health. Take care of yourself for my sake, and don't be so cruelly reckless or you may never recover from such negligence. I embrace you with a tenderness which has no equal—although no offense is meant to anyone else by that statement [the superiority of maternal love over conjugal love to be a leitmotif of the correspondence].

The immortal correspondence had begun; Mme de Sévigné thought she was speaking in the privacy of her boudoir to her beloved daughter, but she was speaking to the world.

XI

By February 9, Mme de Sévigné had received a second letter from her daughter, en route to Provence, and wrote immediately to acknowledge its arrival:

I received your letters, my bonne* *. . . I dissolve into tears when I read them. I feel as if my heart would break in two. Anyone would think that you were writing me insults or that you were ill or had had an accident, whereas it is just the opposite. You love me, my dear child, and you tell me so in such a way that I cannot bear it without weeping copiously. You continue your voyage without incident. And when I hear all this—which is what I want most in all the world to hear—you see the state I am in! So, you enjoy thinking about me, talking about me, but you would rather write me to tell me how you feel about me than to tell me so, face to face. However it is made known to me, it is received with a tenderness and a sensibility incomprehensible to anyone who is not capable of loving as I do. You arouse in me an unsurpassable tenderness. But if you think of me, my dear, rest assured that I think constantly of you. It is what the devout call an "habitual thought"— the way one should think of God, if one were devout. Nothing can distract me from my thought of you. I am constantly with you in thought. I see that carriage bearing you ever farther away, never to return to me. I am always with you on the highroads. Sometimes I grow apprehensive about the carriage overturning. The rains, these past three days, cause me despair. I am strangely fearful at the thought of the Rhône. I keep a map in front of me; I know all the places where you will stop for the night. Tonight, you are at Nevers; Sunday, you will be at Lyon where you will receive this letter.*

The only place to which I could write to you was at Moulins, in care of Mme de Guénégaud. I have received only two of your letters;

---

*"My *bonne*," the mother's and daughter's favorite term of address for one another, is throughout these pages left untranslated for the reason that it is untranslatable: literally, "my good girl"—good in the sense of good friends, in the archaic sense of "my good man, good woman."

perhaps, the third will come soon. That's the only consolation I can hope for; I seek no other kind. I am simply incapable, at this point, of being with crowds; that may come later, but not yet. The Duchesses de Verneuil and d'Arpajon want to cheer me up; I beg them to excuse me, for the time being. I have never seen so many kind souls as in this intimate circle of mine. Saturday, I spent the whole day at Mme de Villars's, talking of you and weeping; she is in total sympathy with my mood.

Yesterday, I went to a sermon delivered by Monsieur d'Agen and then to Evening Service and then to visit Mme de Puisieux and then Mme du Puy du Fou, who sends you a thousand greetings. If only she could be sure that you have a little furred jacket with you, she could stop worrying. Tonight, I am going to supper in the Faubourg, tête-à-tête.* That is how I will celebrate the carnival. I have a Mass said every day for you ... If you really want to please me, take care of your health, sleep in that special little bed;† eat your soup, and make the most of that courage with which you are endowed and I am not.

Later that evening, as was her wont, Mme de Sévigné picked up her letter again to add to it and bring it to a close, since the courier left Paris only twice weekly with the mail for Provence; it was Mme de Sévigné's practice to begin a letter one day, and continue it over the course of the next several days, adding news items as they came to her attention until the day she was ready to seal the letter and send it to the post office:

Before going to the Faubourg, I close my letter and address it to Monsieur the Intendant of Lyon [Mme de Coulanges's father]. The distinction of your letters has enchanted me. Alas, I well deserved that by the distinction of my love for you ... Adieu, my dear child, sole passion of my heart, the joy and sorrow of my life. Love me always; that alone can bring me consolation.

Her letter of Wednesday, February 11 began:

I have received only three of those delightful letters which touch me to the heart; one is still missing. Except for the fact that each one is precious, and that I hate to lose anything that comes from you, I would

---

*With the Countess de La Fayette in the Countess's house near the Luxembourg Palace, on the Left Bank, across the river from the Marais district, where Mme de Sévigné had always lived.

†A portable bed lent to Mme de Grignan by a brother-in-law, useful on the journey where accommodations at wayside inns were apt to be primitive.

feel as if I were missing nothing. There is nothing I could wish for which is not contained in those letters I have received. They are, first of all, very well written, and furthermore, so tender and so natural that it is impossible not to believe them. Had I ever doubted, these letters would have convinced me. They bear that stamp of truth which I always maintain mainfests itself with authority, whereas untruth remains swamped in words which lack the power to persuade; the more insistent they are, the more ambiguous they become. Yours are sincere, and are convincing. Your words serve only to explain how you feel and, in that noble simplicity, they carry an irresistible force. And that, my dear, is how your letters strike me. But what an effect they have on me, what tears I shed in finding myself persuaded of that truth which of all truths I most long to believe—you can well imagine! And that will give you some idea of how I was affected by things which formerly gave me exactly the opposite impression! If my words carry the same power as yours, I need say no more to you . . .

But what I do not like to hear you say is that I was like a curtain which concealed you, cut you off from view. What if I did once overshadow you? You were simply all the more dazzling when the curtain was drawn aside, and you stood revealed. You must be in full view to appear in your full perfection, as we have said a thousand times.

Mme de Sévigné here gives the first hint of the discord which apparently had marred their last months together in Paris, the first hint at the fact that her daughter's inhibitions prevented her from expressing her love verbally, from speaking openly to her mother, face to face. In another letter, some weeks later, Mme de Sévigné gives further evidence of their inability to communicate in person, writing on March 18,

You tell me that you are happy to hear that I am persuaded of your love for me, that you had no such assurance when we were together. Alas, my bonne, with no intention of reproaching you, I must say that all the fault was not on my side. How highly I always prized the least sign of your affection! Did not each one fill me with delight? And how dismayed I was at evidence to the contrary! . . .

What is so curious, so frustrating and so fascinating about the *Letters* is that Mme de Grignan never speaks for herself—all of her letters to her mother are missing; destroyed—purposely so, in all probability. Throughout this correspondence, her voice is never to be heard; at best, only as an echo on her mother's lips. It is Mme de Sévigné's reaction to her daughter's letters, it is her interpretation of her daughter's words that we hear. Mme de Grignan's personality and character are discernible to us solely in her mother's perspective. Mme de Grignan's reproach that her mother overshadowed, outshone her, curtained her off from the world, is one her mother does not even seek to deny. She merely makes light of it. Complex as was their relation, the complexity is further complicated for us by the fact that Mme de Grignan is to be seen and known only through her mother's eyes, her mother's pen—necessarily prejudiced as these were—to be seen, as it were, in distortion, through a maze of mirrors.

If Mme de Grignan has gone down in literary lore as an arrogant, cold, distant, unresponsive, inhibited woman, it is—a supreme irony!—her adoring mother to whom she owes the reputation. What despair it would have caused Mme de Sévigné to know that such was her handiwork! In all fairness to Mme de Grignan, the reader must not lose sight of the fact that she had to struggle fiercely to attain her independence of her mother, that her mother was intensely possessive, reluctant to surrender her daughter to her daughter's husband, reluctant to see her daughter established in a new life of her own, apart from her mother.

Mme de Sévigné's letter of February 11 continued:

> It appears that you are at Moulins today; you will receive one of my letters there. I could not write to you at Briare. That would have meant writing on that cruel Wednesday, the very day of your departure. I was so afflicted, so overcome with emotion that I was incapable of even seeking the consolation of writing to you. Here, then, is my third letter, the second addressed to Lyon. Be sure to let me know whether you have received them. So far apart from one another, one no longer makes fun of letters which begin, "I have received your letter, etcetera"...*
>
> The thought that occurred to you about your going constantly farther away from me, of seeing that carriage recede farther and farther into the distance, is one of those which most torment me. You are moving constantly farther away from me; you will soon find yourself two hundred leagues off...†
>
> I will finish this letter, a little later. Perhaps at Lyon you will be so distracted by the honors paid to you [as Vicereine of Provence] that you will not have time to read all this. Take time to send me news of yourself, of your health, of your dear face which I so love, to let me

---

*These last lines are quoted by Marcel Proust in his La Prisonnière, apropos of his own mother's reproach to him for not having notified her at the receipt of each of her letters to him.

†The two hundred leagues from Paris to Aix, approximately five hundred miles.

know whether or not you will embark on that fiendish Rhône
River . . .

She would finish the letter and date it "Wednesday evening":

*I have just now received your letter from Nogent. It was brought to
me by a very nice man whom I questioned about you as best I could.
But your letter is better than anything anyone could tell me. It is
only fitting, my dear, that you should be the first to make me laugh,
since it was you who made me cry so hard. What you write about
Monsieur Busch is highly original. That is what is called a master
stroke in the style of eloquence. It made me laugh, I admit, and I would
be ashamed, had I not spent the last eight days weeping! Alas, I met
Monsieur Busch in the street when he was bringing the horses here
for your voyage. I stopped him, and, in tears, asked him his name;
he told it to me. Sobbing, I said to him, Monsieur Busch, I entrust
my daughter to you; don't let the carriage overturn, and when you
have safely delivered her to Lyon, come to see me and I will give you
a gratuity. I will do it, too, for what you write me greatly increases my
respect for him.*

*Alas, my dear, you are not mistaken when you imagine that I am
thinking of you even more than you of me, although you seem to be
often doing so. If you could see me, you would see that I am seeking
out those who will talk with me about you; if you could hear me, you
would hear how much! I need only tell you, for example, that I spent
an hour with the Abbé Gueton just to talk about the roads and the
route to Lyon. I have not yet seen any of those people who want, as
they say, to offer me some diversion, because what they really mean is
that they want to prevent me from talking about you, and that offends
me. Adieu, my very dear, continue to write me and to love me. As for
me, my angel, I am entirely yours.*

On Thursday, February 12, another letter:

The Duchess de La Vallière sent word to the King, through the Maré-
chal de Bellefonds, that she would have left the Court earlier—once
she had lost the honor of his good graces—had she been able to bear
the thought of never seeing him again; that her love for him was so
strong that she was scarcely able to bring herself to offer it as a sacrifice*

---

*The title of Duchess had been bestowed by the amorous monarch on his first official mistress.

to God; that it was her intention, however, to give up that love as her penance; that, after having devoted her youth to him, all the rest of her life was not too long to devote to her salvation. The King wept bitterly, and sent Monsieur Colbert to Chaillot* to beg her to return at once to Versailles so that he might speak to her again.

M. Colbert conducted her there. The King talked with her for an hour, weeping bitterly, and Mme de Montespan went out to meet her with open arms and tear-filled eyes. All of this is very difficult to comprehend. Some say that she will stay on at Versailles and at Court; others say that she will go back to Chaillot.

And on Friday, February 13, in continuation:

Monsieur de Coulanges wants me to write to you again at Lyon. I entreat you, my dear child—should you embark on the Rhône—to get off the boat at the Bridge.† You have succeeded so well in convincing me that you love me that it would seem that to please me you would take no risks. Let me know about the boat trip. Alas, how dear, how precious to me that little bark borne off so cruelly by the Rhône!

I have been in such an evil mood that I could not bear more than four people at a time ... I have not yet seen Mme d'Arpajon; she has such a smug air about her that it annoys me. The Mardi Gras ball may be postponed; never has there been such a sad mood.‡ I think it must be your absence which was the cause. Good Lord, how many messages I have for you, how much praise is lavished on you, how many people ask for news of you! I could never begin to name all those by whom you are loved, esteemed, adored! But all that is as nothing, my daughter, compared to what I feel for you. You are never out of my mind. I think of you ceaselessly, and how fondly! I kissed your daughter and she kissed me back, kissed me for you, too. Can you guess how much I love that little one when I think whose child she is?

On February 18, in response to more fond letters from her daughter from along the route, Mme de Sévigné declared herself finally convinced of her daughter's love: "How naughty you have been!" she wrote:

*The Visitandine Convent at Chaillot to which the Duchess had fled for refuge.
†Lest the swift currents of the river dash the bark against the piers.
‡At Court, that is, as a result of Mme de La Vallière's threat to take the veil.

Why do you sometimes conceal from me such precious treasures? Are you afraid that I will die of joy at the knowledge? But, do you not fear even more to see me die of sorrow in believing the opposite? D'Hacqueville* can attest to the state he has seen me in. But let us skip over such sad memories, and let me revel in a happiness without which life is grim and hard. I think I am now somewhat more rational. I am in better control of myself and, sometimes, for as long as four or five hours at a time, I am as normal as anyone, although it takes very little to throw me back into my former state. A memory, a place, a word, a thought too long dwelt upon; your letters, above all; even my letters to you while I am writing, the mention of your name ... those are the reefs upon which I founder, reefs too often encountered ...

Oh, my darling, how I wish I could see you, if only for a moment, to hear your voice, to embrace you, just see you pass by, if nothing more! These are some of the thoughts I cannot resist. It's terrible not to have you with me any longer. This separation racks my heart and soul—I feel it as if it were a physical pain. I cannot thank you enough for the letters you wrote to me, en route. To go to such trouble is very good of you, and is appreciated; nothing is lost on me. You wrote to me at every stop. I was struck by your kindness. It was a labor of love; without that chore, you could have taken more rest, retired earlier to bed. It gave me great consolation. Even now, I impatiently await your letters from Roanne and from Lyon to tell me about your embarkment, whether you got out at the Bridge, about your arrival at Arles, about how you found that furious Rhône in comparison to our poor Loire River which you most kindly complimented. How nice that you think of it as an old friend!† How different everything is, now. I used never to return to this house without impatience and anticipation. Now, no matter how hard I try, I can no longer find you. But how can one live without one's beloved child? How much I want you I will prove to you by the long journey I will make to join you. I received a letter from Monsieur de Grignan. He told me that he will return here this winter; will he leave you there or will you come with him? In such uncertainty, how can I lease your apartment here? We are even now this very day on the verge of concluding the lease. Let me hear from you on this matter.

*The Abbé d'Hacqueville, an old and devoted family friend, the personification of the friend in need, Mme de Sévigné's confidant when it came to problems with her daughter.

†Mother and daughter had gone by barge down the Loire River in 1666 en route to Brittany from Paris.

Monsieur le Dauphin* was ill; he is better, now. Mme de La Vallière is back at Court to stay. The King received her with tears of joy; Mme de Montespan, as well. There have been several tender conversations. All of this is difficult to figure out; best not to talk of it. I must say no more.†

I see your daughter, every day, which is called keeping an eye on the nursery. I want her spine to be straight; that is my special concern. It would be strange, indeed, were a daughter of yours and Monsieur de Grignan's not to be well formed . . . My Lord, that Rhône River! You are on it, at this moment. I think of nothing else! . . .

XII

Mme de Grignan might well have served as model for what Marcel Proust calls "the fugitive": "the figure of flight," in Proust's figure of speech— forever eluding our grasp, forever slipping away from us, forever out of reach, unattainable, inaccessible.

For Mme de Sévigné, the separation from her daughter came as a total shock, touching off an amorous passion in her heart. It was a typically Proustian passion, although that does not imply that she should be seen as a lost soul (the fact that she, one day, in bringing her letter gracefully to a close, bestowed "warm kisses" on her daughter's "fair cheeks and beautiful throat" gave rise, in the dawn of the Freudian age, to suspicious speculation as to the nature of the attachment); it was a Proustian passion, rather, in the sense that Mme de Sévigné's experience serves as perfect illustration for Proust's analysis of amorous passion, as outlined in his *Remembrance of Things Past*; to wit: "One loves only what one cannot wholly possess."

Mme de Sévigné could no longer wholly possess her daughter after her marriage to the Count de Grignan and the Grignans' removal to Provence. Mme de Sévigné had lost her daughter to another life, to another family, to other interests; had lost her, above all, to her husband.

---

*The Dauphin, the King's eldest son and throne heir.

†Mme de Sévigné would say no more for the reason that it was well known that the mails were under surveillance by the government.

Separated from her daughter, Mme de Sévigné would languish of love. Restored to one another's arms, they would relapse into conflict and discord. Mme de Sévigné's letters inadvertently betray the tension and dissension that had troubled their lives together in the months subsequent to the marriage of Françoise-Marguerite and to the birth of Marie-Blanche. The mother-daughter relation had not been ideal; the mother would attempt to idealize it, after their parting. The daughter, for her part, sped joyously to her reunion with her husband—to reign as Vicereine, first lady of Provence, no longer second in importance to anyone, not even her glamorous, dazzling, celebrated mother.

That Mme de Sévigné's passion for her daughter would prove to be an unhappy one serves further to justify Proust's theory that an amorous passion is inevitably unhappy.

What makes the situation so curious is that Mme de Sévigné had never previously had the reputation of being an extraordinarily fond or zealous mother; no reference was ever made thereto by friends or relatives, whereas her hyperactive social life gives proof that she could not have devoted herself exclusively to the upbringing and education of her children. What is more, we remember the impatience in her voice, as late as 1670, at being obliged to go on and on "doing the honors" for "the prettiest girl in France"; that "prettiest girl," her letter to Bussy implied, had been too often a fiancée not yet to be a bride. To arrange a good match for Mlle de Sévigné had been her mother's first order of business: to see her married, to share in her life and her husband's, and in their home. But not to have her out of sight, out of reach, out of Paris! Strangely enough, such a possibility had evidently never even occurred to her.

It is stranger still that Mme de Sévigné—with two children from whom to choose—should choose the aloof, secretive, moody Mme de Grignan as love object. Why not, instead, the delicious Charles, so fond, so warm, so responsive, so eager for her love, so much more her type than his sister? Because, again according to Proust's theory of love and loving, we gravitate to the one most capable of causing us pain. "To love is an unhappy fate," Proust wrote: "It is to come under an evil spell, as with those poor souls in fairy tales for whom there is no hope until the spell is broken."

Proust cites Mme de Sévigné specifically in his theorization on love, putting the words in the mouth of a character in *Remembrance of Things Past*: "The important thing in life," Baron de Charlus says, apropos of Mme de Sévigné, "is not what one loves but that one loves."

Mme de Sévigné may well have been the inspiration for the character of the Princess de Clèves, the heroine of Mme de La Fayette's novel of that name.* The Princess, a woman of moral integrity, stifles her love for the Duke de Nemours throughout the years of her loveless marriage to the Prince de Clèves but, then, surprisingly, refuses the Duke's proposal of marriage when she finds herself suddenly free, at the death of her husband, to marry the man she had so long and hopelessly loved. By the analysis of Mme de La Fayette—herself condemned to a loveless marriage—it is the Princess's sad conclusion that the Duke, no matter how ardent a suitor, may eventually prove a harsh and faithless husband, and so she refuses to risk her newfound freedom and peace of mind. For her to refuse this most love-worthy lover proves the supreme torment. What Mme de La Fayette asserted here, two hundred and fifty years ahead of Proust, was that love hopelessly complicates existence, that "love is a most inconvenient emotion."

The Princess de Clèves rejected love; Mme de Sévigné rejected love—the love of a man, that is—"the other kind of love," as she called it: "that fever too violent to endure," thus making a distinction between amorous passion and affection—affection, a gentle emotion such as she felt (or thought she felt) for her daughter.

Love, however, is an irrepressible force—irrepressible as a volcano—as Jean Cordelier contends: love took its vengeance on Mme de Sévigné for her rejection of one form of love, asserted itself in her heart in another form, that of a passion for her daughter, one as violent, as fervent, as devastating as any woman has ever felt for a man. No love letters ever written to a man could surpass in fervor the Marquise de Sévigné's letters to her daughter. It is a coincidence that the seventeenth century produced another famous batch of love letters, *Letters from a Portuguese Nun*, letters purportedly written by a Portuguese nun to a French officer who had loved and left her.† Mme de Sévigné, who usually read everything as it came off the press, probably read these letters when they were published in 1669, making reference to them more than once in her correspondence. Did she see the similarity between the nun who has lost her lover and the Marquise who has lost her daughter—both writing to express their desolation and their heartbreak at such a desertion? Was it consciously or unconsciously that Mme de Sévigné borrowed the nun's amorous vernacular in writing to her daughter? The nun's letters number five; Mme de Sévigné's, almost a thousand; hers, a thousand times more lyrical, more poignant, more original.

Heartbroken though she was, Mme de Sévigné was too shrewd, too

---

La Princesse de Clèves, published in 1678, is considered Mme de La Fayette's masterpiece.

†Gabriel-Joseph, Viscount de Guilleragues, a friend of Mme de Sévigné, is usually credited with authorship of *Letters from a Portuguese Nun*, first published in French translation in 1669.

discerning a student of human nature to allow her letters to her daughter to become a dirge; she would not risk depressing, annoying or boring Mme de Grignan, lest Mme de Grignan stop reading, stop replying! In order to maintain a lively correspondence, as Mme de Sévigné well knew, both correspondents must enjoy the exchange.

"I must console myself by writing to you," Mme de Sévigné wrote on February 20, some three weeks after her daughter's departure from Paris, and then proceeded to amuse her daughter as well as herself by writing one of her highly entertaining, frequently anthologized letters:

I must tell you that, on Wednesday, the day before yesterday, after returning from Mons. de Coulanges's, where we close and seal our letters on the days the mail goes out, I came home and went to bed, which is nothing extraordinary. What is extraordinary is that at three o'clock in the morning, I heard cries of "Robber!" of "Fire!" and those cries so close at hand that I had no doubt that ours was the house in danger. I even thought I heard something said about my granddaughter, and felt sure that she had been burned! In that fear, I got up out of bed, without a light, and trembling so that I could hardly walk. I ran to her apartment, which is your apartment, and found her sleeping peacefully. But I saw the Guitauts' house on fire, with flames over the house of Mme de Vauvineux, as well. In our courtyard but, above all, in Mons. de Guitaut's courtyard, there was so fierce a glare from the flames as to be terrifying. There were shouts, there was confusion, there were frightful noises, beams and rafters crashing. I ordered my gate to be opened, and sent my people to be of assistance. Mons. de Guitaut sent me a chest containing his valuables which I put away in my desk. Then, I wanted to go out on the street to stand and gape like the others. There I found Mons. and Mme de Guitaut, practically naked; Mme de Vauvineux, the Venetian Ambassador and his staff. The little Vauvineux girl was being carried, sound asleep, to the house of the Venetian Ambassador, along with a lot of furniture and silverware to be stored in safety there. Mme de Vauvineux was having all the furniture taken out of her house. As for me, our house was as on an island,* but I felt terribly sorry for my neighbors. Mme Guéton [Mme de Sévigné's land-lady] and her brother offered very good advice. We were all in a dreadful consternation; the fire burned so fiercely that no one dared go near, and one could only hope for the conflagration to end with the

---

*Its courtyards and gardens isolating it from the flames.

last remnant of poor Guitaut's house. He was pitiful. He wanted to go to rescue his Mother who was trapped on the third floor; his wife was clinging to him, violent in her efforts to hold him back. He was torn between the urge to save his Mother and the fear of causing harm to his wife, who was five months pregnant ... Finally, he asked me to hold on to his wife, which I did. He discovered that his Mother had escaped through the flames, and had been saved. He wanted to go in and get out some papers, but could not get near the room where they were kept. Finally, he came back to us in the street, where I had found a seat for his wife. A number of charitable and well-trained Capuchin monks worked so skillfully that they were able to put out the fire; water was poured over the embers and, at last,

"The combat ended for lack of combatants"*

that is to say, after the first and second floors of the antechamber and of the small room and of the study to the right of the salon had been entirely destroyed. One felt grateful for what remained of the house, although poor Guitaut is bound to have a 10,000 écus loss, since they plan to rebuild that apartment which was painted and gilded. Besides, there were several fine paintings belonging to Monsieur le Blanc, the owner of the house ... not to mention a number of tables, mirrors, miniatures, tapestries and other furnishings ... Around five in the morning, it was necessary to think of Mme de Guitaut. I offered her my bed, but Mme Guéton, who has several furnished rooms, put her in hers. We had her bled. We sent for Boucher;† he greatly fears that such a terrible shock will bring on labor within the next nine days ... So, there she is at poor Mme de Guéton's; everybody is going to call on them and, as for me, I continue my attentions, having started off too well to leave off.

You will ask me how the fire started. No one knows. There was no fire burning in the room where it started. But if anyone had the heart to laugh on so sad an occasion, what a funny sight we must have been! Guitaut naked except for his chemise and hose; Mme de Guitaut, barelegged; one house slipper on, the other missing, Mme de Vauvineux in a short skirt, no robe. All the valets, all the neighbors in their nightcaps! The Ambassador was wearing his housecoat and his wig, fully upholding the honor of the Serene Republic! But his secretary

*A quotation from Corneille's Le Cid.
†Boucher was a surgeon-doctor.

was something to see: talk about the chest of Hercules! His was quite different, entirely bare, white, plump, dimpled—without a sign of a chemise, which had been lost when the cord that held it fell off in the thick of battle! And there you have the sad news of our neighborhood. I implore Mons. Deville [the Grignans' maître d'hôtel] to make the rounds every night to see that all the fires are extinguished. One cannot be too careful to avoid such a disaster . . .

In addition to this local news, Mme de Sévigné used up another two or three pages of the same letter to make a full report of all the Paris gossip, bringing the letter to a close with the following paragraph:

And so, here I go, my poor darling, filling page after page with mundanities and idle chatter. But to tell you always that I love you tenderly, that I think only of you, that you are the light of my life, that no one has ever been as dearly loved as you, why, then, the repetition could not but bore you.

If Mme de Grignan's journey—by carriage, by litter, by boat—was arduous, the thought of its perils—bad roads, mountain passes, turbulent rivers—reduced her mother to a state of tremulous anxiety; she could not rest until she had had word of her daughter's safe arrival at her final destination, Aix-en-Provence. But the mails were slow: four days for the courier to make it on horseback from Lyon to Paris; seven or eight days, from Aix: "Just think, my dearest child," she wrote on March 11, "it has been eight days since I have heard from you. For me, that seems a century!" And, "I am in no mood for diversion of any kind," she had written on February 25, "I do not even want to be distracted from following you in thought on your voyage. I have followed you, step by step . . . as faithful a follower by water as by land . . ." A near-accident, a narrow escape at the Bridge of Avignon only justified Mme de Sévigné's phobia about the "fiendish Rhône." The Count de Grignan, having come to meet his Countess along the road, had encouraged her in her foolhardiness. "I know that the danger is safely past," Mme de Sévigné wrote on March 4,

but it is impossible to think of your life in peril without shuddering in horror, and for Mons. de Grignan to allow you to steer the boat! To vie with you in running risks! Instead of having insisted that you wait until the storm was over! Good Lord, it would have been better for him to tell you that if you were not afraid, he was!—and would not allow you to cross the Rhône in such weather! That Rhône which strikes fear in every breast! That Bridge of Avignon under which no one should ever pass without skillful navigation! A wind storm hurling you against a pier! What a miracle that you were not smashed, drowned instantly! My darling, I cannot bear the thought; I shudder: I startle up out of my sleep, at night, in a panic I cannot control ... I am convinced that it was the Masses I had said daily for you which wrought the miracle ... This letter will strike you as ridiculous: you will receive it at a time when you have forgotten all about the Bridge of Avignon. But I am still thinking of it, at this very minute. That is the curse of communication at such a distance; all the replies seem outdated.

(Time out of joint, or out of synchronization, as she might have said today; the time lag in their correspondence would never cease to dismay her, no matter how many years they were apart.)

A month to the day after Mme de Grignan's departure, her mother's grief was still fresh:

There is not a nook or corner in this house which does not wound me to the heart. Your room kills me. I had a screen put up to block the view from the window out of which I watched you step into your carriage, from which I called to you to come back! I frighten myself when I think how close I came to throwing myself out of that window, for I am sometimes mad ... that small room where I embraced you without knowing what I was doing, those Capuchin Fathers where I went to hear Mass, those tears which streamed from my eyes to the ground, as if water had been spilled, Sainte-Marie, Mme de La Fayette, my return to this house, to your room, that night and the next day, and your first letter, and all the other letters that came, that are still coming, and all my conversations with those who show me sympathy. That poor d'Hacqueville above all others; I will never forget how he took pity on me. These are the depths from which I had to rise. But one must not dwell on such things, one must not give in to one's thoughts or to the pangs of one's heart. I prefer to think about the life you are now leading; that gives me some diversion without however interrupting my concentration on what is poetically termed "the love object." Thus, I think of you and am always hoping for a letter. When I receive one, I yearn for the next. I am presently awaiting one, and will resume this letter of mine when it comes.

"Today is the sixth of March," her letter of that day in 1671 began:

I implore you to let me know how you are. If you are well, then you are sick; but, if you are sick, then you are well! I am hoping that you are not well now, so that you may remain in good health for time to come. This is an enigma difficult to comprehend or divine. I hope that you will clarify it for me.

To listen in on this intimate mother-daughter conversation—carried on, as those two thought, in utter privacy—carries with it some of the stigma of voyeurism, for what Mme de Sévigné is saying, of course, is that she knows that Mme de Grignan's menstrual period is due on March 6, and that she ardently hopes that a pregnancy had not interrupted the rhythm of the cycle.

"That was a divine account you wrote of your official entry into Arles"— the Governor's wife as well as the Governor given a formal welcome by the cities under their governance.

You are being treated like the Queen. She never rests; her life is always much as yours has been recently. Thus, you must adopt her attitude and patiently endure all these ceremonies. I am sure that M. de Grignan is highly pleased at the regal reception tendered you ... We are dying to know if you laughed during those speeches. Knowing your weakness, I only hope you were able to keep a straight face. If you did as well as you say you did, everyone should adore you ... The number of people who inquire about you or ask to be remembered to you are legion. My face would be as weary as yours if I had to kiss them all ... Father Bourdaloue preached a sermon, this morning, greater than all the great sermons he has thus far preached. The Court comes and goes at Versailles. Monsieur the Dauphin and Monsieur d'Anjou [sons of the King] are recovering from an illness. And that is good news.

Mme de La Fayette and her coterie remind you of their friendship and hope you have not forgotten them. Mme de La Fayette says she would really love to play the role you are playing, if only for a change ... Your daughter is pretty. I love her and take good care of her. Mme de Tourville is dead; La Gouville weeps bitter tears. Mme the Princess is at Châteauroux ad multos annos. I feel a tenderness for you, my very dear child, which defies expression ... and I send a kiss to Monsieur de Grignan—in spite of the Bridge of Avignon!

By letter of March 11, she wrote:

In spite of myself I have caught a cold, and have stayed at home. Almost all your friends seized upon that occasion to come to call on me. The Abbé Têtu* begged me to remember him to you. I have never seen an absent person so present in the heart of everyone; that miracle was reserved for you. You know we always used to say that the absent were not missed. You are the exception. I spend my life talking of you; those who are best at listening to me are those whom I seek out the most often. But do not start thinking that I make myself ridiculous—I am very sure of both the people and the place, what should be said and what should not. So, you see, I speak well of myself, in passing—for which I ask pardon of [Fathers] Bourdaloue and Mascaron. I hear one or the other of them preach every morning; even a fraction of the marvels they speak should make a saint of me . . .

I admit, my darling, that I simply cannot accustom myself to think of your being two hundred leagues away from me. I am more upset than when you were on the road; I weep afresh on other counts. I simply cannot see into your heart. I picture, I imagine a hundred things so unpleasant that I cannot tell them to you. I do not even know what M. de Grignan is thinking. My head is in a whirl. I see you overwhelmed with honors, honors paid you primarily because of the name you bear; honored not merely because the Count represents the King there, but because the Grignan name is so highly honored [in Provence]. Nothing is greater, nothing more highly respected. No family can be more pleasant, and they adore you, as far as I can tell . . . But what I cannot tell is how you are bearing up in all that hubbub.

Mme de Sévigné evidently had some misgivings about Mme de Grignan's ability to adapt to provincial life, despite all the honors. "It is a strange kind of life that one leads in the provinces," she wrote.

Everything becomes a major issue. I can see that you are working wonders, but I must know what those wonders cost you, before I know whether or not to pity you. The impression I have of you does not lead me to believe that you can easily adapt to such a way of life. Alas, do I flatter myself by thinking that I could sometimes be of help to you, there?

*A literary and worldly cleric who sighed after the pretty Mme Coulanges.

And, on another occasion, she wrote:

I see you making your curtsies, fulfilling your official duties. You are doing very well, I assure you, but try, my child, to accommodate yourself a little more to what is not really bad, to be tolerant of mediocrity, to be grateful for that which is not totally ridiculous.

What she is saying here is that Mme de Grignan plays her official role condescendingly, making mock of the dowdy provincials who come to pay court to the Lieutenant-Governor and his wife. A portrait of Mme de Grignan emerges gradually from her mother's letters, a portrait subtly and obliquely drawn and, curiously enough—in view of Mme de Sévigné's almost blind adoration of her daughter—the sketch is not entirely flattering. Mme de Grignan comes through as impatient, supercilious, sarcastic; sometimes incapable of maintaining her composure, sometimes awkward in handling social situations—serious drawbacks for a person in a public position.*

Your descriptions are most amusing—your embarrassment, your misplaced civilities [Mme de Sévigné wrote on another day]. Alas, how useful I might be to you there! Not that I could do any better than you at connecting names and faces ... That is not one of my talents, either. I make a thousand mistakes in that direction, but I could help you in making your reverences. Ah, how weary you must be, my poor love, and how exhausting that role must be for Mlle de Sévigné, for even Mme de Grignan, as civil as she tries to be.

Monsieur de Grignan, according to his mother-in-law, likewise expressed misgivings as to his wife's ability to play the role of Vicereine:

The thought never crossed my mind [Mme de Sévigné wrote later in March of 1671] that all was not well between you and M. de Grignan. I do not think I ever implied such a thing. Otherwise, Provence would be unbearable ... but I easily understand that he was fearful that you might languish there, might perish of boredom. We have, he and I, the same apprehensions.

Mme de Grignan, in her letter of March 4, acknowledged receipt of her mother's letter about the fire at the Count de Guitaut's house, to which

---

*The Duke de Saint-Simon would write many years later in his *Mémoires* that Mme de Grignan was far from popular with Provençals.

letter Mme de Sévigné replied in the last pages of her letter begun on March 11:

How very funny, Madame Countess, for you to be showing around letters of mine! But is it not a principle of yours to be secretive about your correspondence, to conceal that which is closest to your heart? Do you not remember how painful it was for you to confide in us so much as the date of a letter from the Count? You think to appease me with your praises, and by treating me as if I were the Holland Gazette. I will get even with you. You conceal the sentimental passages of my letters, you little baggage, whereas I—on the other hand—sometimes show—to certain, special people only—those you write to me. I do not want people to think that I nearly died, that I constantly weep— "for whom, for an ingrate"!* I want people to know that you love me, that if you have all my heart, I have a place in yours ... Here is a passage that you will conceal, for not since Niobe has there been a mother to speak in such a fashion ...

I dine every Friday at Le Mans's,† with Monsieur de La Rochefoucauld, Mme de Brissac and Benserade,‡ who is always the life of the party. Your health is always drunk, and your absence always lamented. If Provence thinks well of me, I am, for my part, very loyal to Provence. Preserve me the honor of her good graces; I will pay her my compliments in person when you wish. I have promised you a voyage there; it is up to you to set the date ...

I love your child because of you. I do not yet have that truly grandmotherly feeling in my entrails.

Goodbye, my very dear child. I am so absolutely, so totally yours that it is impossible to add so much as an iota more. I would ask to kiss your pretty cheeks and embrace you tenderly, but that would start me crying again.

The correspondence with her daughter was to become the mainspring, the mainstay of her life:

To read your letters to me and to write my letters to you are the first order of business of my life. Our correspondence takes precedence over

---

*Quotation from Racine's *Andromaque*: Orestes says, "I become a parricide, assassin, sacrilegious/ For whom? for an ingrate."

†The Bishop of Le Mans, brother-in-law of her good friend Mme de Lavardin.

‡Benserade was the librettist of the royal ballets.

everything; any other correspondence seems trivial. You can be sure that I always write you twice weekly. If I could write twice as often,* I would be just as punctual to that schedule—not out of any sense of duty but because of the pleasure I take in it.

"And here I am at my heart's delight," she wrote on another day, "all alone in my room, writing—undisturbed—to you. Nothing is so agreeable to me as that."

Or, phrased another way:

Finally your letter comes, and here I am, all alone in my room, writing to you in reply ... as I do with the greatest pleasure in the world. When I leave the place where I have dined, I come back here, and when I find a letter from you, I come in and write. There is no greater delight in my life, and I live for the mail-days when I write to you.

"My God, how eagerly I await your letters!" she wrote elsewhere. "It's been almost an hour already since I received one!"

The correspondence was as regular as the irregularity of the mails would permit. The seventeenth century differing little in that regard from the twentieth, complaint about the postal department became a main theme of the correspondence.

"I simply cannot understand the postal service!" Mme de Sévigné repeatedly complained:

It is irregular, and those same obliging fellows who set out at midnight to carry my letters to you will not take the pains to bring yours back to me! ... To come back to those letters of mine which you still have not received: I am in despair. Do you think they are being opened? Do you think they are being withheld?† Alas, I conjure those who are responsible to weigh the small pleasure they can find in reading our mail against the great distress they are causing us. Gentlemen, take the trouble, at least, to reseal these letters so that they will eventually reach their destination!

---

*She could write twice as often if there were four couriers a week to Provence, instead of only two.
†Mail surveillance was commonplace in Old Régime France.

XIII

Late in February, 1671, some few weeks after Mme de Grignan's departure from Paris, Charles de Sévigné makes his appearance on the scene in the *Correspondence.* In her voluminous letter to her daughter, Mme de Sévigné devotes only a scant few lines to her son's arrival: "Your brother returned the day before yesterday [from Nancy where he was in winter quarters with his regiment, the Gendarmes-Dauphin]. I have scarcely seen him. He is at Saint-Germain" [with the Court].

In early March, Charles added a note to one of his mother's letters to Mme de Grignan, congratulating his sister on her "escape from the perils of the Rhône" and on the royal reception tendered her in her "Kingdom of Arles."

The next thing we hear of the dashing young cavalry officer, he is involved in an amorous liaison with—of all people!—an aging, ageless Ninon de l'Enclos—taking up with the famous courtesan where his father had left off. Like father, like son—Charles's mother must have thought, writing with bitterness:

> *Your brother is in the toils of Ninon. I doubt that any good will come of it. There are certain people to whom such experiences are harmful. She blighted his Father's life. We can only commend him [Charles, that is] to God. When one is a good Christian—or, at least, wants to be— one cannot contemplate these irregularities without dismay.*

By mid-March, the situation had further deteriorated: "Your brother is at Saint-Germain, dividing his attentions between Ninon and a comedienne."*

"How dangerous she is, that Ninon!" Mme de Sévigné wrote on April 1:

> *If you only knew how she dogmatizes on the subject of religion, you would be horrified . . . She finds that your brother has the simplicity of*

---

*The comedienne was La Champmeslé, the most famous actress of her day and mistress of Racine, the playwright, and star of his greatest tragedies.

a dove—in which (according to her) he resembles his Mother! It is Mme de Grignan, she says, who has all the salt and spice of the family! ... I am deeply concerned about the harm she may do my son in this respect, but please say nothing to him about it. We are doing our best, Mme de La Fayette and I, to extricate him from the entanglement. He is also involved with a little comedienne, along with Despréaux and Racine, and is paying for all their little supper parties. All in all, it is a devilish business.

On April 8, the news bordered on the sensational:

Let us talk about your brother. He has had his dismissal from Ninon. She wearied of loving without being loved in return. She demanded that her letters be returned to her, and they were. I was very pleased at the rupture. I always managed to say a word or two about God and to remind him of how devout he had formerly been and to beg him not to stifle the Holy Spirit in his heart. Had I not been free to drop a word or two such as this, every now and then, I would not have allowed him to make me such confidences ... But that is not the end of the story: when one breaks off on one side, one might hope to make up for it on the other, but such is not the case. The young marvel [La Champmeslé] has not yet broken with him, but I think she will. Here is why: my son came yesterday from the other end of Paris to tell me about the accident that befell him. A favorable occasion had presented itself, and yet ... dare I say it? "He could not get his dada up at Lerida."* It was a very strange situation: the demoiselle had never before found herself in such a predicament. The cavalier made his exit, in disarray, convinced that he had been bewitched. But what you will find amusing is that he could not wait to tell me about his mortification. We laughed uproariously. I told him that I was delighted that he had been punished for his sins at the precise point of origin! He laid the blame on me, telling me that it was from me that he had inherited his frigidity, that he would gladly have passed up such an inherited characteristic, and that I would have been better off transmitting it to my daughter instead of to my son!

If it was true, as the Count de Bussy maliciously maintained, that Mme de Sévigné's conversation sometimes verged on the risqué, then it is clear—

---

*The quotation came from a scabrous limerick attributed to the Prince de Condé apropos of a mishap he had had in Spain when he failed to function properly in an amorous encounter.

if the above passage is any example—that she handled such questionable material with a deft and delicate touch, and it might be also added, in her defense, that the times of Louis XIII in which she had reached maturity were notoriously libertine.

"He [Charles] wanted [Doctor] Pecquet to restore him," her letter of April 1 continues:

He talked a lot of nonsense, and so did I. It was a scene worthy of Molière! . . . I tried in vain to assure him that the amorous empire is filled with tragic stories; he is inconsolable. The little actress says that she can see that he no longer loves her, and consoles herself elsewhere. In short, it is a malfunction which makes me laugh, and which I hope with all my heart will serve to turn him away from a state so offensive to God . . .

On April 15, Mme de Sévigné wrote again to her daughter:

That was a very good letter you wrote to your brother, as was the one you wrote to Monsieur de Coulanges. I love your letters passionately. You have guessed right: your brother is up to his ears in philandering. No Easter observances, no Jubilee—"swallowing sin like water"! It is all amazing. The only redeeming feature I can find in him is his fear of committing sacrilege. The malady of his soul has stricken his body, and his mistresses are of an ilk unlikely to put up long with such an incommodity. All of God's works are for the best! I am hoping that a trip to Lorraine will break all these vile chains. He is amusing; he gives me much joy; he tries to please me. I know what affection he has for me. He is thrilled, by his account, about the affection you now show me. He is always assailing me, in a laughing tone, about the attachment I feel for you—which, I admit, is great, no matter how hard I try to conceal it from you.

Charles's affairs went from bad to worse, and he spared his mother no details: "My son is not yet cured of that indisposition which makes his precious mistresses doubt his passion," she wrote later in April:

He told me, yesterday evening, that during Holy Week, he had indulged in such awful debauchery that he had been overcome with a dreadful disgust. He dared not think of it: it made him want to vomit. Everywhere around him, he seemed to see baskets full of breasts and thighs ... baskets full of all sorts of things in such abundance that he could not get it out of his mind—nor yet can—and could not bear so much as even to look at a woman! He was like a horse to which hay had become repulsive. He has not yet recovered from this state of mind. I took the occasion to give him a little lecture on the subject. Together, we made Christian reflections. He seems to share my sentiments, at least as long as his disgust endures. He showed me his letters which he had retrieved from the little comedienne. I never read anything so fervent, so impassioned; he was weeping, he was dying of love! He believes it all when he is writing it, and then laughs at himself a moment later. I assure you that he is worth his weight in gold.

Mme de Sévigné's report on Charles's amours was resumed a few days later:

He has broken with the comedienne, after having loved her in his fashion. When he saw her or when he wrote to her, he was in good faith; a moment later, he made mock of it all. Ninon has broken with him. He was miserable when she loved him; he is in despair now that she no longer does, and all the more so for the reason that she now talks disparagingly of him: "His soul is made of mush," she says; "his body of wet paper; and his heart is like a pumpkin fricasseed in snow."

Having retrieved his own letters to La Champmeslé, Charles was about to hand her letters over to Ninon—when his mother stopped him:

I told him it was infamous of him thus to cut the throat of that poor little creature for having loved him, that she had not shown his letters around, as some would have had him believe, but had instead returned them to him, that it would be base treachery on his part and unworthy of a gentleman of quality not to do the same with hers. He saw reason, ran to Ninon's ... and retrieved the letters written by that poor little devil. I had them burned ... My son has given an account of his follies to Monsieur de La Rochefoucauld, who loves odd characters. He agreed with me, the other day, when I said that my son is no fool when it comes to his head; it is his heart which is given to folly. We laughed heartily about all that, and even in the presence of my son, who is very good company, and a good sport. We get along very well together. I am his confidante, and I retain that quality which invites his wretched confidences in order to be able to speak my mind about everything. He

*trusts me as best he can, begs me to straighten him out, which I do—
as a friend. He wants to go to Brittany with me for five or six weeks. If
he does not have to go to camp in Lorraine,* I will take him.*

While Charles had desecrated Holy Week with his debauchery, his
mother had gone to her beloved Livry, on Tuesday of that week, to prepare
herself for Easter. "I left Paris," she wrote on March 24, 1671,

*with the Abbé, Hélène, Hébert and Marphise†—with the intention of
staying in seclusion until Thursday evening, far from the world and its
turmoil. I expect to remain in solitude. I will make a kind of Trappist
retreat. I came here to pray, and to make a thousand reflections. I plan
to fast a great deal—for all sorts of reasons—and to spend as much
time out walking as I do in my room, and, above all, to be bored for
the love of God. But, my poor darling, what I shall do most of is to
think of you. I have not stopped since I arrived here . . . and being
unable to control my emotions, I have set myself down to write to you
at the end of that short shady walk which you love, seated on the
mossy bench on which I have sometimes seen you stretch out to rest.
But, my God, where have I not seen you here? . . . There is no place,
no spot—neither in the house nor in the church, nor in the countryside,
nor in the garden—where I have not seen you . . . No matter where I
turn, where I look, I search in vain: that dear child whom I love with
such a passion is two hundred leagues away from me; I no longer have
her. At which thought, I weep uncontrollably . . . I cannot go on, my
dearest darling . . .*

On Holy Thursday, at Livry, she had picked up her pen again:

*If only I had wept for my sins as I have wept for you since I have been
here, I would be prepared to celebrate Easter and the Jubilee . . . I have
found comfort in the sadness I experience here. A vast solitude, a deep
silence, a sad service, the Tenebrae sung with much feeling‡ (I have
never been at Livry before for Holy Week), a canonical fast, and a
beauty in these gardens which would have delighted you; all of this*

---

*Charles's regiment was quartered in Lorraine.

†The Abbé was her uncle the Abbé de Coulanges, Abbot of Livry; Hélène was her maid; Hébert a
member of her sizeable domestic staff; and Marphise was her little dog, named for a character in Ariosto's
Orlando Furioso.

‡*Tenebrae* are the matins and lauds of the last three days of Holy Week.

was good for me. Alas, how much I wished for you! . . . I will return to Paris tomorrow, out of necessity . . . Had I had the strength to resist writing to you while I was here, and to make a sacrifice to God of all I felt here, that would have been better than all the penitences in the world. But, instead of making good use of my time, I sought consolation in talking to you.* Ah, my darling, how weak and miserable I am!

It was at Livry, during Holy Week, that Mme de Sévigné first became conscious of the conflict raging in her heart between her love for her daughter and her love of God: "love of the Creator," as she would phrase it, versus "love of the creature," the human being. It was a tug of war which would distress her for years. Had she not come to that realization on her own, her visit to Pomponne, on the last day of April—to see her old and dear friend Arnauld d'Andilly—would have revealed the truth to her. (The saintly eighty-two-year-old Arnauld d'Andilly was the father of the Marquis de Pomponne to whom her Fouquet trial letters had been addressed.)

I left Paris rather early yesterday morning, and went to dine at Pomponne. I found our good old friend waiting for me . . . and I found him in an astonishing state of saintliness; the closer he comes to death, the more he is purified. He scolded me severely and, carried away by his zeal and his love for me, he told me that I was very foolish not to give thought to my salvation; that I was an outright pagan, that I had set you up as an idol in my heart, and that that sort of idolatry was as dangerous as any other kind, even though it might not seem sinful to me. In sum, he told me that I had best give thought to my immortal soul, and he said all this so vehemently that I could not find a word to say in reply. So, after six hours of very pleasant if very serious conversation, I left him and came here to Livry where I found the month of May in triumph.

> *"The nightingale, the cuckoo and the warbler*
> *Have heralded the advent of spring in our forests."*

I walked alone, all evening . . . I set aside this time, after dinner, to write to you in the garden where I now sit bewildered by three or four nightingales singing on top of my head!

To read such passages as these is to be reminded of Proust, who gave it as his opinion (speaking through Charlus in the novel *Within a Budding*

---

*Mme de Sévigné regarded the correspondence as a conversation.

Grove) that "the emotion felt by Mme de Sévigné for her daughter could be justly said far more to resemble that grand passion Racine portrays in *Andromaque* or *Phèdre* than did the banal relations between Charles de Sévigné and his mistresses."

Mme de Sévigné found time, that spring, to pay her court at Saint-Germain where the monarchs were in residence: it was the part of discretion to remind them of the absent Grignans; the memory of the Court was notoriously short. She could report a most cordial reception by Her Majesty:

> *The Queen took a step in my direction, and asked me for news of my daughter, remarking that she had heard of your narrow escape from drowning. I thanked her for the honor she did you by her inquiries. She then said to me, "Tell me about how she nearly perished." Whereupon I began the account of your temerity in crossing the Rhône in a high wind, and how you were nearly dashed against the pillar of the Bridge . . . "They were very foolish," she replied in a flurry of Alas!es, concluding with some very obliging remarks about you.*

The Queen deigned to address Mme de Sévigné a second time, that night, inquiring,

> *"Whom does your granddaughter resemble?"—"Madame," I replied, "she resembles Monsieur de Grignan." At which she cried out, "Too bad!" and then said to me most kindly, "She would have done better to resemble her Mother or her Grandmother!" And that is how I pay my court for you, my poor darling.*

The Court was in residence at Saint-Germain in 1671 while the King planned and directed the extensive landscaping and architectural projects at Versailles, to which he would move in 1682. Mme de Sévigné could give Mme de Grignan reports on the progress of the new château, thanks to Mme de La Fayette who had been invited there for a visit:

> *She was received very well, exceedingly well, which is to say that the King invited her to ride in his own carriage with his ladies, and took great pleasure in showing her the beauties of Versailles, much like a private individual whom one visits at his new country house. He spoke only to her and listened most politely and delightedly to the praises she spoke of the marvels and beauties he showed her. You can imagine how pleased she was at such a reception.*

But what interested Mme de Sévigné far more than the wonders of Versailles was the state of her daughter's health the first week of every month. The month of April was no exception, and she slipped her query deftly into a closing paragraph:

Let me know how you were the sixth of this month. Your dresses so well made, that figure of yours so prettily rounded in its natural state— Oh, my God, keep it that way for my visit to Provence!

And there was a message for the Count, as well:

My dear Grignan, if you think your wife so beautiful, then keep her that way! It is bad enough for her to have to endure the heat in Provence, this summer, without being sick. [Mme de Sévigné's word "malade" was a euphemism for "pregnant."]

Mme de Grignan's reply, evidently evasive, inconclusive, was of small comfort to her mother: "I have a very poor opinion of your languors," Mme de Sévigné wrote on April 27:

You can count me among the gossips, and I believe the worst; this is the very thing I feared. But, my dear child, if this mishap is confirmed, take good care of yourself. Do not subject yourself, these first few months, to the jolting of a voyage to Marseille. Wait a bit, and give things time to establish themselves. Think of your delicate health, and remember that it was only by being very careful that you carried to term, last time.

I am already very upset at the thought of the derangement that my trip to Brittany will make in our correspondence. If you are pregnant, be sure that I no longer have any plan except to do what you would like me to. I will be governed by your wishes, and will put aside all other plans, all other considerations . . . I implore you, my child, to tell me truthfully all the news of your health, your plans, what you want me to do. I am very sad at your state. I imagine that you must be, too. I foresee a thousand difficulties, and my thoughts do not make for good company by day or by night.

"How distressed I am at this misfortune," she exclaimed in her next letter, "and yet how clearly I foresaw it!"

One cannot but wonder at the reaction of the Count de Grignan to his mother-in-law's designation of the Countess's pregnancy as "a misfortune." Was it not presumptuous on her part so to characterize it when the entire Grignan family, including the Countess herself, lived in the hope of a male heir—which neither of the Count's two previous wives had been able to produce—to ensure the continuation of that long and noble Grignan line? It is not surprising to note the discord developing between mother and daughter on a matter concerning which they held such divergent views.

XIV

Mme de Sévigné was concerned not only about her daughter's third pregnancy in two years' time, she was deeply concerned, as well, about the Grignans' financial problems. As prestigious as was the Grignans' position in Provence and as great a source of pride as it was to Mme de Sévigné, still she could not but worry about the tremendous expense inherent in the office of provincial governor. It was not unusual for an official to bankrupt himself in the service of the King. The compensation provided by the Royal Exchequer was insufficient to maintain the regal life-style required of a representative of the King; a man had to be independently wealthy to accept the post, much as in the case of the ambassadorial service of many modern nations.

In the capital city of Aix-en-Provence, the ancient Palace of the Counts of Provence and of the fabled King René served not only to house the provincial Parlement but the Grignans and their huge entourage as well: the Count with his Guards and his Gentlemen; the Countess, like the Queen, with her ladies-in-waiting. There, the Grignans held court, open to all Provence, with a constant round of official receptions, with balls and banquets, fêtes and galas, masquerades, musicales, theatricals. Not only that, they literally threw their money out the windows on gala days in Aix; the populace expected just such largesse from the Palace. It was an extreme case of *noblesse oblige*, and it cost the Grignans a fortune. To top if off, the Countess as well as the Count had a propensity for games of chance. There was talk in Paris, as early as March of 1671, about the lavishness of the Grignans' way of life in their governance of Provence. It came to Mme de Sévigné's ears, and she was deeply concerned: "Do not live on so grand a scale. People are talking about your extravagance. Monsieur de Monaco cannot stop talking about it.* But, above all, try to sell a property. There is no other resource open to you."†

"We talk constantly about your problems, the Abbé and I," Mme de Sévigné wrote on March 15:

He is giving you a full accounting, which is why I say nothing on that score. Your health, your peace of mind, your affairs are my main concern. To what conclusions I come, I leave to your imagination . . . You give me cause to be hopeful about that matter.‡ Keep after it constantly, and spare no maneuvering to bring it to a successful conclusion. If you succeed, it will be worth more to you than the sale of a property with 10,000 livres annual revenue. As for your other affairs, I dare not think of them, and yet I do so constantly. You should take charge of everything; that is what might save you. First on the list should be your determination not to cause further ruin by lavish spending, and try to avoid, as best you can, getting into financial straits which would cause you to give up plans to return here. I put my trust in your ability and your good judgment. You have determination, which is the best quality you could have for what you have to do . . .

On another occasion, that spring, she wrote:

The Abbé is very pleased about the attention you are giving your business affairs. Do not lose interest, my darling. Take complete charge of things. It will be the salvation of the House of Grignan.

When it came to subject matter, Mme de Sévigné's letters ran the gamut from the sublime to the ridiculous, from the tender to the caustic, and back again. The topics covered by her letters are as infinite in their variety as the specimens in a botanical garden. Her pen raced at breakneck speed (her own word for its pace) from family affairs to national or international events, from local gossip to literary, musical and theatrical reportage, from the Court Circular to the fashion scene. She devoted several pages, in mid-

---

*The Prince of Monaco had recently visited the Grignans at Aix.

†That resource was not open to them for the reason that the Grignan properties were entailed to their descendants and could not be sold.

‡The matter of the 5,000 livres' annual maintenance for the Count's Guards, whose personal responsibility it would be until payment was voted by the Assembly of the Communities of Provence.

March of 1671, to a new high-style coiffure, known as the "*hurluberlu*" (or "hurlyburly"): the beautiful Duchess de Ventadour (recently married to the most hideous and debauched nobleman in the kingdom) was the first to appear, in Paris, wearing her hair in the new tousled look.

"Her hair was cut short," Mme de Sévigné reported, "and rolled in a hundred curlpapers, causing her to suffer a thousand deaths, all night long [less agonizing, Mme de Sévigné implied, than sleeping with the Duke, to whom she referred as "a monster"!]." "My daughter, it is the most ridiculous hairstyle you can imagine. And you can believe me, for you know how I love fashion."

Mme de Sévigné was so fashion-conscious that, within a few days' time, she expressed herself as "charmed" with the new coiffure, and urged her daughter to try it immediately, "so that you will no longer dress your hair in those hundred tight little curls over your ears, which are not becoming and are now as outmoded as the hairdress worn by Queen Catherine de Médicis!"

"Yesterday, I saw the Duchess de Sully and the Countess de Guiche," she continued:

Their heads looked charming. I have succumbed. This new coiffure is designed just for your face; you will look like an angel, and it takes only a moment to arrange . . . The hair is cut, on each side, in layers— out of which one makes round, loose curls to hang no lower than an inch below the ears. The effect is somehow very youthful and very pretty—like two large bouquets of hair on each side . . . One uses one's ribbons in it, as usual . . . I will have a doll's hair dressed in this fashion, and send it to you. What is certain is that the old coiffure which Montgobert* knows how to arrange is now out of the question. I see you before my eyes, and this new hairdress is made for you. But how ridiculous it looks on some ladies whose age or faces are not suitable!

In that spring of 1671, Mme de Sévigné and her uncle, the *Bien Bon*, were making their plans to go to Brittany: after a five-year absence, her presence there was required in the supervision and administration of her extensive properties. "I am even more fearful than you of my voyage to Brittany," she wrote to her daughter in late March: "I see it as still another separation, a sadness upon a sadness, an absence upon an absence. I am now becoming very distressed about it. It will be in early May."

*Mademoiselle Montgobert was Mme de Grignan's *dame de compagnie*, or lady-companion.

As the time for her departure for Brittany drew near, Mme de Sévigné's dismay mounted: "As if it were not enough to be two hundred leagues away from you," she wrote toward the end of April, "I must now make it three hundred, and every step I take in that direction will be on the third hundred. It is too much. It wrings my heart."

She had been tempted to take the infant Marie-Blanche with her to Brittany "as a diversion for me," but the new wet nurse would not budge beyond the Paris city limits. "As for your child," she wrote Mme de Grignan on April 8,

here is the news: I found her pale, the past few days. I also found that her nurse's nipples never leaked. The thought struck me that she might not have enough milk. I sent for [Doctor] Pecquet, who found me very observant, but told me he would have to wait and see for a day or two. He returned two or three days later, and found that the baby had lost weight. I go to Mme du Puy du Fou's house;* she comes here; she sees what I saw but, since she never arrives at a conclusion, she said we should wait and see. "And see what, Madame?" I asked. By chance, I come across a woman from Sucy,† who tells me that she knows a wonderful wet nurse; I had her come to see me . . . I went to Mme du Puy du Fou, who gave me her approval. As for the little one, on Sunday, I turned her over to the new nurse. It was a pleasure to see her nurse. She had never nursed like that before. Her other nurse had little milk; this one is like a cow. She is a good peasant woman, no airs about her, good teeth, black hair, sunburnt skin, about twenty-four years old. Her child is four months old, beautiful as an angel. Pecquet is thrilled to know our baby will no longer go hungry. We could see that she was . . . always looking for more. I have gained a great reputation, thanks to this incident . . . I was unable to sleep peacefully at night in the thought that the little one was languishing, in the thought that we would have to send away the other nice woman—who was, personally, all one could wish for. The only thing she lacked was milk! I am paying this one two hundred and fifty livres a year,‡ and will dress her, although in most modest fashion. And that is how we take care of your affairs.

I shall leave in about a month or five weeks. My aunt [the Marquise

---

*Mme du Puy du Fou was one of the Count de Grignan's former mothers-in-law as well as an intimate friend of Mme de Sévigné's, and considered by her to be the final authority on child care.

†The village of Sucy in the Paris suburbs where the Coulanges had their summer home.

‡The nurse's wages of 250 livres a year may be compared to the 1,500 livres annually paid by the Grignans for their apartment in the Paris town house.

de La Trousse] is staying here, and will be delighted to have the child;
she is not going to La Trousse this year. If the nurse were a woman
willing to separate herself from her family, I think I would take her to
Brittany with me, but she was reluctant to come even as far as Paris.
Your little girl is growing loveable; I am becoming attached to her.
In two weeks' time, she will be a little kitten white as snow, laugh-
ing constantly. And there, my darling, you have the news in terrible
detail ... Do not thank me for anything. Keep your ceremonial
speeches for your ladies. I love your little family tenderly. It is a plea-
sure to me, not a duty.

Mme de Sévigné's granddaughter was slowly but surely winning her
over: "My little girl has been in my room, all day, dressed in her finest laces
and doing the honors of the house," she wrote. And, in another letter, "She
is pretty, that poor little thing. She comes to my room, in the mornings; she
laughs, she looks about her. She still does not give a proper kiss, but perhaps
time will correct that failing. I love her. She amuses me. I will leave her
regretfully."

Charles would accompany Mme de Sévigné on this voyage, although
Marie-Blanche would not. "I shall take him with me to Brittany," she wrote
in late April, "where I hope to see him recover both his physical and spiritual
well-being. Between us, La Mousse* and I will manage to get him to
confession."

No true Parisienne, in any age, would leave her city without replenish-
ing her wardrobe. Mme de Sévigné was no exception, writing on April 24,
1671:

I bought some fabric much like that in the last skirt you bought, from
which I am having a housecoat made. It is lovely: there is a little green
in it, but violet is the predominant color. I succumbed. They suggested
lining it in a flame red, but I thought that might give it the air of a final
impenitence. The fabric betrays the weakness of my character, but that
red lining would have been positively immoral, so I decided on a white
taffeta, instead. It was not expensive. I do not care about Brittany, but
am having it made with Provence in mind, in order to uphold the
reputation you have given me of an ageless wonder.

*Pierre de La Mousse, a priest, Doctor of Theology, and Cartesian, who had been one of Mme de
Grignan's tutors, had become a household fixture.

Her letter of April 24 began like a Court Circular: all eyes in France were fastened, that week, on the Château at Chantilly where the King and all his Court were to visit the King's cousin the Prince de Condé:

We are now having the most beautiful weather in the world. It began the day before yesterday after dreadful rains. It is the "King's weather,"* as we have often called it, although this time it is the good luck of the Prince de Condé, who had been counting on spring or summer weather when he made his elaborate plans for the King's entertainment. Rain, as on the day before yesterday, would have made all his expenditures ridiculous. His Majesty arrived there yesterday evening, and is there today. D'Hacqueville went too; he will give you an account on his return. I am waiting for a brief report from him, this evening, which I will send on to you with this letter which I start writing, this morning . . .

Her letter continued, dated "Wednesday evening, at Monsieur de La Rochefoucauld's":

I am closing my letter here. I had intended to tell you that the King arrived yesterday evening at Chantilly. He went stag-hunting by the light of the moon; the lanterns provided a marvelous illumination. The fireworks were somewhat dimmed by the brightness of our friend (the moon); but, all in all, the supper, the gaming, everything went along splendidly. The weather yesterday made us hope for more of the same. But here is the news I heard upon entering here, news from which I cannot recover, news which so affects me that I hardly know what I am writing. The news is that Vatel—the great Vatel, the maître d'hôtel of Monsieur Fouquet and more recently of Monsieur the Prince, that man of such outstanding ability, head and shoulders above all the rest, that man whose good head was capable of handling affairs of state—Vatel, that man whom I knew—Vatel, when he discovered, at eight o'clock this morning, that the seafood shipments which he had ordered had not come, could not face the disgrace he knew would be sure to follow— and, to sum it up, he ran himself through with his poignard. You can imagine the horrible dismay that so terrible an accident caused at that

---

*Louis XIV's good luck, his lucky star—his "star"—brought him not only success in battle but good weather for his expeditions, or so a superstitious nation interpreted it.

royal fête. And to think—the seafood shipments arrived just as he was expiring!

The next bulletin began, "It is Sunday, April 26":

The King arrived Thursday evening. The hunt, the lanterns, the moonlight, the promenade, the collation served in a spot carpeted with jonquils—all went off perfectly. The guests supped. There were several tables where the roast was missing because of a number of unexpected guests. This greatly upset Vatel. He says several times: "My honor is at stake; here is a shame I cannot endure." He says to Gourville, "My head is in a whirl. I have not slept for twelve nights. Help me in giving the orders." Gourville comforted him as best he could. The roast had been missing not at the King's table but at the twenty-fifth table, but even so he could not get it off his mind. Gourville tells Monsieur the Prince about it. Monsieur the Prince went all the way to Vatel's room and told him: "Vatel, all goes well. Nothing could have been more perfect than the supper you served the King." He replies: "Monseigneur, your kindness finishes me. I know that two tables had no roast." "Not so," says Monsieur the Prince: "Try not to be upset about it. All goes well." Night comes. The fireworks are not a success; they are veiled in clouds. They cost 16,000 francs. At four o'clock in the morning, Vatel is pacing from place to place. Everyone is asleep. He meets a small purveyor who is bringing him two containers of seafood. He asks that man, "Is that all there is?" "Yes, Monsieur." The man did not know that Vatel had placed orders for seafood at every port. Vatel waits for some time; no other shipments arrive. He becomes very excited. He is convinced that there will be no other deliveries of seafood. He finds Gourville, and tells him: "Monsieur, I will not survive this disgrace. I have my honor and my reputation to lose." Gourville laughed at him. Vatel goes up to his room, places his sword against the door, and runs it through his heart—although not until the third try, the first two wounds not being mortal. He falls dead. The shipments of seafood begin to come in from all directions. They look for Vatel to distribute it. They go to his room. They try to open the door; they burst it open; they find him drowned in his own blood. They rush to Monsieur the Prince, who was in despair ... Monsieur the Prince related the story with great sadness to the King. They said it was because he was a man of honor, after his own fashion. They praised him highly. They lauded and they criticized his courage. The King said that he had put off his visit to Chantilly for five years because he well understood the extreme strain it put on his hosts. He told the Prince that he should have prepared only two tables and not tried to handle the rest; he swore he would never again allow Monsieur the Prince to commit himself to such an undertaking. But it was too late for poor Vatel. Gourville, however, is trying to make up for the loss of Vatel, and succeeding. They dined very well; they partook of a collation; they supped, they promenaded, they gambled, they hunted. Jonquils perfumed the air; there was enchantment everywhere. Yesterday, which was Saturday, the schedule was the same. And that evening, the King left for Liancourt . . .

The Abbé d'Hacqueville, that good family friend who had been among the guests at Chantilly, was to give Mme de Grignan a firsthand account. "But since his handwriting is so much less legible than mine," Mme de Sévigné explained, "I am sending you mine, as well." And well it was that she did: if Vatel is enshrined in culinary history as the premier chef of France—and thus, of the world!—he has Mme de Sévigné's letter to thank for it. No anthology of letters would be complete without it.

XV

To travel still farther away from her daughter at a time when her daughter was pregnant made Mme de Sévigné still further dread the departure for Brittany. Not only had Mme de Grignan, by then, confirmed to her mother the fact that she was pregnant, the news was making the rounds in Paris, as Mme de Sévigné advised her by letter of May 6, 1671:

Monsieur de Marseille* has written the Abbé de Pontcarré that you are pregnant. I made it my duty for a long time to conceal that misfortune, but to do so any longer would make me a laughingstock . . . I embrace Monsieur de Grignan despite his iniquities. I implore him, at least—

*Monsieur de Marseille was the Bishop of Marseille.

since "He who brings on the malady should supply the medicine"—to take extremely good care of you . . .

Mme de Sévigné was very nervous about the trip to Marseille which the Countess de Grignan was planning, apprehensive about the jolting of the carriage, about the reports of smallpox in the area, about the salvos of cannon set off to greet the arrival of the Governor's wife. "I tremble for your health," Mme de Sévigné wrote, fearful that the sound of gunfire might bring on a miscarriage.

"What a madness," she exclaimed in a letter written in mid-May, just before her departure for Brittany, "to go off in a direction directly opposite to that in which one's heart is straining!"

If ever I could see my way clear to go to Provence, I would be transported with joy. The constant desire to get your letters and to hear how you are gnaws at my heart so ferociously that I do not know how I will be able to bear it . . . I am busy giving the instructions necessary to ensure the best mail service possible. I think I have done the best I can.

"I imagine you will want to hear about my equipage," she wrote on May 13:

I am travelling with two barouches.* I will have seven carriage horses, one packhorse to carry my bed, and three or four outriders. I will travel in my carriage, drawn by my two fine horses. The Abbé will ride with me, part of the time. In the other carriage, my son and La Mousse and Hélène; their carriage will have four horses and a postillion. From time to time, the breviaries will be relegated to the second carriage, giving place to a certain breviary by Corneille which Sévigné and I are eager to read . . .

Her last letter from Paris was datelined, "Monday morning, just before leaving, May 18," and begins:

At last, my darling, here I am, about to step into my carriage. All is in readiness. I bid you adieu. I can never speak that word to you without deep sorrow. This departure of mine makes me think of yours. And

---

*Barouches were light four-wheeled carriages.

that is a thought I can scarcely bear, that thought of the eve and day of your departure! My suffering at that hour is something unique in my life, comparable to nothing I have ever known before. What is called tearing one's heart out, breaking it, piercing it, lacerating it—that is what happened, that day, to mine. And this is said without exaggeration . . .

And so I am on my way to Brittany, my very dear darling. I feel the sorrow of putting still more distance between us. Is it possible that we can be going still farther from one another when we are already two hundred leagues apart? Somehow I am finding a way to do it: just as you found that the city of Aix was not far off enough, I find that Paris is too close. You went to Marseille to escape me, and I am going to Vitré* to go you one better!

In all seriousness, my darling, I am very sad about our correspondence, which has been my greatest consolation and my greatest diversion. It will be seriously affected by the increase in distance. Still, I hope, the instructions I am leaving will be effective. My little friend at the postal bureau is very cordial. His name is Mons. Dubois. Do not forget it. When you get to Grignan, you need only notify him of the change of address. The Coadjutor of Rheims recommended our correspondence to his attention . . .

To have news of you is the joy of my life. Do not try to convince me, my little one, that my letters could mean to you what yours mean to me. Alas, what will I have to write to you about from the deep woods? The latest news about Mlle du Plessis and Jacquine?† Won't that be exciting?!

I am very pleased at what you tell me about your health. This pregnancy promises not to be disfiguring or exhausting to you. I have heard it said that Madame your Mother enjoyed just such a pregnancy as you describe. She was susceptible to some morning sickness, but the rest of the day she was in fine fettle. The news here is that you are looking perfectly beautiful. Confidence in your well-being confirms me in my resolve not to try to combine Brittany and Provence in one year . . . But, my angel, in the name of God, if you love me take care of yourself! Do not dance, do not fall, do not hurt yourself, do not push your strength to the limit and, above all, make your plans to be in Aix—where you can count on prompt assistance close at hand—

*Vitré, in Brittany, a few miles from Les Rochers.
†Mlle du Plessis was a nuisance of a neighbor; Jacquine, a peasant maid at Les Rochers.

for your confinement ... Make your arrangements earlier rather than later. Good Lord, what agonies will I not suffer at that time? ...

Hébert returns from Sucy whither I sent him for news of my child before I leave. She is very cute, very pretty, very saucy ... Marie and the wet nurse have nothing to do but watch over her; she is visited by Mme Amelot and Mme d'Ormesson. Everything runs smoothly ...

Monsieur de Coulanges gave a large supper party where all my friends gathered to bid me goodbye.

I am taking your brother with me, removing him from all the shame of his wicked life. You can guess whether or not his mistresses will be inconsolable.

The next paragraph of this letter was addressed to the Count de Grignan:

Ah, my dear, I believe you absolutely. There is no one who would not have done exactly what you did, had he been in your place. Your reasoning is persuasive, and you do it in a tone which merits your pardon but, just the same, remember that the youth, the beauty, the health, the gaiety, the very life of the lady whom you love—all those things will be destroyed by frequent relapses into the "malady" you bring on her.

My darling, now I come back to you, after having said adieu to your husband. Word reaches me here that both of you lose at whatever games of chance you play. Oh, my God, why so much bad luck? ...

Mme de Sévigné's next letter was dated "Saturday, May 23, at Malicorne"—Malicorne, near Mans, the château of Mme de Lavardin, one of her dear friends, one of her "Corps of Widows."* With the accommodations available at the inns along the road devoid of the amenities, the voyager stayed whenever possible at the châteaux of friends along the way.

I arrive here, where I find a letter from you, so well did I arrange things with the post office before leaving Paris. I left with your portrait [a miniature of the superb Mignard oil which hung over her mantel in the Paris house] in my pocket. I look at it very often ... One of my fine horses had to be left behind at Palaiseau; the other six have gone well, thus far. We set out at two o'clock in the morning to avoid the extreme heat ... Never have I seen a more lavish table nor a more delightful

---

*Mme de Sévigné called her group of widowed friends her "Corps of Widows."

house than this. It took all the water I could find here to refresh myself after six days of heat. Our Abbé is very well. My son and La Mousse are a great comfort to me. We have reread the plays of Corneille, and taken pleasure in admiring again what we admired before. We have also read a new book by Nicole. It is of the same stuff as Pascal and The Education of a Prince which is very marvelous stuff. One is never bored with it.

We expect to arrive on the twenty-seventh at Les Rochers, where I should find a letter from you. Alas, that is my only joy. You need not write me more than once a week because the letters will not leave Paris until Wednesday, at which time I would receive two at once. It seems to me that I am losing half my fortune, but I am content because that is some exertion spared you in your condition . . . I must be in very good humor to be willing to see you make the savings at my expense. But, my daughter, in the name of God, take care of yourself, if you love me. Ah, how I regret seeing you lose your pretty figure. Will you never have a moment's surcease? Must you use up your life in that continual fatigue? I understand Mons. de Grignan's reasons but, in truth, when one loves a woman, one sometimes takes pity on her . . .

My son sends you a thousand kisses. He is wonderful at keeping me from getting bored. He does everything to please me. We read, we talk, as you may well imagine. La Mousse makes his contribution to the party and, above all, there's our dear Abbé who makes himself adored because he adores you. He has finally made a bequest to me of his entire fortune. He could not rest until that had been accomplished. Say nothing to anyone; the family would eat him out, but love him tenderly and, on my word, love me likewise. A kiss for that rascal Grignan—despite his heinous crimes.

"And so, here I am, my daughter," her letter of May 31 began, "at sad old Les Rochers. How to see these allées, these inscriptions,* this little study, these books, this room—without dying of sadness? I have happy memories of this place, memories so vivid and so tender that I can scarcely bear it. Memories of you are among this number." (Could those "happy memories" of Les Rochers have included memories of her husband and of their honeymoon spent there?)

A magnificent welcome for Charles and his party had been planned by

---

*The inscriptions were Latin or Italian mottos or quotations carved into the young tree trunks.

the peasants of his Brittany domain: "They had planned a kind of official greeting for my son," Mme de Sévigné continued:

Vaillant [the majordomo of Les Rochers and its dependencies] had put more than fifteen hundred men under arms, all very well dressed, all with new ribbons for their cravats. They assembled in good order, one league from Les Rochers. But here is an unhappy happenstance: Monsieur the Abbé had sent word that we would arrive on Tuesday . . . and then promptly forgot! Those poor people waited on Tuesday until ten o'clock at night, when they all returned home, very sad and very puzzled. We arrive on Wednesday, never dreaming that an army had been put in the field to greet us! This misadventure upset us, but what to do about it? And that is how we made our debut here.

Les Rochers was a smallish, somehow grim and gray medieval château, dating back to the fourteenth century; save for its bristle of turrets and towers, it had the look of a manor house rather than a château. What it lacked in size and elegance, it made up for in the beauty of the park and woodlands in which it nestled. It could boast two courtyards, large stables and manège-ground, a terrace and gardens, a mall, a labyrinth, several broad treelined allées, endless walks and paths laid out through the ancient forest; a river, streams, ponds and farmlands were also included in the great domain of Les Rochers.

Mme de Sévigné's letters of May 31 continued:

My young trees are surprisingly beautiful. Pilois* has seen to it that they are growing up high as the sky and admirably straight. All in all, nothing is more beautiful than those allées which you saw born [planted, that is, in 1666, when mother and daughter last visited Les Rochers].

Alas, my daughter, how uncivilized my letters are! Gone is the day when I could give you the news of Paris, like all the other Parisians. It is only news of me that I can give you here and, yet, see how self-confident I am, feeling sure that you will enjoy news of me better than any other kind.

I have very good company here. Our Abbé is always wonderful; my son and La Mousse get along very well with me; and I, with them. We always seek each other's company, and when business affairs keep

---

*Pilois was foreman of the workmen on the estate.

*me away from them, they are in despair, and think it ridiculous of me
to prefer a farmer's account to La Fontaine's Fables.*

By June 7, the Countess de Grignan's first two letters addressed to Les
Rochers had come to hand:

*I have received two letters from you with a joy impossible to put into
the words of a letter. They reach me here two days after they arrived
in Paris; that brings me closer to you. I had wanted to spare you writing
more than once a week, but since you have so much courage and since
you insist, then, by all means, please continue!*

It was not, as is clear, primarily for their literary quality that Mme
de Sévigné so prized her daughter's letters: they constituted her lifeline
to Provence; the correspondence was the umbilical cord joining her and
her daughter across the miles. Not that Mme de Sévigné did not point to
her daughter's letters as supreme examples of the epistolary art. If the Countess de Grignan was forever apologizing for her letters—as, judging
by her mother's replies, she must have done—then Mme de Sévigné was
forever reassuring her of their excellence. "The letter you wrote to my
son is perfect"; "No one writes better than you"; "You do not like for me
to say it, but your narration is sheer perfection"; "You write deliciously; one
enjoys reading your letters as one enjoys strolling through a beautiful garden." "If I have contributed something to your delightful style of writing,
I did it in the thought that I was contributing to the pleasures of others,
not my own. But Providence, which has decreed our separation at such
great distance, provides me some small consolation in the charm of your
letters."

No valid literary judgment can be pronounced on the Countess's letters
since, unfortunately, none of those to her mother have survived. Only a
handful—three or four letters to her husband, one or two to her daughter,
one or two to friends—are extant. In view of the lack of evidence, in view
of Mme de Sévigné's known prejudice, it would strain credulity to accept
her word for it that her daughter was a nonpareil letter-writer. The few
letters of Mme de Grignan's which have come down to us lack the grace,
the deftness, the dash, the spontaneity, the humor, the lilt—the inspiration!—that distinguish those of her mother's composition.

The scarcity of news in the wilds of Brittany, the lackluster life she led
and the want of a social circle at Les Rochers served not to impoverish the
tenor of Mme de Sévigné's correspondence but, rather, to stimulate her to

flights of fancy and imagination, to feats of ingenuity in letter-writing: "The fact that you enjoy all the nonsense I write from here is proof of your affection," she wrote apologetically to her daughter in June.

Among the huge cast of characters who appear in Mme de Sévigné's letters throughout the twenty-odd years of the correspondence—a cast so huge that only the barest few can be introduced in the fragmented excerpts presented in this collection*—there are several whom she uses (if not invents!) for purposes of comic relief. There is an outrageous, a scandalous Breton nobleman named Pomenars—an original if there ever was one, drawn larger than life—whom she cannot mention without chuckling. In 1671, he is under indictment for counterfeiting and kidnap-rape, both capital offenses in Old Régime France. "Pomenars is always involved in criminal procedures which could cost him his head," she wrote in June of 1671:

> He was wearing a long beard when he visited some of his judges in Rennes, the other day. When someone asked him why he had not shaved, he replied: "I would be a fool to go to all that trouble without knowing to whom my head belongs. The King is demanding it, at this moment. If it is decided that I am to keep it, then I will take the trouble to shave."

Another figure of fun in Brittany was a silly, simpering, snivelling old maid, a perfect pest named Mademoiselle du Plessis (whose family property adjoined that of Les Rochers), who dogged Mme de Sévigné's footsteps whenever she was in residence there, and embarrassed her with attentions and affection. "The worst thing," Mme de Sévigné complained to her daughter, "is that she imitates me—with the effect of a distorting mirror, a reflection that makes me look ridiculous or an echo that makes my words sound idiotic!" This pretentious provincial, with all her affectations, is good for a laugh at her very entrance on the scene—so comic a character that one might suspect that Mme de Sévigné had "made her up" out of whole cloth as an amusement for her daughter; but, no, Charles de Sévigné's stories of their ugly, ungainly, cross-eyed neighbor substantiate his mother's.†

Pilois, the foreman, farmer, woodsman, gardener of Les Rochers, was

---

*The cast is listed in a playbill drawn up by Edward FitzGerald, best known for his translation of *The Rubaiyat of Omar Khayyam.* That prominent Victorian literary figure was a confirmed Sévigniste, and devoted the last years of his life to compiling a *Dictionary of Mme de Sévigné* which was published posthumously in 1914.

†The du Plessis family residing—to this day—on the property adjoining Les Rochers, to this day resent Mme de Sévigné's caricature of their relation.

no figure of fun: "Pilois is still my favorite, and I prefer his conversation to that of many a Breton with the title of Chevalier in the Parlement of Rennes," Mme de Sévigné declared.

Even the miserable Brittany weather was grist to her mill:

"We have had three weeks of constant rain," she wrote on June 21:

Instead of saying: after the rain, comes the sun; here, we say: after the rain, comes the rain. All our workmen have dispersed. Even Pilois went home, and instead of addressing your letter to me, "At the foot of a tree," you should have addressed it, "Huddled by the fireside."

Not that she was totally impervious to the gloom of the Breton mists: "I am overwhelmed by a dreadful sadness. La Mousse is depressed, too. We read, and reading is our life preserver." When the sun emerged, so did she: "I walk a great deal. The weather is fine and warm. This house is very comfortable. When the sun shines in my room,* I go out and walk in the woods where it is always wonderfully cool."

"The good weather has brought all my workmen back," she wrote on June 28:

That gives me much diversion. When I have company, I stitch at my fine altar cloth which you have seen me drag around in Paris. When I am alone, I read, I write, I work on business affairs in the Abbé's study. I wish you could have him with you, occasionally, at least for two or three days.

Walking and reading were the main diversions at Les Rochers:

We read a lot here. La Mousse begged to be allowed to read Tasso with me [she wrote on June 21]. I know it well because I learned it well; it amuses me. His Latin and his good mind will make him a good student, while my training and the good instructors I had make me a good teacher. My son reads us frivolous things, comedies which he acts out à la Molière—poetry, novels, history. He is very amusing; he has wit and understanding; he carries us along with him and has kept us from the serious reading we had intended to do. When he leaves, we will go back to Nicole's fine Essays on Morals. In two weeks, he will return to his military duties.

*Her room at Les Rochers had a western exposure.

The solitude of Les Rochers gave her time to give thought to her immortal soul:

One of the things I most desire is to become devout. I torment La Mousse about this, daily. I belong to neither God nor to the Devil—a condition which disturbs me, even though—just between us—it seems the most natural thing in the world. One is not wholly the Devil's because one fears God and because, basically, one is imbued with religious principles. Neither is one wholly God's because His law is stern, and one is reluctant to punish oneself. That state of mind may be described as lukewarmness. The large number of people who may be so categorized does not upset me; I understand their reasoning. However, they are abhorrent to God; so, one must change, and there is the difficulty.

Lukewarm though she might be about her religion, Mme de Sévigné was a practicing Catholic and, at Les Rochers, missed going to Mass, as was her daily practice in Paris.

"I am here with my three priests [her uncle, the Abbé de Coulanges; the Abbé La Mousse; and the Abbé Rahuel, the concierge of Les Rochers], each of whom fulfills his duties admirably, except for saying Mass; that is the only thing lacking in their company," she wrote. That lack was being rectified: the *Bien Bon* was in the process, that very summer, of building a chapel for Les Rochers where Mass could be said. "Our chapel goes up before our very eyes," Mme de Sévigné wrote delightedly. "The building provides an occupation for the Abbé and a diversion for me."

In mid-June, two of Mme de Grignan's letters went astray, and Mme de Sévigné went to pieces:

"Oh, my daughter [she wrote on the fourteenth], whatever may account for this delay, I cannot begin to tell you what suffering it has caused me. I have hardly slept for the past two nights. I sent twice to Vitré to humor myself with some faint ray of hope, but it was all in vain. This experience teaches me that my peace of mind is entirely dependent on you . . ."

By the seventeenth, with still no word from Provence, Mme de Sévigné let out a wail to her friend and confidant, the Abbé d'Hacqueville:

I write you with an aching heart which is about to kill me. I can write to no one but you because you are the only one kind enough to sympathize with me in the excessive love I bear my daughter. I tremble from head to foot, I have lost my powers of reasoning; I do not sleep or when I do, I wake with a start which is worse than not sleeping at all. I cannot understand why I am not receiving her letters as usual. Dubois advises me that he is faithfully forwarding my mail, but he forwards nothing, and gives me no explanation about the missing letters from Provence. Now, my dear Monsieur, how to account for this? Is it that my daughter does not write to me? Is she ill? Are my letters being intercepted? Impossible to attribute this to postal irregularities; even they could not cause such a disorder as this. Oh, my God, how unhappy I am without anyone with whom I can weep! With you, I would have that consolation, and not all your wisdom would keep me from letting you see my folly. But have I not reason to be in distress? Comfort me, then, in my terrible apprehension, and rush off to those persons with whom she corresponds so that, at least, I can learn how she is. I could better accept the fact that she writes to others than to continue in this anxiety about her health. The fact is that I have not heard from her since the fifth of this month; two letters dated the twenty-third and twenty-sixth of May. So, there we have twelve days' time and two regular mail deliveries from Paris without a letter from her. My dear Monsieur, send me a prompt reply. The state I am in would cause you pity. And try to write more legibly. I have great difficulty reading your letters; although I am dying to do so, I cannot. I make no response to all your news. I simply cannot. My son has returned from Rennes; he spent four hundred francs in three days there. The rain is constant. But all those problems would be as naught, if only I had letters from Provence! Have pity on me. Run to the post office and find out what has kept me from getting my letters as usual. I write to no one else, and would be ashamed to expose my weakness if I did not know your great compassion.

On the twenty-first, she wrote:

Finally, my darling, I can breathe again ... Good Lord, how I have suffered during these two regular mail deliveries which brought me no letter from you. Your letters are essential to my life. Nor is that merely a figure of speech; it is the very truth ... And can you imagine what happened to those dear letters which I await and receive with such great joy? The postal authorities went to the pains of forwarding them on to Rennes because my son was there! ... You can well imagine what a scene I made at the post office!

But the post office was soon forgiven, soon the subject of a paean of praise:

Apropos of Pascal, I cannot but wonder at the diligence of those gentlemen—the postillions—who spend their lives galloping back and forth to carry our mail. There is not a day in the week, not an hour in the day when they are not on the road. Those wonderful fellows! What a marvelous invention is the postal service! And how providential that there are men willing to do such work for money! I am sometimes tempted to write to thank them, and I think I would have done so, had the thought not occurred to me that—as Pascal suggests—perhaps they are tempted to write to thank me for writing the letters which they are paid to deliver.

The correspondence—though it may have come to be the very breath of life to Mme de Sévigné—was still a poor substitute for direct communion with her daughter, as her daughter herself had evidently pointed out: "You put it very well," Mme de Sévigné would write that summer, "when you say that we see and speak to one another as through a heavy veil."

XVI

With the onset of the June heat, the Lieutenant-Governor of Provence and his Lady departed their capital city of Aix to spend the summer aloft, at their Château de Grignan ("above the clouds," as the Countess de Grignan described it), perched on a pillar of rock rising abruptly out of the green and fertile Rhône Valley, a few leagues north of Avignon. The picturesquely situated château was renowned, compared favorably with the royal châteaus of the Loire. Philippe-Emmanuel de Coulanges, that merry, pudgy little cousin of Mme de Sévigné's, who flitted from château to château as the guest of the foremost noblemen of France on their magnificent domains, always referred to Grignan as "the royal château of Grignan"; and Mme de Sévigné, who knew the glories of Versailles, Fontainebleau, Saint-Germain and Vaux-le-Vicomte, referred to her son-in-law's château as "the Palace of Apollidon." Dating back to the thirteenth century, Grignan had been built as high as an eagle's nest, impregnable, battlemented and moated; when it was remodelled in the sixteenth century, its crenellation and machicolation had given way to a more florid Renaissance style. The houses of the village of Grignan clung to the sides of the steep hill, snuggling in the shadow of the château for protection. The road spiralled up from the valley floor to the château gates. The southern Alps served Grignan as backdrop; in winter, the snowcapped peak of Mont Ventoux glittered in the hundred windows of the château's south and west façades.

In June of 1671, the Countess had her first glimpse of her husband's ancestral home, and her letters to her mother evidently glowed with excitement over the "beauty of her château." "You picture it to me with an air of grandeur and a magnificence with which I am enchanted," her mother replied:

> I read, a long time ago, similar descriptions written by the first Mme de Grignan; I never guessed then that all that splendor would, one day, be under your command . . . In truth, it is a great pleasure to be, as you are, a great lady. I can well imagine Monsieur de Grignan's reaction at seeing you admire his château. Indifference on your part could not but have been a great disappointment to him . . . I share in the joy he takes in seeing you so well pleased.

"I can see that the château is really beautiful," Mme de Sévigné wrote from Les Rochers, on another day: "It has an air of the ancient Adhémars about it. I spend more hours there than at Les Rochers!" Mme de Sévigné rejoiced in her daughter's happiness: "You have a husband who adores you. Nothing is lacking to your grandeur. Just try to work some miracle in your financial affairs . . ."

Only financial security was lacking. The Count had been obliged to have recourse again to heavy borrowing:

> What with the Doric orders [of the château] and the Grignan family titles, nothing is left to be desired except order [in your finances] which is up to you to restore, for—without a little substance—everything is difficult, everything is bitter. I pity those who bring on their own ruin. It is the only affliction in life felt equally by all, the only one which augments rather than diminishes.

"The Abbé impatiently awaits a map of Grignan," Mme de Sévigné wrote in July, "as well as a report on the conference with Monsieur d'Arles.*

*The Archbishop of Arles was the Count's uncle and financial adviser.

Above all, he wishes you 100,000 écus to be used to complete work on the château or however it pleases you. I die of fear when I think of all the mouths you have to feed."

Among the many mouths to feed at Grignan, that summer, were numerous members of the Grignan family: the Archbishop of Arles and his Coadjutor, the Bishop of Uzès, uncles of the Count de Grignan; the Chevalier de Grignan and the Chevalier d'Adhémar, two brothers of the Count's; and Mme de Rochebonne, one of the Count's three sisters. It was not them whom Mme de Sévigné grudged their place under the roof-tree of their forefathers: "You have a whole tribe of Grignans with you, my dear daughter," she wrote later that year, "but they are all so delightful that one should rejoice with you at having such good company."

Although her son Charles had departed, Mme de Sévigné was to have good company, too, as the summer of 1671 advanced. Vitré came alive in August when the Duke de Chaulnes, the Governor of Brittany, arrived to open and preside over the annual meeting of the Estates (or States General) of the province. In addition to the twenty-five Royal Commissioners, the three Estates were represented: The First Estate, the Clergy (with twenty-two representatives); the Second Estate, the Nobility (with a hundred and seventy-four); the Third, the Commons (with seventy).

The morning after his arrival, the Duke de Chaulnes sent one of the gentlemen of his suite to Les Rochers to invite Mme de Sévigné for dinner: "We dined at two tables . . . fourteen to a table," wrote Mme de Sévigné:

> Monsieur the Duke presided at one table; Madame the Duchess, at the other. That made a lot of people eating in one room. These are sumptuous repasts: the platters of roast are carried away from the table looking as if they had never been touched. And as for the pyramids of fruit, the doors are not high enough to accommodate them! Our forefathers did not foresee such monstrosities; they built doors scarcely over head-height . . . One of these pyramids . . . composed of twenty pieces of porcelain, toppled as it came through a door —with a crash so loud as to drown out the violins, the oboes and the trumpets!

The dinner was followed by a dance—Breton dances which Mme de Sévigné much admired; and the dance, by a reception for all those in attendance at the States General, some three hundred or more.

"This province is full of noblemen," Mme de Sévigné continued:

Not one nobleman away at Court or in the military service. Only your brother, who may—one day—come back here like all the others . . . I did not care to attend the opening of the Estates, this morning; it was too early an hour. The Estates will not last long; their only business is to ascertain what [taxes] the King requires. There is no protest; it is promptly done. As for the Governor, he receives—to my astonishment—40,000 écus of compensation.* An infinity of funds are allocated—pensions, repair to roads and towns; fifteen or twenty large tables, constant gambling, an eternity of balls, comedies three times a week, elaborate dress—and there you have the States General! I forgot the four hundred large casks of wine drunk here, but if I forget them, the others do not!

"Would to God your Provence were equally liberal"! Mme de Sévigné exclaimed in another letter. "I love our Bretons. They may reek of wine, but their hearts are kind, which is more than can be said of your Provençals, perfumed though they may be with orange blossom! The Grignans excepted, to be sure"!

Her letter of August 19 was written from Les Rochers:

And if you should ask me how it feels to be back here after all that hullabaloo, I would tell you that I am in a transport of joy. I will stay here for at least eight days, no matter what they do to get me back. I cannot tell you in what need I am of rest. Also, I have need of sleep. And I need to eat—for I die of hunger at those banquets. I need to refresh myself. I need to be silent. Everybody came up to talk to me, and my lungs are exhausted. All in all, my darling, I am back with my Abbé, my Mousse, my dog, my Mall, my Pilois, my stonemasons. All of that is uniquely good for me, in the state I am in. When I begin to feel bored, I will go back . . .

On August 23, she could reassure her daughter that boredom was not a problem:

La Mousse has a toothache, so I will walk all alone until nightfall, and God only knows of what I do not think. But have no fear that I will be bored in this solitude. Except for the sorrow in my heart, against which

---

*This was an amount far in excess of that voted the Governor of Provence by the Assembly of the Communities.

I am helpless, I am in no way to be pitied. I have a happy nature which adjusts to and finds amusement in everything, and I am better off here all alone than in the fracas at Vitré. I have been here eight days in a peace and quiet which has cured me of a frightful cold. I have drunk water, I have not talked, I have eaten no supper, and although I have not shortened my walks, I am cured.

("I am convinced," Mme de Sévigné wrote elsewhere—and somewhat inelegantly—on the subject of walking, "that most of our ills come from keeping our rumps glued to the seat of a chair"!)

The Governor and his lady could not do without her, and by the twenty-sixth of the month, she had gone to rejoin them at Vitré, under duress, so to speak: "As a joke, the Duke de Chaulnes sent his Guards to fetch me back, writing me that I had been recalled on the service of the King"!

The Estates had been formally closed on September 5, 1671:

"No matter how good the company, it must eventually disband," the Duke de Chaulnes told the Bretons when he sent them home. The Estates ended at midnight. I went with Mme de Chaulnes and some other ladies. It was a very large, very beautiful, very magnificent assembly.

"Adieu, my dear child," she ended her letter:

Think of me sometimes when you are with your Grignans. I am on my way to Les Rochers, so pleased to be out of here that I am ashamed to think that I can feel so happy in your absence. When I reread my letters, I am always tempted to burn them, seeing what nonsense I write to you. But, tell me, it does not tire you to read them? For, it would be very easy to shorten my letters—without loving you any the less.

A spell of wet and gloomy autumn weather finally succeeded in dampening Mme de Sévigné's spirits:

"Here we are, my dearest darling," she wrote on September 23, "having the most dreadful weather you can imagine":

A storm has raged for four days, without abating. All my allées are drowned out; it is impossible to walk there, any longer. Our masons, our carpenters stay home. All in all, I hate this country, and wish every moment for your sun. But you, perhaps, are wishing for our rain? If only we could get together on this . . .

As it is, I stay in my room, reading, not daring to stick my nose outside. My heart is in repose because I believe that you are feeling well. Without that respite, I would not suffer with impunity the affront offered me by this month of September. It is treason, at this season, when we have twenty men working [in the park and in the chapel].

I am continuing to read Nicole's Essay of Morals which I find delicious. I have as yet come across no formula for bearing up in the rain, but I fully expect to, because this book provides for everything! . . . We are also reading a history of France from the time of King Jean. I want to get it straight in my mind; as straight, at least, as Roman history, where I have no friends or relatives. In French history, at least, one comes across familiar names. All in all, then, as long as we have our books, we will not hang ourselves.

If Mme de Sévigné had been anxious about her daughter's staying on at Grignan—so far from medical assistance—for the birth of her child, she seemed little better pleased at news of the Grignans' arrival at Lambesc, a small town near Aix, where the Assembly of the Communities of Provence would foregather, in September, in sessions over which the Count de Grignan would preside.

"I am sorry to hear that you are leaving Grignan," Mme de Sévigné would write. "You have good company there; it is a beautiful house, with a beautiful view and good air. You will be going to a stuffy little town where there may be illness and bad air. You must be displeased at this voyage."

Impatient though Mme de Sévigné might be with the gloomy weather, she would not yet leave Brittany; she and the Abbé had business to finish. "I will stay here until the end of November," she wrote, late in September,

And then I will go and embrace my little darling and take her home with me and, in the springtime, God willing, I will go to Provence. Our Abbé wants to go with me to see you and bring you back. By then, you will have been in Provence a long time.

("It does not do to allow oneself to be forgotten at Court," Mme de Sévigné would caution, elsewhere.)

Mme de Sévigné had been very upset at her daughter's suggestion that little Marie-Blanche de Grignan be sent south to her parents:

You say in your letter, my darling, that thought must be given to sending your daughter to you. I implore you to look to no one but me, who will surely bring her to you—provided her wet nurse is willing to go along. Any other arrangement would make me very sad. I am counting on having her beside my fire, this winter, as a delightful and well-loved diversion. I urge you, darling, to grant me this small pleasure. I will be so anxious about you that it is only fair . . . that I should have this bit of consolation . . .

By October, the weather in Brittany had improved, but Mme de Sévigné faced a threat worse than rain on her nightly promenades:

By the way [she wrote on October 21], there are wolves in my woods! I have two guards who follow me, in the evening, shouldering their guns! Beaulieu is the captain.* For the last two days, we have paid reverence to the moon, at the hour between eleven and midnight.

Mme de Sévigné had fretted over her daughter's pregnancy from the beginning—over a cold the Countess had contracted in her fourth month, over a fright she had had in her fifth, over the danger of the journey to Lambesc in her seventh. Mme de Sévigné grew more and more anxious with the approach of November: "I have Mass said for you, every day," she admitted. "And so, there you are at Lambesc, my daughter," she wrote on October 18, "and pregnant up to your chin"!

The customs of your country frighten me. So, childbirth is considered a mere trifle there! A girl would not dare complain, and ladies ordinarily have two or three children! I do not like that excessive weight you have put on; at the very least, it must make you miserably uncomfortable.

Listen, Monsieur de Grignan, it is you to whom I am speaking. You shall have only harsh words in reply to all your honeyed ones. You say you are proud of your accomplishment. Instead of having pity on my daughter, you only laugh. It is clear that you do not know what it is to bear a child. But, listen, this is the news I have for you: it is that if—after this boy—you do not give her some rest, I will think that you do not love her, and that you do not love me—in which case I will positively not come to Provence. Your swallows may call, but I will take no heed. And what is more, I will take your wife away from you.

*Beaulieu was Mme de Sévigné's maître d'hôtel, chief officer of her household staff.

Do you think I gave her to you to kill her, to destroy her health, her youth, her beauty? Nor is this said in raillery. At the proper time and place—and on bended knee—I will ask this grace of you. Meanwhile, see what confidence I have in you when I threaten not to come to Provence. That should give you proof that your affection and your words have not been lost on me. We are convinced that you will see whether or not we are people of our word. Meanwhile, take the utmost care of her, and be careful that she does not come to term in Lambesc. Adieu, my dear Count.

The most important of Mme de Sévigné's reasons for staying on at Les Rochers through November was that she wanted to wait there for news of her daughter's confinement:

I cannot make up my mind to leave here [she wrote on November 22] until I have had news from you. That sort of anxiety is unbearable on the road where I would be without mail from you. So, it is you, my daughter, who keep me here.

And as long as she was there, she would continue with her beautification projects:

I do not know what you have done, this morning, but as for me, I have been standing knee-deep in the dew, planting trees. I am laying out return allées all around my park, which will be very beautiful. If my son loves woods and promenades, he will bless my memory.

Not even when the temperature plummeted did Mme de Sévigné desert her workmen:

Did I tell you about the garden I am having planted—the most beautiful one in the world? I plant myself in the very middle of the square, with no one to keep me company because they would freeze to death. La Mousse takes his twenty turns to warm himself. The Abbé comes and goes to talk business with me, but there am I, huddled in my cloak, thinking about Provence—for that thought never leaves my mind.

By the end of November, even she had to make concessions to the weather:

*Winter is here in all its horror. I am in the gardens or beside my fire.
One can find nothing to amuse oneself. I will spend two more Fridays
here,* by which time I hope to have word of your safe accouchement.
It is Mons. de Grignan's obligation to keep me well posted, as I did
him, on a similar occasion.*

"I am wishing time away," she wrote plaintively on a gloomy Sunday
during that interminably long month of November while she waited for
word from Lambesc: "I am wishing time away, and at what price? At the
price, alas, of my life! What a folly to wish for something which will come
inexorably to pass without my urging . . ."

At last, on Sunday, November 29, came word from Lambesc:

*It is impossible, totally impossible, my dearest daughter, for me to
express to you the joy I felt on opening that blessed packet of mail
which brought me news of your safe delivery . . . Finally, shaking like
a leaf, I opened it and read the news I most wanted in all the world to
hear. What do you think a person does in a moment of such extreme
joyousness? . . . Do you know what happens? One feels one's heart
constrict and one weeps uncontrollably. That is what I did, my dearest
daughter, and did it with great pleasure. Those are tears incomparably
sweet to shed, tears to which not even the most dazzling joys compare.
Since yours is a philosophical bent of mind, you must know the reasons
for such reactions. As for me, I only feel things, emotionally, and am
going to have as many Masses said in thanks to God as I had said in
supplication to Him . . . What a marvelous thing it is to give birth to a
son, and to have him named by Provence, for Provence!*

What she meant was that the Assembly of the Communities of Provence—all the deputies of the Three Estates meeting at Lambesc—acted as
godparents to the Governor's son and heir, stood with the proud father at
the font while the infant was baptized as Louis-Provence d'Adhémar de
Monteil de Grignan—the name of the province officially incorporated into
his own.

"Who could wish for anything more?" his grandmother rhapsodized:

*A thousand thanks, my dearest daughter, for the three lines in your
own hand. At sight of them, my joy reached its climax. My Abbé is in*

*Friday was the day the courier from Paris arrived in Vitré.

transports of delight, like me, and our Mousse is thrilled. Adieu, my
angel, I have many other letters to write beside this one.

Many letters, indeed, for Mme de Sévigné's list of correspondents was lengthy: first of all, there was her family: her aunt, the Marquise de La Trousse, the duenna of her merry widow days; her cousins, the Coulanges; her cousin, Bussy; her revered friend, the Cardinal de Retz; her confidant, D'Hacqueville; her bosom friend, the Countess de La Fayette; her "Corps of Widows," as she called them: Mesdames de Lavardin, de La Troche, d'Huxelles, de Moussy, de Marboeuf; along with the Marquis de Pomponne, the Minister of Foreign Affairs; the Duke de La Rochefoucauld; her Burgundian friends and neighbors, the Count and Countess de Guitaut; the Duke and Duchess de Chaulnes; and, last but not least, her coterie of savants: Chapelain, Ménage, Corbinelli.

By December 2, however, she was subject to a post-partum depression, writing.

As it turns out, my darling, after the first transports of joy were over, I
found that still another Friday's mail from Provence was necessary to
give me peace of mind. So many accidents occur after childbirth, and
you have such a nimble tongue, as Monsieur de Grignan says, that I
would not be able to start out lightheartedly until at least nine days
have passed. So, I will wait to receive my letters on Friday, and then I
will be off, and hope to find mail the following Friday at Malicorne. I
am utterly astonished no longer to be feeling anxiety about your
accouchement—it has lain like a pebble, night and day, upon my heart.
I am so grateful that I cannot cease thanking God . . . I have received
countless, extravagant congratulations here in Brittany, and from Paris,
as well, by letter. The baby's health has been drunk for more than
a league around, hereabouts. I put up the drinking money. I served
a supper to my people, no less grand than that of Twelfth Night!
But nothing pleased me as much as the congratulations that came
from Pilois, who arrived this morning, his shovel over his shoulder,
and said to me, "Madame, I come to rejoice with you because I have
heard that Madame the Countess has given birth to a little laddie."
That means more to me than the most elegantly phrased compliments
in the world.

XVII

"I am, at this very hour, leaving to go to Paris," Mme de Sévigné's letter from Les Rochers on December 9 began:

I leave this solitude regretfully, when I think that I will not find you there. I doubt that I would have returned to Paris this winter, were it not for my plans to go later to Provence. This will be a step in the right direction since it is impossible to go all the way from here to there, or to pass through Paris without stopping, as one passes through Orléans ...

On December 13, she wrote from Malicorne, where she was again breaking her journey at the château of her friend Mme de Lavardin:

And here I am, my dear darling, travelling along in the most beautiful weather in the world. I can very easily do one or two leagues on foot, every day, just like Madame* ... We have four horses for each carriage, and rush along like the wind.

She had arrived, she wrote, at the post office at Laval, at the very moment the courier cantered in from Paris:

At that very moment, up rode that fine fellow, that obliging fellow, muddy up to the crotch, bringing me mail from you! I could have kissed him! You can imagine my delight at taking the packet with those two letters of yours from the postillion's muddy hand. He undid his little pouch while I watched. At the same time ... rip, rip ... zip, zip ... I undid my own and learned, at last, my darling, the happy news that you are feeling fine!

---

*Madame, the Duchess d'Orléans, the King's stalwart German sister-in-law, was an inveterate walker like Mme de Sévigné. This was the second Madame, the first having been the English Princess Henrietta-Maria, whose death the previous year, under highly mysterious circumstances, had given rise to suspicion of poison.

"And so, you had colic, you had milk fever, but now you are well again"! she wrote in another letter:

Your son went three hours without pissing ... sending you into a panic! Oh, really, you are very funny, you and your maternal love! How ridiculous! What is there to love about him? He is a blond, that is what you find enchanting; you love blonds. That is not being faithful. Monsieur de Grignan is quite right to be jealous. You "desert" him, he says, for the first fellow who comes along!

The Countess de Grignan had written that the little Marquis de Grignan had his father's big eyes and her small mouth, but that it was too early to tell whether his nose would turn out to be the prominent, hawkish Grignan nose—as was to be feared—or a small, pretty nose like his mother's, as was to be hoped. "Ah my darling, what a fine fellow he is!" Mme de Sévigné replied:

I only hope that his nose will not have long to hover "between hope and fear." How amusingly you put it! That uncertainty is strange: never had a small nose so much to hope for or to fear, although there are lots of noses between the two for him to choose from. Since he has large eyes [like his father], let him think of pleasing you [with his nose]!

Large nose or small, "the good fairies," his grandmother exulted, "had hovered over him in his cradle, according to all the astrologers" whom she had evidently consulted.

The new baby might still be in his cradle, but Mme de Sévigné evidently felt that it was none too soon to be concerned over another pregnancy:

I even begin to think that it is time to remind Monsieur de Grignan of the promise he made me. Just think, this is the third year in a row that you have been in labor in November. It will be September, next year, if you do not control him. Ask him that grace in return for the fine present you have just made him. And here is another reason: you have suffered more than if you had been broken on the wheel ... Would he not be in despair, if he loves you, to be the cause of your suffering such torture every year? Has he no fear, in fine, of losing you? After all these good reasons, I have no more to say except that, on my word, I will not go to Provence if you are pregnant ...

She did have "more to say," much more, such as:

I implore you, my darling, do not be overconfident about sleeping in separate beds. The temptation is still there. Have someone else sleep in the room. Seriously speaking, have pity on yourself, on your health—and mine!

And elsewhere: "I embrace your Count. But I love him better in his apartment than in yours! Ah, what a joy to see you looking beautiful, your figure perfect, in good health, in a condition to come and go, like all the others. Give me the pleasure of seeing you like that!" And yet again: "Mme de Guerchi is dead only because her body was worn out in childbirth. I am amazed at husbands who destroy their wives on the pretext of being in love with them."

Mme de Sévigné's first letter from Paris was dated December 18, 1671:

I have just now arrived, my very dear darling. I am at my aunt's house, being surrounded, hugged, quizzed by all my family and hers . . . Monsieur de Coulanges waits to take me to his house where he tells me I shall be staying because a son of Madame de Bonneuil [to whom the Grignans' apartment had been subleased] has come down with the smallpox at my house.

Mme de Sévigné, along with her little granddaughter and all her domestic staff, would stay with her cousins, the Coulanges, for several months while she looked for another house to lease—one large enough to accommodate the Grignans when and if they returned to Paris. While Mme de Coulanges enjoyed her houseguest—writing Mme de Grignan that "it is delicious to live with Mme de Sévigné"!—the houseguest enjoyed her host and hostess, particularly her host, who had just returned from a visit with the Grignans at Lambesc and could talk endlessly to Mme de Sévigné about her beloved daughter. "It is a stroke of great good fortune that I was brought by chance, to lodge with him here!" was how Mme de Sévigné saw it and said it to her daughter. "I am very happy here," she wrote later that month: "I adore Mons. de Coulanges; we talk constantly of you," and on another day, "I talked fifteen or sixteen hours with Monsieur de Coulanges. I do not think I can talk to anyone else."

"I have received a thousand visits from all your friends and mine," she wrote two days before Christmas: "That makes quite a large crowd"! "I enjoy your daughter," she wrote that same day: "She kisses me, she knows me, she laughs when she sees me, she calls to me. I am '*Maman*' and, as for the one in Provence, not a word"! "Your child is darling," the fond grand-mother wrote on another day, growing fonder daily: "Her tone of voice goes straight to my heart. She has little mannerisms that are appealing. I have fun with her, and I love her, but I still do not understand how it would be possible for my love for her to exceed my love for you."

"Alas, you are right when you say that Provence is my real abode, for the reason that it is yours. I find Paris suffocating, and only wish I were already on my way to Grignan," she wrote at the end of December. The best thing about being in Paris, to her point of view, was the mail service:

Here, I do not have to wait eight days, as at Les Rochers.* For, after all, my darling, you are everything to me, and your letters which I receive twice a week are my one and only consolation in your absence. They are delightful, they are dear to me, they please me. I reread them, just as you do mine but, since I am prone to tears, I cannot read the first few lines without weeping copiously. Is it possible that my letters are as pleasing to you as you tell me they are? I do not find them so when they leave my hands; it must be that they become so, at the touch of yours. In any event, it is very fortunate that you like them, for— seeing to what extent you are inundated with them—you would be an object of pity if it were otherwise. Mons. de Coulanges is dying to know which of your ladies-in-waiting likes them so well. We consider that a point in her favor because my style is so casual that one must have natural wit and a worldly, sophisticated taste to enjoy it.

Was she being coy about her letters, inquiring again in mid-January, 1672:

Could you not be mistaken, my dear daughter, in your opinion of my letters? The other day, at sight of one of my long letters, a rogue of a man asked me if I thought anyone could possibly read all that? I trembled, with no intention however of correcting my faults, and rely-ing on what you tell me, I spare you no trifle—whether long or short— which might amuse you. As far as I am concerned, my correspondence with you is my life, my unique pleasure; everything else comes after that, long after.

I am worried about your little brother. He is very cold, he is in an

*The couriers made it between Aix and Paris in six or seven days.

*encampment, he has been marching toward Cologne for the longest
time. I had hoped to see him here, this winter—but there he is!*

Charles's regiment was part of the French forces being moved in dead
of winter, 1671, toward the Rhine. In the spring of 1672, Louis XIV would
launch his attack on the Dutch States. French national interests as well as
"the just pretensions" of the Bourbon family required that the Spanish
Netherlands be annexed to France. It was not merely the young monarch's
thirst for glory or his overweening ambition that motivated the Dutch War:
the most sober, most astute of the Sun King's Ministers agreed that the
acquisition of the southern Netherlands was vital to the political, military
and economic welfare of the Kingdom.

"Thus it develops," Mme de Sévigné's letter continued,

*that Mlle d'Adhémar is the comfort of my old age. I wish you could see
how much she loves me, how she calls to me, how she kisses me. She
is definitely not beautiful, but she is adorable. She has a charming tone
of voice; she is fair; she is clean. All in all, I love her. You seem to be
mad about your son. I am glad of that.*

A new edition of the Duke de La Rochefoucauld's *Maxims* was off the
press early in the year of 1672. (Pessimistic and moralistic in tone, the
Maxims are models of prose in the Classicist tradition.) "Here are Monsieur
de la Rochefoucauld's *Maxims*, revised, corrected and expanded," Mme de
Sévigné wrote Mme de Grignan. "This is a gift copy from him which I
forward to you. Some of them are divine but, to my shame, there are others
which I do not understand. God knows how you will interpret them."

The winter of 1671-2 proved a thorny time for the Count de Grignan
in his governance: where the other provinces of France meekly subscribed
to the levies specified by the monarch, Provence was reluctant to meet the
demand for an increase in the levy—up from 400,000 to 600,000 livres in a
time of war. The Count de Grignan warned the provincial Assembly at
Lambesc to expect stern measures of reprisal from the throne: dissolution
of the Assembly, *Lettres de Cachet* and exile for the ringleaders of the
resistance. It was thanks to the Count de Grignan's intervention that the
King finally accepted a compromise figure of 450,000 livres.

"We were in a state of great alarm yesterday," Mme de Sévigné wrote
to her daughter on December 30:

*Without Mme de Coulanges, we would not have slept a wink ... But,
finally, Mme de Coulanges most graciously ran to Monsieur Le Tellier**

*Michel Le Tellier was her uncle, Secretary of State and War.

and brought us word that the King had been kind enough, this time, to accept the tribute offered by Provence, that he could understand the reasons, and that he was pleased with Mons. de Grignan. That good news revived us, and we were able to sleep. Rest assured, my darling, that all that has been said on the subject of Mons. de Grignan's zeal and devotion in the service of the King has not been said in vain; it has been said in the right places and has had its effect. The Provençals can rest assured that it is to him that they owe the leniency shown them in the compromise; without him, they would have found out what it means not to give the King blind obedience.

On New Year's Day, 1672, Mme de Sévigné was still fuming over criticism of her son-in-law:

If you knew how certain people blame Mons. de Grignan for having shown too little consideration for his own province in comparison to the obedience he urged, you would easily see that it is difficult to please everybody; had he taken any other course, it would have been worse still. Those who see only the glamour of the post he holds have no idea of the difficulties involved . . .

The Count, on his own behalf, finally obtained from the Assembly—although not without difficulty—a meager gratification of 5,000 livres, the annual subsidy requested for the maintenance of the Governor's Guards.

Mme de Sévigné neglected no opportunity to be of service to the Grignans. She kept up her Court connections for their sake: "I went to Saint-Germain yesterday," she wrote in January, 1672: "The Queen approached me, first. I paid my court in your name, as is my custom. We discussed accouchements, in general; yours, in particular."

Mme de Sévigné well knew that in "that country," as she called the Court, it was a case of out of sight, out of mind: only those close by, within range of the King's narrowing vision, enjoyed his favor and his bounty. Mme de Sévigné would keep the Grignans' memory fresh, as best she could. What she yearned for was a choice Court position for one or both:

Who would not wish to see you established here at Court? Is there anyone here to compare with either of you? My God, my child, how I should love to see Monsieur de Grignan here with a prestigious post, close to his master, in a position to give their walking papers to all those Provençals of yours!

There was talk, that spring, of the Count de Grignan as Governor of Canada, but the assignment went to the Count de Frontenac, instead, and surely Mme de Sévigné must have breathed a sigh of relief when she thought of the mail service. It would have taken months for a letter to go from Paris to Quebec, and vice versa.

It was a fortunate coincidence that the province of Provence fell under the jurisdiction of none other than Mme de Sévigné's fast friend, the Marquis de Pomponne, recently appointed Minister of Foreign Affairs. It was her opinion that "We could not hope for a better friend in that position." "I had an hour's talk with him," she wrote in early February: "His father gave him to understand that he could not better oblige him than by obliging me." (Mme de Sévigné had not neglected going—upon her return from Brittany—to pay her respects to the Minister's father.) "A thousand other reasons, he said, confirmed him in that desire—above all, the reason that the burden of the government of Provence apparently rested on my shoulders!"

For Mme de Sévigné, February was a month of mourning: February 6 would mark the first anniversary of her separation from her daughter. She would observe it in sorrowing, retracing her steps to the garden of the Convent of Sainte-Marie as to a Garden of Gethsemane:

Here I am, my darling, in a place which is the place where I wept more copiously, more bitterly than ever before in my life. The very thought of it makes me shudder. I have been walking for over an hour, alone here, in the garden. All of our Sisters are at Vespers, listening to some second-rate music which I had the wit to avoid. My darling, I can endure it no longer. Memories of you torment me on a thousand occasions. I thought I would die here in this garden where I had seen you a thousand times. I do not want to tell you what a state I am in. You are possessed of a genuine strength and do not understand human weakness. There are days, hours, moments when I am not in control of my emotions. I am weak, although I do not pride myself on it . . .

As part of the dateline of her letter of February 5, 1672, she wrote, "A thousand years ago today I was born." A slight exaggeration: it was not her thousandth but her forty-sixth birthday. The day was significant to her as the anniversary of her daughter's departure for Provence: her eyes, she wrote, had been "streaming, no matter how hard I try to hold back the tears."

In reply to which, the Countess de Grignan must have written to say that instead of weeping over their separation, her mother should put an end to it by coming promptly to join the Grignans in Provence. "You tell me that I weep although I am in command of the situation," she wrote on February 17:

> *It is true, my daughter, that I cannot stop myself from weeping sometimes, but neither can I set the date for my departure at my own sweet will. I wish it could be tomorrow, for example, but very pressing interests of my son's require my presence here, at this time. There are also matters of my own to which I must attend. All in all, it will take me until Easter. Thus, my child, one may be one's own mistress, and yet not be entirely so, and so one weeps.*

Financing her son Charles's equipage for this campaign had necessitated negotiating new loans and renegotiating old ones. This was not easy; the times were bad. "People are in despair," she would write, later that spring:

> *No one has a penny; it is impossible to borrow; the farmers do not pay; one dares not resort to counterfeiting; one does not want to enter into a pact with the Devil, and yet everyone goes off to the army with an equipage. To tell you how it is done is not easy. The miracle of the loaves is less incomprehensible.*

Mid-March came, and still she could not set a date for her departure: now it was the illness of her aunt, the Marquise de La Trousse, which held her back:

> *You talk to me of my departure. Ah, my dear daughter, I languish in that charming hope. Nothing holds me back but my aunt who is dying of misery and of dropsy. It breaks my heart to see the state she is in, and to hear all her words of tenderness and good sense. Her courage, her patience, her resignation are all to be admired. Monsieur d'Hacqueville and I, we see her failing, day by day. He reads my heart and knows what anguish it costs me not to be free, this very moment. I let myself be guided by his advice; we shall see between now and Easter. If her condition worsens, as it has done steadily since I am here, she will die in my arms. If she is granted a reprieve and shows signs of lingering, I will leave as soon as Mons. de Coulanges returns* . . . Our poor Abbé*

---

*Monsieur de Coulanges was to go with his wife to Lyon to attend the marriage of her sister.

is in despair, as am I. We will see how this grievous illness develops in the month of April. I can think of nothing else. Your desire to see me could not equal mine to embrace you . . .

"My son writes me that they are miserable in Germany, and do not know what they are doing there . . . ," the letter of March 16 went on:

You ask me, my dear child, whether I still love life so well. I admit that it holds some searing sorrows. But I am even more dismayed at the thought of death. It seems to me so horrible that death is our only release from the ills of the world that if I could turn time backward, I would ask for nothing better. I find myself in an untenable position, set upon a course which distresses me: I was launched upon this life, though not of my own volition. I must leave this life, and that thought shatters me. And how will I leave it? By what door? When will it be? In what manner? Will I suffer a thousand and one agonies which will bring me to my death in desperation? Will I suffer a stroke of apoplexy? Will I die in an accident? How will I appear in the sight of God? Will it be fear and extremity which will turn me back to Him? Will I feel no other emotion but fear? What can I hope for? Am I worthy of Paradise? Is Hell my just desert? What an alternative! What a perplexity! Nothing is so foolish as to endanger one's salvation, but nothing is more natural, nothing easier to understand. I torment myself with these thoughts, but I find death so terrifying that I hate life all the more because it leads me inevitably there, along such thorny paths. You will tell me that I am asking for eternal life. Not so, but had I been consulted, I would have chosen to die in the arms of my nurse. That would have spared me much anguish and ensured me a sure passage to Heaven. But let us talk of other things . . .

XVIII

Madame de La Trousse hovered, all that spring of 1672, between life and death: if she could not recover from her mortal illness, neither apparently could she die of it. Mme de Sévigné, fond and dutiful and tormented, could neither bring herself to leave the deathbed of her aunt nor go to join her daughter in Provence. Easter would come and go, and Mme de Sévigné would still be marooned in Paris.

"I do not know where I stand, in view of my aunt's illness," she wrote on April 6, the beginning of Holy Week:

The Abbé and I seethe with impatience, but we have resolved—if this proves to be a lingering illness—to go on with our trip to Provence for, after all, even natural goodness has its limits. For my part, I think only of you, and my impatience to see you is so great that my sentiments toward others inevitably suffer.

I am totally crushed not to be able to leave with Monsieur and Madame de Coulanges. That was our plan—save for the pitiable condition in which my aunt finds herself. But we must still be patient; as soon as I can leave, nothing will stop me. I have just bought a new carriage; I am having clothes made. Thus, I can leave on an hour's notice, from one day to the next, and never have I wished so passionately for anything.

Trust me not to waste a moment's time. It is my bad luck to encounter delays where others do not. Sometimes, I feel the impulse to smash china, just as you do!

This is not Mme de Sévigné's only reference to her daughter's temper tantrums: as a little girl, she cruelly pinched the flesh of those who crossed her, again according to her mother. "When it is iron you want to shatter," Mme de Sévigné wrote, on another occasion, "when you find porcelains unworthy of your anger, then I know you must be truly in a fury."

On Good Friday she wrote:

I so long to be on my way that I fear that God will not permit me to enjoy such happiness. Nevertheless, I continue making preparations.

But is it not cruel and barbaric to regard the death of a person one dearly loves as the starting signal for a voyage one passionately desires to make? What kind of world is this we live in? For my part, I find it astonishing. We must make the most of our misfortunes, construe them as a form of penitence.

"I am at this very moment on my way," she wrote on April 22, "to walk for three or four hours at Livry." But as much as she loved Livry, as often as she went there to invite her soul, still the Abbey was haunted with memories of her daughter:

It is difficult for me to revisit that place without you, difficult to look at that garden, those allées, that little bridge, that avenue, that meadow, that mill, that gentle landscape, that forest—without thinking of my very dear child.

Mme de Sévigné reacted with elation to a letter from her daughter to the Count de Guitaut, which bore the line "Send me my Mother!"

How delightful you are, my darling! How well you justify that excessive love that everyone knows I feel for you! Alas, I think only of my departure. Leave it to me ... You are the only one in the world who could bring me to decide to leave her [her aunt] in so pitiful a state ... We will see. I live from day to day, and lack the courage to come to a decision. One day, I am leaving; the next day, I do not dare ...

By mid-May, torn between love and duty, she was clearly indulging in self-pity:

Have pity on our impatience; help us to bear it, and never think that we will lose a minute in leaving, even should there be some slight offense to the conventions. Confronted by so many duties, you can well imagine that I perish. What I am doing crushes me; what I am not doing saddens me. Thus, this springtime—which should restore my life—is not for me.

It was a springtime ominous with war: "Everyone weeps for a son, a brother, a husband, a lover. One would have to be very callous not to be affected at seeing all of France depart"—all of France, including the King, who left on April 27 to join his armies in Flanders and Germany, including even Mme de Sévigné's "little friend" at the post office:

Little Dubois has left to follow Monsieur de Louvois.* I can already notice his absence. Yesterday I went to the post office to try to make new friends, to see whether he had turned me over to someone else there. I find all new faces, unimpressed by my importance.

"But who is it who is not departing, at this hour?" she inquired in the same letter:

It is I! Still, I will have my turn, like all the rest . . . I highly approve of your excursion and your voyage to Monaco, which will coincide very well with the delay in our departure. I should arrive at Grignan shortly after you return there . . .

I am thrilled, my darling, that you are not pregnant! I love Monsieur de Grignan with all my heart for that. Tell me whether this happy circumstance is due to his temperance or to his great love for you, and whether you are, yourself, not thrilled to be able to run around a bit, to go jaunting about that Provence of yours, through allées of orange trees, and to receive me without fear of falling or being seized with labor pains . . .†

Moving into the new house she had leased, in the Marais district, on the Rue des Trois Pavillons, occupied much of Mme de Sévigné's time that spring:

"I have been very busy getting my little house ready," she wrote on May 4:

I will sleep there tomorrow. I swear to you, my darling, that I like it only because it is perfect for you. You will be very comfortable in my

---

*Louvois was the Minister of War.

†In the seventeenth century, to avoid pregnancy was to practice sexual abstinence or *coitus interruptus*. No effective contraceptives are known to have been in use at that time, although there are two or three lines in a letter written by Mme de Sévigné in 1671 which have been interpreted by some biographers and historians as a reference to a contraceptive measure of some kind. This brief passage is not only curious, ambiguous and fragmentary, its authenticity is questioned by Roger Duchêne, the most recent editor of the *Correspondence*. The passage in question appeared in a 1726 edition of the *Letters*, but it was dropped from the Capmas edition of 1876, perhaps out of a false sense of modesty on the part of the editor. The passage reads: "What? Astringents are unknown in Provence? Alas, what becomes of the poor husbands, and poor . . . I do not see how this could be so . . ."

apartment, although without any inconvenience to me. You will not be in your brother's apartment. You will find it greatly to your liking . . . nor will you have need of any furniture . . . I am exceedingly anxious about your poor brother. One feels that this war is so terrible that one cannot be too fearful for those one loves.

Mme de Sévigné gave serious consideration to taking little Marie-Blanche de Grignan with her to Provence, to restore her to her parents, but was discouraged by her friend Mme du Puy du Fou.

Mme du Puy du Fou does not want me to take the little one with me. She says it would be exposing her to danger—at which point, I surrender. I would not endanger her little person. I love her totally. I had her hair cut and dressed in the "hurluberlu" style. That coiffure is made for her. Her complexion, her neck, all her little body is perfection. She knows a hundred little tricks: she talks, she kisses, she slaps, she makes the sign of the cross, she begs pardon, she makes a bow, she kisses one's hand, she shrugs her shoulders, she dances, she flatters, she raises her chin . . . all in all, she is adorable! I amuse myself with her, for hours on end. I do not want anything to happen to that little darling. As I told you the other day, I do not know how one could manage not to love one's daughter!

Mme de Sévigné's daughter was on her way, with her husband, at that time, to visit the Prince and Princess of Monaco. Her reports of the voyage—by land and by sea, by litter and by ship, via the Maritime Alps and the Mediterranean—made intriguing reading for her mother throughout the month of May: "Nothing could be more romantic," Mme de Sévigné exclaimed "than your fêtes on the sea, your banquets on that famous ship, the *Royal Louis!*"*

"Your descriptions are excellent," she wrote on May 15:

I feel as if I am reading a wonderful romance whose heroine is extraordinarily dear to me. I am interested in all those adventures. I cannot believe that your promenade through the most beautiful and sweet-scented regions of the world—received everywhere like a Queen!—this chapter of your life is so extraordinary, so different, so exciting—that I cannot believe you did not enjoy it.

*The *Royal Louis* was the Admiral's ship, then in Toulon harbor.

To be "received everywhere like a Queen" implied a royal retinue, a royal largesse.

I understand, very well, my daughter, the pleasure and the magnificence and also the expense of your voyage [Mme de Sévigné wrote on May 20]. I have spoken of it to the Abbé as a heavy burden to you, even though a necessity. Still, one must ask oneself whether one wants to run the risk of ruin to which such vast expenditure must lead . . .

There was not only the tremendous cost of the royal progress the Grignans were making along the coast, the spring of 1672, there were other huge expenses incidental to the Governorship: a kind of "Court" to be maintained at Aix and at Lambesc, a seigneurial style of living at Grignan. Not only were the Governor's emoluments insufficient to maintain such grandeur, the Royal Exchequer—under stress of war—was slow in meeting its obligations.

I have been to see Monsieur de Bartillat [the Treasurer] about your pension [the Count's mother-in-law wrote to him in May]. I will have to talk to Monsieur Colbert . . . It is necessary, nowadays, to solicit that which was formerly paid as a matter of course . . . What difficult times these are!

Difficult as were the times, the Grignans continued on their course of profligacy: "I dare not think about your affairs," Mme de Sévigné exclaimed. "They are a labyrinth of bitterness through which I cannot grope my way."

In April she sounded like a typical mother-in-law; she had lost her patience over a very costly item of apparel being made in Paris for the Count de Grignan:

Monsieur de Grignan is ordering a very handsome justaucorps. *That is a matter of seven or eight hundred francs! What happened to the very beautiful one he had? . . . In the name of God, try to cut back somewhere on this terrible expense . . .*

But it was the Grignans' gambling which distressed her most: "For a long time, now, your gambling has been ruinous to you. It has greatly distressed me . . ." Worst of all, the Grignans were unlucky gamblers: "Fortune must be blind to treat you as she does!"

"Speaking of écus," she wrote on another day that spring, "what a madness to lose two hundred at that wretched *hoca*,* a cutthroat game which has been banned here . . . You play in hopelessly bad luck; you always lose. That is a great deal of money you are throwing away. I cannot believe that you have enough not to feel these constant losses . . ."

And, then, as if suddenly wondering whether she had gone too far in speaking so bluntly to her daughter and son-in-law, she wrote again, in April: "You do not say whether or not you are displeased about the advice I sometimes give you about your expenses. You should have given me some indication . . ."

Mme de Grignan's silence on the subject spoke volumes, had only her mother listened, had only her mother been more perceptive: her persistent interference in the sex life and financial affairs of the Grignans can only be characterized as insensitive, certain to rankle in the breast of the Countess and her husband.

Even so, scarcely a kind word has been said, throughout the centuries, for Mme de Grignan. The scores of biographers have, with rare exception, worshipped at the shrine of Mme de Sévigné, lavishing praise on the warm, fond, outgoing, the gay and charming mother, at the expense of the cold, the inhibited, the aloof, the grave—the sometimes melancholy, often haughty daughter. The splenetic Duke de Saint-Simon, in his renowned *Mémoires*, set the style in condemning the Countess de Grignan, all his bouquets going to the Countess's mother. Since the Saint-Simon *Mémoires*, along with the Sévigné *Letters*, provide historians with the most vivid, most lively, most precious accounts of the Sun King and his Court, Mme de Grignan has never succeeded in living down the unpleasant reputation given her by the acidulous little Duke. Janet Murbach, author of *Le Vrai visage de Mme de Grignan* (*The True Face of Mme de Grignan*) contends that Saint-Simon was prejudiced, having never forgiven Mme de Grignan for a slight to his sister.

Not even the most prejudiced biographer, not even the most ardent Sévigné admirer could hold her blameless in the tensions that developed in the mother-daughter relation. That extravagant, possessive, obsessive love she bore her daughter—"an excessive love," by her own definition—could not have constituted, in her daughter's eyes, an unmixed blessing.

It is ironic that if Mme de Grignan stands condemned before the bar of literary history, it is primarily from the lips of her adoring mother that the

---

*Hoca, a card game, had been outlawed by the Parlement of Paris in 1658, although the edict was flouted at the royal Court.

indictment comes. It is ironic, too, that a highly secretive, an intensely private person such as Mme de Grignan should have had her privacy invaded— the most intimate details of her marital life, the most embarrassing details of the family's financial problems broadcast, made public!—through the agency of what she considered a totally confidential correspondence. Over and over again, throughout the twenty-five-odd years of their correspondence, Mme de Sévigné had to reassure her daughter that her privacy was being preserved, that she showed only select passages of her daughter's letters to a select few friends.

Mme de Grignan repeatedly cautioned her mother about the secrecy to be preserved in respect to private family affairs: "I have too much respect, too much affection for you," Mme de Sévigné protested, in May of 1672, "not to preserve the confidentiality of what you tell me. When one loves to the extent that I do, one is only too fearful of doing anything to displease or to annoy ... The fear of a reproach is more than enough to make one keep one's mouth closed." How horrified both mother and daughter would have been to know their letters would become public property, printed, reprinted, anthologized, analyzed, annotated!

The supreme irony lies in the fact that it is Mme de Grignan, herself, who—although unwittingly—must be held responsible. Had she not so carefully stored away all her mother's letters in those coffers at the Château de Grignan, why, then, the secrets of the Grignans' alcove might have been preserved.

In the final analysis, of course, it was the worldwide renown of the Sévigné *Letters* that accounted for the invasion of Grignan privacy. Save for the literary fame that attached to her mother's *Letters*, the name of Mme de Grignan would not have survived her generation, would have been forgotten with her moldering bones. Save for the immortal *Letters* written by her mother, Mme de Grignan would have been allowed to die in peace, and have been granted the privilege of oblivion.

XIX

The month of May was running out, and still Mme de Sévigné could only talk of leaving: "My darling," she wrote on May 23, "we talk of leaving":

One day, we say—the Abbé and I—Let us go. My aunt will go on this way until autumn, and we resolve to take our departure. The next day, we find her so low that we say, It is impossible to think of leaving. It would be barbaric. The moon of May will carry her off with it. And, so, we go on from day to day, with despair in our hearts.

Three days later, Mme de Sévigné managed to be cheerful enough to go on a shopping spree. She wrote on May 27:

I went yesterday to Gautier's, to pick up—upon the outlay of a great deal of money—the fabrics with which to make myself beautiful for Provence. I will see to it, my darling, that you are not ashamed of me . . . I came across the prettiest little skirt in the world, very stylish, with a jaunty little jacket. Nothing in the world can stop me from making you a gift of them, and unless you want to displease me mightily, you will say only that you are delighted and think me a kind lady . . .

I am very upset at having no word from my son. The army mails are so deranged that almost no letters are received save by special messenger. I know no news today. I so dislike false reports that I prefer to write nothing. The news I send you is always accurate, and comes from reliable sources.

I am on my way to Livry, at this moment. I am taking my little girl along, and her nurse, and all the rest of the nursery crew. I want them to have a breath of spring. I am coming back tomorrow, not daring to leave my aunt for longer. As for the little one, I shall leave her there for four or five days. I cannot do without her longer than that. She brightens all my mornings. It has been so long since I breathed or walked that I must take pity on myself, for a change, as well as on the others.

Every day, my preparations go forward. My dresses are on order; my carriage has been ready for eight days. In a word, my darling, I have one foot in the air! But if God preserves our poor aunt longer than now seems possible, I will do what you advise me to do—that is, I shall leave in the hope of seeing her again on my return.

The fact that her daughter had gone off leaving her Paris tradesmen unpaid had evidently caused Mme de Sévigné a measure of embarrassment. As in the case of the fabric merchant, Gautier, it was her suggestion that Mme de Grignan send him a little greeting even if she could send him nothing on account: "It is wrong to join silence to the delay in your payment of his bills. If we can give him something out of your pension money, we will do so, although you must have many debts outstanding, to judge only by those I know about."

"So, now," she wrote on May 30, "it is becoming fashionable to be wounded! My heart is heavy because I am very fearful of this campaign. My son writes often; thus far, he is well."

To end her letter on a cheerful note, she had "a story about Livry" with which to regale her daughter, a story about Mme Paul, widow of Monsieur Paul, the head gardener, whose death in the previous year—according to Mme de Sévigné—"had left all the garden looking woebegone":

Mme Paul has lost her head and become wildly enamored of a big booby, twenty-five or twenty-six years old, whom she had hired to do the gardening. He did very well. The woman married him. He is a brute and a fool. Before long, he will beat her; he has already threatened to ... These are all the most violent passions imaginable ... I have amused myself in reflections on the caprices of love.

The denouement came a few days later:

The wife of Monsieur Paul is outraged. A snag has developed in her marriage. Her tears flow as from a fountain. Her great boob of a husband is not very loving; he finds Marie [Mme Paul's daughter] very pretty, very sweet. My darling, no good can come of this. I will tell you frankly: had I wanted to be loved, I would have hidden you away, out of sight! That which is going on here is the stuff from which all the novels, all the comedies, all the tragedies are made.

It seems to me that it is the work of one of those little Cupids who lurk in the forests. To do this one justice, I think he aimed at

Marie. *But even experts miss the mark; his arrow struck the gardener's wife, and the wound is incurable. Were you here, this vulgar affair would amuse you greatly. For my part, I have stepped in, and am taking Marie away with me to prevent her from cutting the grass beneath her mother's feet. Pity these poor mothers!*

"You say that I never tell you anything about your brother," she wrote in the same letter:

I do not know why. I think of him, every minute, and am deeply anxious about him. I love him very much and, in our life together, his attitude toward me is charming. And, as for his letters to me—were they to be found, some day, in my desk—they would be thought to be from the most gallant gentleman of this age! There can be nothing to compare to the gallant and courtly air with which he treats me. So, this war touches me to the quick. He is presently in the King's army—that is to say, in the jaws of death, like the rest.

"I am in a quandary about my clothes," she wrote at the close of the letter of June 2, "torn between the desire to look beautiful and fear of the expense ... Adieu, my dear child, until tomorrow from Paris. I am going now to take a walk and think about you in those beautiful allées where I have seen you a thousand times."

The letter concluded with a separate note, addressed "To Monsieur de Grignan":

You flatter me too much, my dear Count. I can accept only a portion of your compliments—the gratitude you express to me for having given you a wife who constitutes the joy of your life. On that score, I believe I have made a contribution ... You have taken my daughter on the most beautiful voyage in the world. She was thrilled with it, but you took her up and down mountains, exposing her to the precipices of your Alps and the waves of your Mediterranean. I am somewhat inclined to scold you, but not until after I have embraced you tenderly.

No wonder Mme de Sévigné's heart was heavy, no wonder she was depressed, that summer; she was commuting between a deathbed and a sickbed: "Mme de La Fayette still languishes," she wrote—to languish was Mme de La Fayette's status quo; the fragility of her health, proverbial. "And

Monsieur de La Rochefoucauld is still crippled"—after another of his devastating bouts with gout:

Our conversations are sometimes so lugubrious that it would seem that there is nothing left to do but bury us. Mme de La Fayette's garden is the most delightful spot in the world. It is in full bloom, and full of perfume. We spend many evenings there because the poor woman dares not step into a carriage to go anywhere . . . All in all, my daughter, while awaiting the blessed day of my departure, I make my way from the Faubourg to the hearth of my aunt, and from the hearth of my aunt back to the sad Faubourg.

By June 14 came the news that the French had crossed the Rhine, although at a high cost of dead and wounded. Three of the Duke de La Rochefoucauld's sons were casualties: his youngest son, the Chevalier, dead; his eldest, the Prince de Marsillac, gravely wounded; dead, too, his illegitimate son, the Duke de Longueville, love child of a youthful romance between La Rochefoucauld and a Princess of the Blood, Anne-Geneviève de Bourbon-Condé, Duchess of Longueville:

I was at Mme de La Fayette's when they came to break the news to Mons. de La Rochefoucauld . . . That hail struck him in my presence. The tears flowed in the recesses of his heart, but his strength and courage kept them from his eyes. Upon hearing that news, I had not the patience to ask further questions, but ran to Mme de Pomponne, who reminded me that my son is in the army of the King which took no part in this costly expedition.

"You have never seen Paris like this," she wrote on June 20. "Everyone weeps—or fears to be weeping soon . . . May God preserve my son!"

On June 24, Paris was flooded with false reports of peace: "It is easy to believe that all Holland has taken alarm and become submissive. The King's good fortune surpasses all that anyone has ever seen." The King seemed less fortunate when it became known in Paris that the Dutch had opened their dikes, turning victory into stalemate.

After days and nights *in extremis*, Mme de La Trousse breathed her last on the last day of June, 1672:

At long last, my dear daughter [Mme de Sévigné could write on July 1], our poor dear aunt has come to the end of her unfortunate life. The *poor woman brought tears to our eyes on that sad occasion. As for me, tender and quick to tears, as I am, I shed many. She died quietly yesterday morning at four o'clock, her passing unperceived by anyone ... When they approach her bed, they find her dead. They cry out. They open the bed curtains ... They come to tell me. I come running, in a highly emotional state. I find my poor aunt's body cold, but stretched out so peacefully that I realize that the moment of her death must have been the sweetest in the past six months ... I drop to my knees, and you can guess whether or not I wept copiously at such a spectacle. Then I went to see Mademoiselle de La Trousse, whose grief would move a stone to pity. I brought both of them* back home with me ... And so, here I am, ready to leave ... although, no matter how I hurry, I cannot get away for several days ...*

For "those several days," she saw—she noted wryly—"only tears, mourning, services, interments, death." To escape her problems, she ran off, as was her wont, to the countryside, as she wrote on Sunday, July 3:

I am on my way to Livry to take my little one there. Do not worry about her; I am taking the best of care of her, and undoubtedly love her more than you do.

But why do you say, my darling, that I will never get away before winter? I expect to be coming back, by then—bringing you and Mons. de Grignan with me! Our Abbé is courageous enough to be willing to brave the heat, and I fear only for him. Do not stop us from leaving by saying that you no longer expect us!

It appears that our victorious armies are meeting with no resistance. The French are clearly irresistible. Everything must yield to the fearlessness and brilliance of their actions. As valorous as they are, there is no river left to withstand their advance.

On July 8, Mme de Sévigné was back in Paris where, as she wrote, she "still had a thousand matters to attend to":

At last, my darling, you are at Grignan again, and await me on your bed. As for me, I am in all the confusion of departure, but if I had all day to dream, I would not see you so soon ... Be as lazy as you please before I get there, so that all your laziness will be out of your system

---

*Both of Mme de La Trousse's old-maid daughters, Mlle de La Trousse and Mlle de Méri.

by the time I arrive. It is true that our temperaments are somewhat dissimilar but there are many other areas where we are in accord and, then, as you say, our hearts attest to the closeness of our relation, and that should convince you that I did not find you in a cabbage-patch! ... We are still hoping for peace and the total conquest of Holland.

That was hoping against hope. The organization of resistance by William of Orange had begun early in July.

On July 11, more than a week after the death of her aunt, Mme de Sévigné was still writing from Paris:

Let us talk no more, my poor darling, about my trip. We have talked of nothing else for so long that it finally becomes wearisome. As in the case of long-drawn-out illnesses, the protracted hope uses up all the joy of recovery when it finally comes. You will have used up all the joy of seeing me while waiting for me to come ... By the time I get there, you will already be used to the idea of seeing me ...

I was obliged to pay my last respects to my aunt. Then, I needed a few more days, besides. At last, now, everything is in order. I leave on Wednesday, and will spend the night at Essonnes or at Melun. I will take the Burgundy route ...*

I want to congratulate you on not being pregnant, and beseech you not to become so! Should that misfortune befall you in the condition you are in, you would be thin and ugly for the rest of your life.† *Give me the pleasure of finding you as well as when we parted and of being able to run around a bit with me, wherever our fancy leads. Mons. de Grignan owes you and me that mark of his consideration ...*

You write to me about your "Dauphin." I pity you for loving him so tenderly. You will have many trials and tribulations to endure. I love our little Grignan girl all too well. Despite all my previous resolutions, I have brought her back from Livry. She is a hundred times better off here ... I leave her in perfect health, with medical assistance close at hand. Mme du Puy du Fou and [Doctor] Pecquet will have her weaned by the end of August ... Monsieur de Coulanges and Mme de Sanzei [his sister] will give her every attention. And that way, we will all have our minds at ease ...

*Mme de Sévigné would spend seventeen days en route, covering the 156 leagues between Paris and Grignan.
†The Countess had undergone a spell of illness subsequent to her Monaco trip.

(The only possible discord that she could foresee, Mme de Sévigné wrote her daughter, would have to come over the grandchildren—"should you want me to love your son more than your daughter—which I do not think I could do.")

At last, on Wednesday, July 13, 1672, the caravan set off:

At long last, my daughter, here we are! ... I left Paris on Wednesday ... Everybody very kindly assured me that I must be planning to kill our dear Abbé by exposing him to a trip to Provence in the middle of summer! He had the courage to laugh at such talk, and God has recompensed him with ideal weather. There is no dust; it is cool, and the days are infinitely long. One could wish for nothing better. Our Mousse plucks up courage. We travel along rather solemnly. It would have been good to have had Monsieur de Coulanges along to enliven our company. We have found no reading matter worthy of our attention save Virgil—not in the French translation but in the original Latin or the Italian. To be joyous, one must be in joyful company. You know that I adapt to the mood of others, but I do not set the pace.

The last letter written en route is datelined, "Wednesday, July 27, At Lyon":

Monsieur the Intendant [of Lyon]—in company with Madame, his wife and Mme de Coulanges [his daughter]—met me as I stepped off the boat. I took supper with them. Yesterday, I dined with them. They march me around, they show me off; I am the recipient of a thousand courtesies. I am embarrassed; I do not know why I should be so esteemed. It was my intention to leave tomorrow morning, but Mme de Coulanges insisted that I stay one more day, and set that concession as the price for her coming later to Grignan. I thought it would please you to seal that bargain ... Thus, I will not leave until Friday morning. We will spend that night at Valence. I have good boatmen engaged— not the rascals you had! I am to be treated like a princess. I shall arrive Saturday at one o'clock in the afternoon at Robinet* ... Our dear Abbé

---

*Robinet was the port of debarkation for Grignan, some fourteen kilometers away.

is well. Mousse survives. We long to see you. My heart leaps when I think of it.

My carriage has come thus far without mishap, without inconvenience. Yesterday evening, however, they took my horses to drink, and one of them drowned, so that I shall have only five. If that causes you embarrassment, it is not my fault ... I will not have my carriage at Robinet. There are five of us; count on that: our Abbé, La Mousse, the two maids and I ... What bliss to be on my way to you, my beautiful Countess!

X X

On Saturday, July 30, 1672, at one o'clock in the afternoon, at the river port of Robinet on the west bank of the Rhône River, mother and daughter rushed into one another's arms.

Mme de Sévigné, with her talent for evoking time and place and mood, stimulates our imagination to recreate that long-awaited reunion on the banks of the Rhône. One feels the flurry of excitement as the Governor's Guards canter up to the waterside, preceding the carriages of the Governor and his Lady. The villagers are agape as the riverboat from Valence pulls up to the quay, and five passengers disembark: the two elderly black-robed clergymen; the two pert young uniformed maids; the blonde and beautiful, the elegantly attired middle-aged noblewoman.

Mother and daughter tear themselves from one another's embrace to greet and salute the others: the Countess de Grignan hugging her great-uncle, the Abbé de Coulanges, then assuring the humble La Mousse of his welcome; Mme de Sévigné rushing toward her dashing son-in-law to kiss his lips through the luxuriant growth of black beard (for the grooming of which she has brought him a pair of the best tweezers available in Paris).

What of Mme de Sévigné's first glimpse of the Château de Grignan, that "enchanted château," that imposing and ancient pile, high on its rocky eminence? What of her description of the beautiful apartment, set aside months earlier and decorated for her special delectation—the very one, perhaps, pointed out today by Grignan guides as "the suite of Mme de

Sévigné," with its spectacular view across the broad, balustraded terraces of the château, over the verdant valley to the foothills of the Alps? Her rapturous Oh's and Ah's are lost to us through the carelessness of her Paris correspondents, who passed her letters around, from hand to hand, but failed to retrieve them, to file them away for future generations of Sévignistes.

Once the travellers come ashore at Robinet, once greetings and caresses are exchanged, once the baggage is stowed, once the postillions mount their horses and the coachmen crack their whips, once the carriages move off the quay toward Grignan, eight or nine miles distant, the curtain falls! The theater darkens, the drama we have been watching is interrupted.

The hiatus in the correspondence lasts for the duration of Mme de Sévigné's sojourn in Provence, from July 30, 1672 to October 3, 1673. With the flow of letters between mother and daughter temporarily suspended, the narrative fails us, we come close to losing the thread of their lives. Thanks to a handful of letters from Mme de Coulanges and Mme de La Fayette and the Count de Bussy, thanks to letters written by Mme de Sévigné subsequent to her departure from Grignan in October, 1673, some vague outline of the mother and daughter's months together in Provence takes form.

It was not to be a period of unadulterated joy. If only two weeks earlier, Mme de Sévigné had congratulated her daughter on not being pregnant, she arrived at Grignan to discover that her daughter and her husband were expecting a child in the early spring, and were joyous in that expectation: more than one male heir was necessary to ensure the continuity of the ancient and illustrious Grignan line; hope for a second son was cherished by the Countess and the Count, by the latter's numerous brothers and uncles. Mme de Sévigné had, up to that point, at least, shown little understanding of the Grignan point of view. The Countess's fourth pregnancy—in as many years—may well have been a source of discord between mother and daughter.

A second source of discord would have been the Grignans' insolvency. The tactless Abbé, working on their accounts, doubtlessly expressed his dismay at the morass of debt into which the Grignans were sinking ever deeper. His reproaches doubtlessly stung the Count to anger. "You know the interest he takes in your affairs," Mme de Sévigné once soothingly explained, "even though he runs the risk of making himself detested."

Further tensions may have resulted from the fact that Mme de Sévigné found it difficult to come to terms with her daughter's newfound, hard-won independence. The severance of the silver cord is inevitably traumatic. If there had ever been symbiotic elements in this relation, they were no longer present. It may have come as a shock to Mme de Sévigné suddenly to be confronted with her daughter's new persona, to see her involved in a new life, in new roles: the roles of wife and mother, chatelaine, First Lady of Provence—a position of grandeur unfamiliar to her mother. The Countess de Grignan stood no longer in her mother's shadow.

It is unlikely that, save for the bond of blood, these two women would have been close; they had few areas of compatibility. Ironically enough, Mme de Grignan—as extravagantly as Mme de Sévigné loved and admired her—was not really her mother's type: where Mme de Sévigné was warm, open, approachable, expansive, Mme de Grignan was cold, aloof, uncommunicative, undemonstrative—classic examples of extrovert versus introvert. Opposites are said to attract, but temperaments so divergent are apt to jar: Mme de Grignan, languid, lethargic, supine upon her bed for hours and days, in striking contrast to her mother, Mme de Sévigné, with her boundless energy, her hyperactivity, striding miles and miles through the woods, directing workmen and gardeners, keeping pace with the Paris social whirl, writing to her daughter, keeping up with her extensive correspondence, reading omnivorously in her spare time.

It was a filial love—a calm and tranquil affection—that Mme de Grignan felt for her mother; feeling, furthermore, that it should be taken for granted that she felt it. Her mother took nothing for granted, required constant reassurance of love from her friends as well as from her daughter. ("Your mistrust," Mme de La Fayette once told her, "is your only fault, the only thing about you which displeases me.") With Mme de Sévigné, who verbalized as naturally as she breathed, sentiment had to be explicit; with Mme de Grignan, it was implicit. If Mme de Sévigné complained of Mme de Grignan's reserve, Mme de Grignan was embarrassed by Mme de Sévigné's effusiveness—still another source of misunderstanding and conflict. What Mme de Sévigné felt for her daughter more closely resembled a tempestuous passion than a serene maternal love; hers was a love painfully intense, unsatisfied save by a love of equal intensity. Little psychoanalytical insight is required to discern that Mme de Grignan's emotional needs were satisfied in her happy marital relation, whereas Mme de Sévigné's only emotional outlet was through her relation with her daughter.

It may have been these tensions which took their toll on Mme de Sévigné's usually robust good health or it may have been menopausal irregularities which developed in the autumn; at any rate, the all-purpose, the universal medical remedy—a bleeding—was prescribed for her in October, and the foot in which the vein was opened became inflamed, as we learn from a line in a letter of Mme de Coulanges to Mme de Sévigné, dated October 30, 1672: "I am concerned about you, my beauty . . . Why did you have to stand on that leg right after a bleeding?"

A decision was made, in November, to go to consult the renowned medical faculty at Montpellier about the complications of Mme de Sévigné's case. The Countess de Grignan, in the fourth month of her pregnancy, preferred not to travel, but the Count escorted his mother-in-law and her uncle on the ten-day round-trip voyage.

A letter from Mme de Sévigné to her daughter is datelined, "At Montpellier, Saturday, November 25":

> We finally arrived here yesterday, my darling, after having had quite a fright from the high waters at the bridge of Lunel . . . Mme de Calvisson wrote to invite us to her house, but the very thought horrified us, tired as we were. She sent us ortolans, partridge, pheasants, ice cream. We all lay down, though none of us slept . . . The whole town rushes to visit me, but since I do not wish to return these visits, I do not wish to receive any . . . I find the women here pretty and lively; they are witty and they speak French!* I am staying in a divine apartment in the home of a Mme de La Roche. Monsieur de Grignan is paid endless honors. Your name comes up twenty-five or thirty times a day. I think of you constantly; I live and breathe Grignan . . . Our plans are still to leave on Wednesday. The Bien Bon's appetite is ferocious . . . And how are you feeling, my pretty little darling? Has your heart warmed toward me a bit, in my absence? I long to see you, as though it had been forever since we parted. I conceal my love for you with as much care as others take in expressing it . . .
>
> It is the funniest thing about my foot. One day, it is painful; the next day, fine. I shall postpone curing myself of all my ailments until I get back to Grignan. I experienced one ailment here which was the very thing necessary to my good health, one I had eagerly awaited, and am pleased that the bleeding had the desired effect. I have sought much medical advice concerning the future. Adieu, my too dearly, too well beloved.

With the onset of winter, the Château de Grignan became virtually uninhabitable: perched high on its rocky pedestal, it was raked and battered and chilled by the cold and vicious winds howling down the Rhône Valley from the north (by the *bise* and the *mistral*, in the Provençal dialect). In November or December, the Count and Countess abandoned Grignan to the elements and moved to Aix, the capital city of Provence, taking up

---

*A supercilious Parisienne, Mme de Sévigné was surprised that they were witty and that they spoke French rather than the Provençal dialect.

residence in the dark and ancient palace ("that dingy old palace," in Mme de Sévigné's words) erected originally by the Counts of Provence; the abode, in the seventeenth century, of the Governor of Provence and meeting place of the Parlement.

When the Count de Grignan, in late January, 1673, proposed to his mother-in-law that she accompany him on a trip to Marseille and Toulon, where he had been called on official business, she accepted with alacrity, eager to see and travel about the province, as she had hoped to do in the company of her daughter.

Mme de Sévigné's three letters from Marseille have the ring of a typical tourist—one, however, to whom the keys of the city have been delivered, one given highly preferential treatment. The city of Marseille, as the archives show, gave the Governor of Provence and his mother-in-law an official welcome, complete with salvos of cannon, with gifts and welcome speeches intoned by civic and religious notables. The visitors were honored at banquets, concerts and masked balls. ("There was a very pretty little Greek girl there, around whom your husband hovered all the evening, the rascal!") Mme de Sévigné was taken sightseeing by the Intendant of Galleys and the Bishop of Marseille: "I am delighted by the singular beauty of this city," she wrote on January 25:

Yesterday, the weather was superb, and the view from the vantage point to which I was taken—from which I could look out over the sea, the fortresses, the mountains and the city—was breathtaking . . .

Marseille struck her as very "romantic," with its warships and its galleys, its sailors and sea captains, its chain-laden galley slaves. "The crowd of chevaliers" who came to pay their respects to the Count de Grignan—men of the sea, adventurers with their long swords and plumed hats—were "picturesque," "subjects for a painter," she wrote her daughter, and, "as for me, loving romantic novels as I do, I find all this utterly thrilling." "With all due respect to Aix," another letter ran, "Marseille is spectacular, with a population larger than that of Paris, some hundred thousand good souls—although how many of these are really 'good,' I have no way of knowing!"

By January 26, she had had enough of sightseeing, enough of honors and festivities, "enough of Marseille": "I have had my fill, up to here," she wrote, "up to my eyes," and was ready to "leave the next morning at five o'clock" for Toulon, eager to get back to Aix, back to her daughter, by then in the seventh month of her pregnancy.

"I embrace the Countess de Grignan," Mme de Coulanges wrote to

Mme de Sévigné, in late March: "I only wish that that pregnancy had already come to term and that she was safely out of childbed."

She nearly died in childbed, on March 27, 1673, as is revealed in a letter from the Abbé de Coulanges to a friend in Aix:

After nearly two days in labor, Mme the Countess finally found herself, on Monday, at three o'clock in the morning, in the greatest peril imaginable, due to the fact that the child presented itself belly and navel first. You can judge by that, my dear Sir, of what aid she had need, both from God who gave her the courage and the strength to endure the ordeal and from the attendant who was able to bring her safely through the birth—safely, that is to say, for her. Her poor child, a very well-formed boy, large and robust, arrived weak, and drowned in his own waters . . .

The Countess's recovery was slow: on April 19, Mme de Coulanges wrote to Mme de Sévigné:

I am thrilled to learn that Mme de Grignan is no longer so weak. The shock and anxiety I felt at the thought of her peril intensify the joy I feel at her recovery. It is barbaric to want children . . .

But I must not forget to tell you [Mme de Coulanges's letter went on] something that happened this morning:

They came in to tell me, "Madame, here is Mme de Thianges's* lackey." I gave orders that he should be admitted. Here is what he said to me: "Madame, I come from Mme de Thianges who requests that you send her Mme de Sévigné's letter about the Horse, and also the one about the Fields." I told the lackey that I would, myself, deliver them to his mistress, and so I did.† Your letters attract the attention they deserve, as you can see. They are indisputably delicious, and you are like your letters.

Mme de Sévigné's letters were already beginning—even as early as 1673—to enjoy a wide circulation and acclaim: "Mme du Plessis was so charmed with your letter," wrote Mme de La Fayette in May, "that she sent it on to me . . . and I passed your letters on to Langlade, who seemed greatly to enjoy them."

---

*Mme de Thianges was the sister of Mme de Montespan, the King's mistress.
†Mme de Coulanges was careless enough to misplace these letters; neither is extant.

Although Mme de Sévigné so often insisted to her daughter that she enjoyed writing to no one else, that all other letters constituted a chore, her correspondence throughout 1672–3 was obviously extensive. First of all there was her son, with whom she carried on a lively exchange of letters throughout the long months of the Dutch campaign. She was writing regularly and frequently to Monsieur and Madame de Coulanges and to Mme de La Fayette, and expected them to reciprocate. ("Why should you scream like an eagle?" Mme de La Fayette demanded, apparently in reply to a reproach: "What is so terrible about my saying that 'My days are filled to overflowing'? ... You still enjoy writing to all the world whereas I have completely lost the taste for correspondence. If I had a lover who expected a letter from me every morning, I would break with him. So, you should not measure my friendship by the number of letters I write you. I love you no less than you do me, even though I write only one page a month to your one page a day.")

Charles de Sévigné put in an appearance in Paris in the spring of 1673, thanks to his cousin, Mme de Coulanges, who managed to arrange a leave for him from his regiment through the good graces of her uncle, Michel Le Tellier, Secretary of War.

Mme de La Fayette evidently thought it necessary to plead the cause of her son to Mme de Sévigné:

Your son [she wrote] came to tell me goodbye, and to beg me to explain to you his reasons for needing money. Those reasons are so valid that there is no need for me to go into them, for you must realize—even from where you are—the costs of a campaign which goes on and on. Everyone is in despair, everyone is ruining himself. It is impossible that your son should not find himself in the same predicament as the rest. And, furthermore, the great love you bear Mme de Grignan demands that you manifest an equal interest in her brother [as if to remind Mme de Sévigné that she had not jibbed at a whopping 300,000 livres dowry for her daughter]. I leave it to our friend, the big d'Hacqueville, to speak to you further on this matter. Adieu, my very dear . . .

Mme de Sévigné did not turn a deaf ear to her friend's appeal: on March 7, 1673, she guaranteed a loan of 6,000 livres "to be used by the Seigneur, the Marquis de Sévigné, to renovate his military equipage for the present campaign."

If Charles was necessitous, he was also amorous, or fancied himself so. "Your son is head over heels in love with Mlle de Poussay," Mme de

Lafayette wrote on May 19: "What he wants to do is to fall as madly in love as La Fare.* Monsieur de La Rochefoucauld says that it is Sévigné's ambition to die of a passion he is incapable of feeling, for we do not consider him to be made of the stuff from which great passions spring . . ."

Not only Charles de Sévigné but the Count de Grignan, as well, put in an appearance in Paris in the spring of '73, the latter summoned into conference there with Monsieur de Pomponne, the Minister of Foreign Affairs in charge of Provençal affairs. Mme de Coulanges reported to Mme de Sévigné, by letter, toward the end of March: "Monsieur de Grignan shows no signs of provincial rust. He makes a very good impression at Court, but he seems to feel there is something missing. We agree with him; we, too, think there is something missing!" Sorely missed, Mme de Coulanges implied, were Mme de Grignan and Mme de Sévigné. Even without them, the Count stayed on in Paris until the end of May, at which time he took his firstborn child, little Marie-Blanche, back to Provence with him.

The silence that hangs over Aix and Grignan in the late spring and early summer months of 1673 is broken only by an occasional letter from Mme de Coulanges, Mme de La Fayette or the Count de Bussy. If Mme de Sévigné's Paris correspondents were remiss in preserving her letters, her old friend and literary mentor, the Abbé Ménage, was not one of the guilty parties: he did not lose, misplace or destroy the letter she addressed to him from Aix, in June, to acknowledge receipt of his latest volume of published poetry.

"Your thought of me gave me signal pleasure," she wrote on June 23, "and rekindled all the glow of our old friendship":

> Your verses reminded me of my youth, and I wonder why the reminder of the loss of an almost irreparable possession should not sadden me. Instead of the pleasure I felt, it seems to me that there was cause for tears. But, without analyzing the source of the pleasure, I prefer to dwell on the sense of gratitude I felt upon receipt of your gift. You must know how much it pleases me, since it caters to my self-esteem, and since I find myself celebrated in it by the foremost intellect of my time. In justification of your verses, I only wish that I better merited the tribute you pay me. Such as I was, such as I am, I shall never forget

---

*The Marquis de La Fare, from whom Charles de Sévigné had purchased his ensign's commission, was by then a second lieutenant in the Gendarmes-Dauphin. His widely quoted *Mémoires* give some insight into the two great love affairs of his life, the first with Mme de Rochefort, the second with Mme de La Sablière.

your true and steadfast friendship, and all my life I will be the most
appreciative as well as the first of your disciples.

The silence of 1673 is broken again on July 15 when Mme de Sévigné
addresses a letter to her cousin, the Count de Bussy:

And here I am, as you can see, at Grignan. It is exactly a year since I
came. I wrote you a letter, then—a joint letter with our friend Corbi-
nelli, who spent two months with us. Since that time, I have been in
Provence, travelling about, here and there. I spent the winter at Aix,
with my daughter. She almost died in childbirth, and I, along with her,
at sight of her in such a perilous delivery.

"And what do you think," the last line of her letter read, "about the
capture of Maestricht?"

Bussy must have thought, as did all Europe, that the successful siege
of that river stronghold was a masterpiece of military art, a prestigious
victory for Louis XIV, who personally commanded the attack, ensuring
France's control of a section of the Meuse River, assuring France's defense
in that quarter. By then in possession of the Netherlands, the Rhineland, the
Meuse and the Moselle, France could be seen to be the only great military
power on the continent, although the peace conference at Cologne made no
progress. Spain and Austria were forming a coalition against France.

The victory at Maestricht was celebrated throughout France. At Grignan, on July 23, a Te Deum was sung in the collegial Church of Saint-
Sauveur which was attached to Grignan, its tiled roof serving the château as
a vast terrace. *The Gazette of Holland* reported on August 10: "The Count
de Grignan attended the services, along with numerous persons of quality;
and in the evening, as cannons were fired and trumpets sounded, he lit a
huge bonfire which he had ordered laid in the public square."

XXI

October 5, 1673 was a "terrible day," the day Mme de Sévigné left Grignan, the day she parted from her daughter—the agony of this second parting as excruciating as that of the first, in 1671. Perhaps even more excruciating for the reason that Mme de Sévigné had hoped, until the very last, that the Grignans would accompany her to Paris. Their "uncertainty" about the voyage had been due to the uncertain state of international affairs, the threat of war with Spain, which would preclude a governor's leaving his province.

Mme de Sévigné wrote the very night of the very day of her departure—from Montélimar, a town some seventeen or eighteen miles from Grignan:

> *This is a terrible day, my dear daughter. I confess to you that I can go on no longer ... My heart and mind are full of you. I cannot think of you without weeping, and since I think of you constantly, I am in a dreadful state ... My eyes which feasted upon you throughout these past fourteen months are now deprived of the sight of you ... It seems to me that I did not embrace you often enough at parting. Why did I hold back? I did not tell you often enough how happy I am in the love you bear me. I did not sufficiently recommend you to the care of Mons. de Grignan. I did not thank him enough for all the courtesies and all the affection he shows me ... I am already devoured by curiosity; the only consolation I can hope for is in your letters ... In a word, my child, I live only for you. God grant me the grace someday to love Him as I love you. I think of the pichons [a pet name for children in the Provençal dialect]. I can think of nothing but Grignan. I cling to the thought. Never has there been a voyage so sad as this one. None of us says a word ...*

If tensions and misunderstandings had strained relations between mother and daughter, they were now forgotten. In retrospect, the months together had been idyllic. "Never in all my life, my darling," Mme de Sévigné would write, "have I so basked in the warmth of your heart and of your affection as on this recent visit." And again: "It is true that the visit in Provence made me feel closer to you than ever before. Never before had we spent so much time together. Never have I so revelled in your wit and your tenderness."

Travel was arduous, perilous, uncomfortable; one jolted along in springless carriages over bad roads. "Two leagues from Montélimar," wrote Mme de Sévigné, "I had to get out of the carriage, and my horses swam; water covered the floorboards of the carriage." Thinking constantly of the Grignans whom she fully expected—and endlessly exhorted—to follow her to Paris, that winter, she vehemently advocated their travelling "by litter or on horseback."

"I had always hoped to bring you back with me," she wrote from Lyon on October 10: "You know by what arguments and in what tone of voice you cut me off." The argument propounded by the Count de Grignan (and echoed by his wife) was to the effect that a governor's place was in his province in time of war, and rumors of war with Spain were currently rampant. Mme de Sévigné took issue with her son-in-law: it was her opinion that war with Spain would not be declared overnight, and that there were pressing matters upon which the Count needed to consult the monarch and the Council: "I think it would be politically wise for Monsieur de Grignan to appear at Court, sooner rather than later." Her personal motives, she insisted, did not color her thinking, although she would not deny that, "If you can come, this winter, it will give me infinite joy and total consolation . . ."

On October 11, her letter was headed, "From a bitch of a village six leagues from Lyon":

Here I am, my daughter, in a place which would make me sad even if I were not sad already. There is nothing here; it is a desert. I got lost in the fields, looking for a church . . . It is impossible to travel more sadly than I do. This is the fourth time I have written to you; without that, I do not know what would become of me. What is killing me is that after my first sleep, I hear two o'clock strike but, instead of going back to sleep, I put a pot on the fire—a bitter brew which simmers in my mind until daybreak, when it is time to get into the carriage. I am sure, my dear child, that—to relieve my mind—you will tell me that the air of Aix has done you good, that you are not as thin as you were at Grignan—none of which I will believe.

Having made her way into Burgundy, past Mâcon and Chalon, Mme de Sévigné—on October 16, 1673—drove up a treelined avenue to the door of her château of Bourbilly:

At last, my darling, I have arrived at the ancient château of my forefathers. Here it is that they triumphed, in the fashion of their day and time. I find my beautiful fields and meadows, my little river, my magnificent forests and my fine mill just as I left them.* Better people than I have lived here and, yet, on leaving Grignan, after parting from you, I am dying of sadness . . . I am unaccustomed to these constant storms; it rains without stopping . . . I have just gotten in, and am a little tired. When I have warmed my feet, I will write you more.

Nine days later, still at Bourbilly, she wrote:

I am concluding all my business here, today. If you did not have grain of your own, I would offer you some of mine. I have twenty thousand bushels to sell. I am crying famine on a stack of wheat! Even so, I have a guarantee of fourteen thousand francs, and I made a new lease, at the same figure as the last.† These were all the things I had to attend to, and I have the honor of having devised expedients of which even the Abbé had not thought.

On October 25, Mme de Sévigné wrote from Époisses, the Count de Guitaut's château, only a few kilometers from Bourbilly. "This is a place of astonishing grandeur and beauty," she told her daughter:

Monsieur de Guitaut made it his diversion to beautify it, and spent great sums of money in the process. I pity those who cannot afford to indulge themselves in that luxury.‡ We talked for hours on end, the master of the house and I—that is to say, I had the merit of being a good listener.

On October 30, she wrote from Moret, "the eleventh letter," she noted, "written en route":

---

*Mme de Sévigné's last visit to Bourbilly had been in 1644, in company with her daughter.

†The "guarantee of fourteen thousand francs" represented three years of arrears owed by the farmer who had previously leased the Bourbilly lands. His promissory note was based on sale of wheat, but that was so long delayed that Mme de Sévigné was obliged to borrow 6,000 francs against the note. Her plight was typical of the landed aristocracy in seventeenth-century France—the income from the great estates proving insufficient to meet the cost of living of the absentee landlords.

‡She pitied, that is to say, her son-in-law, whose limited means prevented his making the necessary repairs and renovations at Grignan.

*I am close to Paris, my very dear darling. I do not know how I feel about it. I do not look forward to getting there, except to read those letters from you which should be awaiting me. I tell myself that there are things I can attend to for you, messages to deliver to Messieurs de Brancas, La Garde, the Abbé de Grignan, d'Hacqueville, Monsieur de Pomponne, Monsieur Le Camus. Except for that which concerns you, I anticipate no pleasure. It would be what I deserve, were my friends to cudgel me and ship me back whence I came. Would that they could!
. . . Talking of you will constitute my greatest pleasure. But I will choose my words and my audience. I am not naïve, and I know that what is appropriate with some, is inappropriate with others. I have not totally forgotten the ways of the world . . . I beg you to trust me, and not to fear the exorbitancy of my love . . . Even if my hypersensitivity and the unwarranted accusations I made have sometimes caused friction between us, I implore you to make allowances for these failings of mine, for the sake of the sentiment which gives rise to them . . . It is concern about your health that is killing me. I fear that you are not sleeping and that you will fall ill. I implore Mons. de Grignan to do his part—and show his friendship for me—by keeping you in good health . . .*

(By keeping you from becoming pregnant was what she meant—the pleas to avoid pregnancy a constant refrain of the correspondence throughout the years.)

On November 2, Mme de Sévigné could head her letter, "From Paris":

At last, my dear daughter, I am back home, after four weeks of travel which tired me less than the night I spent, last night, in the best bed in the world. I did not close my eyes. I consulted my watch at every hour of the night and, finally, at break of day, I got up—

"For what to do in bed, if not to sleep?"*

We arrived yesterday . . . and stopped first at Monsieur de Coulanges's. First, I see Mons. de Coulanges who embraces me; a minute later, Mme de Coulanges and Mlle de Méri; a minute after that, Mme de Sanzei and Mme de Bagnols; another minute, and there was the Archbishop of Rheims; next, Mme de La Fayette, Monsieur de La Rochefoucauld, Mme Scarron, d'Hacqueville, Mons. de La Garde, the

---

*Mme de Sévigné's adaptation of a line from La Fontaine.

Abbé de Grignan, the Abbé Têtu!* You can hear, even from there, all that is said and the exclamations of joy. "And what about Mme de Grignan?"—"And what about your voyage?" Unanswered questions and answers to unasked questions! Utter confusion! Finally, we go in to supper, then we go our separate ways, and I spend a sleepless night.

I forgot to tell you that last night, before I did anything else, I read all four of your letters, those of October 15, 18, 22 and 25. Your letters are my life—whilst I await a better one.

"Alas!" she sighed on November 10, "I have brought Provence and all your problems back with me. '*In van si fugge quel che nel cor si porta.*' " ("It is vain to try to flee what one carries in one's heart," a quotation from Guarini's *Pastor fido.*)

All Mme de Sévigné's heart and thought and energy were bent, for the next three months, on persuading the Grignans to return to Paris. The correspondence reflects that single purpose. They must come, not for her sake, she insisted, but for theirs! Let them listen—if not to a bereaved and selfish mother—then, to their most trusted counsellors, the Marquis de La Garde (the Count's first cousin), the Abbé de Grignan (the Count's brother) and their good friend d'Hacqueville. This trio represented the Count de Grignan's interests at Court as best they could but, to unravel the snarl of Provençal politics, to counter the machinations of his archenemy, the Bishop of Marseille, the Count de Grignan would have to put in a personal appearance. The Marquis de Pomponne, the Minister of Foreign Affairs, championed Grignan in the royal councils, but the Bishop had powerful friends among the King's Ministers, and sought to foil and frustrate the Lieutenant-Governor at every turn.

Mme de Sévigné hated as she loved—passionately. Her hatred for the Bishop of Marseille waxed so intense as to endanger her immortal soul. "Yesterday I went to confession," she wrote on December 4, "and a very able man refused me absolution because of my hatred for the Bishop."

One ridiculous piece of unfinished business detained the Count in Provence: he was under orders from Louis XIV to lay siege to the citadel of Orange. At war, since 1672, with the United Provinces of the Netherlands— and their general and stadtholder, William of Orange—France had confiscated his tiny principality of Orange, an enclave in the south of France. The

---

*Mme de Sanzei was M. de Coulanges's sister; Mme de Bagnols was Mme de Coulanges's sister. Mme Scarron would become the Marquise de Maintenon, the King's mistress and eventually his morganatic wife.

Governor of the principality, with seventy-odd men, retired into the citadel, and stood his ground against orders to capitulate. The Count de Grignan, as Governor of Provence, marched to the assault, leaving Aix on November 18, with a company composed of a thousand or more soldiers and some two to three hundred Provençal noblemen.

"That siege of Orange distresses me, as it does you," Mme de Sévigné wrote her daughter on December 1, before news of the surrender of that garrison on November 23 could reach her in Paris: "What folly! What expense! I marvel at the Devil's ingenuity in finding ways to cost you money!"

Writing to her friend the Count de Guitaut, she sounded a note of irony:

Of all the ridiculous things imaginable, the siege of Orange takes first place! Monsieur de Grignan is under orders to seize it. The courtiers here seem to think the battle will be fought out with baked apples. Guilleragues calls it a duel between Mons. de Grignan and the Governor of Orange, and calls for him to attack and chop off the other fellow's head—as if it were a case of single combat. All that is very amusing. I laugh as heartily as I can but, to tell the truth, I am worried. The Governor [of Orange] will defend himself; he is a romantic fellow. He has two hundred men with him; he has fourteen cannon; he has gunpowder and wheat . . . He knows he will not be hanged.* There is a kind of small donjon or keep surrounded by moats, leaving only one means of access. The less terrain there is to defend, the easier it will be to do it. That poor Grignan has only a galley-regiment accustomed to marine warfare, inexperienced at sieges. He has a large group of noblemen in fancy waistcoats who will only get in his way. He will have to be everywhere at once; he could very easily be killed in this fine expedition, and people will laugh at him . . .

By December 4, news of the surrender of Orange had reached Paris, and Mme de Sévigné could rejoice with her daughter:

I am greatly relieved to get Orange off my mind . . . You cannot imagine how curious everyone has been about that famous siege; it ranked high in the news. I embrace the conqueror of Orange . . .

---

*The Governor of Orange, as a nobleman, would be beheaded, but not hanged.

And, on December 8, she could report:

The Orange affair enhances Mons. de Grignan's reputation, here. The large contingent of noblemen who followed him out of personal admiration, the huge expense, the resounding success—all that does him honor and rejoices his friends, who are not few in number, here. This widespread interest is most beneficial. At his supper, the King remarked: "Orange has been taken. Grignan had seven hundred gentlemen with him. Fire came from within the citadel but, finally, on the third day, came the surrender. I am very pleased with Grignan."

("The King used the figure 'seven hundred,'" Mme de Sévigné wrote elsewhere, "so 'seven hundred' is what everyone calls it." There had been only two hundred noblemen involved in the action, as Mme de Sévigné noted earlier, but no one took issue with the monarch.)

Mme de Sévigné basked in the glory with which her son-in-law had covered himself at Court:

I have just come from Saint-Germain, my dear daughter [she wrote on December 11], where I spent two whole days with Mme de Coulanges and Monsieur de La Rochefoucauld. We stayed with him. In the evening, we paid our court to the Queen who had the most obliging things to say to me about you ... I found your siege of Orange much talked about at Court.

The Count's victory at Orange was followed by a victory in the Assembly at Lambesc, where his nominee for an important provincial post was elected despite the opposition of the Bishop's faction.

"Now I must go to confession," Mme de Sévigné exulted, on December 22: "This victory has gentled my spirit. I am meek as a lamb. Far from refusing me absolution, they will give it to me twice over."

Twice triumphant, the Count de Grignan was then free to leave his governance and return to Paris—or so Mme de Sévigné thought, until her daughter advised her that there was no real necessity for a trip they could ill afford.

First off [Mme de Sévigné replied on December 28], I want to take up the chapter of your trip to Paris. "There is no necessity," you say, "for coming," and your reasoning on the subject is so forceful, you take so little into account the reasoning of those who urge this voyage on you, that I, for one, am overwhelmed. I know the tone you take, my daughter, and I cannot counter it. But, above all, when you ask "whether it is possible" that I—I "who should give more thought than any other" to the ruinous effect on your financial future—that I should "want to see you embark on an excessive expense which might prove the last straw" to the financial burden under which you already stagger . . . and all that follows. No, my child I want to do you no such harm. God forbid! But since you represent yours as the voice of reason, wisdom, even philosophy, I never want to be accused of being a reckless, an unjust or frivolous mother, who—out of feminine weakness—upsets everything, ruins everything, and prevents you from following your best instincts. Still, I had believed that you could afford this voyage; you had promised me you would come. And when I think of what you will spend at Aix on your Carnival festivities, your banquets and galas, your troupes of actors, I still think it would cost you less to come here where you will not need to bring anything with you. Monsieur de Pomponne and Mons. de La Garde point out to me a thousand matters necessitating your presence and that of Mons. de Grignan . . . I am in a position to provide accommodations for you, here. My heart abandons itself to the hope that you are not pregnant. You need a change of air. I had even allowed myself to hope that Mons. de Grignan would leave you here with me, this summer . . . But none of this seems true or right to you. I yield to the necessity and will take this sorrow—which is not negligible—as a penitence God wants me to make and which I have well deserved. It would be difficult to find one more appropriate, one better calculated to touch me to the heart, but I must make a total sacrifice, and resolve to spend the rest of my life separated from the one person in the world who is dearest to me . . . who loves me more than she has ever done—all that must be sacrificed to God, and with His grace, I shall do it, but I marvel at Providence which decrees that—with all the grandeur and the fine features of your marriage establishment—there are abysses which preclude all the pleasures of life, and a separation which stabs my heart at every hour of the day and at more than I could wish throughout the night . . . I shall make the sacrifice for the sake of my salvation. And now I have finished. I will say no more to you on the subject . . .

Although, of course, she did say more, much more, as on January 1:

I wish that you could have heard La Garde, after dinner, on the subject of the necessity of your coming here to prevent the loss of your five thousand francs [the subsidy for the Governor's Guards still to be voted by the Assembly] and on the subject of what Mons. de Grignan should say to the King . . .

Not only La Garde but the Queen herself had something to say about Mme de Grignan's return, and Mme de Sévigné rushed to quote her: "The Queen said, without hesitation, that it has been three years since you left, and that it is time for you to return . . ."

The Minister of Foreign Affairs was equally vehement, according to Mme de Sévigné: "Monsieur de Pomponne very much wants to see you come, and stresses—even more than we do—the necessity of your presence here."

Monsieur de Pomponne advises me that, as of today, you have your congé. It will be sent to you by the next regular courier [she wrote to her daughter on January 12, 1674]. So, now you are in a position to do whatever you choose, to take or to reject the advice of your friends.

XXII

Paris, Monday, February 5

It was on this day, many years ago, my dear darling, that there came into the world a creature destined to love you above all else in it.

February 5, 1674 was Mme de Sévigné's forty-eighth birthday.

February 4 had marked the third anniversary of Mme de Grignan's departure from Paris, as her mother had by no means forgotten:

It was three years ago today that I suffered one of the cruellest blows of my life: you left for Provence, where you remain. My letter would be very long, indeed, were I to recount all the sorrows I have suffered since that first day of my life. But, enough of this.

Perhaps the birthday accounted for the unwontedly somber mood:

It is true that time passes everywhere, and passes quickly. You deplore the fact because each year carries off something of your beautiful youth. But, for you, much still remains. As for me, it is with horror that I see time pass, see it bringing me ever closer to hideous old age; closer, inevitably, to death. There you have the reflections of a person of my age. Pray to God, my dear, to ask that He help me to profit by the teachings of Christianity.

No matter how old she may have felt, her appearance evidently belied her years:

"Everyone makes a point of telling me that I am looking beautiful," she wrote her daughter, somewhat disingenuously:

They overdo it. I think that they do not know what else to talk to me about. Alas, I have developed a habit of not sleeping until five o'clock in the morning, and my little eyes show the strain but, still, everyone comes along and pays me lavish compliments on my appearance.

Her son, Charles, on leave from his regiment, reached Paris a few days after Christmas, but was recalled the first week of January when the forces of William of Orange began putting pressure on French-held Maestricht.

"Before they have time to pull off their boots, they are back in the mud," Mme de Sévigné wrote on December 29: "French forces are to gather on January 16 at Charleroi ... This is an important development, and our armies are on the move. No one knows where to lay hands on money."

She expressed regret at seeing her "poor son" called back so suddenly to the Dutch War, but his leave-taking caused her no such trauma as had her daughter's. She devoted a scant three or four lines to Charles's departure in her letter of January 5, and then went nonchalantly on to other matters.

No matter how reluctantly she had returned to Paris, no matter how melancholy had been her mood, Mme de Sévigné was soon plunged into the capital's busy social and cultural whirl: opera-going, concert-going, sermon-going, strolling in the Tuileries gardens, visiting friends, attending dinner parties and supper parties. "We took supper again, yesterday, at Mme de Coulanges's, with Mme Scarron and the Abbé Têtu," she wrote that same winter of 1673–4:

We found it amusing, at midnight, to escort Mme Scarron home, beyond the Faubourg Saint-Germain, almost to Vaugirard, in the country: a large and handsome house to which no one has access. There is a large *garden, spacious and fine apartments. She has horses and carriages, a staff of servants. She is modestly but magnificently dressed, like a woman who spends her life with people of quality. She is pleasant, beautiful, kind, unaffected; a wonderful conversationalist. We drove back gaily, along streets lit by lanterns, safe from robbers.**

(Deepest secrecy was still maintained, at that time, concerning the house on the Rue Vaugirard—and Mme de Sévigné would certainly not violate it, especially by letter—but Mme de Grignan knew that it was the house in which Mme Scarron had been installed by the King to supervise the upbringing of his several not yet recognized, not yet legitimized children by his current mistress, Mme de Montespan.)

A cry of joy went up on January 15, at news of the Grignans' decision to come to Paris:

At last, my daughter, you are coming! That is what I most wanted in the world! But I, in my turn, want to say something sensible: it is that I swear to you, protest to you before God, that if Monsieur de La Garde had not found your voyage necessary for your own best interests, I would never have urged your coming—at least, not this year— and not merely on my account . . .

"So, you are coming!" she wrote on January 22:

And I will have the pleasure of welcoming you, embracing you, giving you a thousand little tokens of my love and solicitude. Anticipation fills my heart with a sweet, deep joy. I am sure that you know that, and that you are really not afraid that I will find you too thin, and send you back home!

"Give me your orders, my love," she wrote on January 26,

and you will see how well you will be served. La Garde tells me that he has advised you to bring the smallest retinue possible . . . You should bring no pages; that kind of thing may go over well in the provinces, but not here. He [La Garde] wants you to bring no suite, no officers.† He wants only six lackeys for the two of you . . . You should

---

*Street lights were still something of a novelty, lanterns having been installed in Paris in 1666.
†By "no officers," she meant no maître d'hôtel, no Captain of the Guards.

Mademoiselle Marie de Rabutin-Chantal

Baron Charles de Sévigné

Madame de Grignan

Veüe de
GRIGNAN.
du costé des chastaigners, sur le chemin de
Vaureas.

OPPOSITE, ABOVE: View of Grignan

OPPOSITE, BELOW: Château Les Rochers

BELOW: Hôtel Carnavalet

Duke de la Rochefoucauld

Madame de La Fayette

Courtyard, Hôtel Carnavalet

Madame de Sévigné

travel light, forget the elaborate provincial ritual, turn a deaf ear to the complaint of those who are being left behind. Six horses should suffice for you, along with a few saddle horses ... We have found, nearby, a small house where your staff can be lodged ... There is a carriage-house and a six-stall stable ... You can have it for five hundred francs a year, which is a bargain ...

Her letters were full of warnings and admonitions about the journey: "Travel safely! Take no risks on the road!" "Do not go by carriage along the banks of the Rhône," she wrote in a letter addressed to the Count: "Avoid the high water one league beyond Montélimar ... In the name of God, do not make light of my warnings." "Not a drop of rain could fall" without perturbing her, she wrote, once she thought the Grignans on the road.

"My darling," she wrote on January 29,

I am angry at you. Now, really! You have the cruelty to tell me— knowing my heart, as you do—that you will be inconveniencing me in my own house, that you will be depriving me of my rooms, that you will crowd me out, set things topsy-turvy! Come, now! You should be ashamed to say such things to me. Was it for my sake alone that I took such a house as this? Instead, you should share in my joy, my darling— rejoice in the fact that it is you who are taking over my rooms. Who better than you could ever occupy them? Is it for any other reason that I could be glad to have them available? How could I find happier occupation than in making the minor arrangements necessary for your reception? ... Don't you know me better than that? You should ask my pardon ...

"I am deliciously occupied," she wrote elsewhere, "with the pleasure of welcoming you, making sure that you encounter no slightest inconvenience, that you find everything you need—without even having to ask for it!" "We will buy you a very beautiful housecoat," she wrote on February 2:

You have only to command. I have tried to spare you all the inconveniences of arrival, to make you feel—the day after you get here—as if you had already been here for two weeks!
And I thank you for your assurances that you will take no chances on a carriage along the banks of the Rhône. You prefer to travel by boat. Once you reach Lyon, you will know better than we do here

*which method is preferable. Just so long as you arrive in good health,
that is all I ask. My heart is profoundly moved at the prospect of seeing
you. Let those who wish go out on the road to meet you. I prefer to
await you in your room, thrilled to see you there. You will find the
fires and the candles lit, comfortable chairs, and a heart unsurpassed in
love for you.*

And, so, in mid-February, 1674, with the arrival of the Grignans and
their entourage, a curtain of silence falls again—a silence of some fifteen
months, broken only by an occasional letter of Mme de Sévigné's to a friend
or relative.

Once again, in 1674, as in 1672–3, the intense joy of reunion was
marred for mother and daughter by undercurrents of discord and dissension.
Things must have gotten off to a bad start with Mme de Grignan's
announcement of another pregnancy—the fifth in the five years of the
Grignans' marriage, as her mother would doubtlessly have reminded her.
The fact that the Countess was three months pregnant upon arrival in Paris
is established—not by the correspondence—but by vital statistics records:
Pauline de Grignan was born in Paris on September 9, baptized on September 13 in the Church of St. Paul, with the Cardinal de Retz as godfather and
the Princess d'Harcourt as godmother. (The Grignans may have been bitterly
disappointed in the birth of another girl—the fourth daughter for the Count!—
but, in the case of Mme de Sévigné, this granddaughter was to hold a special
place in her affections, and play a special role in the publication of the
Sévigné *Letters*.)

The old bone of contention between mother and daughter—the Countess's frequent pregnancies, the miscarriage, the stillbirth—was still there,
but it was not the only one to trouble their relation. Other areas of disagreement come to light in the exchange of letters that would follow their separation in 1675.

Five months pregnant in mid-May of 1674, the Countess de Grignan
could not accompany her husband on his return to Provence to preside over
the provincial Assembly. She had no choice but to remain with her mother
in Paris (there to await her husband's return in November).

"We miss you terribly," Mme de Sévigné wrote her son-in-law on
May 22:

*It was always a joy to see you come home, at night. Your company is
delightful and, save for the times one hates you, one loves you extravagantly! . . . My daughter is still languishing. She is sad, but I am*

thrilled with your good reports about my little girl. I appropriate for myself all the caresses you lavish on her . . .

The two children, Marie-Blanche de Grignan, and her brother, the Marquis de Grignan, had been left at the Château de Grignan when their parents departed for Paris in August of 1673.

Sometime during that summer of 1674, Mme de Sévigné—for all her apparently robust good health—suddenly fell ill, as we learn from a letter from the Count de Bussy. In exile on his Burgundian estates, the Count heard rumors that his cousin "had almost died of apoplexy," as he observed in the manuscript version of his *Letters:** "I learned that you had been very ill, my dear cousin," he wrote her on August 5:

That gave me so much concern that I consulted a very able doctor in this region. He told me that hale and hearty women like you, who have been widowed early and who repress their natural instincts, are subject to the vapours. That relieved my fears of a more serious ailment because—with the cure readily available, I cannot believe that you hate life enough not to avail yourself of it, not to take a lover as readily as you would an emetic. You should take my advice, my dear cousin; all the more so, since it is clear that it is disinterested advice because, had you the need to take such a remedy, I could not hope to profit by it when I am a hundred leagues away. Raillery apart, my dear cousin, take care of yourself. Have yourself bled more often than is your custom. It makes no difference how you accomplish it, so long as you stay alive! You remember that I told you, once before, that you are among those people who should never die, just as there are some who should never have been born.

"Your doctor who diagnoses my malady as the vapours and you, who suggest the cure," Mme de Sévigné replied on September 5, "are not the first to prescribe such a specific":

But the same reluctance which prevented my taking the proper preventive measures against the vapours precludes my taking the cure. The fact that your advice is disinterested is less meritorious than it might have been in the first flush of youth. Still, however it is, I am feeling

---

*The first edition of the Count de Bussy's *Letters* was published in 1697.

*well, and if I should die of this malady, it will be in a noble cause, and
I will entrust you with the writing of my epitaph.*

"What do you think of our victories?" she inquired in the next paragraph of her letter:

*Our casualties are so high in our victory [at Senef, on August 11] that
without the singing of a Te Deum and the flags taken to Nôtre Dame,
it might be thought that we had lost the battle. My son suffered a light
head wound. It is a miracle that he survived, along with four squadrons
of the King's household troops, who were exposed for over eight hours
to enemy fire . . .*

The *Gazette*'s August 22 account of the battle of Senef cited Charles's
regiment, the Gendarmes-Dauphin, for bravery, and carried Charles's name
among the wounded. "Our Marquis distinguished himself among the bravest,"
his uncle, the Abbé de Coulanges, wrote to a friend at Nantes, on August 5.

Bussy's reply to his cousin's letter of September 5 was dated September 10:

*Just as I find no one's conversation as delightful as yours, Madame, I
find no one's letters as delightful as those you write me. I must tell you
the truth: it would have been a terrible shame for you to have died.
Your friends would have suffered an infinite loss. As for me, mine
would have been such that whatever respect I may have for your virtue,
I would prefer to see it suffer if that would contribute to your living
forever. For, after all, it is not only for your virtue that I love you, but
because you are the most charming woman in the world!*

Bussy's praise of her talents as a letter-writer elicited a reply on October 15:

*It seems to me that I no longer write so well, but if it was important to
me to take pride in my letters, I would ask you to restore my self-
confidence by your approbation.*

Mme de Sévigné and the Count de Bussy maintained a rather brisk
correspondence throughout the winter of 1674 and into the spring of 1675;
Mme de Sévigné had reports to make to her cousin on the fruitless efforts
of the Cardinal de Retz to alleviate the Prince de Condé's animosity toward

Bussy—a prerequisite, apparently, to the King's rescinding of Bussy's exile order. And the Count de Bussy reported to his cousin on the engagement of his favorite daughter to the Marquis de Coligny—an alliance of which Mme de Sévigné highly approved although she was remiss in her acknowledgment of the announcement.

On May 10, she wrote to make apology:

> I think I must have lost my mind not to have written to send my good wishes on the marriage of my niece.* But I am really in a state, and that is the only excuse I have to offer. My son leaves in three days time for the army; my daughter, shortly after that, for Provence. You can understand that with separations such as these confronting me, I can scarcely be expected to keep my head.

There had been "talk of peace," Mme de Sévigné told Bussy, although "While we wait, everyone goes off to war, and the governors and lieutenant-governors go to their posts in the provinces." The Count de Grignan would return to Provence, and take the Countess with him. "All these separations touch me to the quick," her mother wrote: "I think that Mme de Grignan herself will not leave us without some qualms."

She left them on May 24, 1675—Mme de Sévigné accompanying the Grignans as far as Fontainebleau for the final farewells. "What a day this is, my daughter, this first day apart!" Mme de Sévigné lamented when she sat down at her writing desk at Livry:

> How did it affect you? For my part, I felt all the bitterness and pain I had so long foreseen and feared. What a moment, that of parting! What farewells! What sorrow to go, each in a different direction when there has been such happiness together! I do not want to talk to you further about it, neither to dwell on, nor to "celebrate"—as you call it—all the thoughts which afflict my heart. I want to remember your courage, and all you had to say to me on the subject, all of which makes me admire you. Even so, it seemed to me that you, too, were emotional when you kissed me goodbye.
>
> As for me, I came back to Paris in a state of mind you can well imagine. Monsieur de Coulanges adapted himself to my mood. I went to the Cardinal de Retz's where my grief so intensified that I had to

---

*Mme de Sévigné called Mlle de Bussy her niece although she was the girl's cousin rather than her aunt.

send my excuses to Monsieur de La Rochefoucauld, Mme de La Fayette and Mme de Coulanges who had come there to see me, explaining to them that I was obliged to deny myself the privilege of their company. One must conceal one's weaknesses from the strong. The Cardinal made excuses for mine. I stayed with him until ten o'clock. Do not blame me, my child, for what I felt on returning home. What a difference! What a solitude! What a sadness! Your room, your study, your portrait! No longer to find that delightful person!

The next day, which was yesterday, I found myself wide awake at five o'clock in the morning. I went to pick up Corbinelli* to come here [to Livry] with me and the Abbé. It rains ceaselessly, and I very much fear that the roads through Burgundy will be impassable.† We are reading maxims which Corbinelli is explaining to me. He would very much like to teach me to control my emotions. It would have been a very profitable journey, had I come home with that knowledge. I am going back [to Paris] tomorrow. I needed this moment of repose to regain some measure of composure ...

XXIII

"And how could you expect me not to cry when I read your letter? It takes less than that to set off my tears!" Mme de Sévigné wrote on May 29, 1675:

> In the name of God, my darling, do not start going back over mere nothings. If I sometimes get my feelings hurt, it is I who am in the wrong. I should be confident of your affection and, as a matter of fact, I am. That hypersensitivity of mine is the result of my thinking and caring about nothing but you, so that everything to do with you is of prime concern. But remember that, thanks to that same hypersensitiv-

---

*Jean Corbinelli was a *bel esprit,* an equivocal character of Florentine origin, an impecunious savant, peripatetic philosopher, who enjoyed the patronage of a number of distinguished intellectuals, including Mme de Sévigné, the Countess de La Fayette, the Count de Bussy, the Cardinal de Retz, and the Marquis de Vardes, whose exile he often shared at Montpellier.

†The Grignans' route to Provence evidently led through Burgundy.

ity, all it takes is one word, one smile, one fond gesture of yours to restore my heart and fill me with tenderness . . . I beg you, then, my darling, not to think that you failed me in any regard. Just one word of explanation on your part could wipe out a crime, how much more easily, then, those things so trivial that only you and I would be aware of them. Be sure, my darling, that the disposition of my heart is such that all I can feel for you is a matchless tenderness, a partiality which will end only with my life.

Her friends rallied around her as solicitously as if she had lost her daughter to death: "Mesdames de Lavardin, de La Troche and Villars showered me with letters and attentions." "My friends are overly attentive; they importune me."

Her anguish was only slightly relieved, a week after their parting:

At last, my daughter [she wrote on June 7], here I am reduced to finding my only happiness in your letters. It is true that they are priceless, but when I think that it was you, yourself, that I had—and for a full fifteen months—I cannot contemplate that time without great yearning and great anguish. There are people who wanted to make me think that the exorbitancy of my love embarrassed you, that my eagerness to know and fulfill your every wish annoyed you. I do not know, my dear child, whether this is true. All I can say is that I certainly did not intend to displease you. I simply followed my inclinations, I admit, and was with you as often as I could, for the reason that I lack the self-control to deny myself that pleasure, but I do not believe I imposed on you.

She was grateful for the letter that reached her two-and-a-half weeks later in which her daughter evidently denied that her mother had made her ill at ease. "I thank you, my darling," Mme de Sévigné wrote on June 26,

for taking the trouble to deny that I overwhelmed you with my affection. There was no need for so obliging an explanation. I am as confident of your affection as you could possibly wish me to be; that confidence constitutes the happiness of my life. You explain very well the reason why I could not determine your wishes—for the reason that there was nothing you wished for! I should know you better and, on that score, I will do better, the next time, because I will have a better understanding. At such time as my good fortune brings you

back to me, be sure, my darling, that you will be a thousand times
better pleased with me than ever before.

Who were "the people" who tried to make her think that "the exorbitancy" of her love "embarrassed" her daughter, that she was smothering
her daughter with her affection and her assiduities? Mme de Sévigné did not
mention those "people" by name, neither at this time nor two years later
when those "people" became even blunter, even more outspoken, but it
would seem to have been the Count de Grignan who was closest and surely
most sensitive to the mounting tension between his wife and his mother-in-
law. The Abbé de Coulanges, Mme de Sévigné's uncle, might have been
another who sided against her in this mother-daughter conflict of interests.
D'Hacqueville, too, perhaps, that family friend so close to both mother and
daughter that he could make a judgment on the discord intensifying between
them.

The pangs of separation—on Mme de Sévigné's side—were no less
excruciating in 1675 than in 1670 or 1673. But, to Mme de Grignan—after
fifteen months under the same roof with her doting, possessive, assertive
mother—the parting may have come as a relief, as a liberation, although
she could probably not escape without a twinge of guilt for what she may
have considered a lack of proper filial devotion. Where the Château de
Grignan had been large enough to provide spaces in their togetherness, the
house on the Rue des Trois Pavillons had confined them in too close quarters—the over-fond, over-anxious, over-solicitous mother and the increasingly impatient and resentful daughter, increasingly guilt-ridden at the thought
of denying her mother's demands and needs.

"You are cruel, my darling," Mme de Sévigné protested in her letter of
July 3, "to say that I was inconvenienced by having you here in the house.
Is it possible that you so little know the kind of love I bear you, the keen
joy I took in every moment I saw you here? Really, my darling, I am
astonished that you would say such things to me. I do not deserve it."

Theirs would appear to have been a textbook case of symbiotic relationship. If the condition had been, at one time, advantageous—or even
necessary—to both, it had ceased to be so for the daughter, who was, at
that time, struggling desperately to break the maternal stranglehold in order
to live her life as wife and mother, as herself. (When the association becomes
disadvantageous or destructive to one of the two organisms involved, the
condition is termed antagonistic or antipathetic symbiosis.)

It was the mother who would not, could not relax her hold, who would
not or could not recognize her daughter's desire for independence. She could

not come to terms with the turn of fate that separated her from her daughter. "People come to see me out of charity," she wrote in June, "for it is no longer here that they come for gaiety. I cannot make myself go back into the large room. I am always seeking you there."

"I am back within the circle of my friends," she wrote that same month:

I come and go, but it is when I can talk of you that I am happy, and to shed a few tears gives me my greatest relief. I know the places where I can allow myself such liberties . . .

You seem to be afraid that I am making myself ridiculous, that I am talking too much about you. No, no, my darling, have no fear; I know how to govern that torrent. Trust me a little, and let me love you as I do until such time as God appropriates unto Himself some part of the heart you now totally possess; it is to Him alone that you would yield place. As a matter of fact, I found myself so wholly preoccupied with thoughts of you—my heart so incapable of any other love—that I was denied permission to take the sacrament at Pentecost . . .

Once again, it was the stream of letters to and from her daughter which served as her lifeline:

Instead of going into your room to chat with you, my darling [she wrote on June 14], it is here on these pages that we have our communication. When I am unfortunate enough no longer to have you with me, I find my natural consolation in writing to you, in receiving your letters, in talking about you and busying myself with working on your affairs.

And with gazing at her portrait! "Your portrait is very pleasant to look at," Mme de Sévigné wrote, "although much less so than you, yourself—not to mention the fact that it does not engage in conversation"—a speaking likeness, she implied, that did all but speak. The Mignard portrait of the Countess de Grignan was so lifelike, according to her mother, that "One felt the impulse to embrace it. It seemed about to step out of its frame." (Mignard is thought to have done a portrait of Mme de Sévigné, as well, although some authorities attribute the famous work to Claude Lefebvre, instead. Whichever of the two artists it was, the likeness failed to please Mme de Sévigné, who wished that it had had "less of a bucolic look about it.")

"My God! my darling, how little I accustom myself to your absence!" Mme de Sévigné wrote on July 3:

When I think how we are situated, I sometimes suffer such pangs of anguish that I can scarcely breathe, and no matter how I try to brush aside the thought, it haunts me constantly. And since I am convinced that the love I feel for you has grown even greater since my sojourn in Provence, I find that my sadness is greater, too, at being separated from you by so perverse a fate. The thought comes over me in waves, day and night—beyond my control . . .

Mme de Sévigné managed to get her mind off her grief, that summer, at least long enough to bring her daughter up to date on the latest developments in the amorous intrigues of the monarch. The gentle and unassuming Louise de La Vallière ("a shrinking violet" by Mme de Sévigné's definition: "never another in that mold") had bidden farewell, in June of 1674, to the Court, to her royal lover and their two recently legitimized children* to immure herself in the Carmelite Convent, the strictest and most austere of the conventual orders. "She had drunk the cup of humiliation to the dregs," as Mme de Sévigné reported, yielding place in the King's affection to her onetime friend—more recently her rival—the ruthlessly ambitious, the beautiful and brazen Athénaïs, Marquise de Montespan. As a novice at the Convent, the King's first official mistress had had to shear her crowning glory, her famous silver-blond hair, as Mme de Sévigné also reported with a rather cynical Yes, but!—"But she spared the two fine curls on her forehead!" Not a disparaging word, however, came from Mme de Sévigné's pen when she described to her daughter, in June of 1675, the ceremony at which Sister Louise de la Miséricorde took her final vows—and her black veil from the Queen: "That lovely and courageous person made her profession yesterday . . . in her customary noble and charming manner . . . The entire congregation [tickets of admission were at a premium!] was struck by her beauty . . ."

For those in the know, like Mme de Sévigné, the final hour had struck for Louise de La Vallière the very moment the divorce decree of the new Favorite, Mme de Montespan, became final.† It was high time: Mme de Montespan was about to present the King with their fifth child. From this

---

*Mlle de Blois had been eight, and her brother, the Count de Vermandois, six, when that beautiful stranger, their mother, had left the Court.

†The King had had resort to a special legal process to accomplish the long-desired divorce.

time on, as the *Mémoires* of the Duke de Saint-Simon point out, "Both the pregnancies and the births were public ... At first, the existence of the children had been kept secret ... Gradually, they were brought out of hiding, openly acknowledged ... Eventually, they and their governess were installed at the Court ..."*

As fascinating as Mme de Sévigné found the secrets of the royal alcove, the Grignans' financial affairs gave her cause for mounting concern, if not alarm, that same summer of 1675. A critical situation had developed in the spring during the Grignans' sojourn in Paris: the Duke de Montausier, uncle and guardian of the two Grignan daughters who were the issue of the Count's first marriage bed, insisted that the Count turn over to the girls their maternal inheritance in the amount of 120,000 livres. The Count de Grignan, having dissipated the dowry and fortune of his first wife, had put off as long as he could the evil day of reckoning, but was finally constrained to pledge to reimburse his daughters at such time as they attained their majority, and to pay them—during their minority—the sum of 6,000 livres annual interest. The Countess de Grignan, prompted by love for her husband and by pride in the glory of the Grignan name, voluntarily joined her signature to that of her husband, voluntarily assumed responsibility for her husband's obligation to his daughters. Mme de Sévigné—while she deplored the necessity for what she called her daughter's "heroic signature," could not but admire the "generosity" and the "nobility of soul" which had inspired her daughter's quixotic action.

"I am thrilled to learn that Monsieur de Grignan repays that signal token of your love by taking greater heed of his affairs," she wrote her daughter several months later. "The prudence for which you commend him is the sole token of gratitude you could wish from him." Such prudence was, however, totally alien to the Count's aristocratic insouciance about money. Stagger though he might under his mountainous burden of debt, he continued on his reckless, profligate way. "My hair stood on end," Mme de Sévigné moaned upon hearing that the Count had been seen at the high-stakes gaming tables in Aix. "What madness!" she wrote her daughter in early June. "In the name of God, do not permit it! That is a concession you should be able to obtain from him, if he loves you."

The Count was not only an inveterate gambler (as were most of the French courtiers of the day), he was a collector, a connoisseur of art. A

---

*Of the seven children born to Louis XIV and Mme de Montespan only four would reach maturity. These four were not only established in the Court hierarchy, they were integrated by association and by marriage into France's ruling family, blood brothers of the Bourbons.

Rubens and a Poussin were among the canvases for which he plunged deeper into debt at that time.* To pay off one Jean-François Gassendi, a merchant-banker of Aix-en-Provence, the Count signed over to him all the revenues from two Grignan properties in the region—Peyrolles and Mousteyret—for the years 1675–9. Other creditors had to wait longer still: one upholsterer at Aix could not collect until 1681 on an account run up by Grignan in 1671.

Monsieur de Grignan's mania for borrowing—for paintings and furnishings [Mme de Sévigné fumed by letter to her daughter in mid-July] is something one positively could not believe unless one saw it. How can this be reconciled with his rank, his renown, or with the consideration he owes you? Does he not fear to exhaust your patience or does he think it inexhaustible? Has he no pity on you? What have you done to be so afflicted, to be brought to such financial ruin? Does he think that we will think that he loves you? What a strange kind of love! The love you can count on, my dear child, is mine. Mine will never fail you. Make a test of it in your time of sorrow, and throw yourself into these arms which are forever open to receive you. I did not intend to say this much, but why restrain myself, why hold back the truth? It is by me that you are truly loved . . .

Was this a not overly subtle invitation to her daughter to come home to mother? Had she exceeded a mother's privilege? She evidently had fears on that score: "I have gone too far, my darling. I am destroying myself and you." Another time, she wrote apologetically:

Forgive me, my poor darling, for these tiresome lectures upon which I have embarked. This is a dreadful letter, and utterly pointless because I believe you give thought to all of this, but the distress which I am caused by all these senseless extravagances in which you indulge makes me indiscreet, and I cannot control my fond concern or my pen. I do not often touch on such matters. As for the payment of the back interest you owe which is the most important thing at the moment, you must realize the importance of this all too clearly to let it slip your mind . . .

---

*Mme de Sévigné's cousin "little Coulanges," likewise a collector, encouraged Grignan to "fill up his courtyards with paintings," once the walls of his château were covered: "Paintings are like gold ingots," he wrote. "You will double your money whenever you choose to dispose of them."

The "back interest" to which she referred was that owing the Grignan daughters, not that owing the Abbé de Coulanges on a loan he had made to the Grignans: "I implore you, my darling, on the part of the Abbé, to give no further thought to the back interest you owe him." The proceeds from the sale of a carriage and a desk left behind in Paris by the Grignans for that purpose would more than take care of the interest they owed him, she assured them. And as for the interest due on a loan of six hundred francs made by Mme de Sévigné to her daughter—and for which Mme de Grignan had insisted on giving her mother a promissory note—Mme de Sévigné wanted to hear no more about it! Later, perhaps, but not now! "Never again mention that note you gave me! Do not take advantage of my love for you by saying cruel things to me, things which wound me to the heart."

If there was much talk of the Grignans' financial plight, during the summer of 1675, there was much talk, too, of the Grignan children—far more than was the norm in that day and time. From this time on, the family occupies a larger and larger role in the *Letters*: nowhere else in the seventeenth century does one find so frequent a reference to children as in the Sévigné correspondence. "I was delighted to hear what you had to say about my grandchildren," she wrote, one day that summer:

> *I think you will find it interesting to watch their young minds develop. You do me an injustice to accuse me of loving my little girl* better than the* pichon.† *He must be adorable and very handsome. Tell me about him often. And since you like to hear the mention of my name, make sure that my little girl does not forget me. I would like to see her taught to dance. It is a shame to see how eager she is to learn, without knowing where to begin. I know that it is not a necessity, but it would be a diversion for her while she is at Grignan.*

The Abbé de Coulanges, Mme de Sévigné's uncle, had come, that summer—subsequent to the death of a brother with whom he had previously made his home—to take up residence with his niece in her house on the Rue des Trois Pavillons. She implies that he was not the easiest man to get along with:

"The *Bien Bon* sometimes gets into arguments with Mlle de Méri" [Mme de Sévigné wrote on July 12, 1675, in reference to her cantankerous old maid cousin]:

---

*Mme de Sévigné's "little girl" was Marie-Blanche, who had been left in her grandmother's care in Paris in 1671.

†Mme de Sévigné's grandson was either "the little Marquis," "the Dauphin," or "the *pichon*."

Do you know why? It is the Abbé's precision . . . and when the laws of arithmetic are broken or the Rule of Two Plus Two Makes Four is in some way violated, the good man is beside himself! That is his way. One must accept him on that basis. For her part, Mlle de Méri's style is entirely different. When either from intuition or reason she takes a stand, she cannot be swayed. She insists on her proposition; he feels drowned in a torrent of words. He gets angry and ends up by taking the prerogative of an uncle and telling her to shut up! She tells him that he is impolite. The word "impolite" constitutes a new outrage, and all is lost! They are at loggerheads. The main issue is forgotten; it is the circumstances which have become important. That is when I come on the scene. I go from one to the other, like the cook in the comedy* . . . but I am more successful, because they end up laughing. And, when all is said and done, the next day Mlle de Méri comes back to the good Abbé, and asks him for his advice. He gives it to her, he helps her; the advice is good; he is very good, I assure you. He has his moods, but who is perfect?

We are trying to find some secondhand damask out of which to make your bed-curtains . . . The top bands have been changed skillfully, and we have chosen red satin with varicolored embroidery. This bed will be perfect for Grignan; it has a very noble look, but will not be too expensive. Let me attend to it all . . . There will be enough left to make you a fine winter bed, with the top bands I described to you, in cloth of gold, silver and red, and the curtains made out of the very finest velvet available, with a gold braid trim, and an admirable air of antiquity.

I have just sent a package to you; it will go off tomorrow . . . You will find your order of wools and canvas, costing forty-five livres, five sols, and a pattern by which to work, while waiting for your silks which have not yet been tinted, and will not be ready for another ten or twelve days. I thought you would be impatient without some needle-work to occupy you. You will not yet need your silks. I will try to find someone to bring them to you.

Mme de Sévigné's letter of July 19 contains a frequently anthologized passage, her description of the religious procession bearing the shrine of Saint Geneviève, the first time that saint's treasure and reliquaries—the

---

*The cook in Molière's comedy *The Miser*.

richest in Europe—had been carried through the streets of Paris since 1652 when the purpose had been to ensure the peace and put a stop to the rains.

Have you any idea what a beautiful sight this procession is? All the monastic orders, all the parishes, all the shrines, all the priests of all the parishes, all the canons of Nôtre Dame, along with Monsieur the Archbishop ... who goes on foot, pontifically blessing the people on the right and on the left, all the way to the Cathedral. Actually, he only blesses those on the left because, on the right—preceded by fifty friars— walks the Abbé of Saint Geneviève, barefoot, with his cross and mitre, like the Archbishop, and giving his blessing, too ... Members of Parle- ment in their red robes, and all the sovereign companies follow the shrine—its jewels dazzling to the eye—which is borne by twenty white- garbed, barefoot men. The provost of the merchants and four counsel- lors are left as hostages to Saint Geneviève until that precious burden is safely returned. You will ask why she was removed from her shrine: it was to stop the rains and bring on warm weather. Both things happened the moment the project was undertaken, so that the effect in general being to bring us all sorts of benefits, it is to this we owe the safe return of the King.*

"I await letters from you tomorrow, my very dearest," were her closing lines:

They are my sole joy, my consolation in your absence. This separation is a strange thing, my darling. You have said all that can be said on the subject, but since it is true that time sweeps us along and carries us to death, I find reason to weep instead of laughing as I would if our poor little lives did not run out. I reflect often on this, but it does not do to dwell on it ...

---

*The King, having left the armies under the command of the Prince de Condé, was to return to Versailles on July 21.

XXIV

"It is very warm, today, my very dear darling," Mme de Sévigné began her letter of July 24, 1675, "but, instead of tossing in my bed, I have taken the notion to arise—although it is only five o'clock in the morning—to chat a while with you"—a long "while," as it developed; a long letter, some thirty manuscript pages long, thirty large unmarginated sheets of paper covered by that large, elegant, flowing script, almost totally innocent of punctuation, and not easily decipherable to the uninitiated.* Mme de Sévigné realized that this letter was unusually long, writing, "I have your silks. I wish I could find someone to take them to you. The package is too small to be shipped by coach, too large for the mails. I suppose the same thing could be said about this letter." The superscription read: "For my daughter—who is very patient if she reads all this."

Frequent reference is made in the correspondence, throughout those summer months of 1675, to Mme de Sévigné's plans for visiting Brittany and the extensive Sévigné properties there which were once again in need of her personal attention after a four-and-a-half-year absence. Her departure was delayed from week to week, month to month, to await not only the outcome of a Grignan lawsuit pending in the Paris courts but also further reports from Brittany where bloody peasant uprisings had shattered the peace in recent months.† "I await a little cool weather before I purge myself, and a little peace in Brittany before I go there," Mme de Sévigné wrote in that same long letter of July 24. "Mme de La Troche, Mme de Lavardin, Monsieur d'Haroüys and I discuss our travel plans.‡ We have no desire to rush into the midst of the disorders besetting our province. They spread daily. Those demons went pillaging and burning all the way to Fougères§— and that is a little too close for comfort to Les Rochers."

---

*From those relatively few Sévigné letters that do survive in the original, her script and the size of her notepaper are known, and the relation of the autograph page to the printed page can be determined.

†Brittany was not the only troubled province in France that year. The protracted Dutch War had necessitated the imposition of new taxes at which the already hard-pressed French peasantry rebelled.

‡Mesdames de La Troche and de Lavardin were Brittany friends; d'Haroüys was a Breton relative of the Sévignés, the Intendant-General of the province.

§Fougères was less than thirty kilometers from Les Rochers.

Even had the calm of Brittany been unruffled, it was not there but Provence to which Mme de Sévigné longed to go: "Don't talk to me about coming to see you," she wrote to her daughter, that summer. "You make me forget all about my cruel responsibilities. If I paid heed to my heart, I would follow it to Grignan, and totally disregard all those business affairs of mine." "The Abbé considers the trip [to Brittany] so urgent that I dare not oppose him," she wrote on another day. "I will not always have him, and should profit by his guidance while I do." Resolute she might have been, but not without self-pity: "In all the Court, in all of France, I am the only mother deprived of the joy of seeing so dearly loved a daughter! It is the hand of Providence to which I cannot submit without bemoaning my lot."

That same interminably long letter of July 24 included a paragraph referring to the Grignan nursery, to some mysterious carbuncles or boils appearing on the youngest child's wet nurse:

Those boils you describe—much the same as with the other nurse— seem to me to be a bad sign. Milk of such heat is poisonous. And although it is not a male child in question, it would be a shame to jeopardize our little girl's health—which may be the only fortune she will have to count on in life. If it were up to me, I would send that nurse back [to Paris]—and wean Pauline at one year of age, like a peasant child.

The boils or carbuncles which developed in two of the nurses in the Grignan nursery have come under suspicion—by a consensus of twentieth-century medical opinion—as having been symptomatic of syphilitic contamination—the Count de Grignan having contaminated his wife, his wife having contaminated the children *in utero*, the children having contaminated the nurses who suckled them. The diagnosis of syphilitic contamination in the Grignan case is even more firmly based on the symptoms of the disease known as Hutchinson's Teeth—the half-moon erosion of Pauline's teeth, later described in some detail by her unsuspecting grandmother. More readily explicable in the light of this diagnosis are such symptoms as the rapid deterioration of the Countess de Grignan's health subsequent to her marriage, her several miscarriages, the little Marquis's crooked spine, the stillborn child of 1673, the malformed, short-lived, premature child to which she would give birth in 1676. Although a vitamin deficiency or a calcium deficiency might have accounted for some of these conditions, Pauline's Hutchinson's Teeth offer irrefutable evidence of syphilitic heredity.

In the last week of July, 1675, news of the death of France's greatest military hero, Maréchal de Turenne, sent shock waves throughout the nation. The vivid accounts in Mme de Sévigné's letters put those of French historians in the shade. Generations of French schoolboys know and remember the final moments of the great Turenne, thanks primarily to Mme de Sévigné. Her letter datelined "Wednesday, July 31" was addressed to Monsieur de Grignan:

> It is to you I write, my dear Count, to give you news of one of the most grievous losses France could suffer: it is the death of Monsieur de Turenne. If I am the one who breaks the news to you, I know you will be as moved and as distressed as we are, here. This news reached Versailles on Monday. The King was deeply affected, as one must be at the loss of so great a captain, so great a gentleman. All the Court was in tears ... They were all about to leave for the diversions of Fontainebleau, but all plans were called off. Never has a man been so sincerely regretted. All the part of town in which he resided,* all of Paris, all the people were saddened, emotionally devastated. Everyone gathered to lament the death of this hero. I am sending you a very good account of his activities during the last few days of his life. The last day of his glory and his life comes at the end of a miraculous three-month campaign, one at which the military still marvel. He had the pleasure of seeing the enemy decamp before him. And, on the twenty-seventh, which was Saturday, he went up on a small height [north of Strasbourg] to observe their retreat. He intended to attack their rearguard, and sent word to that effect to the King at noon ... He seals his letter and sends it off at two o'clock. He goes up on that little hill with eight or ten people. A cannon is fired from afar; a random shot rips his body half in two, and you can imagine the cries, the tears of that army! A courier is dispatched, on the instant. He arrives on Monday, as I told you, so that the King—at one and the same time—received a letter from Monsieur de Turenne and another letter giving notice of his death.

On August 6, 1675, Mme de Sévigné addressed herself to her cousin the Count de Bussy-Rabutin:

> I will say no more to you about my daughter's departure, although I think about it constantly, and can never accustom myself to living without her. But that sorrow should be confined to me.

---

*The Maréchal's part of town was Mme de Sévigné's—the Marais district.

You ask me where I am, how I am, and how I amuse myself. I am in Paris, I am well, and I amuse myself with bagatelles. But that sounds rather laconic, and I will enlarge upon it. I would be in Brittany, now, where I have a thousand business matters to attend to, were it not for the uprisings which make it unsafe. Four thousand soldiers under the command of Monsieur de Forbin are on their way there.* The question is what will be the result of this disciplinary action. I am waiting to see what happens, and if these mutineers repent their ways and return to their duties, I will carry out my travel plans, and spend a part of the winter there.

I certainly did have the vapours, and that good health of mine—which you have always seen so superb, suffered several attacks which seemed no less than humiliating to me. I felt insulted!

As for the tenor of my life, you know that, too. It is spent with five or six women friends whose company I enjoy, and in pursuance of a thousand unavoidable duties. What disturbs me is that in doing nothing, the days go by—those very days which compose our short lives, and we grow old, we die. I find that very distressing. I find life too short. Scarcely have we passed our youth than we find ourselves aging. I wish we had a guarantee of a hundred years, with the uncertainty coming after that. Doesn't that strike you as a good idea? ... That poor Madelonne† is in her château in Provence. What a destiny! Providence, oh, Providence!

"That poor Madelonne," her husband and her children were summering at their lofty perch of Grignan, so lofty as to escape much of the heat of Provence. (The *bise*, that cool northeastern wind blowing down from the Alps, was sometimes so violent at the elevation of the château as to shatter the windowpanes of the north façade and rip up the tiles of the terraces.) Mme de Sévigné would have preferred seeing repair to the terrace rather than the painting of the château then in progress: "The painting must be a terrible inconvenience to you, my dearest. What an odor! What a shame to make the château uninhabitable! Has your terrace not been repaired?‡ In my

---

*The peasant masses in Brittany, groaning under an already crushing burden of taxation, took fire at the imposition of a new tax on tobacco. In June and July, mobs had invaded the gardens of the Governor's palace at Rennes, threatening even the Duchess de Chaulnes, the wife of the Governor. The government's response was pitiless repression. When the Breton nobility proved incapable of putting down the insurrection, troops were brought in from outside the province.

†"Madelonne" was a nickname used by Bussy and Mme de Sévigné for Mme de Grignan.

‡The tiled roof of the Church of the Holy Savior served as a vast terrace to the château, which was on a level with the church's roof.

opinion, that is the first thing you should have done—it is your only place for promenades."

"I am very glad that you are staying tranquilly at Grignan until the month of October," Mme de Sévigné wrote:

> Now that you have the company of Mons. de Grignan, the château will be filled with his presence, and you will bring your orchestra to a new pitch of perfection. I could die laughing over what you wrote about that Italian song . . . how your vocalists massacred it! . . . I beg Mons. de Grignan to learn it in its entirety. Tell him to make the effort for my sake. We will sing it together!

There was a paragraph, in almost every letter, about the grandchildren, although Mme de Sévigné was not yet typically grandmotherly in her attitude:

> I warmly embrace Monsieur de Grignan and my grandchildren, but it is you, my darling, who are dearer to me than all the rest of the world put together! Not for me such drivel as most old ladies talk, transferring their love from their children to their grandchildren! My maternal love remains intact, in its initial state, and I only love those little folks because of my love for you . . .

On the subject of "those little folks," Pauline's wet nurse's husband in Paris had made Mme de Sévigné quite a scene:

> Your nurse's husband came here day before yesterday to complain that his wife had complained that she was not being given decent food and that she had been accused of having a disease. He claimed that she stripped off her clothes and stood naked before you to prove that there was no truth to the charge. On the first count, I told him that his wife was the most difficult, most disagreeable, most ill-tempered woman in the world, and that there was no way of pleasing her . . . that at Grignan, the nurse was served all the best the table offered. As for the other matter, I told him he was crazy, and that I did not believe what he said. He went into a rage, and said that his honor was his only treasure, that if his wife had caught a disease, she was a whore, and that he wanted to show me that he was innocent. Whereupon he made ready as if to take off his clothes! I had him thrown out of my room!

By September 6, preparations for the departure for Brittany were finally going forward:

My greatest sadness in leaving is because I will be greatly increasing the already great distance between us, and because our correspondence will be interrupted for several days. To further enhance the pleasure of my trip, Hélène will not be accompanying me. I delayed so long that she is now in her ninth month [of pregnancy].* I will take Marie who is snivelly, as you know.† But don't worry about me. I want to see how I get along without service so skilled as that to which I am accustomed, and to spend a while in solitude. I will test the docility of my spirit and will follow the example of courage and reason you have set for me . . . What a fine thing it would be if I were unable to get along without people who are pleasing to me! I will remember your sermons. I will find my satisfaction in paying my debts and living off the produce of my own lands. I will think about you a great deal, my very dear darling. I will read, I will walk, I will write letters to you and read your letters to me. Alas, life goes by all too quickly! We use it up wherever we are.

Again she feared that her letters from the provinces might seem dull to Mme de Grignan: "All the gossip, all the trivia I usually write you from Paris will be reduced to a bedrock minimum, so that unless you love me, you would do well not to open my letters."

On September 9, she set out from Paris "with the good Abbé and Marie and two outriders and six horses"—with the miniature of the Mignard portrait of her daughter in her pocket. (The original had been confided to her cousin Philippe-Emmanuel de Coulanges for safekeeping during her absence, to be hung in the study where he kept his extensive portrait collection.)

"I carry with me my anxiety about my son," she wrote her daughter on September 11 from Orléans. "It will be distressing for me to be cut off from military news. I wrote him [Charles], the other day, that I feel as if I were sticking my head in a sack where I will be unable to see or hear anything going on in the world!"

"I feel very well, my darling," she reported in that same letter. "I consider myself a fortunate creature in that I think and I read. If it were not for that, our good Abbé would scarcely prove an amusing companion. You know how preoccupied he is with 'the beautiful big eyes of his pocket-book'!" Otherwise, all was well en route: "The weather and the roads are

*Hélène, Mme de Sévigné's maid, had married Beaulieu, the maître d'hôtel.

†Marie was the daughter of the Livry gardener and his widow, whom Mme de Sévigné had taken to Paris with her to get the girl out of the sight of the widow's young husband.

excellent. The days are like crystal wherein one feels neither heat nor cold. With our equipages, we could very well go on by road. It is only as a diversion that we are going by boat."

No sooner did we set foot here in Orléans [she wrote her cousin Monsieur de Coulanges] than twenty boatmen flocked about us, each claiming to have the best boat, the best clientele! . . . It took us a long time to choose. One seemed too young; another, too old. One seemed too eager; struck us as a tramp, with a rotten boat. Another boasted of having had Monsieur de Chaulnes as a passenger. We finally settled on a tall, well-built fellow whose mustache and manner won us over. And so, adieu, my own dear cousin. We are about to set sail on the Loire . . .

It did not prove smooth sailing: the river was low, and the boat went aground, time and time again, on sandbars. Mme de Sévigné now "regretted her carriage which goes along without stopping. One is bored on the water when one is alone . . . But somehow one can never resist the temptation of taking a boat when one comes to Orléans."

The thirty leagues from Saumur to Nantes which they had hoped to make in two days' time proved especially trying. Aground on a sandbar until midnight, they could find only "a miserable hovel" of an inn and had to be grateful "for fresh straw on the floor upon which to stretch out without undressing." They had "reembarked at break of day. Despite wind and tide, we want to get to Nantes. All of us take an oar! I am feeling very well. The only thing I miss is a bit of conversation . . . As you can well imagine, I am most impatient for news from you and from Luxembourg's army. My heart is set on that. I have been nine days, now, with my head stuck in a sack!"

They had come, at last, at nine o'clock on the night of September 19, to Nantes, to the river door of the great château belonging to Monsieur de Lavardin, the Lieutenant-Governor of Brittany (son of Mme de Sévigné's good friend), who rushed out to greet her on the quay with a company of noblemen and flaming torches. "I am sure that from the middle of the river, the scene must have been spectacular, must have given my boatmen a splendid idea of my importance! I heartily enjoyed the supper. It had been twenty-four hours since I had slept or eaten!"

One of her first visits at Nantes had been to the Convent of the Visitation, founded by her grandmother: "I went to see the nuns of Sainte-Marie, who still adore you," she wrote her daughter, "and remember every word you said while you were with them, there." The little girl had been left with the Sisters briefly in 1658. The convent's *Annales* recall that "Mlle de Sévigné spent little time at the Convent. Her mother, who loved her and missed her when they were apart, took her away to bring her up at home."

"The Abbé is feeling very well—and I, better still, if such a thing is possible," she wrote in that same letter of September 20 from Nantes:

> *Monsieur de Guitaut wrote me a letter to announce that his wife was safely delivered of their child . . . He gives me cause to be very suspicious about you. I dare not let myself think long about the possibility of such a misfortune. It is one I dread above any other, and I am sorely afflicted at the very thought.*

The suspicions of the Count de Guitaut, who had recently seen the Grignans on his way through Provence, were well-founded: Mme de Grignan was then in the third month of her sixth pregnancy in the sixth year of her marriage. Mme de Sévigné still regarded her daughter's pregnancy as a "misfortune"; it is the same word she used to characterize the condition in 1671–2. There is, however, a difference to be noted, at this date, in her reaction: she shows more discretion in what she says to the Grignans than ever she did in 1671–2. One can only conclude that the Grignans had given her to understand that they did not appreciate her attitude. Not that they had been eager to tell her the news of this sixth pregnancy; she had had to hear it from a relative stranger. In her letter of reply to the Count de Guitaut, Mme de Sévigné said of her daughter's possible pregnancy: "I have had no news from her on that subject but, as you write, that is not to say that it is not true. I can only tell you that if it is, I will be sorely afflicted."

Again, the word "afflicted" ("*affligée*"), a strong word, used not only in the letter to Mme de Grignan but in the letter to Guitaut, as well. Mme de Sévigné seemed either unwilling or unable to recognize that Mme de Grignan was as eager as her husband and her husband's brothers and uncles to ensure the continuation of that illustrious Grignan line. Marital love such as the daughter knew had been denied the mother. The daughter felt a glory attaching to the Grignan name which she was at a loss to communicate to her mother. Such divergence of opinion between mother and daughter on the subject of family planning could not but have given rise to constant dissension.

XXV

The insurrection in Brittany had been put down by the time Mme de Sévigné arrived in that unhappy province, in late September, 1675. By then, troops had poured in, and the day of retribution was at hand.

Mme de Sévigné has sometimes come under reproach for insensitivity, for callousness or indifference to human suffering, for an aristocratic disdain for the lower classes and their oppression,* for reporting on those tragic times in Brittany in a tone of levity and irony more appropriate to subjects of hers less grim. It would be difficult for even the most devout Sévigniste totally to exonerate her in this instance; he could only explain that she was a product of her age and class, and that it is not realistic to expect a well-developed social conscience in a seventeenth-century aristocrat; he could only point out that what she had witnessed in Brittany had been a class war—with hers, the class under attack: the châteaux of her friends and fellow noblemen burned and pillaged by peasant mobs, a threat to her own. Quite understandably, Mme de Sévigné identified with the ruling class and with authority figures: her son-in-law was Governor of Provence; her good friend the Duke de Chaulnes was Governor of Brittany; her friend and recent host the Marquis de Lavardin was Lieutenant-Governor of Brittany; her cousin Haroüys, Intendant-General of the province. The stones hurled into the garden of the Governor's Palace at Rennes constituted a threat to her son-in-law and his lady in the garden of their palace at Aix.

Sévigné admirers would further remind us that—with the mails under surveillance in those times—she would not have dared to write anything critical of her friend the Duke de Chaulnes, who had taken her under his wing, protecting her estate of Sévigné, just outside the gates of Rennes, sparing her from the burden of penalty taxation being assessed elsewhere. Even if she had sympathized with the victims of the bloody retribution, and there are occasional passages to suggest that she did—she made much of her own delicate sensitivities, describing herself as "tender even when it

---

*Mme de Sévigné's class prejudice surfaces frequently, as in this scornful reference to Beaulieu, her maître d'hôtel, who had miscalculated the date of his wife's accouchement: "She has not yet had her baby. Creatures like that don't even know how to count . . ."

comes to flies!"—even so, she would not have been able to express her sympathy by mail. Later, perhaps, in conversation, face to face with her daughter, she may have been more outspoken in her criticism of the atrocities committed in Lower Brittany.

The fact is that she did report them; many incidents have gone unrecorded save for her accounts. She may have spared the authorities direct censure in these accounts, but her reportage laid bare the horrors perpetrated:

Our poor people in Lower Brittany, according to recent reports, flock into the fields, forty or fifty at a time, and fall to their knees as soon as they see the soldiers, saying mea culpa—*the only words of French they know!* The hangings go on and on in Lower Brittany. Those poor fellows, there, all they ask for is a drink and a smoke before the rope goes round their neck.*

"Twenty-five or thirty men at Rennes," she wrote in another letter, "have been seized at random, and will be hanged." And in still another, "The ruin of Rennes spells ruin for the province ... I am not in fear of the troops, but I share in the desolation and the heartache of the entire province ... Monsieur de Montmoron took refuge at the home of a friend near here so as not to hear the weeping and wailing at Rennes." And elsewhere: "Here I am, sounding like a good Breton, as you can hear. But you can understand that is part of the air one breathes, and something more, because all of us—the entire province—feel the affliction."

The Duchess de Chaulnes, the Governor's wife, on a visit to Vitré in late October, talked for two hours to Mme de Sévigné "about the government's actions over the past six months and about the horrible perils to which she had been exposed":

She knows I have connections in several places, and that I could have heard quite a different story. I thanked her warmly for the confidence and honor she showed me in giving me her version of the situation: to put it briefly, she feels that this province has been guilty of great wrongdoing. Still, it has been severely punished, and to the point where it can never recover ... All these misfortunes are damaging to commerce and bring about economic ruin ...

---

*The Breton language was unintelligible to the French, just as French was unintelligible to the Bretons.

"Would you like to hear the latest news from Rennes?" Mme de Sévigné inquired of her daughter, on October 30:

There are still 5,000 troops there, reinforcements having been brought in from Nantes. A tax of 100,000 écus has been levied on the bourgeoisie, and if the sum is not raised in twenty-four hours, it will be doubled and the soldiers sent to collect it. All the residents of one big street have been evicted and exiled, and it is on pain of death to take anyone in, so there were all these poor homeless creatures—old people, pregnant women, children—wandering about and weeping as they left the town, not knowing where to turn, without food, without a place to lay their heads. Day before yesterday, one of the ringleaders of the revolt was broken on the wheel.* He was drawn and quartered after his death—one quarter for each of the four corners of the town ... Sixty bourgeois were seized, and their punishments will begin tomorrow. An example is being made of this province to serve as a warning to the others—to teach them, above all, respect for their governors and their governors' ladies, neither to insult them nor to hurl stones into their gardens!

Just when the reader thinks to discern a note of compassion in Mme de Sévigné's voice, he comes across a passage in which she sounds her most flippant—a passage such as this one to her daughter: "You write most amusingly about our troubles. Fewer men are now sentenced to be broken on the wheel—only one in eight days, and that one primarily to keep the scales of justice in balance. It is true that the hangings now strike me as a relief..." Or a passage such as this one to her cousin Bussy:

This province is in a state of great desolation. Monsieur de Chaulnes has removed the Parlement from Rennes to punish that town ... The rebels of Rennes have fled, long since. Thus, the innocent will pay for the guilty, but I have no complaint so long as the four thousand soldiers at Rennes ... do not interfere with my promenades in my forests where the trees grow marvelously tall and beautiful.

---

*The victim of this form of torture and execution was fastened—spread-eagled—on a cartwheel, and there subjected to blows which shattered his limbs. In the form of execution known as "drawing and quartering," each of the four limbs of the victim was tied to a different horse, each of the four horses galloping off in different directions and ripping the body apart.

In her forests, along her woodland paths and avenues, she forgot the ugly business of the insurrection. "I have found an extraordinary beauty in these woodlands—and an extraordinary melancholy," she wrote her daughter:

All these trees which you saw as saplings have grown tall and straight and beautiful . . . I suppose there is a trace of maternal love and pride in all this detail; remember that it is I who planted them, and that I saw them—as Molière said of Monsieur de Montbazon—"when they were no bigger than that!" There is a solitude here ideal for revery . . . If my thoughts are not actually somber, they come close to it. I think of you at every moment. I miss you, I wish for you. Your health, your affairs, your absence—how do you think all that affects me at the twilight hour? . . . One must dwell fixedly on the will of God not to despair at the sight of what I see . . . which I will assuredly not go into here.

Not the twilight hour, not even nightfall could keep Mme de Sévigné from her woodland promenades when the moon was full: "I go to pay homage to the moon which, as you know, I worship," she wrote her daughter in October. "I stay with Beaulieu and my lackeys* until eight o'clock. Those treelined avenues hold for me a beauty, a peace, a quiet that never fail to move me."

Accustomed as she was to the brilliant Parisian social season, it is proof of her resourcefulness and self-reliance that she could weather a rural, a provincial winter. At Mme de Grignan's expression of concern about those long and lonely nights in remote Les Rochers, Mme de Sévigné could write reassuringly,

Alas, my darling, I get through those evenings about which you are concerned without being bored. I almost always have a letter to write; otherwise, I read, and before I know it, it is midnight. The Abbé leaves me at ten, but the two hours during which I am alone are no more fatal to me than the others. As for the days, I work on business affairs with the Bien Bon or I am with my dear laborers, or I pick up a convenient piece of needlework. All in all, my child, life goes by so quickly that I do not know how one can become so profoundly disturbed about the affairs of this world. One has time here for reflection, and it is my own fault if my woodlands do not inspire me to it. I am feeling fine. My staff carries out your instructions admirably, going to ridiculous lengths

---

*Elsewhere she referred to Beaulieu and her lackeys as "my infantry."

to take good care of me. Well armed, they follow me [into the woods] at night, ready to draw their swords at the approach of a squirrel!

It was not the long winter evenings at Les Rochers that she dreaded, it was the twilight hour, the dusk. When, in mid-November, there came a brief return of mild weather—"a St. Martin's summer," as she called it—she returned to her woodland glades: "I stay there all day," she wrote, "all alone, with but one lackey in attendance, and I do not come in until nightfall when the torches and the fire brighten my room. Unless I am engaged in conversation, I dread the hour 'between the dog and the wolf,'* and am happier in the woods than in a room alone—which might be called jumping into the pond to avoid the rain!"

The Spartan life at Les Rochers was agreeing with her: "As for me, I am in the pink of condition," she wrote her daughter:

You would be proud of my sobriety, and the exercise I take, and the seven hours I spend in bed—like a Carmelite. I like this hard life; it is typical of the country. I am not gaining weight, and the air is so full of moisture and so beneficial to the skin that my complexion—on which I have for so long received so many compliments—does not change.

"I have just had the waistband of a skirt taken in a finger on each side," she could boast, that autumn. "Would to God you could do the same, my daughter!"

"The same" Mme de Grignan could not do in the fifth month of her pregnancy. Curiously enough, this is one of the few references in the correspondence of 1675 to that pregnancy. Mme de Grignan must have made clear that she wanted to hear no further negative comment from her mother on that subject.

If Mme de Sévigné's correspondence was extensive, she did not allow it to become burdensome:

I am not killing myself writing. I read, I embroider, I walk, I do nothing. "Bella cosa far niente" ["It is a fine thing to do nothing"] says one of my trees. To which another retorts: "Amor odit inertes" ["Love detests the lazy"]. It is difficult to know which one to listen to! But what I do know is that I am not smitten with writing. I love to write to you; I

---

*"The hour between the dog and the wolf" was Mme de Sévigné's curious term for the dusk—the hour, perhaps, when the domestic animal retired, and the wild one roamed the forests.

talk to you, I converse wih you. I could not do without it. But that does not apply to the rest. The rest I do because I am obliged to ...

Mme de Sévigné was grateful, that winter, in the wilds of Brittany, to find the Princess de Tarente (in her Château Madame at Vitré) to keep her company. The Princess's late husband had been the Duke de La Trémouille, the premier duke of France; her niece, Madame, was the second wife of Monsieur, the brother of Louis XIV. The Princess herself was of royal German stock, blood kin to most of the ruling houses of Europe—a consanguinity which condemned her to an almost perpetual state of mourning: it was seldom that the death of one or another of her royal relatives did not oblige her to don garb of black. One day when the Princess—for once, for a wonder—appeared in a colored gown, Mme de Sévigné congratulated her on the "good health of Europe." Mme de Sévigné's peasants were "impressed," she claimed, by the Princess's visits to Les Rochers—as was, perhaps, Mme de Sévigné herself: the Princess was a great lady, entitled to be addressed as "Highness." Best of all, she made good copy for Mme de Sévigné's letters to her daughter: she was a "character" as well as a "Highness." Amorous, highly susceptible to male advances ("a heart of wax," Mme de Sévigné diagnosed it), the Princess's lovers were legion, their tenure transient. The Princess's preoccupation with sex was equalled only by her preoccupation with her pharmacopoeia: she prescribed and dispensed balms, tisanes, elixirs, lotions, unguents and panaceas to all her friends, including Mme de Sévigné. ("She has promised me a totally miraculous essence—three drops of it will cure you of anything!") The Princess's table groaned, as did her dinner guests, especially the Abbé, a notorious gourmand, for whom she provided remedies for flatulence and indigestion. "She has rare and precious concoctions," wrote Mme de Sévigné, "of which she gave us three doses—which have had a prodigious effect!"

The Princess announced to Mme de Sévigné, one day, that she was going to send her a spaniel puppy: "I thanked her," wrote Mme de Sévigné,

but told her of my resolve not to allow myself to become attached to another pet. That was the end of the conversation, and I thought no more about it. Two days later, I see a valet enter with a little doghouse covered with ribbons, and coming out of that pretty little house—an extraordinarily beautiful and perfumed little dog, with silky ears and a sweet puppy breath, small as Sylphide, blond as blond. Never was I more astonished or more embarrassed. I wanted them to take it back, but they would not ... It is Marie who loves it. He sleeps in his little *house, in Beaulieu's room. He eats only bread. I have not yet become attached to him, but he begins to love me, and I fear I will succumb. So, that is the story—which I implore you not to tell Marphise* in Paris. I fear her reproaches. This dog is named Faithful—a name the Princess's lovers have not merited.*

By late October, the leaves had not yet turned at Les Rochers ("Everything here is still as green as in the month of May"), but the Grignans were preparing to leave their windswept eyrie to spend the winter in their capital city of Aix. "I can well understand your regret," the Countess's mother wrote, "at leaving your château with its freedom and tranquillity for the official and ceremonial life to which you are unaccustomed."

Mme de Sévigné expressed some surprise at finding herself still at Les Rochers in November but, in the economic disorder resulting from the insurrection, she and the Abbé had been unable successfully to conclude the business which had brought them to Brittany. Hard times and bad weather trapped them there. "Our accounts are in good order," she reported to the Count de Bussy: "There is only one thing lacking to our satisfaction—that is, to lay our hands on money. Money is what one does not see here. Currency is scarce, and that is a fact. Are times as bad in Burgundy?" (While to her daughter she wrote, "You ask me whether we are ruined: Yes and No. If we wanted to stay on here, we could live for nothing, because nothing is being sold. But it is true that, as for money, there is no more in this province.")

It was the disruption of the mail schedule, however, that dismayed her more than the recession or the onset of winter. "I have received no letters from you, my daughter," she wrote on November 20: "That makes me very sad. Dubut† advises me that this is the result of bad weather, that the courier from Provence no longer reaches Paris in time for his mail to get on the regular Brittany run."‡ By November 27, she was saying, "I must accustom myself to it, my daughter. Your two packets arrive together. The weather has disrupted the postal service, and that is the greatest blow it could inflict on me. I make light of the cold, the snow, the sleet and ice and the season's other hardships."

If only Charles had arrived—as expected—to bring cheer to the remote and isolated château, to the lonely chatelaine! "As for your poor little brother,"

---

*Marphise was Mme de Sévigné's dog.

†Dubut was a member of Mme de Sévigné's Paris domestic staff.

‡The mail leaving Provence on Wednesdays and Saturdays (or Sundays) reached Brittany nine or ten days later, on Mondays and Fridays.

she wrote her daughter on December 1, "I do not know where he has hidden himself. It has been three weeks since I have heard from him." She suspected him of dallying en route with a new light of love: an Abbess, this time—the courtesan and the actress of the previous year having been succeeded by the Mother Superior of a convent. The Flanders campaign had been suspended for the winter, as was then the military custom, and Charles—like the other officers of his regiment—was on leave. His mother impatiently awaited his arrival, and had not long to wait, writing on December 4 to her daughter:

As I returned from my promenade, day before yesterday, there stood your brother, at the end of the Mall! At sight of me, he fell to his knees—feeling so guilty for having been out of touch for three long weeks, singing Matins!*—that he could only face me as a penitent. I had fully intended to scold him, but simply could not get angry enough to do it. I was very glad to see him. You know how amusing he is. He embraced me a thousand times. He offered me the poorest excuses in the world—which I accepted as the best. We talk a lot, we read, we walk, and thus will spend the rest of the year—what little there is left of it.

"I find him the very best of company," she wrote of her son to her daughter on December 29, "and he returns the compliment." Sad to say, she could not wholeheartedly enjoy her son's company for lamenting her daughter's absence: "The length of time required for an answer in our correspondence frightens me and emphasizes the horrible distance that separates us," she wrote in that same letter, at the close of the year 1675. "Ah, my darling, how keenly I feel it, how it devastates my life! Otherwise, would I not be enjoying to the hilt the company of a son as fine as mine?"†

---

*In monasteries and convents, solemn choral services usually sung between midnight and dawn are called matins.

†Mme de Sévigné had, occasionally, the good grace to be embarrassed about the partiality shown her daughter: "I must admit," she had written Bussy earlier that autumn, "to harboring a veritable passion for her. I say nothing about my son. However, I love him very much, and I occupy myself with his interests as painstakingly as I do my daughter's."

XXVI

The year 1676 began inauspiciously. Mme de Sévigné's youthful vigor ("I don't know how I came upon such a Fountain of Youth!") suddenly failed her. Her hitherto rugged constitution ("My health is as good as it was six years ago!") betrayed a weakness—to rheumatism, an attack so crippling that she could not walk, could not wield a fork or spoon or—worse still!—a pen.

The attack began on January 11 with what seemed a simple crick in the neck such as Mme de Grignan herself had recently suffered and described: "Just telling me about it gave it to me!" Mme de Sévigné wrote her daughter on January 15:

> I cannot use my right side—one of those minor ills which earn one no sympathy no matter how loud one moans and groans. In the meanwhile, I embrace you with all my heart—and my left arm ... Your Queen of Hungary lotion will have cured me before this letter reaches Paris ...

Not so. By January 19, she would explain that "the crick in the neck has turned out to be rheumatism, so painful an ailment that it robs one of rest and sleep although offering no cause for alarm." What Mme de Sévigné wanted to make sure was that reports of her illness did not alarm her daughter, then in the sixth month of her pregnancy:

> This is the eighth day of my illness: the fever and sweating will complete the cure. I have had one bleeding, from the foot; abstinence and patience will do the rest. I am perfectly attended by Larmechin,* who does not leave me day or night ... I would happily write you twenty-seven or twenty-eight pages, but I simply cannot manage it. My son will write the rest. I embrace you—and, today, it is with my right arm!

Charles, too, tried to spare his pregnant sister concern about their mother's condition: "I know you will rely upon the Abbé and me to do

---

*Larmechin was Charles's valet.

whatever is necessary to safeguard a health so precious to us all," Charles wrote. "For the first illness in her lifetime, this one has been severe and painful," he admitted on January 21, although hastening to assure his sister that there was no cause for anxiety: "There is a very good doctor at Vitré ... She is surely as well off here as in Paris." And, "We amuse my Mother as much as we can—almost the only thing of which she is presently in need," he wrote on January 19, "because, for all the rest, the illness must take its course, and we expect that to be three weeks. Her fever fell on the seventh day which, as you can see, proves there is no danger. Don't write any letters which might upset her ... A thousand good wishes to Monsieur de Grignan and his beard—impossible as it is to salute the one without the other."

"You can imagine what it means for me to spend sixteen days flat on my back, unable to move," the highly energetic invalid wrote her daughter on January 26: "I settled down in my little bedchamber where I have been devotedly, marvelously well attended. I only wish my son were not my secretary at this moment so that you could learn what he has done for me on this occasion."

The letter of the twenty-sixth contained four brief lines in Mme de Sévigné's own but almost unrecognizable hand which Charles thought might "frighten" Mme de Grignan rather than "reassure her," as the Abbé had thought it might.

On February 3, Charles was still taking dictation from his mother:

It has been twenty-three days since I fell ill. Since the fourteenth, I have been free of fever and of pain and, in that happy state, thinking myself able to walk again, which is all for which I ask, I find my body still swollen everywhere—my feet, my legs, my hands, my arms ... Everyone in Paris writes to express pleasure over my recovery. I have purged myself with Monsieur Delorme's powder which worked wonders for me. I shall repeat the dose; that is truly the cure for all ills. After that, I am promised eternal health. God grant! The first step I can take will be in the direction of Paris. Thus, I implore you, my dear child, to stop worrying about me. You know that we have always written you truthfully. Before closing this letter, I shall inquire of my swollen hand whether it will agree to write two lines to you. Consent is not forthcoming. Perhaps in two hours from now?

February 5, 1676, was Mme de Sévigné's fiftieth birthday, although, strange to say, there was not only no celebration, there was no mention of the occasion by either correspondent.

On February 9, with Charles still acting as her amanuensis, Mme de Sévigné wrote Mme de Grignan, "And, now, although I have recovered, although I walk about my room and go to Mass,* I am still covered with poultices. Truly, the inability to write is very strange, and causes you concern, just as I feared it would."

Madame de Sévigné's own concern mounted at the announcement of the resumption of the Flanders campaign, at the thought of Charles's recall to his regiment:

> I fear that your brother will be leaving me [she wrote on February 9]. That is one of my sorrows. All they talk to him about are reviews, brigades, war. This illness of mine has played havoc with all our little plans† . . . I implore you to take care of yourself and your health. You know that you could give me no greater proof of your love.

"Your brother has been such a tremendous consolation to me that I cannot find words to describe it to you," she wrote on February 15:

> He was sympathetic with all my miseries and, as chance would have it, all his promises were fulfilled, including my promenade of yesterday on which I got along even better than I had hoped. Larmechin, on his part, has watched over me for five full weeks, and I simply do not know how I could have survived without those two persons . . . I await only a little more strength before we set out on the road to Paris, whither my son will travel—to my great regret—ahead of me.

On Friday, February 21, all thought of herself and of her lingering aches and pains was swept from Mme de Sévigné's mind by the arrival of the courier from Provence with the startling news that, on February 9, her daughter had been brought to childbed, prematurely.

Charles's letter dated Sunday, February 23, describes the scene at Les Rochers:

> As gently as you tried to break the news, my Mother was so upset that we were frightened for her. We were playing reversis when the mail arrived: my Mother's impatience was such that it would not permit her to finish the game before opening your letters. She asked Monsieur du

---

*The Christmas Mass had been the first celebrated in the recently completed Les Rochers chapel.
†Their plan had been for Charles to accompany his mother back to Paris in January.

Plessis who was watching the game to open the packet for her. The first one was addressed to me ... and at sight of the word "accouchement" on the outer fold ... she could not control her emotions ... which is one result of her illness.

When she had regained command of her emotions, she wrote—or, rather, Charles wrote for her—on February 23:

You have given birth, my dearest child, at eight months. What good fortune that you came through it safely! But what a shame to have lost another little boy! You, who are so careful, and who scold others, you took a fancy to soak your feet! When one has carried a good work so far, how can one risk it—and risk one's own life at the same time? For it seems that your labor took a bad turn. When all is said and done, my daughter, you came out of it fortunately, by the grace of God. You were in good hands: You can imagine how impatiently I await the next report on your condition, how obsessed I am with and how I go over all the circumstances of your delivery. I thank you for the three lines in your own hand, and I thank you, my dear Count, for the pains you took to inform me. You know what your dear wife's health means to me, but you have allowed her to write too much; such excess is dangerous and, as for soaking her feet, it seems that that is what caused the premature birth. The loss of that child is a shame, and I have need of your Christian reflections to console myself because, no matter what they tell you, you will never save an eight months' child. I would fear that it was the news of my illness which was responsible, had I not known that this occurred two weeks later. Finally, God be praised and thanked a thousand times for the fact that my dear Countess is safe and sound! My life depends on that health: I recommend it into your keeping, my very dear Count, and I agree with all my heart to the rendezvous you propose at Grignan!

By early March, the feeble and malformed infant showed signs of improvement: his spinal column would never properly develop, his bones would never properly serve their purpose in his body, but he would go on living longer than had been anticipated at birth: "I am more astonished than anyone at the improvement in the little child," his grandmother told his mother on March 11: "Still, in the long run it will be a miracle if we save that child."

"And, now, I come to you, Monsieur the Count," Mme de Sévigné wrote in a postscript to her son-in-law:

You say that my daughter should do nothing but have children because she acquits herself so well of that function. Oh, my Lord God, does she do anything else? But I warn you that if you do not give that pretty machine a rest—whether you do it out of love or out of pity—you will assuredly destroy it, and that would be a shame.

There was ambivalence in Mme de Sévigné's attitude toward her son-in-law—and vice versa. If the mother-in-law was occasionally critical of the son-in-law, her reproaches were phrased in a droll or dulcet tone. Their relation, on the whole, seemed genuinely fond, amicable, built upon mutual respect and admiration. Both possessed of all the social graces, they heartily enjoyed one another's company. But the Count perceived more and more clearly that his wife's mother tended to overwhelm and disconcert his wife, tended to invade their privacy, no matter how charmingly, how disarmingly, how beguilingly she went about it. Impressed though she was by the Count's lofty position and lofty lineage, Mme de Sévigné was outraged at the state of eternal pregnancy to which her daughter had been subjected for the past six years—whether by reason of her husband's libidinousness or his obsession with the perpetuation of the Grignan line. There was ambivalence in Mme de Sévigné's attitude toward her daughter's glamorous new role: proud as a peacock, on the one hand, of Mme de Grignan's *grande dame* status ("You are veritably a great lady")—First Lady of Provence ("Queen of the Mediterranean"), chatelaine of Grignan ("with all its grandeurs"); on the other hand, Mme de Sévigné agonized over the financial ruin into which that grandiose Grignan life-style must inevitably plunge them.

Nature-lover and inveterate walker that she was—bedridden and housebound as she had been for weeks, during that spring of 1676—Mme de Sévigné rejoiced at her first outing in early March:

They carried me in a chair into the park where it was divinely beautiful. That makes me feel stronger. I have wrought new beauties there* which I will not have time to enjoy, this year, because my nose is pointed in the direction of Paris.

---

*On this recent trip, Mme de Sévigné had substantially expanded the perimeter of the park surrounding the château, laying out and creating new treelined allées or avenues radiating from the Mall, most of them still maintained today.

By the following week, she was much improved, writing, "I take the air, and walk on my hind legs, like any other. My appetite is good, but I am cutting out supper entirely and forever." She liked the way she looked: "I am thin, but I am pleased about that. There has been no change in my face, and scarcely any in my spirits or my moods. And if someone still sits up at night with me, it is because I cannot turn over in bed, by myself." Had she not become "nervous as a wet hen" about herself since her illness, she would have stayed on, she said, at Les Rochers: "I spend the whole day in the woods where it is already summer," she wrote her daughter, on a mild March day, "but, at five o'clock, the wet hen goes in—enough to make her weep! It is a humiliation to which I cannot accustom myself."* "Goodbye, my very dear daughter," she ended that letter:

> You can believe me when I tell you that of all the hearts over which you reign, there is none so entirely under your sway as my own. And I make no exceptions when I make that statement. Having thus offended the Count, I now embrace him.

(A marvel of tactful tactlessness, this odious and gratuitous comparison of a mother's love to the love of a husband!)

On March 22, she was cross, depressed, discouraged:

> I am so tired of this bitching handwriting of mine that—except for the fact that you would think my hands had grown worse—I would not write to you again until I am cured. This protracted siege of illness is just what was required to mortify a creature who, as you know, was never famous for the virtue of patience. But one must bow to the will of God. It is to good purpose: I was insolent ... Forgive me, my daughter, if I talk constantly about myself and my ailments. I promise you that when I reach Paris I will be better company. That is another of my reasons for going—to clear my head of myself and my recent miseries.

She had still another reason: "I have a thousand affairs to attend to there, business of both yours and your brother's."

And, so, she set out on March 24 ("in warm and beautiful weather") for the capital: "I shall go hobbling along," she wrote, "on short days' journeys," and stopping off often at the châteaux of friends along the route

---

*"It takes a strong constitution," she reflected at this time, "to live in the country and in solitude."

to break the journey and to pick up letters addressed to her there by her daughter.

Arriving in Paris on April 8, she could report enthusiastically:

I am feeling very well; the change has done marvels for me, although my hands are reluctant to acknowledge it. I have seen all our friends. I follow your advice, and stay in my room. From now on, I shall put my health and my promenades ahead of everything else . . .

And a few days later, she could add: "My figure is so marvelous that I cannot imagine it otherwise. And, as for my face, it is ridiculous for me to be looking this well!" On April 17:

It seems to me that my handwriting is no longer so bad. Thank God! At least, that is true for the first few lines because, you must know, my darling, that my hands—that is to say, my right hand will undertake nothing as yet except to write to you, for which I love it all the better. Present it with a spoon—no improvement: it trembles and spills everything.

And, on another day, "At night, I turn onto my left side; I eat with my left hand—that's lots of 'left'!"

At the Easter season, Mme de Sévigné's main complaint was about her sad lack of religious fervor, a state shared by her daughter:

So, there you are, having made your Jubilee, your Stations. You have said all that can be said on the subject. It is not your devotions which have wearied you, it is the fact that you are not devout. Oh, my God, it is precisely that which brings me to despair. I think I feel this misfortune more than anyone. It would seem that everything should bring me to that state, but all my yearning, all my meditations fail to produce the desired result.

It proved the consensus of opinion—family and friends as well as doctors having been consulted—that Mme de Sévigné should go to a watering resort to take the cure in order to eliminate the last stubborn vestiges of rheumatic pain and edema. It remained only to choose between the two most popular spas of the day: Bourbon-L'Archambault and Vichy, both renowned for their mineral waters and therapeutic regimens. "They tell me a thousand good things about Vichy," Mme de Sévigné wrote her daughter, "and I think I would prefer it to Bourbon for two reasons: first, because

Mme de Montespan is going to Bourbon* and, second, because Vichy is closer to you"—so close to Grignan as to make an easy trip for the Countess to come to join her mother, as she had promised to do, for a two weeks' visit.

With the longed-for reunion in the offing, Mme de Sévigné herself perversely spoke the word that prevented its accomplishment, writing to Mme de Grignan on April 10,

> The more I think about it, my darling, the more convinced I am that I do not want you to come for a mere two weeks. If you come to either Vichy or Bourbon, it should be on the basis that you accompany me back here [to Paris]. We will spend the rest of the summer and autumn here: you will take charge of things for me, you will comfort me; and Monsieur de Grignan will come to see you here, this winter and, in his turn, decide where you will go from there. That is how one pays a visit to a Maman one loves, that is the time one spends with her, that is how one consoles her for having been very ill, for having suffered a thousand discomforts, for having lost the sweet illusion that she was immortal . . .

On April 15, Mme de Sévigné—as if astounded at her own temerity—bravely issued an ultimatum:

> Either come back here to Paris with me, or do not come at all. A visit of fifteen days would serve only to upset me while I was taking the waters—all I could think of would be the hour of parting!

Mother and daughter had reached an impasse. Mme de Grignan would not or could not go to Paris to spend the winter with her mother; Mme de Sévigné would not or could not go to Grignan to join her daughter:

> I see no hope of going to Grignan, no matter how I yearn to. The good Abbé does not want to go; he has a thousand business matters to attend to here, and he fears the climate there. I can find no clause in my treaty of gratitude whereby I could leave him at his age, never doubting that such a separation would be fatal to him, heart and soul. And should he die in my absence, my remorse would never let me rest.

*Mme de Sévigné feared that the King's mistress and her huge entourage would overrun the resort town of Bourbon and monopolize the choice accommodations.

XXVII

~

Fate—or, rather, what Mme de Sévigné called Providence ("*cette belle Providence*")—had more blows still in store for her, that spring of 1676: the Dutch War dragged on and, with the vernal equinox, the armies returned to the field, the King and his forces heading back to Flanders in April. Charles de Sévigné, to his mother's distress, rejoined his regiment (embarrassed though he was at being still a lowly ensign). "My son is leaving," she wrote on April 10, "and I am sad about it. I shall feel the separation keenly. All one sees in Paris are military equipages on their way to the front."

By April 15, Charles had gone, as his mother advised his sister: "I am sad, my darling. My poor little chum has just left. He is so richly endowed with all those minor virtues which make up the social graces that I would be sad to lose him, were he only my neighbor."

Another blow came with the news that five-and-a-half-year-old Marie-Blanche de Grignan, the little girl who had won her heart during the many months she had spent with her grandmother in Paris, had been consigned to the Convent of the Visitation of Aix, one of the many founded by the child's great-great-grandmother. Marie-Blanche would never, as it developed, emerge from behind those walls, never see her home again, never rejoin her parents and her siblings. As was the practice of the time, the aristocratic family which could not properly dower its daughters relegated them to the religious life. Just as the younger sons of noble houses automatically went into the army or the church, so the daughters were frequently cloistered.*

"My heart aches for my little girl," Mme de Sévigné wrote Mme de Grignan on May 6:

She will be in despair at being separated from you, at being—as you say—in prison. I wonder how I found the courage to put you in a convent:† the thought of seeing you often and retrieving you shortly

---

*Of the four daughters of the Count and Countess de Guitaut (Mme de Sévigné's Burgundian friends and neighbors), only one was married; the other three were immured in the convent at Avallon, although the Guitauts were in far easier financial circumstances than the Grignans.

†Mme de Grignan, as a girl, had spent some time as a student of the Sisters of the Visitation both in Paris and in Nantes.

strengthened my resolve to that barbaric act which, at the time, was considered essential to your education. But, in the long run, we must bow to Providence which controls our destinies.

By May 10, Mme de Sévigné was making ready for her trip to Vichy:

I am leaving tomorrow at the break of day, but tonight I am having Mme de Coulanges, her husband, Mme de La Troche, Mme de La Trousse, Mlle de Montgoron and Corbinelli* to supper so that they can bid me farewell while eating a pigeon tart.

On May 11, accompanied by two maids and a maître d'hôtel, she stepped into her carriage, and her six horses headed south out of Paris in the direction of Vichy—not, however, by the most direct route through Fontainebleau, for the reason that that town still held painful memories for her as the place where she had parted from her daughter in May of 1675, at the hour of the latter's departure for Provence. The passage of a year had not assuaged the grief of parting or the pangs of separation.

Mme de Sévigné had left the Abbé behind in Paris—"with only a single valet to attend him"—for which she apologized: "He insisted on my taking two of his horses to fill out my six—as well as his coachman and Beaulieu!"

From Nevers, on May 16, she reported:

The weather is wonderful ... I find the countryside lovely, and my Loire River is as beautiful here as at Orléans. It is a pleasure to meet old friends en route. I brought my large carriage so that we are in no way crowded.

Beautiful as the scenery may have been, Mme de Sévigné could not long keep her nose out of a book: in this case, "a short history of the Viziers, of the intrigues of the Sultans and the Harem which," as she commented, "make most agreeable reading. It is a book much in vogue."†

But despite all the distractions of travel and change of scene, Mme de Sévigné could not get her eldest grandchild off her mind:

---

*Corbinelli had stopped writing to Mme de Sévigné after her rheumatic attack: "Corbinelli says I have no wit when I dictate—and no longer corresponds with me. I think he is right. I find my style suffers."

†The book was *L'Histoire des grands vizirs* (*History of the Grand Viziers*), just off the press in 1676.

I am heartsick about our little girl. Poor child, there she is—shut away in a convent! She has somehow concealed her sorrow. I pity her—if you love her and she loves you as much as you and I love one another. But you have a fund of courage which serves you well on such occasions. God would have been good had he favored me with similar fortitude.

Not only her granddaughter, her son was likewise much on her mind; after six days on the road, she felt out of touch with the world, writing, "I am in total ignorance of the news, and I am most anxious about reports from the front. It is not good to begin a cure with such anxiety, but how to avoid it when one has someone in the army?"

The sixth night en route she spent at Moulins, in the Convent of the Visitation, sleeping and writing "in the room in which my grandmother died."

On the eighth day, her six fine horses trotting smartly, she made her grand entry into Vichy: "I arrived here yesterday evening," she wrote on May 19:

Mme de Brissac and the Canon, Monsieur de Saint-Hérem, and two or three others came out to meet me on the banks of the pretty Allier River ... Monsieur de Saint-Hérem, Mons. de La Fayette, the Abbé Dorat, Plancy and still others, followed in a second carriage or on horseback. They greeted me with great joy. Mme de Brissac took me to supper with her ...

I have rested, today, but tomorrow I will begin to drink the waters. Mons. de Saint-Hérem came, this morning, to take me to Mass and to dinner at his house. Mme de Brissac came. They played cards but, as for me, I would not exert myself shuffling. We took a promenade, this evening, in the most beautiful spot in the world. But, at seven o'clock, this wet hen came home to eat her chicken and converse a while with her dear child ... I impatiently await letters from you and, as for writing to you, my dear child, that is my one and only pleasure when I am far from you. And if the doctors, of whom I am highly contemptuous, should forbid me to do so, I would forbid them to eat or breathe— and see how they like that regimen! Tell me about my little girl, and how she is adjusting to the convent. I think about her often ...

On Wednesday, May 20, Mme de Sévigné had her first taste of the waters: "Ah, how nasty they are!" she exclaimed:

One goes at six o'clock in the morning to the springs. Everyone is there. One drinks, one makes a terrible face because—just imagine!— the water is boiling hot and has a very strong, very disagreeable taste of saltpeter. One mills around, one comes, one goes, one takes one's promenade, one goes to Mass, one expels the waters and one talks boldly of how one expelled them. That takes up the whole morning. Finally, one dines. After dinner, one goes to someone's house; today, it was mine. Mme de Brissac played hombre* *with Saint-Hérem and Plancy. The Canon and I read Ariosto . . . Some country girls with a flute came in and danced the* bourrée *to perfection . . . Finally, at five o'clock, everyone takes a promenade through this delicious country-side. At seven o'clock, one eats a light supper. At ten, one goes to bed. You now know as much about it as I do. The waters agree quite well with me. I drank twelve glasses which acted as a mild purgative— precisely the desired effect. In a few days, I will take the showers . . .*

On May 28, she wrote:

Today, I started my showers. They provide a fairly good rehearsal for purgatory. One goes completely naked into a small subterranean cham-ber where there is a pipe of hot water controlled by a woman who directs the flow to whatever part of the body you wish. To go there with not so much as a fig leaf on is a rather humiliating experience. I wanted my two maids with me so that there would be someone there whom I knew. Behind a curtain sits someone to help you keep up your courage for that half-hour; in my case, it was a doctor from Gannat† whom Mme de Noailles always takes to watering resorts with her and whom she likes very much. He is an honest fellow, no char-latan . . . whom she recommended to me out of pure friendship. I retain him—no matter how much it costs me—because the doctors available around here are intolerable. This man amuses me. He has wit and good manners; he knows everyone. In a word, I am satisfied with him. So, he talked to me all the while I was in the torture-chamber. Try to ima-gine a stream of boiling hot water directed at your poor body—all over, at first, and then, on just the affected joints. When it strikes the nape of the neck, it comes as a fiery shock such as you cannot ima-gine. And yet that is the vital center. One must endure it all, and one

---

*Hombre was a card game of Spanish origin, popular during the seventeenth century.
†Gannat is a small town near Vichy.

does, and one is not scalded, and finally, one lies down on a warm bed where one sweats profusely, and that is what accomplishes the cure. Here, again, is where my doctor serves a good purpose because, instead of enduring two hours of boredom inseparable from the sweating, I have him read aloud, and that gives me some diversion. And so, I will follow this routine for seven or eight days . . .

Before that week was out, Mme de Sévigné had won a reputation for herself in the steam rooms: "In a word, I am the prodigy of Vichy for having shown the greatest courage in the showers!"

The medical authorities had apparently diagnosed Mme de Sévigné's problems as menopausal: "The irregularities are regular again," she wrote, "and it is primarily to make this 'adieu' final and to ensure a final cleansing that I have been sent here, and I believe it was the right thing."

"I return to the subject of my health. It is splendid," she wrote on June 12:

I am walking again, like everyone else. I am afraid of regaining weight; that worries me because I like it as I am. I still cannot close my hands, but the warm weather will do the trick . . . I am now eating everything again; that is to say, I will be able to when I have stopped taking the waters. No one has had better results than I at Vichy . . .

"It is as if I had renewed my lease on life and health," she wrote enthusiastically on another day during her Vichy sojourn:

And if I can only see you again, my dear darling, and embrace you again—with a heart full to overflowing with love and joy—then, perhaps, you will be able to call me bellissima madre *again, then perhaps I can reclaim the title with which Monsieur de Coulanges honored me—that of* mère-beauté.* *In fine, my darling, it will be up to you whether I am to be resuscitated in this manner. I certainly do not say that it was your absence which brought on my illness. But it is true that to spend my life without seeing you casts a sadness and a bitterness over it to which I cannot accommodate myself.*

"The twenty-fourth of this month† was a black day for me," she continued in the same vein on May 28:

---

*Bellissima madre, Italian for "most beautiful mother." Mère-beauté, French for "mother-beauty."
†May 24, 1675, was the date on which Mme de Grignan, on her way to Provence, had parted from her mother at Fontainebleau.

I observed the anniversary sorrowfully, my darling. Days such as that are not easily forgotten, but it would be cruel of you to take that as a pretext not to see me again—cruel to refuse me the joy of being with you in order to spare me the agony of an adieu. I implore you, my darling, to drop that line of reasoning and to allow d'Hacqueville and me to arrange for a leave of absence which will allow you as much time as you want at Grignan and still leave time enough to come here . . . It is true that to have had you make this trip for two weeks would have meant a hardship for both you and me. But, if instead of doing all that philosophizing, you had had the good grace to come, to accord me freely the time I asked of you, it would have been a signal proof of your love . . .

Could Mme de Grignan have been so "cruel" as to suggest that they avoid reunions in the future as the only way to spare her mother the agonies of parting? Clearly, she was critical of her mother for dwelling on the pangs of separation. A note of acrimony sounded in the letters, growing more and more pronounced—undisguised and endless reproaches from Mme de Sévigné's lips rankling in Mme de Grignan's heart. If Mme de Grignan was "cruel," Mme de Sévigné was tactless, harping eternally on Mme de Grignan's failure to join her in Vichy—even when the time had passed for all save recrimination. Of which there was no lack. Neither mother nor daughter could resist rehashing the steps by which they had arrived at that sad pass. If Mme de Grignan reminded her mother, over and over again, that it was she who had vetoed her daughter's suggestion of a two weeks' visit to Vichy ("You are still talking about how harsh it was of me not to have allowed you to join me in Vichy"), Mme de Sévigné rehearsed her reasons for the veto; time and time again, justified her rationale. When Mme de Grignan was joined in the attack by Mlle de Montgobert, her *dame de compagnie*, Mme de Sévigné begged for mercy: "Do not make fun of me, I implore you, and explain to Montgobert what my sad reasons were, so that she will understand and pity rather than scold me."

The Grignans had, by then, left their capital city of Aix and were summering at their eyrie of a château. "I can understand how much you are enjoying the beauty of the improvements being made at the château of Grignan," Mme de Sévigné wrote in July of 1676. "They are a necessity in view of the fact that you are now spending so much time there." She was shocked, however, when she realized the scope of the renovation, the lavish program of embellishment under way, that summer. If the Count had forgotten his brave resolutions to economize, to mend his extravagant ways, she would not hesitate to remind him of them, through her daughter:

Your description of the beautification going on at Grignan astonishes me. Am I wrong when I say that Monsieur de Grignan, for all that gentle manner of his, does exactly as he pleases? Wild as are all his wails about impending financial disaster, he goes right on with his purchases of furniture, paintings, marble mantelpieces! I have no doubt that they are all splendid; that is not the question. Where does he find the money, my daughter? Does he do it by black magic?

No matter how she deplored the Count de Grignan's profligacy, she yearned to revisit Grignan and its glories: "It is my fondest dream to find myself once more in my life in that château, with all my *pichons* and all the Grignans in the world! There cannot be too many for me!"

Apropos of her "*pichon*"—the little Marquis de Grignan—she declared that she was "overjoyed to hear that he might, one day, have a true Grignan physique!" (There had apparently been some concern about a crooked back, a spinal weakness, and frequent discussion of corrective methods such as metallic corselets and exercise programs.) "From your description, he must be very bright, very loveable," she wrote, early in June:

Your concern about his being timid was evidently unwarranted. You take an interest in his education, and that should prove a lifelong blessing to him. The course you are following promises to make a great gentleman of him. How right you were to put him into breeches. They remain girls as long as they are kept in dresses.

"Kiss my *pichons* for me," she said in another letter that same month:

I love that saucy little Pauline. And as for the baby, is he determined to live despite the prognoses of Hippocrates and Galen? If so, I predict that he will turn out to be an extraordinary man . . . And as for our other little girl, she no longer—thank God!—thinks of her Father or her Mother! Alas, my darling, she has not inherited that trait from you! You love me too much, and are overly anxious about my health. It has given you grief enough.

As assiduously as she had besought her daughter to commit herself to coming to Paris for the winter ("Thank you for the hope you give me of seeing you in Paris, this winter! In the name of God, do not disappoint me!"), she was horrified at the suggestion that the Grignans might prefer a roof other than her own over their head, might set up a separate establishment. The Grignans, in 1675, had shared Mme de Sévigné's house on the Rue des Trois Pavillons, but that was before the Abbé de Coulanges had come to make his home with his niece. Now, the Grignans evidently feared that Mme de Sévigné's house could not comfortably accommodate the three households.

"The Abbé is terribly upset at the thought of your not returning to your little apartment in our house," she wrote:

> *Alas, my darling, I only chose it, only keep it for that purpose. In the name of God, never talk about staying anywhere in Paris except with me! I adore the good Abbé for all he has said to me on the subject, for the burning desire he has to see me welcome so cherished and so happy a company!*

And, "As for my poor little house," she wrote elsewhere, "nothing could upset me except to have you refuse to stay there."

Having completed her "cure" at Vichy, Mme de Sévigné set out for Paris on June 13, breaking the trip at the château of the Abbé Bayard at Langlard, at the Convent of the Visitation at Moulins, at Vaux-le-Vicomte, the once splendorous château of the once splendorous Fouquet, where she was received by his son:

"I spent the night at Vaux," she wrote on July 1,

> *intending to refresh myself beside those beautiful fountains and to eat two fresh eggs. As it turned out, the Count de Vaux was expecting me, and gave me a very good supper, but all the fountains were silent, without a drop of water because they were under repair. I had to laugh! We talked at length, comparing the fortune he once enjoyed with that with which he must be satisfied today . . .*

Despite all the pleasant stopovers en route, the trip was long and arduous, the weather "extremely hot": "We start out at four o'clock in the morning; we take a long rest at dinner time, we sleep on straw and on the carriage cushions to avoid the discomforts of summer."

Her carriage clattered into Paris and up the Rue des Trois Pavillons on Sunday, June 28, 1676: "We finally got here. At my door, I found Mesdames de Villars, de Saint-Géran, d'Heudicourt who had come merely to inquire when I would arrive," she wrote on July 1:

> *A moment later there were Monsieur de La Rochefoucauld, Mme de La Sablière who had come by chance, the Coulanges, Sanzei, d'Hacque-*

ville ... Great drops of sweat poured off us. Never have the thermom-
eters been put to such a test. There are crowds at the river. Mme de
Coulanges says one can bathe there only if one has a ticket ... As for
me, I am still sweating; I never stop, and change my chemise at least
three times a day. The good Abbé was thrilled to see me again, and not
knowing what to say to please me most, expressed the hope that the
sight of you would soon provide me a joy equal to his in seeing me.

XXVIII

Once Mme de Grignan had committed herself to coming to Paris ("You
overwhelm me with joy when you speak of your trip to Paris as a certainty!"),
there remained only the question of when. "When will you come?" "When?"
"When?" the letters asked, over and over and over again, the question
phrased in a thousand different ways: hopefully, plaintively, querulously,
bitterly, indignantly, resignedly.

Originally, in a grand gesture of filial devotion, Mme de Grignan had
given her mother the privilege of setting the date for her coming—then and
there, in early July, should her mother say the word. Her mother, in a grand
gesture of maternal selflessness, did not say the word; set the date, instead,
for the relatively distant month of September—"September probably being
the month when Monsieur de Grignan will be making ready for the Assembly ..."*

"That way," Mme de Sévigné expatiated,

You can please everyone. You are the soul of Grignan, and you need
not leave your château or your pichons until you would have left them
to go to Lambesc—at which time you will come here to give me back
my life again, give me the greatest joy this world can provide ... Like
you, I am sure that Mons. de Grignan will appreciate my denying
myself the pleasure of your company, here and now, in order not to

---

*The Governor presided over the Assembly of the Communities of Provence, a legislative and tax-
raising body which met annually at Lambesc in the autumn.

deprive him of the pleasure of having you at Grignan for the summer. After that, it will be up to him to come chasing after you, and he will, and we will be happy to see him arrive. The only thing I ask of you— or, rather, of him—is that he allow you to arrive here in a state of good health which, in my opinion, can be the only basis for a truly enjoyable visit ...

"Come in September" was the gist of the last few lines—"but, in Heaven's name, do not come pregnant!"

If only Mme de Sévigné could have gone into a state of estivation— like a bear or snail—dozing away the summer months, awakening only in time to greet Mme de Grignan upon her arrival in the autumn!

Those summer months she spent, instead, commuting between Paris and Livry, her bucolic suburban pleasure-ground. ("How convenient that it should be so close!") Paris might mean the breath of life to a true Parisienne but, at times, Mme de Sévigné felt as if she might "smother" there: "I have need of air and exercise," she wrote in August: "I need to go to Livry or, at least, I think I do."

In one day, there [at Livry], I found myself able to invite my soul, as I cannot here [in Paris] in two weeks' time. I prayed, I did a lot of reading, I talked about the next life and the ways and means to attain to it. The Father-Prior* has more sense than I gave him credit for ... But, here I am again, today, back in the maelstrom.

The maelstrom, that is, of Paris: with errands and business to attend to, much of it in behalf of the Grignans (a trousseau to be selected for a Grignan bride, government bureaus to be visited to remind the proper authorities of the Count's gubernatorial pension, already far in arrears), Paris with a frenetic social schedule: dinner parties, supper parties, visits to her legion of friends ("I spent the evening with d'Hacqueville in Mme de La Fayette's garden," she wrote on July 29: "There is a *jet d'eau*—a fountain spouting high in the air, a little covered study ... the prettiest spot in all Paris in which to enjoy the open air").

Her friends "scolded" her, she said, for spending so much time in the country: "They cling to me without really knowing why, but I came back [to Livry] on Wednesday morning, which was yesterday, and I am walking

---

*The Father-Prior was the monastic superior at the Abbey of Livry.

in my garden, here, before they have so much as given me a thought in Paris."

When she absented herself too long from them in Paris, her friends followed her to Livry: Mme de Coulanges came, Mme de Sévigné said, "not out of complaisance, but because she adores it here. She is good company, and we are never in danger of boring one another. Corbinelli is here often, Brancas,* Coulanges, and a thousand others who come and go ..."

The Count de Bussy-Rabutin was one of those who came to spend several halcyon summer days with Mme de Sévigné at the Abbey—a joyful reunion for those two cousins. After ten years of exile on his Burgundian estates, Bussy had obtained special permission from the monarch to spend a few months in Paris to attend to legal matters. "I found Bussy gayer, happier, more amusing than ever," Mme de Sévigné wrote her daughter in July. With him, as usual, was his favorite daughter, the apple of his eye (or something more, it was whispered), the recently married, recently widowed Marquise de Coligny. (The extravagance of their love for their daughters constituted another bond between the cousins.)

> My niece de Bussy—or, rather, de Coligny, is a widow [Mme de Sévigné wrote later that month]. Her husband died, in Schomberg's army, of a horrible fever. Bereft but not grieving, she says she scarcely knew her husband, and had always wanted to be a widow. He leaves her all his fortune, so that she will enjoy some fifteen or sixteen thousand livres a year income ... She is nine months pregnant ...

The only drawback at Livry was the dearth of news which, in Mme de Sévigné's opinion, diminished the entertainment value of her letters to her daughter.

"I hope that those who are in Paris will have written you the news," Mme de Sévigné wrote from Livry, one August day: "I know none, as you can see. My letter is redolent of the solitude of the forest, although even in that solitude you are loved and cherished to perfection."

From Paris, on the other hand, Mme de Sévigné could fill her letters with news sure to hold her daughter's interest, and made a point of doing so: "I am going, now, to make the rounds to see if I can hear something amusing to tell you." "You know how I love to pick up gossip for your diversion."

She made a point of being in Paris on July 17 so as to give Mme de

---

*The Count de Brancas was one of Mme de Coulanges's several ardent admirers.

Grignan a firsthand account of the Marquise de Brinvilliers's execution—the gruesome finale to the months-long trial which had horrified and fascinated the capital. A mass-murderess, this winsome little monster had gone to Paris charity hospitals to try out her poisons on the hapless patients, in order to learn how to best do away with her brothers, her father and her husband, along with various and sundry other persons whom she considered obstacles to her happiness. Tried by the two high courts of the Parlement of Paris—a privilege reserved for the nobility of the kingdom—she was brought to justice on July 17.

"Now, at last, it is over and done with," Mme de Sévigné reported on the seventeenth:

La Brinvilliers has gone up in smoke … Her poor little body was tossed, after the execution, into a raging fire, and her ashes scattered to the winds! So that, now, we shall all be inhaling her! And with such evil little spirits in the air, who knows what poisonous humor may overcome us?

At six o'clock she was taken, naked under her chemise and with a rope around her neck, to make the Honorable Amend at Nôtre Dame.* Then she was put back in the tumbril where I saw her, flung upon her back on the straw, wearing a chemise and a mobcap, the priest on one side of her, the executioner on the other. To be honest, I trembled at the sight. Those who witnessed the decapitation say that she mounted the scaffold very bravely. As for me, I was standing on the Nôtre Dame Bridge with the good d'Escars.† Never has Paris seen such a crowd of people. Never has the city been so aroused, so intent on a spectacle. But if you ask me what people saw, I can only tell you that all I saw was a mobcap!

Later that month, Mme de Sévigné paid a visit to Versailles—her first in almost a year, her first glimpse of the recently completed wonderland wrought there by the hand of Louis XIV. On July 29, she wrote to her daughter to describe the château and its marvels. To see Versailles with Mme de Sévigné on a sunny summer day in 1676, shortly after the Sun King had established it as the official royal residence, is to see it in all its glory— thousand-windowed, golden Versailles, its splendor proof against the attrition of time, the neglect and the abuse of three long centuries:

*Crucifix and candle in hand, upon her knees in front of the central door of the Cathedral, she performed the Honorable Amend, which consisted of enumerating her sins and expressing her penitence.
†Her good friend Mme d'Escars.

On Saturday, I went to Versailles, and here is how the day was spent ... At three o'clock, the King, the Queen, Monsieur and Madame and the Grande Mlle, all the Princes and Princesses, Mme de Montespan and all her retinue, all the courtiers—all, in sum, the so-called Court of France gathers in that handsome apartment of the King's which you well know. The furnishings are divine, utter magnificence everywhere.* Gambling is the principal attraction. A game of reversis was the main event ... There sits the King, with Mme de Montespan holding his cards; there are Monsieur, the Queen and Mme de Soubise; Mons. de Dangeau and company; Langlée and company.† Thousand-louis gold pieces are scattered across the table, no other tokens ... I saluted the King ... and he returned the salutation as gallantly as if I were young and beautiful ... The Queen chatted with me as lengthily as if my illness had been a case of childbirth, and had several words to say about you ... Mme de Montespan talked to me about her trip to Bourbon, and asked me to tell her about Vichy, and how I liked it. She had gone to Bourbon, she said, in hopes of a cure for a pain in the knee, but had come back instead with a toothache ... I found her quite flat again in the rear end ... but seriously speaking, her beauty is breathtaking ... While losing weight, she has lost none of her radiance ... her skin, her eyes, her lips all aglow ... Her costume was a mass of French lace, her hair dressed in a thousand ringlets, the two at her temples quite long, falling against her cheek, her coiffure topped with black velvet ribbons and jeweled pins, her famous pearl necklace ... caught up with superb diamond clips and buckles. In short, a triumphant beauty to show off, to parade before all the Ambassadors ... This delightful hubbub in the King's apartment goes on from three to six ... when the gaming ends ... and then, they are off in their carriage: the King, Mme de Montespan, Monsieur, Mme de Thianges ... The Earthly Paradise! ... Later, everyone amuses himself according to his fancy ... Some go out on the Canal in gondolas, again to the sound of music ... At ten o'clock, they all come in for the performance of a comedy ... At the stroke of midnight, supper is served ... And that is how Saturday is spent at Versailles ...

---

*The ceilings were frescoed by Le Brun, the walls covered with Leonardos (including the Mona Lisa), with Titians, Raphaels, and Rubenses. A hundred thousand candles blazed in giant silver candelabra and silver chandeliers.

†Claude de Langlée and Philippe de Courcillon Dangeau were highborn semi-professional gamblers who banked the palace games.

Athénaïs de Montespan—her five children by the King now openly acknowledged at Court—claimed the title of official mistress to the King (*"maîtresse en titre,"* the French having a word for everything), but signs and portents pointed to a change. The royal liaison was in its tenth year: His Majesty seemed restless, his eye had begun to roam, possible rivals were named, if only in a whisper—the Princess de Soubise, Mesdames de Théobon, de Louvigny, de Ludres, La Montespan's own beautiful nieces, the Thianges girls. Rumors flew, and were promptly discredited. "Never has Quanto's sovereign sway been so firmly established," Mme de Sévigné noted that summer, using her favorite code word for the royal Favorite. "The rumor about La Théobon is totally unfounded." As for the two teen-age Thianges, daughters of Mme de Montespan's own sister, she "no more feared those two little snot-nosed nieces of hers than if they had been carbonized!" Far more likely, Mme de Sévigné thought, that it was their aunt herself who had introduced "the wolf into the lamb-fold," purposely tempting the jaded royal palate with those tender morsels of female flesh. "Her [Mme de Montespan's] beauty is at its most glorious, her attire matches her beauty; her gaiety matches her attire." And yet,

> It is said [Mme de Sévigné reported in late August] that there is a scent of fresh meat in Quanto country . . . although no one is quite sure just where it comes from. A lady is named whose name I have already mentioned, but since this clique is oh! so subtle, that lady may not be the one, after all. The one sure thing is that the Cavalier [the King] is gay and sprightly whereas the Demoiselle [Mme de Montespan] is sad, mortified, and sometimes tearful.

Mme de Sévigné's pen could not keep up, so rapid were the developments at Versailles. On September 2:

> The Mme de Soubise episode has passed like a shooting star across the summer sky. The reconciliation is complete. The other day, I am told, Quanto was seen at the gaming table, leaning her head, as cosily as could be, on the shoulder of her Friend. This was an affectation to be interpreted, "Never have I been in higher favor!"

But that may have been mere bravado on Mme de Montespan's part, as Mme de Sévigné pointed out a few days later:

> Everyone is convinced that the Friend is out of love, and that Quanto is in a quandary—unable to decide which she most fears—the conse-

*quences of the return of the royal attentions or the dangers of with-
holding her favors . . . and seeing her royal lover turn elsewhere. Certainly,
she has not yet adjusted herself to the idea of a mere friendship. So
much pride and so much beauty are not easily reconciled to second
place.*

But who was it who was moving into first place? Was it the Favorite's
old friend, Mme de Maintenon, into whose care the five royal bastards had
been entrusted? Was Mme de Maintenon the outsider, the dark horse in the
royal sweepstakes? "She is in very high favor, indeed," Mme de Sévigné
remarked, that autumn. "They say," Mme de Sévigné went on, "that that
friend of the Friend is no longer what she once was, and that one cannot
count on anyone's keeping a cool head in the whirlpool of the Court."

According to Mme de Sévigné's letter of September 8, the finale was at
hand: "Everyone believes that Mme de Montespan's star is fading. There
are tears, there is melancholy; there are affectations of gayety, there is
sulking. In sum, my dear, it is all over."

Until they could be absolutely certain that it was, indeed, "all over,"
the courtiers continued, throughout the summer and autumn of 1676, to pay
court to the royal Favorite, to lavish gifts upon her. Dangeau and Langlée,
the King's cardplaying cronies, set out to outdo one another in the way of
gifts as in the way of wagers. Dangeau had the novel idea of founding the
menagerie at Clagny, Mme de Montespan's magnificent new château, not
far from Versailles—a news item promptly reported by Mme de Sévigné to
her daughter: "At a cost of more than 2,000 écus," she wrote, "he bought
up the most passionate of all turtledoves, the plumpest of all piglets . . . the
curliest lambs, goosiest geese, duckiest ducks . . . and paraded the lot into
Clagny."

Not to be outdone by his rival, Langlée devised a unique and splendorous gift, described in detail by Mme de Sévigné for her daughter's
delectation:

*Monsieur de Langlée has given Mme de Montespan a golden gown,
gold on gold, fitted over a golden brocade sheath, which was cross-
woven with threads of various shades of gold—all of which adds up to
the most heavenly fabric imaginable! Fairies must have woven it on
some secret, mysterious loom of their own! Human hands could never
have wrought it. The donor wanted to give the gift in a fashion as
mysterious as its manufacture. So, Mme de Montespan's dressmaker
came, one day, to deliver a dress she had ordered. It was a ridiculous*

misfit. *What shrieks and scoldings went on, you can well imagine! The dressmaker spoke in a tremulous voice: "Madame, since the time is pressing, please look at this other gown to see if it might not suit you as well as the one you ordered." Whereupon the golden gown was brought forth. "Oh, what a glory! What a fabric! Was it made in Heaven?"—The gown is tried on. It fits to perfection . . . It is a picture! The King comes in. The dressmaker says: "Madame, this gown was made to order, especially for you."—It becomes clear that this is a gallantry on someone's part. But whose?—"It is Langlée's doing," says the King: "Only he would be capable of so magnificent a gesture."—"It is Langlée," everyone starts saying. And all the world takes up the refrain: "It is Langlée!" Even the echoes agree, and repeat, "It is Langlée!"—Even I join the chorus, and chime in with the rest to tell you, my dear daughter, "It is Langlée!"*

It is not surprising that Mme de Grignan hung on her mother's every word from Versailles; that she delighted in her mother's letters reporting on the amorous caprices of the Sun King and his mistresses; generation after generation of Sévignistes, of history buffs and literary buffs have done the same. No matter that historiographers superciliously categorize such material as *petite histoire* or boudoir history: it is not Voltaire's formal history, *The Century of Louis XIV*, it is the *Letters* of Mme de Sévigné—along with the *Mémoires* of the Duke de Saint-Simon, another non-professional writer—which bring the Splendid Century to life.

The Splendid Century owed part of its splendor to Louis XIV's military might—without which French hegemony could never have been extended over Europe.

In early August, 1676, Paris thrilled to news of a French victory at Aire,* one in which—to his mother's delight—Charles de Sévigné had distinguished himself. "The Chevalier de Nogent, who returned to bring the news of the capture of Aire, says that the Baron was everywhere in the thick of battle, appearing in the trenches wherever the fighting was most furious . . . He was cited to the King for valor in action."

The capture of the fortress of Aire compensated, to some extent, for what seemed the imminent loss of Maestricht, for many months under siege. By late August, to Mme de Sévigné's dismay, Maréchal Schomberg's army—in which Charles served—was on its way to relieve that beleaguered fortress. "The Baron writes me that, in his opinion, no matter how they hurry, they

---

*Aire is in northwest France, just south of Lille, close to the border of present-day Belgium.

cannot possibly reach there in time. God grant he is right!" ("I ask pardon of my beloved country," she wrote in her letter of August 28, "but I hope that Monsieur de Schomberg finds no occasion to enter the fray.") Her beloved country would have no need of either Monsieur de Schomberg or Charles de Sévigné to save the day at Maestricht: it was part of what Mme de Sévigné called "the King's luck" that the enemy forces besieging that fortress faded away at the approach of Schomberg's army. But until the news reached Paris, Mme de Sévigné was on tenterhooks of anxiety about the safety of her son. "I have been in the most dreadful state of anxiety imaginable," she wrote on September 2: "I sent messengers to inquire at Mme de Schomberg's house, at Mme de Saint-Géran's and at d'Hacqueville's, and learned these glad tidings. At last, the long siege of Maestricht is over!"

Maestricht had been saved for France, Aire had been taken, but the campaign of 1676 could not be considered successful: with the loss, on September 9, of Philippsburg on the middle Rhine, France had lost control of both the Rhine and the Meuse, a severe blow to French power and prestige.

XXIX

The month of September would come and go, without a word from Mme de Grignan as to the date of her departure: "What about your voyage, my darling? Is it not your intention to begin your trip when Monsieur de Grignan sets out on his?"

"I was generous enough not to have insisted upon your coming in the summer, as I was privileged to do," Mme de Sévigné wrote somewhat huffily in September, "but now I should be rewarded for such complaisance, and without further shilly-shallying, you should start out, as it was agreed between us you would do, on the day Monsieur de Grignan leaves for his Assembly . . . I shall say no more . . ."

Although, of course, she did, to wit: "I implore you, my darling, not to delay further . . .to remember that today is October 2. Firewood has already been stacked in our cellar." ("The weather is marvelous," she wrote on October 9: "These are the crystal clear days of autumn, no longer hot, not yet cold . . . I stay out from ten o'clock in the morning until five in the afternoon.") "I am dying to have you set the date for your departure!" she implored on October 21.

Mme de Sévigné had cause to wonder at the vagaries of Providence whereby her daughter—whom she had been expecting momentarily since September—had not yet put in an appearance in mid-October, whereas her son—whom she had thought to be attached to his regiment in Charleville—announced that he was to be expected shortly. The Baron, who had thumbed his nose at enemy cannon, turned tail at the first twinge of rheumatism, and urged his mother to intercede at the Ministry of War to arrange sick leave for him.

Before she could comply, Charles appeared on her doorstep: "We embraced, we talked about a thousand different things at once," she wrote on October 23:

We asked questions of one another without ever waiting for or ever hearing the answers. In short, the reunion was marked by all the joy and confusion typical of such an occasion. However, Monsieur limps a bit, Monsieur groans, Monsieur claims to be suffering from rheumatism of the hip—although never in front of me! In my presence, he appears embarrassed, does less complaining.

Her air of nonchalance and sarcasm notwithstanding, Mme de Sévigné appeared thoroughly to enjoy the companionship of her son at Livry, where it was thought he was least likely to attract the attention of the War Office.

"The *frater* is still here," she said in her letter of October 28,

still waiting for documents from his regiment declaring him unfit for duty. He hobbles about, he takes medicine. We talk and we read. My little chum, who can guess that I stay on here for his sake, feels guilty about the rain, and makes every effort to amuse me—at which he is highly successful. Aware as we are of the severity of army discipline for deserters, we live here inconspicuously, hoping to escape a hanging!

In reply to what must have been repeated expressions of concern by Mme de Grignan in regard to her mother's health, Mme de Sévigné more than once took occasion to assure her daughter that she was feeling fine—except for the stubborn swelling in her hands. Not that she had not tried everything her numerous doctors had suggested as a cure: she had dipped her hands into fresh-pressed wine; she had plunged them into the warm red throat of a freshly slaughtered cow. Now, she was being advised by certain authorities to return to Vichy for further therapy, while others in her stable of doctors contended that this was the wrong season for the spa. "What could be funnier," Mme de Sévigné inquired of her daughter, "than such a diversity of opinion? It is true, of course, that if one looks hard enough, one can find medical authority for almost anything! I consult doctors in order to make fun of them . . . I shall take their advice when it suits me."*

The presence of Mme de Sévigné's son at Livry—happy company though he might be—could not long console her for her daughter's absence. "I am surprised to hear," she wrote on October 28, "that the Assembly is not yet in session . . . So, you will spend La Toussaint [All Saints' Day] at Grignan. But, after that, my daughter, will you not be thinking of coming here?"

The Assembly of the Communities of Provence was not yet in session, as had been expected, but had been twice postponed: first, from September to October; eventually, to November—in view of which, it was understandable that Mme de Grignan's plans had been subject to change, along with her husband's. But why should she, at that late date, have suddenly expressed misgivings about the propriety of her visiting Paris without her husband? "My God, my darling," her mother cried, "is it possible that you could believe that public opinion would be critical of your coming to visit your Mother? Your friends might find it even more difficult to explain your *not* coming!" (Could it have been that the gossip said by some contemporaries to have attached to Mme de Grignan's name prior to her marriage made her fearful of defying the conventions in any form?)

"I implore you, my darling," Mme de Sévigné wrote on October 21, "to hesitate no longer about making the visit you promised me . . . Make ready, and come, my darling! Come! . . . Make up your mind for once and for all. Do not make me languish longer, and spare me any epilogue on the impropriety of your coming alone."

Throughout October, and well into November, the dismal dialogue went on—Mme de Grignan's, the voice of reason; Mme de Sévigné's the cry of the heart: "I shall say no more about your departure. The date should be decided now—or never! You cannot doubt how I long to see you. I imagine that, by now, Mons. de Grignan has left for the Assembly. If so, you should be on your way."

Mme de Grignan was not on her way because ominously dark clouds could be seen to be gathering on the political horizon of the province under her husband's governance. The continuing military campaigns to which the

---

*As to the menopausal symptoms with which she had been plagued, she quoted a young doctor who attended her at Livry as saying that "in view of my robust constitution, I can expect such irregularities to continue for another three years."

nation was committed necessitated the imposition of ever larger taxes on the provinces. Provence, suffering from a recession like the rest of France, was disinclined to comply with the huge increase demanded in 1676 by the Royal Treasury—twice that of 1675, which the Assembly had voted only under protest.* This session promised to be even stormier; a confrontation seemed inevitable between the representatives and the Governor, and the Governor's lady considered it her duty to be there at his side.

Mme de Sévigné might burst into tears at this latest disappointment, but she could not conceal her admiration for the nobility of her daughter's character: "Having so well done your duty in Provence, I believe that you will be constrained, next, to think of me," she wrote on November 13:

> *I cannot but marvel at my connection with public affairs. As it develops, the additional tax burden imposed on Provence falls on my shoulders! As soon as I heard about it, my heart sank because, knowing you as I do, I knew you would not want to leave Mons. de Grignan. It is, as you say, one of the most important issues to confront a province, and you will be very useful to him, at this hour. I greatly fear those deliberations [in the Assembly]. When I think of how difficult it was for Mons. de Grignan to get them to vote for the 500,000 francs assessment, I cannot imagine how he will manage to induce them to double that amount. I hope that you will soon return to your original travel plans. If you continue on the way you started out, you will find yourself at Rome instead of Paris.†*

"Having given Mons. de Grignan this proof of your devotion—of which I heartily approve in such a crisis," Mme de Sévigné wrote on November 18, "you should now make up your mind to come on without waiting any longer for him. Make your decision, and come—in good heart and with good grace, to afford me the greatest joy in all the world." Her son-in-law, Mme de Sévigné felt sure, would approve: "It is upon Mons. de Grignan that I pin my hopes, convinced that it will be to him that I will owe the thing in all the world which I most passionately desire!"

Within a week, the word she had so long and so eagerly awaited was

---

*In 1676, upon hearing the King's request for one million francs, the Assembly proposed sending a deputation to the monarch "to convey their humble remonstrances." In response to the Assembly's counter-proposal—a tax contribution of 600,000 francs—the Count de Grignan informed them that His Majesty, in view of the province's economic woes, had decided to reduce his demand from one million to 800,000 francs—an amount upon which the Assembly was not slow to compromise.

†Starting out for Lambesc, the Countess had travelled south from Grignan rather than north, in the direction of Paris.

brought to her by special messenger, by the hand of Pommier, a young officer in the Count de Grignan's Guard, as she dramatically describes in a letter dated, "Wednesday, November 25, At Livry":

I am taking a promenade along the avenue when I see a courier coming. Who can it be? "It is Pommier!" Ah, truly, that is wonderful! "And when is my daughter coming?"—"Madame, she should be on her way, by now."* "Come, let me embrace you! And what about your Assembly's tax vote?"—"Madame, they have voted an 800,000 francs contribution."—"That is very good, indeed" . . .

So, now, you are on your way, my very dearest one. And the weather is fine! I will send a carriage to meet you wherever you prefer. I am going to send Pommier on his way so that he can reach Versailles before nightfall.†

Whereupon, Mme de Sévigné—in a transport of joy—could begin to count the days, although her letter of December 13 betrays some pangs of conscience at the thought of the perils, the hardships and the discomforts of a twenty-day voyage in midwinter:

How can I ever make it up to you for all your pains, your fatigue, your long, hard days of travel in cold and ice, for all the inconveniences of the trip you are taking to come to me? I feel as if I had suffered through it all with you. You have not been out of my mind for a moment . . . Good God, what a trip and what a terrible time of the year for it! . . . I will not go to Melun to meet you . . . But I will meet you for dinner at Villeneuve-Saint-Georges. There, you will find awaiting you a bowl of hot soup and—I say this without meaning to step on anyone else's toes—the one person in all the world who loves you with utter devotion. The Bien Bon will be waiting for you at home, in your apartment—with all the candles burning bright and a fire roaring on the hearth!

*Mme de Grignan had returned to the Château de Grignan from Lambesc to pick up her baggage, and had departed Grignan for Paris on December 2.

†Pommier was on his way to Versailles to deliver the Count de Grignan's report on the action of the Assembly to the Marquis de Pomponne, the Secretary of State in charge of Provençal affairs. "The news of the 800,000-franc appropriation greatly pleased the King and all his Ministers," as Mme de Sévigné could advise her daughter in her next letter.

XXX

Mme de Grignan, suffering from exhaustion and a heavy chest cold, drove into Paris on December 22, 1676, and when the wheels of her carriage rolled into the courtyard of her mother's house on the Rue des Trois Pavillons, their correspondence ended—a blanket of silence falling across the next five-and-a-half months, the duration of Mme de Grignan's visit.

Far from the blissful occasion to which Mme de Sévigné had so long and so eagerly looked forward, the reunion degenerated into a contest of wills, a clash of personalities breeding misunderstanding and resentment, activating hitherto latent areas of conflict, verging on disaster, on open rupture—to the horror not only of mother and daughter but of intimate friends and family (as comes to light once the correspondence is resumed on June 8, 1677, the date on which the Count and Countess de Grignan left Paris to return to Provence).*

The resumption of the correspondence reveals a desperate attempt on the part of both mother and daughter to salvage the relationship and prevent a permanent breach. Mme de Sévigné's letters, over the next six months, endlessly rehearse, endlessly deplore the tragic developments of the preceding six: those letters of hers survey and lament the injuries the mother and daughter inflicted on one another, seek both to probe and to bind up the wounds and, finally, to assess the blame—Mme de Sévigné absolving herself, and fulminating against those persons to whom she refers only as "they"— those family members and intimate friends who prescribed separation as the only remedy for the desperate situation. (Who were "they"—those shadowy, ominous figures who recommended tearing a daughter from a mother's arms as the only solution to the predicament? It can only be assumed that "they" denoted the Count de Grignan, for one; the Abbé de Coulanges, for another, along with those most intimate friends and confidants, such as the faithful d'Hacqueville, such as the eminently rational Mme de La Fayette, never one to mince her words.)

But how had they come—mother and daughter—to such a predica-

*The Count de Grignan had reached Paris a month or so later than his wife, joining her at her mother's house in January, 1677.

ment? The two prime issues of controversy were not new: the prodigal Grignans' rushing headlong to financial ruin; Mme de Grignan's six pregnancies in six years' time—taking their toll on her health and beauty. ("God's punishment is visible on you," Mme de Sévigné declared with some asperity: "After six children, what have you to fear?" And again: "I never saw a woman as brilliant and beautiful as you who seemed so to relish self-destruction!")

It was the personality clash between the two women which was apparently more pronounced than ever: Mme de Sévigné demonstrative, effusive, possessive, overbearing, overwhelming, exacting confidences her daughter was reluctant to make, demanding expressions of love of which her daughter was emotionally incapable. Confronted by this invasion of privacy, this challenge to her hard-won independence, this threat of envelopment by her mother's overpowering personality, Mme de Grignan could evidently find no defense save that of withdrawal. Angered at her mother's demands, guiltsick at having failed to meet her mother's needs, Mme de Grignan vented her frustration in outbursts of rage ("going to pieces over mere nothings," as her mother called it). It is, furthermore, not impossible that some element of female jealousy or rivalry entered into Mme de Grignan's fierce resentment: It may well have rankled to see her mother's beauty undiminished at age fifty-one; her own, fading fast at thirty-one.

No sooner had the Grignans' carriage disappeared down the Rue des Trois Pavillons than Mme de Sévigné seized her pen to begin a letter, heading it, "Paris, Tuesday, June 8":

> No, my bonne, I shall say nothing, nothing at all. You know all too well your hold over my heart, and what you mean to me. I cannot manage wholly to conceal from you the fact that your health gives me some concern ... I pity you for harboring similar concern for mine. Would to God I had as little cause in that regard as you!

Concern for each other's health appears to have been one of the chief sources of conflict between the two—each insisting that the other exaggerated the danger, each annoyed at what seemed the other's unwarranted solicitude.

"As for me, my dear," Mme de Sévigné's letter continued, "I am in the best of health. Tears cause me no harm. I have dined, and am now going to call on Mme de Vins and Mlle de Méri. Adieu, my dear children. Alas, all I can see is that carriage bearing you away! It is constantly in my mind's eye."

("In His own good time," she would later write, resignedly, "God will give me peace of mind on your account.")

By June 11, Mme de Sévigné's irrepressible sense of humor occasionally leavened her lament:

It seems to me that if only I had the weak chest and you had the headaches, we could both laugh about it, but I am anxious about your chest, and you worry about my head. Very well, then, I will treat my head with more respect than it deserves, if you will reciprocate by wrapping up that little chest of yours in cotton batting! I am angry that you wrote me such a long letter upon your arrival at Melun; it was a good rest you needed more. Think about yourself, my dear child; do not conjure up "dragons"!* Think about coming back to finish your visit because destiny—or rather, Providence—and for a variety of reasons—cut so short the one you had planned to pay me . . . What a day! What bitterness! What a parting! You wept, my very dear one, and that is quite a thing, for you! It is otherwise with me; it is my nature to weep. The fact that you are in ill health greatly adds to my distress at parting. It seems to me that I could bear a not overlong separation with equanimity, but to see you so thin, your voice so weak, your face sunken, that beautiful throat of yours unrecognizable—that is more than my heart can bear!†

The dirge was interspersed, occasionally—perhaps methodically—with news and gossip of Court and Capital, so dear to the exiles in far-off Provence. The June 11 letter included the latest report of the amours of the amorously volatile monarch, the last word on the last chapter of the Montespan affair:

Ah, my daughter, what a triumph at Versailles! What pride redoubled! What a solid reestablishment of favor! . . . There is evidence of added zest in the relation—all the sweeter, now, after lovers' quarrels and reconciliations. What a reaffirmation of possession! I spent an hour in her—Mme de Montespan's—chamber . . . the very air charged with joy and prosperity!

---

*A "dragon" was the family name for *bête noire*, bugaboo, bogey.

†Mme de Grignan was evidently quite pleased with her loss of weight, even though a slender figure was not as stylish in the seventeenth century as it is in the twentieth. Mme de Sévigné notes that the Count's brother, the Coadjutor to the Archbishop of Arles, had told her how much Mme de Grignan "feared getting fat."

"I have an advantage over you when I write you a letter," Mme de Sévigné remarked in her letter of June 14: "You cannot answer back, and I can finish what I have to say without fear of interruption." "What a shame," she continued in that same letter,

> that you wasted your sympathy and anxiety on my health which is now totally restored to normal, and can only suffer harm from such harm as you do your own . . . As for me, I do have anxiety about your health, an anxiety that is only too well founded: it was no figment of my imagination—the state you were in at our parting. Monsieur de Grignan and all your friends were frightened by it. I hit the ceiling* when they come and tell me, "You two are killing each other! You must be separated." Now, there, to be sure, is a fine remedy, one likely to put an end to all my woes—although not in the manner intended! They read my mind, and could see that I was distressed about you. And how could they expect me not to be? Never have I seen such grave injustice as has been done me, in recent weeks. It is not you I am accusing. To the contrary, I implore you, my daughter, not to think that you have anything with which to reproach yourself. Our only problem was with your unjustified alarm about my health—a fault of which you must correct yourself . . .

By June 15, there came good news from the voyagers: "I have just received your two letters from Auxerre," wrote Mme de Sévigné:

> D'Hacqueville was here, and he was thrilled to hear your news. What gratitude do I not owe to God for the improvement in your condition! At last, you are sleeping again, you are eating something, you are relaxing. You are no longer exhausted, tense, debilitated, as you were those last days here . . .

On June 16, Mme de Sévigné cautioned her daughter about letting her imagination run riot: "not to think me ill when I am feeling fine," "not to dwell on the past" (the rheumatic attack by which Mme de Sévigné had been stricken the previous year), "not to brood over the future"—the thought of her mother's advancing age and death:

---

*A translation which—if not literal—adheres strictly to Mme de Sévigné's words: "*Je saute aux nues quand on vient me dire . . .*": "I jump up to the clouds when they come to tell me . . ."

If you do not make up your mind to that, the prescription at which they arrive will be one forbidding you ever to see me again! I do not know whether this remedy will be good for you. As for me, it would indubitably end my life. Give thought to that. When I worried about you, I had only too good reason ... The dismay of your friends and the change in your appearance confirmed only too well my fears and my alarm. So, spare no effort to heal yourself, body and soul. It is up to you to do everything in your power to make your return [to Paris] as pleasant and joyous as your departure was grim and sad. As for me, what have I to do? To feel well? I feel fine. To take care of my health? I do, for your sake. Not to worry about you? That is what I cannot promise, my dear girl, as long as you are in the state in which I saw you last. I speak to you sincerely. Make every effort to recover your health. And when they come to me, and say, as they do presently, "You see how well she is feeling, now, and you, too—you are both at peace, you are both well again" ... what they are really saying is that for the two of us to keep well, we must remain 200,000 leagues apart! And they dare to tell me that, to my face! Enough to make my blood boil, to make me hit the ceiling! In the name of God, my darling, let us reestablish our reputation by another reunion at which we will show ourselves more reasonable—that is to say, that you will! So that they will never again say to us, "You are killing each other!" I am so devastated by such remarks that I can no longer go on. There are other, kinder ways of killing me ...

When she wrote on June 27, Mme de Sévigné had still not recovered from the shock of that precipitate departure, that cruel parting:

Oh, my God, will we never see one another again to bask in one another's love and affection? Will we not pluck out the thorns, will we not prevent their ever saying to us again—and with a cruel barbarity to which I cannot accustom myself: "Ah, how much better off you are, five hundred thousand leagues apart! You see how well Mme de Grignan is doing, now. She would be dead if she had stayed on here. You will be the death of one another." I do not know how you react to such remarks; as for me, I find them crushing ... So, let us do better next time, my darling! ... Let us restore our good reputation. Let us show them that we are sensible enough to live together when Providence decrees. I am outraged at the blame that has been heaped upon me, in recent weeks. I cannot see where I have been at fault. Seeing you looking so ill, how could I be expected not to be upset? In short, my daughter, let us correct our faults, let us see one another again, let us not give our love the appearance of hatred and dissension. Let us do honor to our feelings which are profound and fond. Why distort them? But I am being foolish. What is past is past. I will not bring it up again. This all comes from the fact that dear d'Hacqueville has been lecturing me . . .

"So, there you are, at last, at Grignan!" Mme de Sévigné wrote on the last day of June, 1677:

The letters you wrote me all along the way give me constant proof of your devotion. I can assure you that you are right when you say you think that I have need of such consolation; nothing is more necessary to me. It is true, as I so often think, that your presence would have been an even greater comfort than your letters, but you were in such an extraordinary mood that when you decided to leave, I could only accept your decision, and stifle all my feelings. It was a crime for me to be perturbed about your health. I saw you perishing before my eyes, but was denied the right to shed a tear. To do so was to kill you, to assassinate you! I was supposed to choke back everything I felt. Never have I seen so unusual, so cruel a form of torture! If instead of that constraint which only heightened my misery, you had been disposed to admit that you were languishing, if only your love for me had expressed itself in complaisance, if only you had evidenced a genuine desire to follow doctors' orders, to eat, to follow the regimen prescribed, to admit that the air and peace and quiet of Livry would have been beneficial to you—why, then, that is what would have truly consoled me . . . relieved my mind . . . Oh, my daughter, at the end, we had come to a point where we had no choice but to do what we did . . . There, now, it has been said, once and for all. But let us make our reflections, each on her own side, so that when it pleases God for us to be reunited, we will never again come to such a pass! . . . I had to write all this, this once, to unburden my heart, and to urge that when the opportunity comes, we never again put ourselves in such a position that they will come to pay us the abominable compliment of recommending that the best thing for us both is never to see one another again! I marvel at anyone patient enough even to listen to advice so cruel!

"I hope that this letter will not seem too long," Mme de Sévigné wrote on July 9, apologetic about the voluminousness of her letters which had, by then, incurred Mme de Grignan's reproof. Mme de Sévigné went on to explain that she did not tire her hand, writing "only a few pages at a time" and those "at her leisure," insisting that "it is my paper and my handwriting that make my letters seem so excessively long. There is more on one of your sheets than on six of mine!" The length of her mother's letters had given Mme de Grignan concern, early in July; by the end of the month, she evidently expressed concern at their brevity—somewhat to her mother's amusement: "I had to laugh at you, my *bonne*," Mme de Sévigné wrote on July 30. "When my letters to you were too long, you were anxious lest the effort have a deleterious effect on my health. When I write short letters, you think me ill! You know what I shall do? Exactly as I have always done! When I begin a letter, I never know whether it will be long or short; I write as it pleases my pen to write. That is the deciding factor . . ."

No matter how humorous her declarations of independence, the nameless and amorphous "they" continued to alarm her mind and heart: "Now that they have told us we are better off two hundred leagues apart," she wrote in her letter of July 9, "will the next step be to impose an embargo on our correspondence?"

Clearly, she was fearful for their future; her letters, in the course of the following days and weeks, returned again and again to the question that nagged at her heart and mind: how had such a debacle befallen their reunion? how to prevent a reoccurrence?

Vowing repeatedly not "to dwell on the past," to look only to the future, Mme de Sévigné persisted nonetheless in bitter retrospection: "You tell me wonderful things about your health," she wrote on July 19.

You are sleeping, you are eating, you are relaxing, free of duties, free of visitors. Free of a doting mother! You forgot that item, and it is the most essential! In conclusion, my daughter, I was forbidden to worry about your condition. All your friends were disturbed about it, but I was supposed to be unconcerned. I was wrong to have predicted that the air of Provence would be harmful to you. You were neither sleeping nor eating, but to see you perish before my eyes was supposed to be a trifle unworthy of my attention . . . And, instead of trying to reassure me by a course of action calculated to restore your health, all they could talk about was separating us. It was I who was killing you; I who was the source of all your ills! When I think how I struggled to conceal my fears, when I think of how violently you reacted to the few words of caution which escaped my lips, I must conclude that it is forbidden me to love you . . . Thanks be to God, the air and the quiet at Grignan have wrought a miracle, at news of which I experience a joy proportionate to my affection. Monsieur de Grignan has won his case, and should now fear—as strongly as he loves your life—to see me come near you. I can see him smile; I can hear your banter on the subject. It strikes me that you have won all your bets. You are feeling well, you say; you laugh about it with your husband. How could you be mistaken with such good evidence?

I shall make no comment on your plans for the winter. I can well understand that Monsieur de Grignan wants to take advantage of the short time remaining to him. Monsieur de Vendôme is on his traces.* You will make your plans according to your best judgment, and could make no mistake. As for my plans, if you are strong enough to withstand the strain of my presence—and if my son and the good Abbé would be willing to spend the winter in Provence, I would be well pleased, and could not wish for a more delightful sojourn. You know how much I enjoyed being there. And, indeed, when I am with you— and you are well!—how could I ask for anything more in all the world?

There seemed no doubt that Mme de Grignan was well again; she had shown rapid improvement since her return to Grignan. ("Can you imagine what joy it will give me to see you again with that lovely face I so admire, to see you again at a sensible weight, some flesh on your bones, to see you in a gay mood which is a sign of good health!") To have these facts confirmed by Mlle Montgobert (the Countess's *dame de compagnie*) was reassuring. "At last, my daughter," she wrote on July 28,

I am convinced of your good health. I know that Montgobert would not deceive me. But, tell it to me once again. Write it to me in verse and in prose! Repeat it to me, thirty times over! Let all the echoes ring with the joyous tidings! If I had an orchestra like Mons. de Grignan's, I would make an opera of it!

But, as late as August, more than two months after their anguished parting, mother and daughter were still not done with recriminations. The bitterest words of all remained to be written by Mme de Grignan. Her letters having been lost, her voice is to be heard only as an echo in the letters of

---

*The Duke de Vendôme had held the title of Governor of Provence and enjoyed the lion's share of the remuneration of the post without thus far performing any of its functions. Rumor was current in 1677 to the effect that he would finally go to Provence to assume the responsibilities which had hitherto devolved upon his Lieutenant-Governor, the Count de Grignan.

her mother, when she is quoted by her mother, as in this letter of Mme de Sévigné's dated August 11, in which Mme de Sévigné makes clear that she is quoting Mme de Grignan verbatim:

I reread the last lines of your letter, my daughter. They are devastating: "Now that you no longer have me with you, you no longer run the risk of stirring up hornets' nests. I caused the disorder in your mind, in your health, in your house. I am absolutely not good for you." What words! How could you even think them? How can I bear to read them? What you are saying is worse even than all that went before and so distressed me, worse even than all the cruel things they said to me, at parting. It was as if they had wagered among themselves to see which one could destroy me first! Now, you continue in the same vein. I could laugh at the others as long as I believed you were on my side. Now I see that you are part of the conspiracy. My only answer is to repeat to you what you said to me, the other day: "When life takes a turn in a certain direction, then let it come to its conclusion as it must." Even, I would add, the sooner the better. That is how I wish it.

XXXI

That melancholy summer of 1677 had been made more melancholy still by the death of the Grignans' youngest child, the premature and malformed infant born in February of 1676. "Alas, my dear, how sorry I am to hear about your poor little baby!" Mme de Sévigné condoled with her daughter: "It is impossible not to be distressed. Not, as you know, that I had had any hope of his living. From what you had told me, I deemed it a hopeless case but, nonetheless, it is a loss for you. That makes three you have lost. May God preserve the one son remaining to you!"

Mme de Sévigné urged Mme de Grignan to seek consolation in the children remaining to her: above all, not to send three-year-old Pauline to join seven-year-old Marie-Blanche in a convent! "Love, oh, please love Pauline!" she pleaded: "Give yourself that pleasure. Don't play the martyr by depriving yourself of that little creature . . . You can place her in a convent later, if you find it necessary. Allow yourself the experience of maternal love." ("Why should anyone be afraid of having too much fun with her children?" she inquired elsewhere of her daughter.)

"I would adore to see the little Marquis," his grandmother wrote, "and I am dying to kiss Pauline's plump cheeks! Ah, how pretty she must be! I promise you that she will look like her mother. A naturally curly blond head is a wondrous thing! Love her, love her, my daughter . . . Don't hold back . . . You have given your Mother love enough . . . from now on, it can only become tedious . . ." (Pauline might someday resemble her mother but, at that point, she had "a little squared-off nose" like her grandmother's—"a strange feature to find in that family of yours!"—a large, hawkish nose acknowledged as a Grignan characteristic.)

As for the little Marquis, "he must be very handsome," his grandmother concluded from what she had been told: a sound, bright boy for whom they must find a good tutor—a quest frequently to be discussed in the correspondence.

There was frequent discussion, as well, of a return trip to Vichy for further treatment of Mme de Sévigné's still swollen hands; another pilgrimage to the waters constituting a point upon which Mme de Grignan insisted.

Originally, Charles de Sévigné had proposed escorting his "darling *Maman*" there, himself inclined to try the therapeutic effects of the spa for a heel wound which he had suffered in action against Dutch and Spanish forces near Valenciennes in early March,* but he was obliged to forego that plan in order to rejoin his regiment in Flanders.†

Deprived of the escort of her son, Mme de Sévigné had to rely on that of her uncle, the Abbé de Coulanges, with whom she departed Paris on August 16, with Vichy as their final destination. Taking the Burgundy route, they were to stop off at Bourbilly, Mme de Sévigné's estate in that province, to attend to business matters. Setting out "at break of day" in their fine carriage, the two travelled along at a fast clip ("My coachman is marvelous," Mme de Sévigné exclaimed, "and our horses are spirited!"), travelled along "in the most perfect weather, through the most beautiful countryside, along the best roads in the world."

---

*With Mme de Sévigné's *Lettres* suspended at this point, the report of Charles's wound in March comes from *Lettres historiques* by Paul Pellisson, on duty in the same battle area.

†"The heel wound I told you about," Mme de Sévigné wrote in a letter to Bussy at the end of July, "did not heal until two weeks ago. The flesh is still so red, so bruised, so tender that he can scarcely put any weight on it. Even so, he wants to go to the army." Charles's mother had financed the purchase of a second-lieutenant's commission for her son in the Gendarmes-Dauphin Regiment—the sale of his ensign's commission having formed part of the transaction.

Too loyal openly to belittle the Abbé as a travelling companion, the most Mme de Sévigné would allow herself to say was that "Ours may not be the gayest of parties, but we have our books." "We are reading a history of the Emperors of the Orient," she wrote on August 18.*

It is a very entertaining history, but without prejudice to Lucian† whom I continue reading ... Although what I prefer above all other reading matter, my darling, are your letters. Nor do I say that because I love you. Ask those who are around you. Speak up, Monsieur the Count! Monsieur de La Garde, Monsieur the Abbé, is it not true that no one writes as well as she does? Thus, I have brought along three or four of your letters to reread: your commentary on a certain woman of our acquaintance is worthy of publication.

Mme de Grignan's letters in recent weeks had suggested that her mother continue south from Vichy to Lyon, a relatively short journey, and from Lyon to Grignan, another relatively short journey. "You urge me to come to Grignan; you tempt me by telling me of your melons, your figs, your muscats. Ah, I would feast on them, but it is not God's will that I should make that delightful trip, this year. Perhaps another time!" The Count himself picked up a pen to address his mother-in-law an invitation: "Monsieur the Count," she replied on August 18,

you could not be any more eager to welcome me to Grignan than I to go there to embrace you! In the name of God, do not blame me for this barbarity. I am sick at the thought of it; my heart aches. You must know that there is nothing I so passionately desire, but I am attached to the Abbé who finds so many poor reasons not to make this trip that I have no hope of seeing him change his mind.

The Abbé may have thought it too soon to risk another reunion between the two women. The wounds were still fresh; Mme de Grignan's words still festered in her mother's heart: "You will never persuade me, my darling," Mme de Sévigné wrote on August 28, "that I am better off not being with you. I never thought anyone could have convinced you of anything so ridiculous, but there are lines in your letter which I can never forget. In

---

*Alexiade ou Histoire d'Alexis 1, by Princess Anne Commène, translated and abridged by Louis Cousin from L'Histoire de Constantinople, published in 1672–4 in eight volumes.
†Lucian, the Greek satirist and humorist.

which case, you and I are to be pitied, should your affairs [bring you to Paris and] oblige you to see me again."

Mme de Sévigné and her uncle, as dispirited as their horses after an exhausting eleven-hour journey from Auxerre, drove across the drawbridge, over the moat, and into the vast Court of Honor of the Count de Guitaut's magnificent château at Époisses, on August 21. "You know the master of this beautiful house," Mme de Sévigné wrote her daughter, upon arrival, "and the superb manner in which he greets those of whom he is fond ... Our conversations go on endlessly. He loves to talk, and when it comes to that, I am no slouch, either."

Mme de Sévigné had been unable to stay at Bourbilly which was then undergoing extensive reconstruction. "Everything is topsy-turvy at the château of my ancestors," as she had explained to the Count de Bussy in the letter announcing her arrival. She and the Abbé were critical of the farmer to whom her properties were under lease, as she explained to her daughter on August 22:

We have already begun to scold about the eight thousand francs' worth of reparations under way, and about the sale of my grain three days before the price increase. Precipitate action cost me more than 200 pistoles, but I do not fret about it. That is the hand of Providence. When what happens is not my fault, when there is nothing to be done, I refuse to allow myself to be distressed.

Proceeding from château to château on their Burgundian odyssey, Mme de Sévigné and the Abbé de Coulanges arrived on August 30 at the Count de Bussy's Chaseu, near Autun—"a very splendid, beautifully situated château," as Mme de Sévigné described it. As usual, the two cousins found one another infinitely amusing. ("Either we should never see one another," Bussy would write her, nostalgically, two weeks later, "or we should never part!")

Leaving Chaseu on September 1, the voyagers finally rolled into Vichy on the fourth, finding the spa filled with familiar faces, Parisian friends and acquaintances: "Never has there been such a crowd, here!" Mme de Sévigné wrote her daughter on September 6: "Never has the weather been so perfect! September is an independent kind of month, taking its cue from neither summer nor winter, and this is the most beautiful September I have ever seen."

"Everything runs on schedule, here," she reported on September 7:

Everyone dines at noon; sups at seven; goes to bed at ten; goes to drink the waters at six [in the morning]. I wish you could see the way two or three of the local belles have taken to dressing up—the change in their coiffures and costumes!—since the arrival of Termes and Flamarens.* By six o'clock in the morning, they are bustling about, their hair curled, powdered and dressed in the hurluberlu *style, rouge and beauty spots on their cheeks, little dangling coiffes and bonnets à la bascule . . . fans; long, tight bodices! You would die laughing!*

And, by letter of September 13: "The company, here, is of the best. The weather is fine, the countryside beautiful. One lives exceedingly well." (The Abbé, perhaps, too well: "The good Abbé drinks the waters to purge himself of all those big dinners he eats, paving the way so that he can eat heartily for the next ten years!")

By September 22, Mme de Sévigné had completed her "cure":

Tomorrow, I wind up all my affairs, here. I am taking the last of my medicine. I have drunk the waters for sixteen days, but I took only two steam baths, two hot showers. I could not stand the heat; it made me dizzy . . . Drinking the water was all I needed, and that worked miracles . . . As for my hands, my daughter, they are better . . .

As a matter of fact, Mme de Sévigné was in somewhat of a hurry to get back to Paris to conclude negotiations and sign the lease on a house large enough to accommodate the Grignan family and staff as well as all her own and the Abbé's. The joyful news that family business was to bring the Grignans to Paris for the winter had reached Mme de Sévigné in Vichy. "The end of your letter delighted me," she had replied ecstatically. "Come, then come, my darling, and without any dragon eating on your heart, since the good Archbishop† makes the pronouncement *ex cathedra* to the effect that your voyage is necessary to the best interests of the family." The family interests would best be served, it appeared, by bringing the Count's two daughters from his first marriage to live with their father and stepmother. The Mesdemoiselles Grignan—"the Grignettes," as Mme de Sévigné called them—had hitherto resided with their maternal uncle and guardian, the Duke de Montausier. The theory was that the Count, in providing a home

---

*The Marquis de Termes and the Chevalier de Flamarens, Parisian men-about-town.

†The Archbishop of Arles, patriarch of the Grignan family, chief counsellor to his nephew, the Count de Grignan.

for his daughters, would be able to reduce the annual interest payments due the girls on the estate bequeathed them by their mother. The main purpose of the Grignans' trip to Paris in late 1677 was to complete these arrangements with the Duke de Montausier.

One would have thought that since the experiment of sharing a house had proven such a dismal failure in 1676, neither mother nor daughter would have been eager to risk a repetition in 1677. As surely as they were devoted to one another, just as surely they were incompatible. Was it not tempting fate to recreate the conditions which had developed into disaster the preceding year? In so doing, they must have vowed sedulously to avoid the old pitfalls. Mme de Sévigné sought to convince herself that all would be well, if only the two of them were hale and hearty, if only neither made a to-do about the other's frailties. Quite simply, Mme de Sévigné could not live without her daughter; she had to run the risks of living with her.

Mme de Sévigné made clear that, in her opinion, it behooved Mme de Grignan to make a supreme effort, this time, to be at her best—rather than, as in the previous year, at her worst: "My darling," she besought her daughter in a letter in September, "hold fast to all your endowments, and remember of what you are capable when you so choose—what sweetness and amenity of temper is yours when you are not being devoured by all your dragons! But when you wish to, my daughter, oh, my God, what a paragon you are! What a charmer, what an enchantress you can be!" "If you will only arrive here feeling as well as I do," she wrote in October, "I promise not to bedevil you about your health!" "In the name of God," the peroration ran, "let us not be guilty again of saying all those cruel things to each other!"

Not that Mme de Sévigné expected all the concessions to be made by her daughter: she herself was prepared to concede far more than she had ever done before, to make a declaration of abnegation so abject as to be startling: "It seems to me," she wrote in September,

that it will be a great convenience for us and spare us much inconvenience not to have to seek each other out. For those under the same roof, there are hours of the morning and the evening which one would never enjoy if one had to run from house to house to find one another. I think you feel the same way about it as do I, and that if the right house can be found, we could not hope to do better for this winter. I expect, my darling, to have you occupy the apartment set aside for you in this house—unless you have already located a house to be occupied by you alone. I will conform to your specifications, I will consult your preferences, I will try to read your thoughts. It will be my pleasure to please you. I will change my mind to come to a meeting of the minds with you. I will change my plans if they do not coincide with yours. I will go on the theory that what I had in mind was a mistake if it fails to meet with your approval. Above all, I want to see you happy; my happiness will have its source in yours.

"The anticipation of your arrival, the hope of seeing you and welcoming you does me a thousand times more good than all the waters of Vichy!" she wrote in exultation at the announcement of the Grignans' departure date.

Happily—and thanks to the families' faithful and indefatigable friend, d'Hacqueville—the perfect house to accommodate the two families had been located, and was put under lease, that autumn. It was a large and handsome, an imposing town house on the Rue Culture Sainte-Catherine (renamed, today, Rue de Sévigné), in the Marais district, Mme de Sévigné's favorite part of town, and within a stone's throw of the Place Royale where she had been born. This house was known as the Hôtel Carnavalet*—the word *hôtel* denoting not a public hostelry but a family mansion. (To Mme de Sévigné, with her penchant for nicknames and pet names, it became "The Carnavalette"—Carnavalet being the corruption of a Breton name, Kernevenoy, which was that of one of the hôtel's early owners.) Dating back to the early sixteenth century, the Hôtel Carnavalet underwent extensive reconstruction in the early seventeenth century at the hands of the master architect François Mansart. The hand of the renowned sixteenth-century architect-sculptor Jean Goujon is visible in the stunning bas-reliefs which ornament the second-story façade of the beautiful courtyard—twelve larger-than-life classical figures representing the signs of the Zodiac.

"Thank God, we have the Carnavalet!" Mme de Sévigné could write on October 7, 1677:

It is really an excellent deal: the house will accommodate all of us, and in high style. Since one cannot have everything, we will have to forego parquet floors and the small new fireplaces now in vogue, but we will have a beautiful courtyard, a lovely garden and a fine neighborhood! . . . and we will be together, and you love me, my dear child!

They would be living together but "not in too close quarters," as she made clear: the Grignans would take the first or ground floor, she would

---

*It is known today as the Carnavalet Museum, a storehouse of Sévigné memorabilia.

have the second; the Grignan girls and Mlle Montgobert, the third; the Abbé would have "a very suitable wing of the house unto himself." It was a spacious, gracious structure: in addition to the grand marble Mansart staircase, there was a service stairway to the rear. There was "a stable to accommodate eighteen horses and four carriages."

The chore of moving was no easier in the seventeenth than in the twentieth century: "Everything is up in the air," Mme de Sévigné complained on October 15:

> All my staff is busy moving. Your furniture is being taken out first. I camped in my room. Now I am in the Bien Bon's room with nothing in it but the table upon which I write you. That is enough! I think we will be very pleased with the Carnavalette. I am happy to be going there.

So happy that she verged on the euphoric: "Our garden is very beautiful. I may sleep there!" "Adieu, my darling," she ended that letter of October 16, "Adieu, my dear Grignans, male and female. I love you and I honor you. Love me a little, too. They are taking out my writing-portfolio, my paper, my table, my chair! Oh, go ahead, and move out anything you like! Here I am, standing up!"

"I must talk to you a while, my daughter, about our Hôtel Carnavalet," she wrote on October 20:

> I will be moving in in a day or two, but since we are very comfortably installed at Monsieur and Mme de Coulanges's house, and since we can see that they are pleased to have us, we are getting everything into place, we are furnishing your room, and these days of leisure spare us most of the inconvenience and disorder of moving. We will go tranquilly to spend the night there, as one goes to a house where one has been living for three months ... I find it a diversion to arrange things so that you will be spared all discomfort—at least, upon your arrival ... In the midst of all this confusion, I have a thousand callers ... and sometimes I receive them in the courtyard of the Carnavalet, sitting on the carriage-shafts!

She had only one request to make of Mme de Grignan: "Please, my love, do not bring such a terrible amount of luggage! When I think of the thirty-two pieces you brought, last time, I shudder!"

The first week of November, Mme de Sévigné ran away to Livry to escape the final throes of moving, confessing to Bussy on the third:

I have come here to enjoy the last of the good weather, and to say goodbye to the leaves. They are all still on the trees; they have merely changed color. Instead of being green, they have taken on tones as varied as the dawn, as varied as a magnificent, golden brocade which we are inclined to think even more beautiful than the green—if only for the sake of change.*

I am settled at the Hôtel Carnavalet. It is a large and beautiful house. I hope to stay there a long time, because the moving wearied me greatly. I now await la belle Madelonne, who will be happy to know that you still love her.

The good Abbé sends you a thousand thanks. We speak often of [the château at] Chaseu, of its beautiful situation, its luxury—and last but not least, of the good company there. It is a shame that we should be separated almost all our lives.

By mid-November, the Grignans were on their way to Paris and, with their approach, the correspondence between mother and daughter was broken off once again. The only known letter written by Mme de Sévigné in the last month of the year 1677 was addressed to her cousin the Count de Bussy-Rabutin, dated "Paris, this 8th of December":

La belle Madelonne *is here, but since there is never one moment of unadulterated pleasure to be expected in this world, my joy in seeing her was greatly diminished by distress over the grievous state of her health. Just think, my poor cousin, that pretty little creature—for whom you have so often expressed your admiration—has become so thin and frail as to seem altogether another person! There is such deterioration in her health that no one who cares about her can escape anxiety. And that is what God in His goodness had in store for me when He restored my daughter to my arms.*

---

*"I commend your taste, Madame," Bussy replied (keeping copies of all his letters to his cousin and all hers to him), "and I endorse your preference of the variegated autumnal colors to the springtime greens, although I think I detect a trace of vanity in that judgment. It implies that there is greater merit in your mature age than in callow youth. And, upon my word, you are right, for youth has only the spring green tones; we others of the more advanced season, have a thousand shades, one more beautiful than the other."

The chief element of discord which had devastated the reunion of 1676 was present again in 1677: mutual fears for one another's health would once again wreak havoc. The reunion, which would last almost two years—from December, 1677 to September, 1679—was doomed from the beginning.

XXXII

All was not well at the Hôtel Carnavalet in 1678—all Mme de Sévigné's high hopes for the reunion with her daughter were dashed.

Mme de Grignan, after a long and arduous midwinter journey, arrived in Paris wan and weary, emaciated, nerves on edge, and coughing so hard that she could scarcely speak. Mme de Sévigné went to pieces at the sight of her. The sparks began to fly as they had at the reunion of 1676.

There was undoubtedly cause for alarm on Mme de Sévigné's side: it was "the Countess de Grignan's ill health," as she wrote the Count de Guitaut, two days before Christmas, 1677, which caused her "a thousand and one pangs of sorrow, daily. She grows thinner and thinner, and that pretty face we knew has become almost unrecognizable." And to Bussy, on January 4, 1678: "I must confess that the ill health of that Provençale fills me with sadness. I tremble at the delicacy of her chest: as a result of the cold weather, she lost her voice for three hours yesterday, and had such difficulty breathing, I almost died!"

As for Mme de Grignan, she may have made too much of a brief spell of illness suffered by her mother in mid-November, 1677: an attack of "bilious and nephritic colic," as Mme de Sévigné herself had characterized it by letter to the Count de Guitaut. (Thanks to a bleeding, a purgative, and "other remedies as numerous as the sands of the sea," she had been up and about before the week was out—"just pale enough to prove to my friends that I had merited their attentions.")

Concern for each other gave rise on both sides to admonition, to exhortation, to nagging solicitude—resulting, on both sides, in impatience, annoyance, indignation.

But there were other more basic causes of dissension between the two women, at this reunion: the contrariety of their temperaments, their person- alities, their humors had never been so pronounced. Tension between them reached such a pitch that communication became impossible. By the spring of 1678, Mme de Sévigné had to resort to letter-writing to reach her daughter, who was as close as the other side of the door, no more than a step away. They could no longer trust themselves to spoken words; words too easily exploded into anger. Mme de Sévigné and Mme de Grignan could no longer carry on a conversation without the flare of temper.

As stormy, as thorny, as distressing as those months proved, even so, Mme de Sévigné showed panic at the thought of their coming to an end. When Mme de Grignan, in May of 1678, seized upon the threat of war as an excuse to escape from Paris and her mother—to follow her husband back to Provence (where his presence, as Governor, was required in time of national emergency)*—Mme de Sévigné had to take up her pen to plead her case: "My letters succeed better than I do, in person," she wrote plaintively:

Where my heart is so deeply involved, I express myself more felicitously by the written than by the spoken word. I hear you say that you are leaving. I am not the only person to disapprove of the plan. It seems to me that it would be more sensible, more natural for you to wait here to see whether we are to have peace or war. If it is peace, Mons. de Grignan would return to get you and take you back with him. If war, your stay in Provence will be lengthy enough; there is no need to rush away when you should stay here and devote another two months to regaining your health. No matter what you say, the air of Grignan is deadly for you, and has brought about the state you are in. By putting off your departure until September, you will avoid spending the summer months there—and devote your time here to rest and to [therapeutic] baths. It is even possible that Mons. de Grignan will spend very little time at the château; he will not be able to get far from his Mediterranean.† So, here is what I ask of you. Common sense, reason, all your friends, your health—you, yourself, if you could see it objectively—would convince you that this is the sensible and natural course to follow ... I am familiar with all your counter-arguments, but three months pass quickly, and you will be under no expense here, if only you allow yourself this respite.

And that, my darling, is what I am constantly thinking—yet dare not talk to you about. I fear your outbursts. I cannot bear them; they leave me dumbstruck and devastated. If you think me a stupid woman,

---

*The Count de Grignan had joined his wife in Paris early in January, 1678, only to turn around almost immediately to return to his post.

†It was the Governor's responsibility to maintain a watch over the southern coasts.

you are right. Face to face with you, I always am—obsessed with you as I am. I implore you to make no reply to this letter. Say nothing to me. Instead, just reflect for a few moments on all I have said. But if I mean anything to you, you must know that there is nothing in all the world I so much want as to have you resolve to spend the summer with me.

The same roof sheltered mother and daughter at that hour, but, to judge by the total lack of communication, they might have been at the far ends of the earth. Mme de Sévigné had learned of her daughter's plans to go to Provence only when the latter revealed the news to others in her mother's presence ("I *hear* you say that you are leaving," Mme de Sévigné had written in the letter printed above). "I can tell you nothing about the length of my daughter's sojourn here," Mme de Sévigné wrote in plaintive tones to the Count de Guitaut on April 28: "The letters she receives from Provence are kept so secret from me that I know nothing of their plans."

Eventually—by the end of May—Mme de Sévigné would seek to enlist the support of the Count de Grignan in the contest of wills in which she was engaged with her daughter:

I want to report to you on a two-hour consultation with Mons. Fagon, a very celebrated physician.* It is Monsieur de La Garde† who brought him here; we had never seen him before. He is highly intelligent and skilled in his science. He speaks with an astonishing amount of knowledge and authority ... Unlike most other doctors who prescribe a thousand remedies, his only prescription is good nutrition. He finds my daughter exceedingly thin and frail. He would, above all, like to see her drink milk but, as strong as is her aversion, he would not insist. Instead, he prescribes demi-baths and nourishing bouillons ... When she told him that her weight loss was insignificant—that having once been plump, one then becomes thin—he told her that she deludes herself, that her loss of weight was the result of the dryness of her lungs which had begun to wither, and that she could not go on as she is, that she must take steps to recover her health or her loss of weight would become serious; that her languor, her lassitude, her loss of voice, were proof that her illness came from her lungs; that he prescribed peace and quiet, rest, a gentle regimen—with, above all, no writing!—that he

*Guy Fagon was "an excellent physician and fine practitioner," according to the *Mémoires* of the Duke de Saint-Simon. In 1680, he became the physician of the Queen and the Dauphin; in 1681, of the King himself.

†The Marquis de La Garde was the Count de Grignan's cousin and trusted adviser.

hoped that, on this regimen, she would recover, but that if she failed to take such steps, she would go from bad to worse. Mons. de La Garde was witness to all this; send him my letter, if you like.*

I asked Mons. Fagon if rarefied air was bad for her; he said it was very bad, indeed. I told him that it was my hope to keep her here during the hot weather, so that she would not leave until autumn, and then go for the winter to Aix, where the air is good; that you wanted only what was best for her health, and that it was with her alone we had to contend to prevent her leaving at once. That is how we left it. Mons. de La Garde was witness to it all. I felt that it behooved me to report to you on what had happened, making it clear to you that my desire to keep her here longer—greatest pleasure of my life though that might be!—is not, however, what brings me to take up this subject with you, again—but, rather, I felt that you would have reason to complain had I allowed you to go on thinking that her ailments are no more serious than they were thought to be. It is all the more serious because it has been going on for over a year; it is the duration of the condition which causes concern. You will tell me that I should keep her here. To which I reply that I have no influence over her, that it is only you or Mons. de La Garde who could resolve her doubts. Should her peace of mind not result from that, there is no hope and, without hope, it would be better for her to go ahead and risk her life. She feels a strong and proper attachment to you and to her marital responsibilities. Unless she can find—in the thought of pleasing you—the same tranquillity she would find in going to join you, her staying on here would do her more harm than good. And so, Monsieur, it is you who are the sole master of the life and the health of a being entirely devoted to you ... I embrace you with all my heart.

I am not surprised that you are unaware of the state she is in; it is her whim always to say that she is feeling fine. Would to God that were true and that she was with you, now! That the opposite is true will be attested to by the Abbé de Grignan† and Mons. de La Garde, as by all those who see and take any interest in her.

For once, the Countess de Grignan speaks for herself: of the few letters of hers which are extant, two date from the spring or early summer of 1678,

---

*In view of the repeated references to the Marquis de La Garde as witness in substantiation of the accuracy of her statements, one can only conclude that Mme de Sévigné's objectivity as regarded her daughter was sometimes questioned.

†Louis de Grignan, the Abbé, was the youngest brother of the Count; he became Bishop of Évreux in 1680; Bishop of Carcassonne in 1681.

both to her husband: the first, for the most part, running to trivialities, mundanities; the second (written probably in May subsequent to the signature of the peace treaty with England), sounding a note of desperation:

So, here I am in this place [Livry] which recalls so many happy days spent together ... as well as those grim ones you suffered with colic. Those, in truth, I would not wish to relive, but I would the others, and wish that by some magic formula, we could have you here with us this summer to breathe this sweetest, best air in the world. There is talk of peace and truces but, since there is still uncertainty, and since—even if it proves true—I do not know whether you would prefer coming back here for the summer to spending the summer and fall at Grignan, I think of nothing but going to join you, and have made arrangements with La Garde to be there by the end of June. I will be very happy, my dear Count, when I have the pleasure of being reunited with you— never again to part! I want you to know that I am firmly resolved and will stand by the resolution, and I beg you to declare your own, so that we may stand together on this point, so essential and so beneficial to the peace of our lives ...

You gave me much pleasure by telling me that you could see a difference in Mons. de Louvois's letters to you.* I would consider myself fortunate if I contributed to the improvement in his attitude. It amused him to say that I had charmed but not persuaded him, but I see by the results that I succeeded, instead, in persuading him, which is of far more benefit to us. My very dear Count, I heartily approve your determination to make your regiment† one of the best; its standards must be maintained. We have a little Colonel to put at its head; it would be a shame to lose that post. As for me, I am convinced that he will be luckier than we are, and that while we seem unable to attain—even to hope for—personal gratification, we will obtain it for that little son of ours. I wish he were already old enough to be appointed as your successor.‡ I have a feeling that he will be. In the meanwhile, your service will further assure it; thus, the recompense will be all the more certain ... I am fairly well pleased with the way your establishment is running ... It is true that your household has never been better regulated. Express your satisfaction to the staff and let them know you

---

*The Marquis de Louvois, son of Le Tellier, whom he succeeded as Secretary of State and of War.

†The Regiment of Provençal Infantry, formed in 1674, of which the Count de Grignan was Colonel.

‡Appointment of a minor child to succeed to his father's post at the time of his father's death was common practice in Old Régime France.

hope it will continue. Do not raise Anfossy's stipend* ... I am well pleased with that young man ... I have written Bonrepaus about the reparations at the [Governor's] Palace [at Aix] ... Under the circumstances, I will not bring you a maître d'hôtel. You seem satisfied with the way things are going; that suffices. You are so discriminating that I can trust your taste ... I sent you a suit ... There is a Venetian satin vest which I think will please you. If, in addition, you want a Chinese silk camisole, I will bring it to you, but let me know in your reply to this letter. I hope, before my departure, to be able to give you definite news of peace ... Your little girls are very happy here; I warn them they cannot expect such beautiful gardens at Grignan. We are determined, the Abbé de Coulanges and I, to add rooms here to accommodate your family which is large and for whom we are hard pressed to find place ... Finally, my Count, hurry and give me your orders, for I am waiting here—it might be said—with one foot in the stirrup! ... I embrace you with all my heart, my very dear Count. I am all yours, and love you with the greatest tenderness imaginable. I beg you to believe me on that score and to continue to say that you have a very pretty person devoted utterly to you. I wish I could be as sure of the "pretty" part as I am of the devotion! You have not gone to see my daughter;† you owe her some attention. I long to see her, the poor little thing—and Paulinotte and my son and all our little household of whom I think so fondly. My Mother and your daughters and the Bien Bon send you a thousand greetings and assure you—that is to say, your daughters assure you—of their respect. I leave you to go walk among the nightingales, who call to me and whose song would delight you. Oh, my God, will there never come a year when I can go to join my husband without having to desert my Mother? How I wish it would! But if I must choose between you, I will not hesitate to follow my very dear Count whom I love and embrace with all my heart ...

She had no choice but to choose between them, that summer of 1678. The fact that she did not follow her husband, as she had so vehemently declared she would, suggests that her mother exerted extraordinary powers of persuasion. Having won the support of Dr. Fagon and the Marquis de La Garde, Mme de Sévigné managed to prevail upon Mme de Grignan to remain in the Île de France for rest and recuperation from the ailments she had suffered during the winter.

*Anfossy was the Count's secretary.
†Marie-Blanche, the eldest Grignan child, who had been left at the Visitandine Convent at Aix.

There is evidence that Mme de Grignan's Paris sojourn was not a rest cure, in the strict sense of the word: the Countess, in another letter to her husband, refers to "the fast-paced life," the "long, busy days" she was putting in in the capital: the sermon-going, the round of visits to friends and relatives and government ministries (in pursuance of Provençal political objectives), the nightly games of chance at high stakes (*"bassette, the rage of the season"*).

A letter from a Mme de Senneville, a correspondent of the Count de Bussy's, indicates clearly that Mme de Grignan did not live as a recluse: the letter, which appears in Bussy's published *Letters*, is dated April 25, 1678, and reads:

> *I cannot close my letter without telling you that your beautiful de Grignan cousin appeared recently at [the Church of] Saint Antoine, glittering from head to foot in gold and silver—in open defiance of the strictly enforced sumptuary regulations, bringing down upon her head—to everyone's astonishment and her own great embarrassment—a reprimand and a warning from the Commissioner. It was imprudent of Mme de Grignan to expose herself to such an affront, nor do I under- stand why the Commissioner confined himself to a warning and did not impose a fine. That woman has wit, but wit of a bitter kind, and her pride is insufferable. She will make herself as many enemies as her mother has friends and admirers.*

Had Mme de Sévigné exaggerated the seriousness of her daughter's physical condition? In the opinion of the Count de Bussy, the Countess de Grignan's ailments were imaginary: "I think the *belle Madelonne*'s prob- lems all originate in her head," he had made so bold as to write her mother, early in the year: "As long as she was the prettiest girl in France, she was the healthiest . . . If she really wanted to get well, she would not resist the advice of men skilled in such matters." Mlle de Scudéry, the popular, prolific and prolix novelist, seemed to agree with Bussy that his cousin's problems were psychosomatic, writing, "I met Mme de Sévigné, the other day, and she is, in truth, still beautiful. They say that Mme de Grignan no longer is, and that the loss of her beauty causes her such distress that she may die of it."

If Mme de Sévigné's campaign to hold Mme de Grignan in Paris seemed to absorb all of her thought and energy that year of 1678, other events could not but have had strong impact on her life and emotions.

Admittedly "obsessed" with her daughter, Mme de Sévigné often tends in her *Letters* to neglect her son. After a long absence from the scene, Charles suddenly reappears in the summer of 1678 in the role of hero: according to the August 30 issue of the *Gazette*, "The Marquis de Sévigné, sub-lieutenant of Monsieur the Dauphin's Gendarmes Regiment, was exposed for more than two hours to heavy enemy fire. He held firm throughout, although forty men under his command were lost." "Where is your son, my cousin?" Mme de Sévigné had inquired by letter of the Count de Bussy on August 23: "As for mine—having escaped death ten or twelves times near Mons—he should live forever!" The engagement near Mons was the last of the 1678 campaign, taking place on the very eve of a truce between Louis XIV and William of Orange: "The King has chosen to restore peace to the Christian world, this year, instead of taking over the rest of Flanders—which he will leave for another time," as Mme de Sévigné reported airily in another letter to Bussy.

The sudden death of the Abbé d'Hacqueville (Mme de Sévigné's dear friend and confidant and right-hand man) on the last day of July, 1678, after a brief seven days' illness, must have cost her many tears: a grievous loss, that of a man so dedicated to the service of his friends, so indefatigable in that service that Mme de Sévigné referred to him in the plural, as "*les d'Hacqueville*"—the implication being that one man alone could not have encompassed such efforts, such feats in behalf of those to whom he was committed in friendship. It was to d'Hacqueville that she confided her problems with her daughter, to him she turned for sympathy and for counsel, for representation at Court, for assistance in arranging the lease on the Carnavalet—for every- and anything! With Mme de Grignan in Paris at the hour of his death—on hand to stanch her mother's tears—poor d'Hacqueville was cheated of his memorial (the elegiac letter bemoaning his loss which Mme de Sévigné would otherwise have penned to her daughter). To neither the Count de Bussy nor the Count de Guitaut, with whom Mme de Sévigné was in correspondence that summer, did she mention her friend's demise. News of it comes, instead, from another correspondent of Bussy's, in a letter from François Roger de Gaignières, dated August 5, which appears in Bussy's published *Letters*.

The year 1678 may not be memorable, historically, as the year of the Abbé d'Hacqueville's death, but it is memorable, literarily, as the year of publication of what might be called the first French novel in the modern sense of the word—Mme de La Fayette's *La Princesse de Clèves*, the only seventeenth-century French novel to withstand the test of time; the forerunner, so to speak, of all important French psychological novels—from those of the Abbé Prévost to those of Marcel Proust.

"It is a small volume off the press of Barbin, two days ago," Mme de Sévigné wrote enthusiastically to Bussy, "which seems to me one of the most charming things I have ever read. I imagine our Canoness [the Canoness of Remiremont, another of Bussy's daughters] will send it to you shortly. I will ask your opinion of it when you and our dear widow have had time to read it ..." Mlle de Scudéry—fearful, perhaps, for her own laurels as première novelist of the decade—somewhat wryly notified Bussy of the publication, erroneously citing the Duke de La Rochefoucauld as a co-author: "Monsieur de La Rochefoucauld and Mme de La Fayette have collaborated on a novel dealing with a romance at the Court of Henri II. They are at an age [the Duke, sixty-five; the Countess, nineteen years his junior] when to collaborate would seem to be the only thing they could do together."

Bussy's hostility toward the Duke, whom he believed to be a co-author, may have affected his literary judgment; he gave credit, grudgingly, to the first volume; the second he characterized as "contrived," "improbable." Mme de Sévigné, perhaps unwilling to point to herself as the model for the heroine, perhaps reluctant to rise to the defense of the skills of her bosom friend; perhaps for a variety of reasons, chose to pretend to agree with Bussy: "I agree with what you said about *La Princesse de Clèves*. Your critique and mine were formed in the same mold." To which Bussy gallantly replied, "You could not be more pleased than I, Madame, to discover that we think alike. I consider myself highly honored. Our criticism of *La Princesse de Clèves* is that of people of quality endowed with wit."

Her correspondence with her daughter in abeyance in 1678, Mme de Sévigné more sedulously maintained that with the Count de Bussy:

Are you at Chaseu, my cousin?—that pleasant spot! The countryside, there, lingers on in my mind's eye, and I will keep it there as I do the pleasant Father and pleasant Daughter, who have their place in my heart. That makes a lot of "pleasants," but that is part of that negligence of mine which I seem unable to correct. I hope that if my letters merit rereading, there will be some person charitable enough to correct such failings.*

Bussy promptly protested—as she may have expected him to do—that, on her part, "negligence" was a virtue rather than a failing: "Your way of

*Mme de Sévigné was aware of the fact that Bussy planned to publish his correspondence.

writing—free and easy—pleases me far more than the formality of the gentlemen of the Academy. Yours is the style of a woman of quality who is blessed with wit, who can carry off frivolities and enliven serious subjects."

"The Court is at Saint-Cloud," Mme de Sévigné advised Bussy in October:

The King wants to go Saturday to Versailles, but it appears God is not willing, because it is impossible to put the buildings in shape to receive him. This is a result of the prodigious mortality rate among the work-men—cartloads of corpses carried off nightly from Versailles, as from the Charity Hospitals. This grim transport is being concealed in order not to frighten off the work force, in order not to decry the air of that "Favorite without merit," as Versailles is described in the bon mot, *as you may know.*

No, Bussy said,

I did not know that Versailles was known as "the Favorite without merit," but nothing could be truer or better said. Kings can—upon the outlay of vast sums of money—give the earth a shape and form other than its natural one, but it is not in their power to change the quality of water or the air. It would be a strange misfortune if, after the outlay of thirty millions at Versailles,* it should prove uninhabitable.

In October, Mme de Sévigné wrote to Bussy, from Paris, to tell him "We have returned from Livry sooner than expected because one of the Mesdemoiselles de Grignan ran a fever. We have reaccustomed ourselves gradually to this fair city, but we almost wept when we had to leave our forest ... The good Corbinelli has a cold and is confined to his room ... The health of my daughter—for which we earlier had hope of improvement—is failing again; that is to say, it is extremely delicate." By late December, just before the New Year, winter weather had set in, and Mme de Grignan suffered:

That poor beautiful Madelonne feels the bitter cold so terribly that she has asked me to make her excuses and to send her fond greetings to you and to Mme de Coligny. Her chest, her ink, her pen, her thoughts—

---

*From the seventeenth century on, there has been conjecture as to the amount of money poured into the construction of Versailles.

all are frozen! All except—let it be said—her heart! I can say as much for mine, my dear children. When I want to think of something pleasant, I think of you two . . .

XXXIII

With the New Year of 1679, the Countess de Grignan was happily reunited with her husband and their eight-year-old son, the little Marquis de Grignan. Once peace with Holland had been signed, once the Assembly of the Communities of Provence had risen from its final session, the Count de Grignan found himself free to leave the province under his command and head for Paris—and his wife—as he did in late December.

With his arrival (and that of his son and their entourage), even the spacious, three-story Hôtel Carnavalet was filled to capacity: in residence there were Mme de Sévigné, Charles de Sévigné, the Abbé de Coulanges, the Count and Countess de Grignan, "the Grignettes" and Mlle Montgobert, the little Marquis—and all the domestic staff in attendance on their households: maîtres d'hôtel, chefs and sous-chefs, valets, lackeys, maids, tutors, equerries, secretaries, coachmen, outriders, stable-boys.

"Poor Madelonne is still languishing," Mme de Sévigné sighed, writing to Bussy on February 27: "Her ill health constitutes the greatest sorrow of my life." The severity of the winter weather she deplored primarily as a threat to Mme de Grignan's delicate chest: "We have had unbearably heavy snow and ice," her letter continued: "Only within the last few days have the cobblestones of the street become visible again—a sight as welcome to us as was the olive branch that signalled the waters receding from the earth." She could not close her letter without giving her cousin the latest news bulletin from Pignerol: "Have you heard about the relaxation of the prison regulations in the case of Messieurs de Lauzun and Fouquet? Permission to mingle with the personnel of the Citadel and to see each other, to eat and talk together may be one of the greatest joys they can expect."*

---

*Released at last from solitary confinement in Pignerol, the two victims of royal displeasure did not long enjoy the privilege of each other's company: when Fouquet's wife and daughter received permission to join him, Lauzun promptly attempted to seduce the daughter—to Fouquet's indignation.

Were it not for Mme de Sévigné's correspondence with the Count de Bussy and the Count de Guitaut—sporadic as it was, in both instances—little would be known about her life and that of the Grignans during the first six months of 1679. After almost three months' silence, Mme de Sévigné addressed her cousin on May 29:

We have been here at Livry for the past ten days enjoying the most beautiful weather in the world. My daughter has been fairly well. She has just left with numerous Grignans. I will follow her [back to Paris] tomorrow. I surely wish that she would stay with me all summer. I think her health demands it, too, but she has an austere way of reasoning which makes her put her duty above her life. We stopped her from leaving, last year, but since she is in better health, this year, I fear that she will slip away from us.

Although Mme de Sévigné may here appear reconciled to the thought of her daughter's departure, actually she had not yet abandoned hope of holding her longer in Paris, as she reveals in this letter to the Count de Guitaut, dated "Paris, June 1":

My daughter begins to talk of nothing but going to Époisses en route to Grignan, but since her health is not yet good enough to consider so strenuous a journey, and since the Court is here, I am hoping that Monsieur de Grignan—with no urgent business to attend to in Provence, and loving his wife as dearly as he does—will not rush their departure.

"They had wanted to leave in two weeks," she wrote to Guitaut in another letter that month, "but I have just stopped them by telling them that we will all be leaving on the sixteenth of August—they, for Provence; I, for Brittany—and that it would be unfair of them to leave ahead of me when so short a time is in question. Thus, we will spend the summer together: '*chi ha tempo ha vita.*'" (Another of Mme de Sévigné's Italian quotations: "Who has time, has life"—with time, that is to say, things may change.)

She was justified in her optimism: "*La belle Madelonne* will not leave until the month of September," she could write jubilantly to Bussy on June 27. When she wrote, she asked his pardon for her delay in replying to his letter of June 12 in which he had reproved her for her long delay in replying to his preceding letter:

I cannot find a word to say in reply to your strictures, except to say that Livry is my favorite place for letter-writing. I am at peace, there—body and soul, and when I have a letter to answer, I put it off until my next visit. But that is a bad habit, and causes delays of which I want to correct myself. I always say that if I could only live to be two hundred, I would become the most exemplary person in the world! I am pretty good at self-improvement, and find that as I grow older, I am even better at it. I know that the charms of youth may expect a leniency which is denied, once youth is over. After that, no allowances are made . . .

Most of that summer of 1679 Mme de Sévigné and the Grignans spent in the green glades and gardens of their beloved Livry, whence Mme de Sévigné wrote, one halcyon summer day, to Mme de Grignan, who was in Paris:

Everything has been raked, everything has been trimmed and pruned, everything is clean; everything awaits your arrival! Here is your carriage, drawn by my horses! Everything I possess is at your disposal; take charge, make your plans, give your commands, for—loving you as I do—it is my fancy to do your will in preference to my own, to carry out your plans rather than mine.

Your son is merry, and eats like a little demon in this forest air. The Bien Bon *embraces you.*

On the surface, things were deceptively smooth; below, the waters were roiling. "How amusing it would be," to use a favorite metaphor of Mme de Sévigné's, "to be able to see the underside of the cards!" Another letter of Mme de Sévigné's written to Mme de Grignan during that same summer gives us the rare opportunity of seeing the face of the cards usually so carefully concealed by the players in the game under way at the Carnavalet:

You who know, my darling, how my imagination runs away with me, should have spared me the ugly phantasmagoria evoked by the last words you spoke to me. If I do not love you, if I am not happy to be with you, if I prefer being at Livry to being with you, then, I must confess, my darling, that I am the most astonished person in the world to hear it! I did my best to forget your reproaches, and had little difficulty in finding them unjust. Stay on in Paris, and you will see whether I do not come running back even more joyously than I came

*here. I tried to console myself for leaving you by thinking of all you
had to do in places where I would not be. You know that you have
little time to miss me,* but that is not the case as far as I am concerned.
You know that I love to look at you, want never to be far from your
side as long as you are with me, here, where the months seem so long
to you. So they would seem to me, too, if I felt always as I feel now...*

There are other letters of Mme de Sévigné's, written that summer,
which reveal the same symptoms of acute incompatibility evidenced in the
reunion of the previous year: the same dire symptoms of mistrust and
misunderstanding, of recrimination and resentment, of contention and
contrition were present again in 1679. With these developments, there came
the realization (at least on the part of Mme de Grignan) that they were
impaled on the horns of a dilemma—unable (at least on the part of Mme de
Sévigné) to live apart, unable to live together.

"I slept poorly. I was crushed by your words, last night," Mme de
Sévigné wrote dolefully one morning of that tormented summer, as this
undated letter shows:

*I could not bear the injustice you did me. I, more than any other,
recognize the admirable qualities God has given you. I admire your
courage and your conduct. I am convinced that, basically, you care for
me. All these are well-established facts—especially among my friends.
I would be very annoyed if—loving you as I do—you did not respond
with love. What is it, then? Just this: that it is I who am guilty of all the
failings of which you accused yourself, last night, and that, as chance
would have it, I complained to the Chevalier [de Grignan] that you
were sometimes intolerant of my shortcomings, to the point that I was
sometimes afflicted and humiliated. You also accuse me of talking to
persons to whom I never breathe a word of these intimate family
affairs.† On that score, you do me a crying injustice. You are carried
away by your prejudices. When they are that strong, truth and reason
suffer. I spoke about this to no one but the Chevalier. He seemed to
agree with much of what I had to say, but when I see that . . . you
accuse me of finding my daughter to be a mass of imperfections, full of
faults—all those things you said to me, last night—whereas that is*

---

*The Grignans had gone to pay their court to the monarch at Saint-Germain.

†Other letters in the *Correspondence* make clear that the persons whom Mme de Grignan mistrusted—
to whom, in her opinion, her mother talked indiscreetly about "intimate family affairs"—were the
Countess de La Fayette and Corbinelli.

positively not what I said nor what I thought—to the contrary, the thing of which I complain is that you are overly critical of my faults, why, then, I ask: what has brought about this change? And I feel the injustice of it all, and I cannot sleep. But, this morning, I feel quite well, and will now drink my coffee, if you don't mind.

Mme de Sévigné's pillow might nightly be soaked with tears, but the dawn would see her waiting eagerly at her daughter's door. She never gave up hope that the next day—the next week, the next month—things would go better between them; that Mme de Grignan's health would improve and, with it, her disposition, her mood, above all, her attitude toward her mother. ("My darling," Mme de Sévigné wrote pleadingly, "if only in the future, you would treat me as you would a friend, our relations would be wonderful! But if your nature which, as you say, is inclined to be uncommunicative, still prevents you from giving me that pleasure, I will love you none the less.")

"I must allow myself, once and for all, my darling, to tell you how I feel about you," she wrote her daughter on another wakeful night, that year of 1679:

I do not have the wit to say it to you; face to face, I become nervous and clumsy. So, take this letter from my hand, instead. I shall not touch upon the infinite tenderness I feel for you; it is prodigious. I cannot tell how you are affected by what you call the contrariety of our temperaments; that contrariety must be less pronounced as concerns our sentiments toward one another. Either that, or there is something very strange about me, since my attachment to you is undiminished. It would seem that I want to overcome these obstacles, and that that increases my devotion rather than lessens it. To sum it up, then, it seems impossible to me for anyone to love more perfectly. I assure you, my darling, that I think only of you—or of things having to do with you—saying nothing, doing nothing except what I think might be beneficial to you.

"Yesterday, you said, most cruelly, my darling," that letter of lament continued, "that I would be only too well pleased to get away from you, that you caused me a thousand heartaches and constant frustration!"

My heart winces with pain, I burst into tears at the very thought of your words. My dearest, you cannot know how I feel about you if you do not know that all the heartaches in the world that may be caused

me by my excessive love for you are sweeter to me than all the plea-
sures of the world apart from you. It is true that I am sometimes hurt
by being kept in total ignorance of your sentiments, by being excluded
from the circle of your confidence. I know your friends are treated
otherwise. But, after all, I tell myself that that is my misfortune, that
that is the way you are, that people do not change. But, even more
important, my love, remember the vulnerability of true love; by which
I mean that it requires only the sight of you, only one kind word from
you, only one warm smile, only one fond gesture to win me back and
make me forget all that has gone before. Thus, my darling, feeling a
thousand times more pleasure than pain ... imagine how I suffer to
think that you could think that I could possibly be happy without you.
You could never believe that if you knew the infinite tenderness of my
love for you ... Any other emotion is transitory, lasts no longer than a
moment; basically, my heart is as I have described it to you. How do
you think I would adjust to an absence which relieves me of minor
heartaches of which I am no longer even conscious while depriving me
of a creature whose presence, whose least expression of affection
constitutes my life and my only pleasure? Add to this my anxiety about
your health, and you would not be cruel enough to do me so grave an
injustice. As for your departure, give it thought, my darling, but do not
hasten it. The final decision is in your hands.

My poor darling, this is an awful letter. I have indulged myself in
the pleasure of talking to you and telling you how I feel about you. I
could go on talking until tomorrow! I want no reply. God forbid! That
is not my purpose. All I want you to do is to embrace me and to ask
my pardon—pardon for having ever thought that I could find solace in
your absence.

Mme de Sévigné was to suffer two grievous losses by the end of the
summer: one would come with the Grignans' departure for Provence; the
other, with the death of her dear friend and relative—that highly controversial prelate, the Cardinal de Retz. "Alas, my poor Monsieur," she addressed
the Count de Guitaut on August 25,

what news you are about to hear! What sorrow I have to bear! Monsei-
gneur the Cardinal de Retz died yesterday, after a seven days' fever ...
My daughter is affected, as well she might be. I cannot bear to speak
about her departure. It seems to me that everyone is deserting me, and
that the very worst thing which can happen to me—which is her

absence—will soon strike me down. Monsieur and Madame, do you not feel pity for me? These two blows have prevented me from being properly grateful for the recovery of our good Abbé who has returned to us from death's door.

"We had been friends for thirty years," she wrote of the Cardinal in a letter to Bussy, that same day, "in the course of which he gave me unfailing proof of the tenderness of his affection . . . I am touched to the bottom of my heart . . . Our good Abbé de Coulanges almost died. The remedy of an English doctor resuscitated him. It was not God's will that the Cardinal de Retz should take that remedy, although he repeatedly asked that it be given him. The hour of his death was decreed, and nothing can change that." (Year by year, more and more, Mme de Sévigné was coming to regard Providence as a doctrine, as the explanation of the enigma of life on this earth; was coming to see it and accept it—in resignation—as the will of an almighty Jansenist God dispensing justice and working out an order beyond the comprehension of the human mind.)

The Cardinal had died on August 24; the Grignans left Paris on September 13. The fourth period of separation had begun; the pangs of separation, on Mme de Sévigné's side, no less acute than at the first, in 1671. If Mme de Grignan, on her way home to the Château de Grignan with her gallant husband and little son, breathed a sigh of relief at leaving Paris and her mother, her mother felt herself totally bereft (left all alone, in Paris, with only her son, her uncle, her cousins and a wide circle of friends to keep her company!).

No matter how strained their relations when she and her daughter were together, to be apart was utter agony—at least, for Mme de Sévigné. With so much good will, with so much love on both sides, she reasoned, they could surely—the next time, if not this!—work out their problems, minimize their contrariety, compose their incompatibility. The next time! Thought of their next reunion could be her only solace at their parting: before the month of September was out, she would write to urge the Grignans to approve the renewal of the Hôtel Carnavalet lease.

After a well-nigh two years' interruption, the correspondence recommenced. Facing what was apparently no permanent separation, Mme de Sévigné was nonetheless racked with grief, a grief that may seem, to some, as excessive, as abnormal as her maternal passion. Grief welled up in her heart and overflowed her letters, as in this one written the very night of her daughter's departure (addressed to Auxerre where the Grignans were to disembark from the boat on which they had sailed from Paris, up the Seine):

How to tell you, my darling, how I have suffered? How to put into words the anguish of such a parting? I do not know, myself, how I bore it . . . I stood watching your boat move away, recede into the distance, thinking of what precious freight it carried away from me, of how many days would pass before I saw again that person and that family I so love and honor, for its own sake as well as yours. Once your boat was out of sight, I turned for comfort to my philosopher-friend, Corbinelli, who too well knows the human heart not to respect my sorrow. He allowed it to express itself and, like a good friend, made no foolish attempt to silence me. I went to Mass at Nôtre Dame and, then, back home to that hôtel, the very sight of which—with its rooms, its garden— caused me anguish such as you may not understand because you are strong, but which is a torment to the weak, such as me . . . All in all, my dearest, I do not know how I will accustom myself to the solitude of this house, to being in it without you. I am so full of you that I can bear looking at no one else, at nothing else. I can only hope that, in time, I will again be able to pick up the threads of normal social intercourse . . .

On September 15, the threnody continued:

And so, here we are again up to our ears in letter-writing! At least, I need not reproach myself for not having enjoyed to the hilt the pleasure of your company. I need not rue having missed a single moment I could be with you, or having mismanaged those precious hours. Life seemed to pass in a flash, so fast I could not fully savor it . . . It is your absence which brings me to the realization of how long life is, of how the days drag by . . .

Mme de Sévigné could not make the adjustment to life without her daughter because she refused to face the fact that her daughter's place was with her husband, and that his place was in the province under his governance, his natal province of Provence, the site of the Grignan domains.* Instead, Mme de Sévigné pinned her hopes on the Grignans' return to Paris, on the Count's appointment to a position of prominence in the royal Court. Did not all their friends and relatives with Court connections—the Duke de

---

*The departure of her daughter, Mme de Sévigné now concluded, had been the doing of her son-in-law: "Since you sought to read and interpret Mons. de Grignan's wishes—as in olden times they did the entrails of their victims—and saw that he wished you to go with him—shrugging aside all concern for your health—it was inevitable that you should have gone, as you did."

La Rochefoucauld, the Countess de La Fayette, Mme de Coulanges, the Marquis de Pomponne—all promise to exert their influence to that purpose, to use their good offices in behalf of the Grignans? So they are quoted, time and time and time again, by Mme de Sévigné in her letters.

Five days after their parting, Mme de Sévigné was already beginning to idealize the reunion which had been anything but ideal:

> I remember nothing about you that is not delightful because, when it comes to you, my heart is attuned in such a way that it takes only one word of explanation, one caress, one touch of your hand to disarm me and heal my wounds—as if by miracle ... I have often told you this, and now I repeat it; it is the truth. I am convinced that you do not mean to take advantage of it, yet it is certain that it is you—and you alone—who, in one way or another, work havoc in my soul ...
>
> Would to God, my daughter, that you were back in the Hôtel Carnavalet, not for a week, not to do penance there, but so that I could embrace you and show you clearly that I cannot be happy without you, and that whatever distress my love for you may have caused me, I still prefer it to being bored in the doldrums of a life without you. If only you had opened your heart to me a little more, you would not have been so unjust: for example, was it not cruel to have accused certain people of trying to make me love you less, and to say harsh things to me on that score? And how was I to divine the cause of your displeasure? You claimed that it was well founded, but it was all in your imagination, my daughter. Whereupon your conduct was such as to have effected the very thing you accused them of trying to do—as if such a thing were possible! ... And when you saw that my love for you was unwavering, why did you continue in your unjust thought? Why did you not try instead to show me that you loved me? It was difficult for me not to answer your charges; I deserve praise for my self-control, but I remember two or three evenings when you said things that were incomprehensible to me, at the time. Never again allow yourself to do me such injustice. Speak out, explain yourself; it is impossible to guess your thoughts.

On September 20, a week after Mme de Grignan's departure, the first batch of her letters reached her mother and were promptly acknowledged from the latter's desk at Livry:

> I have received, my very dear one, your daily letters written along the way, including the last one from Auxerre ... Never tell me again that I

have no reason to miss you. Do you not know that I have every reason in the world? ... Never doubt, my dear, that my love—which you call your "treasure"—could ever be lacking to you. Would to God you could be equally sure of keeping all the other things you call your own!

The closing paragraph was addressed to her son-in-law and to his two eldest daughters, the "Grignettes":

My dear Count, if you will only safeguard that delicate health [her daughter's], I will be more grateful to you than for anything you could possibly do for me! Mesdemoiselles, you are often in my thoughts. I call out to you—to one of you, in the garden; to the other, on the swing. There is no reply. You play a part in my sadness. My dear little Marquis, do not forget your Grandmother.

"I think of you constantly," she wrote her daughter from Livry on September 22, "and since I have few distractions, that makes a lot of thinking."

My thoughts are many. I am alone here. Corbinelli is in Paris ... My mornings will be solitary. I still have the feeling, my daughter, that I will not be able to go on living without you ... Separation is a strange thing. I feel it, my dear, far more than you, who have so little leisure, and I already feel—all too keenly—a terrible longing for you, the full sorrow of a year apart. It all seems more than I can bear. I spend every morning in that garden you know so well. I search for you every-where—and feel a stab of pain in all the places where I have seen you.
 Your dear letters are my only consolation. I reread them often. And here is what I do: I no longer remember what seemed signs of your estrangement or indifference. I tell myself they could not have emanated from you. Instead, I take your every loving word—whether written or spoken—as the true expression of your heart toward me ...

XXXIV

Fate had still another blow in store for Mme de Sévigné in the autumn of 1679. Surely she pondered the ways of Providence at news of the Marquis de Pomponne's precipitous fall from grace: occupying a seat of power, serving Louis XIV as Minister of Foreign Affairs on November 17; summarily dismissed from office on the eighteenth, denied so much as a word of explanation from the monarch.

"My darling, I am going to astonish and dismay you," Mme de Sévigné wrote to Mme de Grignan on Wednesday, November 22:

> *Monsieur de Pomponne has been disgraced! He was given orders on Saturday night, as he was returning to Saint-Germain from Pomponne, to resign his post . . . He wrote to the King to express his deep sorrow and to declare that he had no idea what he had done to bring on his disgrace . . .*

Mme de Sévigné, having spent that weekend at Pomponne, was still in a state of shock when she broke the news to the Count de Guitaut: "We saw him leave that house as a Cabinet Minister; he returned to Paris the same night, stripped of all his offices, a simple private citizen!"

"I went to their house toward evening," Mme de Sévigné wrote her daughter from Paris on November 22:

> *They were not receiving, but I went in, and found the three of them [M. de Pomponne, his wife and his sister-in-law, Mme de Vins]. Mons. de Pomponne embraced me without being able to speak a word. The ladies could not restrain their tears; nor I, mine . . . It was a sad spectacle. How different the circumstances from those in which I had seen them the previous Friday at Pomponne! . . . Poor Mme de Vins, whom I had left so radiant, was scarcely recognizable—scarcely recognizable, I tell you! A two weeks' fever could not have wrought such a change! . . . We spoke of the dire consequences of such a disgrace. They are dreadful . . . Oh, God! what a change in their lives! What retrenchments! What economization for that household! . . .*

How to account for the thunderbolt of royal displeasure which had struck him? Mme de Sévigné heard and reported numerous versions: "It is said that he went too often to Pomponne"; "It is said that he was somewhat lax in the performance of his duties, that he kept couriers waiting . . ." The courier he should not have kept waiting was the one who arrived from Bavaria on November 17, and who was impatiently awaited by the King because he was bringing news of the outcome of the diplomatic negotiations then under way to arrange the marriage contract of a Bavarian princess with the Dauphin, the heir to the French throne.*

"I simply cannot accustom myself to the downfall of this minister!" Mme de Sévigné exclaimed. What distressed her so greatly in this close friend's fall from favor was that her son-in-law had lost a champion at Court. "It is another of my sorrows," she wrote the Grignans,

> to be entirely useless to you in the future. It is true that it was through Mme des Vins that I was most effective, but we managed very well between us. But, after all, my darling, that is how things go, that is the way of the world. Mons. de Pomponne is better able than most to sustain his misfortune with courage, with resignation and Christian philosophy.

"In the last analysis," she wrote in another letter to her daughter, "one must always come back to Providence, a doctrine of which Pomponne is a disciple . . . How to face life without that divine doctrine? Without it, one would be tempted to hang oneself twenty times a day. Even with it, one must struggle against the impulse!"

A man who lost favor in seventeenth-century France was a man who lost his friends. Mme de Sévigné was atypical in the steadfastness of her friendship: she stood by Bussy and by Fouquet although they had incurred the royal displeasure. "Misfortune shall not make me shun their house," she wrote of the Pomponnes to Guitaut: "I have been a friend of Mons. de Pomponne's for thirty years, and pledge my loyalty to him to the end of my life, in times of misfortune even more than in times when fortune smiled."

As resilient as her spirit usually was, Mme de Sévigné could not quite shake off a cloud of depression hanging over her, that autumn. Once a genuinely social creature, happiest in the midst of the social swim, she came

---

*Mme de Sévigné prided herself on the accuracy of any news she relayed to the Grignans. In this instance, the hearsay is substantiated by Louis XIV's own words. In his *Reflections on the Métier of King*, Louis XIV made reference to Pomponne's "weaknesses" in the Cabinet post, his "stubbornness" and "lack of application."

more and more, that year of 1679, to seek out solitude: "How I wish I could see you, my dear child, and spend the evenings with you," she wrote in November: "I come home sadly to this big house, sometimes between nine and midnight. I have no more company here than I do at Livry, but I prefer the restful silence there to all the soirées to which I am invited, here. I simply could not run around at night."

News of her grandson's illness further disturbed and depressed her: "You can imagine, my darling," she wrote on November 15,

> *what a shock it was for me to learn that you were at Saint-Andiol* with your poor little boy gravely ill—a high fever, all the signs of either smallpox or measles! And just as I would not have asked you not to worry on the day you wrote to me, so I know you will not ask me not to worry until I know that your child's life—and your own—are out of danger. To be so far from one another is a terrible thing. I was still at Livry when he fell ill; and when I receive your letter, eight days have passed since it was written, so that all is changed again. By now, all is well or all is ill. It is like the thunder: by the time we hear the noise the damage has been done.*

The time lag in the correspondence was one of the things that most distressed Mme de Sévigné about their separation. "My dearest darling," she wrote upon receipt of Mme de Grignan's next letter,

> *I have, this moment, received your letter of Wednesday, the eighth. I opened it with extraordinary emotion and, although I found all I could hope for in it, I could not hold back my tears. My heart swelled with joy at the knowledge that that dear child has been saved—and you, consequently, as well—from death!†*

Not only the little Marquis but the Abbé de Coulanges, too, had been "snatched back from the door of death," as Mme de Sévigné had written the Guitauts earlier. It was because of her uncle's illness that all thought of a trip to Brittany had been abandoned: "My plans," she wrote the Guitauts, "are to see to it that the good Abbé does not stir from the corner of his

---

*Saint-Andiol lies between Grignan and Lambesc, whither the Grignans were going to attend the annual session of the Assembly of the Communities of Provence.

†The little Marquis's illness had proved to be measles rather than the dreaded smallpox. "What a miracle you did not catch the measles!" Mme de Sévigné wrote her daughter. "Her son nearly died of measles," she wrote the Count de Guitaut: "She nursed him; she was luckier than she was wise."

hearth, this winter. I wrote you that he had recovered from a fever; he is now suffering from a heavy cold which gives me some concern."

Her son had been in Brittany for some time, awaiting her arrival. "My son keeps in constant touch," his mother had written his sister:

He has given a good account of himself at the Estates [General]; he has made himself respected. I only fear that he may become a confirmed Breton. He speaks to me of you with great affection.

"He has served on several minor committees," she wrote to Mme de Grignan on another day that month,

assignments such as are made to honor newcomers. We will hope for something better, later. I begged La Marboeuf [her friend, Mme de Marboeuf] to arrange a marriage for him, there. He will never again appear to such advantage as he does, this year. After ten years at Court and on campaign, he has a reputation, and this first year of peace he has devoted to his province. If he does not make a good match this year he never will.

One of Charles's letters to his mother dealt humorously with what he evidently considered his schizophrenic state of mind concerning her:

My son writes me a great deal of foolishness: he tells me that one side of him adores me, while another side would like to strangle me, and that there was a struggle to the death between the two sides, one day last week, in the Mall at Les Rochers. My reply was that I wished that one had destroyed the other, so that I should not have three children; that it was the second side which was the bane of a mother's existence, and that if he would strangle it, I could get along very well with the other two.

It was, as usual, her daughter rather than her son whom she so sorely missed. She lived for the day of Mme de Grignan's return to Paris, to the house on the Rue Sainte-Catherine on which they were even then arranging to renew the lease. "So, now, we are all in agreement about the Hôtel Carnavalet," she wrote:

The first thing the Bien Bon did was to go into the plans for the changes you want made in your apartment . . . He needed time to write

Monsieur de'Agaury [the landlord] in Dauphiné to get his permission to tear out that old relic of a fireplace ... They say one hundred écus should cover everything.* You can be sure that we will be happy to take care of all this for you. But since, to my regret, we have only too much time to arrange it, we will try to rent your apartment until the Saint-Rémi. That should mean some relief to you, and one often finds people in Paris who are looking for short subleases ...

She was apparently undismayed by their last experience under the same roof: "I confess to you," she wrote her daughter, "that I would be grieved, would find it impossible not to live together. To share a house large enough to accommodate us all seems to me the perfect solution."

Their reunion, she hoped, would come in the year 1680. "May God give you a healthy, happy year, my very dearest," she wrote on January 3, 1680,

and may He give me the ultimate bliss of seeing you in better health than you are presently. I assure you that I am very worried about you. Perhaps it is freezing at Aix as it is here, and your chest is affected. I implore you fondly not to write so often, not to reply to all the baga-telles I write you. Just let me go on, just read what I write, just think of it as a gazette!

Mme de Sévigné's "gazette" carried accounts of the two important weddings of the season: the first, that of young Mlle de Blois, the King's favorite daughter (borne him by his first official mistress, Louise de La Vallière) to a Prince of the Blood.†

"The Court is utterly delighted over the marriage of little Mlle de Blois to the Prince de Conti," she wrote her daughter:

It is a love affair such as you read about in novels. The romance has been a great diversion to the King. He spoke tenderly to his daughter, telling her that he loved her so much that he wanted to keep her close by him. The little creature was so affected and so pleased that she wept, whereupon the King told her that he could see that she must have an aversion for the Prince de Conti. Whereupon she redoubled her tears,

---

*Mme de Grignan wanted to modernize her apartment in the sixteenth-century Hôtel Carnavalet by installing a stylish new small fireplace and newly fashionable parquet floors.

†Through this marriage, which took place on January 16, 1680, Louis XIV established one of his legitimized bastards in France's first family, the House of Condé.

her little heart unable to contain all her happiness. The King described this little scene, and everyone was touched. As for the Prince de Conti, he was in a transport of joy, knew not what he said or did, went rushing—sweeping everyone in his path aside—on his way to Mlle de Blois. Mme Colbert did not want him to see her until the evening.* He forced the door, threw himself at her feet, and kissed her hand. She, without further ado, embraced him, and started weeping again. That dear little Princess is sweet and darling enough to eat! ... He [the King] amused himself by giving the Prince a fright, sending word that it would take so much time to draw up all the articles [of the marriage contract] that the wedding would have to be put off until the following winter. Whereupon the Prince almost falls down in a faint, and the Princess assures him that she will have no other. Such a happy ending would not be expected so early in a novel but, actually, no novelist has ever devised a better one. You can imagine what delight this marriage—and the way the King has gone about it—has brought to a certain place.†

Although Mme de Sévigné had not been included among the guests when the King gave his daughter in marriage to the Prince de Conti, she had been invited to the second most important wedding of the winter season, that of Mlle de Louvois (daughter of the powerful Minister, Secretary of State and War), and would not have missed it for the world—if for no other reason in the world than to describe it to her daughter in detail, and in what some critics term her "cinematographic" style:

I went to Mlle de Louvois's wedding. What can I tell you about it? Magnificence, celebrities, all of France, costumes dripping with gold, jewels in profusion, braziers of flame and of flowers, a traffic jam of carriages, shouting in the street, fiery torches, carriages backing up and running over people! All in all, a turmoil, an extravagance, questions asked—the answers unattended; empty compliments paid by people oblivious to what they are saying; cordial salutations addressed to those one does not even know, heels caught up in other people's trains! From the midst of all that tumult came several inquiries about your health, to which—not finding myself sufficiently pressed to reply, I made none,

---

*Mme Colbert, wife of the chief Minister of Commerce and Internal Affairs, had been placed in charge of Mlle de Blois's household and upbringing.

†The "certain place" was the Carmelite Convent to which Louise de La Vallière had retired six years earlier.

*remaining silent while those who had inquired remained uninformed—
and indifferent. Oh, Vanity of Vanities!*

Mme de Grignan's health was anything but a matter of indifference to
her mother: if Mme de Grignan informed her mother of her ailments, her
mother agonized over every symptom; if Mme de Grignan was evasive or
minimized her health problems, her mother was suspicious, reproached her
for not being forthright—and so on and so on, and back and forth, and
round and round in a vicious circle: "The coldness and numbness in your
legs which you make light of—at least, with me—worry me terribly . . . It
is not living, my dear child, to live with as many discomforts as you do!"
"Would to God your health were as good as mine! My sturdy constitution
withstands even my terrible anxiety about you." "Those swollen veins and
arteries of yours, won't they cause you to cough up blood as you have
before?" "Is it your lungs? Is it your chest? Is it what you write about your
nerves and your swollen veins? Is it your blood which causes all the disorders? And do you think I can live when I think of you exposed to that *bise*
which blows at Grignan? My darling, you must pardon me if I agonize over
everything which postpones your return."

To spare an enervated Mme de Grignan the exertion of writing, Mme
de Sévigné was prepared to renounce even that which was the breath of life
to her, her daughter's letters—threatening to break off the correspondence
(which was her lifeline!) unless Mme de Grignan curtailed the number and
the pages of her replies. To allow her daughter to continue the correspondence at such a pace, she exclaimed, was tantamount to "killing you with
my own hand!" "My very dear darling," she wrote,

> *imagine that I am on my knees before you and that, with tears running
> down my cheeks, I beseech you never again to write me a letter [so
> lengthy] as the last! I can reproach myself for the painful and perilous
> state you are in! I, who would give up my life to save yours, will be
> the cause of your collapse . . . the very thought sets me trembling . . . I
> swear, I protest to you that if you write me more than one page . . . I
> will not write to you at all . . . If you love me, strike my name from the
> list of those with whom you feel obliged to correspond . . .*

The biographers who diagnose Mme de Grignan's diverse pains and
aches as psychosomatic, do so on the theory that she was constantly tormented
not only by a sense of guilt over her relations with her mother, but also by
a desperate, gnawing anxiety over the specter of bankruptcy confronting the

House of Grignan. That was how her mother saw it, although the word "psychosomatic" was, of course, unknown to the seventeenth-century vocabulary. "It is easy to understand your distress over the plight you are in; nothing could be more of an affliction," she wrote her daughter early in 1680:

How can anyone even bear to think of the chaos [of the Grignan finances], of the decline and fall of a House and a name so cherished? And to see a person [such as you] buried beneath the ruins! What a decree of Providence! And what bitterness does one not feel despite one's resolve of submission! I do not know whether you are correct in thinking that there is no way to regulate your expenses. I would have to be at Salon to hear what Monsieur the Archbishop has to say about it.* It is true that the gambling frightens me. Mons. de Grignan hates bassette, *but he loves* hombre—*although he obviously does not know how to play the game since he loses constantly at it. Is not that tantamount to doubling your necessary expenses? That is what I dislike . . . I cannot keep myself from giving advice to Mons. de Grignan. I must try to talk about something else, for all I am doing is to add to your distress . . .*

Expenses at the Governor's Palace escalated at the Carnival season: "I imagine you in the midst of Carnival, my daughter," Mme de Sévigné wrote on February 9, 1680: "You are giving small supper parties for eighteen or twenty ladies. I know that life and the great expense you are under at Aix. It is a dreadful thing to endanger your affairs still further in Provence—instead of improving them." "Furthermore, my dear child," she continued in another letter in the same vein, "is it not a hard thing to have to retrench for six months to make up for having spent the winter at Aix? If it served to enhance your family prospects, I could better understand but, conversely, it is more apt to work against you, here. The Intendant can talk of nothing but your magnificence, your air of grandeur, your sumptuous banquets!"

Mme de Sévigné's Paris life was lived at a far slower pace and on a far less sumptuous scale, as she pointed out:

I lead much the same life as when you were here, either in the Faubourg [Saint-Germain] or with my good friends, the widows; dining some-

---

*"In no other family," she said of the Count's uncle, the Archbishop of Arles, "do I know of a patriarch so worthy of respect and devotion."

times here, sometimes at Mme de Coulanges's to share her chicken,
but always happy in the thought that time is passing and carrying me
along with it and, so—closer to reunion with you.

Mme de Grignan's letters must have given her mother hope that she
would return to Paris before winter: "But I count on your leaving, this
autumn, as you said you would."

Presently, my darling, I live and breathe only to see you again, to be
able to keep you here, and take care of you myself. As for the days that
intervene, I want no part of them; anyone who wants is welcome to
them; the more quickly they go by, the better! The springtime—and
the summer even more so—seems a century away; I feel as if I will
never see the last of it. I sleep in a hurry; I am impatient to get to
tomorrow which may bring a letter from you, and to the next one after
that, and the next ... I am careful not to make such a confidence to
anyone; no one would understand but, sometimes, in the midst of a
thousand other things, I feel the need to tell it all to you. I do not often
take advantage of the liberty your absence gives to me.

Whatever liberties she may have taken with her daughter, she had taken
liberties greater still with her son-in-law. Her censure, a few weeks earlier,
of his profligacy and his gambling had been unwontedly acerbic, uncharac-
teristically blunt. "Are Monsieur de Grignan and I on speaking terms again?",
"Has Monsieur de Grignan made up with me?", she asked repeatedly of her
daughter in the weeks that followed her attack. The inquiries were humorously phrased, but she evidently sensed that she had overstepped her privi-
leges as a mother-in-law.

Seizing on the opportunity of praising a letter of the Count's addressed
to Mme de Coulanges, Mme de Sévigné coaxed her daughter to effect a
reconciliation:

Be sure to point out to him my heartfelt affection for him which, in
itself, should constitute an excuse. Whatever I said I said out of love,
out of interest, out of esteem for a name and a house which no one
could honor more than I, honoring it perhaps even more than he does.
See what your skill can do with so much good material because, to tell
the truth, I am somewhat embarrassed to be on bad terms with a man
who writes so well ...

(As concerned the opinions of the three on each other's skill in the epistolary art, theirs was a mutual admiration society. Mme de Sévigné lavishly praised the letters of her son-in-law, praised those of her daughter to the sky; while the Grignans, with doubtlessly better reason, returned the compliment: "I find myself extremely honored," Mme de Sévigné once wrote her daughter, "by Monsieur de Grignan's predilection for my letters. I had not had so exalted an opinion of them, but since you two like them so well, I can hope for nothing better.")

By February 2, the reconciliation between Mme de Sévigné and the Count de Grignan was complete: "I embrace Monsieur de Grignan," Mme de Sévigné wrote her daughter on that date, "since you have—at last, and with such tact and perseverance—prevailed upon him to pardon me."

By the end of the month, she felt secure enough to risk teasing her son-in-law, writing her daughter on March 1, "I want to tell you about the opera (*Proserpine*, by Quinault and Lully,* which had had its première before the King on February 5)":

I have not seen it (I am not eager for diversion), but they say it is sheer perfection. Many people said it reminded them of you and me. I did not tell you because they made me out as Ceres, and you as Proserpine—leaving Monsieur de Grignan in the role of Pluto, and I feared he might sing out in reply—to the accompaniment of his entire orchestra—the lines: "Can a mother be compared to a husband?" It is that line I wished to avoid because, as for the preceding line—"Pluto's love is greater than Ceres'"—I could have made light of that!

Mme de Sévigné's relations with her son-in-law were nothing if not ambivalent, as she herself recognized in a May 1 letter to her daughter:

No one concedes more readily than I to Monsieur de Grignan's complaisance. He exhibits facets of nobility, of courtesy, of even a profound tenderness. There are other aspects too shocking to believe. He can be incredibly sweet and kind, and when it comes to the social graces, he is incomparable. One loves him, one scolds him, one admires him, one criticizes him, one wants to kiss him, one wants to slap him!

---

*In the opera, as in the myth, Pluto steals Proserpine from her mother, Ceres, and carries her off to the underworld to be his bride.

XXXV

It was March which proved the cruellest month for Mme de Sévigné in 1680, bringing the loss of friends—the first, a close friend and constant companion. "I fear that this time we shall lose Monsieur de La Rochefoucauld," she wrote on March 15:

Yesterday morning, he did not see Mme de La Fayette because she was weeping and he was taking extreme unction. He sent, at noon, to inquire about her. Believe me, my daughter, it is not in vain that he did so much thinking all his life; approaching his last hours on earth in the same manner, they held nothing strange or new for him.

On Sunday, March 17, she wrote:

Although this letter will not go off until Wednesday, I cannot restrain myself from beginning it today to tell you, my dear, that Monsieur de La Rochefoucauld died tonight. My mind is so full of this sorrow and of the terrible grief of our poor friend that I simply have to talk to you about it . . . Monsieur de Marsillac [the Prince de Marsillac, eldest son of the Duke] did not leave him for a moment; he died in his arms, in that chair you have seen him in so often. He is utterly grief-stricken but, my darling, he will go back to the King and the Court; he will find all his family there. But where will Mme de La Fayette find another friend, another such wonderful companion, another so tender, so delightful, so trustworthy, so considerate of her and of her son? She is an invalid, she never leaves her house, never runs the streets. Monsieur de La Rochefoucauld was sedentary, too. That made them indispensable to each other. There is nothing to be compared to the trust and the devotion they had for one another. If you think about it, my darling, you will see that it is impossible to suffer a greater loss, one which time will not heal. I have not left her side, these last few days . . .

"Never has a man been so well wept," she wrote of the Duke on March 26: "His death is a public loss, but we have personal reason to feel it"—one reason being that the Duke had undertaken to forward the interests of the Count de Grignan at Court (doing so through the good offices of his son, the Prince de Marsillac, who was Master of the Royal Hunt, one of the monarch's closest friends and favorites). With the death of the Duke, the Count de Grignan's prospects for a suitable Court appointment went glimmering.*

"Don't you marvel at the fact that God has deprived me of even the comfort of discussing your interests with Monsieur de La Rochefoucauld?" she asked plaintively in the same letter. "He was most obliging, and showed great interest in what concerned you. So that having already lost Monsieur de Pomponne, I now feel I can never be helpful to you again."

"As for me, my child," the letter continued,

I think of nothing but seeing you again. The more Monsieur de La Rochefoucauld's death makes me think of my own, the more I long to spend what remains of my life with you. Mme de La Fayette has fallen from the clouds. She never forgets for a moment what a loss she has suffered. Everyone else will find consolation, but not she. Monsieur de La Rochefoucauld has now returned to his duties. The King sent for him; there is no sorrow he cannot console.

As rhapsodically as Mme de Sévigné had described the relationship between her two dear friends, she gave no clue as to whether or not she thought it had been a platonic one—a question which had tantalized the pair's contemporaries since 1669 or 1670 when the liaison had become open.†

The second of Mme de Sévigné's friends who died in March of 1680 was one she had not seen in nineteen years, but whose loss she mourned: "And here is more sad news, my daughter," she wrote on April 3. "Monsieur Fouquet is dead. I am very touched. Never before have I suffered the loss of so many friends!"‡

Such consolations as Mme de Sévigné could find, that spring, she found in the blessings which befell—the signs of royal favor shown to two young-

---

*An effort by the Duke de La Rochefoucauld to have the Count de Grignan named Captain of the King's Guards had been unavailing.

†There had been no sign of an open rupture when the Count and Countess de La Fayette had gone their separate ways, not too long after their marriage, the Count retiring to his estates, leaving the Countess in Paris to her own devices—and eventually to the Duke de La Rochefoucauld.

‡The *Gazette* of April 6 reported that Fouquet had died of apoplexy on March 23 at the fortress of Pignerol where he had been imprisoned since early 1665.

er members of the Grignan family: the Abbé de Grignan named Bishop of Évreux (with a handsome stipend and imposing bishopric) and the Chevalier de Grignan named *menin* or companion to the Dauphin, "one of eight or ten men of quality and merit," as Mme de Sévigné put it, "assigned to the Dauphin's retinue," at a fine pension of nine thousand livres a year. "This has been, in truth, a very good little week for the Grignans!" she wrote jubilantly to her daughter: "If only Providence chose to do as much for the eldest Grignan, we would see him attain to a splendid post!"

If only the eldest were also at Court—as was the burden of her song— in proximity to the monarch from whom all blessings flowed—instead of in far-off Provence! "The King's largesse is immense," as she had noted, earlier:

> *So, actually, we must not despair. Even if one is not his valet, it could happen that while one pays one's court, one might find oneself in the way of the golden shower. What is certain is that in the case of those far away from him, their services go unrewarded. In the olden days, the opposite was true.*

Mme de Sévigné showed some impatience with the Grignans' air of resignation, of despair as concerned their prospects. "You should never for a moment doubt your own worth, no matter how unkind Fate may be," she admonished: "If, in truth, Fate so willed, Monsieur and Mme de Grignan would hold their own in any position at Court."

"But what I cannot understand," she wrote on March 3 to rally their flagging spirits,

> *is that both of you should consider yourselves out of the running, no longer eligible for good fortune or the favor of His Majesty. And why should you eliminate yourselves? How old, pray tell, are you? . . . And where did you get the idea of burying yourselves like Philemon and Baucis? Are you not well liked? Are you not likeable, both of you? Are you not of the right caliber to present to the King? Is your name not well known? Is it not a name more than ever likely, now, to stand you in good stead? With such grace as has recently been shown your family, does not that imply that you may hope for it, as well? Do not times ever change? Do not people ever change? Is this not a period of great liberality? So, why should you count yourselves out, and put your only hope in the distant future, that of the little Marquis? I do not know whether it is because I can have little hope of sharing in that distant*

future or whether I am simply not one of those grandmothers who look beyond their own children to their grandchildren, but I confess that you cut me short, and that I cannot bear the way you look at things . . .

If Mme de Sévigné's daughter gave her little pleasure that spring, her son gave her even less. Like a bolt from the blue came Charles's announcement that he had had enough of campaigning, and had decided to sell his commission in the Gendarmes-Dauphin Regiment, at any price—as eager, by then, to sell as he had been, only three years earlier, to buy! His mother had financed the purchase of the sub-lieutenancy at great sacrifice, hypothecating properties of her own to secure the loan. ("At least," she wrote her daughter, "I know that I put his career above my own personal interests, and have no reproach to make myself on that score.") She knew, too, that to leave the armed forces eliminated the possibility of a Court career: "The King cannot abide those who leave the service," as she noted. "And, once my son has no more Court affiliation, I will advise him to return to his province rather than to fritter away his life running to operas and comedies."

"My son has just arrived from Douai," she wrote Mme de Grignan on April 3: "It was his turn to take command of the regiment, there, during the month of March."

Charles returned to Paris and had the effrontery to complain to his mother and her uncle about the disarray of Sévigné affairs in Brittany, and to insist that they go to oversee the family properties in that province. "The good Abbé is unwilling to listen longer to reproaches, no matter how tactfully made," she wrote somewhat indignantly. "It is true that our properties are in disorder, but that is a result of the hard times there. Even so, we will go and do our best, if only to satisfy our conscience. The thought of putting even greater distance between us makes me shudder."

In response to Charles's continued pressure, plans were formulated for the voyage, although with no good grace: "As for me," she wrote in April,

I will go dashing off to Brittany, much as I dread the thought. I am going to be going, to spend a short time there, to be able to say I went, and thus put an end to the matter. Next to the loss of health—which I consider the greatest of disasters—nothing is so disturbing as miscalculation and derangement of business affairs. Thus, I submit myself to the cruel necessity. You can imagine my distress when you know how upset I am over so much as a two-hour delay in the mail schedule!

"I must be out of my mind," she wrote on another day, "to be going still farther away from you!" It would be as if they were "on different continents," she moaned. Not only that: written from the provinces—out of touch with Court and Capital—her letters could not but diminish in interest and entertainment to her daughter.

Until the day she departed Paris, she would regale Mme de Grignan with the latest news, would keep her Court Circular up to date. The arrival of the Dauphine—the Bavarian Princess chosen as bride for France's heir to the throne—was the major event of the vernal season.

"Apropos of the Court," Mme de Sévigné wrote in mid-March, "I am sending you the latest reports:

> Madame the Dauphine is greatly admired. The King was so curious to know what she looked like that he sent Sanguin, whom he knows to be a truthful man and no flatterer.* "Sire," that man told him, "once you get over the first impression, you will be delighted." And that is very well said because there is something about her nose and forehead which is too long in proportion to the rest, and that creates a poor first impression. But they say that she is so graceful, has such a beautiful figure and neck, such beautiful arms, hands and hair, so much wit and warmth, that she is so gracious without being mawkish, so cordial and yet so dignified—in sum, so many attributes that one readily forgives her that first impression . . .

Not even the marriage of his eldest son and heir could long distract the Sun King from his philandering—certainly not when "the most extraordinarily beautiful blonde to be seen in many a year at Versailles" made her Court debut.† Marie-Angélique de Fontanges, at the tender age of seventeen, not unexpectedly caught the roving eye of the insatiably amorous forty-two-year-old monarch. (Her noble but impecunious provincial kinsfolk had taken up a purse to finance a Court debut to promote their promising candidate in the competition for the King's favor. She had been "destined by her parents since early youth to attain to this illustrious position," this glorious dishonor traditionally reserved for ladies of noble birth.)

"Mlle de Fontanges is extraordinarily beautiful," Mme de Sévigné wrote: "She appears in the gallery [of the Royal Chapel] like a divinity . . . Mme

---

*Sanguin, the King's maître d'hôtel, was sent ahead with the official party to greet the Dauphine as she travelled from Bavaria to France.

†The quotations in this paragraph are from a report to the Elector of the Palatine, written by Ezekiel Spanheim, his Ambassador to the Court of France.

de Montespan, on the other side, another divinity . . ." (her beauty, at age forty, conspicuously less dewy than that of her latest rival).

"I am going to tell you a piece of news which is no longer a secret, although you will have the pleasure of being among the first to hear it," Mme de Sévigné reported proudly, on April 6, to her daughter:

> *Mlle de Fontanges has been made a Duchess with a 20,000-écus-a-year pension; she accepted congratulations yesterday, lying on her bed. The King paid her an official visit. Tomorrow she takes her tabouret and then goes to spend Easter at an Abbey which the King has given her sister.* This kind of separation will do honor to the confessor.† There are some who say that honors of this kind presage a rupture. I know nothing about that; only time will tell. What I do know is that Mme de M[ontespan]‡ is in a rage. Yesterday, she wept copiously. You can well imagine what a martyrdom this is for anyone with such pride as hers. Her rage is even greater at the sight of the high favor being shown Mme de Maintenon. His Majesty goes very often to spend two hours of the afternoon in her chamber in friendly conversation, and with an air so free and easy as to make that chamber the most desirable spot in the world!*

By April 12, Mme de Sévigné could finally give her daughter a first-hand report on the Dauphine:

> *It is true that I was curious to see her. So I went with Mme de Chaulnes and Mme de Kerman. She was at her toilette; she was talking Italian to Monsieur de Nevers. We were presented; she greeted us graciously, and I could see that, given the proper opportunity and opening, she would easily enter into conversation . . . But still and all, my darling, that world there is not for me. I am no longer at an age to think of establishing myself there or to think of being accepted. If I were young, I might hope to please that Princess but, good God, by what right would I ever think of returning there?*

It is this letter—along with another written a few weeks later—which gives us some insight into Mme de Sévigné's personal attitude toward the

---

*Mlle de Fontanges's sister, a nun, had been installed as Abbess of Maubuisson.
†On high holy days, the King's mistresses absented themselves so that he could take communion.
‡Constantly aware of the possibility of mail surveillance, Mme de Sévigné often used initials rather than name names.

Court; her biographers seldom agree as to how she really felt—in her heart of hearts—about the courtier's life. Did she sometimes wish that she had been a part of that "glorious," "glamorous," "treacherous," "cruel" world? (The adjectives are among those she herself applied in description of it.) As disdainful as she may seem, at times, about "*ce pays-là*," "that country, there," that world unto itself, as she called it—still, we have her own word for it that her caustic comment may have been a case of sour grapes. She prayed, literally as well as figuratively, for Court appointments for her son-in-law and her daughter. There is ambivalence in her relation to the Court as in that toward her son-in-law.

She makes crystal clear, however, that she would have been unwilling to subject herself to the embarrassment Mme de Coulanges suffered as a hanger-on, an outsider looking in on a Court of which she was not—and, because of her lack of a title, could never hope to be—a part. The Marquise de Sévigné knew no such drawback, could lay claim both by birth and by marriage to proud and ancient titles such as were requisite to Court entrée. Given the proper friends or family in high places—as, at one time in her life, she said she had—a Marquise de Sévigné might well have expected appointment to a Court post. It had been the sudden disgrace—the exile, banishment, imprisonment—of those friends and relatives—Bussy, Fouquet, Retz, Pomponne—which had dashed whatever hopes she may have had of a place in the sun at the Sun King's Court.

"Did I tell you how well received Mme de Coulanges was at Saint-Germain?" Mme de Sévigné inquired in that same letter of April 12 quoted earlier:

> *Mme the Dauphine told her that she already knew her through her letters, that her ladies-in-waiting had spoken of her wit, and that she was most eager to judge for herself. Mme de Coulanges lived up to her reputation; all her replies were scintillating; she spouted epigrams, and the Dauphine appreciated all she said. She was invited into the study after dinner by her three friends*—to the indignation of the other ladies in the retinue. You can understand that, through her friends, she is on a footing of intimacy with the Princess. But what can all that lead to? And how embarrassing when one can be included in neither the carriage rides nor the dinner parties!† That would spoil all the rest. She*

---

*Mme de Coulanges's three close friends at Court were Mme de Maintenon, Mme de Richelieu (Dame d'Honneur to the Dauphine) and Mme de Rochefort.

†The only ones who might ride in the carriage of the King or the Queen were those who could produce patents of nobility dating back several centuries to the genealogical "Mists of Time."

*feels the humiliation keenly. She spent four days partaking of those
pleasures and displeasures.*

"Her wit gives her standing in that Court," Mme de Sévigné wrote her
daughter elsewhere. "If true merit in addition to wit counted there, you
would have—and I do not mean to flatter you—good reason for acceptance."

With the advent of the month of May, the dreaded trip to Brittany could be
put off no longer: "Here I am, still in Paris," Mme de Sévigné wrote on May
3, "but in the midst of all that confusion of departure with which you are
familiar. I am a responsibility to everyone I know. I no longer have a
carriage, and yet I have too many! Everyone prides himself on his generosity
and thoughtfulness in taking me places . . ."
   "I am going off like a Fury," the letter continued,

*to make people pay me what they owe me! I will listen to neither
rhyme nor reason. I will just keep saying over and over again, like
[Molìere's] the Miser, "Money, money, money—ten thousand écus are
what I want!" And I might very well have them if only I could collect
what is owing me in Brittany and Burgundy.*

"I feel the pangs of separation all over again and the anguish of putting
still more distance between us," she went on. It was, she said, as if they
were "trying to go to the far ends of the earth from one another!" "For two
people who are drawn to one another, who always long for one another,
this is the strangest destiny I ever saw!" Only the theory of Providence
could explain it for her:

*Whoever tried to deprive me of my belief in Providence would deprive
me of my only comfort . . . I need to believe that it is the Creator of
the Universe who disposes of our lives. When it is with Him that I
must take issue, I no longer take issue with any other, and so I can
submit. My heart is wounded, but I endure the pain as part of the will
of Providence. It is the will of Providence that there should be a Mme
de Sévigné who loves her daughter more than any other mother in the
world, that she should often be separated from her, that her greatest
sorrow in this life should be caused her by that beloved daughter. I
hope that Providence will work in another direction, and that we will
be reunited, as we have already in the past.*

Mme de Sévigné made ready for her voyage to Brittany in an unwontedly somber mood: "I miss all of you terribly," she wrote the Grignans on May 6, the eve of her departure: "I have lost touch with music and gaiety. No matter how I tap my foot, my life is monotonous and sad, spent either in that depressing Faubourg [with a mourning Mme de La Fayette] or with those cautious widows. Monsieur de Grignan is very necessary to me, for there is a spark of folly in my heart which is not yet extinguished."

XXXVI

Once Mme de Sévigné had told family and friends goodbye ("So many came to bid me adieu as to astonish me!") and left Paris behind, the excitement of travel caught her up, as usual: she responded to the thrill of rushing along "like the wind," as she put it, in a fine carriage drawn by spanking horses, and to the perennial beauty of the French landscape unfolding before her eyes. "And so here we are at Orléans," she wrote on May 8,

> *after an uneventful trip in fine weather over excellent roads. Our equipage is splendid; my son lent me his horses, and escorted me this far. He brought great good cheer to our somber cavalcade. We talked, we argued, we read. The days are so long that we will not even have need of that glorious moon which will accompany us on the Loire upon which we embark tomorrow.*

The correspondence took on the nature of a travelogue; her next letter was headed, "Thursday, May 9, Blois" (where she "sat writing romantically," she said, "upon the river bank"):

> *I want to write you every night, my dear child; it is my sole diversion. I move about, I walk, I pick up a book but, no matter how hard I try, I am bored, and it is my writing case I need! I have to talk to you, and even though this letter will go off neither today nor tomorrow, I will write you every night to tell you of the day's happenings.*
> *We embarked at six in the morning in the most perfect weather*

imaginable. I had them put aboard the body of my large carriage, and placed it at such an angle as to avoid direct sun. We lowered the windows. The opening at the front frames a marvelous picture while, with the view from the portieres and the side windows, we can see out on all sides. There are just the two of us, the Abbé and I, in these snug private quarters, seated on soft cushions, with plenty of fresh air, very comfortable! All the rest [the domestic staff] sprawl like pigs on the straw. We have had our soup and boiled meat, served good and hot. There is a little stove; we eat on a plank in our carriage, like the King and Queen!* Just see how luxurious things have become on the Loire!

"Our Loire is orderly and majestic," she pointed out in another letter that week—"no fury" like the Rhône or the Durance. And she "never tired," she said, "of the beauty of the landscape."

From Saumur, she could report that "the good Abbé is feeling fine. He is delighted with this route. No one has ever made this trip as we are doing; it is too bad that we are so solitary." ("We talk, the Abbé and I," she wrote elsewhere, "but the conversation cannot be said to be amusing." The Abbé was as a rod and a staff to her; he comforted but he could not entertain her. Not that she was not deeply appreciative of his devotion: "I am touched by the kindness of the good Abbé who is ready, at age seventy-three, to travel by land or by sea to take care of my affairs.")

By the time their chartered boat had reached Tours, on May 10, Mme de Sévigné began to worry that her letters might suffer the blight of boredom as a consequence of the dearth of news in the hinterlands. (She wrote more than once to the Count de Bussy about her fear of provincial dry rot, of "the danger of growing rusty" out of the social and cultural mainstream.) "*La belle Fontanges* was expected at Court the day after my departure," she wrote her daughter, "but now it will be up to the Chevalier to keep you posted. I will no longer have anything of interest to write you. If you did not love me, you would do well to burn these letters without even opening them."

She continued, nevertheless, to write them; the next, dated "Saturday, May 11, from Saumur":

This morning, we left Tours, where I posted a letter to you. Whoever would deprive me of the faculty of thinking would greatly discommode

---

*She had even, she wrote, "taken along a small supply of our best aged Burgundy wine to quench the Abbé's substantial thirst."

me—above all, on this voyage. I spend as much as twelve hours a day
in that strategically placed, many-windowed carriage I told you about.
Some of those hours I spend eating, some drinking, some not drinking,
some reading. Many are spent looking out, enjoying the scenery, but
still more are spent dreaming and thinking of you, my love.

After five such long days on the Loire, Mme de Sévigné confessed
herself to be "impatient to reach Nantes," partly because that town was the
final destination of the river journey, but primarily because mail from her
daughter was to be expected there. Mme de Sévigné had posted letters to
Provence all along the way, but it had been agreed that Nantes should be
the only address at which Mme de Grignan would try to reach her mother
en route to Les Rochers.

"That packet of mail from you was the only joy to which I could look
forward here," Mme de Sévigné wrote upon arrival at La Seilleraye, the
château of her cousin d'Haroüys, Treasurer of the Estates General of Brittany. Her joy was short lived: Mme de Grignan had chosen, for some strange
reason—inexplicable, unless out of some lingering sense of guilt—morbidly
to rehearse the circumstances of her precipitous departure from Paris, the
preceding year. Nothing is to be found in Mme de Sévigné's letters of
previous weeks to have provoked the outburst. What had prompted Mme
de Grignan—nine months after the altercations had subsided—to rehash the
whys and wherefores of that acrimonious parting in 1679, accusing her
mother of having been "one of those who wanted her gone"? As usual, with
Mme de Grignan's letters missing from the correspondence, only the echo
of her letter is audible in her mother's reply; the only words of hers to reach
us are those quoted by her mother: sentences and phrases of Mme de
Grignan's quoted verbatim by Mme de Sévigné.

"To begin with," Mme de Sévigné began her reply to her daughter's
accusations, rejecting the blame and laying it at the doorstep where she
thought it properly belonged,

I really wish, my dear, that you would not include me in the number of
those who wanted to see you leave. For me, your departure constituted
one of the great sorrows of my life. Every separation shortens it;
nothing is so cruel, so painful to me as your absence. I know who it is
you are really talking about . . .

(It was "the good Abbé," as Mme de Sévigné well knew, who was the
real target of her daughter's attack. She herself had been incensed at his

suggestions that the Grignans were not paying their fair share of the Carna-valet expenses.)

He denies it [her letter continued], and swears that it was never his idea that your leaving would relieve your and my problems because, by his own admission, he only said all those things out of ill humor (over which he has no control) . . . things said unreasonably and unjustly to you, my darling, who are the soul of reason, of justice, of discretion, of generosity—that is what killed me! But that poor man does so much to compensate for all that, and since everyone has his faults, one must try to forget all the rest.

In the last analysis, my darling, you must do yourself the full honor you deserve, and admit that it is because you love Monsieur de Grignan (as he, so well, in truth deserves) and love to please him. I have often even felt that you never really relax when he is far away from you. He has so suave a way about him—one more likely to succeed with you than any other in the world—that you would follow him to the Indies if he beckoned! Letting you think you are the mistress of the situation, it is actually he who remains the master. This maneu-ver comes quite naturally to him, but were there an art in touching a heart like yours, he would have been the one to discover it. You saw through his polite pretenses to what he really wanted . . . You were motivated by your desire to please him. Thus it is up to him to decide when a voyage will be ruinous to you or up to you to state your position more forcibly . . .

"I think I have struck upon the real reason for your departure," she declared.

Even so [she concluded blithely], they will begin work on your little apartment [at the Carnavalet] in accordance with your instructions: all the orders have been given for the partition, the fireplace, the parquet floors, the casement windows . . . I have more than enough money of yours to cover all the construction costs. You always forget that small sum of money of yours I am keeping for you . . .

"I have been here eight days," she wrote her daughter from Nantes on May 21, "and I am very bored." Only business affairs kept her there: "I want to make those who owe me pay me off so that I can pay off those whom I owe," she wrote in a letter to the Count de Guitaut on May 18:

"That thought consoles me for all my boredom." "You will ask me," she wrote her daughter on May 25, "whether no one else could have taken care of these matters for me; the answer is no. My presence was required as well as the influence of my friends."

Charles's trip to Nantes earlier in the year had done more harm than good: "I went yesterday," she wrote on May 27 to her daughter, "to Buron [one of the Sévigné estates a dozen kilometers west of Nantes], and came back in the evening."

> I thought I would weep to see the damage done there. Those were the most ancient woods in the world. My son, on his last trip, put them to the axe. He also wanted to sell off another quite beautiful grove of trees. It is pitiful to see. He got four hundred pistoles in return, of which not so much as a sou remained to him a month later. It is impossible to know what he is doing or what his Brittany trip cost him, although he lived like a vagabond, having sent his lackeys and coachman back to Paris, keeping only Larmechin [his valet] with him in this town where he spent two months. He has found a way to spend money with nothing to show for it, to lose money without gambling, to pay without obtaining credit: a constant thirst, constant need for money in time of peace as in time of war ... but his hand is like a sieve through which money spills ... All those displaced dryads that I saw yesterday, all those woodland nymphs who knew not where to go for refuge, all those ancient ravens nesting for two hundred years in those woods, all those owls whose doleful cries, in that obscurity, announce the doom of mankind—all these came to me yesterday to make moan, and touched me to the heart ... That was un luogo d'incanto.* I came back much saddened; the supper party given in my honor by the First President [of the Parlement of Brittany] and his wife failed to cheer me ...

She was writing that night, she explained in her letter of May 28, because she was "leaving, thank God, early tomorrow morning":

> We will not even wait to get your letter to reply to it, but will leave a man on horseback here who will bring it to me by dinner time, and I will leave this letter here to go off with the next courier so that— insofar as possible—the rhythm of our correspondence will not be interrupted.

*An enchanted spot.

Her next letter was datelined "Friday, the 31st, last day of the month, at Les Rochers":

We arrived at Rennes on the eve of Ascension Day [May 29]. That good Marboeuf [her good friend, Mme de Marboeuf] wanted to swallow me up alive, to put me up at her house and keep me there. I wanted neither to take supper nor to sleep at her house. The next day she gave a large luncheon-dinner to which the Governor and everyone of importance in the town ... were invited to visit me. We left at ten o'clock, everyone telling me that that gave us plenty of time, that the roads were "as smooth as the floor of this room"—that being always the simile. They proved to be so much like the floor of this room that we did not get there until twelve midnight! Everything under water! The road from Vitré here, over which I have travelled a thousand times, was totally unrecognizable, covered with mud! ... Finally, finding that we could see nothing and that we must try to make it along the road, we sent to Pilois to ask for help. He came with a dozen strong fellows. Some of them held us up, others lit our way with torches of flaming straw, and all of them spoke with Breton accents so thick that we thought we would die laughing! Finally, thanks to that illumination, we arrived here, our horses exhausted, all our people soaking wet, my carriage broken, all of us rather weary. We ate very little, slept a lot and, this morning, awoke at Les Rochers, although still in confusion and disorder. Knowing what a filthy rascal the Father [Father Rahuel, the concierge of Les Rochers] is, I had sent Rencontre [one of her lackeys] ahead to clean up, so as not to return to an accumulation of four years' dust. At least, we were neat and clean. We were greeted by many people from Vitré—Mlle du Plessis is in tears over [the death of] her mother, but I was not happy until everyone had left, about six o'clock, and I could spend some time in the woods with my friend Pilois. All those allées are very beautiful, my darling; there are more than ten which have been planted since you were here. Never fear that I will expose myself to the night dew. I know how displeased you would be and, furthermore, my dearest, the very sight of that alcove in the room in which I was confined to bed during my illness gave me a twinge of pain which will not fail to remind me to take care of myself for fear of another attack.

The Château de Grignan was a far grander, far less isolated place than Les Rochers. ("This hostelry is a far different place from yours," Mme de

Sévigné would say, comparing the two.) "It requires a great deal of energy to entertain all the visitors you have had," she wrote her daughter in her May 31 letter: "Twenty extra people at table staggers the imagination! In truth, your hostelry is one of the most popular." ("The idea of fifty servants seems preposterous!" she wrote elsewhere. "We have trouble even counting them!")

As for Grignan, "I do not understand why you should want anyone beside your family there," she wrote on one occasion:

> *I remember that with just the family, we were a hundred in your château! I found that enough. You cannot possibly believe that such a great number of people does not disrupt any idea you might have had of economizing and living off the produce of your lands. That is something you never seem to understand . . but when you not only double but quadruple the number of mouths you feed, your cost of living goes as high as in Paris.*

"It's a republic, it's a world, that château of yours! I have never seen such throngs," she would exclaim, one day. "I pity you, my darling, when I think of all the guests you have to entertain,"* she wrote at another time, on the same subject:

> *When I think of your château, my dear, filled with all your large family and all the chance-comers, and all the musicians and entertainers Monsieur de Grignan brings there, I do not see how you can avoid enormous expenditures . . .*

"My son says there are constant diversions at Fontainebleau," she wrote on May 31 in what must have been—from her daughter's point of view—a welcome change of theme:

> *The Court is charmed with Corneille's comedies. I write my son that it must be a great privilege to be obligated to appear at Court, to have a master,† a position, a connection—and that, as for me, had I had one I would have much enjoyed that world; that it was only because I had none that I withdrew; that it was out of spite and envy that I spoke*

---

*Many travellers en route to and from Italy or Spain, whether on official or unofficial business, passed through Provence, and were apt to stop at the château of the Governor at Grignan.

†The Dauphin was the "master"—Charles de Sévigné being an officer in his Gendarmes-Dauphin Regiment.

deprecatingly of the Court, as Montaigne did of youth [when he had grown old], and that I marvelled that he would prefer to spend his post-prandial hour between Mlle du Plessis and Mlle de Launay (as I am doing) instead of in the midst of all the best and finest in the kingdom. I speak of myself, but I am thinking of you, my darling. Never think that if you and Mons. de Grignan had posts such as you deserve, you would not accommodate yourselves very well to that life. But Providence does not will you to have grandeurs other than those you already have. As for me, there were moments when the most glamorous opportunities in the world seemed within my grasp, but Fate stepped in, and suddenly there were imprisonments and exiles. Do you think my fate has been a very happy one? I am well enough satisfied, and if I sometimes murmur in discontent, it is not on my own account.

But was she being honest with her daughter—or with herself? Was she grieving over what might have been—the glamorous Court appointments that might have been hers, had only such friends and relatives as the Count de Bussy, the Cardinal de Retz and Fouquet not suddenly lost their favor with the monarch? She went so far as to compare, somewhat self-pityingly, her role and place in life to that of her daughter, the Vicereine of Provence, the chatelaine of "royal Grignan": "It should be said to our credit, that you accommodate yourself very well to your glamorous sovereign position in the public eye, as do I to my own undistinguished place, to my obscurity and to my forests . . ."

XXXVII

Even the weather conspired to dampen Mme de Sévigné's normally high spirits, that summer of 1680. "The rain never stops," she wrote dolefully on June 2, and the end of the month saw little improvement: "If I find the days so long, it is because they are not only long but cold and dreary," she complained on June 26. "I am wearing a quilted housecoat, and light a fire every night."

Not only was the weather depressing, Brittany was in the throes of a recession: "Times are hard here," Mme de Sévigné wrote lugubriously on June 9: "Our properties decrease in value while yours enhance.* I see only people who owe me money but have no bread, who sleep on straw and weep. What would you have me do about that?"

Mme de Sévigné seemed more than usually conscious of the isolation of Les Rochers; the solitude, for once, weighed heavily on her. The company of her nearest neighbor could not be construed as a blessing: "Mlle du Plessis is in deep mourning,† scarcely leaves my side . . . She is impertinent; I am actually embarrassed by the friendship she shows me. She talks constantly, but God is good to me as He is to you in similar circumstances, and spares me from hearing a word she says."

"I am like a doe in the wildwood, far removed from the world of polite society," Mme de Sévigné wrote in mid-June, wallowing in self-pity. "I no longer know whether there is any music or laughter there. What would I have to laugh about?"

"I pity myself for being here while you two are in Paris," Mme de Sévigné wrote the Count de Bussy and his daughter, Mme de Coligny, on June 19:

I am here in total solitude and, for one who is unaccustomed to it, I am adjusting quite well . . . I return again and again to that same thought of Providence which disposes of our lives as it wills. It was not easy to understand that a demoiselle from Burgundy, raised at the Court, should somehow end up in the wilds of Brittany.‡

The days seemed "interminably long" to Mme de Sévigné (to judge by this letter addressed to her daughter):

It seems that they will never end; even at seven, eight or nine o'clock at night, they still drag on . . . When I have visitors, I quickly pick up my needlework. I do not consider these mesdames worthy of my woods . . . I show them out . . . and when they drive off to supper, I go for my

---

*The economic depression spreading across France had not yet affected Provence.

†"Did I tell you," Mme de Sévigné wrote of her neighbor, "that she pretended to be deeply grieved, but all the while was filching from her mother's purse while she lay dying?"

‡What is interesting about this passage is that Mme de Sévigné saw herself as "a demoiselle from Burgundy" although she was Paris born and bred, and had spent relatively little time in her father's natal province. Interesting, too, that she should think of herself as "raised at the Court" whereas her association with the Court had been minimal.

*promenade. I want to think about God. I think about you. I want to
say my Rosary. I dream. I find Pilois, and talk to him about three or
four new allées I want to lay out. And then, for fear of displeasing you,
I come in as the dews of night begin to settle.*

The company to which she turned with unfailing pleasure was that of
her books: "I brought along a great quantity of carefully selected books,"
she wrote on June 5:

*I have just arranged them on the shelves. There is not a one you can
pick up without wanting to read it through. There is one whole shelf
of devotional books . . . Another is devoted exclusively to good histories. Another to poetry and to novellas and memoirs. The long novels
are now scorned, and have been relegated to small closets. When I go
into that study, I wonder why I ever leave it.*

She spent much time in that small tower room overlooking the garden.
"I am often in my study," she wrote on June 15, "in such good company
that I say to myself, 'This little room is worthy of my daughter. There is not
a book in it which she could not pick up with pleasure' "—this despite the
fact that she recognized their literary tastes to be dissimilar, as she makes
clear in a letter of June 9:

*I will always be attracted to some light reading because I have lowbrow
tastes like your brother. Abstract thoughts come naturally to you, but
not to me. With our literary tastes so divergent, my darling, it is a
wonder how well we get on together. To the contrary, we have the
attraction of novelty to offer one another, and when all is said and
done, all I ask of this life is to see you again and revel in the pleasure
to be found in the bosom of a family as agreeable as mine. Monsieur
de Grignan makes clear that he wants to have his place in that family
circle, and be reassured that he constitutes a valuable addition to it.*

In addition to Mme de Sévigné's books, there were her woodlands to
serve her as diversion. Not even nightfall could always confine her to the
château:

*The other evening, they came to me and said, "Madame, it is warm in
the Mall; there is not so much as a breath of wind . . . and the moon is
making magic there!" I could not resist the temptation. I called up my*

infantry, and put on a mass of bonnets, headgear and cloaks which were totally unnecessary. I went to the Mall where the air was as warm as in my chamber. I saw a thousand phantom shapes ... white- and black-robed monks, gray- and white-robed nuns, sheets draped here and there, black men, men buried up against tree trunks, little men hidden so well that only their heads were showing, priests who dared not come too close. After having laughed at all those shadowy forms, and being convinced that they were what we call spirits—using our imaginations as their stage—we came back without stopping anywhere, and without having felt so much as a drop of moisture. My darling, forgive me, but I felt obliged—as did the Ancients—to pay my respects to the moon.

With an imagination as vivid as hers, Mme de Sévigné was never at a loss when it came to creating her own diversions. Marcel Proust saw Mme de Sévigné's romanticism, her taste for the bizarre, the picturesque and the hallucinatory—this passage, in particular—as an expression of what he called her "Dostoievskan side."

There were Mme de Sévigné's books, her woodlands and—above all— her letters to her daughter to occupy her heart and mind at Les Rochers:

Finally, my darling [she wrote on June 5], during this eternal separation of ours, while I await other, greater consolations which constitute the high hope of my life, I find some cause for gratitude in the fact that your letters reach me within nine days after you have written them. They arrive in Paris on Saturday, and are tossed into the mail pouch for Brittany, where I receive them on Monday morning.

"Those letters are read and reread with all the emotion they deserve," she wrote on June 12:

You keep me busy all the week. On Monday morning, your letters reach me. I read them, and go on with my replies until Wednesday. Thursday I spend waiting for Friday morning to come—when I can expect another mail packet from you. That one will sustain me in the same way until Sunday. And so the days go by, and I yearn for the time for which my heart prompts me to hope, without knowing how or when it will come ...

And now I am going to tell you a funny thing, which is that the first time I read your letters, I am so emotional that I do not see half of

*what is in them. Rereading them at my leisure, I find a thousand things
I want to talk to you about . . .*

Madame de Sévigné's letters reveal that the Grignans lavishly admired
her letters, as she acknowledges somewhat coyly on June 15:

*I make no reply to what you have to say about my letters, my darling.
I am thrilled that they please you, but had you not told me so, I would
never have thought them even passable. I never have the courage to
read them through in their entirety, once I have finished them, but
sometimes I say to myself, "My God, how I pity my daughter having
to read all this rubbish!"*

"I cannot understand," she wrote on another day that summer, "how
that Monsieur de Grignan of yours can find my letters so amusing."

*They often contain whole chapters on business affairs, melancholy
meditations, reflections on expenses. What does he make of all that?
He would have to skip around to find passages to entertain him. In this
part of the world, those are referred to as "wastelands"; one must cross
many of them in my letters to reach the green meadows.*

What she seemed to have hoped for, by then, at Les Rochers, was to
have her faith to comfort her:

*I read my books of devotion because I wanted to prepare myself to
receive the Holy Ghost. Oh, my darling, this would have been the very
place—here, in this solitude—to have hoped to have it descend upon
me. But that Holy Spirit manifests Itself only where It wills, decides in
which hearts to dwell . . .*

She envied those with faith, thought her friend the Count de Guitaut
"very lucky" to be "devout." "I am somewhat more struck by the thought
of Eternity than you are," she wrote her daughter toward the end of June,
"but that is because I am closer to it. And yet that thought in no slightest
degree increases my love of God."

She had reason repeatedly to rue her intellectual approach to religion,
what she called her "enlightened mind and ice-cold heart."

Before the summer was out, however, she had shaken off her melancholy, and reverted to her customary good humor, reassuring her daughter, who had evidently expressed concern over her mother's isolation:

> It is most kind of you to be wishing for companions for me, but I really need none. Here I am now quite well adjusted to the solitude. I have workmen who amuse me; the Bien Bon has his own. Only his mania for construction and renovation can win out over his thrift.
>
> It is true that he costs us little, but the expense would be still less if he would restrain himself. It is these woods which are my delight. Their beauty is astonishing. I am often alone there with my cane and Louison.* I need nothing else.

Not that she did not yearn to be at Grignan where her favorite people were gathering:

> Little Coulanges will be coming to visit you. He turned down Monsieur de Chaulnes and Brittany in favor of Lyon and Grignan. I would do the same, my darling. What I would like best in all the world is to be there with all of you! . . . Yours will be, in truth, a wonderful company! You will be a very large and very distinguished number. Grignan is a city, not a château!

"You have such a distinguished company at Grignan," she wrote on another occasion that summer, "so grand a scale of living, so fine an orchestra, so excellent an art collection that—in that beautiful château of yours—there can be no such thing as solitude. It might be said to be the most delightful of republics—were it not for the bise and the horrors of winter."

The Grignans' prominence, their viceregal way of life, the magnificence of their château gave Mme de Sévigné cause for both infinite pride and infinite concern. (The governorship, she wrote, was "a role you have played most worthily for ten years in a row. I would not have wanted to have missed seeing you in your kingdom.") They had lived in a grandeur she had found enormously impressive, although it was a grandeur far beyond their means. "I can understand, my darling, that you dare not inquire into the state of your finances," she wrote sorrowfully, that summer:

> It is like a house of cards upon which one dares not breathe lest it collapse. There must be some kind of sorcery you practice in connec-

---

*Louison was another of Mme de Sévigné's maids.

tion with the magnificence of your château and the high life you lead ... I think you must resort to black magic, as must those impecunious courtiers. They never have a sou, but they go on every voyage, on every campaign; they dress in the height of fashion, take part in all the balls, all the tilting tournaments, all the lotteries, and are constantly on the go, no matter how bankrupt they may be ... Their lands decrease in value; no matter, they go on just the same. If it proves necessary to go to meet Monsieur de Vendôme,* one will go, one will find the money somehow. Must one refuse a present? Must one rush out to greet Monsieur de Louvois as he passes through? Must one mount an expedition to patrol the coast? Must one revive—at Grignan—the ancient sovereign state of the Adhémars? Must one have an orchestra? Does one see pictures one desires? One undertakes, one manages to do it all. It is one of the things I do not understand, but since I take an interest in your affairs, I am very concerned about them, even more than about my own, and that is the truth. But, my darling, let us not dwell on such matters in our letters. They come to my mind only too often in the middle of the forest, in the middle of the night.

One way to change the subject was to talk of the Court, to relay the latest reports from her numerous Paris correspondents; even at second hand, she managed to make the gossip lively. ("Really, my darling, I am thrilled that my letters and the news from my friends which I relay to you, amuse you as much as you say they do.") The Court was at Fontainebleau for the month of June; Charles de Sévigné was among the courtiers in the suite of the Dauphin, and kept his mother posted:

I hear that there is a constant round of pleasure, but not a moment of genuine enjoyment [Mme de Sévigné wrote her daughter]. Mme de Maintenon's favor increases constantly, while that of Mme de Monte-span perceptibly decreases. That of the Fontanges is at zenith.

They write me that His Majesty's conversations with Mme de Maintenon grow longer and longer, more and more fascinating [Mme de Sévigné wrote Mme de Grignan toward the end of June]; that the daughter-in-law [the Dauphine] sometimes goes there for a short visit where she finds them seated, each in a large chair, and that as soon as

*The Duke de Vendôme, Governor of Provence, was expected to visit the province in 1680, and the Count de Grignan, as Lieutenant-Governor, would have been expected to welcome his superior along the way.

she leaves, the thread of the conversation is resumed. My friend tells me that no one any longer approaches the lady without fear and respect, and that the [King's] Ministers pay court to her as other people pay court to them.

By July, the Court had removed to the Palace at Saint-Germain, as Mme de Sévigné noted in her letter of the seventeenth:

Mme de Coulanges wrote me upon her return from Saint-Germain. She continues to be astonished at the degree of favor Mme de Maintenon enjoys. No other admirer is so solicitous, so attentive as he to her. She writes me what I have so often said, myself, that she introduces him to a world he had never before known, that of friendly interchange, of conversations without constraint and without guile. He appears charmed by it.* Mme de Fontanges has left for Chelles.† She had four carriages, drawn by six horses, each; her own carriage, drawn by eight, and all her sisters with her, but all so sad that it was pitiful to see—that great beauty losing all her blood,‡ pale, changed, overwhelmed with sorrow, despising the 40,000 écus annual pension and the tabouret which she has, and wishing for her health and the heart of the King which she has lost.

By July, the Princess de Tarente—Mme de Sévigné's favorite neighbor—was back in residence in her Château Madame at Vitré and, shortly after, she persuaded Mme de Sévigné to accompany her on a short visit to Rennes, the ancient capital of the Duchy of Brittany and the Parliamentary seat. "I must tell you about the reception tendered Mme the Princess de Tarente in this town, yesterday," she wrote on August 6, from Rennes:

To begin with, Monsieur the Duke de Chaulnes dispatched forty Guards with a captain at their head to greet us, a full league beyond the town. A little later, there appeared Mme de Marboeuf, two [Parliamentary] presidents, some friends of Mme the Princess de Tarente, and finally

---

*The relationship was evidently less platonic than Mme de Coulanges and Mme de Sévigné envisaged at that time. Mme de Maintenon had the honor of becoming Louis XIV's morganatic wife—or the last in his long line of mistresses.

†The King, in 1680, had installed Mme de Fontanges's sister, the Abbess of Maubuisson, as the Abbess of Chelles.

‡Mme de Fontanges had been subject to hemorrhaging since being brought to bed of a child which did not survive.

Monsieur de Chaulnes, Monsieur [the Bishop] of Rennes, Messieurs de Coëtlogon, de Tonquedec, de Beaucé, de Kercado, de Crapodo, de Kenpart, de Keriquimini ...* Everyone stops, everyone kisses, everyone sweats; no one knows what anyone is saying. The carriages roll again, to the sound of drums and trumpets ... With no vanity on my part, I advise stopping a few minutes at Mme de Chaulnes's. We found her with a retinue of at least forty noblewomen or girls—not one who did not bear a good name. Most of these were relatives of the men who had come out to meet us on the road. I forgot to tell you that there were six carriages with six horses each, and more than ten with four horses. To return to the ladies: I met three or four of my "daughters-in-law"†—red as fire, so fearful they were of meeting me! I saw nothing to prevent me from wishing them other husbands than your brother! Everyone kissed everyone, male and female alike. It was a strange procedure ... Toward the end, one could not pull oneself loose from the cheek one touched; it was total union; sweat sealed us together! Finally, we got back in our carriage, looking unrecognizable, and came to Mme de Marboeuf's ... We shut ourselves in our rooms, and you can guess what we did. As for me, I changed my chemise and my costume, and without meaning to appear vain, made myself so beautiful as totally to eclipse my daughters-in-law!

Dinner that evening was at the Governor's brilliantly illuminated Palace—"everyone seated at two large tables of sixteen covers each":

Every night, the routine is the same. After supper, there are games and conversation, but what I found most annoying was the sight of a very pretty young lady—certainly no brighter than I am—who twice check-mated Monsieur the Duke de Chaulnes, doing it with such dash and such skill as to make me green with envy!‡ We returned here for a delicious night's sleep. I awake this morning, and am writing to you, my darling, although my letter will not go off until tomorow. I am sure that I will be telling you of the most elaborate dinner, most elaborate supper—the same thing, over and over again: a great din, trumpets, violins, a regal air! So that, all in all, you may rightly deduce that this is a very splendorous government, this one here in Brittany. However,

---

*Mme de Sévigné loved to roll the exotic Breton names on her tongue and pen.
†Breton girls to whom Charles de Sévigné had been attentive.
‡Card games held little attraction for Mme de Sévigné, but she was intrigued with chess, and could not understand why—with a mind as quick as hers—she could not become more skillful at it.

I saw you in your little Provence accompanied by just as many ladies, and Monsieur de Grignan followed by just as many gentlemen, and received at Lambesc just as impressively as Monsieur de Chaulnes could be here. The thought came to my mind that, there, in your governance, people were paying court to you while I have come here to pay mine. It is thus that Providence ordains . . .

By August 7, Mme de Sévigné had had a surfeit of large crowds, small talk and rich food: "It's banquet after banquet!"—"I am passionately eager to get out of here, where they overwhelm me with honors. I hunger to go on a diet and to be silent." "Tomorrow, please God," she wrote on August 12, "I will be back at Les Rochers"—back to what she called "the peace and the silence of my forests."

XXXVIII

Charles de Sévigné's prospects struck his mother as dismal, at that juncture: "I foresee such problems in your brother's future that I simply cannot talk about it," she wrote on June 21, 1680. Somewhat to the surprise of the reader, Mme de Sévigné's letters during the summer of 1680 manifest almost as much concern for her son as for her daughter. Both his military and his Court career had gone awry. At odds with his superior officer and dissatisfied with his subaltern post, Charles was still determined to sell his commission—at any price. Indifferent to the splendors and pleasures of Versailles, Fontainebleau and Saint-Germain, he dreamed only of retiring to his estates in Brittany. His mother would not so much have minded paying the substantial interest on the money she had borrowed to finance the purchase of that commission, "if only," as she put it, "he had been happy in his career."

"I continue to receive the gloomiest letters from my son," she wrote Mme de Grignan on July 3:

What other men would hail as their good fortune and their joy, he refers to as his chains and his slavery. If ever a man seemed cut out— by personality as well as by wit—to fit perfectly into that world, and to gain distinction in it—I would have thought Monsieur de Sévigné to be that man. The very opposite is true.

It is one of the games Providence plays to prove to us how fallacious are our judgments [she wrote on another day, that summer]. There is every pleasure to be found in the world in which he finds himself . . . It is his misfortune that he does not take advantage of his opportunities. How he would have hankered after that life, had it been denied him!

If both of her children were profligate, Mme de Sévigné could better understand her daughter's profligacy than her son's:

You are not so inept as he [she told her daughter] because you, at least, have something to show for your miscalculations: your splendorous purchases, your large domestic staff, your equipages, the air of grandeur in your household, your lavish expenditures on every side—large enough to make you feel the pinch, although not enough to satisfy Monsieur de Grignan's tastes. But, as for my son, no one would ever give him credit for having a sou. He gives no gifts, no dinner parties, he is not generous in his gallantries, owns not so much as a horse on which to follow the King or the Dauphin on the hunt, never risks so much as a louis on the gaming table. But if you knew the amount of money that passes through his hands, you would be surprised. I compare him to the mosquitoes in your part of the world which cause so much discomfort without ever being heard or seen. As a matter of fact, my darling, it is not my ineptitude my children have inherited. I have no business acumen, but I am provident and amenable to reason.

The Grignans might have something more to show for their prodigality than poor Charles, but that did not mean that they were exempt from censure: "Your château must be simply overflowing with guests, this summer," Mme de Sévigné wrote rather testily:

Two tables of twelve each set in your Gallery! I am to blame for having told you of Monsieur de Chaulnes's. But, my darling, to have to put up beds in the Gallery! That seems to me to be carrying things so far that I cannot but think that your expenses are excessive, too, and when you tell me that it costs you nothing to live at Grignan, then I must say that I cannot believe it. I know only too well how costly it can be, and what a drain on your provisions. And, as for the gambling, do you really *expect me to believe that you and Monsieur de Grignan are suffering no losses? I am convinced that this exceeds normal expense ... But, then, my dear, some people are born to spend lavishly, just as others are born to break their necks. Nowhere can they escape temptation, nothing can stop them ... They attract people, pleasure, expense—as amber attracts straw ...*

In mid-July, according to a letter to Mme de Grignan, Mme de Sévigné heard from her Paris correspondents that her son "was being seen constantly in the company of the Duchess de Villeroy," spending more time at her "great, very great house" at Fontainebleau than at the château. "You know very well, my dear," Mme de Sévigné added, "that this is not the way to pay one's court."

She was, as she wrote Mme de Grignan, puzzled by the letters she received from Charles, later in the month: "Apropos of some money he won from her, he said, 'Would to God that was all I had gotten from her!' What the devil does he mean by that?"

By the end of July, she had discovered "what the devil" he meant by that: it was a case of venereal disease he "had gotten" from the Duchess. Paris buzzed with the scandal:

It is my son who told Mme de La Fayette and ten or twelve of her friends about his misfortune—a little secret to be shared by the fifteen of us! I was astonished to see how nonchalantly he treated this slight indisposition of his. I would have thought he would have died rather than open his mouth about it but, seeing him so forthright on the subject, I am, too.

By the end of August, the stricken Lothario tottered into Les Rochers. His mother was livid with rage at the confidences he made her: "My daughter," she wrote, "there are women whose heads should be bashed in by the general public!"

Do you understand what I am saying to you? Yes, they deserve to be mobbed! Perfidy, treason, insolence, effrontery are common practice with them, and vile deceit is the least of their faults. Furthermore, they lack so much as a shred of sentiment. I do not use the word "love" because they do not know what it means. They have not a shred of decency, charity or human kindness. All in all, they are monsters, monsters who speak and have wit, brazen creatures above all reproach who enjoy taking advantage of human weakness. Put a frame around this picture, and you have the portrait of a lady I do not wish to name . . .

"To be honest with you, your little brother is not feeling well," Mme de Sévigné wrote in late August:

He is only too happy to be here in peace and quiet. For my part, I am not satisfied about his condition. I think it is a great comfort for him to be able to complain to me, and I am glad to be able—despite my remonstrances—to be helpful to him in this bizarre situation. To tell the truth, it would have been better for him to have been "fricasseed in the snow," as Ninon expresses it, than in a sauce so highly seasoned as this one! It strikes me that you find nothing extraordinary about this adventure, and that you think that the loved one—or, rather, the hated one!—is no more perturbed, no more embarrassed than if the complaint were a simple head cold!

(Indignant as she was, Mme de Sévigné could not but chuckle at Mme de Coulanges's comment that a cure for the Duchess would constitute "cause for public rejoicing.")

With no specific remedy for venereal disease available in the seventeenth-century pharmacopoeia, Charles languished late into the summer: "As for your little brother," Mme de Sévigné wrote his sister, "he is in a bad way, but since there is no real danger, I beg you, my child, not to be alarmed . . . about him or me. His is not an ailment I will contract by reading or chatting with him."

"Let's talk about your poor brother," she wrote, on another day:

A rascally Paris surgeon—after having tried numerous remedies on him—assured him that he was cured, and prescribed nothing but whey to refresh him. Your little brother took it with utter confidence, but in the meanwhile precious time was lost. Finally, he found himself in such a state as to curse the whey. As a result, he saw that doctor I told you about who is very skillful, and who is now treating him as the ailment ought to be treated—without, however, quarantining him. We hope that, in time, he will regain his health. We console him, we amuse him—Mme de Marboeuf, a pretty woman from Vitré, and I. Sometimes our neighbors come to play hombre with him. He is very patient, and amuses himself with games and books, for which he has not lost his *taste. You are going to say to me, "But, Mother, don't they suspect what is wrong with him?" Oh, yes, my daughter, certainly they do; it is not difficult to make out. But he is patient, and what is so funny about it is that he is less embarrassed because it is a Duchess—on her dais*—who is responsible for the damage, rather than some camp-follower on the ramparts! . . . All in all, my daughter, you would pity that poor little brother of yours if you could see him. He is in constant pain. I think I could never find a better opportunity to repay him for all the care and attention he gave me. God does not wish me to be indebted to him . . .*

If Charles was "very patient," his mother was not. She felt that they had given the local doctor ample opportunity to effect a cure, and that it was time to consult the renowned medical faculty of the capital: "I am most concerned about my son. I have strongly urged that we go to Paris, the source of all good and evil, but he has resisted, making light of this disease, and putting all his confidence in that doctor I told you about. I have no influence over my children," she complained on October 16:

He likes being in this peaceful spot. He comes down every morning, and sits at the corner of the hearth in his housecoat and furred bonnet. With his Capuchin's beard, his big eyes and regular features, his despondency, and faint aroma of unguents, he would make us think of our wounded heroes—if we did not know the underside of the cards! . . . We read, we chat. He is glad to have me here, and I—for a thousand reasons—am glad to be able to give him comfort . . .

For Charles, as well as Mme de Grignan, to be in poor health was almost more than their mother could bear: "You are both of you so old and broken in health that I spend my life nursing you!" She could never really feel easy about Mme de Grignan's health; it was, at best, delicate. Mme de Sévigné inquired repeatedly about her daughter's "lassitudes and languors," her "colics," her respiratory problems, her "over-heated blood," and other disturbing symptoms which Mme de Grignan had evidently reported. "My poor darling, aren't you alarmed about your cold, numb legs? Aren't you afraid it might end up in paralysis?" Mme de Sévigné fretted over her daughter's weight loss, only to learn that the latter liked being slim: "My

---

*The dais, like the *tabouret*, was a symbol of the highest rank in the feudal hierarchy of France.

God, my daughter, how I would scold you for being pleased about being so thin!" Mme de Sévigné fumed: "If you were simply resigned to it, I could better understand; but to be pleased about it, that is unreasonable!" "You say that you are feeling well," she wrote Mme de Grignan, that autumn: "I hope that is true, for I simply could not face the thought of both my children being ill!"

Just then, in the early autumn, on September 11—almost a year to the day since mother and daughter had parted—came tidings so glad as to dispel the miasma of gloom and fog overhanging Les Rochers:

I would never have believed, my dearest dear [Mme de Sévigné addressed her daughter on September 11], that a letter telling me you would be in Paris for the winter, and that I would see you there, could make me cry, but that is the effect the assurance of such joy had on me ... No, surely, it is not always sadness that makes us cry; emotions of all kinds are capable of bringing on tears. You have often laughed at me for being stirred by sentiments which did not even affect me personally. Imagine, my darling, how moved I am by those wondrously wise and saintly words of Mlle de Grignan's! What resolution! What courage! How I admire her!

Those "wondrously wise and saintly words of Mlle de Grignan's" to which Mme de Sévigné refers so rhapsodically were those in which the twenty-year-old girl* had couched the announcement of her decision to take the veil. Mme de Sévigné's elation reflects the fact that if the girl renounced the world, her worldly goods—some 70,000 livres bequeathed her by her mother, but not yet paid her by her father—could be expected to revert to the Grignan coffers. It was unthinkable that she might prefer to endow the convent she would enter rather than to assist her necessitous family. It is unfair categorically to characterize Mme de Sévigné's attitude in the matter as entirely opportunistic. Certainly, she was not unmindful of the great financial benefits that would accrue to her son-in-law and his family, but she may well have been sincere when she spoke of Mlle de Grignan's vocation as "miraculous" and the girl herself as "a treasure of grace, a predestined soul." The Catholic tradition in which Mme de Sévigné had been reared

---

*Louise-Cathérine de Grignan, the elder of the Count de Grignan's two daughters by his first wife, Angélique d'Angennes, announced her decision to take the veil as early as 1680, but did not enter the Carmelite order until 1686.

represented the Bride of Christ as one of God's Elect, the celibate life as one of far greater perfection than the marital.

"What gratitude my heart feels toward you, my dear darling," Mme de Sévigné wrote her daughter on September 15, as the full impact of the announcement of the Grignans' imminent arrival in Paris dawned upon her, "for having put my heart at rest by giving it the right to hope to see you, this winter! I have read and reread, time and time again, that dear letter of yours for which I had so fondly hoped, and I say to myself, 'It is she herself who writes and tells me that she will be coming to Paris shortly after All Saints' Day!'"

So, there you are now, my darling [she wrote], having arrived at your decision, thanks to the most important, most advantageous thing that could have happened to your family! It is a brilliant stroke of fortune, and it is on an occasion such as this that one must make a journey . . . in ogni modo. You will find the money somehow, for Monsieur the Archbishop has never had to resort to the Devil to find means of subsistence for you; he has always found it by natural means†. . . . In this instance, anything you do would be justified by the importance of the matter which obliges you to it, and by the marvelous advantages which will result from it . . .*

In truth, my darling, if all this ends as I believe and hope it will, it should prove a great joy to you, as well. It strikes me that you have even contributed to it by the good example you have set, by your kindness, and by your line of conduct with that saintly girl. You have imbued her with love for her House and her name. Her goals and visions on a loftier plane, she is pleased to think that those closest to her should benefit by what she leaves behind and spurns. Don't you really think that vocations such as hers—so long meditated and so steadfast—are miraculous?

"My God, what a credit all this will be to you, my darling," Mme de Sévigné exclaimed in another letter to her daughter, "to you, in particular! And how clear it will seem that it was you who managed and directed it all for the benefit of your House! In all justice, you are due high praise!"

Justly or unjustly, succeeding generations have heaped not praise but censure on Mme de Grignan's head for her role in her stepdaughter's deci-

In ogni modo—by one means or another.
†Family account books show that the Archbishop of Arles made a loan to his nephew on October 11, 1680, presumably for the Paris journey.

sion to enter a religious order. In the twentieth century it has become popular to condemn Mme de Grignan as cold and calculating, a conniving woman who exerted pressure on a naïve, impressionable young girl entrusted to her care to immure herself in a nunnery so that her father might be spared the expense of paying her the substantial sum still due her from her mother's estate. What twentieth-century biographers sometimes forget is that it was common practice in seventeenth-century France for the nobility to relegate their daughters, willy-nilly, to the convent—often at an early age. (Had not the Grignans immured their own five-year-old Marie-Blanche in the Convent at Aix-en-Provence? Had not the Count and Countess de Guitaut—of far better financial status than the Grignans—deposited four of their seven daughters in the Convent at Avallon?)

As has happened before, a letter of Mme de Sévigné's intended as a panegyric redounds, instead, to her daughter's discredit. It happens again in a letter written within a week of the foregoing, and was obviously intended as a reassurance to her daughter, who had evidently deplored her own inability to make and keep friends: "You are very unjust, my dear girl," Mme de Sévigné wrote on September 22, 1680, "when you sit in judgment on yourself":

> You say that, first off, people think you amiable enough, but that when they know you better, they no longer care for you. The exact opposite is true. In the beginning, people stand in fear of you. You have a somewhat disdainful air about you. People are discouraged from trying to make friends with you ... But when one comes to know you, when one attains to the circle of your friends and wins your confidence, one adores you and becomes a fast friend. If someone seems to break off with you, it is because that person loves you, but despairs of ever being loved by you as he or she would like to be. I have heard people rave about the pleasure of being included among your friends, and confess their own shortcomings as the cause for having forfeited that privilege.

Few voices have been raised, across the centuries, in Mme de Grignan's defense. As late as the 1920's, Thornton Wilder contributed to the bad press by which the Countess de Grignan has been plagued for the past three hundred years. The Marquesa de Montemayor, one of Wilder's leading characters in *The Bridge of San Luis Rey*, is none other than the Marquise de Sévigné—borrowed from real life and transplanted from Paris to Lima—writing out her heartbreak in exquisite love letters to her unworthy, unresponsive (what Wilder calls her "cold and intellectual") daughter, Doña Clara, in far-off Spain.

XXXIX

The decision to leave Brittany was sudden.

At Les Rochers, Sunday, October 20 [1680]:
> *By the time you receive this letter, my darling, you will be able to say, "My Mother is in Paris!" I am leaving tomorrow morning, taking my son to the great city where he is sure to find relief. The doctors everywhere else are ignorant, and one can say of Paris,*
> *"Just as it causes all the ills, so it provides all the cures."**
> *...And so, my dear, we are leaving ... What it might have taken us a month to do, we have accomplished in a moment; our baggage is ready. And, as Providence would have it, it is not for your sake that I am rushing back. I am always dashing off to the one who needs me most, and I can look forward to the joy of seeing and embracing you only after I have brought our poor invalid—not to our house—but to safe harbor.† I will arrive before All Saints' Day, and will have time to see that your apartment is in order, and to welcome you upon your arrival with all the love you know I feel for you.*

"Adieu, adieu," she wrote, as she came toward the close of that very long letter:

> *I amuse myself chatting with you, but I have a thousand things to do. I am going now to help the good Abbé, and sign a thousand papers. I had farewell visits from that good and obliging Princess, and all the rest of the neighborhood ... The roads are very good. God, I hope, will guide us ... I feel sure that we have made the right decision, darling, and feel certain that in Paris we can look forward to a total cure ... My darling, you should avoid the bad weather. You no longer have a pretext for delay, now that I am back in Paris.*

---

*Mme de Sévigné quotes from a verse by Benserade.

†Charles would not go to the Hôtel Carnavalet upon arrival in Paris, but to the house of the doctor in charge of his case.

Her next letter was headed, "At Malicorne. Wednesday, October 23," and began:

So, here we are, on our way, my darling, with a keen desire and a great need to get to Paris. We have no time to lose in finding relief for this poor boy. The pains in his head and the constant fever which is the result of the pain—along with his Lauzun beard—render him unrecognizable . . . Tell me about your plans . . .

On Wednesday, October 30, she wrote from Paris:

I arrived here last night, my dear one, in perfectly wonderful weather. If you are wise, you will take advantage of it, and not wait until next month when you may run into rains and bad roads.

The improvement in Charles's condition cheered her: he had already been restored "to his natural state"; "no more fever, no more discomfort, regaining strength." "I found the Chevalier [de Grignan] in perfect health," she continued: "I am thrilled to have him here,* and wish he could stay on . . . He and I went to look at your apartment. It is really going to be very pretty, and you will be pleased with it."

Mme de Sévigné had learned, to her great disappointment, that her six-year-old granddaughter, Pauline, would not be coming to Paris with her parents and her brother, the little Marquis, who was nine, but that she would be going, instead, to the Convent at Valence, where her aunt was Abbess. "We would have liked it far better had you decided to bring her with you," Mme de Sévigné wrote her daughter. "Oh, Good Lord, how we would have enjoyed that! You will be my consolation but, in truth, nothing less would do."

"I have seen all of my poor friends," Mme de Sévigné continued:

Mme de La Fayette spent the entire day here, after dinner . . . It did not strike me that Mme de Schomberg had as yet usurped my place† . . . Do you remember our talking once about the pleasures of budding friendship—of showing off one's merchandise before new acquaintances? Nothing could be truer. Everything is new, everything is

---

*The Chevalier had asked for temporary lodging at the Carnavalet while he looked for a house to rent in the neighborhood.

†Mme de Schomberg had become intimate with Mme de La Fayette during Mme de Sévigné's absence in Brittany—much to the latter's displeasure.

admirable, everything is admired. One decks oneself in all one's riches; one outdoes one another in praise. There is much more vanity in a friendship like this than there is confidence or devotion. In short, I do not feel that I have yet been thrown out with the garbage.

If you want me to speak frankly and reasonably, my daughter, Monsieur de Grignan should have you leave without waiting for the ceremony of welcome to be tendered to the Duke de Vendôme.* That would throw you into the month of January—and that would be deadly . . .

Mademoiselle de Méri, that hypochondriacal, cantankerous old-maid cousin of Mme de Sévigné's, having spent the summer at the Carnavalet while all its occupants were away, lingered on after they returned, trying Mme de Sévigné's soul, as was her wont. "Mlle de Méri is still here," Mme de Sévigné wrote Mme de Grignan, who was very fond of the lady, and thought her mother less than patient:

She will take a long time about moving; she is in no hurry. She seems in better health [Mme de Sévigné wrote in early November]. She talks, and is capable of listening. We have long conversations, every evening. Oh, my child, how easy I am to live with! How far a little kindness, a bit of sociability, a touch of confidence go with me! I really think no one is more disposed than I to live amiably with people. I wish you could see how things go when Mlle de Méri meets me halfway.

We are putting the finishing touches to your apartment. All is in place; only you are missing! Come with a light heart. Remember that this voyage betokens a stroke of great good fortune for your House. Don't bring along any of your "dragons." Don't resist, this time . . .

On November 8, Mme de Sévigné reacted sharply to Mme de Grignan's announcement that their visit would be brief:

We are all strangely hurt at the idea of your leaving us again in the month of May . . . It is positively ruinous to go to the expense of leasing a house, making renovations, and shipping baggage for a mere three months' stay . . . As much as I long to embrace you, I would advise you not to come if you are spending so short a while . . . My love for

---

*The Duke de Vendôme, Governor of Provence, had been expected in the province that year, but never reached there.

you, my darling, seems to flow in my bloodstream. I feel it in the marrow of my bones. It has become my very self . . .

These were the last lines of Mme de Sévigné's letter of November 8, 1680. Almost four years would pass before she penned the next one to her daughter. Mme de Grignan's talk of spending only three months in Paris was premature. With France at peace, the Count de Grignan was not obliged to spend much time in the province he served as Lieutenant-Governor. He made annual visits to preside over the Assembly of the Communities of Provence at Lambesc, but Mme de Grignan did not accompany him. She and "the Grignettes" and the little Marquis remained at the Hôtel Carnavalet in Paris with her mother and the Abbé de Coulanges. Her brother, Charles de Sévigné, joined his family there when he was dismissed by his doctor.

When it is said that Mme de Sévigné's letter of November 8 was the last one she wrote to her daughter in the winter of 1680, it should be made clear that it is the last letter known to us. Since Mme de Grignan did not reach Paris until early in December, it is only logical to assume that her mother— as regular as was her writing schedule—addressed at least six more letters to her daughter during that period of time but, if so, they have disappeared, and are missing from the collection. At such time as Mme de Grignan was in residence at her château, she stored all her mother's letters in special coffers. The six addressed to her just before she left Provence and along the road to Paris must have been misplaced or lost.

It is from a letter to the Count de Bussy that the date of Mme de Grignan's arrival in Paris is established: "I wish you a good day and a good year, my poor cousin," Mme de Sévigné wrote on January 2, 1681:

I left Brittany on October 20, somewhat sooner than I had expected, to go to Paris. A month later, I had the pleasure of welcoming my daughter, although it was not on her account that I had come home. I found her in better health than when she left. That pernicious air of Provence which might well have been devastating to her, proved not to be. She is as enchanting as ever, and I defy the two of you to see and talk to one another without loving one another . . .

With Mme de Grignan "in better health" and "as enchanting as ever," the reunion was off to a good start. The reunion of 1680–84 was halcyon, as can be ascertained through letters written subsequent to their separation in 1684. Mme de Sévigné had been determined to make it so, to preserve it from the discord which had plagued the reunions of previous years. Mme de Sévigné, for the first time in the correspondence—for the first time, very probably, in their lives—acknowledged that she might have contributed to their problems, and vowed to correct such failings of her own as she had identified. If she had failed, that summer at Les Rochers, to find the blind faith for which she yearned, she had, at least, arrived at a state of utter submission to the decrees of Providence and, in so doing, had attained to an equilibrium, an emotional stability that would go far toward eliminating confrontations with her daughter.

Mme de Sévigné was full of good resolve: "I hope to put into practice all the resolutions I made in the course of my meditations," she wrote. "I will become perfect by the end of my life. What consoles me about the past, my darling, is that you see into my innermost being—my too tender heart, my too lively temperament, my mediocre intelligence."

"It seems to me, as it does to you, my darling," she had written Mme de Grignan from Les Rochers upon receiving news of the Grignans' impending visit, "that our relationship will never again be clouded by misunderstanding or mistrust. I said this to you, just the other day. I even think that as far as I am concerned, you will find me less importunate in my attentions. This is what has made me yearn more than ever to see you again, my most loveable child."

Mme de Sévigné would pattern herself after Monsieur de Grignan:

Monsieur de Grignan, who is a perfect example of that imperturbability, that nonchalance which you admire, would be a good model for me to follow. But it seems to me that I have already corrected myself of that silly excitability of mine, and I am certain that I will make still further progress on that road along which you lead me by convincing me that I need never doubt your love for me.

Never to doubt each other's love—that was the keystone of the entente that was thenceforward to distinguish the once troubled mother–daughter relation. Confident of each other's love, each could make allowances for the other's foibles, sidestep controversial issues, avoid stepping on one another's toes. The happy reunion of 1680 was evidently the result of a concerted effort, of a determination on both sides to live harmoniously together. Mme de Sévigné, having already promised to be "less importunate in her attentions," may also have striven to appear less anxious, less effusive, less intense—to be as cool as Monsieur de Grignan; while Mme de Grignan may have set her mind on being more open with her mother, more forthcoming, more demonstrative, less reserved, less inhibited.

In previous years, conflict had arisen between the two women over the organization of the household they shared. Mme de Sévigné would try to make sure that their reunion, this time, would not be blighted by controversy over living arrangements. Better to go into detail in advance than to risk friction later. "Now, let us talk a little about the advice you asked of me," she had written on September 22:

I do not advise your bringing kitchen utensils; it is too much trouble, and you won't need them. You can use mine; I can use the Bien Bon's *... As for napkins, I will lend you some of mine, to start with. Bring a few, and tell the Chevalier ... that if he has contacts in Flanders, to order fifteen or twenty dozen for you. They cost only nine or ten francs, and are very pretty, and last a long time ... I would advise you, my dear, to stick with your everyday menus. I am convinced that you will save money that way. You have a large staff; your household is large. At very little extra cost, you will find that you can save on the more than ample amount you pay me so meticulously for your share of the household expenses. When you do not want to come upstairs, you can eat in your antechamber which is large and handsome and provided with screens. We will eat our main meal separately. The good Abbé likes to eat at more regular hours than you do, and I am expected to keep him company. But, in the evening, I will bring my hen to your table, and we will not see any the less of one another. You always bring a cook and a maître d'hôtel ... As for furnishings, you can always count on my old tapestries; if you do not dislike them, they are yours to use ... But if you don't want to use mine, you have only to say so. And so, here, my darling, you have my first thoughts on the subject. See how they strike you. If you do not approve, you have only to change things, and tell me what you prefer ... and we will have no arguments, for your ideas are often better than mine ...*

I don't think, my darling, that this is a letter you will want to frame. It would be like a picture by Bassan who always paints humble subjects of everyday life. You might do better burning it! Still, it might be useful to you in making your plans ... Can't you guess the reason why I go into all this? This way, there should be no clouds, no misunderstandings ...

XL

With the regular flow of letters between mother and daughter suspended for the duration of their reunion, we almost lose track of their lives throughout the years 1681–4. The little that is known of what went on in the Hôtel Carnavalet for those four years is known thanks to a scattering of letters addressed by Mme de Sévigné to three men with whom she corresponded intermittently: her cousin the Count de Bussy; the Count de Guitaut, her friend and neighbor (and "liege lord," as she facetiously called him); and Philippe Moulceau, presiding judge of the Montpellier tax court (with whom she had evidently struck up a warm friendship during her visit to Provence in 1672–3).

These three, fortunately for Sévignistes—and for various reasons of their own—meticulously preserved her letters. The Count de Bussy, supremely confident of the historical value of his correspondence, and with publication in mind, made copies of every letter received by him and of his reply. The Count de Guitaut regularly filed away his correspondence in the Château d'Époisses's Archives Room (where some sixty or more Sévigné letters constitute the largest cache of holographs extant today). Moulceau's motive in preserving the letters of his friend is unknown; he may simply have so much enjoyed them that he held on to them to reread, and repeat the pleasure.

In a letter dated January 12, 1681, Mme de Sévigné described her daughter's health as "delicate enough to make all those who loved her tremble." She was writing to Bussy in reply to a letter of his in which he proposed sending some of her letters along with some of his to King Louis XIV, who had enjoyed the first chapters of Bussy's *Mémoires*, and had requested more. "I would never have guessed the third party to our correspondence," Mme de Sévigné wrote. She appreciated the compliment, but confessed to some misgivings:

> *Do you think those letters of mine are worthy of inclusion? I only hope that you have edited them wherever necessary. Do you think my style—which reflects the intimacy of our friendship—might not be subject to misinterpretation? I never saw a letter written by one person*

to another which might not be taken amiss by a third, and that would
be a great injustice to the naïveté and the innocence of our longtime
friendship.

("I have not touched up your letters, Madame," Bussy jauntily made
rejoinder, "any more than Le Brun would have retouched an original Titian,
even had that master been guilty of some negligence.")

Months had passed, and it was the Easter season before Mme de Sévigné
again wrote to Bussy, a gossipy letter with a dateline of April 3, brimming
over with the latest news of Court and Capital for the exile's delectation: "I
don't know whether you have heard that the beautiful Fontanges is in a
convent, not so much to spend the holy days there as to prepare herself for
the voyage to eternity." "Life is short," she mused, again in a letter to Bussy,
"It is soon over. The current of the stream which carries us along is so swift
that there is scarcely time for us to show ourselves. And there you have my
moralizing for Holy Week."

By the last of June, the beautiful twenty-two-year-old mistress of the
King had embarked on that "journey to eternity": "*La belle Fontanges* is
dead," Mme de Sévigné wrote succinctly on the last day of the month: "*Sic
transit gloria mundi.*"

Her letter to the Count de Guitaut, in the early summer, was a letter of
congratulations on the birth of a son—the first after six daughters: "So,
finally, Monsieur, you have a boy! Take good care of him because you are
unable to produce one at will." "My daughter is writing to you," she continued, "and will doubtlessly mention her concern about her son, who has a
heavy cold. Since she is always borrowing trouble, she considers his illness
far more serious than it really is. But her poor little face—even though less
thin and drawn than when you saw it last—shows her anxiety—despite the
fact that she feels better than she did."

The autumn months of 1681 were spent, as was Mme de Sévigné's
custom, at her beloved Abbey of Livry, as her letter to Philippe Moulceau
confirms: "We did not return [to Paris] until yesterday," she wrote on
November 26: "We stayed on out of gratitude for the beautiful weather and
for my daughter's health which showed so much improvement during her
sojourn there."

Mme de Sévigné's next letter to the Count de Bussy-Rabutin—one
dated December 28, 1681—was written to assure him that, as a loyal member
of the Rabutin family, she stood squarely behind him and his beloved daughter, Mme de Coligny, in the face of the sordid scandal attaching to the latter's
name. Mme de Sévigné's expression of family solidarity was occasioned by

the rumors rampant in Paris on the subject of Mme de Coligny's secret liaison and subsequent marriage to a man posing as a gentleman—in fact, the son of a lackey. In 1679, Henri-François de La Rivière—an impostor whose real name was François Rivier, with no claim whatsoever to the "de," the particle of nobility—visited Bussy's château in Burgundy and seduced his widowed daughter. After a torrid two-year love affair—conducted somehow under the very nose of her unsuspecting father—the pair were wed in June of 1681 in the chapel of the bride's château at Lanty. When it proved that her husband had deceived her as to his name and lineage, Mme de Coligny repudiated him, and instituted suit to have the marriage declared null and void on the grounds that it was not only unconsummated, but further invalidated by various legal technicalities. The groom countered by insisting that she had borne him a child clandestinely, prior to the wedding ceremony, and eventually—cad that he was—resorted to blackmail, threatening not only to publish her impassioned letters, but also to expose what he referred to as the incestuous relations between her and her father unless she abided by the marriage contract. Scornful of the varlet's threats, the Count de Bussy and his daughter took their case to the courts of Parlement.

"As for the rest, my cousin," Mme de Sévigné began her letter of December 28, 1681,

> *I admire my de Coligny niece for her courage in undertaking to secure her peace of mind even at the price of the notoriety this kind of affair will bring upon her, and despite all the unpleasantness she will have to face to carry it through. But one must extricate oneself from such a plight and when—upon good counsel—one has so resolved, I heartily approve her determination to go through with it. She has need of you, my cousin; you will find great comfort in each other's love. Each of you will play his part, and all your friends and relatives will be zealous in their duty.* *

Mme de Sévigné had made a point of family solidarity in her December letter to her cousins, but the one she wrote to the Count de Guitaut, a few weeks later, may more accurately reflect her reaction to the imbroglio. In her opinion, as she told Guitaut, it took a lot of courage on the part of Bussy and his daughter to face up to the ugly scandal their course of action was sure to bring about; it was the courage, not the course of action she admired:

---

*Mme de Grignan, less zealous than her mother, used her ill health as an excuse for not calling on father and daughter when they came to Paris a few months later.

It takes courage, courage of an unusual kind [she wrote on January 23, 1682] for, as far as I am concerned—poor little female that I am—if I had made such a mess of things, I would simply have made the best of it ... That poor Coligny admits to a folly, to a passion nothing can excuse but love itself. In that vein, she wrote all those "Portuguese" letters;* you have seen them ... But what is there to learn from that save that she loved a man, although with this difference, that she had wanted to—or did—marry him. If all husbands could read the love letters written at one time or another by their wives, they would doubtless find that their wives had granted similar favors with perhaps less ceremony, but that poor Rabutine was scrupulous and naïve because she believed that Monsieur de La Rivière was a gentleman. He had the approval of her father; he has wit; on that basis, she became involved. Suddenly she finds that she has been deceived, that he is of lowly birth. What does she do? She repents. She is touched by her father's lamentations and reproaches ... She learns at the same time that there were other invalidities in her supposed marriage. She cannot stay as she is; she must be released from those bonds. She decides to be quit of them rather than spend the rest of her life with a man whom she now hates as once she loved him ... She knows that we have consulted legal authorities who believe the marriage to be null and void. And he, what does he do? He goes into a rage over her want of loyalty. He forgets that it was he who first practiced deceit. He says abominable things about her. He attempts to intimidate her. He threatens to say in public that she has slept with her father, that she has poisoned her husband, that the child she claims to be his [Coligny's] is one she has substituted. Those are the little peccadilloes of which he accuses her. She, in her turn, now becomes infuriated. Modesty goes by the board. She wants to sever all relations with such an insolent calumniator. And that is how things stand presently. There will be a rush of lawyers to both sides. We will lower our coifs,† and try to free ourselves from such odious chains. So, then, we have loved a man; that is a mistake, and we have been foolish enough to marry him; that, in the eyes of the world, is even worse. We write letters aflame with passion; that is because our heart is aflame, as well. What more can they say about us than that which we admit— which is having married him? That says it

---

*See page 84 for footnote on *Letters from a Portuguese Nun.* De La Rivière published Mme de Coligny's letters to him in pamphlet form; they were republished in a collection in 1743.

†The coif was a seventeenth-century headdress; the veil could be pulled down to cover the face.

all ... So, now, what does this Rivière set out to do? What would he want with such a Fury, such a Bacchante, even if he could get her back? Would it not be far better to hush this thing up and try to settle it?

In April of 1682, Mme de Sévigné rejoiced to see Bussy return to Paris in response to a message from the King, who had relented to the extent of giving the exile an audience at Versailles, as Mme de Sévigné was pleased to relate to Moulceau in a letter dated April 17:

And here is Monsieur de Bussy, back again after eighteen years! He has seen the King who received him most graciously. This is a period of justice and mercy. Pleasure is taken in doing not only that which is good, but that which is exceedingly good.

The families at the Hôtel Carnavalet were well, she could likewise advise Moulceau in that letter:

My daughter is feeling much better than when you were last here; her face would remind you of the one you saw at Grignan. Monsieur de Grignan, his daughters and his son, and our good Abbé are all of them very well ...

By midsummer, the Count de Grignan had left his family at the Hôtel Carnavalet, as Mme de Sévigné reported to Moulceau on July 28: "Monsieur de Grignan has left for Provence"—ostensibly to perform·his gubernatorial functions at Aix and Lambesc.

On August 7, Mme de Sévigné wrote to Moulceau to announce the birth of a throne-heir—one who would not live to reach the throne—first son of the Dauphin, first grandson of the monarch:

Mme the Dauphine gave birth yesterday, Thursday, at ten o'clock in the evening, to a Duke of Burgundy.* Your friend [Corbinelli] will tell you of the Court's outburst of joy, of how they all went rushing to express that joy to the King, to Monsieur the Dauphin, to the Queen— what noise, what bonfires lit in celebration, what a flood of wine, what a dance by the two hundred Swiss [Guards] at the palace gates, what shouts of Long Live the King!, what a din of church bells and cannon

---

*It was the Duke of Burgundy's son who would succeed to his great-grandfather's throne as Louis XV.

in Paris, what a rash of congratulations and oratory, but all that will soon be over.

The autumn months of 1682 found Mme de Sévigné, as usual, in her woodland retreat at Livry, as is announced by her in still another letter to Moulceau, dated October 29:

I have been here five weeks with my daughter, often with my son, with my good Abbé, with the Mesdemoiselles de Grignan, with the little Grignan [the Marquis], and sometimes with the Chevalier. If you could know, Monsieur, how happy a household this is, you would easily understand my lack of impatience to return to Paris. Even so, we will have to go back like all the others by Saint Martin's Day. *

Her letter went on to explain to Moulceau why their mutual friend, Corbinelli, was missing from that happy household:

He was very uncomfortable here: he fears the evening dews, and the house is a bit crowded; for these reasons, he keeps to Paris. But you would no longer recognize him! Please be advised, Monsieur, that he is now wearing a wig like every other man! That curly little head of his— none other like it in the world—is no more! You have never seen such a change. I trembled for our friendship. Gone was that head of hair to which I have been devoted for thirty years; my secrets, my confidences, my lifetime habits hung in the balance. He looked twenty years young- er! I no longer knew where to look for my old friend. Finally, I grew more accustomed to that stylish head, and managed to find—behind it—our good friend Corbinelli!

The letter concluded with a few lines concerning Mme de Grignan:

You would be pleased at the state of my daughter's health; its greatest defect is its delicacy, at which we tremble. My God, how fragile every- thing in life is! How little it is in our best interests to allow ourselves to become so attached to it!

By the year's end, Mme de Grignan's delicate health had once again given them cause to tremble: "My daughter has been very ill," she wrote on

*St. Martin's Day fell on November 11, the day that the Parlement of Paris regularly convened.

December 23, 1682, this time to Bussy, "but she has recovered—and I, along with her—because we wince, you and I, at our daughters' every ache and pain."

By January, 1683, the Count de Grignan had returned from Provence, as can be known through a letter addressed to the Count de Guitaut:

> *Your good wishes for the New Year were greatly appreciated, and that Grignan lady intended to write, yesterday evening, to thank you, but her husband has arrived, and now I don't know what has become of her!*

The other important news to be communicated to Guitaut at that writing was the sale—at long last!—of Charles de Sévigné's commission in the Gendarmes-Dauphin Regiment. "I want to tell you," she continued in her letter of January 12, "that my son has disposed of his sub-lieutenancy to Monsieur de Verderonne":

> *He is losing forty thousand francs thereby,* but there has been a considerable decline in the price of commissions. He made clear that it was his desire to stay on in the service, requesting the King to allow him to purchase a sub-lieutenancy in the monarch's Light Horse Regiment. He has no idea whether he will get the post. If so, we will be better off than we were; if not, we will console ourselves by paying off our debts.†*

The choice of the King did not fall on Charles for the post of sub-lieutenant in his cavalry regiment—an eventuality for which Mme de Sévigné seemed prepared: "As for me, I am satisfied," she told Guitaut by letter on February 12: "but my son would like to be upset about it, for the reason that he always has to have something to be upset about."

"I have just returned from Versailles," she wrote in that same letter to Guitaut:

> *I saw those beautiful apartments. I was charmed with them. Had I read about them in some novel, I would have dreamed about seeing them for myself. And now I have both seen and spent time in them. They*

---

*Mme de Sévigné had paid 122,000 livres for Charles's commission, which was sold in January of 1683 for 84,550 livres.

†They would be paying off the debts incurred in purchasing the commission.

are an enchantment . . . It is all on the grand scale. It is all magnificent, and the music and the ballet are utter perfection. I concentrated on those two things and, having some expertise in both fields, paid my court in praise of them. But what is of sovereign pleasure is to spend four whole hours in the company of the sovereign, to take part in his diversions—as he does, in ours. That is enough to satisfy an entire kingdom which passionately loves to see its master . . . I really wished for you, there. I was a newcomer; they took special pleasure in taking me everywhere, showing me all the most unusual features. I had no regret for having taken this little voyage . . .

She had still another story about Versailles to relate to Guitaut on March 5:

You know about the King's having given a two thousand livres annuity to Mlle de Scudéry. The happy news was announced to her in a letter from Mme de Maintenon. She went to thank His Majesty one day when he was receiving, and was accorded a most gracious reception. It was quite an affair to welcome that marvelous Muse. The King spoke to her and embraced her to prevent her from embracing his knees. Their little conversation was simply perfect. Mme de Maintenon served as interpreter. All of Parnassus is in a stir about writing to felicitate both the hero and the heroine.

The stream of letters from Mme de Sévigné to Guitaut in the winter and spring of 1683 reflected her need to consult him on problems confronting her in what she called her "poor little properties" in Burgundy: his advice on whether or not to renew her contract with an unsatisfactory tenant farmer at Bourbilly was of extreme importance to her.

She wrote, too, to commiserate with him on the loss of his four little daughters recently consigned to the convent at Avallon: "I know the merit of those little persons, and the importance of the role they play at Époisses." "Let me know, my dear Monsieur," she wrote elsewhere, "how you are bearing up under that terrible blow you dealt yourself when you gave up all your delight and amusement by separating yourself from those darling little friends of mine."

The Carnavalet household was under some strain, that winter, as a result of the Chevalier de Grignan's recent bout with gout: the Count de Grignan had given up his bedroom to his ailing brother, and gone to share that of his wife—to the alarm of his wife's mother. "Proverbially," Mme de

Sévigné wrote to Guitaut, " 'He who has a good neighbor has a good morning' but, in this instance, I have my doubts. In this instance, such proximity might prove highly dangerous." In February, she commented— again to Guitaut —"I hope the only ill effects this move may have on my daughter will be the noise of the snoring. That is bad enough!"

There were rumors of the Grignans' leaving Paris. "It seems to me that I hear talk of Provence," she wrote Guitaut in March:

Should that prove to be the case, I would take off for my Brittany. I would rather be in my woods, and be bored there, than to stay here, [moving] from house to house, dragging out my life without her. The good Abbé is just finishing his vintage wine,* while I drink down my Chablis.

In April, she succumbed to a cold so severe—so complicated with fever and chest pains—that she had to submit to a bleeding, a highly popular medical procedure which she dreaded: once the doctor had found a vein, "he did a good job," she conceded (in still another letter to Guitaut): "It took him an hour to discover how carefully Providence has concealed my veins from even the most skillful surgeon!"

Still another letter went off to Guitaut after Easter:

If I have not properly made my Easter devotions [she wrote on April 20, 1683], it is not the fault of Father Bourdaloue. He has never preached as well as he has this year. Never has his fervor been more triumphantly expressed. I am charmed, I am transported by it but, even so, my heart remains cold, and my mind—for all the illumination he brings to it—is not capable of effecting my salvation. So much the worse for me! This is a state which often frightens me.

---

*The good Abbé's wine came from Burgundy, from the Count de Guitaut's vineyards.

XLI

As always, Mme de Sévigné was overjoyed at being reunited with her cousins the Count de Bussy-Rabutin and his daughter, when they drove into Paris in the spring of 1683 to institute legal action in the annulment of Mme de Coligny's marriage to La Rivière.

Bussy had not appeared on Mme de Sévigné's doorstep the day of his arrival, because—as he explained by note the day after—an attack of rheumatism had confined him to his bed.

> *Alas, my poor cousin [she wrote in immediate reply], I pity you getting rheumatism just when you need all your faculties to take charge of our affairs—for that is how I refer to them. [It was Mme de Coligny's marital-legal embroilment to which her editorial "our" had reference.] My son and I will come to see you tomorrow. I did not send to your house to inquire about your arrival because I had a feeling that any minute I would see you walk in my door to embrace and dine with me!*

When Mme de Sévigné next wrote to the Count de Bussy, autumn had come, and he and his daughter had returned to Burgundy, where she addressed this letter (dated October 23), which began:

> *How lucky you are, my poor cousin, to be in your châteaux where you can find rest for body and soul after all the trials and tribulations of your last trip here.* I was more disturbed about your ailments—and their cure—than I let you know and, as for my attentions to you during your illness, I am only too happy to know that you were pleased by them . . .*
>
> *There are times in life almost too difficult to bear, but your courage surpasses that of other men and, as the proverb says, "God gives the cloak to suit the weather." As for me, I don't know why you claim me as a Rabutin. I am a little wet hen, and I sometimes wonder, "If I*

---

*Bussy had suffered not only a rheumatic attack but had also undergone surgery for hemorrhoids during his Paris sojourn earlier in the year.

had been a man, would I have brought disgrace on my house in which valor and heroism are hereditary?" When all is said and done, I don't think so, and I base that opinion on the influence of education. As long as women are expected to be weak, they will unscrupulously take advantage of the privilege, whereas men—who are brought up to believe that it is the love of glory which will prove their distinction—make that their main goal in life—which, to some extent, explains the French renown for bravery.

Mme de Sévigné's next letter to Bussy, dated some six weeks later, struck a happier note—the announcement of her son's engagement, couched in words of delight and astonishment. In 1683, matrimonial prospects for Charles de Sévigné—without army rank as without Court connections—struck his mother as dim. If Charles was unmarried at thirty-five, it was not for lack of trying. The correspondence, across the years, contains half a hundred references to the matchmaking efforts made in his behalf. His sister as well as his mother and his mother's friends had all tried their hand at finding a bride for Charles, but the financial provisions of the wedding contracts invariably proved a stumbling block. Always a suitor, never a groom, Charles had finally found a jewel of a fiancée in Brittany, as his mother triumphantly announced to her cousin on December 4:

If you could know, my poor cousin, what it means to marry off one's son, you would forgive me for not having written you in so long a while. I am caught up in a very brisk correspondence with my son who is in Brittany and on the verge of marrying a young lady of good family whose father is a Counsellor in Parlement, and rich by more than sixty thousand livres' revenue. He is giving two hundred thousand francs to his daughter. In times like these, that is a good marriage.* There were many problems to work out before we came to the signing of the preliminary agreement, as we did four days ago . . .

On December 8, Mme de Sévigné addressed the Baron de Mauron, father of the bride, with whom contractual negotiations over the past two months had been stormy:

It is impossible [she wrote him] that upon reflection—in the light of what has transpired in the past two months—you would not be convinced

---

*"Two hundred thousand francs constitute a good marriage in these times or any other," was Bussy's rejoinder.

that I have never so much desired anything for my son as the honor of this alliance with you. This letter would be far too long if I took the time to express to you the sincere and veritable joy that hope arouses in me. I cannot refrain from flattering myself that when you know me better, you will see me differently. We will have conversations which will give you the opportunity to know my heart and the esteem and respect I have for your worth.

She had sent him, she went on to say, "the preliminary documents with all the necessary signatures affixed save that of the Countess de Grignan who had to await permission from her husband who was in Provence and temporarily out of reach." Mme de Sévigné was making gift to her son of several of her Brittany properties and, to this, the Grignans' consent was requisite. In compensation, Mme de Grignan was to receive as gift her mother's Burgundian estate. (In both the gift to Charles and to Mme de Grignan, the usufruct of the properties was reserved to Mme de Sévigné for her lifetime.) As best can be determined from the legal documents and records available, Mme de Grignan had, if anything, the best—not the worst—of the bargain: the very large cash dowry provided by her mother at the time of her marriage, in 1669, made her portion at very least the equivalent of that provided Charles under the instruments drawn up in 1683. Mme de Grignan, nonetheless, only grudgingly relinquished any rights she may have had in her father's estates in Brittany: her objections and delays in compliance infuriated both her brother and the Baron de Mauron.

Speaking for her son-in-law, Mme de Sévigné assured the Baron de Mauron that

there is no lack of good will on his part. My daughter herself will write to tell you of the delight she takes in sending you her consent. I assure you that all the necessary papers will be forthcoming shortly . . .

I implore you, Monsieur, to believe that nothing in the world would give me greater joy than to come to Brittany to witness the one thing in all the world I have most wished for for my son, were it not for the fact that I am duty-bound to stay with my uncle whose age of seventy-six and more years makes it impossible for him to consider making the trip at this season. I hope that you will find this reason to be valid . . .

Does it strike even the most objective reader as a valid reason? Did Charles de Sévigné and his fiancée's family accept it as such? This much can be said in Mme de Sévigné's favor, that at least she was consistent in her claim that the Abbé was dependent on her: if he kept her from going to Brittany to attend the wedding of her only son, he likewise kept her from what is known to be her heart's desire—going to Provence to visit her daughter when the Grignans were in residence there. With this one difference: Mme de Sévigné's expressions of regret at missing Charles's wedding are mild compared to those to which she gives voice when she is faced with foregoing the visits to Provence.

She wrote again to the Count de Bussy on December 13 to request a proxy so that his signature, as a member of the bridegroom's family, could be affixed to the marriage contract. "Finally," she wrote, "after many difficulties, I will be marrying my poor boy":

> One should never despair about one's luck. I thought that my son— after so many storms, so many shipwrecks, without a position of any kind and without any prospect of success—had lost his chance to make a good marriage. But while I gave myself over to such gloomy thinking, Providence had in store for us a marriage so advantageous that, even in the days when my son could have hoped for it, I could not have wished for a better match for him. Thus it is we live and stumble along like the blind—unable to see where we are going, unable to see that what seems good to us is actually bad for us, and that what seems bad to us is actually for our good—and always in a total ignorance.

The "many difficulties" in the way of the marriage (to which she had referred in her letter to Bussy) are clarified in a very touching letter addressed by Charles de Sévigné to his mother, early in January, 1684:

> I have just now returned from my last journey, my very dear Madame. All went exceedingly well, and whatever hope Monsieur de Mauron may have cherished of my breaking my neck has now been dissipated.* He must, at last, make up his mind to give me his daughter . . .
>
> I have received your two letters. So, you want to go on talking frankly? Very well, then, let us talk, my very dear Madame. Is there something else still to be said? Come, then, let us comfort one another. First of all, you are always mistaken when you take what Monsieur de Mauron says as if I said it, myself. I write you that Mons. de Mauron

---

*Charles's journey had taken him to Vannes, where the Maurons lived—the implication being that he might have broken his neck en route, in the deep of winter.

says that my sister scorns him, and that it appears that she considers this alliance as prejudicial to her. For my part, I only tell you this to show you that it is necessary that my sister write to him. You reply by pointing out to me that it is Monsieur de Mauron's actions which are discourteous to you. Well, to tell the truth, I know this, and agree with you. But it is not I who need to be persuaded nor is it I who should be punished, and that is what my sister did by not writing. She is displeased with Mons. de Mauron; she does not exactly know why but, on that basis, she refuses to write two letters which I very much need to have, and the lack of which are causing me infinite trouble in a family into which I am only too happy to marry . . . Her reasoning escapes me—with due apology to Monsieur Descartes's logic!* Please remember, my very dear Madame, that I never spoke for myself when I spoke to you of the scornful attitude of which Mons. de Mauron complained. I resent his action toward you and toward me—as I should—but, in the last analysis—as you yourself have said—the name of the game is marriage. Thus, marry we must. Those who have my interest at heart should try to facilitate it and to imitate you, my very dear Madame, who thought only of me throughout all this, who wrote when I asked you to write, who did not make a fuss over a lame point of honor, who did not make me suffer for Monsieur de Mauron's eccentricities, who regards with some indifference whatever Mons. de Mauron does—just so long as he gives me those two hundred thousand francs and his daughter!

(In the very nick of time, just when Monsieur de Mauron threatened to break off the engagement, then and only then did Mme de Grignan oblige with a letter of compliance.)

Charles concluded his lengthy—nine or ten page—letter with fond acknowledgment of his mother's generosity (as well he might: she had stripped herself, invaded and depleted her own once handsome estate to provide for her two children). Charles expressed himself as "overwhelmed with gratitude for what you are doing for me on this occasion—more than you did for my sister, in view of the difference in the economy and the financial straits in which you find yourself presently . . ."

"You are going to tell me that Monsieur de Mauron's conditions were neither just nor reasonable," Charles's letter went on to say:

But put yourself in Monsieur de Mauron's place: give 200,000 francs to your daughter, and then have Monsieur de Sévigné come along with

---

*Mme de Grignan fancied herself as a disciple of Descartes.

all his papers in a bundle, and see if you wouldn't expect him to come up with at least 13,000 livres a year income, and then tell me whether he is greatly in the wrong . . .

My heart aches when you call your room at Les Rochers your "former room." Have you, then, given it up, my very dear Madame? Is it your intention to break off all relations with your son after having done so much for him? Do you want to estrange yourself from him, punish him as if he had failed in his duty to you? My marriage could not compensate for such a misfortune, and I love you a thousand times better than all the rest of the world put together. Let me hear from you about this because I have, in truth, a heart so heavy that if there were not people in my room at this hour, I could not keep back the tears. Adieu, my very dear Madame. Do not renounce your son. He adores you, and wishes for your happiness as ardently as for his own salvation.

The wedding, as reported in the April, 1684 issue of *Le Mercure Galant*, took place on February 8:

A marriage of great importance took place in Brittany: it was that of Monsieur the Marquis de Sévigné, from one of the noblest houses of that province. He was married, in the month of February, to Mademoiselle de Mauron, daughter of Monsieur de Mauron, a Counsellor in the Parlement of Brittany, and possessed of more than 70,000 livres of annual income. The couple, having come on the tenth of the month from Rennes to their house of Les Rochers, near Vitré, were greeted by a troop of more than a thousand of their vassals, all under arms. This troop, which had gone out along the road to meet them, was led by Mons. Vaillant, the Sénéchal, who delivered a very witty address of welcome to the newly wedded pair. They were accompanied by the Marquis de Châtelet, who had met them a league beyond [Vitré] in the company of many gentlemen and bourgeois from that town, all very well mounted and preceded by a trumpeter. Many ladies went along in the carriages, and after they had met the Marquise de Sévigné, who was accompanied by many other carriages filled with persons of quality, Monsieur the Marquis de Sévigné mounted his horse and joined the cavaliers who saluted the bride, sword in hand. Then the horsemen went to ride ahead of the carriage which they escorted back to Vitré, and passing through the park of the Princess of Tarente, they went all the way to the château of Les Rochers where a sumptuous collation awaited them.

By March 1, when Mme de Sévigné wrote to Philippe Moulceau, she had sufficiently recovered from the strain of Charles's several matrimonial crises to sound her exuberant self again: "It is true that I was remiss in not advising you that my son's marriage had finally taken place. But just ask our friend Corbinelli what it is like to do business with someone from Lower Brittany!" "I should make the rounds of the Hôtel Carnavalet, I think, Monsieur," she wrote in conclusion, "and send you greetings from all the apartments":

My daughter is feeling well. She still does not know whether she will go to Provence or whether a lawsuit in which she is involved will keep her here. The destiny of Mlle d'Alérac is still uncertain. We believe, however, that the name of Polignac is inscribed along with hers in the Heavens.* Mlle de Grignan could tell us, if she wished, what to expect because she is in constant communion with the celestial spheres. The little Marquis shows a promise which will surely not disappoint us. The good Abbé is still the Bien Bon. The other Grignans are still worthy of your esteem . . .

The next letter of the Marquise de Sévigné's of which there is any record is one dated June 6, 1684, again addressed to Moulceau, and giving news of the families' comings and goings:

I am not in Brittany, Monsieur. I am still in Paris, and will be here some time longer. It will be interesting to watch the denouement of several matters on which my daughter's departure hinges. If she does go, I will be going shortly after—going, that is to say, in exactly the opposite direction. If she does not leave Paris, I will perform the heroic act of leaving her because a thousand reasons force me to go to Brittany . . .

She would have been reluctant, in any event, to leave Paris while the Coligny-Rivière divorce case was being fought out in the courts of the Parlement of Paris. The decision—in favor of La Rivière—was handed down on July 13, and Mme de Sévigné hastened, the very next day, to send the news to Moulceau:

---

*A marriage between Mlle d'Alérac, the younger of the Count de Grignan's two young lady daughters, and the Viscount Scipion-Sidoine de Polignac had been under discussion between the two families for months, but would not eventuate.

Monsieur de Bussy yesterday lost his case on every count: his daughter obliged to recognize both the husband and the child, and condemned to pay amends of one hundred francs ... Bussy hit the ceiling. His daughter lies frantic in her bed. So God has willed it through all eternity. Amen.

On Monday, September 3, Mme de Sévigné penned a little farewell note to Mademoiselle de Scudéry, whose latest work, entitled *More Conversations*, had come off the press in July:

I might use a hundred thousand words to say it, but I would succeed in telling you one truth only, and that reduces itself to assuring you, Mademoiselle, that I will love and cherish you all my life. No other words can express my opinion of your extraordinary merit. I speak of it often, and of the happiness I feel in enjoying the friendship and esteem of a person such as you. Since constancy is a virtue, I feel sure that you will never change toward me, and I dare to pride myself on the fact that I will never be so godforsaken as to change in my feelings for you. In that confidence, I leave for Brittany where a thousand business matters await my attention. I bid you adieu, and embrace you with all my heart ... I am taking a copy of your Conversations *to my son; since I was charmed by them, myself, I intend that he should be.*

XLII

The parting between mother and daughter came on September 12, 1684, the sixth time this mother had wrenched herself from this daughter's arms, and the most agonizing time of all, perhaps, for the reason that this parting was of Mme de Sévigné's own volition. This time, it was she who had chosen—or, rather, been constrained—to leave Paris and her daughter, rather than vice versa, as had almost always been the case.

Mme de Sévigné and her uncle were to take the same route as on their two previous journeys to Brittany,* via Étampes to Orléans where they would embark on a week-long boat trip down the Loire River.

*The journeys in 1675 and 1680.

At Étampes, the love letters began again. But, this time, they tell a different story. Just as the exchange of letters subsequent to the previous partings revealed the stress and strain of preceding reunions, so the exchange of letters subsequent to the parting in 1684 reveals that between 1680 and 1684 the two women lived together in what was apparently perfect harmony. The stormy weather of the mother-daughter relationship was over; the skies were serene. Mme de Sévigné and Mme de Grignan had made the necessary concessions and allowances, adjusted to each other's way of life, and reached an accord. There are biographers who see the year 1680—those months spent in solitude and meditation in the forests of Les Rochers—as a turning point in Mme de Sévigné's life, who see 1680 as a year of significant religious development for her. If she did not attain to the state of grace for which she longed and prayed, she did come to find an inner peace—she no longer railed at fate, she bowed to it—and from the year 1680 on, there came a marked improvement in her relations with her daughter.

Mme de Sévigné's first letter to her daughter in 1684—after a four-year hiatus in their correspondence—was written from Étampes on the first night out of Paris.

You can well believe, my darling [that letter began], that despite all your good advice, I found myself, at the moment of parting, exposed to a thousand sword-blades upon which one wounds oneself, no matter how hard one tries to escape. I dared not think, dared not speak a word. My emotions reached such a pitch that I could scarcely bear it. But, all in all, I have done the best I could. I feel very well; I have slept, I have eaten, I have attended to the Bien Bon, and here I am. I have made myself go back over my reasons for making this trip. As I reviewed them, I found them so valid that I could understand what brought about my decision, but since the anguish of leaving you temporarily erased them from my mind, I needed to remind myself in order to endure your absence with any degree of equanimity. I have not yet reached that stage . . . I am overwhelmed with longing to see you again . . . I am thrilled to think that you are at Versailles . . . I hope you will have good luck, there. How could they possibly refuse your request?*
. . . I remind you not to neglect your health. It is a great consolation to me to think of you with those pretty plump cheeks I left you with. Keep them that way for me. I thank Mlle d'Alérac's pretty eyes for the

---

*Mme de Grignan had gone to the Court to seek compensation for the extraordinarily heavy expenses incurred by the Count de Grignan in recent months: the Count had been obliged to call up the nobility and the militia to patrol France's Mediterranean coast in the face of threats by the Genoese and the Spanish.

tears they shed for me but, my God, what thanks do I not then owe to you for such tenderness and such anguish as you showed [at parting]? Ah, let us not dwell on that! But, remember, my heart is indisputably yours; you hold sovereign sway there.

In Madame de Sévigné's second letter, datelined "Saturday night, September 16, at Amboise," she could report herself as "feeling very well; no sign of the vapours," and then proceeded to apologize for it:

In fine, I am living without you, and ashamed of it because I cannot get over having left you in a place where it is natural for us to be together. That cuts me to the heart, and I had to force myself to yield to the reasons which drove me to it ... I feel that I am forfeiting one of the most precious seasons of my life. It may have been a mistake but, then, I confess that my business affairs frighten me. Oh, my beautiful darling, how I need you to comfort my heart and sustain my courage!

From Saumur on September 18, Mme de Sévigné wrote that adverse winds were delaying them and that the boatmen were obliged to resort to their oars. "Looking at the beautiful countryside constitutes my only diversion," she commented:

We spend fourteen or fifteen hours a day aboard, the good Abbé and I, seated in our carriage* ... We look forward to our dinner as the main event of the day. We are served hot food, and our terrines compare favorably with even those of Monsieur de Coulanges. I have been reading, but I am distracted, and have counted waves instead of concentrating on my history book but, God willing, I will get back to it.

Disembarking at Angers on September 20, she wrote,

I found, at the end of the bridge, a six-horse carriage which I took to be my son's. It was his carriage, but it was the Abbé Charrier whom he had sent to meet me because a minor indisposition had kept him at home. I was well pleased with the Abbé: he is somewhat familiar with Grignan through his father, and through having seen you—which so raised him in my estimation that I could not have wished for a better

*Their carriage had been put aboard the riverboat as on the previous trip.

escort. *He gave me your letter written from Versailles, and I made no effort to restrain my tears in his presence* ...

Mme de Grignan, in that letter from Versailles, had evidently confessed—philosophical though she usually was—to missing her mother sorely. "I could see," Mme de Sévigné replied, "despite your effort to repress it, that same tenderness, that same anguish which made us shed so many tears at parting."

Ah, my darling, how my heart responds to your love! I am so sure of it that I am angry when you say, even in teasing, that I should have had a daughter like Mlle d'Alérac, and that you are far from perfect. That Alérac is certainly kind to miss me as she does, but never wish me any daughter other than yourself! You are all in all to me, and never has a mother been so well loved by a well-loved daughter as I by you. Oh, my darling, how once you veiled such boundless treasures from me! Even so, I assure you, my darling, that I never really for a moment doubted that you loved me, but now you heap all those riches on me— riches of which I am unworthy save for the infinite love I bear you, a love so great as to defy definition in words.

I have just opened the letter you wrote my son. What tenderness for me you express there! What sweet attentions! ... I was glad to see you say that you hope he appreciates my leaving [Paris] at this season, but God only knows whether the financial straits in which I find myself and the fear of a worse disorder in my affairs were not the real reasons for my coming here! There are times when resources become so depleted as to make it incumbent upon anyone who has a conscience or a sense of honor to prevent things from going any further.

By September 24, the travellers had arrived at their destination, the Château of Les Rochers, as Charles took up his pen to advise his sister:

My joy at welcoming my Mother and the Bien Bon helps me to gauge your sorrow at losing them ... I forgive you for envying me, now, but it was only fair that she should share between us the pleasure of her company. Don't hate me, my pretty little sister, and follow my example by loving your rivals. Mme de Coulanges once recognized me as such, or so she said, and that is how—in my heart of hearts—I have always thought of you.

"At long last, my daughter," Mme de Sévigné could sigh with relief as she began her letter of September 27, "here are three letters from you!"

I marvel at what that comes to mean when one has no other consolation. It becomes one's very life, one's excitement, one's occupation, one's nourishment! ... All that you write me is so tender, so touching that I would be ashamed to read your letters without weeping, just as I will be ashamed, this winter, of being able to go on living without you.

Let's talk a little about Versailles. The lack of response could be interpreted favorably. I cannot believe that you will be refused so reasonable a request at a time of great liberalities ... What pride would it not give you if—through your efforts and your solicitations—you should obtain this small grace. Nor could it come at a more appropriate time because I have an idea—and that is yet another of my anxieties— that your affairs are in serious disorder. As for me, I am convinced that I would never have been able to recover from the disorder of my affairs, had I waited another six months.

We lead a rather dull life here, but even so, I do not think anything more exciting would please me any better. My son is troubled with some kind of boils. My daughter-in-law is given to only moments of gaiety because she suffers from the vapours. She changes her expression a hundred times a day without finding one that is becoming to her. Her health is extremely delicate. She practically never takes a walk. She is always cold. By nine o'clock, she has faded away completely. The days are too long for her, and the need she has to rest leaves me the liberty to do as I please, and I return the favor. This suits me perfectly. One would never guess that this house has a mistress other than me. Although I don't take charge, I am served as if upon little invisible orders ...

This little woman is pitiful. Theirs is not a very sprightly ménage. The two of them send you a thousand messages. No great effort is made to win my affection; that would be very displeasing. No overtures are made to me. There is nothing to discourage me; nothing to encourage me, either. That is exactly how I wanted it.

"Although my letter is dated Sunday," she wrote on September 30,

I am writing it on Saturday night. It is only ten o'clock, but everyone has retired. It is an hour I can devote wholly to the thought of you, uninterrupted by the people who are in and out of my room at other times. Today is my eighth day here; that is moving right along. The Abbé Charrier is the only person with whom I can talk of you. He understands me. I tell him how much I love you. No one will be able to take his place when he leaves. He shares my sentiments; he is surprised at yours, and at the fact that the distractions of Paris and Versailles have not consoled you for my absence. I must disagree with what you said about your taking our close companionship for granted, as one does one's health—and missing it only when one loses it. I think you fully appreciated the sweetness of our time together—my five or six visits a day. As for me, I have nothing with which to reproach myself on that score: there was not a single moment in which I was not supremely conscious of the joy of being with you; every time I came in from Mass or from the city or from the Bien Bon's apartment to yours gave me exquisite pleasure.

Is it possible that I have written so many pages without yet having said a word about Mlle de Grignan? I am more annoyed than surprised to hear about her flight.* We were a burden to her; our conversations displeased her.

On Sunday, October 1, Mme de Sévigné sat down at her desk to resume writing the letter she had begun the night before:

Here is where I stopped last night ... My son has just left for Rennes. He wants to make sure his boils are nothing serious. His wife hovers about me, understanding very well the game I play of not seeing her today. I spent hours in the woods with my Abbé Charrier. Now it is her turn to go there, and I am going to write. I assure you that this is very convenient. She has some very good qualities, at least I think so, although now, in the beginning, I do not find myself disposed to praise her except in the negative: she is not "this"; she is not "that." Later, perhaps, I shall actually come to say, "she is thus and so." She sends you a thousand pretty greetings. She would like to be loved by us, but she is in no hurry about it—no hurry, at all. That is my impression of her, up to now. She does not speak Breton, has no trace of a Rennes accent.

I feel strongly that my seal should read simply Madame de Sévigné.

---

*Without so much as a by-your-leave to anyone in the Hôtel carnavalet, Mlle de Grignan had fled to a Benedictine convent in Gif and taken refuge there.

Nothing more is necessary. No one will confuse me with anyone else during my lifetime, and that's enough.

Her next letter bore the date October 4:

Thanks to my arrival, my son has rid himself of the undesirable company with which he was overrun. And I am thrilled because I am intolerant when it comes to certain impertinences and since, unlike you, I am not lucky enough to be able to escape into daydreams, I grow impatient and say rude things. Thank God, we have now been left in peace. I read; at least, I intend to begin a book suggested to me by Mme des Vins on the English Reformation. I write and receive letters. My correspondence with you takes up nearly all the days of the week. Your letters arrive on Monday and, until Wednesday, I write in answer. On Friday, I receive more letters from you, and spend the time until Sunday on my reply. That keeps me from feeling the long time between mails. I do a great deal of walking, both because we are enjoying the most marvelous weather in the world and because I foresee with dread the terrible winter ahead of us.

I saw the Princess [of Tarente] who speaks of you, who understands my sorrow, who loves you, who loves me, and who drinks twelve cups of tea, daily! She prepares it by infusion, as we do, and then adds at least half a cup of boiling water. It nearly made me vomit. That cup, she insists is the cure for all her ills. She assured me that the Landgrave [of Hessell-Cassell] drinks forty such cups daily.* "But, Madame, don't you perhaps mean thirty?" "No, it's forty!" He was dying, and this is clearly what brought him back to life!

"All in all," Mme de Sévigné concluded her chapter on the Princess of Tarente (who amused her when she did not exasperate her), "I am now perfectly informed on the affairs of Germany. She is dear and kind in spite of all that . . .

In late September, the Countess de Grignan's tonsillitis diverted Mme de Sévigné's attention from the affairs of Germany. "Oh, my dear child, you have been ill!" her mother lamented on October 4. "Swollen tonsils are a very painful thing. You make light of it so as not to alarm me . . ."

"My son returns today from Rennes," she wrote on October 8:

---

*The Landgrave was a nephew of the Princess's.

During his absence, I have talked with his wife. I found her full of good common sense, interested in all our past history, like any reasonable person, remarkably so for a Breton. It means a lot to see things without prejudice, to see things straight.

The October 4 letter ended with the exclamation, "As for the month of September, it seems to me to have been six months long! I cannot believe that I have been here only two weeks!"

The three bleedings prescribed by the Paris doctors to cure Mme de Grignan's tonsillitis put Mme de Sévigné into a frenzy of anxiety, although her letter of November 5 began with the reassurance that she was maintaining her calm: "I promise you not to become alarmed over your illness . . . but I implore you always to tell me how you are." Nothing would do but that the Abbé Charrier, on his way to Paris, should take the Countess a vial of *Baume Tranquille*, one of the wonder drugs compounded by the monks of the Capuchin monastery at Rennes, renowned for their pharmacopoeia and medical skills. "You put eight drops on a warm plate," Mme de Sévigné instructed her daughter on the use of this famous Balm,

and apply it to the spot on your side where you have the pain. To the eight drops of Balm an equal number of drops of essence of urine should be added. Rub it in gently, then cover the area with a warm cloth. It is known to have worked miracles.

As for me, I can sincerely say that my health is perfect. I walk whenever the weather permits . . . My daughter-in-law does not go out at all; she is under treatment by the Capuchins; that is to say, she is drinking a brew they prepare, and taking herbal baths which have fatigued but, thus far, not helped her . . . The good Abbé feels some discomfort from overeating and gas pains—complaints to which he is accustomed. The Capuchins have prescribed a dose of powdered shrimp every morning, and promise him relief . . . As for me, I am free of the vapours. I think they came over me only because I was apprehensive about them; now that I scorn them, they have gone off to frighten some other silly soul!

By November 15, the harsh Breton winter was upon them: "The weather has been so dreadful for the past two weeks," Mme de Sévigné wrote plaintively, "that we have not even been able to think of our allées or our promenades . . . I am out of the habit of my daily walk . . . and stay in my room working on the needlepoint for my little Coulanges's chair."

*You speak of my being away from you, my darling [the letter contin-
ued], and ask me why. Alas, how easy it would be for me to explain if
I wanted to sully my letters with the reasons which forced me to this
separation: the hard times in this region, the money owed me here, the
way it is paid, the money I owe elsewhere, and how I would have been
swamped and suffocated by my affairs if I had not come to this decision,
painful as it was to me. You know that I was glad to put it off for two
years, and did so unhesitatingly but, my darling, there are limits beyond
which one cannot go without risking the loss of everything. I can no
longer afford to run such risks. My holdings no longer belong to me.*
One is obliged to finish one's life with the same honor and probity of
which one has always made profession. And it is this, my darling,
which has made me tear myself temporarily from your arms, agonizing
as that was to do.*

"I am thrilled to hear that you liked my portrait," she went on to say
in that same letter. "Hang it in a good light and look, from time to time, at
a mother who adores you ... who loves you infinitely, beyond all words."
(The portrait to which Mme de Sévigné refers in this letter in 1684 might
have been any one of the several portraits she had sat for or a copy of any
of them.†)

December 13 was observed as an anniversary of their parting: "Try as
they might," she wrote on that date, "no one could ever convince me that it
was only three months yesterday that I bid you goodbye and shed such
bitter tears, my dear Countess. No, I would never believe it!"

It seemed much longer. Time dragged at Les Rochers in the winter. In
late November, the *Bien Bon* had come down "with one of those dreadful
colds of his," she noted: "He is in his little alcove; we can take better care
of him here than in Paris." "When the weather is good," she wrote on
November 26, "I go out at two o'clock in the afternoon and walk as far as I
can. I don't stop. I pass and repass workmen cutting wood, who look just
like those one sees in paintings of winter scenes." Charles managed so well,
she commented, "that there is nearly always a game of *hombre* going on in

---

*One of the provisions on which Charles's father-in-law had insisted for the marriage contract was
that Mme de Sévigné should pledge to leave Charles her properties unhypothecated.

†Mme de Sévigné had commissioned several artists to do her portrait throughout the years, as was
the custom in her social circle in seventeenth-century France, and the artists she had chosen were among
the best of that day. The most renowned of her portraits is the one that hangs today in Paris's Musée
Carnavalet—formerly attributed to Mignard, more recently to Lefebvre. Other portraits are to be seen
at Versailles Museum and at Château Les Rochers.

my room, and when he has run out of neighbors, he goes back to reading aloud and to discussions of the books being read ... If one is fortunate enough to enjoy that amusement, one is never at a loss."

"I thought often of you on Christmas night," she wrote on December 27:

I pictured you at the "Blues"* while we were gathering so quietly in our chapel. Your brother has become extremely devout. He is a learned man, he is constantly reading saintly works, he is deeply touched by them; he is a convert. A day will come when one will be grateful for having been nourished on such Christian teachings. Death is frightful when one is devoid of all that can console us at that hour. His wife shares his convictions. I am the most wicked, but not enough so to be considered contraband. He was pleased to read the passage [in your letter] in which you expressed yourself as pleased with him. You have a way of saying things so well, and you are so amiable that it makes me feel all the more keenly the distress of being far from you. And the foreseeable future frightens us. You can be sure that that sorrow is no less painful for me than for you, but I must find courage. Too short a sojourn here would be useless; I would only have to do it all over again. The whole dose must be swallowed down.

Over and over again, Mme de Sévigné explained to her daughter—and to herself—the reasons for her self-imposed exile:

"What I am doing here," she wrote, "will stand me in the stead of your 12,000 francs gratification." (The 12,000 francs were the gratification granted the Count de Grignan by the King in response to the Countess de Grignan's petition for reimbursement of extraordinary expenses incurred in his governance.)

Being here [she continued], where I have no expense, and where my son is only too happy to repay me in this way, I send my revenues to Paris. What else could I have done? You understand my problem only too well, but I have thought about it a thousand times. What would you have done, yourselves, had not that relief been forthcoming? You should now be in fairly comfortable circumstances.

*The convent she referred to as the "Blues" was the one adjoining the Carnavalet where the nuns wore blue robes.

XLIII

In a carriage accident, early in the new year, 1685, Mme de Sévigné suffered what appeared to be minor cuts and bruises to her leg, and congratulated herself for having escaped serious injury. Congratulations proved to have been premature; complications developed: laceration to varicose veins in her leg resulted in an ugly, open sore, red and puffy, sometimes pustulous, which stubbornly refused to heal. Neither the Capuchins' "sovereign remedy" nor the Countess de Grignan's "Powder of Sympathy" nor even her "Black Unguent" could effect more than temporary relief. Having, from the first, minimized the damage in order to spare her daughter from concern, Mme de Sévigné had to apologize for each relapse. "It is true," she wrote on February 4, "that we thought, in the beginning, that it would be a matter of a few days. We have been mistaken, that is all, and it has been two weeks."

> But, finally [she continued], a scab is forming ... My leg is neither
> inflamed nor swollen. I went to see the Princess, I took a walk, I
> certainly do not look like an invalid! Don't think of your bonne as a
> pitiful hospital case. I am looking beautiful ... All in all, my bonne, it
> is not on that count that you should pity me but, rather, because I am
> away from you, because I can attend your dinner parties only meta-
> physically,* because I am losing this precious time ...

As she thought of the "precious time" they might have had together, Mme de Sévigné was moved to a celebration of their love:

> At four o'clock, this afternoon [she wrote on Monday, January 29,
> 1685], I receive your letter written on Saturday, which is only the day
> before yesterday. That is a speed which would bring me a measure of
> consolation for any absence save yours ... But, my dear child, happy
> as we are together, as perfect an understanding as exists between us, it
> is impossible for me not to dwell tenderly, as do you, on the misfortune
> of being apart.

*The word *métaphysiquement* is underscored by Mme de Sévigné.

344

I have just read the letter you wrote to my son. I am touched, and I marvel at the way you explain your reasons for loving me. No one can equal you when it comes to the dialogue of the heart. Save all those treasures for me so that, one day, I can enjoy them to the full . . .

A letter of Mme de Sévigné's written that same winter gives us a glimpse—an astonishing glimpse!—of Mme de Grignan in a moment of utter abashment in the presence of the King: "Is it possible," Mme de Sévigné inquired in astonishment, "that in your conversation with the King, you found yourself totally disconcerted by that awesome majesty of his . . . forgetting everything you had meant to say? I simply cannot believe that my beloved daughter, with all her wit and all her presence of mind, should have found herself in such a state."

In justice to Mme de Grignan, it must be said that she was not the only one to be disconcerted in the presence of the *Grand Monarque* (the Great Monarch, as he was known throughout Europe). Even ambassadors coming to present their credentials had been known to be struck dumb, dazzled by their first sight of the Sun King. What makes Mme de Grignan's loss of poise in his presence seem so strange is that she had known the man and the monarch for twenty years, was said to have flirted with him, had danced on the same stage with him, had appeared with him in numerous Court ballets in the 1660's. It is upon such an incident as this one described by Mme de Sévigné that biographers base their claim that Mme de Grignan suffered from an inferiority complex; that the haughty air and the arrogance for which she was widely criticized by her contemporaries were merely a reflection of her basic insecurity; that she wrapped herself in her hauteur and her disdain to shield herself from rebuff or rejection.

"When all is said and done," Mme de Sévigné went on to say in the letter dealing with her daughter's embarrassment before the King, "the important thing is whether or not your requests will be granted."

I must admit that from what you told me about His Majesty's saying that he wishes to do something for Monsieur de Grignan, I did not take it to mean that he meant merely recompensing him for the extraordinary expenses which he was called upon to make in Provence recently but, rather, that reply of the King's struck me as meaning, "Madame, the gratification for which you ask is relatively insignificant; I want to do something more than that for Grignan." And that I interpreted as an assurance that you could count on the reversion . . . [An assurance, that is to say, that the Count de Grignan's post of Lieutenant-Governor of Provence would pass—or revert—to the little Marquis de Grignan upon the death of his father, as was the hope then cherished by the Grignan family.]

As for the little Marquis, who was being groomed to succeed his father, "this was to be a great winter for him," as his grandmother noted proudly in reply to a letter from Versailles in which Mme de Grignan had described the boy's introduction to the Court. "Our little man has been admired by all the world!" Mme de Sévigné exclaimed in pleasure at the news conveyed to her by letters from her friends as well as from her daughter:

Mme de La Fayette and her son write me marvels about him! His life is being rushed along in such a way that, had you made allowance for his childhood as one used to do, you would not have been this far along the way. You have been moved to act in accordance with his destiny. At fourteen, he is expected to play an important role; for that reason, he must be in the public eye two years earlier. There will be talk about him; he must show his little self. Your stay in Paris can be seen as the work of Providence in the furtherance of its designs. Had it not been for you, he would have been shut away in his room, but you will have contributed—both by your presence at Court and by the way you have raised your son—to his establishment and his fortune. I have long thought this to be so, but especially this winter, when he has appeared in such a very good light. He has come before the King; he has been well regarded. He is well built, he looks distinguished. If people's thoughts have been put into words, you must have heard some very pleasant comment. You can well imagine how much this means to me.

The fourteen-year-old youth had been scheduled late in February, to appear in Indian costume at a masquerade ball at Versailles, which had to be called off at the last minute upon receipt of news of the death of King Charles II of England. Mme de Sévigné wrote to console her grandson:

My Marquis, you must be very disappointed at having so extraordinary an event interfere with your plans ... You had consolation, however, that same day. The billiard party, the festivities in the King's apartments, the King's Mass and all the praise given you and your pretty costume should have cheered you without depriving you of the hope that the masquerade had only been postponed ...

"My *bonne*," she wrote on the next line, turning her attention back to her daughter,

I understand better than anyone else how you feel. Yes, it is true that one lives vicariously in the lives of one's children, and even more vividly than in one's own. How familiar I am with such emotions, and what a pleasure it is to experience them through some pretty little creature who is worth the trouble, who attracts attention everywhere. Your son is extremely attractive; there is something piquant and pleasing about his face. One cannot pass him by, as one might another; he holds one's eye.

When the masquerade finally took place, a week later, Mme de Sévigné sent another message to her grandson, "My Marquis, I want to kiss you and rejoice with you over your successes. A handsome little Indian who dances perfectly, who holds his head high, who is brave! My imagination delights in the thought!"

Mme de Sévigné could pride herself, in 1685, on not only a handsome grandson but on a radiantly beautiful daughter: "People talk to me of nothing but your beauty," she wrote Mme de Grignan in February:

Since you are not yet middle-aged, enjoy that pretty face of yours which did you so much honor even when you were ill. It can only become more lovely, now that you are in good health. Regular features and good proportions—in a word, beauty—must be seen as a blessing.

Despite all her good intentions to try to extricate herself from debt, Mme de Sévigné had apparently sunk in deeper, and had been obliged in recent months to secure another loan which—on account of the provisions of Charles's marriage contract—she could not accomplish without Charles's signature. "Your brother agreed most graciously and willingly to sign for me," she noted gratefully. Writing to her daughter, on another day, on the subject of the division of her estate, she had this to say:

It does not seem to me that you will ever have any trouble in dealing with your brother. He wants peace; he is a Christian, and you do him justice when you say that you have as much reason to be satisfied with him as to be dissatisfied with his father-in-law. It never occurred to him to do anything to prevent your sharing equally in the estate, and that is the truth. At last, I see peace reigning in all the hearts where I hoped it would.

If the mother and daughter had, by 1685, reached a new accord, living happily and peacefully together under the same roof for the past four years, it was probably in some part due to the fact that Mme de Sévigné had come, at last, to see her daughter (in her thirty-ninth year in 1685) as a mature woman, a responsible and capable *mater familias*, worthy of full autonomy—out, at last, from under her mother's shadow. Occasionally, however, some outrageous excess in the chronic Grignan extravagance provoked Mme de Sévigné to an outburst, such as in this letter dated February 25:

What folly, my bonne, *to have four people in your kitchen! Why so many, and what's to become of you with such expenses? Would not just two be adequate to serve your table? Lachau's airs and wigs cost you dear.* I am very displeased at such extravagances. Can't you control things better? It is very costly to live in Paris. And, on top of that, to have three valets! In your household, it is always double or triple anyone else's! ... Could Monsieur de Grignan approve such outrageous expenditures? My darling* bonne, *I cannot restrain myself from speaking forthrightly to you on this matter. If I have scolded you like a mother, allow me now to hug you tight to show me that you are not annoyed.*

While she was on the subject of staff and cuisine, she could not resist a comment on that of Les Rochers:

You have an idea that my son is a gourmet, that he knows his sauces, understands good service. My bonne, *he knows nothing at all! Larmechin, still less, and the cook, less still!† It is not surprising that a cook who was once good has been completely ruined. And, as for me— whom you so disdain—I am considered an authority, and no one ventures an opinion until it can be seen how I like it! You owe this long and silly discourse to my pride in being able to tell you that I reign supreme over ignoramuses!*

By the end of February, the worst of the Brittany winter seemed behind them, much to Mme de Sévigné's delight:

---

*Lachau served the Grignans as maître d'hôtel or majordomo in 1685.
†Larmechin was Charles de Sévigné's valet.

Good Lord, what weather! It is perfect! From early morning until five in the afternoon, I am out in those beautiful allées ... I wear your beautiful Brandebourg which is my adornment.* My leg is healed. I walk, like anyone else! No need to pity me any longer, my dear bonne. I would die if I were shut up inside in weather like this!

But by mid-April, the woodland promenades had to be renounced: Mme de Sévigné's leg was giving her trouble again. Charles de Sévigné had tried to induce the Capuchins to come from Rennes to Les Rochers to treat his mother's leg and his wife's vapours, but when the monks begged off it was decided that Mme de Sévigné should go to them in Rennes for treatment.

"They urged me so warmly to come," she wrote her daughter on April 15, "and Mme de Marboeuf offers me so comfortable a room that I am leaving tomorrow."

It seems to me that this is what you want me to do, what you advise, and that you will be pleased to see me have a change of air, and since my treatment will be by skilled hands, I should be able to look forward to a real cure. I am going alone with only Marie,† two lackeys, and a small carriage drawn by six horses. I am leaving my poor Bien Bon here with my son and his wife. I will return as soon as I can, for it is not without great regret that I leave the peace and quiet of this solitude and the greening of the trees which has rejuvenated me, but I feel, too, that it is simply ridiculous to go on being deceived again and again about this healing, and that finally I should follow your advice. Just when this little sore seems to have healed up, it breaks open again. A masterly hand is needed to bring me out of this long misery during which I have been sustained only by hope which has led me to believe twenty times that I was cured ... Mme de Marboeuf is so thrilled to have me, she manifests such eagerness and affection that it is embarrassing to me. When the feeling is not mutual, how does one respond?

In a letter written from Rennes two weeks later (on April 29),‡ Mme de Sévigné expressed herself as hoping against hope that the Capuchin Fathers would succeed in healing her leg:

*A Brandebourg was a newly fashionable kind of cloak.
†Marie was one of Mme de Sévigné's maids.
‡Three letters are missing from the correspondence at this juncture. Two dozen or more letters are missing from among those written by Mme de Sévigné to her daughter during her sojourn in Brittany in 1684–5, mislaid or lost when Mme de Grignan transferred them from Paris back to Provence in 1688 to add to the collection she stored so carefully there.

Like you, I said to myself: if my leg is healed after so much pain and so many disappointments, thanks be to God! If it is not [healed], and I am forced to go to Paris for help—there, also, to see my dear and darling daughter!—God be blessed! Thus it was that while I could calmly await the decree of Providence, my heart yearned for the continuation of my ailment because that would mean that I would see you three months earlier . . .

I availed myself of Mme de Marboeuf's generous offers [offers of a room in her house at Rennes] which are as sincere as they are sound, and I would unhesitatingly have availed myself of them again [offers to lend Mme de Sévigné money to make the trip to Paris] had not my leg—as if through malice!—shown every sign of healing. But you know, too, how difficult it is to try to repay what it is so easy to borrow. So, I am going back to Les Rochers to observe the condition of this leg which is presently free of any sores or swelling.

What gave Mme de Sévigné even more concern than her leg was the thought of Mme de Grignan's leaving Paris for Provence within a few weeks of her mother's return in the autumn:

But you told me something in passing—as if what you were saying was unimportant—which gave me a terrible shock. What you said was that if I return because of this leg, you will not run the risk of going away while I am there. My daughter, what are you saying? Do not deceive me on this matter; that would be a sorrow I would be unable to bear. You assure me that I will find you there the beginning of September, that you will still be involved in your affairs, at that time. As for me, I hurry to dispose of mine without the loss of a moment's time. I have to renegotiate the lease on one property; I have a thousand things to attend to, too many to mention. But in an emergency, I would do—in order to see and embrace you—what I would do for my leg. So, out of your wisdom and your love, tell me what to do. You know the state of my affairs, you know how much I love you, and you also know your plans, so tell me what to do . . . I put my trust in you, and confide my destiny into your hands.

With twelve letters missing here—those of May, 1684, and of early June—the next to appear in the *Correspondence* is dated "Wednesday, June 13," from Les Rochers, to which Mme de Sévigné had returned on May 2.

She was still using the herbal packs prescribed by the Capuchins and, to that date, all was going well.

With the Estates General of Brittany scheduled to convene that summer, both Mme de Sévigné and her son were prompted to give thought to their wardrobes, and turned to Mme de Grignan in the fashion capital of France for assistance in making themselves ready for that gala occasion.

Find out something, my bonne, about what the men will be wearing, this summer. I shall ask you to send me a pretty fabric for your brother, who implores you to turn him into a fashion plate at minimum cost, to tell him how cuffs are being worn, also to choose the trimmings for him, and to send it all in time for the Governor's reception. My son has a very good tailor here. Monsieur du Plessis* will give you some of the Abbé's money for the ribbons, because—with a little note I am writing to Gautier†—to whom I owe nothing—he will wait until my return to be paid ... I must ask you, too, to consult with Mme de Chaulnes on the summer dress I will need in Rennes ... I have a gown of quilted brown taffeta with a silver trim on the turned-up sleeves and the hem of the skirt, but I think that it is no longer fashionable, and one cannot risk looking ridiculous at Rennes in the midst of all that magnificence. I will be thrilled to have a dress of your choice—so long as we keep modesty and economy in mind. I want no part of Toupris; none but the good Mme Dio, for me; she has my measurements.‡ You will know better than I do the date for which the gown is needed because you will know when the Chaulneses depart§—at which time I will be going to Rennes to see them.

That letter of June 13 was a long one, rambling on for pages and pages:

They tell me [Mme de Sévigné went on to say]—and this is fuor proposito‖—*that the Minim Fathers of your Provence have dedicated a thesis to the King in which he is compared to God—although in such a manner that it is clear to see that God is only the copy! It was shown to Monsieur [the Bishop] of Meaux, who showed it to the King, saying that the King should not permit it. He agreed. It was submitted to the*

*M. du Plessis was the Marquis de Grignan's tutor.
†Gautier was a popular Paris fabric merchant.
‡Toupris and Dio were popular Paris couturières.
§The Duke de Chaulnes, as Governor of Brittany, would come to preside over the Estates General.
‖*Fuor proposito*: totally irrelevant.

Sorbonne for an opinion; the opinion was that it should be suppressed. Too much is too much!

Some biographers have accused Mme de Sévigné of fawning upon majesty, but this paragraph makes clear that her admiration of the monarch—abject though it might have been—was yet not limitless.

XLIV

In the summer of 1685, a peer of the realm—a duke, no less—made Mme de Sévigné, then in her fifty-ninth year, a proposal of marriage. It could not but have presented a temptation to her, impressed as she seemed to be—as who was not in that day and time and social structure?—by the glamour of lofty rank with its prestige and its privilege. A duke ranked above all the rest of the feudal nobility, and yielded precedence only to the six ecclesiastical peers of France and the Princes of the Blood (the Bourbons of collateral branches). It was the Duke de Luynes, twice a widower at age sixty-five, who sought Mme de Sévigné's hand in marriage, who offered her not only financial security but a prominent position at Court—after which, in recent years, she had seemed to hanker.

Mme de Sévigné had arrived, thirty or more years earlier, at a decision not to take another husband—"another master," as she phrased it—but to retain her independence, her control over her own life, and she stood firm in 1685 when this flattering offer of marriage came her way. In view of the financial straits in which she found herself since Charles's marriage, the prospect of wedlock to a wealthy peer of the realm must have been tempting, but not even the thought of a ducal equipage more resplendent even than the one she had so recently and regretfully been obliged to relinquish could shake her resolution. When, however, she enunciated her refusal to the Duke, surely it was couched in her most dulcet tone of voice and most gracefully turned phrase. (Her cousin the Count de Bussy said she had a way of taking the sting out of rejection.)

Although, in all probability, the Duke's proposal of marriage and the discussion pro and con formed the subject of many a letter in the mother-daughter correspondence that summer, only one brief reference to it is to be found in the relatively few letters extant from the year 1685.* "We will talk, some day, about Monsieur de Luynes," was how Mme de Sévigné approached the matter in this letter to her daughter:

Oh, what a folly! Mme de Chaulnes agrees with us. If Mme de La Fayette had chosen, she could have told you about—or shown you—a letter I wrote to her in which I set forth all the valid reasons I have for remaining as I am. She and Mme de Lavardin both praised me for my decision.

(The flurry of excitement over the Duke de Luynes had died down by midsummer when he took as his third wife the Marquise de Manneville, a widow less strong-minded, less jealous of her freedom of action than Mme de Sévigné.)

In June of 1685, Mme de Grignan and her family were rusticating in the green glades of Livry, as she advised her mother on the thirteenth. "How happy I am, my daughter, that you are enjoying the little Abbey!" Mme de Sévigné wrote in reply on June 17. The Abbey of Livry was to prove as great a delight to daughter as to mother.

How happy I am, my very dear bonne [Mme de Sévigné's letter continued], to know that you are at Livry—with all thoughts of Paris banished from your mind! What joy to be able to sing my song, if only for eight or ten days! You have a thousand sweet things to say, my bonne, about your fond memories of the good Abbé and of your poor Maman. I don't know how you always manage to think and say precisely the right thing. It is because, in truth, it is your heart which speaks; it is your heart which never fails you, and despite what you used to say in praise of the mind when it gainsays the heart,† it is the mind which falters, which errs, which constantly flounders . . .

But, my God, what do you mean, my bonne, . . . when you say that you were not really certain of being able to stay on in Paris to wait for me . . . until Mlle de Grignan announced that it would be September before she would reach a firm decision about taking the veil? . . . Oh, Saint Grignan, how much obliged I am to you for that certainty!

---

*As has been noted, Mme de Grignan lacked the facilities in Paris to stow her mother's letters as securely as she could at the Château de Grignan.

†What Mme de Grignan used to say in the days of their misunderstandings.

But let's get back to Livry. You seem to be enchanted with it. You have inherited all my predilections . . . But where do you get the idea, my bonne, that one hears nightingales on June 13? Alas, they are busy making ready for their little ménages. It is no longer a question of singing or making love; they have more practical things in mind . . .

I implore you, my bonne, not to go back to Paris to take care of the commissions with which your brother and I have importuned you. Send Anfossy to Gautier's,* and let him send the samples to you . . . Finally, my bonne, there is no need to rush, don't inconvenience yourself. You have plenty of time: it takes only two days to make my coat, and my son's clothes will be made here. For Heaven's sake, don't shorten your stay there. Enjoy that little Abbey while you can, while you have it.

On July 1, Mme de Sévigné could give her daughter a good report on her health: "So, my leg is completely healed; it has been six weeks since there has been any kind of sore. I walk as much as I want. I use an Emerald Water which has so pleasant an aroma that if I did not put it on my leg, I would put it on my handkerchief!"

It was to her cousin the Count de Bussy-Rabutin that Mme de Sévigné wrote on July 22 to acknowledge receipt of his work *Généalogie de la maison de Rabutin* (*A Genealogical History of the House of Rabutin*), which had been dedicated to her:†

One would have to be perfect [she wrote], that is to say, to be free of vanity not to be susceptible to such highly seasoned praise. It is praise so gracefully and expertly phrased and stated that if one were not careful, one might be seduced into thinking one deserved at least part of it—no matter how exaggerated. You should always have been prejudiced in my favor because I always loved you and never deserved your hatred. But let us talk no more of that. You compensate only too well for the past, and in a manner so noble and natural that I forgive you all the rest.

My daughter could not take the book in hand without reading it through, and found herself so agreeably treated that it has doubtlessly increased the esteem she has for you and for our family . . . My son is

---

*Anfossy was the Count de Grignan's secretary; Gautier, the fabric merchant.

†It was Marie de Rabutin-Chantal, Marquise de Sévigné, Bussy said somewhat patronizingly in his dedication, who would prove to be "the most illustrious of the Rabutins." So she would, although it would have astonished both him and her to know it.

less well pleased. You leave him an ensign without mentioning the commission of sub-lieutenant which he held and in which he served as commander-in-chief of the Dauphin's Gendarmes ... His wife is from one of the best houses of Brittany, but that is unimportant.

I hope to see my daughter before she returns to Provence, where it appears she would like to spend the winter ...

In a letter written the same day to her daughter, Mme de Sévigné's comment on Bussy's genealogical work was far less flattering:

Had only Bussy talked a little less about himself and his heroine of a daughter—the rest being true—it might have been considered good enough to deserve a place at the back of a bookshelf, if nothing else. He treats you very handsomely. He is too eager to make up with praise for his abuse of me earlier—neither of which I deserve. My son is treated cavalierly, left dangling cruelly for all eternity as an ensign. And he [Bussy] could have spoken more respectfully of his [Charles's] wife, who bears one of the proud names of that province. But, to tell the truth, my son has never gone out of his way to be polite to him, has indeed treated him so discourteously that—once having recognized him as a member of the family—he could well have skipped the rest. You showed yourself more friendly, and he returned the compliment.

"It is true," Mme de Sévigné went on to say in that same letter, "that having said to you at least twenty times, 'I am cured,' ... you have the right to laugh at anything I say on the subject." This time, however—this twenty-first time—the cure was certain, beyond the shadow of a doubt. The latest medical authority to be consulted was always, for Mme de Sévigné, the most convincing. The Capuchins by then—by July, 1685—out of favor, it was the Princess de Tarente who was in ("The Princess is the best doctor in the world!"), and it was the Princess's "good and skillful nurse" ("who comes daily to dress my leg") who was "the first to diagnose the ailment, to give it a name." (The name given it was "erysipelas ... although not the kind which comes as the result of natural causes; this has come about through accident, through severe injury."*) It was this Charlotte "who cures everyone in Vitré ... whom God did not want me to know about sooner because He wanted me to be mortified in that part of the body most miserable for me ... I am convinced that God now intends these minor ills to subside."

---

*Twentieth-century medical practitioners suggest the complication might have been phlebitis.

It was Charlotte who had her walking and who assured her that she was well enough to make the journey to Dol to greet the Governor and his Lady upon their arrival in Brittany. " 'You will see Mme de Chaulnes, and you will enjoy that,' " Mme de Sévigné quotes Charlotte as saying to her:

"You need diversion; you need to get out of your room where you have spent a week at my direction" . . . She asks me to keep my leg loosely bandaged, and to pamper myself a bit. She promises me that if I follow these instructions, I will go back to you with a leg "à la Sévigné," sure to please you because with both legs now a bit less plump, they are close to perfection! And that's more than enough about me . . .

I will be thrilled to see the good Chaulnes and little Coulanges,* but I assure you that if I were not in condition to go, I would not do it because what I want most in all the world is to be well enough to leave here at the very beginning of September.

It is you, my very dearest one, who will set the blessed date to fit in with your Court calendar. I feel sure that you will be at Fontaine-bleau until the Court moves on to Chambord. Your brother gives no thought to leaving home. His affairs do not permit him to think of Paris for several years. He has taken a notion to pay off all his debts, but since he has no reserves to draw on to accomplish that, it can only be achieved, little by little, out of his annual income. As for me, I have no hope of settling up all my debts, but I am waiting to see a farmer who owes me 11,000 francs which is almost more than I can hope for. But, no less impatient than you to end this sad and cruel separation, I will allow nothing to prevent me from keeping the date we have set.

At this point in the correspondence, at least three letters are missing: the preceding letter was dated "July 22, from Les Rochers"; this next one bears the date "Wednesday, August 1, from Les Rochers," and begins,

I returned last night, my dearest girl, from my big trip. I said goodbye to our Governors on Monday morning at eight . . . I confess that I was thrilled to have made this little journey in their honor. I owed them this mark of friendship in return for all those they show to me. Your

---

*Mme de Sévigné's cousin "little Coulanges" had accompanied the Duke and Duchess de Chaulnes to Brittany.

*health was toasted. They embraced me for you. They shared my joy in
the knowledge that I would soon be seeing you . . .*

 *So, I left on Monday morning, and my dear little Coulanges was
determined to come here to spend ten days with us, and my son did
not pass up the opportunity to return with him, so that here they are,
the two of them, to stay until the eighth of the month; then they will
go to spend the last two weeks [of August] attending the Estates
General; after which my son will come back here to kiss me goodbye.
He implores me on bended knee to wait for him, but I might leave on
a moment's notice. That will be, my bonne, on one of the very first
days of September in order to arrive on the ninth or tenth, without fail,
at Bâville*. . .*

 *I came home via Rennes to see that good Marboeuf for a moment
and, while passing through Vitré, to see the Princess, so that I can now
enjoy my little Coulanges, undisturbed. I told you how pretty my gown
was; I wrote you that from Dol . . .*

As for her "poor little Coulanges," they were "wearing him out," she
went on to say. "He has a thousand funny things to tell us . . . He is always
such good company; he is so lively and amusing that I am not surprised that
he is loved in all the places where there is love of joy."

 By August 15, "little Coulanges" had left Les Rochers with Charles de
Sévigné for Dinan (where the Estates General of Brittany were in session
from August 1 to August 23), while Mme de Sévigné, alone with her uncle
at Les Rochers, was packing and counting the days until her departure for
Paris, as she wrote her daughter:

*You can see, my bonne, that we are now counting only by days, no
longer by months nor even weeks! . . . I will not be ashamed of my
equipage. My children have very handsome ones; mine was once like
theirs. Times change. I now have only two horses, along with four
rented ones from the coach house at Mans. I will not be embarrassed
to arrive in that state.*

 To the contrary, it seems clear that she was precisely that, "embarrassed" and "ashamed." The equipage was one of the most conspicuous
status symbols of seventeenth-century France; Mme de Sévigné had been

---

*Bâville was a country estate belonging to Chrétien-François de Lamoignon, a family friend whose
Paris town house, the Hôtel de Lamoignon, still stands just across the street from the Hôtel Carnavalet.

very proud of her fine carriage and fine horses, her expert coachman, her postillion and outriders. She more than once expressed her delight in travelling along at a fast clip over good country roads—"a sensation like flying," she called it. The loss of her equipage was, to her, perhaps, the most painful symptom of her reduced circumstances.

The four rental horses trotting smartly in harness with her own two, Mme de Sévigné's carriage bore her and the *Bien Bon* from Les Rochers to Bâville in twelve days' time—the details of the journey unknown to us for the reason that Mme de Sévigné's letters written en route are among the many missing in 1685.

The account of the joyful reunion at Bâville we owe to letters written by Mme de Sévigné to the Count de Bussy and to President Moulceau.

Her letter to Bussy is dated October 5, 1685:

I got back from Brittany on the fifteenth of last month. I went straight to Bâville where Monsieur de Lamoignon had arranged for me to meet my daughter and all the Grignans. It has been a long time since I have known so great a joy . . .

Caught up in a flurry of excitement at her homecoming, Mme de Sévigné put off giving the news to her friend Moulceau until late November: by then, she said, she had to catch up with a fifteen-month hiatus in their correspondence:

And so, at last, Monsieur, after having been in a carriage accident and nearly drowned, and having done my leg an injury which has healed only in the last six weeks, I left my son and his wife, who is very pretty, and arrived at Bâville on the tenth or twelfth of September.* There I found my daughter and all the Grignans, who welcomed me with much joy and affection. To make my happiness complete, my daughter is staying with me here for the winter!

---

*Mme de Sévigné's memory has failed her here: writing to Moulceau more than two months later, she had forgotten that her arrival date had been September 15, as confirmed in her letter to Bussy.

XLV

Another reunion, another hiatus in the mother-daughter correspondence; a hiatus, this time, of three years' duration: from September 15, 1685 to October 6, 1688.

The little that is known of the lives of the Sévignés and the Grignans throughout those years is known through random letters addressed by Mme de Sévigné to her cousin the Count de Bussy-Rabutin in Burgundy and to her friend President Moulceau in Montpellier.

Late in October, 1685, a month or more after her return from Brittany, Mme de Sévigné wrote again to the Count de Bussy, this time from Livry where she had gone, as was her custom, to enjoy the glory of the autumn foliage:

> *I am here, my cousin [she wrote], with my daughter, her son, her stepdaughter, the good Abbé, and the most beautiful weather in the world! Only our friend Corbinelli is missing; he would spark and stimulate our company, but one cannot always get him when one wants him. He has other friends, he has business affairs, he likes his freedom, and we accept him on that basis.*

Six months later, in a letter to Moulceau dated April 3, 1686, Mme de Sévigné announced in some surprise that she was heir to the ills of the flesh, like everyone else! "It was ten days ago, Monsieur," she wrote, almost indignantly, "that my gloriously good health showed signs of failing me: a hint of colic, a nephritis, a bilious attack—some of those ailments, in sum, which make us realize that we are mortal!"

In a letter to Bussy, that same week in April, she spoke of "a touch of rheumatism, a touch of the vapours"; at the end of June, she had more to say:

> *It is true, my dear cousin, that this spring I had made plans to go to Vichy in the autumn because of an attack of rheumatism, but since I no longer have it and am now completely cured, I will not force myself to*

make a voyage which is always an embarrassment to anyone like me
who no longer has an equipage such as I once had.

A new name appeared, that summer, on Mme de Sévigné's list of correspondents, that of Jean d'Herigoyen, a man from Nantes, in Brittany, to whom she gave, in 1686, a six-year contract to manage and farm out her Buron properties. Their correspondence proved rather brisk but, dealing strictly with business, it provides little insight into Mme de Sévigné's personal life beyond the fact that she was more and more hard-pressed financially. In her generosity to her children, Mme de Sévigné had divested herself of everything but the usufruct of her Burgundy properties (whose revenues had dwindled from 4,000 to 3,200 livres annually) and her dower rights to the produce of Buron (with its revenues of some 4,000 livres annual income). From this total of approximately 7,200 livres annual income, 3,000 livres of interest was to be deducted, leaving her approximately 4,000 livres net income.

One thinks to hear a note of desperation in her voice:

I give my wholehearted consent [she wrote to her new steward, d'Her-
igoyen], to your making the necessary repairs to the mills, the small
farms, the moats and the meadows. My God, how could you think that
I don't want to put my property back into condition so that it can be
farmed out again? That is to my best interest. So, proceed along those
lines. Don't wait for my son ... You know more than he does about
such matters. Once confidence is established between us—as it already
has been on my side—I will give you the power to do, in good conscience
and honor, whatever you think necessary. Begin on that basis, and try
to lease the mills, the small farms and the meadows. There is not a
moment to lose.

October of 1686 found Mme de Sévigné back at Livry, this time with her son, who—evidently still plagued by the venereal disease he had contracted in 1680—had come to the capital for medical aid, as she related to Moulceau on October 25. "Let's talk for a moment about that poor Sévigné," she wrote:

I would be sad if I could not tell you that after five months of terrible
suffering brought on by remedies which purged him to the marrow of
his bones, that poor boy has finally been restored to perfect health. He
spent the whole month of August with me here in this retreat you

know so well. We were here alone with the good Abbé. We had infinitely long talks, and this close communion restored us to our old intimacy, rekindled our affection. He has gone home, a devout Christian philosopher with a touch of the anchorite about him—and, with all this, an infinite love for his wife, by whom he is loved in the same fashion, which makes him one of the most fortunate men in the world because he will be able to spend his life doing what he likes best.

In a letter to Moulceau dated January 6, 1687, there was mention of another invalid:

Extreme old age is frightful and humiliating. Day by day, we have a sad example before our eyes—Corbinelli and I—one to afflict us both. It is the poor Abbé de Coulanges, whose great weight and discomforts make us wish not to live that long.

On January 15, 1687, Mme de Sévigné wrote to Bussy in a happier vein:

A good day and a good year, my dear cousin. A good day and a good year, my dear niece. May this year be a happier one for you both than those that have just passed. [It gave promise of being happier because Mme de Coligny at last found herself free from that cad of a husband of hers, who had agreed to renounce his conjugal rights in return for the use of the bride's château at Lanty and the usufruct of those estates for his lifetime.] . . . Mme de Grignan is still in Paris, busy with many matters. She had the pleasure of seeing Mlle de Grignan make a gift to her father of all he owed her, which amounted to not less than forty thousand écus, and had constituted a heavy burden on that family. The gift comes as a great relief to the Grignans. That saintly girl, having taken the white veil at age twenty-five at the Carmelite Convent, and having left because of the delicacy of her health (which could not stand up to the rigors of life of that order), wanted to give a mark of love to her house when she went as a pensionnaire to another convent where the expense was small. You are fond enough of your cousin, I think, to share her joy in this matter; she worked wonders [in bringing it about].

In a letter of May 31 Mme de Sévigné availed herself of the opportunity of consulting Bussy about her properties in Burgundy:

I don't know the condition of your properties. As for mine, my cousin, the revenues from my Bourbilly estates have gone down to next to nothing due to the decline in price and the sluggish market for corn and other grains. The only way to get along is to live on one's own estates, but when one's life lies elsewhere, it is impossible to transport one's produce from those lands.

(Mme de Sévigné here gives a capsule analysis of the dilemma then confronting the landed aristocracy which could not—or would not—live on its own lands as it had been expected to do by the terms of the original feudal contract. It had been the express design of Louis XIV to weaken the power of the great and fractious feudal lords by drawing them to his Court where he could control them and make them totally dependent on his favor and his bounty. He succeeded in strengthening the central authority by this stratagem, but he brought about the ruin of the nobility who could not survive as absentee landlords.)

Bussy replied on June 4 to Mme de Sévigné's letter of May 31:

I get better returns proportionately, Madame, than you do from Bourbilly because I am living on my lands and you are not. As you say, Madame, one can live on one's revenues when one eats them, oneself—whereas, if one lives elsewhere, they amount to almost nothing.

When next Mme de Sévigné wrote to Bussy—a month or two later, on September 2—she wrote, as she told him, "overwhelmed with sadness," out of a grief which was still fresh:

Ten days ago [the letter began], I watched my dear uncle die. You know what he meant to his beloved niece. There was no benefit he did not provide me, whether it was leaving me all his worldly goods or whether it was conserving and reestablishing those of my children. He rescued me from the abyss into which I had fallen at the time of Monsieur de Sévigné's death. He won lawsuits for me, he restored all my properties to good order, he paid our debts, he made the property on which my son lives into one of the prettiest and pleasantest in the world. He married my children. In a word, it is to his unfailing care that I owe the tranquillity and the security of my life. You can well understand that such deep obligations, such long association cause excruciating pain when the time comes to say an eternal farewell . . . I am filled with sorrow and with gratitude.

By the middle of September—prompted by some physical and emotional disorders—Mme de Sévigné was on her way to the spa of Bourbon-L'Archambault with the Duchess de Chaulnes, in the Duchess's fine equipage ("a tremendous convenience for the little boat to be in tow to the big one!").

And with Mme de Sévigné's departure from Paris on September 16, the mother-daughter correspondence was resumed, if only briefly, for the five weeks (September 16–October 19, 1687) of Mme de Sévigné's absence. Only seven letters from this period have come to light.*

From them, it is clear that even in the magnificent equipage of a Duchess, travel in seventeenth-century France was arduous: "What a day!" Mme de Sévigné exclaimed on September 22 upon her arrival in Bourbon:

We drove from dawn to dusk without stopping except for exactly two hours for dinner. A constant rain, fiendish roads, often on foot for fear of the carriage overturning in the fearful ruts, the longest fourteen leagues imaginable!

Mme de Sévigné was "very pleased with the doctor chosen at Bourbon" to supervise their "cure": he thought the hot showers too much of a shock for her nerves, and advised her to confine herself to drinking the hot mineral waters, to taking the hot, aromatic baths, and to a strict diet ("no sauces, no ragouts," she grumbled). "We are the healthiest people here, Mme de Chaulnes and I!" she wrote exultantly, after one look at "the lame and the halt, the half-dead who seek relief in the boiling heat of these springs." "In comparison, I find myself in such good condition that I should never leave a place where I stand out as the most fortunate." "The opinion here is that my fears were far greater than my minor ailments warranted."

But, after three weeks at Bourbon, Mme de Sévigné was ready to come home. "We will arrive in Paris, as arranged, on the nineteenth," she wrote Mme de Grignan on October 7:

I want to embrace Mme de La Fayette and Mme de Lavardin, and then go with my dear daughter to Livry, to breathe, to take long promenades, to get a bit of exercise . . . If you come back to Paris, my darling, to meet me,† you well know that I will be thrilled, but avoid the fatigue

---

*It is reasonable to assume that Mme de Sévigné would have availed herself of every courier available between Bourbon and Paris, and would, accordingly, have written three times a week during her three-week stay at the spa. She also wrote at every stopping place en route to and from Paris.

†To meet her mother upon her arrival in Paris, Mme de Grignan would come back to Paris from Fontainebleau, where she had gone to pay her court.

*of coming out on the road to meet us on our way in. My only thought
is to be reunited with you and to spend as long a time together as God
will grant us ... I hope my friend Corbinelli will come to see us at
Livry. We will enjoy it to the very last moment—until they push us
out by the shoulders!*

Mme de Grignan was as assiduous a correspondent as her mother,
addressing letters to her at her every stopping place en route back to Paris.
"Everywhere I go I find tokens of your thoughtfulness and love," Mme de
Sévigné wrote from Milly on October 18: "I wrote to you from Maison
Rouge, six leagues back, so you will see that I did not forget you, either."

Mother and daughter again reunited on October 19, 1687, their correspondence again lapsed.

To Mme de Sévigné's delight, the Countess de Grignan would allow
the Count de Grignan to return without her to Provence; she and her son
would stay on at the Hôtel Carnavalet in Paris with her mother, for another
year. It was the Aiguebonne lawsuit against the Grignan family that dragged
on and kept her there again, as it had for the past several years.*

The good Abbé was still much on Mme de Sévigné's mind when she
wrote to the Count de Bussy on November 13, a letter even more elegiac,
more eulogistic than the one she had written him shortly after her uncle's
death:

*I keep going back over the last days of the life of my dear uncle, the
Abbé, to whom—as you know—I had infinite obligations. I owed him
the sweetness and ease of my life. It is to him you owe whatever joy I
brought to our association. Without him, we would never have laughed
together; you owe him all my gayety, all my high spirits, my vivacity,
the gift I have of understanding you so well, the intelligence which
allowed me to understand what you said and to divine what you were
going to say. In a word, the good Abbé, in rescuing me from the abyss
into which I had fallen at the death of Monsieur de Sévigné, made me
the person I was, the one you knew, worthy of your esteem and
affection.*

*I would never have left him as long as he lived. But, seeing by the
fifteenth or sixteenth of September that I was only too free, I decided*

*The lawsuit brought by Guichard d'Urre de Cornillon, seigneur d'Aiguebonne, against the Gri-
gnans concerned some properties in contest between the two families for over a hundred years. The case,
having come to trial originally in the Parlements of Grenoble and Toulouse, was eventually heard in the
courts of the Parlement of Paris, where the verdict pronounced in 1688 was in favor of the Grignans.

to go to Vichy* if for nothing else but to relieve my apprehension about some kind of spasms in my left hand and about the vapours to which I was subject which made me fearful of apoplexy . . . They [the doctors at Bourbon] mocked at my fears, told me that it was all in my imagination, and sent me home with a clean bill of health.

It is three weeks since I came back from Bourbon. Our pretty little Abbey had not yet been given to another, and we spent twelve days there. It has just now been turned over to the old Bishop of Nîmes, a very saintly prelate.† I left there three days ago, heartsick at saying adieu to that delicious retreat I loved so well. After having wept for the Abbé, I weep for the Abbey.

One of the few of the Countess de Grignan's letters extant is addressed to the Count de Grignan in Aix-en-Provence, and dated, "Paris, January 5, 1688." "All your family wishes you a good day and a good year," she wrote. She had just come back to Paris, she said, from Versailles where she had gone to pay her court. She had received many compliments, she told her husband, on a skirt she had worn there:

It is the most magnificent skirt in Versailles, and so very beautiful that Monsieur said to me, "Madame, you did not buy that fabric; you are too practical." I confessed to him that it was a gift from you; I gave you full credit. You tell me that I am never satisfied with my son's wardrobe, but I buy him only what is necessary. I admit that I very much want to see him dance at the ball. He is handsome, he has an air about him, he dances well. There could be no better time for him to appear and make a good impression. So, I would very much like for him to be dressed in a fashion worthy of him. I think I will go to that expense. Otherwise, all I can tell you is that I am dying to be back . . . at Grignan and to give up all this. Were it not, alas, for our lawsuit, you and I would be hidden away together in our château. I would not let you leave it often, and we would economize so as to provide for our child and show him off in a good light. That is my main purpose in life.

---

*The Duchess de Chaulnes had persuaded her to go to Bourbon instead of to Vichy, as originally planned.

†The Abbé de Coulanges had enjoyed possession of the Abbey of Livry since 1624, some sixty-three years. A new abbot was named as his successor in November, 1688.

Six months later, on June 15, 1688, Mme de Sévigné addressed a letter to the Count de Bussy, who had written to apologize for a long silence: "We didn't know what had become of you!" she began,

> We said to each other, Corbinelli and I, "If it was anyone else, we would be fearful he had hanged himself!" but we could not believe anything so doleful of a temperament like yours. And, indeed, there you are again, in the best of health!
>   The Countess of Provence is very nervous as the trial begins.* All the Grignans have come from wherever they were to lend their support.

On August 13, Mme de Sévigné could report to Bussy that her daughter had emerged victorious from the legal fray:

> I should tell you, too, that my daughter won her case by a unanimous decision, and with all court costs paid! That is remarkable. With that decision, a great burden is lifted from the shoulders of the family. It was a "dragon" which had harried them for six years. But that "dragon" is now succeeded by another—the thought of our being separated! Is it not what I said about the ways of Providence? And, so, we must bid each other adieu, my daughter and I, the one on her way to Provence, the other to Brittany. That is very probably how Providence will dispose of us.

By September 22, the evil moment was upon her, as she mourned to Bussy:

> I am very sad, my dear cousin. Our dear Countess of Provence whom you love so dearly is leaving Paris in a week. That separation tears the soul out of me, and determines me to go to Brittany. I have lots of business to attend to there, but I suspect that there is a trace of amorous spite in it. I want no more of Paris without her; I am angry at the whole world. I will go and bury myself in a desert!

A letter of lamentation went off to Moulceau on the same day:

> Pity me. My daughter is leaving for Provence. I am overwhelmed with sorrow. It is so natural to become attached and accustomed to the company of a person one loves—and by whom one is loved in return—

*The Countess of Provence was another of her mother's pet names for the Countess de Grignan.

that it is, in truth, a martyrdom to be separated. Even if we could look forward to being reunited, one day, at Grignan, that would be some consolation but, alas, that time is far off in the future, and the adieu is close at hand.

XLVI

Clinging tenaciously, holding fast to her daughter to the very last, putting off the evil moment of parting as long as possible, Mme de Sévigné accompanied Mme de Grignan as far as Charenton, where their adieus were said on October 3, 1688. From Charenton, Mme de Grignan's carriage headed south toward Provence while her mother's turned back to Paris, to the emptiness of the cavernous Carnavalet.

The letters written by Mme de Sévigné after this seventh parting from her daughter vary significantly from those of previous separations: there is sadness, there is loneliness, there is longing, but there is no longer evidence of so cruel an anguish as heretofore. A plaintive note still sounds, but the wailing has grown faint. Their separations like their reunions, Mme de Sévigné has come to see, are in the hands of that "*belle Providence*" of hers. Not only has Mme de Sévigné learned submission to fate, she finds separation easier to face now that she feels secure in her daughter's love. She and her daughter are apart, but they are at one. Her letters in 1688 are given to fond reminiscence; they speak of close companionship, of supremely happy days, months, and years at the Hôtel Carnavalet between 1680 and 1688. Mme de Sévigné's Love Letters (her *Lettres d'amour*, as Roger Duchêne, the editor of the most recent edition of the *Correspondence*, calls them) are less impetuous in 1688, less insistent, less hysterical, less strident than in previous years—testimony to the fact that mother and daughter alike, by then, knew their love to be reciprocated. Mme de Sévigné had come, what is more, to recognize her daughter's strength, her judgment, her skill in handling not only the Grignan household and family, but Grignan legal and financial affairs, and this recognition had brought about a subtle change in their relation: the mother came to defer to—even to lean upon—her daughter rather than to attempt to dominate her.

Mme de Sévigné's first letter to Mme de Grignan is dated "Wednesday,

October 6, in Paris" and is denoted as "in reply" to a letter from Mme de Grignan from her first stopping place en route south:

And how can you expect me not to cry in the face of such fond attention, such devotion, such affectionate letters? ... All we do is love and praise you. Monsieur the Chevalier and I seek each other out so naturally, my dear bonne, *that you cannot be surprised to learn that that little room [of his] is where I spend most of my time.*

The Chevalier de Grignan—the only Grignan remaining to Mme de Sévigné in the Hôtel Carnavalet—occupied a small room in the ground-floor apartment of his brother and sister-in-law, having taken up residence with them several years earlier after an attack of the crippling gout which was to blight both his military career (as Colonel of the Grignan regiment) and his Court career (as *menin* or gentleman-in-waiting to the Dauphin). Thus incapacitated, the Chevalier could no longer serve his family as liaison with the Court and the War Department—a loss repeatedly lamented in the letters of Mme de Sévigné that year. His invalidism, she wrote her daughter, could be considered as "a great misery for him, a great misfortune for you. What good offices might he not have performed in your behalf at Versailles— in behalf of both your son and your other affairs!"

"We take our meals together," she wrote of the Chevalier and herself in that first letter to her daughter:

We are in perfect accord, and it is true that the better one knows Monsieur the Chevalier on that footing, the more one loves and esteems him. It seems to me that my company does not displease him. In sum, that little room is my destiny; there is no other place in the world where you are more perfectly loved and admired, not to say honored.

Your portraits are all around us [she continued], but they cannot make up for your absence. It is our dear Countess whom we need, whom we cannot find ... at which point our eyes begin to redden. All is lost. Even the honor of being served first when it is time for coffee distresses me rather than consoles me, so indifferent is my heart to the grandeurs of this world.

("Ours is becoming a fast friendship, the Chevalier's and mine," she wrote later in October, "but never be jealous, my dear child; we love each other in you, because of you, and through you.")

The celebration of the beloved had become a concelebration in 1688, the voice of the Chevalier chiming in with that of Mme de Sévigné in a paean of praise for Mme de Grignan.

"Adieu, my dear *bonne*," the letter of October 6 concluded: "I know nothing more to say about my love for you. It has all been said, it has all been felt, all believed. I am confident of it." "I had your novenas* said," she had assured her daughter on another page of that same long letter. "I have no doubt they will ensure for you the safety of your child . . ."

It was the safety of her only son, the young Marquis de Grignan, over which the Countess at that hour agonized: he was, at age sixteen, on campaign in Germany with the Dauphin, a volunteer assigned to the Regiment of Champagne (in which his father had once served as Colonel), at that hour involved in the siege of Philippsburg.

Mme de Sévigné was concerned about her daughter as well as her grandson: "I have worries of my own," she would say, "but I worry more about your worries than my own." It was hard for Mme de Grignan, her mother knew, to be so far from Paris, so far removed from the nerve center of the War Department: "You are cut off, alone," Mme de Sévigné wrote, "tête-à-tête with a 'dragon' which gnaws at your heart, lacking all distractions, trembling at every sound, unable to bear your own thoughts, and fearing the worst. That is a cruel, an unbearable state . . . You are in greater danger than your child."

"Up to this point," she wrote on October 18,

> *your son is in fine fettle. He is accomplishing marvels. He sees, he hears cannon and cannon fire without any show of emotion. He has mounted guard. He sends reports of the siege to his uncle like a veteran officer. He is loved by all the world. He often eats with Monseigneur [the Dauphin] who speaks to him and gives him the* bougeoir *to hold.†*

"Are your youth and health still holding up under the strain of your 'dragons,' your fears, your cruel nights?" Mme de Sévigné inquired of her daughter on October 29:

> *It is the thought of that which is killing me because I know nothing more devastating. But you are far from the source of the news; your imagination runs riot. If you were here, you would get the news every*

---

*A novena is a series of nine Masses which are said for a particular purpose; as, in this instance, the safety of the Marquis.

†The *bougeoir* was the golden lamp which lighted the Dauphin's sleeping quarters; noblemen vied for the honor of holding it at the Dauphin's bedtime.

day, like the rest of us. You would see that that little fellow has made a good adjustment. There he is, making headway in the profession he is to follow. He writes blithely and spiritedly. He has gone twice into the trenches . . . He is doing very well. It is not believed that his regiment will go a third time into the trenches . . . What a joy it will be for you, my dear Countess, when we write you "Philippsburg has been taken! Your son is safe!" Then, please God, you will breathe again, and so will we.

"My letter was sealed," Mme de Sévigné wrote, "when I received your letter written 'On the boat beyond Mâcon' ":

You can rest assured that I will not leave Paris as long as the siege of Philippsburg goes on, as long as the Chevalier remains here. Quite naturally, I find myself deeply involved in those two things. Your memory is bright, all pervasive. Never has a person so permeated all the places she has been, and never have I so thoroughly enjoyed the privilege of living in the same house with you. Our mornings together—were they not wonderfully pleasant? We had two hours together before other women even awakened. I have nothing with which to reproach myself on that score: I lost no time, no opportunity to be with you. I was greedy, never wanted to miss out on a moment of time I could spend with you. I never went out of this house without yearning to return, never came home without being conscious of the joy of finding you here and spending the evening with you!

"You want me to tell you about my health and my life," Mme de Sévigné wrote her daughter:

I eat very well, my dear bonne. Never think that I am foolish enough to allow myself to starve to death. In the evening, we have a small fowl of some kind; in the morning, a good soup, either chicken or veal, and good cabbages. To please you, I will add some rice. On the whole, my bonne, it is not on that score that I am to be pitied. Not that I was not a thousand times better off at your hostelry [at the Grignans' table]. I was, in truth, far better nourished . . . both body and soul, but it is God's will that we be separated for some time . . . As for my life, you know how that goes: often in that little room downstairs where I am as if destined to be. I try, however, not to take advantage, not to be an inconvenience. It seems to me that my appearance is welcome there.

We talk constantly of you, of your son, of your affairs. I go to Mme de La Fayette's, to [Mme de] Lavardin's; they all still talk of you, love you, hold you in esteem; another day, to Mme de Moussy's, yesterday to the Marquise d'Huxelles . . . There is no one in Paris. One comes home in the evening, one goes to bed, one gets up, one goes to Mass. Life passes quickly because time passes quickly. Mlle de Méri feels very comfortable with us, here, and we with her. Do not think that I would ever take money from her [for rent], but if she will give me a quittance in return, I would accept that. If not, I will pay it [the pension] to her.

(The Abbé de Coulanges had left Mme de Sévigné his entire estate out of which, according to his will, she was to pay Mlle de Méri a pension of 250 livres a year. It was this amount which Mme de Sévigné hoped to receive as quittance in lieu of rent.)

Mme de Sévigné's financial straits had forced her to take in paying guests at the Hôtel Carnavalet during the Grignans' absence. Not only her cousin Mlle de Méri but her old friend Corbinelli had taken an apartment on a sublease there. In October, the Abbé Bigorre moved in. "You are very kind," Mme de Sévigné wrote her daughter, "to agree to my getting some relief by subletting to the Abbé Bigorre. If I had not had need, I would not have had him here. You can be sure that it is only out of necessity that I seek relief of that kind."* (By November, she was enjoying the Abbé's company: "The Abbé Bigorre is really the best friend and most agreeable guest anyone could wish for." By the spring of 1690, he was beautifying the premises: "The Abbé is sanding our garden and planting a thousand flowers and a thousand little trees—all that in addition to his thirty gold *louis*!")

"So, there you are at Grignan," Mme de Sévigné wrote exultantly on October 26, "and in good health, and although that is a hundred thousand leagues away from me, I must rejoice. Such is our destiny. Perhaps God will permit me to join you soon. Let me live in that hope. You draw a pretty picture of Pauline. I recognize her; she has not changed, as Monsieur de Grignan told us. She is a very darling little creature, one easy to love! If I were in your place, I would enjoy her company which should provide you an occupation and a diversion." (Pauline had not accompanied her parents to Paris in 1680, having been put in the care of her aunt, the Abbess of the Convent of Villedieu at Aubenas. Mme de Sévigné's letters in 1688 repeat-

*Mme de Sévigné and the Grignans paid 1,800 livres a year for their lease on the Hôtel Carnavalet. The Abbé Bigorre paid 400 livres a year for his apartment; Mlle de Méri's apartment was estimated at 250 livres; there is no record of the amount paid by the Chevalier or by Corbinelli.

edly urge her daughter to keep this winsome thirteen-year-old girl at home with her rather than to commit her to conventual life, thus sparing her the fate of her sister, Marie-Blanche.)

"I am very pleased that the Chevalier speaks so well of me," Mme de Sévigné continued in her letter of October 26:

> My vanity is flattered to know that I am not displeasing to him . . . I do not know, my daughter, how you can say that your moods are like clouds which hide your love from me. If that was true in the past, you have surely lowered the veil in recent years, and no longer make a secret of the most tender, most perfect love that ever was. God will recompense you with that of your children, who will love you—not perhaps in the same way, of which they might not be capable—but to the utmost possible to them, for which one must be content.

(Mme de Sévigné considered her daughter's love nothing short of prodigious: "I implore you to go on loving me as a daughter has never before loved a mother, because that is true, and I am astonished to have been destined to the pleasure and the good fortune of enjoying such a prodigy.")

On November 1, All Saints' Day, a courier galloped into Fontainebleau from the German front, and the King interrupted a sermon in progress in the Royal Chapel to announce a victory. By nine o'clock that night, the news had reached Paris, and Mme de Sévigné rushed to her writing-table to relay it to her daughter: "Philippsburg has been captured, my dear child! Your son is safe! . . . Now, you can breathe again, my beloved daughter."

On November 10, Mme de Sévigné could report to Mme de Grignan that

> the Chevalier's health has improved and will permit him to go to Versailles. That will be very fortunate for you and for the Marquis, who should be here shortly. Now you can sleep, my dear child; you no longer need live in cruel anxiety. We could have hoped for nothing better. Our fondest hopes are realized, as concerns both the Marquis's safety and his budding reputation.

Feeling that she deserved a vacation, Mme de Sévigné accepted an invitation to her cousin's country estate at Brévannes:

> Mme de Coulanges has been asking me to come for six weeks, but I had Philippsburg to capture. Now, however, I am going to spend a few

days there . . . I will do some walking, because it is when I take exercise that I find relaxation for both body and soul for all that I have suffered in my anxiety over both you and your child.

On November 15, she rushed back to Paris from Brévannes on a summons from the Chevalier, writing to Mme de Grignan at five o'clock that afternoon:

Monsieur the Chevalier left yesterday for Versailles, sending me these two letters of yours to Brévannes. I was sure that there was one in which you would speak to me of your joy at the news of the capture of Philippsburg but, my dear daughter, you will be no less content at the news of the capture of Mannheim where our child ran some risk as the result of a slight contusion on his hip, subsequent to which he wrote me this letter which I am herewith forwarding to you—in which you will see that he is very lucky to have gotten off so lightly, and Monsieur du Plessis [the Marquis's tutor] will tell you with what composure he sustained the wound—for which he was praised, as you will see. Monseigneur reported the wound to the King, and Dangeau reported it to the Chevalier de Grignan, rejoicing with him at the news . . . Thus you need have no concern about your dear child, for you can clearly see that he is feeling fine, and that he is very lucky. To have sustained such a wound before his seventeenth birthday . . . must be considered as still another auspicious and advantageous landmark in your son's career.†

(She referred to the wound as "that very good little contusion which does him great credit, I assure you, because of the cool composure he exhibited upon being struck.")

She could not close and seal her letter of the nineteenth without a word of congratulation to the Count de Grignan:

My very dear Count, I still have to say a word to you about this little fellow. This campaign is of your doing. There is every reason for you to feel that you used good judgment. I do not say it to flatter you, but

---

*Philippsburg, which controlled the middle Rhine, was a natural target for Louis XIV in his effort to secure French frontiers. With the capture of that strategic site, Alsace would be safe from attack from the north.

†The *Gazette* reported on November 20, 1688, that "the young Count [sic] de Grignan had suffered a slight contusion after being struck by a shell fragment."

all the world speaks well of your son. People speak of his zeal, his sangfroid, his bravery, even his daring.

Throughout November, Mme de Sévigné's letters bubbled over with excitement over the family's little hero. It was the proud grandmother who wrote: "I have never seen so auspicious a debut into the world and the war! His courage, his determination, his cool head, his wisdom, his conduct have all been widely praised, especially at Versailles." "This child's reputation is made, and can only grow." Monsieur the Chevalier, she wrote on November 19, "is being overwhelmed with congratulations at Versailles, as I am here. I am thrilled when he is there because he so perfectly serves all the family interests. He told me the Marquis was the talk of Versailles, and in the most favorable terms. Mme de Maintenon congratulated him* . . . The entire Court responded to the good news."

On Wednesday, December 8, Mme de Sévigné could at last report the young hero's return to Paris:

The scatterbrained little rascal, after writing us that he could not reach here before Tuesday (yesterday), arrived the day before yesterday, at seven in the evening, before I had come in from my rounds of the city. His uncle greeted him, and was thrilled to see him, and I—when I came in—found him looking handsome and in high good humor. He embraced me five or six times with very good grace. He wanted to kiss my hand; I wanted to kiss his cheek; that brought on a struggle. Finally, I took his head in my hands and kissed him at my pleasure. I wanted to see his contusion but since it is—pardon my saying so—on his left hip, I did not think it appropriate to make him take down his pants. We spent the evening talking with this little fellow . . . We are thrilled to see him, and only regret that you cannot have the same pleasure.

In his mother's absence, the Marquis's grandmother stepped in as his social arbiter, writing her daughter:

When you are here, my dear bonne, *you give your son such good advice that I am filled with admiration but, in your absence, I step in to teach him the art of conversation which it is important for him to know . . . I preach to him about being attentive when other people talk*

---

*Mme de Maintenon had, by then, in the opinion of most historians, become the morganatic wife of Louis XIV, the ceremony having been performed in secret in 1684.

*and about the importance of presence of mind in order to understand
and to reply promptly—all of which is of great importance in this
world.*

And while his grandmother strove to indoctrinate the little Marquis in
the social graces, his uncle (the Chevalier de Grignan) held forth on what
Mme de Sévigné called "the major themes of honor and reputation":

*He covers every angle; he is interested in everything, and wants the
Marquis to handle his money, himself; to write, to calculate, to avoid
useless expenditures. Thus, he tries to communicate to him his own
sense of propriety and economy in order to eradicate that air of the
grand seigneur—of "what difference does it make"—that air of ignorance and indifference which leads to such grave injustices—and,
eventually, straight to the poorhouse!*

If the Marquis had inherited his father's insouciance about money, he
had not inherited his father's physique: "He will never have a fine figure
like his father's," Mme de Sévigné ruefully conceded: "No use thinking
about that." (Not even the metal corselets into which the little boy had been
strapped at an early age had succeeded in correcting what was evidently a
slight curvature of the spine.)

Not only Mme de Sévigné and the Chevalier but also Monsieur du
Plessis bewailed the fact that the young man had no taste for reading. "Since
we all feel deeply about this matter," Mme de Sévigné wrote her daughter,
"we bring it up often. We overlook no opportunity to try to inspire him
with so suitable a taste." ("The hubbub of his youth is deafening to him,"
she said elsewhere in defense of her grandson: "He can hear nothing else.")
"I pity those who do not like to read," she would say in another letter:
"Your son is, thus far, among that number, but I hope—like you—that he
will see that this constitutes ignorance on the part of a soldier who has so
much to read about the feats of others ... It is through reading, furthermore,
it seems to me, that one learns how to write."

Mme de Sévigné did not fail to pay tribute to her daughter for the role
she had played in forwarding her son's military career: "This is what you
wished for," she wrote:

*Here he is ... already a veteran musketeer, a volunteer who experi-
enced a fine siege, and Captain of a Cavalry Company! But I find it
very amusing that it is you to whom the credit goes for having put that*

company together . . . So, you have many capabilities. It is not only a
trial you handle so wonderfully well.

(In order further to advance the Marquis's career, the Grignans had put
together a company of light cavalry as part of the Grignan regiment of
which the Chevalier was the Colonel and the commandant. The newly
constituted cavalry company was to be under the command of the young
Marquis, who would hold the rank of captain. Mme de Sévigné gave Mme
de Grignan the credit for choosing not only the men but the horses forming
the new unit: "That company [she wrote]—the fruit of your exertions—
which is presently the finest in the whole army!")

"Like you, I found the month of November quite long, quite full of
important events," Mme de Sévigné wrote her daughter in early December,
1688: "But I admit that the month of October seemed far longer, far more
trying to me. I simply could not accustom myself to not being with you
every moment. It was a sorrowful time." "You know my life," she wrote on
another day, that winter: "The days pass, some sadly, others gaily, but finally
one comes to the very last. I will go on loving you, my very dear Countess,
until that final day."

XLVII

The year 1688 was to prove, on several counts, a most propitious one for
the Grignans. First of all, it was the year in which the Marquis de Grignan
underwent his baptism by fire alongside the Dauphin, the heir apparent to
the throne of France, both young men furnishing proof that they had been
bred to valor. Secondly, the Count de Grignan was named by his monarch
to that select company known as the Order of the Holy Ghost, France's
version of England's Order of the Garter.

The third honor to be enjoyed by the Grignan family in 1688 came as
a result of Louis XIV's displeasure with the Pope over what the French
monarch construed as an anti-French bias on the Supreme Pontiff's part vis-
à-vis the European political chessboard. In a huff, in October of that year,
the Sun King sent troops to occupy the city of Avignon, which had been a

papal see since the fourteenth century. To replace the Papal Vice-Legate, who had administered the affairs of that walled city on the River Rhône, Louis XIV appointed the Count de Grignan. Happily, the appointment was not an empty honor: The King accorded Grignan—as always necessitous—the handsome sum of 40,897 livres for his year's incumbency.

Mme de Sévigné shone in the reflected glory; her letters glowed with pride: "That post has its distinction and its grandeurs." "It is true, my dear Countess, that the Avignon appointment comes as a great blessing," she wrote, "a sign of benevolence and grace toward you on the part of Providence, for which I am duly grateful."

"Congratulations pour in for you . . . as many as when you won your trial," Mme de Sévigné told Mme de Grignan on December 6:

> *You cannot say, my daughter, that the past three months have been unlucky for you. I begin with your victory in the lawsuit; next, the preservation of your son's life; his splendid, outstanding reputation, his contusion, the beautiful company you put together for him; the Avignon appointment, the* Cordon Bleu* . . .

"All in all, my dear child, people talk of nothing but you and your Grignans!" Mme de Sévigné exclaimed elatedly on December 8.

The year 1688 ended in bitter cold in Paris, and Mme de Sévigné could not resist comparing her winter to her daughter's:

> *I wrote you yesterday, I think, that your heat and your fleas were proof that the same sun does not shine on you and me. Last week, here, it froze hard enough to break rocks; it snowed on top of that, so that yesterday it was impossible to keep one's footing. Now, it is pouring in such sheets that one cannot tell whether there is a sun in the world.*

"Here I am seated at the corner of my hearth," she wrote on December 15, "a little table in front of me, laboring for two hours over business letters to Brittany . . . But now I am going to relax and refresh my mind by writing to my dear daughter."

("Is it possible, my dear daughter," she wrote on another page, "that I write so well? I write so fast! But if you are pleased, I ask no more!" "It is true that I love my little squiggles," she said, once, about the strange little lines or strokes with which she marked or underscored her letters. "They

---

*The *Cordon Bleu* or Blue Ribbon was the insignia of the Order of the Holy Ghost.

are there to call things to your attention. They invite reflection, request an answer. Sometimes they serve as epigrams, sometimes as satire. In the last analysis, one makes of them what one wills." "My little strokes," she explained elsewhere, "point out the passages to which you are to reply.")

Christmas in seventeenth-century France was observed in solemnity: "This is a day for devotions, my dear Countess," Mme de Sévigné wrote on December 24, 1688: "You know that I will go tonight to our good 'Blues' [the blue-robed nuns of the Order of St. Augustine in the Church and Convent of St. Catherine de la Culture, just down the street from the Hôtel Carnavalet]. The Marquis and Monsieur du Plessis want to go to Catherine [the Church of St. Catherine de la Culture in the parish of St. Paul], but they will come back here to eat my soup and boiled chicken."

The letter continued:

Your child went alone to Versailles. He has gotten along very well . . . has paid his court at all the levers, at all the couchers [the formal ceremonies of arising and retiring observed morning and night in the royal households, and attended by the courtiers]. Monseigneur [the Dauphin] chose him to hold the bougeoir.

So, there he is launched in the world! He has acquitted himself very well. He is in vogue. He could not have made a better debut nor enjoyed a better reputation universally, for I would never finish if I named to you all those who speak well of him. It saddens me that you cannot have the pleasure of seeing and embracing him every day, as do I.

With the Grignans at Aix-en-Provence in December, Pauline needed a wardrobe befitting a *jeune fille* of fourteen:

You are right to order a dress and cornette* *for that pretty Pauline [her grandmother wrote]; she cannot do without them. But, in the meantime, if I were you, I would keep her with me. That is the best place for her. I see no reason why she should be banished to the attics. She is still Mlle de Grignan; that name is an adornment. But, considering the expense you are under for your son and his company, strict economy is indicated not only in regard to her, but also in regard to your table and your retinue.*

---

*The *cornette* was a seventeenth-century hair ornament.

On December 31, 1688, Mme de Sévigné's letter ended with the words, "Adieu, my very dear one. I embrace you a thousand times, and wish you a happy year, '89."

January 7, 1689 was observed by Mme de Sévigné as an anniversary, the anniversary of their parting, three months earlier (on October 7, 1688):

> *Like you, I find the time infinitely long since your departure, so long that it seems to me like three years! . . . I have missed you so, miss you more every day! I cannot accustom myself to not seeing you—accustomed as I was to so long and happy a time together! That painful day at Charenton is still vivid, still poignant.*

By January 10, Mme de Sévigné appeared in a happier frame of mind, thanks to some pleasant social diversions:

> *Mme de Coulanges gave a very delightful supper party for the gouty [she wrote]. There were the Abbé de Marsillac, Monsieur the Chevalier de Grignan, Monsieur de Lamoignon (whose nephritis served him in place of gout), his wife, and The Divine Ones [Mme de Frontenac and Mlle de l'Outrelaise], always complaining of inflammation of the chest, and I—included out of consideration for my rheumatic attack twelve years ago—and also Coulanges, who is a candidate for gout!*

(Mme de Sévigné was correct in her prognosis: By February 4, little Coulanges had succumbed—"like any little debauchee"—to an attack of gout: "He shrieks. They carry him about on their backs. He sees visitors. He suffers. He does not sleep. But all this goes on as if for laughs. Not even pain does he take seriously!")

Mme de Sévigné had come to respect her daughter's strength and judgment but her lectures on economy continued. If the Countess had flirted with the idea of accompanying the Count to Avignon, her mother discouraged it:

> *The Chevalier, with all his good common sense, does not consider a trip to Avignon—with all the expense involved—appropriate. You have shone for twenty years in Provence. The expense to which you are committed for your son is your primary responsibility . . . I fear that this fact is not yet clear to Monsieur de Grignan, that he will judge the future by the past; that he will continue, in the future, the way he has gone in the past. Such a hope is futile and deceptive. We have talked at*

length about all this, the Chevalier and I. However it may be, my daughter, dispense with any hope of reconciliation with the Pope, and take as much as the King permits out of Avignon, but think of it as a blessing sent you by God to maintain your son—not as a means to indulge yourselves in high living, because if you do not have the courage to retrench, as you have resolved to do, this gift of Providence will prove useless to you. And there, my daughter, you have the conversation of a Maman who loves you as sensibly as she does tenderly.

Such blessings as Providence bestowed on the Grignans, on the one hand, Providence snatched from them, on the other hand. Mme de Sévigné was shocked at news of the damage sustained by the château in the winter storms. She saw "the gales, the whirlwind, the hurricanes as devils unchained, intent on carrying off your château! There's a thousand écus expense you had not been expecting ... God preserve you from ever having to spend a winter there!"

On Friday, January 21, Mme de Sévigné's letter to her daughter began with a celebration of mutual love: "I have never known a love so strong, so tender, so delicious as that you harbor for me. I sometimes think how that love—the sweetness of which I presently savor—has always been the one thing in the world for which I longed most passionately." (Harking back to the days when she had been less certain of her daughter's love, Mme de Sévigné wrote, on another day that month: "Never compare your heart, my dear child, to any other. God gave you yours in a perfection. Thank Him for it. Your moods were merely a mist, a fog that concealed the sun."

In February, Court and Capital were agog over Racine's new drama presented under the auspices of Mme de Maintenon at Saint-Cyr, the convent founded by her for the education of indigent young ladies of quality. It was these young ladies who composed the cast of *Esther*, a tragedy based on the Old Testament book of that name. "Racine has outdone himself!" Mme de Sévigné rhapsodized on February 7, before she had ever seen the play: "He now loves God as he once loved his mistresses. He is now intent on the sacred as he once was on the profane. The play adheres meticulously to Holy Scripture." "The King and all the Court are charmed with the tragedy of *Esther*," she reported to her daughter. "It is one of Racine's masterpieces. If I were devout, I would long to see it."

Devout or not, she jumped at the opportunity when she received an invitation to attend the last performance on February 19: "I paid mine [my court], the other day, at Saint-Cyr, more agreeably than I had ever thought to do," Mme de Sévigné wrote on Monday, February 21:

We went out there on Saturday, Mme de Coulanges, Mme de Bagnols, the Abbé Têtu and I. Seats had been reserved for us. An usher told Mme de Coulanges that Mme de Maintenon was holding a place for her beside her own. You can imagine what an honor that was! "As for you, Madame," he said to me, "you may choose your location." I sat beside Mme de Bagnols in the second row behind the Duchesses. The Maréchal de Bellefonds came, by choice, to sit on my right . . . I cannot speak too highly of that drama. It is one which is not easy to produce, and which will never be imitated. There is such a total, such a perfect rapport between the music, the words, the songs and the characters that nothing is left to be desired. The girls who play the roles of the Kings and other personages seem made for the parts. One listens with rapt attention; one's only disappointment is to have so delightful a play come to an end. There is an innocence and a simplicity about it, a sublimity and a poignancy. The fidelity to the Holy Book evokes respect . . . I was charmed by it, as was the Maréchal who left his seat to go to tell the King that he had greatly enjoyed it and that he had sat beside a lady who was worthy of having seen Esther. The King approached our seats, and after having turned, he addressed me, saying, "Madame, I have been told that you were pleased." Maintaining my composure, I replied, "Sire, I was charmed. What I felt is beyond words." The King said to me, "Racine has great talent." "Sire," I replied, "he does, indeed, but—in truth, so do these young ladies; they play their roles as if they had been doing it all their lives." The King said, "Ah! as for that, I agree." And then His Majesty moved away, and left me the object of envy. Since I was almost the only one who had not seen it before, he took some pleasure in my sincere and simple expression of admiration . . . Mme de Maintenon stopped to see me for a fleeting moment, then was gone in a flash, leaving with the King . . . We returned to Paris, that night, by the flare of torches. I took supper with Mme de Coulanges, to whom the King had also spoken . . . That night, I saw Monsieur the Chevalier. I gave him, quite naïvely, an account of my small successes, having no good reason to make a mystery of them . . . I feel sure that, as a result, he found me neither foolish nor vain nor guilty of a bourgeois ecstasy* . . . I pitied you for not being there. But, how could that be, my dear child? You could

---

*The Count de Bussy, in that scathing pen-portrait drawn by him of Mme de Sévigné in his *Amorous History of the Gauls*, had accused her of fawning on royalty like some bourgeoise, going off into transports of joy at so much as a word from the King or Queen.

not be in two places at once. You were at your opera in Marseille . . .
Since Atys *is delightful, it is impossible that you were bored by it.*
Pauline must have been thrilled to see such a spectacle; she could not
have hoped for one more perfect. I have such wonderful memories of
Marseille that I feel sure you could not have found your time there
dull . . . and I would wager that you found far more diversion there
than at Aix.

"Your sojourn in Marseille seems to me to have been most enjoyable,"
Mme de Sévigné wrote on February 25, evidently in reply to a letter from
Mme de Grignan from that city:

As for me, I must admit that it would not have been my nature to have
been bored in the midst of such spontaneous demonstrations of public
respect as you are shown throughout your governance. I know many
people to whom such honors and tribute paid by people of quality and
high repute could never be disagreeable. I witnessed them, and was
both surprised and touched. But each to his own taste.

(Mme de Sévigné's "*Chacun à son goût*" makes clear that although
she and her daughter had come, in recent years, to a meeting of the minds,
had learned to live amicably together, their temperaments were nonetheless
radically dissimilar.)

If Mme de Grignan had originally not appeared the type to adapt to a
life in the public eye, she had evidently proven a success as First Lady of
Provence—at least, in the opinion of her mother: "I can well understand
how pleased your *Cordon Bleu* of a husband is to see you comport yourself
so graciously at public functions," she wrote in that same letter of February
25:

He seemed to fear, when he was here, that you would always remain
aloof and grave, but I said to him, "Ah, Monsieur, give her a chance.
She is incapable of embarrassing you; she could not but acquit herself
creditably." And, in truth, you have played your role with nobility and
great good grace.

"One thing which truly disturbs me," Mme de Sévigné wrote her
daughter on another day that month,

is the terrible condition of your château, thanks not only to the wind-
storms but also to the mania of Monsieur the Coadjutor, who is causing

as much damage as the hurricanes!* Clearly, my daughter, you should come to Paris, having nowhere else to go for refuge. I cannot believe that Monsieur de Grignan will allow you to spend the summer there under conditions so uncomfortable for you, so inimical to your health.

With the first stirrings of spring, the armies of Europe prepared to take the field again. "Our two Grignans returned from Versailles an hour after I had made up my mail packet," Mme de Sévigné wrote on February 25:

Monsieur the Chevalier will have written you, my bonne, *how that little captain took his leave and how affably the King behaved toward him . . . He bid goodbye to all the Court, and showed the way to those who will follow after. But he has the honor of being the first, of setting the example. Such zeal on the part of a novice is most becoming. He jested very wittily with those who asked him why he was leaving so early, replying that he had a colonel who had chased him off. That colonel bandies words very deftly, too, and I can assure you that he could have taken no step to do him greater honor at smaller cost, because he has no business to keep him here, and he is thrilled to go and prove himself a good officer. This will give him time to rest up at Philippsburg and to give his equipages a rest, as well, so that they will be completely refreshed when the time comes to move on. He is awaited with impatience by his officers. His lieutenant will serve as his equerry, and take care of his equipage and personal affairs, while Montégut† and the others will act as his guardians and watch over him, exclusively. Monsieur the Chevalier feels very comfortable about all this, and we must follow his example. I will be greedy about spending all the time I can with this little fellow, as is natural when there are only a few days remaining. He takes his meals with me. I will take him to dine at Mme de Coulanges's and Mme de Chaulnes's to bid them adieu, and I will dispose of the seven or eight days left to us to be together. But, my darling, as far away as you are, do not let your imagination run riot. There is as yet nothing about which to be concerned. For your child to be in garrison will be no different from being here. It is only fifty leagues away.‡*

---

*The Count de Grignan's brother, the Coadjutor of Arles (future Archbishop of Arles) had a mania for building, and had undertaken extensive construction projects in 1689 on the Prelate's Wing of the Château de Grignan, wreaking havoc there.

†Montégut was in command of the Grignan regiment in the absence of the Chevalier, who was its colonel.

‡Fifty leagues were the equivalent of 200 kilometers, 125 miles. Mme de Sévigné was mistaken about the distance: Philippsburg is actually 300 kilometers from Paris.

"Your child has stayed here with me," Mme de Sévigné wrote on February 28:

I do not leave him. He is pleased. He will go to say goodbye to the little Castelnau girls. His heart is not yet involved. He is preoccupied with his duties, his equipages, his accounts* . . . There is still no talk of action, anywhere. We will not go on the attack; we will not seek battle. We are on the defensive, but in such strength as to cause our enemies to tremble. There may have been some king of Persia, but never before a king of France to see himself with three hundred thousand men under arms!

It was Louis XIV's idea, even as early as 1689, to walk softly and carry a big stick: "We hope," wrote Mme de Sévigné on March 2, "that the Irish war will create a powerful diversion, and prevent the Prince of Orange from harassing us by attacks.† In that way, our three hundred thousand men under arms, everywhere so strategically deployed, will serve solely as a warning of the King's strength so that no one will dare challenge him."

On March 5, the Marquis was off to join his regiment in garrison at Philippsburg, as Mme de Sévigné advised his mother on Monday, March 7:

You would have wept on Saturday, my daughter, along with me, had you seen your dear child depart. It could not have been otherwise. However, it must be borne in mind that this is nothing but a journey, that there is no question of anything else, at this time. He was sharp, gay, teasing me, and totally preoccupied with his equipage which is in excellent condition. Monsieur du Plessis is with him, and will take good care of him until he has delivered him into the hands of the officers of his uncle's regiment, who—on his side—will exert every effort to be in the same army. All the young men are following the good example set by your child. I urge you to fortify yourself like the others, and to be confident that God will bring him safely back to you . . .

On March 18, 1689, it was a letter of condolence Mme de Sévigné addressed to the Grignan family:

---

*"Your child is very loveable, very sprightly," his grandmother wrote on another day: "He takes an interest in all his affairs. He directs, he haggles, he calculates. Too bad Monsieur his Father did not do the same."

†James II, onetime King of England (deposed in the Glorious Revolution of 1688), had gone to Ireland to try to rally support for an attack on England and an effort to recapture the throne then occupied by James's daughter, Mary, and her husband, William, Prince of Orange.

You are right, my dear daughter, in thinking that I would be grieved by the loss of Monsieur the Archbishop. You cannot imagine how much the true merit, the rare virtue, the fine mind and perfect heart of that great prelate make me regret him. I cannot think of his kindness to his family, his tenderness for all in general—but for you and your son in particular—without seeing a great void in your family circle.

The Archbishop of Arles, the patriarch of the Grignan family, the last of his generation, had served his nephew the Count de Grignan as benefactor and counsellor. "My dear Count," Mme de Sévigné wrote in a paragraph addressed to her son-in-law:

Please accept my sympathy. You were a beloved friend of that great man's. He loved his name, his family, and he was right; they are worthy objects ... There goes the last of that earlier generation. We will be the next to go, my dear Count. Meanwhile, I embrace you, weeping as if I had the honor of bearing your name.

XLVIII

With the Marquis de Grignan in garrison at Philippsburg, with the Chevalier de Grignan planning his departure for Provence, Mme de Sévigné made ready to leave for Brittany in the company of her friend, the Duchess de Chaulnes, who was on her way to join her husband, the Governor of the province, at Rennes.

Mme de Sévigné was anything but enthusiastic at the prospect: "Alas, my dear *bonne*, there is no attraction for me there save only my business affairs." Could it be that business alone took her to Brittany? Not her son—whom she had not seen in some four years, not since her departure from Les Rochers in 1685? Of course, the letter does go on to say: "Neither my son nor his wife is at Les Rochers; they are tied down at Rennes with that ridiculous little mother [of hers]. My son may become involved with that nobility" (the last, a reference to the home guard of noblemen from the Rennes and Vitré region, who had selected Charles as their commander).

"We will not leave until after Easter," Mme de Sévigné announced in early March.

Easter in 1689 fell on April 10: on March 28, Mme de Sévigné reported a festive Lenten supper she had attended:

Yesterday, we took supper at the Abbé Pelletier's: Monsieur and Madame de Coulanges, Mons. and Mme de Lamoignon, Mons. Courtin, the Abbé Bigorre, Mlle Langlois and your Maman. No one had eaten dinner; we devoured everything in sight. It was the most wonderful Lenten repast you ever saw: the best fish prepared in the best fashion, the best ragouts, the best cook—never a supper so splendid! We wished most sincerely for you, but the Saint-Laurent wine so vividly evoked the memory of you that there was a clinking of little glasses to prove that that wine came from your vineyards.*

On Good Friday, April 8, Mme de Sévigné prepared to go to confession. "I will not wait for your letters today, my dear daughter," she wrote: "I want to go on retreat tonight. Tomorrow I will make my Easter duty. You are the very one whom I must banish, at least temporarily, from my thoughts."

Writing on April 11, in reply to a letter from her daughter, Mme de Sévigné showed herself little pleased at the announcement that the Grignans had departed the palace at Aix to take up residence in their château:

At last, my daughter, you have left Aix; you seem to have had it there—up to your eyes! You are at Grignan. Do you feel better in that solitude, despite all the difficulties that have developed? It strikes me that that craving of yours to be alone is simply another example of your indulging your taste for melancholy and despair. You prefer to have nothing to distract you from your anxiety about your child, once he runs the slightest danger . . .

I think that we will leave in the morning, the day after tomorrow. I am ridiculously sad about a trip I want to make and need to make, and that I am making in the greatest comfort imaginable. Mme de Kerman is going along, too. She is a most agreeable woman. A large retinue, two six-horse carriages, a baggage wagon, eight outriders; in a word—in high style! We will stop to rest at Malicorne. Could I hope for a more delightful opportunity? You will address your letters to me

---

*Saint-Laurent is a hamlet on the left bank of the Rhône, part of estates belonging to the Count de Grignan in Languedoc.

to Rennes, and I will tell you when to change the address to Vitré. I will soon be tired of the hubbub at Rennes; I am going there only to greet Monsieur de Chaulnes.

Monsieur the Chevalier is leaving at this hour for Versailles . . . I am distressed to part from him. It is a great consolation for me to talk with him about you and your affairs. This community of interests makes for a close relation. We meet to talk about the things dearest to our hearts. The Chevalier is strong; I am weak. He will get along without me; it will be otherwise for me. I will retreat into myself, and I will find you there, but I will miss that support from him which was so pleasant and so necessary for me. One must wrench oneself loose and do without everything.

"Even so," she complained on April 13, "I am leaving with that lingering trace of sadness I told you about":

How to think of your financial dilemma without real sorrow? The loss of Monsieur the Archbishop is still another blow for you. I fear, without quite knowing why, that your impatience to return to Grignan may have cost you dear. The Chevalier was somewhat annoyed that you had left Aix without concluding arrangements for your loan. There are some matters one cannot drop; they slip through one's hands if one fails to follow up on them.

The Grignans' financial status went steadily from bad to worse. Mme de Sévigné, herself, was vexed by financial problems—her generosity to her children having made serious inroads on her estate, its revenues were no longer sufficient to maintain her in the style to which she had been accustomed. She was having trouble making ends meet, but the Grignans teetered ever closer to the brink of disaster. Obliged to borrow to pay even the interest on the huge burden of debt they had accumulated through the years, they had by then reached the point of no return in their odyssey toward financial ruin. Mme de Sévigné's mind boggled at the figures quoted by her daughter: "I make no reply, my child," she wrote on April 4, "to the accounting and the computations you have made—to those horrifying advances, those unrestrained expenditures, those 120,000 livres!

There are no longer any limits . . . I have no words to tell you what I think. My heart is too full. But what will you do, my child? I simply cannot understand it all. What will you live on? On what can you base *the present and the future? What does one do when one has reached a certain point? We were computing your revenues, the other day; they are large. You should have been living on the emoluments of your office, and using the revenues from your properties to pay off your indebtedness* . . . It is easy to see that, as far as Provence is concerned, your profligacy has ruined you there. All in all, this is enough to finish you off, especially since there is no remedy. God knows how your expenses at Grignan—with all those countless guests who pour in on you from every province in addition to all the members of the family up to their chins at your table, with all their retinues and their equi- pages—God knows how all that has contributed to the dissipation of your resources! . . . I must put all these thoughts out of my mind, my dear* bonne, *for they will surely keep me from my sleep . . .*

"And here I am at Chaulnes, my dear daughter," she wrote on Sunday, April 17, from that château, "and still sad at the thought of going still farther away from you."

I left on Thursday, my dear Countess, with Mme de Chaulnes and Mme de Kerman. We went in the best carriage, with the best horses, the greatest number of equipages, baggage wagons and outriders, in the safest and most comfortable way possible. The roads are terrible, but this house is very beautiful and has an air of grandeur about it even though it is unfurnished and the gardens are neglected. Scarcely a trace of green is yet to be seen, and not yet a nightingale. In other words, it is still winter on April 17!

(Mme de Sévigné could not look upon any of France's outstanding châteaus without making comparison to Grignan: "This château is very beautiful," she would say of Chaulnes, "but the elevation of yours makes it more like a Palace of Apollidon.")

"This is a very pleasant house," she wrote from Chaulnes on April 22:

One enjoys a great deal of liberty. You know the good and solid qualities of the Duchess. Mme de Kerman is a very agreeable person.

---

*In addition to the 3,000 livres a year allotted by the Royal Treasury to the Lieutenant-Governor of Provence, that province allowed him 18,000 livres a year, in addition to the 5,000 livres for the Gover- nor's Guard. In addition to this, there had been a royal grant of 12,000 livres in 1684 to compensate for extraordinary expenses in the province. The revenues from the far-flung Grignan properties amounted to some 40,000 to 50,000 livres a year.

*I tested her. She has far more worth and wit than she lets you know.
She is far from being as ignorant as most women. She has an enlightened mind, and daily more so, thanks to the good books she reads.*

Mme de Kerman evidently improved on acquaintance: "She knows a
little something about everything," Mme de Sévigné wrote of that lady,
later: "Since I have a smattering of knowledge, too, our superficialities
accord well with one another."

"Adieu, my very dear one," Mme de Sévigné concluded her letter of
April 22:

*I embrace you tenderly . . . I understand your anxiety about your son.
I feel anxious about him whom I love and about you whom I love still
more. That makes my anxiety doubly keen.*

"We left there [Chaulnes] on Monday, my dear *bonne*, and spent the
night at Amiens, where Mme de Chaulnes is honored and revered as you
are in Provence," Mme de Sévigné's letter of April 27 began. She was
writing from the Château de Pecquigny, which she promptly compared to
Grignan, describing it as "an old structure rising above the town, like
Grignan, with a very fine collegiate church—like the one at Grignan—with
a dean and twelve canons. I do not know if the foundation is as fine, but
there are terraces overlooking the Somme River as it winds its way in a
hundred twists and turns through the fields—something not to be seen at
Grignan."

If their caravan made its way through the valley of the Somme in a
manner as leisurely as the river itself, its dawdling pace was a matter of
indifference to Mme de Sévigné: "This delay does not bother me," she wrote
on April 27, "because I am under no expense—or very little—and I manage
to send some money to Beaulieu."* "The thing that does bother me," she
continued, "is that we have letters awaiting us at Rouen which will have to
wait another two or three days, and I am very sad to have had no news of
you or of the Marquis of whom I think so often." Mme de Grignan's letters,
her mother wrote, "constitute to such great extent the essential subsistence
of my heart and mind that I languish without them."

On Monday, May 2, her letter was headed "Pont-Audemer." Having
followed the Seine River from Rouen, she described that valley as "the most
beautiful countryside in the world":

*Beaulieu, Mme de Sévigné's maître d'hôtel, was to distribute those funds among her creditors.

I saw all the beauties, all the bends of that beautiful Seine and the most beautiful fields in the world. Its banks—for the four or five leagues I rode along them—compare favorably with those of the Loire. They are gracious, ornamented with houses, trees, small willows, and small canals which have been channeled out of the great river. It is truly beautiful. I did not remember Normandy; I was too young when I saw it.* Alas, there is perhaps no one left of those I once knew; that is sad. Even the Sotteville cream is no longer served in the same pretty little faience plates which delighted the eye.† It is now served in pewter bowls. That does not appeal to me.

"Mme de Chaulnes sends you a thousand greetings," her letter of May 2 ended: "What good care she takes of me! Much too good! Impossible to travel in a lovelier springtime or more comfortably or more luxuriously or more easily. Adieu, my darling. Enough from Pont-Audemer. I will write again from Caen."

She wrote again from Caen, as she always had and always would from every stopping place along her way. Beyond Caen, at Avranches, on May 7, a world-famous sight—a perennial tourist attraction—loomed up in her window: "From my room, I could see the ocean and Mont-Saint-Michel," she wrote her daughter on May 9 from Dol, "that lofty mount which you saw rise so proudly from the sea, as it saw you in all your beauty. I thought fondly back to that trip. We dined at Pontorson, do you remember? We spent a long time on the shore, looking at that mount—my thoughts, all the while, returning to my darling daughter."

"We arrived here yesterday, my dear *bonne,*" she wrote from Rennes on May 11:

That makes exactly one hundred full leagues we made in eight and a half days of travel.‡ The dust is irritating to the eyes, and the thirty women who came out on the road to greet Mme de Chaulnes—and whom we had to embrace in all the dust and sun—along with thirty or forty gentlemen—tired us far more than the voyage. Mme de Kerman collapsed under the strain, because she is delicate. As for me, I bore up

---

*According to Gérard-Gailly, editor of the 1953–7 Pléiade edition of the Sévigné *Letters,* Mme de Sévigné had made a trip to Normandy in 1640, at age sixteen, in company with her uncle and guardian, Philippe de Coulanges.

†At Sotteville, the thick cream (for which Normandy is famous) was served with sugar and cinnamon.

‡It was some 450 kilometers (about 270 miles, or 140 leagues) from Pecquigny to Rennes, a distance they had covered in some ten days' travel time.

without difficulty . . . I sought out my son in the throng, and we joyfully embraced. His little wife was thrilled to see me . . . I went to my son's to change my chemise and to freshen up. And, from there, to supper at the Hôtel de Chaulnes, where there was too much supper. There, I found the good Marquise de Marboeuf, to whose house I went later, and where I stayed . . . in a beautiful room . . . furnished with fine crimson velvet, decorated in Parisian fashion, with a good bed in which I slept wonderfully well; a good woman who is thrilled to have me, a good friend with a properly high regard for you. So, I am settled here for a few days, because my daughter-in-law is flirting with the idea of Les Rochers, dying to go there—as am I—to rest and relax. She cannot long bear up under the turmoil caused by Mme de Chaulnes's arrival. We will find our opportunity. I found her as lively as ever, very pretty, loving me dearly, very impressed with you and Mons. de Grignan; her penchant for him amuses us greatly.* My son is as loveable as ever; he appears very happy to see me. He is very attractive, personally; he enjoys perfect health, is lively and witty. He is really astonished to hear about his "princess"!

(The "princess" was Charles's pet name for Mlle d'Alérac, the younger of the Count de Grignan's two daughters by his first wife, who—having attained her majority at age twenty-five—had married the Marquis de Vibraye, against the wishes of both her father and her uncle the Duke de Montausier.)

"Suffice it to say," said Mme de Sévigné, "that it was a very foolish marriage":

Had the family had large means, as once they did, that would have been a valid reason. Had he been outstanding for his military prowess or enjoyed some special favor—but, from every point of view, he is insignificant, a mediocrity or worse. Is it possible that she lusted after that dreadful boy? See how cunningly she tried to trick or force her father into giving his consent! I could talk for a year about this; you are far from boring me on the subject.

On May 25, Mme de Sévigné was still at Rennes ("having stayed here for two weeks," as she apologized, "for the sake of the Duke and Duchess de Chaulnes"):

---

*Charles's wife had at that time not yet met the Count de Grignan, but professed to admire him extravagantly.

As far as I am concerned, I am so worn out by visits and duty calls that, in all good faith, I can endure no more. I feel a veritable need for rest and silence in those lovely forests of Les Rochers ... Last night, we took supper at Monsieur [the Bishop] of Rennes's. These are banquets; this is the land of good living; of fine meats, well larded; the land of La Prévalaie butter* ... Mme de Chaulnes had tears in her eyes and a catch in her voice when she bid me adieu ... She is, in truth, a very loveable friend, one who acquits herself divinely well of all the roles Providence has set her to play ... I will let you know when I go to Nantes, and when my son goes to take command of his regiment of noblemen. All I have in mind is to press myself to economize in order to send money to Beaulieu, who will try to satisfy my most pressing creditors ... That is how it stands; those are my plans. I will make arrangements with the Abbé Charrier about Nantes ...

To his mother's delight, Charles de Sévigné had made many improvements at Les Rochers, contributing to the beautification of the park: "There is one *Place* which is very beautiful," she wrote on May 29:

It straightens out the angle at the entrance to the park. One comes into the parterre which has been laid out according to a design by Monsieur Lenôtre†; it is well planted, in full bloom, completely sanded. One sees an iron grille and, beyond that, a long allée leading through the cabbages and the fields. On the right, there is another gate which leads straight into the first of the broad woodland avenues; on the left, another gate, leading to the fields. The effect is very beautiful. All this semicircular area is full of orange trees in tubs, many of which have been brought from Provence ... We do a lot of reading, we walk separately; we meet for meals, and eat well but sensibly. We are at peace, and that poor Duchess de Chaulnes would like to be with us!

"Oh, how many Grignans you have there," the letter went on, "without having all those you need!"

---

*The Château Thierry de la Prévalaie, near Rennes, was famous throughout Brittany for its butter. Mme de Sévigné had it sent to her from there when she was in Paris.

†Lenôtre was the outstanding landscape architect of the Splendid Century, renowned for his design of the gardens at Vaux-le-Vicomte and Versailles.

Let us take a look, my bonne, at where that little Grignan is going: to Germany!* Aren't you impressed with how capably and how seriously he performs his duties? I think of him a thousand times a day, and about the reputation he is making for himself, everywhere ... God keep him safe!

On Whitsunday, which fell on May 29 in 1689, Mme de Sévigné wrote her daughter from Les Rochers:

So, I reached here on Wednesday, my bonne, with my son and daughter-in-law ... My God, what peace and quiet, what a stillness, what a freshness! ... All those saplings I planted have grown so tall that I can scarcely believe that we can all be alive at the same time! Still, their beauty does not seem to interfere with mine. You know about my beauty. Everyone in this country admires me; they all assure me that I have not changed at all. I try my best to believe what they tell me.

If she looked so well, it was because she felt so well: "As for me, my dear child," she wrote that summer, "I have told you how perfect my health is":

I no longer wake up with a start in the night. No more trouble with my hands ... I am astonished at the state of my health, and following your example, I am almost making "a dragon" of it. I keep thinking that it is impossible that such a state can continue much longer, and that I must expect some of the usual human disabilities.

"Pauline is very fortunate to be acting as your secretary," Mme de Sévigné exclaimed in a letter to Mme de Grignan dated June 1:

She will learn how to think, how to compose her thoughts—by watching you. She will learn the French language, which most women do not know. You will go to the trouble of explaining words to her which she would otherwise never learn and, while you are teaching her so many things, you will relieve both your mind and mine, because my mind is at rest when yours is. The strain of dictating is in no way

---

*The Marquis de Grignan had been placed under the command of Boufflers; the corps to which he was assigned was delegated to protect the flank of the French forces in Germany. In their wake, he was to take part in the systematic scourging of the Palatinate, a wanton destruction for which Louis XIV stands condemned by history.

comparable to that of writing. So, do go on with this project which is both so educational for your daughter and such a relief to you and me.

"There has been no rain in six weeks," the letter of June 1 concluded:

It has been very warm but, all of a sudden, despite the lack of rain, it has turned cold, and we have fires. I told you that all the nobility of these cantons—five or six hundred gentlemen, in all—have chosen your brother as their commander. That is considered a great honor, but it will mean a senseless expense. He has no orders, as yet, to mobilize; we are hoping that such a useless sort of exercise will not prove necessary.

(The expense to which Charles would be put in this matter preyed on his mother's mind: "My God, my daughter," she moaned on July 6, "what are you talking about? You think that the King or the province will contribute in some way to my son for the maintenance and training of the noble home guard? Nothing at all, I assure you! It is all too great an honor!")

Money matters were very much on Mme de Sévigné's mind: "I can understand how much Avignon means to you," she wrote her daughter on June 5:

It is Providence which grants you such relief. I give much thought to you and to your affairs. I give much thought to my own, and take the necessary measures, but the main thing is to stay here, and to put aside some money. It is difficult to lay one's hands on any in this country, overrun as it is with troops. We are taking every precaution possible, as if the Prince of Orange thought only of us . . . but the one thing we can count on is that there will be desolation in this province. My son is still with us. We tremble lest Monsieur de Chaulnes order him off at the head of his nobility . . .

("The Attila of his time!" was Mme de Sévigné's scathing epithet for William III of England.* "What the devil kind of man that Prince of Orange is! When one thinks that, thanks to him alone, all of Europe is on the march!")

In a letter dated June 8, Mme de Sévigné applauded her daughter's

---

*William, Prince of Orange, and his wife, Mary (Protestant daughter of the deposed James II of England), were installed on the throne of England in 1689.

decision to accompany her husband to Avignon, where official business was to take him, that month.

That is a good decision you have made to visit your "land" of Avignon, to see the people who give so generously to their Vice-Legate. It is fitting that they should have the pleasure and the privilege of seeing you; you could not make better use of your time. After that trip, you will be free, and need not leave your château again until you wish to. You will have a rather good group there. Indeed, my dear bonne, you will already have it by the time this letter reaches you. What? Is it possible that Monsieur the Chevalier is already there? How lucky you are! And how lucky he is, too! Will my turn never come?

Mme de Sévigné followed the Grignans in thought to that picturesque and storied city on the Rhône, addressing them at Avignon on June 12:

Here, we are in a state of utter, of perfect relaxation, in the midst of a peace, a silence which is the very opposite of what you are experiencing at Avignon. You may still be there, today. That city is beautiful and splendorous, I imagine. You will have been received there with acclamations. I have followed you throughout these festivities; because of your position, there must have been constant fêtes. I will be happy to get your first letter from Avignon. I think you were wise to show Monsieur de Grignan this consideration; when he is right, he should not be opposed. You did the proper thing . . .

She could not but be struck by the difference in their destinies. Like so many mothers, Mme de Sévigné lived vicariously through her daughter, but occasionally one thinks one detects a trace of envy for her daughter's glamorous life, as in this message dated June 15:

What a difference, my bonne, between your life at Avignon, on the grand scale, exciting, diverting, lavish—and the life we lead here: drab, simple, solitary! That is the order of things, the order of God, but I simply cannot believe that—despite your anchoritic tendencies—you could find such respect and such honors—paid you, as they are, by people of quality and of standing—to be displeasing. In truth, it would be unnatural not to enjoy, occasionally, a position superior to that of others.*

---

*According to a manuscript in the Avignon archives, when the Count and Countess de Grignan returned on June 15 to their château, it was "to the great regret of the entire city and especially that of the ladies whom Mme had entertained lavishly during her sojourn there."

"I passionately love your letters from Avignon, my dear *bonne*," Mme de Sévigné began her letter of June 19:

I read and reread them. They rejoice my imagination and the silence of our forests. I feel as if I am there with you. I share your triumph . . . I enjoy your beautiful sun, the charming banks of your beautiful Rhône, and the softness of your air, but I positively refuse to play bassette* because I am afraid of losing!

"My son has just left for Rennes," she continued in her letter of June 29:

He will return tomorrow but, in a week, he will leave to form the squadron of the nobility and give them a martial air. My son is furious to have to return to a profession he had determined to abandon.

They were losing their "companion," she complained, their "indefatigable reader." ("That makes us very angry.") Mme de Sévigné's daughter-in-law did her best to make up for her husband's absence: "She thinks only of how to keep me entertained," Mme de Sévigné wrote fondly of the young Marquise: "She is an attractive woman." "We will be alone," she went on, "but the good weather comes to our aid, as do good books and needlework and lovely promenades and the passage of time—time which races by, flies by, and carries us off in its flight. So God wills it, my dear *bonne*, for that is my constant refrain. I know no other, but I will love you utterly and devotedly to the end of time."

Bassette was a game of chance popular in seventeenth-century France. "I dare not ask you what your trip cost you," Mme de Sévigné wrote her daughter, later in the month, "or how you came out at *bassette*, although I am keenly interested."

XLIX

"We live so well-regulated a life," Mme de Sévigné wrote from Les Rochers on June 29, 1689, "that it is almost impossible not to keep well!"

We arise at eight o'clock; very often I go to enjoy the cool air of the woods until nine o'clock when the bell rings for Mass. After Mass, we dress, we bid each other good morning; we come back to pick orange blossoms; we dine; we do needlework or read until five o'clock. Since my son is no longer here, I do the reading aloud in order to spare his wife's little chest the strain. At five o'clock, I leave here. I go out into those lovely forests. I have a lackey who follows me. I take books, I move from one place to another, and I vary the course of my prome-nades. A religious book, another of history; I change around; that is a diversion. I daydream a bit about God and about His Providence; I invite my soul, I think of the future. At last, at eight o'clock, I hear a bell; it is suppertime. Sometimes I am rather far away; I join the Marquise in her beautiful parterre. We are good company for one another. We have our supper at the hour "between the dog and the wolf." Our people have their supper. I go back with her to the "Place Coulanges" in the midst of the orange-trees ... I enjoy this life a thousand times more than that at Rennes. This solitude—is it not most appropriate for a person who should think of herself, one who is—or wants to be—a Christian?*

(Mme de Sévigné's daughter-in-law added a page to this letter of June 29: "You thrill me, my dear sister," she wrote in addressing Mme de Gri-gnan, "when you tell me that Mme de Sévigné loves me. My taste is good enough to appreciate the value of her love, and to love her with all my heart.")

July 3, 1689, marked the anniversary of their parting, as Mme de Sévigné would remind her daughter:

---

*The parterre or garden area was located between the château and the Place Coulanges. "The scent of jasmine and of orange blossoms is so strong in the evening," Mme de Sévigné wrote that summer, "that I think I am in Provence."

It is nine months to the day, a Sunday like the Sunday that I left you at Charenton, with so many tears—more even than I let you see. These adieux are bitter and painful, above all when one has no time to lose ... Thus it is nine months that I have not seen you, not embraced you, that I have not heard the sound of your voice. I have had no illness, no serious problems. I have seen beautiful houses, beautiful countrysides, beautiful towns. Still, I confess to you that it seems nine years to me since I parted from you.

A letter from the Countess had brought her mother news of the Chevalier's arrival at Grignan—more crippled than ever; to which news Mme de Sévigné reacted with characteristic empathy, in a reply which was dated July 6:

How could you not be touched at the sight of his being carried into those apartments? You bring tears to my eyes. I have long reflected sadly on that subject. What a man! At what an age!* Where is he? Where should he be? What a reputation! What a career, blighted, suffocated! What a loss for your son!

I am greatly obliged to your large company for having thought of me, having wished for me. I admit that I often wish myself in that big, beautiful house whose occupants I know so well. I send a thousand greetings to the latest arrival ... Write me about everything that goes on at Grignan; it may not be the most important theater of action in Europe, but it is the one in which I take the greatest interest. When I think of the number of people gathered at Grignan, and that that is what you call taking refuge from expense in your château, I would laugh if I could, and I say, "She is swept away on a terrible wind which she cannot escape, which follows her wherever she goes; it is her destiny." But, at the same time, I can see that God proportions your courage to your destiny, and works some miracle whereby you are always in the air, and manage to fly without wings.

As for me, my dear child, I fall flat on my face, and when I have nothing, I have nothing. My affairs at Nantes are going badly; all chicanery and litigation which could drag on for twenty years.†

---

*The Chevalier de Grignan was forty-eight years old.

†A new overseer had taken over Buron, Mme de Sévigné's property near Nantes, but it was proving difficult to compel former tenant-farmers to pay back rents they owed.

Mme de Sévigné's letters, that summer of 1689, returned again and again to the theme of the cruel fate that separated her and her daughter, the economic necessity that pinned them down—the one in Brittany, the other in Provence, hundreds of leagues apart! "When I take an overall look at the long separation to which we are condemned, I admit that I shudder at the thought," she wrote on July 13:

> But, if taken day by day, it is clear that it must be endured for the sake of our affairs, and I realize that my trip here would have been in vain if I did not stay on for the winter ... As for you, my daughter, you calculate that you will be able to live six months outside of Grignan, the other six months "hidden away" at Grignan. Can you really call your sojourn there, with all its inherent grandeur, being "hidden away"?

"You give me a pleasant picture of your days," the letter rambled on:

> What good company you have there! It is even nice not to be tempted to leave your beautiful terraces. And that is a bit of good luck for the gouty. I am not familiar with that terrace where you are spending so much time; it is in great use because it is sheltered from the north wind. You have wonderful views in all directions. I remember the view of Mont Ventoux.* I adore all those amphitheaters, and am convinced, like you, that if ever Heaven had any curiosity about the sights here below, its inhabitants would choose no other spot than that as the best vantage point from which to view the world and, at the same time, you have—incontestably—the most magnificent view in the world.
>
> My son has gone to Saint-Malo to see Monsieur and Mme de Chaulnes ... We hope that it will soon be possible to disband the nobility; it can be recalled by a whistle blast, should the need arise ...

"It gives me pleasure to think of the life you lead, my dear Countess," the Countess's mother began her letter of July 17:

> I rejoice my woods with news of it! What good company! What a fine sun! You would suffer less patiently the continuation of our rains, but they are over, and I resume my lonely but pleasant promenades.

---

*The sheltered terrace to which Mme de Sévigné referred would appear to be the one beyond the south wing of the château, known as the "Wing of Francis I." Mont Ventoux, a peak in the southern Alps, visible from the main terrace, lies to the west of Grignan.

Mme de Sévigné reacted rather sharply to her daughter's criticism of those "lonely promenades," those long walks upon which she set out without her daughter-in-law. "What are you saying, my child?" she inquired:

What? You find it strange that—having gone to Mass together, having dined together, having worked or talked together until five—we should not have two or three hours to ourselves? She would be annoyed, as would I. She is a very bright woman; we get along well together, but we both have a pronounced taste for liberty, and for meeting later. When I am with you, my daughter, I admit that I never part company with you without distress, and that I do it out of consideration for you. With everyone else, however, it is out of consideration for myself.

In late July, Mme de Sévigné and her daughter-in-law unexpectedly enjoyed a change of scene. "At Rennes, this Wednesday, July 20," Mme de Sévigné's letter began:

This dateline will surprise you, my dear child, as it surprises me, since I was not expecting to leave Les Rochers so soon . . . It is true that it is only for a few days that we have come, but Monsieur and Mme de Chaulnes urged me so strongly, so kindly to come to see them here, where they have come to see my son at the head of his regiment of nobility, that—Madame, the Colonel's wife, having also been invited, of course—we came here, the next day, which was yesterday. Here, we found my son. I have perfect accommodations at the Marquise de Marboeuf's . . .

Four days later, on July 24, she wrote again, from Rennes:

I cannot tell you with what joy and affection those good Governors welcomed me, with what gratitude for my having come from Les Rochers to see them! They had me attend a review of the regiment of nobility; that regiment is very fine, and fairly well trained. My son accepted all the praise in a manner which pleased me but, actually, I kept thinking that it was not for this purpose that I had financed and forwarded his military career . . .

"Monsieur and Mme de Chaulnes send you a thousand greetings," the letter continued:

Sometimes I think I am with you at Avignon: two large tables, twice a day, and the inevitable game of bassette without which no one can do. This country is somewhat different. Mme de Chaulnes has seen Avignon. She was as mad about it as you; she did not want to leave. She was received there as the Ambassador's wife. She understands the charm it has for you. May God preserve it to you!

We will part company in three or four days, my dear child. Please don't worry about that. This life is too trying for me; I am made over too much. I cannot get away for a moment; I become overheated. Everyone who goes to Mme de Chaulnes's comes here. I do not have a minute alone. Do not suggest that they lure me from my solitude; I would be ill if I continued this way of life for very long.

The very next day, the twenty-fifth, Mme de Sévigné had to eat her words, explaining to Mme de Grignan why she was not returning to Les Rochers, as she had intended: "I am leaving tomorrow morning at daybreak with Mons. and Mme de Chaulnes on a two weeks' journey," she would write:

Here, my daughter, is how this came about. Mons. de Chaulnes said to me, "Madame, you should come with us to Vannes to see the First President.* He has shown you consideration in this province; it is a kind of duty of yours as a woman of quality to go to see him." I could not see that: "Monsieur, I am dying to get back to Les Rochers, to a kind of repose of which one has need when leaving here . . ." The next day, Mme de Chaulnes said to me in a low voice, at table: "My dear, you should come with us. There is only one overnight stop between here and Vannes; sometimes, one needs to turn to Parlement. From there, we will go to Auray, only three leagues farther on. There, we will not be overwhelmed with attentions. We will return in two weeks."

I replied, a bit too forthrightly: "Madame, you do not need me; it is a kindness on your part. I see no reason for me to pay my respects to those gentlemen. I am going back to my solitude, of which I have a veritable need." Mme de Chaulnes turned away rather coolly. Suddenly, the thought struck me: what do I mean by refusing these people to whom I owe a thousand kindnesses, a thousand favors? I use their carriage and them whenever it suits my purposes, but I refuse to take a

*René Lefebvre, Seigneur de La Faluère, was First President of the Parlement of Brittany.

short trip with them, one on which my company might be meaningful to them ... They ask me this favor hesitantly, candidly, while I— although in very good health and without any valid reason to refuse them—do this at a time when they are trying to arrange to have my son appointed deputy, an appointment in Mons. de Chaulnes's power to make this year.* All of this flashed through my mind. I saw that I had been wrong. I said to her, "Madame, I thought at first only of myself, and had little desire to go to see Monsieur de La Faluère, but could it be possible that my presence would give you the slightest pleasure?" She blushed, and said to me with sincerity, "Ah, you may well believe that!"—"That is all you need to say, Madame. I assure you that I will go with you." She made it clear that she was truly delighted, hugged me, and left the table, saying to Mons. de Chaulnes, "She is coming with us!" He said, "She refused me, but I hoped she would not refuse you." Thus, my dear daughter, I am leaving, and I am convinced that I did the right thing, not only out of a sense of gratitude to them for their constant friendship but also because it is the politic thing to do, as you would surely have pointed out to me. My son is thrilled, and thanks me for having agreed.

Mme de Sévigné's next letter to Provence was datelined "At Auray, Saturday, July 30," and began:

Take a look, please, my dear bonne, at where I am. I am here on the south shore [of the peninsula of Brittany], at the ocean's edge. When was the time that we were together in that little study in Paris, only steps apart from one another? We can only hope that we will be reunited there! Meanwhile Providence has cast me up on this shore ... We came in three days from Rennes to Vannes (that is six or seven leagues a day). Finding our suppers and our dinners ready and waiting for us makes it a very easy kind of trip. Everywhere we go, the communities await us with the same kind of welcome speech and commotion to which your grandeurs have accustomed you. Here, there are also troops and officers and regiments to be reviewed, which gives everything a martial air ...

We arrived Thursday evening at Vannes ... I cannot begin to tell you the honors Monsieur de La Faluère paid me. He could not look at

---

*Charles de Sévigné wanted to be appointed deputy of the nobility of Brittany to the Court of Versailles.

me without exclaiming, "What? That is Mme de Sévigné there? What? It is she herself?" To which Mme de Chaulnes replied, "Monsieur, it was the desire to pay her respects to you that drew her forth from Les Rochers. Save for that, I could never have persuaded her to come."

From Auray, the Governor and his party made expeditions around the peninsula (as much a tourist attraction in the twentieth as in the seventeenth century). On August 12, Mme de Sévigné wrote her daughter:

During the last three days, we have made the prettiest voyage imaginable to Port Louis which is a very beautiful spot, which has—as you will remember—a view of the open sea. The day after that, which was Thursday, we went to a place called L'Orient, one league inland. It is there to which the merchants from the Orient come, with their merchandise. We saw a lot of the imports, the porcelains and fabrics. They are quite pretty. Were you not the Queen of the Mediterranean, I would have looked for some fabric from which to make a dressing gown for you, but I feared to do you an injustice. We came back in the evening, with the tide, in delicious weather, to Hennebont. You can follow our itinerary on your map . . .

That halcyon seaside excursion was cut short by the arrival of a special courier from the King, summoning the Duke instantly to Versailles into conference.

Writing from Rennes, on "Wednesday, August 17," Mme de Sévigné had bad news for her daughter, news from Rome: the Pope was *in extremis*; a conclave of cardinals would be summoned to the Vatican to choose a successor. Louis XIV would send the Duke de Chaulnes as his ambassador to Rome to represent the interests of France at that crucial hour. "In truth, my dear daughter," Mme de Sévigné's letter began, "I have many things to tell you and to reply to":

I go back to the courier who came to Hennebont to find Mons. de Chaulnes. He brought a letter from the King, which I saw—all filled with demands to obey promptly, to rush, to do the impossible! We recognized the style of Monsieur de Louvois [the Secretary of State], who does not ask, "Can you make the trip to Rome?" He will brook neither delay nor refusal; he foresees every eventuality. The King advises that "He has resolved to send him to Rome because he deems him the only man capable of giving the Church a head who can, at once, govern

*the Church and satisfy all the world, in general—and France, in
particular."*

Monsieur de Chaulnes—according to Mme de Sévigné—was "torn
between his pride at being the monarch's choice, at being recalled from the
farthest reaches of Brittany to receive the honor of so prestigious an embassy,
and his regret at having to miss the meeting of the Estates [General of
Brittany] where important matters were sure to arise, matters in which he
could likewise have been of service to the monarch." Mme de Chaulnes—
again according to Mme de Sévigné—could not but have been flattered at
such an honor paid her husband, but even so, "she weeps and sighs" (in
Mme de Sévigné's version), because she saw it as "a long voyage for a man
of his age."

Mme de Sévigné herself could have wept and sighed at the news of the
Pope's grave illness: France's reconciliation with the Vatican spelled the
return of Avignon to the Holy See, the end of the Count de Grignan's term
as Vice-Legate, the end of the handsome revenues he had derived from that
post. God had not "preserved" it to him for long.

"Mme de Chaulnes will leave two days after his [the Duke's] departure," Mme de Sévigné's letter of August 17 went on:

*The Duchess wants to take me with her; she says that is what you
would want. She is really distressed to leave me. We reflected on the
ways of Providence. We were all to have spent the winter, here; I was
to have spent a month at Les Rochers, but had promised to go at the
beginning of October to Saint-Malo for the Estates, then back for a
while to Les Rochers. I had promised, too, to go to Rennes at the
beginning of Lent, to stay until after Easter—instead, in four days'
time, all is changed. Mons. and Mme de Chaulnes will not remain in
this province, and I will go to Les Rochers with your brother and his
wife, and spend the winter there more agreeably than anywhere else,
since the Governor and his wife are no longer here. I send, and will
continue to send, a little money to Paris. What I look forward to is
meeting you, there, next year. That is my hope, but it will be at God's
pleasure, for I have become disillusioned about the plans made by men.
Thus my companionship with that good Governor and his wife comes
to an end. It is lucky that I love Les Rochers and those who are its
masters and the life led there. Thus, I am back on my own terrain from
which I will not stray except for you.*

"So, here I am back at Les Rochers which you so dread for me, but which has nothing dreadful about it," her letter of August 21 began:

Neither the Duke nor Duchess is any longer here; they were very sad to leave me. They wanted to take me back whence they had brought me, and it cost me a great pang to refuse them, but my trip here would have served no purpose had it been cut so short, and since I am already here, I took it upon myself to make it serve its purpose. On such occasions
"The heart says Paris; the head says Brittany."*
So, my daughter, what is done is done. It cost me many a tear to see that good Duchess leave ... Monsieur de Chaulnes told my son that as far as the deputation was concerned, he might be able to accomplish more during his audience with the King on the matter of Brittany than he could have done had he stayed on here for the Estates General. Thus, we wait for news from him. If it is good, then it will be my son who will take me to Paris in the spring.

("You need have no fear that I will become an anchorite," she reassured her daughter in that same letter: "My son will see to that; a thousand people will be coming to see him, perhaps too many. The weather is glorious. I will resume my way of life, my reading, my promenades.")

By August 28, news of the death of the Pope had reached even far-off Brittany, much dismaying Mme de Sévigné: "God in His goodness has not saved the Pope, important as he was to your life and your welfare. You will lose the County of Avignon which had proven so beneficial, so useful to you." If the Marquise had become resigned to the dictates of Providence affecting her own life, she still complained about a fate unkind to her daughter: "We are not so resigned to the thought of your losing your beautiful land of Avignon. What a pleasant place to sojourn! To spend the winter! What a blessing were those revenues which you put to such good use! What a loss! What a disappointment!" "I weep for the Pope," she wrote elsewhere, "I weep for the County of Avignon. God has given; God has taken away."

God could also be expected to watch over the Marquis de Grignan, his grandmother felt sure: "And what God watches over is well watched," she promised the Marquis's mother. Their young cavalry officer was with Boufflers's army in Germany, that summer. ("I am overcome with emotion at the

*Mme de Sévigné has paraphrased a line of Boileau's.

very mention of Boufflers's name!" Mme de Sévigné confessed.) The Marquis had been in the thick of the action at Valcourt: "That little rascal!" his grandmother exclaimed in her letter of September 11:

> To go in, sword in hand, and force his way into the château, to kill or carry off eleven or twelve hundred men! Just think for a moment of that child grown to be a man, a man of war, a scourge to the country-side! . . . In truth, my dear Countess, you are right when you say that I am not indifferent to that child or to your affairs. I am more than interested; I share your concerns—I am up to my eyes in them! And where else would I be? It is that which makes me know that I am still alive!

("Could we ever have guessed," she wrote elsewhere on that same subject, "that this work—this profession, that is to say—would have been to his taste, and that he would have become so totally involved in it? A zeal, a vigilance, an ambition to distinguish himself, an intrepidity—everything, in fact, and no trace of laziness! He is a loveable and bright and commend-able boy. May God preserve him!")

"Our weather today is frightful," she continued in her letter of September 11:

> One would think that the winter was already about to begin. To dry myself out, I think of your warm sun in Avignon. Oh, God, let us not talk about that! . . . I dare not think of the revenues which came to you from there or of what you will do without that relief.

The loss of the Avignon revenues had evidently not yet dimmed the splendors of the Château de Grignan, where the Duke de Chaulnes and his entourage—en route to Rome—had been expected in early September. Mme de Sévigné's letter of September 18 makes clear that she was, as usual, at once impressed and distressed at the thought of the lavish life-style at Grignan:

> Let us talk at once about that good Duke de Chaulnes, of the warm and magnificent welcome you gave him. Your great house with its air of grandeur, your splendid table—your two tables, served in high style, like those in Brittany—your large company . . . free of any interference from the north wind! . . . It appears that Flame [the Grignans' maître d'hôtel] is expert, that his service is smooth and smart. I envision all

this with a pleasure I cannot express to you. I wanted him [the Duke de Chaulnes] to see you in all the glory of your country life, for that at Aix is even grander, and I wanted him to eat at your house something beside our chicken and our bacon omelettes. Now he knows what you are capable of . . .

Monsieur de Coulanges, Mme de Sévigné's beloved, chubby little cousin—having been invited by the Duke de Chaulnes to accompany him on his diplomatic mission to Italy—had been a member of the house party at Grignan, as Mme de Sévigné took note:

So, Coulanges, too, played his role very well. He has suffered no diminution of spirits. I fear any change in him in that regard because his gaiety constitutes a large part of his charm. He was there, it strikes me, to his heart's delight, interested in everything that happened, and enchanted by Pauline! You always accuse him of exerting himself only for dukes and peers, but I have seen him highly amusing with us, and you told me about supper parties, five years ago when I was here, at which you found him most amusing. Monsieur de Chaulnes has written me; here is his letter. You will see that he is well pleased with all of you and at the manner in which you do the honors of your house . . . You spoke of me many times; you drank my health. Coulanges climbed up on his chair. I find that a very dangerous stunt for a little fellow round as a ball and clumsy. I am grateful to learn that he did not take a tumble while he toasted me!

"Coulanges seems to me to be charmed both by you and by Monsieur de Grignan and your château and your magnificence," Mme de Sévigné wrote on September 25, evidently upon receipt of a letter from her little cousin:

Your way of doing the honors of your house really impressed him. He recognizes you as the Duke and Duchess of Campo-Basso,* to say the least. All in all, my dear Countess, what can you not accomplish when you want to? And with what an air and what a grace!

---

*The Count de Grignan laid claim to the title of Duke de Termes (or Termoli) and of Campo-Basso by reason of the marriage of an Adhémar ancestor in the fifteenth century to a daughter of the Count de Campo-Basso and de Termoli.

"And so you want to know about our life here, my dear child?" Mme de Sévigné inquired, that same autumn of 1689:

Alas, it is like this. We arise at eight o'clock; Mass is at nine. Whether or not we go for a promenade—each of us, often, on our own— depends on the weather. We dine very well. A neighbor comes in; we talk of the news. After dinner, we do needlework, my daughter-in-law at a variety of things; I, at the two bands of tapestry Mme de Kerman gave me at Chaulnes. At five o'clock, we separate; we go for our promenades, either together or separately. We meet at a very pretty "Place." I take a book along, I pray to God, I daydream about my dear daughter; I build castles in Spain, in Provence, sometimes gaily, some- times sadly. My son reads very interesting books to us; we have one book of devotions, several history books; that keeps us busy and amuses us. We discuss what we have read. My son is indefatigable; he would read for five hours if we wished. Attending to our mail—receiving letters and answering them—is a major occupation of ours, of mine in particular. We have had guests, and will have more. Not that we wish for company, but when someone comes, we enjoy it. My son has workmen on the grounds; he has the large allées "groomed," as they say here; they really look beautiful. He is having the parterre sanded.*
All in all, my daughter, it is strange that—with this way of life as lackluster and almost melancholy as it is—the days rush by and escape us, and God knows what else escapes us at the same time! Ah, let's not talk of that! I think about it, however, as one should. We have our supper at eight o'clock. After supper, Sévigné reads to us—but never anything serious, lest we fall asleep. They leave me at ten o'clock. I rarely go to bed before midnight. And there you have the schedule of our convent. Written on our door are the words, "Holy Liberty, or Do As You Please."† I like this life far better than that of Rennes; it will be time enough to go there for Lent for the nourishment of body and soul.

---

*The "grooming" consisted of weeding the allées and then lining them with rake marks. There was a new or second parterre to be sanded.

†A reference to Rabelais's Abbey of Thélème in the novel *Gargantua*.

L

At Les Rochers, Sunday, October 2 [1689]:
It will be a year tomorrow, my dear bonne, since I have seen you, since
I have embraced you, since I have heard the sound of your voice, a
year since we parted at Charenton. My God, how that day stands out
in my memory! And how I long for the one which will mark the day
of our reunion, my dear child, the day when I will be with you again,
take you in my arms, cling to you forever, finishing my life with the
one who has been its main preoccupation ... object of a true love
which has filled my heart and all my life. That is how I feel and what I
have to say to you, my dear bonne, even though I had not meant to
say this much, and say it only in solemnization of this one-year anni-
versary of our separation.

The mother-daughter love, by then acknowledged on both sides, and
by then no longer troubled by conflict or by doubt, by then no longer
required vehement protestations of affection and good will. If, in striking
contrast to earlier years, Mme de Sévigné now appears somewhat reticent
about explicit expression of love and devotion, it is no longer for fear of
displeasing her daughter by her demonstrativeness, but because a mutual
affection as satisfying as theirs has become requires less verbalization.

Disagreement between them no longer degenerated into rancorous
dispute, as is evidenced in another paragraph of the anniversary letter:

In fact, my bonne, we are in no wise angry at our good Governors. I
am thrilled at that, because I was in despair to think that they had
wronged us. All our friends agree that it would have been improper on
the part of Monsieur de Chaulnes to have said so much as a word about
Brittany or the deputation. The conference was confined to Rome.

When Mme de Grignan expressed her displeasure with the Duke de
Chaulnes for having failed to secure the deputation for Charles de Sévigné,
Mme de Sévigné insisted that she could see the justification for his course

of action—or, rather, inaction. Her respect for her daughter's judgment was profound, but so was her loyalty to her friends, and the correspondence over the following months gives evidence of her staunch defense of the Duke and Duchess de Chaulnes against sharp attack by Mme de Grignan: "Very well, then, my *bonne*, be angry at Monsieur de Chaulnes; as for me, I simply cannot." "Ingratitude is my pet hate," she would exclaim. And, again, "I will not amuse myself by hating people who are, I am convinced, as upset about this as I am. Consider it a closed chapter." "Thus, we no longer count on it," she wrote elsewhere, "and should it work out in our favor, it would be a miracle, but that is not the greatest disappointment brought about for me by the death of the Pope when I think about the loss it means to you."

"Your letter begins, my daughter," Mme de Sévigné would write later, "by saying important things in the fewest words: 'Ottobon, *Pope*;* the County [of Avignon] *restored* [to the Holy See]; the King and Monsieur de Chaulnes *triumphant*; Mme de Grignan, *ruined*!' "

On October 9, Mme de Sévigné reported herself alone at Les Rochers: "My son has gone to Rennes to see the Maréchal d'Estrées; my daughter-in-law, to see her mother. Tomorrow I expect a woman from Vitré whom I find quite pleasant." A week later, she was "still alone: my son and his wife are still at Rennes; my friend from Vitré has gone home. I am quite all right; don't feel sorry for me . . . Don't be upset about my solitude; I do not dislike it. My daughter-in-law will be returning soon . . ."

On October 23, she wrote:

I am still alone, my dear child, but I am not bored. I have my health, a choice of books, needlework and good weather—with only a modicum of good sense, one should go a long way like that. Despite what my son and daughter-in-law write me, I can see that they are thrilled to be in Rennes and, knowing that, I truly want them to stay. I forbid them to come home; I can even see that they are right. There is good company at Rennes; it is a joyful place. No thought is given to the millions that will be demanded of the province; all they can think about is the return of Parlement to that poor town. The Estates convene in the most beautiful palace in France; there is none more magnificent.

On October 24, Mme de Sévigné's daughter-in-law drove unannounced into Les Rochers, evidently to her mother-in-law's surprise and delight, as the following letter to Mme de Grignan attests:

*Cardinal Pietro Ottoboni had been named Pope (Alexander VIII) on October 6, 1689 subsequent to the death of Innocent XI.

*She left Rennes in the face of much opposition and despite the many
attractions of the town, to come—she said—to be near me, preferring
that pleasure to all those of the Estates General. That surprised and
would have upset me, had I not been able clearly to see that she is well
pleased with her decision, and that it was out of love as much as out of
consideration that she took this action. Dumesnil arranged for a
production of the opera Atys* in Rennes ... She attended one performance, and liked it, but likes being here still better. She said to me,
"Everyone at Rennes scolded me when I talked of going back to Les
Rochers but, Madame, when I explained that it was to be with you,
they could readily see that I had good reason" ... So, here she is! It
struck me that this little account would not lower her in your estimation ...*

Mme de Sévigné was not unappreciative of her daughter-in-law's sacrifice in returning from Rennes to keep her company, but her heart and mind
yearned toward Grignan: "I think constantly of Grignan, of all of you, of
your terraces, your superlatively beautiful views," she wrote wistfully from
Les Rochers, one day in that autumn of 1689:

*I emerge from my forests to take a promenade with you, but in this
flurry of thoughts, some cause me to cry out in pain, for how can I
forget that they are working in Rome to deprive you of your beautiful
County [of Avignon]! But let us not talk of that, my daughter ...*

They would talk, instead, about Mme Reinié, Mme de Grignan's Paris
couturière who had suddenly and unexpectedly burst into Grignan demanding payment on past-due bills. "Let us talk for a moment about Mme
Reinié," Mme de Sévigné wrote on October 26:

*What a Fury! You must have thought she had died and that it was her
ghost come to persecute you after death as she had in life! I would
have been petrified with fear and made the sign of the cross, although
I think it would take something more than that to exorcise her. How
can anyone travel 150 leagues to demand money of a person who is
dying to pay, and who pays on account whenever possible? I can think
of no one whose arrival at Grignan could have more greatly astonished
me than hers. I let out a shriek! You were right, however, not to have
mistreated her; you were entirely reasonable. But how will you extri-*

---

*The opera *Atys* had its première in Paris in 1676. Dumesnil was a renowned operatic star.

cate yourself from her claws—and get away from that deluge of words under which one thinks one is drowning . . . ?

When letters from Mme de Sévigné's cousin Monsieur de Coulanges sang the praises of Pauline de Grignan, that young lady's grandmother beamed with pride: "I really dote on Coulanges's wholehearted praise of Pauline," she wrote the girl's mother:

If that Count de Grignan had only been willing to pass on to her just his eyes and fine figure, and leave the rest to you, Pauline would have "set the world afire."* But beauty that great might have been embarrassing; this nice combination is a thousand times better, and surely makes for a pretty little creature. Her vivacity reminds me of yours. Your intelligence penetrates to the core, as you say of hers, and that is a great compliment. She will learn Italian in no time, thanks to a schoolmistress far better than yours.† My dear child, you well deserved a daughter as utterly loveable as the one I had.

"I must tell you about a letter I had from Mme de La Fayette," Mme de Sévigné wrote Mme de Grignan on October 12:

Sounding like a decree handed down from the Supreme Council, she spoke primarily for herself, but also for Mme de Chaulnes and Mme de Lavardin, and threatened to stop loving me if I refused to return at once to Paris, insisting that I would be ill if I stayed on here, that I would die, and my mind would degenerate—and finally, I must come, without argument; they will not even listen to my miserable excuses! All this, my daughter, with a zeal and a fondness which give me pleasure. And then she goes on; here is how it is to be done: I am to go to Malicorne in my son's equipage; Mme de Chaulnes will send her husband's there to meet me. I am to come to Paris. I am to stay with the Duchess. I am to buy no horses until the spring. And here is the best part: I will find a thousand écus at my house, placed there by someone who has no need of them, who makes the loan without interest, and who will not press for repayment. But I am to leave immediately! . . . I replied gratefully, but jestingly, assuring her that I would be only slightly bored here with my son, my son's wife, my

---

*A phrase that had been used in description of Mme de Grignan at the time of her Court debut.
†Mme de Sévigné had been Mme de Grignan's Italian teacher.

books and the hope of returning next summer to Paris, without being lodged at someone else's house, and with no need for someone else's equipage for the reason that I will have one of my own, and with no need of being in debt for a thousand écus to a generous friend whose kind heart and consideration for me would constitute a pressure more distressful than all the policemen in the world! And that, furthermore, I would give her my word neither to be ill, nor to age, nor to babble, so that she could love me forever, despite her threats. That is the reply I made to those three good friends. Someday I will show you the letter; it will please you. My God, what an idea—to stay at someone else's house rather than my own, to be dependent, to have no equipage of my own, and to owe a thousand écus! Really, my child, there is no comparison; I far prefer staying here. It is only from afar that the idea of a winter in the country appears so horrifying; close up, it is different. Write and tell me whether you do not agree with me. If you were in Paris—ah, that would be a compelling reason, but you are not there . . .

Mme de Sévigné's reply to her friends has disappeared. Mme de La Fayette, unfortunately, failed to save her correspondence. But Mme de Sévigné forwarded Mme de La Fayette's letter to her daughter, who filed it away with those of her mother.

"My style will be laconic," Mme de La Fayette's letter dated October 8 reads:

What I want to tell you, my belle, is that you positively must not spend the winter in Brittany, no matter what! You are old. Les Rochers is in the deep woods. You will fall prey to colds and pneumonia. You will be bored, you will be sad, and become depressed. This is inevitable, and material considerations are nothing in comparison to things such as these. Don't talk to me about money or debts. I don't want to hear a word out of you about that. Monsieur de Sévigné will have his horses take you to Malicorne; there, you will find Monsieur de Chaulnes's horses and his calèche. So, there you are in Paris! You will go to the Hôtel de Chaulnes. Your house is not ready; you have no horses; that will come later. At your leisure, you will arrange to return to your own house. Let's get down to facts: you pay Monsieur de Sévigné a pension; you have a staff here; put all that together, and it amounts to money because you still have your house under lease. You will say, "But I have debts, and in time I will pay them off." You can expect to find a *thousand écus here with which you will pay on all those debts you consider urgent, and this sum will be lent to you without interest charges, and you can pay it back later, little by little, as it is convenient for you. Don't ask where the money comes from or who loans it; you will not be told. But they are people who have no fear about being reimbursed. No discussion, now! Why waste time on words or letters? I absolutely refuse to read anything you write me. In a word, my belle, you must either come here straightaway or forfeit my friendship, that of Mme de Chaulnes and of Mme de Lavardin. We want nothing to do with a friend who willfully insists on growing old, on killing herself. You have brought misery and poverty on yourself.* You must come the moment the weather permits!*

("A fond conspiracy" was Mme de Sévigné's characterization of the proposal made her by her friends—one which she infinitely appreciated, but categorically rejected.)

It was Mme de Sévigné's purpose to dispel not only her friends' but also her daughter's fears about the grim Brittany winters: "You must not think of me in a dark and lonely wood with an owl on my head!" she replied indignantly to some remark of Mme de Grignan's. Certainly, the tenor of life at Les Rochers brightened perceptibly in mid-November when Charles de Sévigné headed home from Rennes—with numerous guests in tow—to join his wife and mother at that many-turreted château. "My son has returned from the Estates," Mme de Sévigné wrote on November 16: "He is happy to be with us again. Mme de Marboeuf has come for a visit, as has the Abbé of Quimperlé, whose only thought is to oblige me . . ."

She was even more obliged to the Abbé Charrier, another guest brought to Les Rochers by Charles. "I am most obliged to that Abbé," she wrote: "He is taking over all my business affairs in lower Brittany, which are not few and which I could never attend to from Paris." "We have spent two days, the Abbé Charrier and I, straightening out accounts with our monsieur the farmer," she wrote late in November:

He is an honest man, but the one who preceded him ruined my property. Nothing but reparations and damages. I will never get my hands on the thousand pistoles he owes me, and for the last two years, the revenues have been used to put things back in shape . . .

---

*Mme de La Fayette reproaches Mme de Sévigné for having stripped herself financially to give to her children.

"Whenever the sun shines, it penetrates our woods," she wrote on November 29:

The ground is dry, and the "Place Madame" gets the midday sun, while one end of the Long Allée enjoys the marvels of the setting sun. But when it rains, a nice room with a roaring fire; often, two gaming tables, as now. We have a number of guests, but they do not inconvenience me. I am free to do as I please. When we are alone, however, we are even better off because reading gives us a pleasure greater than any other. We enjoy Mme de Marboeuf; she shares all our tastes, but we cannot keep her forever. I wanted to give you some idea of how things are, so that you need have no concern about me.

It was not Mme de Grignan who needed to be concerned about her mother's wintering in Brittany; it was Mme de Sévigné who was concerned about her daughter's wintering—for the first time—at the Château de Grignan: "So, you have decided to spend the winter at Grignan," Mme de Sévigné exclaimed in dismay in early December, "making clear the reason which prevents your holding court at Aix for three or four months, as Monsieur de Grignan was accustomed to do." (The reason, clearly, was the Grignans' insolvency; their retirement to Grignan was open acknowledgment that they could no longer afford the expense of the winter season in the capital.)

"You have told me so much about the *bise* at Grignan in the winter that I am frightened," Mme de Sévigné wrote in another letter to her daughter:

I think Monsieur de Grignan will find it difficult to make up his mind to forego spending those three months at his good city of Aix, but sometimes one must face up to the impossible. How sad it is, and what a misfortune to find oneself bankrupt when one has such need not to be!

"But tell me, my dear Countess, how you will adjust to spending the winter at your château, on your windswept mountaintop? I tremble at the thought," she wrote on another day, that winter. "It is a miracle that your mirrors were not broken!" she moaned after reading her daughter's report on a hurricane wind that had battered the château early in November. There had been floods in October: "You are not accustomed to such a deluge," Mme de Sévigné had written in commiseration with her daughter: "According to your description, your château is in a dreadful state. I would be grieved if you were unable to save those beautiful furnishings of yours—especially those in the study which were worthy of Versailles."

It was a harsh winter; still, there came news to cheer them in November: "You spare me much anxiety, my dear child," Mme de Sévigné wrote on the twentieth, "by giving me the news that our Marquis is now a Colonel—in command of his uncle's splendid and beautiful regiment!"

Nothing could be more advantageous for him. At age eighteen, one could not be further along one's way ... I defy you—with all your propensity in that direction—to find anything with which to reproach yourself in this connection. The only question, now, my dear Countess, is how to maintain that rank, which implies greater expense than that of captain. Monsieur the Chevalier must be paid; how much will that be? We can only hope that you will obtain permission to sell your fine company, your very own handiwork.* In fine, my daughter, there are advantages and disadvantages. Honors increase expense ...

"My little Colonel wrote to me and to his uncle ... to tell us about his promotion," Mme de Sévigné advised by letter of December 11:

He had not yet received our letter of congratulations. He frankly admits that he is thrilled to find himself at the head of so fine a troop, and to be able to speak of "my regiment"—that may sound somewhat immature, but he is only eighteen.

"Will not your Colonel come to see you?" Mme de Sévigné inquired of the officer's mother. "It seems to me that he would have time enough." It seemed to her, likewise, that it was time for their Colonel to think of making "a good marriage." The prospect of being a great-grandmother dismayed her not at all: "Were he to have a child by the end of the year, I would be thrilled!" (By a "good marriage" Mme de Sévigné meant a marriage financially advantageous to the well-nigh bankrupt Grignans, their only hope for a financial recovery. To every member of the Grignan family, it was clear that the Marquis should marry young, and provide sons and heirs to ensure the continuation of the line.)

---

*Only the Secretary of War could authorize the sale of military units; only he could approve a purchaser, once a purchaser was found. The cavalry company captained by the Marquis de Grignan was sold in April of 1690 for a sum of 12,000 livres. The Count de Grignan paid his brother the Chevalier the sum of 8,000 livres for the regiment to be commanded by the Marquis.

As assiduous as was the mother-daughter correspondence, it was fortunate, indeed, that they so admired one another's letters: "I am always interested in anything concerning Monsieur the Chevalier," Mme de Sévigné wrote on November 29, "not because he chooses to read and to admire my letters—on the contrary, I take the liberty of making fun of him—but because his head is as marvelously sound as his heart."

But how can it be—if he likes that kind of reading—that he does not avail himself of the privilege of reading your letters before you mail them? They are worthy of his esteem. When I show them to my son and his wife, we are well aware of their beauty ... All in all, my daughter, it is fortunate that my letters please you; otherwise, you would be subject to oft-repeated ennui.

Another paragraph of that letter made reference to Mme de La Fayette's letter of October 8, and harked back to an adjective she had used in description of Mme de Sévigné:

So, you were struck by the word Mme de La Fayette used about me—spoken, though it was, affectionately? [The word that stuck in their minds was "old": "You are old," Mme de La Fayette had told Mme de Sévigné baldly.] Although I do not allow myself to forget this fact, I admit that I was astonished, because I am, as yet, conscious of no deterioration which might remind me of it.

However, I am much given to reflection and to reckoning, and I find the conditions of life rather harsh. It seems to me that I have been dragged, against my will, to this fatal point where I must submit to old age. I can see it. I am there! And I would certainly like to find a way to stay where I am, to advance no farther along the way that leads to the infirmities, the miseries, the loss of memory, the disfigurements which are about to outrage me, but I can hear a voice that says, "You must continue on, despite yourself or, indeed, if you do not wish to, the alternative is to die, which is another extremity repugnant to nature. That, however, is the fate of all those who go a bit too far. But the thought of God's will and of that universal law by which we all stand condemned restores our reason and induces patience.

"At Les Rochers, this Sunday, the first day of the year," the superscription of Mme de Sévigné's letter of that date reads. The new year was 1690, first year of the last decade of the seventeenth century. The new decade—the transition from the 1680's to the 1690's—was somehow disconcerting to Mme de Sévigné: "You are right," she would write her daughter, later in the month, "I can't accustom myself to the new dateline." Still later, she would call it "a year of ignominy.")

"You have had a wonderful spell of weather in the midst of your winter," Mme de Sévigné commented in her New Year's Day letter to Mme de Grignan:

> Weather so fine that Monsieur de Grignan could not resist going hunting, weather so fine that you deserted your invalids, so fine that you preferred the pleasure of a promenade to that of letter-writing! Ah, how right you were! One must not miss such enchanted days. We have had horrible weather, the kind of weather in which to huddle by the fire, in which to avoid sticking one's nose out the door, in which there is not a drop of fog which does not carry the threat of frost or ice— weather, in short, the very opposite of yours; a time, however, when my son had five or six neighbors in, playing games and making quite a racket in this room.

A week late, Mme de Sévigné sent New Year's greetings to her cousin Philippe-Emmanuel de Coulanges in Rome, heading her letter, "At Les Rochers, Sunday, January 8":

> What a dull dateline compared to yours, my darling cousin! But it suits a solitary soul like me, while that of Rome suits you, with your wandering star . . . What a lovely life you lead, and how kindly Fortune has treated you, as you say . . . Always loved, always esteemed, always the purveyor of joy and pleasure, always the favorite of some important friend whom you adore—a duke, a prince, a pope (I bring in the Holy Father for the

rarity of the occasion),* always in good health, never a burden to anyone, under pressure from neither business affairs nor ambition! But, above all, what an advantage not to grow old! That is the height of good fortune . . . All in all, having given it much thought, I consider you the luckiest man in the world! This last trip of yours to Rome seems to me the most wonderful adventure you have ever had: to go there with an adorable Ambassador on a great and important occasion, to revisit the fairest city in the world, one to which everyone always yearns to return! I love the verses you wrote about it . . . They are good, they are clever, and we will sing them . . . Ah, how I would love to make the trip to Rome, as you suggest I do! But it would have had to have been with the face and the air I had many years ago, and not as I am today. It is unwise to rattle old bones—those of women, above all . . . During my youth, however, I would have been carried away by such an experience . . .

I was delighted to hear of all Monsieur de Chaulnes's triumphs, but you seem to fear exactly what is feared by his friends, that since he is the only one capable of filling the place he occupies, he will be kept there a long while . . . With a genuine fondness and without fear of disrespect, I will take the liberty of embracing my dear Governor of Brittany, my dear Monsieur the Ambassador. All his great titles do not intimidate me; I feel sure he will always love me. May God keep him, and bring him home! And there you have my wishes for the New Year . . .

Mme de Sévigné had written to Mme de Grignan upon receipt of Coulanges's last letter from Rome:

Coulanges wrote me a very long and very amusing letter . . . He sent some verses which I admire because he apostrophizes all the beauty spots of Rome which I also admire.† He is gay, he is happy; he is a favorite of Monsieur [the Prince] de Turenne's. He is in love with Pauline, and asks the Pope to give him permission to marry her and to give her Avignon, which would thus be restored to the family! That would make her the Countess of Avignon! And, finally, he says that

---

*"They tell me that Monsieur de Coulanges is a great favorite of the Pope's," Mme de Sévigné had reported to her daughter in November.

†A volume of Coulanges's verse, published anonymously in 1694, contains the lines about Rome to which Mme de Sévigné refers: "What? I see again that famous Coliseum/After thirty years, I see the Pantheon again/Nero's Palace, the Arch of Constantine."

old age is all about him. Certain calculations give him some doubt, but he insists that he does not feel old in any way, neither in body nor in mind, and I admit to you, in my turn, that I find myself almost like him, and that it is only when I think about it, that I realize my age.

"It is when they come into your hands, my dear child, that my letters turn to gold," Mme de Sévigné told her daughter in a letter written when the new year was one week old:

When they leave mine, I find them so thick and so full of words that I say, "My daughter will never have time to read all that!" But you give me great reassurance, although I cannot in good conscience believe all you have to say about them. So, take care; such praise, such approbation is dangerous. I can tell you, at least, that I prefer your praise to that of anyone else in the world!

Another letter on the same subject was sent by Mme de Sévigné to her daughter during the following month: "You praise my letters so far beyond their worth that if I were not convinced that you would never again leaf through them or reread them, I would be fearful of seeing myself suddenly, one day, in print, through the treachery of one of my friends."*

If Mme de Grignan admired her mother's letters, Mme de Sévigné returned the compliment, writing in early February,

I read and reread your letters with all the emotion they deserve, according to the various subjects upon which they touch, but sometimes you say things so amusing that I have to laugh, despite my broken heart.

Mme de Sévigné's heartbreak had come with recent news from her daughter. The year 1690 was ill-fated for the Grignans; the Count had been dealt a grievous blow by the bankruptcy of Jacques Le Blanc de Valfère, the Treasurer of the Estates of Provence, to whom Grignan was heavily indebted. A letter from the Count de Grignan, dated January 14, 1690, and addressed to Pontchartrain, the Comptroller General of Finances, gives some idea of the desperate circumstances in which he found himself:

---

*It is this passage which has led some biographers and critics to contend that Mme de Sévigné was conscious of the literary value of her letters, and would not have been surprised to see them published. Roger Duchêne, on the other hand, the foremost Sévigné scholar of this generation, discerns a distinct irony in the Marquise's words.

Monsieur: My affairs would have to be in extreme disorder for me to dare to speak of them to you at a time when the needs of the State so justly claim all your attention but, Monsieur, since you give thought to everything which is of importance to the good of the services, I flatter myself that—because you have seen me serve the King for so long a time in a great and important province, obligated to great expense not only for the government of the province but also for my son who heads a regiment—you will include me among those whom you deem worthy of some relief by means of special assistance.

Thus confident, I most humbly beg you, Monsieur, to accord me your protection so that I may obtain from the King a grace which will cost him only a word: that is, that he should create a post of King's Lieutenant, below that which I hold as Lieutenant-Governor, and to be so kind as to make me the beneficiary of the emoluments of such a post. Such a post exists in both Brittany and Normandy. There is more reason to establish it in Provence than anywhere else, for the reason that there are so few officers in command here. Provence pays only two [the Governor and the Lieutenant-Governor]; a slight increase such as this will prove no burden, and will save me from the abyss which looms before me. I will not weary you with explanations of the need I have for prompt assistance. However, Monsieur, let me call to your attention the fact that a state of emergency has developed here; that is to say, the Treasurer of Provence has gone bankrupt. He had advanced me almost three years of the emoluments due me as Lieutenant-Governor, as well as making me other loans. His creditors will collect what is due them by taking over the revenues accruing to me presently, and I will be left without any means of support. If I could make you understand the predicament in which I find myself, I feel almost assured, Monsieur, that—out of justice and out of kindness— you would add your voice to the humble prayer I address to His Majesty.

The Count de Grignan, it developed, owed a total of 44,000 livres to Le Blanc for the advance of his emoluments over the next three years, and thus could look forward to no more revenues from Provence until 1693. Grignan was furthermore obliged to sign an agreement with Le Blanc's creditors, pledging to them the revenues from his properties for the years 1692–1704—revenues for the years 1690–92 already under pledge to other creditors.

Mme de Sévigné was in despair at the very thought of such a debacle. "You will never catch up with your revenues!" she groaned:

Good God, what a horrible miscalculation! '90 and '91, and as far beyond that as the eye can see! Never was there such reckless expenditure! One is sometimes financially embarrassed, but to ruin oneself and to indebt oneself into the far distant future, such a thing as that should never be allowed to happen. It is difficult to talk at such a distance about matters like this, because replies are needed, but one can sigh over it, and no matter what sorrow one feels, one would not want to live in ignorance of the facts. I need, as you say, a map and a key to your sentiments. It is essential that I share your distress. Love would have it thus. I do understand that the only remedy available to you is a pernicious one—bad for both your affairs at Court and for your reputation in the province. You know better than anyone else that it is not in this fashion that one would fill one's post if one could do otherwise, and that it is certainly not hidden away in one's château that one should spend all the winter, not knowing how or when one can ever come out of it.

"My God, what a disastrous state you are in! In what a critical condition!" she lamented, on another day, "and with what anguish I share your concern!" If only she could have been of some assistance to the Grignans in this crisis! The realization that—financially embarrassed as she was, herself—she could make not so much as a gesture in their behalf was a torment to Mme de Sévigné:

How futile, my daughter [she wrote], how inane expressions of sympathy must sound on such occasions! And how useless it is for me to tell you that if I still had—as once I did—any available funds of my own, they would be at your command! I find myself, in a minor way, overwhelmed and threatened by my creditors, and don't even know how I can satisfy them all, as I had hoped to do, because I am swamped by the need to pay, quite soon now, the sum of five thousand francs owing for the lods et ventes* due on the properties I bought from Mme d'Acigné, so as not to have to pay ten thousand francs if I put it off another two years. So, that is how it stands, although I tell you this only to explain to you my sorrow at finding it impossible to be of help to you. Your brother seemed very sympathetic to your plight, and I am sure that he would be quicker to do his duty than your rich prelates, if*

---

*Lods et ventes were a form of feudal tax which were owing on the lands Mme de Sévigné had acquired from Mme d'Acigné.

only the times were as they used to be, and one could still arrange to borrow money.

"What I marvel at," Mme de Sévigné wrote Mme de Grignan, "is how God preserves your health amid such overwhelming difficulties. How I pity you! And how prejudicial this state of affairs must be to the establishment of your poor child!"

That "poor child" had finally arrived in Paris from the winter quarters of his regiment in Kaiserslautern. "I am very eager to hear how he acquits himself of all his responsibilities at Court and in Paris, for you have friends there whom he should see. I instructed Beaulieu to write me everything he says and does, everything about his little person." "I do not think he will have time to go to see you," Mme de Sévigné wrote the Marquis's mother:

That grieves me for both your sake and his. They write me that he is heavy, and that we must give up hope of his having a fine figure like his father's. People speak well of him. He is gentlemanly, he is bright. But it is a misfortune that during his first season at Court ... the little Colonel should have the support of none of his family. In view of the fact that he had to do it all on his own, I think he handled himself wonderfully well.

"Today, we begin our Carnival season," Mme de Sévigné wrote on February 5:

That consists of assembling a group of five or six men and women from the neighborhood; they will play games; they will eat; but if our sun should come out again, as it did yesterday, I would gladly go off on a promenade. We can already hear the wrens, the warblers and the titmice, and there is a hint, a breath of spring in the air.

"We had very sensible people here," Mme de Sévigné told Mme de Grignan in her letter of February 8, "and at no inconvenience to me":

They played games constantly, but I was free to go my own way. Yesterday evening, just before supper, and without a word of warning, my daughter-in-law left the room and, suddenly, the servant who waits on table comes in very cleverly disguised, and tells us that supper is served. We go into the dining room which we find brightly lit, and my daughter-in-law masked, in the midst of her people and mine—all of *whom are in masquerade: those who hold the basins in which we wash our hands, those who hand us the napkins, all the household officers, all the lackeys! That amounted to more than thirty, so charmingly costumed that—what with the surprise in addition to the spectacle— there were shrieks, there was laughter and excitement which greatly gladdened our whole supper party, for it was impossible to tell who was serving us or who was pouring our beverages! After supper, every- one danced; there were bagpipes;* they danced all the* passe-pieds, *all the minuets, all the* courantes *popular in the village, played all the games of the local fellows. Finally, midnight sounded, and there we were in the Lenten season. Do you remember, my darling, the Mardi Gras we spent together, when we went to bed early, before Lent had begun?*

Lent proved little of a hardship in Brittany, according to Mme de Sévigné's letter of February 19:

*We enjoy a very good table here. We don't have your Sorgue River,†
but we have the ocean. We do not lack for fish, and I love the delicious butter from La Prévalaie which is sent to us every week. I love it, and eat it as if I were a Breton. We eat countless slices of bread and butter, some of the slices cut from round loaves. We always think about you when we are eating them. My son's tooth-marks in the bread prove that he has not lost a one and, to my great pleasure, I mark all of mine as well. Soon we will add* fines herbes *and violets to the buttered bread. At night, a soup with a little butter—in the Breton way; some good prunes, some good spinach. All in all, this cannot be called fasting . . .*

("I am feeling very well," she remarked elsewhere that season; "the sobriety of Lent is very healthful.")

"Adieu, my *belle,*" she wrote on the last page of her letter of Febru- ary 12:

I am convinced that there is no one whose love compares with yours— unless it is mine. But a mother's love is so natural a thing, whereas the

---

**Sonnoux,* the word used by Mme de Sévigné, was the regional word for a wood instrument, probably a Breton bagpipe, which was used as accompaniment for regional dances.

†The Sorgue River, which flows from the Fountain of Vaucluse and empties into the Rhône, was famous for its fish, especially its trout.

love of children is so unusual that while I am doing what I should be doing, you are a prodigy.

The Sévignés reached a decision to go to Rennes for Holy Week and Easter, as Mme de Sévigné advised her daughter by letter of Wednesday, March 15:

We are going to Rennes on Monday to spend two weeks. Since we do not have a venerable chapter as you do,* we want to partake of something of the church ceremonial. We also have some business matters to attend to, there. La Marboeuf awaits me in transports of joy . . . Don't change your usual address. I will be back before your reply to this letter could reach me.

Mme de Grignan's letters addressed to Les Rochers were forwarded to her mother in Rennes, who wrote from that town on April 2:

You are very unlucky not to have been able to sell your company for ten thousand francs.† What a misunderstanding! You will lose a thousand francs on the transaction—and that means cash, because the nine thousand will be paid you on credit, and with bad grace.

"On Monday we go back to Les Rochers," she wrote on April 5, manifesting her customary ambivalence about the bucolic versus the metropolitan way of life, "and despite the many banquets, I confess that I am thrilled to be returning to my solitude."

"To get back to your services," she went on in that same letter of the fifth, "and to your fine, your magnificent chapter":

I would find that tradition of holy grandeur very impressive and, since it is already established, it is preferable to ten thousand livres of income. It must be considered a great distinction. I wish I could have attended Tenebrae *there. I have a high opinion of Monsieur de Grignan's orchestra. At Saint Peter's [Cathedral in Rennes], the services were simple.*

Mme de Sévigné must have wondered how the grandeur of the Easter services—the grandeur of life in general—at the château could be reconciled

---

*The chapter of the collegiate church attached to the Château de Grignan included a dean, a canon-sacristan, six canons, a deacon and assistant deacon, two cantors and two choirboys.
†The cavalry company over which the Marquis had command as captain.

with the bankruptcy and ruin confronting the Grignans. "It seems to me, my *bonne*, that you lead a fine life at Grignan," she wrote her daughter on April 26:

> *Despite so many storms, so many shipwrecks, I see only abundance and magnificence there. It is very convenient to put off mending one's ways, and wait for time to pass. But how will you work out of the terrible complication in your affairs brought on by the advances made you by the Treasurer?*

If Mme de Sévigné's letters had implied that it was the Count de Grignan's extravagances which had brought them to the brink of ruin, Mme de Grignan's replies made clear that her love for him was undiminished by his financial irresponsibility. "You give me a very interesting insight into your love for Monsieur de Grignan," Mme de Sévigné remarked: "It accounts for the fact that you cannot stay angry with him for long." How long would it take Mme de Sévigné to learn that her daughter would never join her in a denunciation of the Count de Grignan's profligacy? If Mme de Sévigné had sought "a key and a map," as she phrased it, to her daughter's "sentiments," they were to be found in her daughter's deep and abiding love for her husband. She took infinite pride in the grandeur of his house and his name; not even bankruptcy could disenchant her. Mme de Grignan was no more likely to indict the Count for the economic disaster that had befallen them than to have denied him his conjugal rights, even though these had cost her a yearly pregnancy or miscarriage. Historians agree that the marriage of convenience was generally a loveless one; the Grignans' was evidently an exception—the point Mme de Sévigné had difficulty in understanding.

Mme de Sévigné had returned from Rennes to Les Rochers in time to preside over the rites of spring. "I come back again to you, my *bonne*," she wrote on April 19, "to tell you that if you want a detailed report on spring, you must come to me."

> *My own knowledge had been very superficial but, this year, I observed it carefully from its very earliest beginnings. What color do you think the trees have been for the last week? Answer me! You will say, "green." Not so! They are red! There are little buds, all ready to open up, which are truly red, but then they all unfurl and make a little leaf, and since they do not come out all at once, the effect is a lovely mixture of red and green. All this is hatched out under our very eyes. We bet large sums—not that we ever pay up!—that this end of the allée will be*

green within two hours. Someone bets it will not. The bet is on. The elms have their way of going about it; the beech, another. All in all, I am as well informed on the subject as anyone in the world!

"The weather, thank God, is really marvelous," Mme de Sévigné resumed:

I have managed so well that spring is here in all its beauty! Everything is green. It was no easy task to see to it that all those buds unfurled, that the red all turned to green. When I finished with all those elms, I had to go on to the beeches, then to the oaks. That is what gave me the most trouble, and I still have another week to go before I can claim to have made a perfect job of it. I begin to enjoy all the pains to which I went, and I really think that not only did I not interfere with all that beauty, but—in a pinch—I would know how to manage a springtime, on my own, so carefully did I observe, so critical an examination did I make of this one, something I had never done so meticulously before. It is my great leisure I have to thank for this opportunity and, in truth, my dear bonne, it has been the most delightful experience imaginable.

"So, you want to know about my correspondence?" Mme de Sévigné inquired of Mme de Grignan another day that spring:

First of all, there is the one with my daughter, which takes precedence over all the rest. Mme de Lavardin writes me faithfully, once a week, enclosing all the best news sheets, and ending always with a page of personal messages, in her own hand. Mme de Moussy and the others keep in touch through Mme de Lavardin, who is the leader of the Corps of Widows ... I have just written a letter of condolence to the Marquise d'Huxelles on the occasion of the death of her saintly mother. Mme de La Troche, now that she has come to Paris, writes me at length about other news events which are highly entertaining, and which I am thrilled to hear about. You know about my "little Bigorres."* Mme de La Fayette writes when she is feeling well, but I see little of her handwriting—at the most, a line, saying "Here I am," and that only once in the last two months. Mme de Vins, Mme de Coulanges. And all that at the price of only a letter in reply. So, these correspondences are very nice, very agreeable, without being a burden to me. Mme de Chaulnes is far from forgetting me, either ... And there, my dear

*Her "little *Bigorres*" were newsletters distributed by the Abbé Bigorre.

bonne, *you have an idea of my letter-writing, my only occupation, helping to pass away the time—and my life, along with the time.*

Having successfully ushered in the spring at Les Rochers, Mme de Sévigné began making her plans for the winter:

And so [she wrote], I have decided not to go to Paris this coming winter, since you are not going, because—had you been there or should you change your mind about going—I would surely go.

And had we gone together, I would have proven to you that you could have helped me to keep up appearances—by allowing me to stable two of your horses which you would use far more than I would— with the result that no one would have noticed that I had none. On the other hand, without you, I cannot keep up appearances. Therefore, I will not go and, although it is a long way off, I am thinking about taking a litter, in September, and going direct from Vitré to Grignan, to spend the winter there with you, my dear bonne, and then returning with you to Paris at the end of the following summer, or going ahead of you to Paris in order to show myself again as a woman who is neither running away from anything nor pursued by anyone, but rather one who has put her affairs back in order at a time when her daughter was doing the same. That is my plan, which satisfies both my love for you and my sense of values. I implore you at the same time, however, to say nothing of this to anyone in Paris—so that, that is, none of my friends there learn of my plans. They love me, and their disappointment would color their letters, which would distress me instead of diverting me, as their letters usually do. So, let's say not a word, I beg you, but remember, instead, that all our plans are subject to the will of God, Who often brings them to naught; that my health must continue to be as perfect as it is now and, also, from another point of view, that Providence's plans must coincide with mine—or, rather, that mine should coincide with those of Providence—in which event, we will spend the winter together, whether in Paris or at Grignan—because, as I have already told you, you would make it possible for me to go to Paris, should you change your mind. . . . What brings me to the deci-sion not to spend the winter here, although I still greatly enjoy being here and although my son and daughter-in-law are very pleased to have me, is that I do not want to impose further on their love and consideration for me. They have a house in Rennes; they have family there; they like being there. I kept them away from there this past winter; that is enough. And as for me, I do not like to spend more than two weeks at a time in Rennes. That is how I have reasoned things out, and with no fear of the length of the voyage from Les Rochers to Grignan. Dixi.*

LII

"It will be a year tomorrow that I arrived here," wrote Mme de Sévigné under the dateline of "Les Rochers, this May 24 [1690]":

I enjoyed the spring of the year at Chaulnes, where the nightingales compare favorably with yours, about which you tell me such marvels ... Alas, it has been a year, too, since you enjoyed your triumphs at Avignon whence you sent us such charming descriptions. You returned from there to welcome Monsieur the Chevalier. Good Lord, how time flies, carrying us along with it, carrying us off!

In reply to Mme de Grignan's reply to the above letter, Mme de Sévigné wrote on June 11:

And so, as you say, my dear bonne, *here's another year gone by—to be followed by another, and another still, and you can see where that will take us! I simply cannot accustom myself to the rapid passage of time, and it is even more astonishing in my case than in yours because, there, you are always in a hustle and a bustle, whereas here there is often a veritable solitude. I don't know, my dear* bonne, *whether it is this life we lead—as regular as clockwork—or the gentle and healthful exercise which accounts for the perfection of my health, but it is certain that I have never felt so well. This sometimes surprises me, and I ask myself what has become of all those ridiculous little ailments of mine— as you so amusingly referred to them. Not a one now troubles me, but since I have never heard it said that, as one ages, one can hope to*

---

*I have spoken.

remain in perfect health, I am constrained—unless I include myself in the ranks of the immortal—to fear some betrayal, without knowing from which direction it will come.

In another letter, Mme de Sévigné specified "those little ailments" to which she had previously been subject: "I have had neither vapours in the night," she would write on June 25, "nor those small sores in my mouth, nor that cramp in my hands, and no nephritis. We drink white wine which I consider very beneficial, even better than a tisane."*

With the mild spring and summer weather, Mme de Sévigné's customary complaints about the mail service conspicuously diminished: "Our mails are now so well regulated that I receive a letter by every courier," Mme de Sévigné commented gratefully. It was "something of a miracle," she thought, that "a letter which left Vitré on Sunday, June 4, at ten o'clock at night should arrive at Grignan in six days' time, on Saturday, the tenth, at two o'clock in the afternoon. That was, as I said, my *bonne*, thanks to the good weather, the good roads and the moonlight." Good weather or bad, she invariably wrote, as she said, "on Wednesdays and Sundays."†

Her letters were evidently eagerly awaited, warmly greeted at the Château de Grignan, or so Mme de Grignan told her mother, if one is to judge by Mme de Sévigné's letter of April 23:

And so, you always open them, my bonne, with a joy and a tenderness which you think Saint Augustine and Monsieur du Bois‡ might find somewhat excessive? You call them "your dear bonnes"; you say they "are necessary to your peace of mind." It is up to you, then, whether to consider that such an attachment is a sin. You will, nevertheless, you say, "continue to love me with all your heart, and far more than you do your neighbor whom you love only as well as you love yourself" . . . And that, my dear bonne, is what you tell me. If you think that those words only touch my heart superficially, you are mistaken. I feel them keenly. They have taken up their abode in my heart. I say them to myself, over and over again, and even take delight in repeating them back to you, as if thus to renew your vows and pledges. The words of people as sincere as you carry great weight. Knowing that they are spoken in good faith, I live happily and contentedly. Indeed,

*A tisane is a medicinal tea.
†With that schedule so precisely defined, the dates on the remaining letters of the correspondence make clear that many written during the summer of 1690 are missing.
‡Philippe, Seigneur du Bois, was the author of various works on and translations of Saint Augustine.

it is too great, too intense—that love of yours. It seems to me that, out of a sense of justice, I have no right to so much, because a mother's love does not ordinarily set the standard for a daughter's, but, then, you are not the ordinary daughter! Thus, I will enjoy without scruple the treasure you bestow on me.

Mme de Sévigné had come to see her daughter's role as nothing less than heroic in coping with the problems besetting her husband and their family, had come to see her as a tower of strength in the storms that shook the family château and the family exchequer. In her mother's eyes, the Countess de Grignan served as the gracious First Lady of Provence, as the gracious and competent chatelaine of Grignan, as devoted wife and mother and sister-in-law, as family bookkeeper and estate manager.*

"For a long time now, my *bonne*," Mme de Sévigné wrote on May 21,

*I have observed and admired you. I see you as "The Strong Woman,"†
totally dedicated to your responsibilities and making an admirable use
of the full scope of your intelligence ... If Rome could be saved, you
would save it, as one of the Ancients put it‡ ... What don't you do?
You borrow money to repay important debts; you appease your minor
creditors; you wield everything from the scepter to the trowel! You
cope with it all. You have a business acumen which astonishes me.
One can have a great intellect without having intelligence of that kind.
I admire it all the more because it is so far above my head! You know
those to whom I have turned for assistance. You can be thankful to
God, for certainly such gifts do not come from you. When a beautiful
and amiable woman receives them from Heaven, like you, it is a marvel.*

"You sacrifice yourself in all your youth, to the austerity of your duty," Mme de Sévigné wrote, on another day that spring, on the same subject:

*You leave the world and the Court. You are at Grignan, engaged in
doing what is best for your house and your son ... You are there in*

---

*One of her account books is still extant.

†Mme de Sévigné's reference is to the strong woman of the Scriptures. The King James version of *Proverbs* refers to "a virtuous woman—her price far above rubies," who "girdeth her loins with strength" and who is further described as wife, mother, mistress of the household.

‡The "Ancient" so loosely quoted by Mme de Sévigné is Virgil—a reference to Troy, not Rome, from the *Aeneid.*

your château where you say it is not costing you "three sous." That is
something I cannot believe. Your way of life there is too magnificent.

By June, 1690, the Marquis and his regiment were back with the Army
of Germany: "Our Marquis," according to a letter of Mme de Sévigné's
dated June 11, "is by now part of that large and beautiful and superb army,
and you speak a great truth when you say that he is surely in God's hands."

You ask me whether my submission to Providence is complete enough
to give me comfort on such an occasion as this. Oh, my God, my
bonne, I have not yet reached that point! Far from it! Only too often I
realize that I am paying only lip service to that holy doctrine.

Both mother and daughter could breathe a sigh of relief once they
made sure that the name of the Marquis did not appear on the long list of
casualties suffered by the French forces in the battle of Fleurus, in Flanders,
on July 1, when the Maréchal de Luxembourg's army defeated that of the
coalition forces under the Prince von Waldeck. "Think, my *bonne*," Mme
de Sévigné wrote on July 9, "of that great battle won by Monsieur [the
Maréchal] de Luxembourg, where God watched over your child, and kept
him safe. He had not as yet arrived there, and you are assured of his safety.
Here are the names of those who perished . . ."

"It was a great day," she exulted again in her letter of July 12:

What a glorious, what a full, what a complete victory, and one which
could not have come at a more opportune moment! I am sure that as
soon as you were no longer anxious about the Marquis—whose regi-
ment, I believe, was not included in the detachment sent there by
Monsieur de Boufflers—you must have been extraordinarily excited! I
know I was, not really knowing about whom I was concerned, because
I did know that our child was either not there or was not one of the
casualties. So great an event, when one least expected it! To know of
so many people afflicted! To think that the war is still not over!

To Louis XIV, the war must have likewise seemed interminable. The
Dutch War of the preceding decade, followed by the years of expensive
construction at Versailles, had constituted a great drain on French resources.
The monarch's motive, in the war begun in 1688, had been to establish a
defensible northern frontier, to strengthen France's borders against the prin-
cipalities of Germany. He had envisaged it as a short and limited action

because it had been his hope that the Hapsburg Emperor would continue locked in the struggle against the incursion of Islam into the Danube Valley, and that William of Orange would be locked in a struggle with James II for the crown of England. Instead, the Ottoman Empire met defeat at Buda, and William of Orange, ascending the throne of England as William III, could bring that nation—along with his native Netherlands—into the War of the Grand Alliance against France. By the summer of 1690, France stood alone, faced with a coalition including all her neighbors: the Emperor of the Holy Roman Empire, the Kings of Sweden, Spain and England, the Stadholder of the United Netherlands. The war of 1688–97 became what one historian calls "The First World War."*

Like any patriotic Frenchwoman in the Splendid Century, Mme de Sévigné believed in the Sun King's "lucky star" which, in July of 1690, appeared to be in the ascendant again. "Such victories, my *bonne!*" Mme de Sévigné exclaimed on July 19: "And such alarms! Victory on land, victory at sea!"—these being references to the battle of Fleurus on July 1 and the naval victory of July 10, off the Normandy coast, where the French fleet defeated the combined forces of the English and the Dutch.

The safety of the Marquis de Grignan was quite naturally of primary concern to his grandmother at that hour, but she did not overlook her other grandchild. Scarcely a letter from her pen went off to Provence without some reference to Pauline. "You draw us a picture of Pauline which lets us see her clearly," Mme de Sévigné wrote in reply to a letter of Mme de Grignan's describing her sixteen-year-old daughter: "She is very pretty, very amiable, very gracious; her manner is very noble, her heart is kind. I see her! There she is! It is she, herself!" "And aren't you wonderful not only to form Pauline's mind but also to serve as her dancing teacher!" Mme de Sévigné wrote in praise of Mme de Grignan's maternal solicitude. "You are better than Desairs, because she need only look at you and imitate you. Is she tall? Is she graceful? I thank her for not having confused me with all the other grandmothers whom she hates. I am saved, thank God!"

Pauline and her grandmother sometimes exchanged greetings:

My dear Pauline [Mme de Sévigné wrote], I am thrilled to see your handwriting again. I feared that you had forgotten me in the midst of your good fortune. That is what it is to be on good terms with your dear Mother, and to have become worthy of her—enough to turn a little head like yours! I advise you to continue to work on your budding

*John B. Wolf, in *Louis XIV*.

perfections which will preserve your Mother's love for you, and put you on the road to winning the esteem of the world.

In the spring of 1690, reference is made in the *Correspondence* to a health problem of Pauline's which was apparently of some concern to her mother, but far less so than it would be to a twentieth-century parent. "I don't understand about the half-moon shape of her teeth," Mme de Sévigné wrote in puzzlement in reply to a letter from her daughter: "What does that mean, my *bonne*?" Mme de Grignan did not have the answer to her mother's question. The answer would not be forthcoming until three hundred years later when medical research would be done on the phenomenon known as "Hutchinson's Teeth"—a half-moon erosion of the dental enamel—and would prove it to be symptomatic of hereditary syphilitic contamination.

Suddenly, in midsummer of 1690, Mme de Grignan—perhaps in response to protest on the part of Mme de Sévigné's Paris friends—began to express misgivings about the wisdom of her mother's undertaking so extensive a journey, and to suggest that she make it, instead, in two stages, going from Brittany to Paris, and stopping over there for the winter, before starting south in the spring. To put across her point, Mme de Grignan must have hinted that she might find herself unable to spend the entire winter with her mother at Grignan, that she might have to accompany her husband to Lambesc for the Assembly, perhaps even to Paris, should he be summoned there. Mme de Sévigné dealt with these objections in her letter of July 9, writing,

> *Such questions as that, my very dear* bonne, *we will allow time to decide for us. If you say "Paris," I will answer like an echo: "Paris!" If you say "Grignan"—"Grignan" it shall be! And even, my* bonne, *should you say "Lambesc," I will reply "Lambesc!" I am not making this trip to inconvenience you or to stand in your way. I am going to see you, to love you, certainly not to make you miserable—as you would be at being separated from Monsieur de Grignan. So, my* bonne, *be sure that if God preserves my health, I will follow your every step, and answer to your call. I ask you only one favor: please do not write about this to Paris. My friends are already beginning to question me. To inject that kind of discord into our correspondence would make it unbearable. So, there, my daughter, that is all I can tell you. My son and his wife, for their part, do everything in their power to keep me here and to shorten my trip, but I receive with affection these tokens of their affection without wishing to take advantage of it. My decision has been made.*

"It is dear and kind of you to be giving thought to my apartment, and to welcome me with such love and pleasure," Mme de Sévigné wrote happily to her daughter in midsummer:

Not that the love I bear you is comparable to any other—God knows that as does all the world—but it is so daring an undertaking I contemplate that I owe it to my friends who are all cautious and set in their ways to explain that there are two reasons for it: the condition of my finances as well as my desire to spend with you the time it will take me to pay off my indebtedness. I owe them that in the name of friendship, particularly in view of the fact that these are ladies who never leave Paris and will consider this as risky as an overseas voyage ... The pleasure, the comfort and the delight I anticipate in being with you almost frightens me, but I banish the thought because it seems to me that no one is allowed to be that happy in this world.

For Mme de Sévigné and the Grignans, the outbreak of hostilities with Piedmont, that summer of 1690, had the effect of bringing home their young Marquis. When the Duke of Savoy and Prince Eugene joined the coalition against France, several regiments—including that of the Marquis de Grignan—were detached from the Army of Germany, and dispatched to the south of France to defend the Piedmontese borders.

"God preserve the little Colonel! We will welcome him home with great joy," Mme de Sévigné exclaimed on July 30—by which she meant that she hoped to have reached Grignan in time to join in the family welcome to the Marquis before his orders took him away again.

Not only the junior but the senior Grignan was to be called upon to counter the Piedmontese threat to France's Mediterranean littoral: the Count de Grignan took command of the recently mobilized Provençal home guard. "I find that Monsieur de Grignan cuts a very fine figure in Provence, at the head of his little army," his mother-in-law declared proudly.

By early August, the little Colonel was at the château. "I scold you, my *bonne*, for taking the time to write to me," Mme de Sévigné wrote her daughter in a letter dated August 16:

When you have your dear child with you, you are "not in good form for letter-writing." That I can well believe! ... My bonne, *you speak very well of his mind; it is certain that he has one but it is, as you say, in the back of his head because you know that, as soon as one rouses him, one finds him responsive ... and he gives very good answers to one's questions ... But it is true that sometimes, to my despair, he seemed silent and distracted—as if ten thousand leagues away—a fault just as surely as presence of mind is a virtue ... So, he told you that he would have given anything in the world to have seen action at Fleurus? ... As far as I am concerned, I am thrilled that he has come through this campaign unscathed.*

And I am very relieved to learn that Monsieur de Grignan is leaving his war to return to his château. It lasted all too long, and that damnable expense further complicates your affairs. I hope that the King will take note of this, and do you the same justice, grant you the same grace as he did once before, on a similar occasion.*

As for me, my dear bonne, I begin to give a little thought to my great voyage. I have already explained to my friends in Paris that it will be impossible for me to return to Paris. It is simply a question of getting them to swallow the idea. The knowledge that I will find the Abbé Charrier at Moulins is a real comfort to me, and greatly brightens the prospect of that long trip in a miserable rented litter.

Her son and daughter-in-law continued to voice their regret at her departure: "Monsieur and Mme de Sévigné say all that can be said to express their sorrow and their fear of losing me and, in truth, I give them so few problems, so little trouble that I believe what they say."

The correspondence has given ample proof that Mme de Sévigné—although she had stood back, aloof and critical, in the early days of her son's marriage—had come to be genuinely fond of her daughter-in-law and to enjoy her company. The young Sévignés' was a happy home, a happy marriage. "I can tell you," Mme de Sévigné had written the Grignans earlier that year, "that he [Charles] had never experienced true love until he married, and that makes for the happiness of his wife and his own."

On August 27, Mme de Sévigné dedicated her letter to the celebration of a final victory in the Aiguebonne case; a second appeal had been decided in the Grignans' favor: "You won your case, my dear *bonne*, and won it by a unanimous decision!" The stubbornly litigious Aiguebonne was "even condemned to pay an amend! This is all you could have wished for!" Mme de Sévigné gloated.

The next page of the letter offers proof that, although Mme de Sévigné respected her daughter's opinion, she did not easily relinquish opinions of

---

*In 1684, the King had made the Count de Grignan a gift of 4,000 écus to compensate him for the expenses incurred in patrolling the southern coasts of France with Provençal militia and a corps of noblemen in response to invasion threats from Genoa and Spain.

her own: "And, now, let's talk about that 'overseas' voyage which so alarms you but to which I was so well reconciled."

I am going to answer you like "a dear bonne*" who loves you with all her heart and who is convinced of your love, who is neither angry, nor ill-humored nor perverse. I want to correct you in your theory that the air here is unhealthy. It is not. I am in perfect health. I lead a quiet and well-regulated life. You know at least half of the people I am thrown in contact with here. You must, therefore, my* bonne, *put out of your mind the thought that I will fall ill here, rather than somewhere else. You want me to go to Paris, and have me borrow money from this one and that one, including the Abbé Charrier. That, my dear* bonne, *is what I positively cannot do, and I implore you not to say a word to him about it. I know his affairs; his mother controls the funds . . . The poor man has trouble keeping himself going. His good will exceeds his purse. As for my Paris friends, ah! my dear* bonne, *please forget all that and do me the favor of rejecting all their propositions. I positively do not want to use Mme de Chaulnes's horses. Anyone who returns from Brittany after an extended absence and borrows horses and money would strike me as the kind of person who rises from the dinner table and dies of hunger. That is not what one would expect from people who have just returned from their estates. I will not expose myself to humiliation or ridicule . . .*

That leaves the question of you, my dear bonne. *I can clearly see that my coming inconveniences you, but I say that without rancor. You may have to go to Paris. I would not want to go there before the end of summer or keep you from making the trip; important family matters might make it imperative for you to go. Should you not go there, you might have to go to Marseille or to other of your properties, as might be necessary for a mistress of the household as skillful and zealous as you. You say you would not want to leave me, whereas I would not want to keep you from such important missions. Things, then, just do not work out.*

You want me to go to Paris for the winter, and if you do not come there, to grease my travel boots in the month of May, and come to see you in Provence. I confess my heart would will it so, but my common sense and judgment forbid . . .

Mme de Sévigné's long letter of August 27 went on to rehearse her daughter's objections to Mme de Sévigné's plan of travelling from Brittany direct to Provence that autumn:

And so, you cannot accept the idea of so long a journey? So, things are not working out as we had hoped they would? Well, then, my dear bonne, let me stay here, where I am faring very well, and I promise you that if you go to Paris, I will join you there, but I will not go there to wait for you because I would be doing for your sake what I would do under no other circumstances. That would bring on financial difficulties which could not be overcome in six months' time. I have arranged to set aside the revenues from my estates—whether to pay off my Paris creditors or the lods et ventes I owe—until after St. John's Day. By August 1, I will have all that behind me; from that time on, my income will be my own again, to do with as I please.*

To go deeper into debt would complicate my affairs for the rest of my life. By being patient for only a little longer, now, I will find myself in possession of a somewhat smaller income, but mine to use as I choose, whereas any other procedure would involve me in problems that could not be solved as long as I live. To sum it up, I positively do not want to borrow money. I will not go to Grignan because it is clear to see that I would tie you down. I will not go to Paris without you before August or September [1691] but, if you go there, I will promise you to go, too, and I will manage the impossible for your sake alone, but I will not go to spend five months in Paris, and then get back on my horse and set out on a second journey . . .

Mother and daughter had apparently reached an impasse on plans for the winter of 1690–91. As smooth as their relations had been over the past several years, this disagreement threatened to disrupt the *entente cordiale.* By September 17, Mme de Sévigné was in receipt of Mme de Grignan's reply to her letter of August 27, and promptly addressed a letter designed to heal the threatened breach:

You are angry at me, my bonne. You call my letters "bitches." You say that "I have taken what you wrote me the wrong way." We will discuss all this at Grignan—God willing!—a week after All Hallows' Eve! I think that I would win this case, as you did the Aiguebonne case, and that you would be condemned to an amend! You were under pressure from my "darling friends," as you call them. You wanted to make me give up the thought of going to Grignan in order to make me go to Paris; you succeeded, your arguments proving more convincing than

---

*St. John's Day falls on June 24.

you had expected! You made me think that you would be in Paris; I wanted to let you reach there before coming to see you. Save for that, I would not have considered going. You have a horror of the air of this region, while I do not. I suffered no ill effects from the winter last year; this year's would have been no different. My first reaction was to laugh about those voyages in Provence you wanted to take, because it would have been no misfortune for me to have spent that time with Monsieur de Grignan! But, upon reflection, I decided to write artlessly to tell you, as I did, what I had in mind, and then wait to see whether or not your case came to trial. I feared, as you did, that it might be postponed but, my bonne, since you have won it, and have changed your tune, have I shown even a moment's hesitation? Have I not—with a veritable joy—reinstated all my original plans? Have I not written to the Abbé Charrier to do the same? Are these plans not, once again, firm? . . . Have I not set October 3 as the day of my departure? Will I not arrive at Moulins on the fourteenth? . . . Will I not be in Lyon three days later, which will be something like the nineteenth? Will I not be able, after a short rest, to embark on the Rhône on the twenty-first? And to reach Grignan on the twenty-second? Will I not be in a transport of joy at seeing and embracing you? Will I not embrace the Count as well—and prove to him that I am no provincial? . . .

To make my happiness complete, my bonne, I received a letter from Mme de La Fayette—one written even before she had received my letter telling them of my plans—in which her advice to me was to go spend the winter in the beautiful land of Provence! Mme de Lavardin says the same thing! I am sending their letters on to you. They seem to me to have been aware of my intentions and, prompted by both courtesy and affection, they offer me the approval I seek before I ask for it.

Mme de Sévigné cared deeply about Mme de La Fayette's approval: "The better one knows her, the more one loves her," Mme de Sévigné said of her lifelong friend: "She is an amiable and an estimable woman, a woman one cannot but love, once one has had experience of her intelligence and her reason." Happily, Mme de La Fayette's letter written early in September told Mme de Sévigné everything she longed to hear:

You will have seen [she had written] by both my letter and Mme de Lavardin's that—since you were not coming to Paris—we wanted to see you go to Provence. That is the very best thing for you to do. The sun is far warmer there. And you will be in good company—even aside from that of Mme de Grignan, which is considerable—you will be in a large château with many people. All in all, to be there will be to be living!

By October 7, Mme de Sévigné was on her way, addressing a letter to her daughter, on that date, from Tours:

And here I am, my bonne, *in perfect health, and well pleased with travel by litter. It can go anywhere; one has fear of nothing. It is said that this method of travel is depressing; I find it wonderful because one need not be afraid.*

I slept the first night at Laval, then at Sablé, then at Lude, then here. Those are not barbaric names, but what is barbaric, my bonne, *is death. I wanted to walk, at night, at Lude . . .*

These lines were Mme de Sévigné's admission to her daughter that she had made a sentimental journey to one of the great châteaux of the Loire, that of the late Duke du Lude, late Grand Master of Artillery, a onetime suitor of Mme de Sévigné's, the one upon whom, in all probability—according to the Count de Bussy's scurrilous *Amorous History of the Gauls*—she had looked most favorably out of the many who had flocked about her in her days as a merry widow. Mme de Grignan had teased her mother about having made numerous visits to the Duke's house to inquire about his condition in the course of a grave illness he had suffered in 1680. Whether or not Mme de Sévigné had yielded to his advances, she evidently revelled in the memory of that brief but ardent interlude. She had gone out of her way to pause at his tomb:

I began [she wrote], at the church. There I found the poor Grand Master. It was sad! I carried my memories into his beautiful house. I wanted to familiarize myself with those magnificent terraces and with the air of a château which is infinitely magnificent. Everything weeps, everything shows a sad neglect. A hundred dead or dying orange-trees offer proof that five years have passed since they have seen either master or mistress.

I leave in an hour, my very dear bonne. *The weather is divine. I still hope to be in Moulins on the fourteenth.*

And here is the Archbishop of Tours coming to call on me. I am in a rush. And here's an ink spot on my paper! This will be my last letter sent via Paris, but I embrace you. And that's enough for now.

From Lyon, on October 19, she wrote:

I arrived here at noon, my bonne, *with my friend the Abbé Charrier, who has been of great assistance to me in every way over a route with which I was unfamiliar.*

I do not tell you that I love you, that I long for you. It seems to me that my footsteps will tell you that and, in the past few days, I have taken many a step! Tonight we hope for a letter from you telling us what day to expect your carriage at Robinet because, in truth, my very dear child, I suspect that the drive there, as short as it is, will be very inconvenient for you. Send me Pauline and her little nose, so that I can have some idea of how I get along with her. You must know that she is the one I worry about—nervous as to the impression she will have of me. You will find that difficult to believe when there are so many important persons who do me the honor of awaiting my arrival and of wishing for me. Nonetheless, it is true.

I shall stop now, and finish this letter later. I feel so perfectly well that I myself am surprised. I am not at all tired, and want only to board ship on Saturday or Sunday . . .

LIII

Yes, we are together, loving one another, embracing one another joyfully—I, thrilled to have my Mother come so courageously to join me from the ends of the earth, from the land of the setting sun to that of the rising sun! Only she in all the world would be capable of carrying out such an undertaking to be near her child!

Here is Mme de Grignan herself, for once, writing one of the few letters of hers that have come down to us, voicing her joy at the mother-daughter reunion—a letter written a few weeks after her mother's arrival at Grignan, and posted along with a letter of her mother's addressed to their cousin Philippe-Emmanuel de Coulanges, at that hour still in Rome with the Duke de Chaulnes.

Disembarking at the small Rhône River port of Robinet on October 24, involved in all the excitement of arrival, of reunion with her daughter and all the Grignans—male and female, young and old—at the château, Mme de Sévigné did not find time to write to her cousin the Count de Bussy-Rabutin until November 13:

When you see the date of this letter, my cousin, you will take me for a bird! I came bravely all the way from Brittany to Provence. If my daughter had been in Paris, I would have gone there but, knowing that she would spend the winter in this beautiful land, I decided to come here to spend it with her, to enjoy her bright sun, and then to return with her to Paris, next year. I decided that after having given sixteen months to my son, it would be only fair to give a few to my daughter, and this voyage which seemed so difficult to make was not too trying for me. It took me three weeks to make the journey, by litter and [by boat] on the Rhône. I even had time for a few days' rest, en route. And, finally, I was welcomed by Monsieur de Grignan and by my daughter, with an affection so cordial, with a joy and a gratitude so sincere that I found I had not travelled far enough to come to see such good people, and that the 150 leagues I had covered had not tired me in the least. This house is of such a grandeur, such a beauty, and of such magnificence in its furnishings that I must talk to you about it, someday.* I wanted to notify you of my change of abode so that you would no longer address me at Les Rochers, but here instead where I am basking in a sun capable of rejuvenation by its warmth. At our time of life, we should not neglect such small benefactions, my dear cousin.

We learned, the other day, of the death of Monsieur de Seignelay.† How young he was! What a fortune he possessed! What establishments! Nothing was lacking to his happiness. It seems to us that splendor itself is dead. What surprised us is that Mme de Seignelay should have renounced the common property because her husband owed five

---

*An inventory of the Château de Grignan furnishings is to be found in the Aix-en-Provence archives, but that of the château's precious objects is missing. The value of the furnishings of the château was established at 41,000 livres, a considerable amount.

†The Marquis de Seignelay, the Secretary of State for the Marine, was the son of the powerful Jean Baptiste Colbert, Minister of Commerce and Internal Affairs subsequent to the disgrace of Fouquet.

thousand. That shows that vast revenues are useless if one spends two or three times as much. In short, my cousin, death is the great equalizer. That is where we catch up with the lucky ones. Death deflates their pride and joy, and thereby consoles those less fortunate. A word or two of Christian philosophy would not be amiss at this juncture, but I don't want to make this into a sermon; I want it to be a cordial letter to my dear cousin to ask him for news of himself and of his dear daughter, to embrace them both with all my heart, and to assure them of the esteem and services of Mme de Grignan and her husband . . . and to urge them to keep on loving me—there is no point in changing after all these years!

A letter written that same month (November, 1690) to Philippe Moulceau bubbles over with a joy as exuberant as that which suffuses the previous-quoted letter to the Count de Bussy. She and her friend from Montpellier* had apparently been out of touch for some time, but now that she was back in his neighborhood again, she was eager to reestablish contact. "And where do you think I am, Monsieur?" she asked:

Had you not heard that I was in Brittany? Corbinelli should have let you know. Having spent sixteen months there with my son, I decided that the thing to do was to spend the winter here with my daughter. The idea of this 150-league journey seemed, at first, a castle in the air, but love made it so easy that I finally managed to make it between October 3 and 24, when I arrived at the port of Robinet where I was received with open arms by Mme de Grignan, and with such joy, such affection and such gratitude that I felt I had come neither soon enough nor far enough. After that, Monsieur, can you say that affection is not a wondrous thing? It is that which has made me so often think of you, made me hope to see you here once more in my life.† We will be here all the winter and all the summer. If you cannot find a moment to come to see me, I will think you have forgotten me. You will not recognize this house, it has been so much embellished, but you will find the master and mistress as full of esteem for you as ever—and me, Monsieur, imbued with a friendship strong enough to enrage our friend,‡ but well-deserving of your visit.

*Moulceau was a presiding judge in the Montpellier Tax Court.
†Moulceau had visited at Grignan during Mme de Sévigné's visit to Provence in 1672–3.
‡Corbinelli, through whom Mme de Sévigné had probably met Moulceau originally, pretended to be jealous of him.

In mid-November, Mme de Sévigné and the Grignans left the château for Lambesc, where the Assembly of the Communities of Provence would convene between November 16 and November 29, the annual autumnal session over which the Count de Grignan, in his role of Governor, would preside.

In a letter datelined "At Lambesc, this December 1, 1690," Mme de Sévigné made reply to the Count de Bussy's letter of November 19 (which had been written in reply to hers of the thirteenth:

> I am very glad, my dear cousin, that you approve of the voyage I made from Brittany to Provence. Had I made the trip solely for the sun, it would have been well worth the effort. One cannot come from too far away to spend the winter in this land; it is certainly the most agreeable thing in the world. In addition to that, la belle Madelonne is here—a circumstance which means more to me than all the sweetness of spring.
>
> We will spend the winter very quietly at Grignan. Monsieur de Grignan will go to Paris when he has recovered from a fever and a violent colic which struck him here ten days ago. He sends you a thousand greetings, and my daughter as many fond messages. As for me, my dear cousin, you know how I feel about you. It is too late to change that ... If you wish sometimes to write to me, address your letters to me, "At Grignan, via Montélimar." They will reach me, and bring me great joy.*

Sunday, December 1, 1690, must have found Mme de Sévigné at leisure in Lambesc, for she wrote still another letter on that day, the second addressed to her cousin Coulanges, who had spent more than a year in Rome with Ambassador de Chaulnes:

> What has happened to us, my darling cousin? It has been about a thousand years since I have heard from you! I wrote you last from Les Rochers ... since then, not a word from you. We must start all over again, now that I am in your neighborhood. What do you think of my courage? It is a fine thing to have! After having spent sixteen months in Brittany with my son, I decided that I owed a visit to my daughter, too, knowing that she was not going to Paris this winter, and I have been so warmly welcomed by her and by Monsieur de Grignan that if

---

*The couriers passed through Montélimar with the mail; a rural mail carrier brought it from there to the Château de Grignan.

I had suffered some fatigue, I would have completely forgotten about it, but I felt only joy and pleasure at finding myself reunited with them. This voyage was disapproved by neither Mme de Chaulnes nor Mme de La Fayette nor Mme de Lavardin, of whom I voluntarily sought counsel, so that nothing has been lacking to the happiness and pleasure of this voyage. You will provide the finishing touch by coming back via Grignan where we will be awaiting you.

The Assembly of our little Estates is over. We are here alone, waiting until Monsieur de Grignan is well enough to go on to Grignan and, from there, if he is able, to Paris ... We will stop only momen- tarily, at Aix to see our little Grignan nun,* and a few days later we will be at Grignan where we will spend the winter, and where our little Colonel, whose regiment is in winter quarters near Valence, will come to spend six weeks with us. Alas, that time will go by all too quickly! I begin to sigh sadly at seeing it rush by so fast. I see it, and know the consequences. You are not yet at an age, my cousin, for making such sad reflections.†

With the voluminous mother-daughter correspondence suddenly at an end, with only an occasional, casual letter addressed by Mme de Sévigné to a friend or relative, a kind of silence reigns where once there was a babel of familiar voices. The close contact with the households of Les Rochers, Grignan and Carnavalet to which the reader has become accustomed, across the years, is suddenly lost. Henceforward, he catches only a word, here and there; only a glimpse, now and then, of this cast of characters whom—in the course of some twenty years—he has come to know so intimately.

Mme de Sévigné may have earlier waxed lyrical about winter in that southern clime, but January of 1691 came roaring into Provence like a lion— "a killing cold," Mme de Sévigné would call it: "I warn you that the winter here is more cruel than anywhere else in the world!" The Château de Grignan, on its rocky eminence, buffeted by storm and wind, with only great, gaping fireplaces to warm its vast and drafty chambers, must have been miserably uncomfortable. The Grignans had never spent a winter there, were there in the winter of 1690–91 not by choice but out of stark necessity—and Mme de Sévigné with them. Mme de Grignan, in a letter addressed to Coulanges in December, in anticipation of his visit to Grignan,

---

*Twenty-year-old Marie-Blanche de Grignan had been placed at the Convent in Aix at age five; she had taken the veil in 1688, at age sixteen, at which time her father had borrowed 4,000 livres to be contributed to the convent for her lifetime maintenance.

†Coulanges was fifty-seven, Mme de Sévigné sixty-four, in 1690.

confessed, "I warm my rooms as best I can but, to you, coming from Rome, they will seem like ice."

The advent of spring must have come as a great relief.* In April of 1691, French armies were on the move again, the King himself leading the attack on Mons. It was Louis XIV in person, as Mme de Sévigné wrote Coulanges on April 10, who "took Mons with a force of 100,000 men, in a most heroic manner, dashing here and there—everywhere!—exposing himself all too often to danger."

She had news that day for Coulanges from another front, much nearer home: Maréchal de Catinat's army—to which the Grignan regiment was attached—had laid siege to Nice on March 26, the town capitulating as soon as the trench was opened; the citadel surrendering on April 2. Mme de Sévigné could take personal pride in that engagement:

Our little Marquis took part in the siege of Nice, like an adventurer vago di fama.† Monsieur [the Maréchal] de Catinat put him in command of the cavalry for several days ... but that did not stop him from dashing about, into the thick of the battle, coming under enemy fire which was very heavy at first ... We now await the arrival of that little Colonel of ours who comes to make ready to go to Piedmont, for the expedition to Nice was only a prelude to the full-scale attack. He will no longer be here by the time you come through, but do you know whom you will find here? My son, who is coming to spend the summer with us ... coming ahead of his Governor,‡ but on the heels of his Mother.

Apropos of mother and son, do you know, my dear cousin, that I have been, these past ten or twelve days, in a state of sorrow from which you alone can rescue me, while I write to you. I am speaking of the grave illness of the dowager Mme de Lavardin, my close, my long-time friend. That woman of such good, sound mind, that illustrious widow who had gathered us all up under her wing, that most merito-rious person was suddenly stricken by a kind of apoplexy. She is coma-tose, she is paralyzed ... All in all, my child, I could not have suffered a greater loss in the realm of friendship. I feel it keenly ... Hers is a recognized merit; everyone is interested, as in a public loss. Imagine how her friends must feel! ... Adieu, my dear cousin. I can write no

---

*There are no letters between January 19 and April 10, 1691.

†An Italian phrase meaning "avid for glory."

‡Charles de Sévigné's Governor was the Duke de Chaulnes, whose long absence in Italy had not cost him his title of Governor of Brittany.

more. I have an aching heart. If I had begun with this sad subject, I would never have had the courage to go on with this letter . . .

Mme de Sévigné was vociferous in her complaints about the postal service to Rome: "There is simply neither rhyme nor reason to the operation of the mails," she declared in April. "I cannot understand why you don't receive our letters," she wrote Coulanges on June 12, "but I understand still less why you don't elect a pope!"*

To see how you started out, it would have appeared that there was nothing easier, but we see now that, to the contrary, there is nothing in the world so difficult. I think that, finally, the Holy Ghost will have to take a hand. So, hurry up, and bring that about, because we are very eager to see you . . .

There is, at this point, a hiatus of a month in the correspondence. Perhaps Grignan was besieged by visitors from June 12 to July 12, 1691. Perhaps there was a series of banquets in the stately Hall of the Adhémars and a series of *fêtes champêtres*—highly elegant picnics—at the Grotto of La Rochecourbière, at the edge of the village of Grignan, whither the guests of the château were conveyed by carriage to be entertained *al fresco*, to the sound of music by the Count de Grignan's own excellent orchestra. However it was, Mme de Sévigné allowed her correspondence to lag for at least a month, that summer. The next letter of hers to be found in the collection is dated July 12 and addressed to the Count de Bussy-Rabutin, with whom she had been temporarily out of touch:

I received your letter of May 29. You had addressed it to me in Paris, in care of poor Beaulieu, whom you knew. I must tell you, my dear cousin, that that young woman and her husband, who was a bright fellow, are both dead within six weeks of one another.† I deeply regret the loss because they were people who served me well . . .

It has been eight months since I arrived here. I wrote to tell you about the courage I displayed in coming here from Brittany. I have not regretted it.

---

*A pope would finally be chosen on July 11, after five months of conclave: Cardinal Pignatelli, who would become Pope Innocent XII. Alexander VIII had died in 1691 after two years as Supreme Pontiff (1689–91).

†Beaulieu, Mme de Sévigné's maître d'hôtel, was married to Hélène, her maid.

*"I would do it again if I had it to do."**

My daughter is charming, as you know. She loves me deeply. Monsieur de Grignan is possessed of all those qualities which make his society agreeable. Their château is very beautiful, very magnificent. The house has a grandeur about it, they live extremely well, and one sees a thousand people come and go. We have spent the winter uneventfully save for the illness of the master of the house—a fever which not even quinine could alleviate . . . But, at last, he is well again. He made a trip to Aix where they were thrilled to see him again.

If Mme de Sévigné, in her letter to the Count de Bussy, played up the grandeur of loftily perched Grignan, it was to play down the financial quagmire into which that house was precipitately sinking. The situation was critical, that summer of 1691, to judge by several letters in the hand of Mme de Grignan, addressed to Pontchartrain, the Comptroller General, and beseeching relief for her husband, the Lieutenant-Governor of Provence, in the desperate financial straits in which he then found himself. Mme de Sévigné shows herself again as ambivalent about the Grignan splendors: they never failed to impress her, ruinous though she knew them to be.

"On the other hand," Mme de Sévigné's letter of July 12 to Bussy continues, "my son has come here from Brittany to take the [mineral] waters in this country, where the good company—which he augments by his presence—does him more good than any other remedy."

So, we are all here together. There is one little Grignan whom you do not know, who holds her own very well with all the rest. She is sixteen years old; she is pretty; she is witty, and we will see to it that she is more so still. All of this adds up to a very good life—even too good, perhaps—because I find that the days pass so quickly—and the months and the years!—that I, my dear cousin, can no longer hold onto them. Time flies by and sweeps me off, despite myself, and that thought frightens me greatly. You can guess the reason why.

The little Grignan spent the winter with us. He had a fever in the spring. He left here only two weeks ago to go to rejoin his regiment . . . The date of our return to Paris is still among the secrets of Providence. My daughter is much occupied by the affairs of her house, where she accomplishes marvels . . .

You are planning to go to Fontainebleau to pay your court, as you

*Mme de Sévigné is quoting from Corneille's *Le Cid*.

are very wise to do. You would be very fortunate to please His Majesty, in whatever fashion that might be. I received your letter of December 10 in February, by then so out of date that I thought it best not to reply to it. I ask your pardon, and do not love you any less. So, here is a letter to put us back in touch, and to pick up the thread of our interrupted correspondence.

I saw Monsieur Larrey here, the son of our old friend Lenet with whom we used to laugh so hilariously, for there was never a youth so blithe as ours.

Adieu, my dear cousin, I ask pardon of a great wit like you for a letter so pedestrian as this, but sometimes we must write one like that.

A letter written by Mme de Sévigné, dated July 24 and addressed to Coulanges in Rome, was in reply to a letter from him in which he had described a long and painful attack of gout. "It almost made me cry," she said sympathetically:

Impossible to think of you sick in bed, with pain in every part of your little body, in all your joints, with your nerves inflamed, unable to move, hand or foot! The thought is killing us! But when we learn that, miserable as you are, my poor cousin, you have written a song about your misery . . . then we are greatly relieved, for that proves that you have not lost your jollity. That siege of gout has succeeded only in causing you a few melancholy moments . . . but has failed to make any permanent impression.

Monsieur de Chaulnes wrote to us on the fifteenth, by the same courier who carried the news of the election. His first thought is of coming to see us; he will spend two weeks here. So, that is how it stands, my cousin: you are well again, you are leaving, you are coming here. A thousand embraces!

With the installation of Innocent XII as Supreme Pontiff, the French Ambassador was preparing to leave Rome for Paris—via Grignan—with his friend Coulanges in tow. Mme de Sévigné, nonetheless, addressed another letter to her cousin in Rome as late as August 14: "I was eager to hear what you thought about Monsieur de Pomponne's return to the Ministry. Here, we all rejoice at the news!"

As well they might. The Marquis de Pomponne, after years of exile and disgrace, was back in favor, named a Minister of State, restored to the precincts of power in which the Grignans rejoiced to find a friend.

Joy reigned at Grignan in October in response to word that Coulanges could be expected to reach Marseille on the eleventh. Charles de Sévigné set out at once to meet his genial cousin there, and escort him back to Grignan. The Duke de Chaulnes joined them at the château a week later.

Mme de Sévigné, in a letter to the Count de Bussy dated October 27, gave him the news, listing the persons at the château who asked to be remembered to him: "Here are greetings," she wrote, "from Monsieur de Grignan, from my daughter, from my son, and from Monsieur de Coulanges who is on his way home from Rome."

Coulanges and the Duke de Chaulnes, making their way from Grignan to Paris in November, were not long on the road ahead of their hosts: Mme de Sévigné, the Count and Countess de Grignan and Pauline arrived in the capital sometime in December. No exact date for their arrival is to be found in the correspondence, but it could not have been earlier than the fifteenth in view of the fact that the Count is known to have presided over the Assembly of the Communities of Provence in session at Lambesc, November 13–27.

"We arrived here, my dear cousin, at the end of the year," is how Mme de Sévigné states it in a letter addressed to Bussy from Paris on January 27, 1692, "in time for Monsieur de Grignan to be installed as a Chevalier,* but not in time to have the honor and the pleasure of seeing you."

I remembered the line from the opera: "Even had I made haste, I would not have arrived in time."† Actually, you left when you had said you would,‡ and I know, through Mme de Montataire,§ that you are in your châteaux or at Autun, enjoying in peace and quiet the grace the King has shown you.‖

Monsieur de Grignan and my daughter ask me to assure you that they are your humble servants. They have with them here a little daughter who, although lacking her mother's beauty, has so well mitigated and softened the Grignan characteristics that she is really very

---

*The installation of the three Chevaliers (including the Count de Grignan) who had been unable to attend the ceremony of the preceding year, took place at Versailles on New Year's Day, 1692. These were Chevaliers of St. Michael, Order of the Holy Ghost.

†The line is from Quinault's *Alceste.*

‡Bussy, in his letter of November 5, 1691, had advised Mme de Sévigné that he would be leaving Paris before the bad winter weather set in.

§Mme de Montataire, a daughter of Bussy's, was the Canoness of Remiremont.

‖Louis XIV had granted a handsome and much-needed pension to Bussy when he paid his court to the monarch at Fontainebleau in October.

pretty. You will judge for yourself, some day, I hope—as I hope, too, that you will go on always loving me as much as I do you.

Mme de Sévigné and Mme de Grignan, back in the capital after years in the provinces, were getting back into the swim. "We found, my daughter and I," Mme de Sévigné admitted to Bussy, "that we were a little rusty, but we begin to feel at home again, and our friends are eager to know us again." There was danger in burying oneself in the wilds of Brittany or Provence for years on end, as these two sophisticates, these two habitués of Paris society and the Versailles Court well knew. They were grateful to breathe the air of Paris again; to Parisiennes like them, it was the breath of life.

LIV

With Mme de Sévigné and Mme de Grignan together in Paris, together at the Hôtel Carnavalet, during the years 1692 and 1693—with their correspondence at an end—little is known of their lives at that period. Few if any letters survive from other correspondences. The only letter known to have been written by Mme de Sévigné between January and October, 1692, is addressed to the Count de Bussy-Rabutin, and dated April 12. It is brief and, for once, of little interest to anyone save a contemporary familiar with the ramifications of Paris society and the Court: "If you come here, this fall, my dear cousin, I will truly rejoice," she wrote, "but a lot can happen between now and then."

Everywhere, armies are on the march ... The King himself will lead one of his. The names of the ladies who are to accompany him have already been announced. His [Cabinet] Ministers will also be included in the journey. May God bring the war to a successful conclusion for France, one to redound to the glory of the King!

Bussy, an excellent correspondent, shot back a letter dated April 17, but six months and more would pass before Mme de Sévigné would again take up her pen to reply to him, datelining her letter, "Paris, this last day of

October 1692." The first lines were addressed to Bussy's daughter the
Countess de Dalet*:

> *There appeared before me, my dear niece, a very handsome boy, well
> built, with a noble mien, and from the few words he spoke, I would
> wager that he has great wit, and that you and my cousin have taken a
> hand in his education and supervised the formation of his morals. He
> is at the perfect age to enter the Academy† ... I will keep my eye on
> things and report to you. Let me know if your son's estate is substan-
> tial, for it seems to me that, thanks to his great name alone, arrange-
> ments for his marriage on that basis should be begun.*
>
> *And next I turn to my poor cousin whose health does not permit
> his coming to Paris, this winter. You are right, Monsieur the Count,
> not to come here if you are ailing. You will make a speedy recovery in
> the peace and quiet of your château, and you will still find us all here
> in the spring. I applaud my niece for not leaving you ... I beg you to
> keep me posted about your health in which I take a great interest for
> so many reasons.*

Not one but two letters to Burgundy went out from Mme de Sévigné's
desk in October, the second addressed to the Countess de Guitaut, widow
of the Count de Guitaut, whose death had occurred in 1685. "I have counted
on my fingers," Mme de Sévigné wrote on October 29, "and it seems to
me, Madame, that you should have arrived home by now."

> *I was just about to send to your house to inquire when a very nice
> person, coming up to me here on the street by my house, mentioned
> your name and, as if by inspiration, told me exactly what I wanted to
> know. So, there you are back in your beautiful château, with your
> handsome children, your chapter church, your canons ... and grain in
> your granaries, despite which you may perhaps cry famine, although it
> will be your fault if you do not make money, with prices as high as
> they are everywhere.*
>
> *However, Madame, there is not a day that passes that I do not
> miss you; above all, in the morning at our Mass, where I thought*

---

*In 1690, Bussy's daughter the Countess de Coligny took the title of Countess de Dalet, having
inherited the lands of Dalet and Malintras at the death of her father-in-law.
†There were, at that time, two Academies in Paris, offering education in the sciences and the arts
appropriate to young noblemen. Bussy's grandson was sixteen years old in 1692.

myself fortunate to see you for a moment and to be only two steps
away . . .

A month later, in November, 1692, Mme de Sévigné—having had no
reply from her Burgundian neighbor—wrote again, this time to inquire why:

*I wrote you a little note, my dear Madame, to ask about your health,
and how it felt to be back in your château. You have made no reply,
but I learned from the young lady who lives at your house that you
were suffering from severe headaches. That is all too good an excuse
[for not writing], but I hope that you are now free of them and that,
with a kindness worthy of a Mme de Guitaut who reigns supreme in
our region, you will be good enough and charitable enough to take the
time to listen to what Hébert, my collections agent, and Boucard, my
former superintendent, can tell you about how I am to be paid by the
said Hébert the more than 12,000 livres due me for the year 1691,
along with all of 1692 . . . When you have made a judgment in the
matter, I will send you my thanks, and ask you a thousand pardons . . .*

Much as Mme de Sévigné might deplore the Countess de Guitaut's
headaches, she would spare her not one detail relative to agricultural and
marketing problems at her Burgundian properties of Bourbilly and Sauvignon. Her correspondence with that lady accelerated—to, at times, a weekly
basis. The *Letters* list twenty-four letters to Mme de Guitaut over a period
of sixteen months, between October, 1692, and February, 1694. Laced though
it was with lavish compliments, spiced though it was with choice tidbits of
Paris gossip and ecclesiastical reports calculated best to appeal to the recipient, this was essentially a business correspondence. It is interesting to note
that during the lifetime of the Count de Guitaut, Mme de Sévigné—while
never failing to include greetings to the Countess—addressed all her letters
to the Count. It was the Count with whom she had laughed and talked and
drunk—the Countess, perhaps, more at ease in the chapel or the nursery or
the countinghouse than in the library or the salon.

Mme de Sévigné's letters to Mme de Guitaut, during the years 1692–4,
are filled to overflowing with thanks for past favors and appeals for new
ones.

*"I ask you a thousand pardons, and go right on burdening you with
my miserable affairs." "Are you still suffering from headaches? I pity
you, and have great hesitation in importuning you about my affairs."*

453

"Really, now, are you not the kindest and most charitable person in the world? For, it is surely charity on your part to help me out of the plight I am in." "Are you not too kind, my dear Madame, to involve yourself in all this tedious business of mine?" "Good Lord, you are a hundred leagues beyond me when it comes to business acumen!" "I am thrilled to hear that you will handle my affairs along with your own." "I place all my hope in you." "This, my dear Madame, is what I expect of your charity, that you see to it that I do not have to wait too long in January to get my money!"

To read Mme de Sévigné's exchange of letters with Mme de Guitaut is to see the charming Marquise in a less attractive light than usual. If she appears here to exploit a friendship, it can only be said in her defense that she felt herself helpless and desperate. ("It does not do to be poor in this good town [of Paris]!" she remarked bitterly in late 1692 to her correspondent in Burgundy.) Far removed from her properties—the revenues from which represented a substantial portion of her annual income—Mme de Sévigné found herself at a terrible disadvantage, that of the absentee landlord. She sorely needed someone *in situ*—especially at a time of agricultural crisis—to assist her with personnel, with supervision and with collections, and clutched at Mme de Guitaut as that someone.

Mme de Sévigné was a clinging vine, clinging first—and fast!—to her uncle the *Bien Bon* for guidance and assistance in business affairs; in Brittany, in recent years, it had been the Abbé Charrier about whom she had woven tendrils of dependence; now, it would be the Countess de Guitaut to whom she would attach herself in Burgundy.

In January, 1693, she wrote Mme de Guitaut that her collections agent "must close the deal, must send me all he can, as soon as he can! I am in great need!"

I assure you that it appears that the princes' only interest is in making war. There is no talk of peace. So, Madame, let us sell our grain, as soon as the Intendants permit.* As I wrote you, everyone advises this. It is now a question of when we are permitted to do so. Let us lose no time when that permission comes. The sooner we can sell, the better. That is the advice my friends here give me. Grains will never go higher than they are now, and could go down.

---

*With the nation at war and harvests poor, the government took measures to halt rising prices of grain.

When Mme de Sévigné wrote to the Countess de Guitaut on Wednesday, June 3, 1693, it had not—for once—to do with business. It was, instead, in response to a letter of condolence from the Countess. Mme de Sévigné's letter begins:

I had left you to your silence, Madame, out of respect and consideration for your poor head, contenting myself with obtaining news about you elsewhere. You could not have broken that silence, Madame, on an occasion more significant to me.

The occasion so significant to Mme de Sévigné was the death of Mme de La Fayette, which had occurred on May 24 of that year. "You well knew Mme de La Fayette's great merit," Mme de Sévigné wrote in reply, "knew it either through personal experience or through me or through your friends. On that score, you could have believed all you heard. She was worthy of your friendship, and I considered myself very fortunate to have been loved by her."

("You can believe me, my dear one," Mme de La Fayette had written Mme de Sévigné in a note dated January 24, 1692, "when I tell you that you are the person I have most truly loved in all my life.")

"There never came so much as the smallest cloud to shadow our friendship," Mme de Sévigné's letter to Mme de Guitaut continued:

Long years of intimacy had never dulled my appreciation of her merit. The pleasure I took in her company remained strong and fresh. If I was very attentive to her, it was at the prompting of my heart rather than at the dictate of the conventions to which friendship obliges. I was assured that I provided her her tenderest consolation, and so it has been for forty years. That is a shockingly large number, but it accurately dates our liaison. Her infirmities over the past two years had become extreme. I always defended her when people said that she was mad to refuse to go out of her house. She was pervaded by a mortal sorrow. "What madness!" it was said of her on this point, too. "Was she not the most fortunate woman in the world?" She could not deny that, but as I said to those persons who were so precipitate in their judgment, "Mme de La Fayette is not mad!" and stood my ground. Alas, the poor woman is now only too well justified: she had to die to prove that she was not crazy to be sad and to refuse to go out. One of her kidneys had a stone in it; the other was purulent. Scarcely a state in which one could go about. There were two polyps on her heart, and

the point was withered. Was all this not reason enough for the desola-
tion of spirit of which she complained? Her colon was hard and full of
wind and the colic of which she constantly complained. That was the
condition of the poor woman who used to say, "Someday they will
find"—precisely what they found!

In other words, it had required an autopsy to prove to the world that
Mme de La Fayette had not been a hypochondriac.

"Thus, Madame," Mme de Sévigné concluded, "she was right while
she was alive; she was right after she was dead; she was never without that
divine reason of hers which was her outstanding characteristic."

The spring of 1693 had proved a season of mourning, of profound grief
for Mme de Sévigné. The death of Mme de La Fayette in May had been
preceded by that of the Count de Bussy-Rabutin in April. These were two
grievous losses she had to sustain, not to mention that of Mme de Lavardin
who was lost to her as well—in a state of living death since the spring of
1691. These had been the three persons nearest and dearest to Mme de
Sévigné's heart, outside her immediate family and that of the Coulanges.

The year 1693 was to prove in many respects an unfortunate one for
Mme de Sévigné: still another blow was in store for her, that summer, when
a wind and hail storm destroyed her crops in Burgundy and damaged her
château at Bourbilly. "Who would have dreamed that on July 7th—once all
the heavy rains were over—that one was not safe? And that there would
come the kind of storm that would cost one all one's crops—severing the
stalks of the grain, blighting the hay, breaking windows and roof-tiles on
one's château?" It was to Mme de Guitaut that Mme de Sévigné wrote in a
wail on July 24, concluding with the lines, "If I receive no revenues at the
Christmas term or at the St. John's, I will be in serious—and I do not
exaggerate when I say 'serious'—difficulties, but I will resign myself to it if
Mme de Guitaut tells me it must be so."

In the summer of 1693, there was occasion for national mourning and
for national celebration in which personal problems were, at least temporarily, put aside: "My God, Madame," Mme de Sévigné's letter of August 7
began, "how many dead, how many wounded, how many condolence calls
to make, and how that battle which was at first seen as an advantage that
cost us too dear, now proves to have been a signal victory!" (It was the
battle of Neerwinden, in Brabant, of which Mme de Sévigné wrote, where
the Maréchal de Luxembourg had defeated the coalition forces under the
Prince of Orange and the Elector of Bavaria.)

We have taken so many cannons [the letter continued], so many kettle-
drums, so many flags, so many standards, so many prisoners that never

has a pitched battle in the last fifty years produced so many trophies. The army of the Prince of Orange is no longer intact, there are only remnants scattered here and there, so that Monsieur de Luxembourg could—if he would—march on Brussels, unopposed. In a word, all the armies are on the move. We tremble for the Marquis de Grignan, who is in Germany where, doubtlessly, Monseigneur [the Dauphin] intends to give battle.

The Marquis's regiment, as it developed, was not to become involved in the campaign that summer, but Mme de Sévigné could not but have been relieved to see the year 1693 come to an end, and the year 1694 begin; "And here is another one, my dear Madame, I see beginning," she wrote to Mme de Guitaut on "This first day of the year 1694":

What I wish, above all, for myself, is that state of grace of which I am so in need that I may love God better than anything else in the world, convinced as I am that that alone is desirable, and disdaining to desire all else. But to get around to you—for, indeed, I think of you—what I wish for you is the continuation of that state of grace you already enjoy, and its augmentation, since it cannot be too great.

But 1694 dawned little more propitiously than 1693 for Mme de Sévigné. She reeled in shock at the announcement of a tax to be levied on her Burgundian estates by the high-handed parish priest at Bourbilly. "A decree from on high has been issued, Madame," she wrote indignantly to Mme de Guitaut on February 2,

by Monsieur the Abbé Tribolet, who taxes me twenty bushels per month to be given to the poor of my villages. He does not specify that it is until the harvest only, but I suppose that is what he means, for it would be a strange thing and reduce me to the condition of those to whom I am supposed to give, were it to go on for long. He assures me that if I make appeal to your tribunal, I will not get off more lightly. That does not prevent me from trying while submitting myself wholly to your ruling. Consider, then, my dear Madame, whether a person who has not fared too well in the revenues from her properties, a person who is not without debt, and who can scarcely see her way clear to the end of the year, should give blind obedience to a parish priest ... You have only to command, my dear Madame, and to say what you wish me to contribute each month, and it will be done.

Without meaning to brag, I will point out that I have various small charities to which I am obliged to contribute here in this part of the world but, no matter, you have only to speak, and you will be promptly obeyed. That is the reply I make to my parish priest . . .

Mme de Guitaut made her pronouncement, and Mme de Sévigné made meek rejoinder on February 12:

How wholeheartedly I obey you, Madame, and how touched I am by the stories you tell me about those poor people who are dying of hunger! I could tell you stories more pitiful still,* and many of them, but one must address oneself primarily to those whom one can and should help, and since it is not easy to live on hope under such conditions, I send you a letter for Lapierre† [instructing him] to give Monsieur, the parish priest—to whom I am writing—twenty bushels of wheat and rye, half of one, half of the other.

Meanwhile, she inquired piteously on February 25, could not Mme de Guitaut use her good offices to ensure that the payments due her by her farmer and her agent were forthcoming? (They were "rascals who enraged me," she fumed.) "And I cannot wait until Easter," she insisted, "because my need is as urgent as that of the parish poor to whom I donate the grain! . . . Finally, Madame, have pity on me, give me some crumb of comfort, or exhort me to fasting in order to diminish my needs."

For some sixteen months—from October, 1692, to February, 1694—it had been Mme de Guitaut alone to whom Mme de Sévigné had addressed herself by letter. Save for these two dozen letters, dealing primarily with agricultural and financial problems at Bourbilly, the Hôtel Carnavalet was shrouded in silence. What little light is shed on the households there—and it is very little, indeed—comes from this same series of letters to Mme de Guitaut.

Then, suddenly, on March 29, 1694, the correspondence between Mme de Sévigné and Mme de Grignan was resumed. After a Paris sojourn of three years and three months, Mme de Grignan journeyed back, with her daughter Pauline and a large entourage, to Provence to join her husband

---

*Things were worse in Paris than in the provinces, according to a letter of Mme de Sévigné's to Mme de Guitaut in November, 1693: "If I were in Brittany or Provence or Époisses, I assure you, Madame, I would never come here."

†Lapierre was the man to whom Mme de Sévigné had given a contract to farm her Bourbilly property.

who had preceded her there.* For mother and daughter, this separation was to be their ninth—and last—and brief.

Mme de Sévigné's first letter to her daughter in 1694, written on the very day her daughter departed Paris, is missing from the collection found at Grignan; the first letter on record is dated "Monday, March 29, at Paris," and begins:

I wrote you on Friday, my dear bonne, addressing the letter to Briare. All I could talk about was the sadness and sorrow I felt—despite myself—at parting, and of how I dreaded coming back to this house. I told you how distressed I was, and that if I could not look forward to going to join you momentarily—and it will only be a moment until I do!—I would fear for this perfect health of mine which you so prize. I could talk of nothing else, and it was in that frame of mind that I received your letter from Nemours, last night—your first, I think—in which I could not find a word about what we suffered at parting. Monsieur the Chevalier noticed this, too, but at that very moment, your letter from Plessis came into our hands, and there we found precisely what we had been wishing for. You forget nothing, my bonne, of what is pleasing. You express such devotion that while already loving you more than anything in the world, one finds that one does not love you well enough! . . . I will take your advice, my dear bonne, and follow the one I love. My only thought, now, is to prepare to leave early in May. Monsieur the Chevalier would like to make it earlier but, in truth, I cannot do it without a haste which would detract from the pleasure of my departure. You know that I do not lack the courage to go to find you.

Paris news takes up pages and pages of this letter:

I dined Saturday at the Abbé Pelletier's . . . Monsieur du Coudray was there . . . I dined yesterday at the Duchess du Lude's; she sends you fondest greetings . . . Monsieur de Chaulnes is back . . . Mme de Chaulnes and Rochon will return next week. I went, after dinner, to Mme de Verneuil's, who has finally arrived, and to the Abbé Arnauld's where I

---

*The Count de Grignan had evidently gone regularly to Provence to perform various gubernatorial duties during the three years the Grignan family had remained in Paris. Dangeau's *Journal* notes that he had presided over the Assembly at Lambesc in the autumn of 1692, and had been granted an extra 12,000 francs by the King "in reward for his good services that year."

met Monsieur and Mme de Pomponne, Mme de Vins, Mademoiselle Félicité and Monsieur du Coudray . . . [Etcetera, etcetera . . .]

"I pity you, my *bonne*," the letter went on, "for having had to leave your Marquis.* Such an adieu that was! I thought he should have gone to Grignan. My dear Pauline, I kiss your pretty cheeks. No one has ever left so universally fine a reputation here as you have . . ."

Mme de Sévigné's last words, of course, were for her daughter: "You are our soul, my dear *bonne*. We would not know how to live without you."

Ten days later,† she wrote:

As for me, my bonne, *I am determined not to allow myself to be sad or blue. I think you were perfectly right to go. You had a valid reason [for going], one you had forgotten, and one that precluded our objections. And, then, you are going to see Monsieur de Grignan; you go running to him, and we will come running after you! The only thing I have to do now is to pay off those small accounts that I have been struggling with, and then get ready, by slow degrees, to leave in early May. So, you can see, my bonne, that there is absolutely no time to miss you—that would slow up my departure! When sadness overtakes me—at the sight of your apartment or on my return to mine—when I feel pangs of pain at no longer seeing you, no longer hearing that charming woman who fills and lights up all our lives, who is so essential to our family circle and whom I love so naturally, I banish such thoughts from my mind, and remind myself that I am going soon to join her, that everything I do is toward that end. Now, my dear bonne, that is my present state of mind.*

Easter in 1694 fell on April 11. Mme de Sévigné feared that Mme de Grignan might find it difficult to observe Lent properly in the course of her travels: "I hope you have obtained permission everywhere along the way to eat fresh eggs,"‡ she wrote on March 31: "I am afraid of carp; they are bony."

---

*The Marquis de Grignan went from Paris to Besançon to assemble his regiment in preparation for joining the army of Maréchal de Lorges in May.

†A ten-day hiatus in this correspondence between Mme de Sévigné and Mme de Grignan was unlikely. Thirteen of Mme de Sévigné's letters during this brief separation in 1694 are deemed to have been lost or misplaced, and thus to be missing from the collection at Grignan.

‡Dietary dispensations had to be obtained from local bishops.

Corbinelli is thrilled that you liked his book* [that letter continued]. He sends you all kind of messages telling you how he adores you. I always tell him that you would love to have him at Grignan. He dined with Monsieur the Chevalier; since it was not a fast day, they could have a young hare from Bâville. As for me, I had a noble fish, and I sometimes invite guests to dine—not as splendidly as one dines at Monsieur du Coudray's, but all too splendidly for someone whose crops were hail-damaged, like mine.

Mme de Sévigné's letter of April 19 began with an inquiry concerning the whereabouts of Monsieur de Grignan, who had been obliged to leave his château to go on patrol along the coast when an Anglo-Dutch fleet suddenly appeared in the Mediterranean, posing a threat to Provence.

I believe I am right, my bonne, in thinking that, by now, you can give Monsieur de Grignan a hug for me. The miracle just wrought by Heaven in the destruction of that fleet which was on the verge of picking up those [Piedmontese] mountain troops to turn them loose to ravage Provence convinces me that Monsieur de Grignan has returned to his château where he surely found a happy company.

It was not until today that Monsieur the Chevalier deigned to confirm to me that we would positively leave together. I was really overjoyed, and make ready to make the voyage as I had hoped to do. Without him, I assure you I would not have attempted it. I know the perils of travelling alone . . . Here is a letter from Corbinelli. He is very sad about my going, but I say to him, as you said to me, "Let him who loves me, follow me!" I am sending a thousand things to my son so that he can dazzle the eye at Nantes!†

"We marvel, my *bonne*," Mme de Sévigné wrote on April 21,

at the vagaries of fate—by which you set out on a trip for the sole purpose of seeing Monsieur de Grignan—and have not yet done so! You know, my bonne, that we have given the order for our litters, and that we have one foot in the air, ready to go. You give me great joy when you tell me of your joy, and of the love you have for me. If it resembles that which I have for you, ah, my bonne, that is good reason

---

*Corbinelli's book *Les Anciens historiens latins réduits en maximes* had just been published.
†Charles de Sévigné had been named King's Lieutenant for the county of Nantes in 1692.

for me to be content! Embrace Monsieur de Grignan for me—if you can!

On April 25, Mme de Sévigné wrote to explain to the Countess de Guitaut why she could not accept her invitation to come to Époisses on her way south:

Alas, my dear Madame, if it were up to me, I would like nothing better than to go to Époisses, and could make a long sojourn there without ever being bored—while the pleasure of being paid for the St. John's term would be of only secondary importance. But here are my plans: I am committed to the Chevalier de Grignan who did not leave with my daughter in order to wait for me when it developed that I could not leave until early May. She felt that that arrangement ensured my coming to Grignan, and that I would never have the courage to make the trip alone. That is the thought of someone who wants me, and since I also love the Grignan country, the château and the environs, and the repose I find there, I am determined to go to take cover there for some time, at least until the storm which strikes at us from all sides here has passed.* I lost my two best friends, Mme de La Fayette and Mme de Lavardin. I leave others here whom I love and esteem, but since it is not to the same degree, and since they have other friends beside me, I leave them with a bearable regret. As for the Chevalier de Grignan, he may be reduced to eating bread made of leaves and ferns, having nothing in the world but his menin's pension which is no longer paid him.† He has no choice. Thus, we are having two litters brought from Lyon, and with some mounted men and his wheelchair, we are leaving on the eighth of May. And there, my dear Madame, you have my very valid reasons for not going via Époisses.

Mme de Sévigné had hoped to be in her litter, on her way to Provence before Monday, May 10, the date of the last letter addressed by her from Paris to her daughter:

It is infamous not to have left on Saturday! A Mass to be heard tomor-row—there's a fine reason for you! It is, however, the Chevalier's

---

*Mme de Sévigné makes reference here to the bad times in Paris, the population decimated in 1694 by famine and disease.

†The Chevalier had been a *menin*, a member of the Dauphin's household, a duty he had been obliged to forego because of his crippling gout. Mme de Sévigné seems to have forgotten, however, that he still enjoyed a pension from the bishopric of Évreux.

reason ... So, it is to be Monday, then? Mme de Coulanges and other friends take it upon themselves to stop us because I am hoarse. Thus, I spent the whole day at her house, with all my friends who do not want to leave me until I step into my litter, as I will finally do tomorrow morning, and will not recover [my voice] until I stop talking. You can easily see by what I write that this voyage is all I have on my mind ...

So you will have a Chinese cabinet [she wrote on another page]! It will cost you little. It is larger and handsomer than the one you approved. Your clothes kept going down in price; your two cabinets are out of style and, together, brought less than five hundred livres. So we had to add another two hundred francs to make up the seven hundred the cabinet cost ... Finally, my bonne, I am thrilled that you are satisfied.

To tell you the truth, it is a strange thing to leave and sell off everything, as we are doing. One feels sorry for oneself. There is nothing left, but I am more than happy to be going to see you, to embrace you—and to leave a place where everyone will die if this drought continues another week ...

LV

"At Grignan, July 20, 1694," the superscription reads on Mme de Sévigné's letter to the Countess de Guitaut—the first notice she had given the Countess of her arrival in Provence:

I am closer to you here, Madame, than I was in Paris. This letter, however, must go back there in order to be sure to reach you. I left the eleventh of May; I arrived at Lyon on the eleventh day, and spent three days there to rest. I boarded a boat on the Rhône and, the next day— on the banks of that beautiful river—found my daughter and Monsieur de Grignan, who gave me so warm a welcome and led me to a land so different from that which I had left and through which I had come that I thought myself to be in an enchanted castle! Surely you would think so, too, Madame, because here one sees neither misery nor famine nor illness nor poverty. One thinks oneself in another world, but one does not forget one's friends and, since in that wretched world from which I came it is always a question of money and, since I assigned that which was due me for the Midsummer term to people to whom I was indebted and who impatiently await payment in the month of July, I am writing to Monsieur Boucard to send me the 1,391 livres owed me by my farmer—because of his payment of 2,009 livres at the Christmas term, he owes me only the above-mentioned sum.* If there are no difficulties—and there should be none—he will not pester you, and will send me my money via Dijon. If he has anything to say, I refer him to you, my dear Madame, and beg you on bended knee to consider the matter and come to a decision . . . So, my dear Madame, assemble your council—that is to say, the Abbé Tribolet—and do not refuse me the continuation of your kindness and your charity, for I have only you.

I told you, Madame, how happily I arrived here. I think I have also told you of the lovely life I lead here: a collegiate church with a gallery in it for me to put to marvelous use;† a freedom of action which ensures my having always at least three hours a day to read and to do as I please. When I join the others, I find my daughter and her daughter, Monsieur the Chevalier de Grignan, Monsieur the Marquis de La Garde, whose piety and whose company are both much to be admired; Monsieur [the Bishop] of Carcassonne and Monsieur [the Archbishop] of Arles are expected in two or three days—a beautiful château with a fine air about it, beautiful terraces, a table that is all too lavish! It is a life that is all too sweet, the days pass all too quickly, and one fails to do one's penance.

I don't write you any news; you know as much as we do. I never know any news when I am in Paris but, in the provinces, one reads everything, one knows everything! My daughter holds you in great esteem and honors you and I, my dear Madame, I embrace you and ask you a thousand pardons, and implore you to take pity on my poor affairs . . .

There can be no doubt that Mme de Sévigné did not wait until July 5 to write to Monsieur de Coulanges, but her letter of that date is the first

---

*The lease of the Bourbilly properties called for 3,400 livres a year from the farmer. The 2,009 livres payment mentioned was for the year 1694.

†High on the left wall of the collegiate Church of the Holy Savior (which is attached to the base of the Château de Grignan), there is a tribune or gallery directly accessible to the château by means of a few steps leading down from the terrace (which is built upon the church's roof).

addressed from Grignan to her beloved cousin to come down to us in print. The others are missing. Monsieur de Coulanges did complain, in a letter dated June 23, that Mme de Sévigné had been dilatory as a correspondent, but undoubtedly she had written to him and to his wife more than once since her departure from Paris in early May.* To judge by the dates on the Coulanges's letters to Mme de Sévigné—copies of which do exist—the correspondence was assiduous, letters twice or thrice monthly. The fact that so many of Mme de Sévigné's letters to the Coulanges from Grignan in 1694–6 are missing is not, in all probability, because the Coulanges tossed them away; they speak repeatedly of how they treasure every page she wrote ("Everything turns to gold at the touch of your pen," Mme de Coulanges said of her husband's cousin's epistolary art). In all likelihood, it was the demand of friends to share those delicious pages that explains why they are missing from the collection; they were borrowed from the Coulanges, and never returned. Certainly Mme de Sévigné had given the Coulanges news of her journey and of her arrival at Grignan on May 26 or 27 in letters written prior to July 5. Her very brief letter of July 5 refers to Mme de Coulanges's lingering illness:

> *You allow me to breathe again when you tell me that Mme de Coulanges is better. Her last letter so distressed me that I went to pieces. . .*
>
> *Monsieur de Grignan is somewhere in the vicinity of Nice with a large body of troops mobilized to repel—in the case of attack—that [English] fleet which was turned back at Brest.† You know how the lieutenant-generals of the provinces are presently serving as lieutenant-generals of the army—much to their delight and to their financial ruin. There are always people stopping off here, and playing hombre. I read, I spend time in my room. And that is how the days go by. Our little troupe loves and embraces you.*

The collection contains several letters addressed by the Coulanges to Mme de Sévigné during July and August, 1694, but none in reply from Mme de Sévigné until September 9:

> *I have received your many letters, my dear cousin; none of them has been lost. It would have been a terrible shame if they had: each has its special merit and, all together, they constitute the delight of our society.*

---

*Coulanges's letter of May 24 even makes mention of a letter of Mme de Sévigné's written to him from Moulins on her way to Grignan.

†Admiral Russell had brought the English fleet into the Mediterranean to rally the Spanish squadrons and to protect Barcelona, which had been threatened by a French fleet under Maréchal de Noailles.

The address you put on the last one—"To the royal château of Gri-gnan"—made you no enemies here. That line caught our eye and gave us all reason to believe that—despite all the many beautiful places you see—the memory of this one, which is not commonplace, remains in your mind's eye, and that, in itself, is reason for pride. Since you admire it so much, I will tell you a few things about it. That ugly staircase by which one reached the second courtyard—to the shame of the Adhé-mars!—has been completely torn down and replaced by one of the handsomest imaginable. I do not say either large or magnificent because, since my daughter did not want to tear up all those apartments contig-uous to it, it was necessary to confine it to a certain area within which a masterpiece was achieved. The vestibule is beautiful, and will accom-modate large dinner parties. A flight of stairs leads up to it. The Gri-gnan coats of arms are emblazoned on the doors; you admire them; that is why I mention it. The prelates' wing, of which you saw only the salon, is quite well furnished, and wonderful use is made of it.* While we are on the subject, let's talk about the sinfully fine fare served here, day in, day out—actually, only what is eaten all around here. Partridges—nothing extraordinary about that, but what is extraordinary is that they are all like those which cause people in Paris to smell them and exclaim, "Ah, what an aroma! Take a sniff!" We discourage all such exclama-tions. All of these partridges feed on thyme and marjoram and all the other herbs that make up our herbal bouquets. No need, here, to pick and choose. As much can be said for our plump quail which we expect to be so tender that the thigh pulls loose at the first touch (it never fails), and the turtledoves, all perfect, too. As for the melons, the figs and the grapes, it is a strange thing, but if we took a sudden mad fancy to find a bad melon, we would have to send to Paris for it! None could be found here. The sweet white figs, the grapes like edible grains of amber which, however, would go to your head if you ate enough of them because it is like taking sips of the most exquisite Saint-Laurent wine! What a way of life, my dear cousin!

A glamorous way of life it always seemed to her. Even too glamorous, may she not have thought occasionally? Surely, she was overjoyed in May of 1694 to be reunited with her beloved daughter and darling granddaughter in magnificent, high-perched Grignan, but that did not mean that she did

---

*Work on the prelates' wing of the château, begun in 1688, had not been completed when Coulanges stopped there en route home from Rome in 1691.

not worry about the ways and means of maintaining it. The emoluments paid to the Count de Grignan by state and province for his services had proved woefully inadequate in comparison to the expenses incurred by him in exercise of his duties as Governor and Lieutenant-General of Provence. Grignan had never been fortunate enough to enjoy the royal largesse or appointment to a lucrative Court position. By the early 1690's, the Governor of Provence could no longer afford to put in an appearance at his capital city of Aix, and was obliged to retreat to his château for the winter. He might have resigned the governorship and lived modestly as a private gentleman on the revenues from his vast landholdings, but service to monarch and to province was a tradition in the Grignan family, and he continued zealously and unstintingly to serve them both—to a great extent, at his own expense. *Noblesse oblige* was the motto of the *grand seigneur*, although that species— like the diplodocus—was headed for extinction.

Thanks to occasional grants from the Royal Treasury, he might some-how have managed to survive for a while in the seigneurial way of life, had not Julie-Françoise de Grignan—the younger of the Count's two daughters by his first wife—begun to press for the restitution of the sum bequeathed her by her mother's will, which—with the interest compounded throughout the years—had more than doubled, increasing from some 60,000 livres to well over 120,000. Julie-Françoise—or, rather, Madame de Vibraye, to give her her married name—had brought things to a head in 1694 by demanding immediate settlement. The Count de Grignan could not hope to raise such a sum. He was faced with ruin. To save the House of Grignan, that illus-trious name would have to be sold to the highest bidder: the Marquis would have to marry for money.

The search for an advantageous match for the Grignans' son and heir had been going on for years—thus far, in vain. Not even friends such as the Lamoignons, the Oraisons, the d'Ormessons or the Lavardins would give their daughters and their money to the son of a family drowning in a sea of debt. Writing to her daughter from Paris in April, 1694, Mme de Sévigné had gone over the list of eligible brides for the Marquis, and been obliged to mark off one after the other. "Unless by some miracle," she concluded, "such as the sale of a property which would turn stones into bread, I do not think there is any choice between a match which would ensure the future of your son and your house—and one which would finish you off."

Since there was no prospect of a wealthy bride in the ranks of the *noblesse d'épée*—the old nobility, that of the sword—nor even in the ranks of the *noblesse de robe*—the more recently ennobled parliamentary and judicial families—the Grignans squirmed on the horns of a dilemma: they had to choose between nobility without wealth and wealth without nobility. There was no way out but to accept some richly dowered financier's daughter as the future Marquise de Grignan. If it came to a question of blood versus gold, the Chevalier de Grignan—according to Mme de Sévigné's letter of April 21—expressed himself vehemently "in favor of gold!"

Gold was what a tremendously wealthy tax-farmer from Montpellier had to offer. In desperation, and choking on their pride, the Grignans agreed to take his daughter Anne-Marguerite de Saint-Amans as the Marquis's bride—along with a dowry in the amount of 400,000 livres, 300,000 of which were to be paid in cash upon signature of the marriage contract, and would serve to pay off the groom's father's most pressing debts.

It is not surprising that tongues wagged. Mme de Grignan's cousin Philippe-Emmanuel de Coulanges wrote from Paris, in June of 1694, urging her to pay no attention to the gossip. "Go ahead, and go through with this match. You are right and public opinion is wrong." Coulanges appeared to be the only member of the family who had not forgotten his bourgeois origins. Perhaps he sought to remind Mme de Sévigné that there had been similar dismay among the Rabutins at the thought of a scion of that ancient chivalric line marrying the daughter of an upstart tax-farmer named Coulanges; no Rabutin had deigned to sign the marriage contract. "Follow the course that suits you best," Coulanges counselled Mme de Grignan in his letter of June 28:

> But if you want to prove public opinion in the wrong, then assure yourselves so large and fine a sum of cash as to relieve your financial pressures. A really good marriage settlement will justify your course of action ... Get, as I said, the most cash you can ... Take your precautions, and console yourselves for a mésalliance both by the relief you will feel at no longer being harassed by creditors when you sojourn in your large, beautiful, magnificent châteaux ... and also by the satisfaction of being able, occasionally, to indulge yourselves in the superfluous which, in my opinion, constitutes one of the greatest joys in life.

Coulanges had not minced words: "mésalliance," he had said, without flinching, as the Grignans would have to learn to do. If the bride is rich enough, little Coulanges insisted, it makes no difference what people say or think.

"Nothing, now, I think," Mme de Sévigné wrote Mme de Coulanges on November 17, "can prevent the marriage from going through. Everything has, at last, been settled. All the parties on both sides, I believe, will assemble from all directions within the next two weeks."

Or sooner, as it developed: the marital contract was to be signed in Paris the very next day, November 18, 1694, by the father of the bride and the legal representatives of the father of the groom. It was ill health which had prevented the Count de Grignan from making the trip to Paris. "Monsieur de Grignan has had dizzy spells," Mme de Sévigné wrote Mme de Coulanges on November 17, "which frightened us because of the terrible fall he had had.* It was a miracle he did not break his head, and three weeks later, he had the vapours, as I said, but we are assured that it is nothing serious."

A letter from Mme de Coulanges dated November 19 gave Mme de Sévigné news of the publication of a book of verses by Monsieur de Coulanges on November 15, of which Mme de Coulanges commented somewhat acidulously, "A book of his poems was published and, in the front of the book, highly complimentary remarks about him personally. It was said that he was born with a capacity for both serious and frivolous pursuits. Proof was given of the latter." She was happy, she told Mme de Sévigné, to think of them all at Grignan rejoicing over the Marquis's marriage:

> *Monsieur the Abbé de Marsillac [she wrote] had many good things to tell me yesterday about Monsieur and Madame de Saint-Amans and their daughter the future Marquise de Grignan. He says they are the nicest people imaginable, and that they raised a masterpiece for you.*

In December, Mme de Sévigné wrote to the Countess de Guitaut to give her news of the impending nuptials, although the first several pages of her letter were, as usual, devoted to pleas for assistance with her affairs at Bourbilly:

> *For nearly a year, now [she wrote], there has been talk of a marriage for the Marquis de Grignan. It is the daughter of a farmer-general named Saint-Amans. You will not find it hard to believe that he is very rich. He had the franchise for provisioning for Marseille. His elder daughter is eighteen years old, pretty, amiable, sensible, well brought up, extremely practical. He is giving 400,000 francs to this girl, with more to come to her in the future. He has only one other daughter. It was thought that such a match would be good to sustain the grandeurs*

---

*The Count de Grignan had fallen on a staircase at Sorgues, just north of Avignon, and broken his nose.

of this house, which is not without indebtedness, a major portion to Mme de Vibraye who is pressing for payment ... The contract was signed in Paris where the father of the bride had gone ... The father and the contract are both here; his wife and daughter have come from Montpellier and, finally, Madame, after having seen and admired more than 50,000 francs' worth of lingerie, clothes and jewels of which he also generously makes a gift, the Marquis and that girl—after an eight- or ten-day sojourn here to get acquainted—will be married on Sunday, the second day of the year '95. So, that, Madame, is how we are spending this winter, without ever leaving our château, where there are only the two prelates and Monsieur de Montmor, who started the whole thing.* I am going to make you give up a quarter of an hour of your time to read this long letter, and tell you how it has pleased Providence to dispose of the fate of this house and our sojourn in this land.

On Sunday, January 2, 1695, in the collegiate church attached to the base of the château, and in the presence of a large company, the Bishop of Carcassonne performed the marriage ceremony uniting his nephew the Marquis de Grignan and Anne-Marguerite de Saint-Amans. Twenty signatures, in addition to those of the bride and groom, were appended to the marriage certificate; an even larger number of people had signed the marriage contract on the evening preceding the nuptials.

It is a misfortune that Mme de Sévigné's letters describing the wedding and the attendant festivities are lost. Addressed to the Coulanges, these letters must have been passed from hand to hand around Paris—around Versailles, perhaps, as well—and disappeared. The Coulanges's replies, their comments on her letters give some idea of their content, and serve to whet the reader's appetite for the originals, as when Mme de Coulanges writes to Mme de Sévigné on January 14: "I thank you, my friend, for having let me know the conclusion of your romance—because all you tell me is romantic. The heroine is charming; the hero we already know." (It is curious to find such words as "romantic," "hero" and "heroine" employed by those familiar with all the purely pragmatical aspects of that marriage: a bride and groom who had not met until after the marital contract had been signed, had not laid eyes on one another until a week before their troth was to be plighted. But then, Mme de Sévigné was hopelessly romantic: influenced by the

---

*Jean-Louis de Montmor, Count de Mesnil, Intendant of Galleys at Marseille and an old friend of the Grignans, had had dealings with Saint-Amans, who had the provisions franchise there, and was the one who had suggested the match.

novels she had devoured, by the plays she had seen or read, she gravitated to the romantic or dramatic element in real life. To her, the Prince de Conti's and Mlle de Blois's was "a storybook love affair," the Chevalier de Grignan was "as handsome as the hero of a novel"; the Princess de Tarente's tales appealed to her because of "their romanesque style." It was Mme de Sévigné's inclination to embellish reality, to escape from reality into fantasy—as in this instance, to glamourize a shocking mésalliance. Describing the pomp and ceremony of the occasion, she may have become intoxicated by the resonance and the flow of her own words, her romanticization of the wedding intended less to deceive the Coulanges than to deceive herself. Mme de Coulanges, recognizing her friend's propensities, played along.)*

"I am glad to know that Monsieur de Grignan is well again," Mme de Coulanges's letter of January 14 continued:

That circumstance could not but have contributed to the pleasures of the occasion ... Yesterday, I told Mme de Chaulnes, who had just arrived, about your wedding. "Jesus God, so they are married!" she exclaimed, as if she had never heard it mentioned before. Monsieur de Coulanges spends all his time at the Court, now. No one could say of him that it is his interests which take him there. He is motivated solely by pleasure, but he is happy. Who needs more?

To which letter, Monsieur de Coulanges—evidently back in Paris from Versailles, at least for the moment—added several pages of his own, such as this:

My God, what good letters you write, my very dearest governess, and what pleasure all the details gave me! I could see your nuptials as clearly as if I had been there! I could see that beautiful château illuminated, and all the guests that filled it, the beautiful gowns and all the

---

*Robert Nicolich, in his *Mme de Sévigné and the Problem of Reality and Appearances*, remarks that "Mme de Sévigné, it is evident, clearly thought of reality in terms of the dramatic and the poetic, in terms of the fantastic, adventurous literature she devoured, and her statements are frank avowals of this. Her next step was to see practically everyone in terms of the hero and heroine ... For her, the division between fantasy and reality easily disappeared." She was much given to fantasy, seeing grotesque figures—black and white garbed nuns and monks, black men—lurking in the moonlit woods of Brittany. If there was someone far off whom she longed to see, she imagined that he might come "blowing in on a gust of wind," and she refers repeatedly to "the hippogriff"—a fabulous animal, half-horse, half-bird—on which one might fly from Brittany to Provence, or vice versa. There was also a magic pair of spyglasses about which she fantasized: one end permitted her to see people she wanted to avoid at a great distance; the other end allowed her to bring up close those whom she longed to have with her.

adornments of the bride, those three tables so sumptuously set out in the Gallery, all those bright-lit, richly furnished apartments! I could even hear the music! . . . I attended the nuptial banquet with no complaint except that of having eaten too much, for never did I enjoy a better repast. You really acquitted yourself marvelously of the detailed account, but who will advise me whether we really have a Marquise de Grignan, and whether we can expect nephews worthy of their ancestors?

As for me, my charming Marquise, my life is always the same, part of the time at Versailles, part of the time in Paris, but always in the best of company.

On February 3, Mme de Sévigné answered the joint letter from the Coulanges, concluding with a reprimand for him:

*You certainly succeeded in visualizing the magnificence of our pastoral nuptial ceremony. Everyone here appreciates your praises, but we don't know what you mean about "that first night." Alas, how vulgar you are! I was charmed by the dignity and decorum of that evening. I spoke of it in my letter to Mme de Coulanges. The bride is conducted to her apartments; her dressing table is brought there, along with her lingerie and her hair ornaments. She takes down her hair; she is helped to disrobe; she goes to bed. No one knows who comes or goes in that chamber. Everyone goes to bed. Everyone arises the next morning; no one goes near the newlyweds. They arise and dress. No one asks them silly questions: "Are you my son-in-law?"—"Are you my daughter-in-law?" They are what they are. No wedding breakfast is arranged. Everyone does, and everyone eats what he pleases. All this goes on with modesty, without chatter. No one leers at the bridal couple; no one embarrasses them; no ribald remarks are made, and that is something which I had never seen before, but which I find the most seemly behavior in the world.**

"People are still coming to pay wedding calls," Mme de Sévigné continued in her letter of February 3, a month after the ceremony:

There are ladies like Mme de Brancas and Mme de Buous, ladies of distinction whom we had implored not to make the trip over these icy

---

*The wedding customs of Paris and Brittany evidently compared unfavorably, in Mme de Sévigné's eyes, with those of Provence, which she found far more decorous.

roads, who broke the ice to come, who almost slipped and fell, who risked life and limb to come to offer their congratulations. That is what friendship is like in this part of the world. Would people do as much in Paris?

Mme de Chaulnes writes to tell me how lucky I am to be under this warm sun. She thinks all our days are spun of gold and silk. Alas, my cousin, it is a hundred times colder here than in Paris! We are exposed to all the winds. There is the meridional wind, there is the bise, there is the devil—whichever chooses to assault us; they vie among themselves for the honor of shutting us up in our rooms. All our rivers are frozen over. The Rhône—even that wild, furious Rhône— cannot hold out against the ice. Our inkwells are frozen; our fingers, being frozen, cannot direct our pens. We breathe only snow; our mountains are beautiful in their excess of horror. I wish every day for an artist to paint that beautiful and dreadful scene. And that's how it is here with us. Explain this to our dear Duchess de Chaulnes who pictures us out in the meadows with our parasols, taking our promenades in the shade of the orange trees.

The cold numbs my hands, and the pen drops from my fingers. Where are you? At Saint-Martin, at Meudon, at Bâville?* Which place is lucky enough to lay claim to that young and charming Coulanges? I have just expressed myself savagely to Mme de Coulanges on the subject of avarice. When I think of the vast wealth left by Mme de Meckelbourg, it makes me happy to know that I will die without any cash on hand, but without any debt, as well.† That is all I ask of God, and that suffices for a Christian.

---

*The Abbey of Saint-Martin belonged to the Cardinal de Bouillon; Meudon was the great estate belonging to Mme de Louvois, later exchanged by her with the King for that of Choisy; Bâville, the Lamoignons's country estate in the Île de France.

†"Oh, don't even talk to me about Mme de Meckelbourg! I renounce her," Mme de Sévigné exclaimed by letter to Mme de Coulanges, in response to news of the death of that enormously wealthy onetime friend: "Miserly toward the poor, miserly toward her servants to whom she left nothing, miserly toward herself, allowing herself almost to starve to death!"

LVI

Had it not been for Mme de Sévigné's correspondence with the Coulanges, the Château de Grignan and all its inhabitants would have been lost from sight in the mid-1690's. With the Count de Bussy-Rabutin and Mme de La Fayette and Mme de Lavardin gone, Mme de Sévigné's cousin and his wife were almost the only correspondents left her. If she was reduced to those two alone, she could not have hoped for a pair better renowned for their epistolary talents and scintillating wit. (Mme de Sévigné kept in touch, beyond the shadow of a doubt, with her son Charles de Sévigné—and, very probably, with his wife, as well—but it was evidently not their practice, as it was Mme de Grignan's, to save her letters.)

Mme de Coulanges's letter of February 12 was, she explained, in the hand of her new secretary—Monsieur de Coulanges, himself! "I am trying out a new secretary," she began. "Let me know if you can read his handwriting." The series of "magnificent dinner parties at the Duke de Chaulnes's," she advised, were the talk of the town: "I went to the first one, but when it came to the second, I sent my son, who goes by the name of Monsieur de Coulanges. As the number of my years increase, his decrease—so that I find myself almost too old even to be his mother!" Her ill health persisted: a colic that not even a stable of doctors could succeed in curing. ("I don't like to see her running from empiric to empiric," her husband complained, in a letter of his own.) "My stomach has become so delicate," Mme de Coulanges explained, "that even the sight of a good dinner makes me ill"; later adding, "I find that I have to have a very good reason to leave my bed."

"I would be consoled for the loss of your little secretary," Mme de Sévigné replied to Mme de Coulanges on February 22, "if the new one you took in his place was entirely at your service. His handwriting is excellent, his style is good but, from what I hear, you are apt to lose him at any moment. He is a libertine; he sleeps around the town.* With that in mind, my friend, use him if you like. I advise you to give him a trial."

Mme de Sévigné was still complaining about the Provençal weather in

*Monsieur de Coulanges often spent the night at Mme de Louvois's Paris hôtel as well as at her various châteaux in the country. There was a family joke to the effect that Mme de Louvois was his "second wife."

February: "A bitter cold and lots of snow, as you know; freezes on top of that, and more snow and frost, so that, altogether, we have had a worse winter than yours in Paris." Bad weather and a series of unpleasant menopausal symptoms afflicting Mme de Grignan in early 1695 may have served to depress the usually ebullient Marquise de Sévigné. "I bring my letter to a close, my darling," she wrote in the last paragraph of her letter to Coulanges; "I have no amusing little odds and ends to sprinkle across my pages, today. It might be better if a gust of wind came along and blew them all away! . . ."

At this point there is a two months' hiatus in the Sévigné-Coulanges correspondence—at least, at Mme de Sévigné's end of it. All of her letters between February 22 and April 26 are missing.

"I take really great pleasure in your letters to me, my darling cousin," her letter of April 26 began:

They are as charming as you are, and I read them with a delight that is shared by many. Everyone loves to hear what you have to say, everyone approves, everyone admires in proportion to his affection for you. When you do not write to me, I do not fuss and fume, I do not sulk; I say, "My cousin is in some enchanted palace. My cousin has no time to himself. Someone has doubtlessly carried my poor cousin off!" And I patiently wait for you to think of me again, without ever doubting your love for me, because how could you not love me? To love me was the very first thing you did upon opening your eyes . . . Just as it was I who made it fashionable to love you! A friendship so firmly founded does not fear the depredations of time. It seems to me that time, which wreaks such havoc on the heads of others as it goes by, leaves yours unscathed. You say that you do not believe your baptismal certificate; you are convinced that a serious error was made in the date. The Chevalier de Grignan says that they added all the years to his certificate which they subtracted from yours, and he is right; that is how his age should be computed. As for me, there is nothing as yet to remind me of my age. I am sometimes surprised at my good health. I have been cured of a thousand minor ailments I had earlier. Not only do I move along into old age as slowly as a tortoise, sometimes I think I should say as slowly as a crayfish. However, I try not to allow myself to be deceived by appearances, and when you are several years older than you are now, I would advise you to do the same.

Mme de Sévigné's next letter to her cousin was dated May 28. "I received your two letters from Chaulnes, my dear cousin, and we were charmed with your poems," she wrote:

We sang them with great pleasure, as more than one person here will tell you, for you should not be unaware of the admiration we have for all your verse. You may back away from your baptismal certificate, but you move ahead when it comes to gayety and high spirits. No one could ask for more, and it is that which makes everyone seek you out. Who does not enjoy your company? With whom do you fail to get along? . . .

By May 28, the terrible winter was finally over, and Mme de Sévigné basked in a Provençal spring:

Our early spring weather has been beautiful [she wrote], but for the last two days, the rain—which no one likes here—has been as widespread as in Brittany or Paris, and they accuse me of having brought it with me. It interrupts our promenades, but cannot silence our nightingales. All in all, my dear cousin, the days go by too quickly. We get along very well without the tumult of the great world. Those who make up our company would not displease you, and if ever a gale of wind should blow you into this "royal château" . . . but that is to fantasize! We must hope to see one another elsewhere in a more natural and likely way . . . We still have all the summer to write to one another . . .

That last line suggests that Mme de Sévigné and the Grignans had made plans to spend the summer at Grignan and go to Paris in the fall. On the last page of Mme de Sévigné's May 28 letter, Mme de Grignan added a postscript for their cousin:

I note with pleasure, in your letters to my Mother, that the memory of our rock lingers in your mind. The epithets you use to honor it are eternal monuments to the glory of the Adhémars. If their château deserves a place in your opinion alongside all the many other magnificent, superb and extraordinary châteaux which you visit, this must constitute its greatest eulogy. It is even more beautiful than when you saw it, and if we could only hope to see you here again, we could wish for nothing more.

Mme de Sévigné was homesick for her cousin, too: "Yes, my child," she wrote in June,

I am in that room of mine with its lovely study where you saw me, surrounded by all those beautiful views.* Monsieur de Grignan has gone on a tour of inspection of the coasts. His absence makes itself sadly felt in this château. We were expecting Monsieur [the Bishop] of Carcassonne, but he will not arrive for another two or three days . . . You are much loved by all the inhabitants of this château. You know the life we lead here—what lavish fare we enjoy at table, what a society, what liberty of action! The days pass too quickly; that is what kills me, from every point of view. If you go to Vichy, you must come to Grignan . . .

On June 5, Mme de Sévigné wrote to her friend Philippe Moulceau, presiding judge of the Assize Courts in Montpellier, reproaching him for his silence and neglect:

I intend, Monsieur, to bring suit against you. Here is how I shall proceed. I intend to have you judge it yourself. It is more that a year since I came here to be with my daughter for whom I still feel a strong affinity. You must, doubtlessly, since then, have heard talk about the marriage of the Marquis de Grignan to Mademoiselle de Saint-Amans. You have seen her often enough at Montpellier to know what she is like. You will also have heard talk about her father's great wealth. You must have heard that the wedding was elaborately celebrated in this château with which you are familiar. I suppose you have not forgotten that visit which gave rise to the high esteem in which you are still held here. With that in mind, I judge your reaction by my own, and reason that if we have not forgotten you, you should not have forgotten us. Not to mention Monsieur de Grignan, whose friendship with you dates back still further than ours. In view of all this, I find myself offended, and hereby register complaint. I complain about it to all your friends; I complain to our dear Corbinelli, jealous confidant and witness to all the esteem and affection we feel for you. And, finally, I make my complaint to you, yourself, Monsieur. What accounts for this silence? Have you forgotten us? Is it indifference on your part? I know that you are in good health. What do you expect me to think? What is the meaning of your conduct? Give it a name, Monsieur. And that is the

---

*The suite or apartment in the southwest tower of the façade François I which is shown today at the Château de Grignan as Mme de Sévigné's is probably the one built expressly for her at the time of her first visit in 1672.

suit I bring against you. It is for you to judge. I consent, as you can see, to your being both judge and defendant.

This letter, which was among Moulceau's papers, is signed "Marquise de Sévigné" and bears a postscript reading, "My daughter is at one with me in the composition of this letter, and is no less distressed than I am at your coolness."

"It is tantamount to winning the case, Monsieur, when you lose it as you do," Mme de Sévigné wrote on June 29 to Moulceau, in reply to his reply to her letter of June 5:

I cannot refrain from telling you that—despite your intention of breaking off with all your correspondents—your epistolary style, which we remembered and found as delightful as ever, gave us the kind of pleasure we had not experienced since you last wrote to us. We read and reread your letter several times, my daughter and I; it is delicious, and you may not have realized all its merit. How fortunate you are, Monsieur, to retain that sort of wit even when you have become so devout and serious-minded . . . We were gripped by so keen a desire once again to have the honor of welcoming you to this château that my daughter cannot understand why—since your health is good—you would not consider paying us a visit, why you might not still plan on coming, this autumn?

By the time autumn came, however, a guest would have been less welcome at Grignan, as Mme de Sévigné's letter of August 6, addressed to Coulanges, suggests: for one thing, the campaign in Flanders had, by then, come to a head, with the French army—under the direct command of the monarch—laying siege to the fortress of Namur (at the confluence of the Meuse and the Sambre). "My God, how much blood shed at Namur!" Mme de Sévigné's letter of August 6 to Monsieur de Coulanges begins: "How many tears! How many grieving widows and mothers! Things are relatively peaceful in our Germany; that is the front which gives us our principal concern." (It was Germany to which the Marquis and his Grignan regiment had been assigned.)

"Goodbye, my dear cousin," her letter to Coulanges concluded:

Did I not warn you that this letter would prove dull? One sometimes worries, and for good reason. I spoke of this to Mme de Coulanges. My daughter sends you love. You wonderfully diverted her with your songs and chitchat, because your letters are actually a conversation. I distributed your greetings to all the apartments, where they were warmly welcomed and warmly reciprocated. I hug you, my amiable cousin, and exhort you always to live deliciously in celebration of polygamy which, in your case—instead of being a hanging offense—constitutes the chief delight of your existence!

The "worries" to which this letter refers, and for which there was "good reason"—worries about which she said she had already written to Mme de Coulanges, in a letter missing from the collection—were attributable, primarily, to Mme de Grignan's worsening health and, secondarily, to worsening relations with Monsieur de Saint-Amans. Mme de Grignan, at age forty-nine, was experiencing menopausal difficulties, and Saint-Amans was making difficulties about certain clauses of the marriage contract. Mme de Sévigné's letter to Charles de Sévigné, dated September 20, reveals the tensions. "So, there you are at poor Les Rochers,* my dear children," the letter begins, "where—free of all duties and responsibilities—you find a peace and quiet which will permit our dear little Marquise to breathe again."

My God, how clearly you describe her condition, her extremely delicate health! I am deeply touched, and enter so tenderly into your thoughts that my heart aches and my eyes fill with tears . . . But I want to believe that that dear person—given the proper care—will have as long a life as anyone else . . . You do me justice when you say that you fear to tell me how upset you are. You are right; I am profoundly distressed. I only hope that this reply finds you better satisfied and in a more tranquil state of mind. You do not seem to have Paris in mind for our Marquise; you speak only of going to Bourbon in the spring. Keep me advised of all your plans, and keep nothing from me which affects you.
  As for the health of your poor sister, it is certainly not good. She is no longer flooding; that has stopped. But she does not regain her strength. She is still so changed as to be unrecognizable, because her stomach is no better, and she does not assimilate her food, and that is the result of the bad condition of her liver, of which—as you know— she has long complained. That ailment is so severe that I am terribly disturbed. There are remedies which could be prescribed to help the liver condition, but these would be bad in view of the excessive menstrual flow which it is feared may recur, and which aggravates the liver prob-

*She may have referred to it as "poor Les Rochers" because she felt she might never see it again.

lem. *Thus, the two ailments, for which the remedies are exactly opposite, have a dire effect. It is hoped that time will correct the disorder,
and should this blessing come, we would go immediately to Paris. That
is how things stand here, and those are the things to be worked out—
about which I will faithfully keep you posted.*

*That weakness and lethargy account for the fact that there is no
talk about the return of the warriors from the war. However, I have no
doubt that the match will be made; things have gone too far.*

The "match" in question was that of Pauline and the Marquis de Simiane, the "warrior" whose return from the battlefront could be expected
momentarily, at the return of autumn. Grignans and Simianes had lived on
cordial terms for generations, their lands contiguous; the Simiane château
at Valréas, only a few miles from Grignan.

*But it [the wedding] will be celebrated joylessly [the letter went on],
and even if we go to Paris, we would leave there two days later to
avoid the air of a wedding and the round of wedding visits of which
we want no part: "a burnt cat," etcetera.*

*As for the problems with Monsieur de Saint-Amans, of which
there has been much talk in Paris, they arose because my daughter—
having proved by documents she showed us all that she had paid her
son nine thousand francs out of the ten thousand the contract called
for her to pay—sent him only one thousand, upon which Monsieur de
Saint-Amans declared that he had been cheated, that they were trying
to put all the burden on him, and that he would give absolutely nothing
more ... and that it was up to Monsieur the Marquis to look for relief
from the other side of the family. You can well imagine that if "the
other side" had had to pay, it would have caused quite a few complications, but all that is over now. Monsieur de Saint-Amans soon came to
the conclusion that it was not a good idea to be on bad terms with my
daughter. And so, he came here, meek as a lamb, seeking only to please
and to take his daughter back to Paris, which he did, although, in all
justice, she should have waited for us. But the advantage of having her
lodged with her husband in that beautiful house of Monsieur de Saint-
Amans's—with all their fine furnishings, all their living expenses paid—
made us consent without hesitation to her going to enjoy such a privilege, although it was not without tears that we saw her leave, because
she is very pleasant, while she herself wept so copiously at bidding us
farewell that no one could have guessed that she was leaving to go to*

begin a wonderful new life in the lap of luxury. She had shown a definite taste for our society. She left on the first of this month with her father.

The *Mémoires* of the Duke de Saint-Simon offer an entirely different version of the story, showing us the poor little Marquise left alone and ill at ease at Grignan in the spring of 1695, subsequent to the departure of her husband and his return to his regiment. The Countess de Grignan, according to Saint-Simon, made her daughter-in-law's life a misery, humiliating her in front of all and sundry. Here is Saint-Simon's account:

Mme de Grignan, when she introduced her to people, made excuses for her, and—pretending in her affected way to make light of it— explained that it was necessary, from time to time, to add manure to the finest soil in the world. She seemed very proud of this bon mot, which everyone, with good reason, found inappropriate coming from the person who had made the match—but she repeated it over and over again to one and all, in the presence of her daughter-in-law. Saint-Amans, her father, finally heard of the remark, and was so insulted that he cut off the flow at the faucet.

Between the two versions of the story the truth is difficult to discern. While the Duke de Saint-Simon is known to have looked upon Mme de Grignan with a jaundiced eye as a result of the ill will existing between her and his half-sister, the Duchess de Brissac, Mme de Sévigné is known to have been blind to the shortcomings of her daughter.

However it was, Monsieur de Saint-Amans would seem to have been justified in taking his daughter with him to Paris in September, rather than allowing her to wait to make the trip with her mother-in-law, who had suffered a relapse by October, as Mme de Sévigné's despondent letter of October 15 to Coulanges reveals:

I have just written to our Duke and Duchess de Chaulnes, but I excuse you from reading my letters; they are not worth the trouble ... The best thing you could do for me, my amiable cousin, would be to send us—by some feat of magic—all that vigor, all that strength, all that good health and all that joyousness of which you have an overabundance to give to my daughter by transfusion. For three months, now, she has been overwhelmed by a kind of illness which they say is not dangerous but which I find the most depressing and most frightening of any one could have. I admit to you, my dear cousin, that it is killing me, and that I no longer have the strength to bear up under all these sleepless nights she puts me through. Her last attack was so violent that a bleeding was prescribed, from the arm—a strange remedy to drain more blood from someone who has lost so much already. That is burning the candle at both ends. That is what she said to us, because— even as weak as she is and as greatly changed—there is nothing to equal her patience and her courage.

If we could regain our strength, we would immediately take the road to Paris. That is what we hope to do, and then we will present our Marquise de Grignan to you, whom you should already have met if you had followed the lead of the Duke de Chaulnes who forced her door, and gave a very enthusiastic report of her. Even so, my dear cousin, never stop loving us, no matter how unworthy we may be of it, in our state of depression. One must love one's friends with all their faults—illness being one of the greatest. God preserve you from it, my darling! My letter to Mme de Coulanges is on the same plaintive note which is habitual with me, now. For how could I not be sick at heart— seeing that Countess of mine sick of body, day in, day out? Mme de Coulanges is lucky to be out of it.* Mothers should not, it seems to me, live long enough to see their daughters come to such a pass. I make respectful complaint to Providence.

The young Marquise de Grignan was to be presented at Court and to Paris society by her mother and father-in-law as soon as they arrived in the capital. Until that time, the young woman evidently lived in seclusion, fearing to associate with people of whom the Grignans might disapprove, unacquainted with those of the Grignans' aristocratic circle. "People here are talking about the solitary life led by Mme the Marquise de Grignan," Mme de Coulanges wrote Mme de Sévigné on October 28. "Her life is intolerable because she must either see the right people or no one at all. You see in what great need she is of your return and of that of her mother-in-law."

By the first week of November, 1695, the Marquis de Grignan had joined his wife at her father's elegant town house on the Rue des Vieilles Haudriettes, and went promptly to call on his cousin Mme de Coulanges, as she reported to his grandmother on November 7:

---

*Mme de Coulanges had no children, no ailing daughter to break her heart.

Monsieur the Marquis de Grignan came to see me; he is certainly not as fat as he was, on which I complimented him. Mme his wife did me the honor of coming here yesterday. I found her looking so greatly improved that she seemed an entirely different person. She had gained weight, her face is prettier, her beautiful eyes so bright that I was dazzled . . .

The very next day, Mme de Coulanges wrote again to Mme de Sévigné, again urging that she and the Grignans return to Paris:

Your return is necessary for so many reasons—the change of air for Mme de Grignan, one of the most important. Her daughter-in-law is lost here without her. And there is Monsieur de Sévigné's arrival imminent! How many reasons, my darling, for you to come back to see us!

Mme de Sévigné's "*belle Providence*" willed otherwise. Mme de Grignan grew worse instead of better. The long, arduous trip from Grignan to Paris was out of the question. Not only that: Pauline's fiancé, the Marquis de Simiane, had returned home from Flanders, and the marriage contract had been signed. The ceremony was scheduled to take place at Grignan before the month of November was out.

Only two letters of Mme de Sévigné's describing the Grignan-Simiane nuptials are extant. One was addressed on November 14 to her old friend the Marquis de Pomponne and was preserved among his papers, along with all the other letters she had written him. (The opening lines refer to the death of his eldest son in 1693 and to Mme de Grignan's illness.)

How much I would have to say to you, Monsieur [her letter begins], if I wished to touch on all the sorrows of your life and of mine! My respect, my fear of renewing your sorrow . . . above all, my confidence that you knew my heart and how sensitive it is to anything concerning you, imposed a silence which I believe you understood. I break it, today, Monsieur, because Monsieur de Grignan does not deem the marriage of a daughter significant enough to call to the attention of a Minister like you, and because my daughter is as yet unable to use her pen, and dares avail herself of no other than mine; I find myself, by slow degrees, the secretary for both. I know that you love Mademoiselle de Grignan. She would not dare change her name without giving you notice of it; that of Simiane is not unknown.

The wedding, she went on to tell Pomponne, would be held at the family château "without fanfare of any kind, as is appropriate to the weakened state of my daughter's health": it was solemnized on November 29 in the Church of the Holy Savior at Grignan, with the bride's uncle the Archbishop of Arles officiating. According to a letter of Mme de Coulanges's written on December 23, the bride's mother had been unable to attend: "You gave me an idea of how ill she was when you told me that she was too weak even to be carried to the chapel to see her dear Pauline wed."

Mme de Sévigné's second letter concerning Pauline's marriage was addressed to Philippe Moulceau in Montpellier:

When I accept the compliments offered me on the marriage of Mme de Simiane [she wrote], it can only be for having heartily approved what my daughter so wisely arranged a long time ago. There can never have been a more appropriate union. All is noble, fitting, and advantageous for a daughter of the House of Grignan who found a man and a family who placed all their emphasis on her merit, on her person, and her name—and none at all on her worldly goods, which is all that counts in other regions. So, we profited joyously by a sentiment so rare and so noble.

It was a good marriage for a girl who was not an heiress. It was better than that: it was that rarest of rare things in seventeenth- or eighteenth- or nineteenth-century Europe, it was a love match.

LVII

The Assembly of the Communities of Provence having been called into session December 9–December 20, 1695, the Count de Grignan set out from Grignan for Lambesc to deliver the opening address, as was the duty of the Governor of the province. When his carriage rolled across the drawbridge and the moat, down the steep, winding road from the château to the village of Grignan and into the valley, his mother-in-law rode with him. The Countess de Grignan, having been too weak and ill even to attend the wedding of her daughter on November 29, could not have considered accompanying her husband. But she was evidently feeling somewhat stronger, showing some improvement, however slight, or her mother would not have left her for the pleasure excursion upon which she had embarked.

It is entirely possible that Mme de Sévigné felt she needed a little vacation, a change of scene, after such close confinement to her daughter's sickroom over the past six months. It may have been that the Count de Grignan—or the doctors summoned into consultation at Grignan—deemed it expedient to separate mother and daughter for a week or two to relieve the tension, as had been necessary during Mme de Sévigné's previous visit to Provence in 1672. Much of the friction between them in years past had stemmed from Mme de Sévigné's extreme anxiety over Mme de Grignan's health. With Mme de Grignan seriously ill in 1695, Mme de Sévigné's solicitude could, once again, have rasped Mme de Grignan's nerves. The harmonious relation established between the two in recent years may have been imperilled in the emergency by what Mme de Grignan considered nagging on her mother's part.

Only two letters addressed by Mme de Sévigné to her daughter during that two-week absence in December of 1695 are extant. The superscription of the first of those two reads, "At Lambesc, Sunday [December 11, 1695], at eleven o'clock at night." It cannot have been the first because Mme de Sévigné refers to previous letters which she hopes have "provided some diversion" to her daughter. To anyone familiar with Mme de Sévigné's letter-writing schedule in her correspondence with her daughter, it is clear that a number of letters from that period are missing. "I leave tomorrow at six in the morning, my very dear one, for Marseille," the letter dated December 11 begins: "All my days have been carefully allocated. I will spend only one day in that beautiful town, and two at Aix." Marseille had been included on her itinerary not only because she had friends there, but because she remembered it, from her previous visit there in 1672, as a "beautiful" and "romantic" spot. The two days allocated to Aix were to be spent visiting with her elder granddaughter, Marie-Blanche de Grignan, at the Convent of the Visitation. (The conventual archives make reference to this visit by the granddaughter of the saintly founder of the Order.)

"They regret, here, to see me leave," Mme de Sévigné's letter of December 11, written from Lambesc on the eve of her departure for Marseille, continues:

Monsieur de Grignan adjusts quite well to my company. Saint-Bonnet left four hours ago for the Court.* We are having the kind of weather I

---

*Henri de Saint-Bonnet, Captain of the Governor's Guards, had left for Versailles to report that the Assembly had voted to make a tax contribution of 700,000 livres to the Royal Exchequer.

always find here. I am tormented by fleas and lice. I hate wearing my velvet dress; the lavender one is too heavy. That is how rigorous a winter we are having! I hope that this mild weather will restore your strength ... that you won't go on looking like the shadow of your former self. You don't tell me enough about yourself. I had hoped for a note from Martillac.* I hope my letters have provided you some diversion ... Sollery† will tell you what a gala life we lead here ... A big banquet today at the Archbishop's with whom I talked yesterday for two hours, tête-à-tête ...

"Adieu, my very dear *bonne*. I will be even gladder to get back to you than I was to leave you!" the closing lines of the letter read—lines that speak volumes as to the nature of the parting. Happily, after a few days' holiday, Mme de Sévigné could joke about what had evidently been a tense moment.

Only one other letter survives of those addressed by Mme de Sévigné to her daughter during her two-week tour of Provence in December, 1695. It was written after her return to Lambesc from Marseille and Aix. It carries the dateline, "At Lambesc, Tuesday, December 20, at ten o'clock in the morning," and begins:

When one makes one's calculations without taking Providence into account, one runs the risk of miscalculating. I was all dressed at eight o'clock; I had had my coffee and heard Mass, all my goodbyes had been said, the luggage-mule was loaded. The mules' bells reminded me that it was time to get into my litter. My room was full of people who were imploring me not to leave because it had been raining hard for several days, had rained the day before without letup, and was raining still, at that hour. I bravely resisted all the talk, intending to stand by the resolve I had made and all I had written you by yesterday's courier, wherein I advised you that I would arrive on Thursday—when suddenly Monsieur de Grignan, wrapped in an omelette-colored dressing gown, began to lecture me very seriously about the foolhardiness of my undertaking, warning me that the muleteer would not follow me, that my mules would fall into the ditches, that my people would be drenched and unable to rescue me—all this resulting in my changing my mind,

---

*Countess de Grignan's companion and housekeeper.

†Boniface Sollery, a gentleman from Avignon, was likewise an officer in the Governor's Guards, and often served as courier to Versailles.

that very minute, and yielding to his sage remonstrances. Whereupon the trunks were brought back in, the mules unharnessed, the maids and lackeys dried themselves off after having only crossed the courtyard, and a messenger was sent off to you—in view not only of your fond concern for me, but mine for you while you are ailing, and so that man will bring me back news of you, whether I am still here or on the road back . . . In short, my daughter, here I am. You are no longer to expect me. I will surprise you, but I will run no risks for fear of worrying you—and myself, as well. Adieu, my very dear and darling daughter. I fume at being a prisoner at Lambesc, I can assure you. But who would have guessed that there would be rains such as have not been seen in this country in the last hundred years?

Mme de Sévigné, in typical tourist fashion, had addressed a letter to Mme de Coulanges from Marseille, as is shown by this reply from Mme de Coulanges from Paris, dated December 23:

How lovely to dateline a letter "from Marseille"! How lovely to feel well enough to travel about! How lovely to be always as charming as you are! But how wicked of you to deceive me! For, my friend, you have deceived me. You are not coming back. I know it from people who are well informed . . .

It may be supposed that the skies at Grignan cleared in time for Mme de Sévigné and the Count de Grignan to have returned to the château before Christmas, although there is no letter extant to confirm the supposition. The next letter of Mme de Sévigné's on record is addressed to Philippe Moulceau from Grignan, and dated January 10, 1696. His letter was not found in the collection at Grignan, but we know from Mme de Sévigné's reply on the tenth that Moulceau had written to send good wishes for the new year to his friends at the château, to wish Mme de Sévigné a long and healthy life. Mme de Sévigné's response is redolent of a melancholy unsuitable to the season. The élan that enlivens her letters from Lambesc is missing here. One can only conclude that, upon her return, she found Mme de Grignan's health precarious; the hoped-for recovery, an illusion. Had Mme de Sévigné, by then, lost hope in her daughter's recovery? She would seem to have lost heart along with hope, to have lost her once irrepressible zest for living as well. "It is *you* to whom a long life should be wished," she wrote pointedly to Moulceau, "you, who have so much still to offer to the world."

As for me [the letter continued], I am no longer good for anything. I have played my role in life, and had I been consulted, I would never have chosen so long a life. One rarely comes to the end—to the dregs of life—without finding humiliation. But we are fortunate that it is the will of God by which this, as all other things in this world, is decided; everything is better left in His hands than in ours.

A glance at the chronology suggests that these morbid reflections on old age might have been inspired by the imminency of Mme de Sévigné's seventieth birthday—February 5, 1696—less than a month from the day on which she wrote her world-weary note to Moulceau.

When next she wrote him, two weeks later—the fewest of lines, only a dozen on less than a page—she was panic-stricken. Mme de Grignan had evidently suffered a relapse; complications of some kind must have overtaken her.

I replied to your last letter early in the year [the letter began]. This note is solely to implore you to ask Monsieur [Doctor] Barbeyrac* to read these records of the consultations on my daughter's condition, to beg him to use even more dispatch than usual in giving us his advice which we value so highly, and to send it to us at the very earliest moment possible. I make my appeal to your heart, Monsieur, which has surely not forgotten how deeply involved mine is in anything that concerns my daughter. On so important an occasion, I would fear to offend you if I made the slightest excuse or included so much as a word of formal compliment.

Moulceau and Barbeyrac must have rushed to oblige, to judge by this next letter of Mme de Sévigné's, addressed to Moulceau on February 4, some ten days later, its mood as blithe as that of the first was somber:

I was not deceived, Monsieur, when I thought that you would be touched by my grief, and that you would make all the haste possible to assuage it. Monsieur Barbeyrac's prescription and your letter took wing, as you had hoped they would, and it appears that the low-grade fever— which had shown signs of lingering—took flight, as well, at the very

---

*Charles Barbeyrac was the most renowned doctor in Montpellier, long renowned for its medical faculty. Doctors had been called into consultation at Grignan, and it is the record of those consultations which was forwarded to Barbeyrac in Montpellier.

mention of the name of Monsieur Barbeyrac! All in all, Monsieur, there is something miraculous about so rapid a change, and I have no doubt that your good wishes and your prayers contributed to it. You can gauge my gratitude by the effects. My daughter asks to be included in all I say to you, here; she sends you a thousand thanks and implores you to share them with Monsieur Barbeyrac. We are only too happy to follow the prescription of being patient and taking our rhubarb, which agrees with her very well.* Thank God, both on your part and ours, for we cannot doubt that you are interested in our gratitude and, then, Monsieur, think of all the inhabitants of this château, and imagine how grateful they are to you!

"You are not yet rid of me, Monsieur," Madame de Sévigné wrote Moulceau on February 29:

It is easier never to enter into correspondence with you than to break off this one which I started up again, as irregular as it is. Honesty obliges me to tell you that we are angry that, during this time when we are so ill (for I always speak in the plural!), you took the liberty of falling ill, too!

We think that the least we owe the rhubarb—and we are mightily obliged—is not to allow it to be condemned without a trial. That is the gist of the report I have drawn up for Monsieur Barbeyrac. Out of respect, I do not address it to you, but because of my friendship for you and because of that I flatter myself you have for me, I implore you to read it, and help him to understand it. I am not sealing it, because I do not write methodically, and it is you alone who can explain it to him. It would be a real act of charity on your part, Monsieur, to do this for me. You will not have to search too hard to find in your heart all the kindness which we hope will ensure your excusing the liberties we take with you.

There is a third reason for writing you. I must send you a letter that I finally extracted from our dear philosopher, Corbinelli. He reminded me of the name of "scoundrel" which I had forgotten, but which you so well deserve.† Adieu, then, illustrious "scoundrel"! Never has such

---

*Rhubarb, which came from China via Persia, was thought to contain two substances, one purgative, the other, astringent. It was a remedy universally prescribed, primarily in control of dysentery.

†The nickname of "scoundrel" for the eminent jurist was a longstanding joke among the three friends.

*a quality been so highly esteemed by both mother and daughter as this
one is in you ...*

Thanks to the rhubarb and the improvement in her daughter's health,
Mme de Sévigné had recovered her sense of humor—or pretended to have.

The correspondence with Coulanges was brisk in February and March:
three letters from him to his cousins at Grignan in the month of February
are extant; there are two in March, the first, dated the fourteenth, the second,
the nineteenth. In the first, a very long letter, he kept them posted on the
social activities of the Paris Lenten season, on a rash of marriages at Court
and in the Capital.

His letter of March 19 begins:

*The chapter of marriages is finished; now, it is the chapter of deaths
which begins. Mme de Guise departed this world on Saturday, at noon
... She died at Versailles, fully conscious and fully resigned ... The
King saw her two hours before she died ... She instructed that she be
buried without ceremony, and preferred interment in the Carmelite
Convent to all the ostentation of Saint-Denis, alongside the kings* ...
Poor Blanchefort is dead at twenty-seven years of age, with unpara-
lleled courage. It is a great loss to his house, but especially to his
mother, who will die of grief—if anyone actually dies of grief—and
Mme du Plessis-Bellière will die of the death of her daughter. And who
do you think died suddenly yesterday? It was Monsieur de Saint-Géran,
who had gone to confession on Wednesday in order to complete his
jubilee ... and yesterday, feeling fit and fine, he went to his parish of
Saint Paul where, as he entered the confessional, he suddenly fell dead ...*

Coulanges's obituary column went on and on, but it was the death of
young Blanchefort, the son of old friends, which came as such a shock to
Mme de Sévigné, and to which she responded so emotionally in her reply
to Coulanges which was datelined, "At Grignan, March 29":

*All else aside [she wrote], I weep and cry aloud at news of the death
of Blanchefort, that charming boy—so utterly perfect, an example to
all our young people! His reputation already made, his valor recognized
and worthy of his name: good-humored, fortunately for him (for to be
ill-humored is a curse), a joy to all his friends as to his family, respon-*

---

*The Duchess of Guise was entitled by reason of her Bourbon blood to burial in the royal crypt at
the Abbey of Saint-Denis, but chose instead to be interred at the Carmelite Convent in Paris.

sive to the affection of Mme his Mother and Mme his Grandmother, loving them, honoring them, appreciative of their merit, taking pleasure in letting them know his appreciation, and thereby repaying them for the excess of their love; a good mind and a fine face, never inebriated with his youth, as so many young people are, those who seem to have the devil in the flesh—and that darling, amiable boy disappeared in a moment's time, like a flower blown away by the wind, with no occasion to account for it, neither war nor pernicious air. My dear cousin, where can one find words to speak to the grief of those two mothers, or to make them understand what we are thinking, here? We are not thinking of writing to them, but if the occasion should arise, and you find the proper moment to mention my name and that of my daughter, along with those of the Messieurs de Grignan, you know how we feel about their irreparable loss . . .

The numerous other deaths reported by Coulanges were touched on only lightly by Mme de Sévigné, in response:

I pay due respect to the saintly and modest sepulture of Mme de Guise, whose renunciation of that of her royal ancestors merits an eternal crown. I find Monsieur de Saint-Géran very fortunate and you, as well, to be obliged to console his widow. Say to her, on our behalf, whatever you deem appropriate. And, as for Mme de Miramion, that mother of the Church, hers will be a public loss.*

Adieu, my dear cousin, I would not know how to change tone, at this point. You have made your jubilee. No sooner had you shed the sackcloth and ashes you told me about than you were off on a delightful excursion to Saint-Martin. The good life presently enjoyed by Monsieur and Mme de Marsan entitles them to the pleasure of your company occasionally, and being added to your list of favorite hosts. As for me, I deserve to be inscribed on the list you reserve for those who love you, although I fear you may keep none for the latter.†

When Mme de Sévigné laid down her pen—on March 29, 1696— having signed and sealed this letter to Coulanges, she could not have dreamed

---

*Mme de Miramion, as a young, wealthy and pretty widow in 1648, had been abducted by the Count de Bussy-Rabutin, who had been misled into believing that she welcomed his matrimonial advances, whereas she chose to devote her life to her salvation.

†The last lines of Mme de Sévigné's letter refer to another family joke: it is not, precisely speaking, "a list of favorite hosts" kept by Coulanges; it is, rather, a "basket"—a special kind of basket strapped to one's back, like a knapsack—into which Coulanges pretended to tuck the names of the favorite people on his list. "I put the whole d'Armagnac household into my basket," he wrote in a letter dated December 31, 1694.

that she was never to pick up her pen again, that this letter to Coulanges was to be her last.

A week later, on April 6—Holy Week of 1696—she felt flushed, grew feverish, and took to her bed in her apartment on the second floor of the southwest corner tower of the François I façade of the château, its windows opening out upon the green valley, far below, and beyond, to the foothills of the Alps—"the beautiful view" by which, as she had written Coulanges, her apartment was "surrounded."

Five days later, on April 11, a priest from the château's collegiate Church of the Holy Savior was summoned to administer extreme unction.

On April 17, the twelfth day of her illness, Marie de Rabutin-Chantal, Marquise de Sévigné, was dead.

On April 18, clad in a gown of blue brocade, the corpse was sealed into its lead coffin for interment in the subterranean Grignan family crypt to the left of the high altar in the Church of the Holy Savior, in the shadow of the château.

The blue brocade gown in which Mme de Sévigné was buried implies that Provençal funeral customs were observed—the casket left open, the corpse adorned—despite the fact that the deceased had voiced vigorous objection to those customs in a letter to her daughter, dated December 13, 1688:

> My God, my daughter [she had written eight years earlier], how silly your women are, there, alive and dead! You horrify me by your description of those ribbons in their hairdress. What a profanation! It reeks of paganism! What folly! Oh, my child, I would hate to die in Provence! The least you can do is to promise me that you will never send for the coiffeur along with the casket-maker!

The interment and the funeral services took place on April 18, 1696, on the day following Mme de Sévigné's death. That much is known—the facts established by the Parish Register of the Church of the Holy Savior; the death certificate signed by the Curate. So much is known, no more. The rest is conjecture; conjecture that one of the Grignan prelates—either the Bishop of Carcassonne or the Archbishop of Arles—said the Requiem Mass, and that the immediate family was in attendance: the Count de Grignan, the Chevalier de Grignan, the Marquis de La Garde, Pauline de Simiane and her husband, all in mourning garb, all taking their places in the Gallery, high on the left wall of the Chapel. All the family, with the exception—or so it would appear—of the Countess de Grignan, the daughter of the deceased.

LVIII

Was it a conspiracy of silence by which the news from the sickroom during the twelve days of Mme de Sévigné's fatal illness was suppressed? And if so, by whom and why? What had the family to conceal? Legend has a way of cloaking the death of the famous in mystery. The death of Mme de Sévigné is a case in point and, in her case, the family contributed mightily thereto. Biographers, essayists and monographists have sought for three centuries to penetrate the mist shrouding that tower room at Grignan during Easter week of 1696. Mme de Coulanges was puzzled by the silence, complaining to Pauline de Simiane, as early as May 2, about the paucity of news supplied them in Paris: "I still know none of the details of that fatal illness. My persistence in ferreting them out gives proof that I am not yet in control of my emotions."

Such few letters as are extant shed little light on the nature or the course of the illness that struck Mme de Sévigné so suddenly. Smallpox it was not, although a rumor to that effect had wide circulation for a century and a half. The rumor was false, some confusion having probably arisen from the fact that the death of the Countess de Grignan, in 1705, was attributable to that most dread and widespread disease of the seventeenth century. Not that there was any shame attached to it: Mme de Sévigné did not die of it, but if she had, the disease would have been no cause for secrecy. The seventeenth century was a time, however, in which great significance was attached to the deathbed scene, especially if it was edifying— Mme de Sévigné herself describing at great length that of her saintly uncle Saint-Aubin. ("That is where one learns how to die," had been her comment.) In view of this attitude, the Countess de Grignan's reticence about the deathbed of her mother is especially curious.

Family tradition had it that the cause of death in the case of Mme de Sévigné had been "*une fièvre continue*," a constant, an unabating, unremitting fever, the same diagnosis made in the case of the Cardinal de Retz and the Abbé de Coulanges, among so many others. This was the term of reference in seventeenth-century France for any infectious malady beyond the diagnostic capability of the medical faculty. The term included all the bacterial and viral diseases for which the pathology of the day had no proper designation. There is surmise that, in Mme de Sévigné's case, it was a form of grippe or influenza or pneumonia. So her family thought, according to the Chevalier Perrin, the editor of the first authorized edition of *The Letters of Mme de Sévigné*, his information as to her illness and demise—like his authorization for the publication of her letters—coming from his friend Pauline de Simiane.

The infection struck at an hour when Mme de Sévigné's resistance was low, according to Perrin, which means according to Pauline, Mme de Sévigné's granddaughter. "It is easy to imagine what Mme de Sévigné suffered," Perrin wrote in his Preface to the first four volumes of the *Letters* published in 1734:

> *She could not have lived in constant fear for the life of her daughter— as she had done for six months running—without damage to her health. Arising in the middle of the night to go to see if her daughter was sleeping, she neglected herself in her concern over Mme de Grignan. Succumbing, at last, to stress and strain, she fell ill on April 6, 1696, of an unremitting fever ...*

Not only had the sleepless nights and long vigil at her daughter's bedside taken their toll of Mme de Sévigné's robust health, her will to live had been sapped by her anxiety and her consuming fear that she might outlive her daughter. That thought had come to be her greatest dread:

> *If my heart were only made of crystal [she had written her daughter in 1680] wherein you could discern the excruciating pain that filled it when you expressed the wish that my life span should exceed yours, you would know how ardently I pray that Providence will not reverse the natural order of things which made me your Mother and brought me into the world long before you; that is the rule and the good reason, my bonne, whereby I should be the first to go, and God—for whom our hearts are an open book—well knows and perfectly understands how ardently I ask of Him that that order be observed in my case.*

With Mme de Grignan convalescent, but still too weak to pick up her pen in April of 1696, the duty of notifying Charles de Sévigné in Brittany and the Coulanges in Paris of the death of Mme de Sévigné devolved upon Pauline de Simiane, herself too shattered by the loss to do more than dictate to a secretary. Pauline's letters to Charles and to the Coulanges are missing, but Coulanges's letter in reply to Pauline's is extant. Datelined "Paris, April 25," it begins:

Far from finding you remiss, Madame, for not having written in your own hand, I am surprised that you even thought of me on an occasion so cruel and so grievous as that in which we find ourselves ... My God, Madame, what a blow for all of us! As for me, I am lost in the realization that I will never again see that poor cousin of mine to whom I have been so tenderly attached since the day of my birth, and who reciprocated my affection with her own—equally tender, equally constant. If you could see, Madame, all that transpires here, you would be still more aware of the reputation your grandmother enjoyed, the esteem in which she was held, for there could have been none greater. She is widely regretted, and tribute is being paid her everywhere, as is her due ...

Tribute was paid to Mme de Sévigné by even so generally harsh a critic as the Duke de Saint-Simon, who made this entry in his *Mémoires* for the year 1696:*

Mme de Sévigné, a most amiable woman and the best of company, died ... at Grignan, at the home of her daughter, whom she idolized—despite the fact that such idolatry was scarcely merited. I was a very close friend of her grandson, the Marquis de Grignan. This woman, thanks to her easy manner, her natural graces and her scintillating wit, had the knack of making anyone with whom she conversed—even the dullest—appear to great advantage. In addition to all that, she was extremely kind, and possessed of a great fund of knowledge, although she never flaunted it ...

Coulanges's April 25 letter, addressed to Pauline, continues:

Mme de Coulanges is in such a state of desolation that I fear for her health. From the day we learned of the cruel malady which finally took her [Mme de Sévigné] from us, we have not had a moment's ease. It is killing Mme the Duchess de Chaulnes, and poor Mme de La Troche ... We come together to weep and to mourn our loss ... In the midst of such distress, our anxiety over Madame your Mother's

---

* The Saint-Simon *Mémoires* were not published until the nineteenth century.

health is not one of the least. Do not impose on yourself the task of writing again, but ask one of your people to keep us posted ... I will not write to Mme your Mother for fear of augmenting her grief by my letters ... I will not show your letter to Mme de Coulanges. Please pass along my condolences to Monsieur de Simiane, to Monsieur the Chevalier de Grignan and to Monsieur de La Garde. Good God, what a scene in that "royal château!" And how much I pity poor Mlle de Martillac, who so well acquitted herself of all the duties of a kind and tender friendship!

Letter by letter, bit by bit, the story unfolds: through Coulanges's letter of April 25, we learn that it was Mlle de Martillac, the Countess's *dame de compagnie*, who took over the sickroom, who served Mme de Sévigné as nurse in her last illness. Not her daughter. The Count de Grignan came frequently to his mother-in-law's sickbed, as subsequent letters indicate. Pauline de Simiane evidently commuted from the nearby Simiane château at Valréas to Grignan to the bedside of her beloved and loving grandmother. Is it possible that the Countess de Grignan did not put in an appearance in that sickroom? Was it her absence which the family found embarrassing, which they went to some effort to conceal?

The Count de Grignan, on the other hand, was attentive, climbing the stairs day after day to her tower apartment, as is made clear in this reply of his (dated May 7) to a letter of condolence from the Marquis de Pomponne. The Count's is the briefest of notes, a dozen or so lines, the most significant of which are these:

In truth, Monsieur, everyone who was attached to Mme de Sévigné by bonds of blood or friendship is to be pitied; above all, those who saw her during the last days of her life, and recognized the full extent of her sterling worth and intrinsic virtue. I hope, some day, to have the honor of telling you in detail of those days, for it could not but win your admiration.

The Count de Grignan, in the above letter to Pomponne, only hinted at the touching deathbed scene he had witnessed; in his letter to Moulceau, dated May 28, he is more expansive:

You understand better than anyone, Monsieur, the extent of the loss we have suffered, and my own personal sense of deprivation. You were well aware of Mme de Sévigné's sterling worth. It is not only a mother-in-law I lose, it is a staunch and tender friend, an enchanting compan-

ion. But what is even more deserving of our admiration than our regret is that she was a woman of strength.* From the earliest days of her illness, she faced up to the approach of death with astonishing firmness and resignation. That woman who was so weak and tender when it came to those that she loved, found herself possessed of great courage and faith when she had reached the point where she felt she should concentrate on herself and on her own salvation. We were bound to realize—by the use to which she put the store of knowledge she had amassed—how useful and important it is to fill one's mind with good things and with the devotional literature for which Mme de Sévigné had such a surprising avidity. I give you a report on all these details, Monsieur, because they coincide with your sentiments and with the affection you had for her for whom we weep . . .

Here, at last, is the detailed report of the exemplary death so dear to seventeenth-century hearts. It had taken Monsieur de Grignan a month to recover his equilibrium and write to Moulceau the most revealing letter of the lot.

The Countess de Grignan, when she finally brings herself to write, ten days after the funeral, to Philippe Moulceau—in reply to his letter of condolence—is far more reserved than her husband, far more chary of details. Her letter—one of the few of hers to survive—is dated April 28:

As considerate as you are, Monsieur, you need not fear to reopen my wounds by speaking to me of the sad loss I have suffered. The thought of it is never out of my mind; it is graven so deep in my heart that nothing could augment or diminish it . . . You have lost a friend of incomparable merit and loyalty. And I, Monsieur, what have I not lost? . . . For a loss so deep and so irreparable, there is no hope of relief save that of tears and moans. I have not, as yet, the strength to lift my eyes sufficiently high to find the source whence comfort comes. I can, as yet, only look about me—and, there, I can no longer see that person who showered me with benefactions, whose only thought was to give me daily tokens of her affection, along with her companionship. It is indeed true, Monsieur, that it requires a superhuman strength to sustain so cruel a separation and deprivation. I was in no way prepared for it: the perfect health which I had seen her enjoy, the year of illness which imperilled mine a thousand times had led me to believe that the order of Nature would not prevail in our case. I in-

---

* Another reference to "the strong woman" of the Book of Proverbs.

dulged in false hope when I hoped that I would never have to suffer so grave a loss. I suffer it now, and feel it to its full intensity . . .

Mme de Grignan's letter to Pomponne, in acknowledgment of his expression of sympathy, is little more enlightening than that to Moulceau. Dated July 15, it begins:

You are well aware, Monsieur, of the terrible misfortune which has befallen me. You know what a fond association, what an intimate union was broken off, what bonds were severed. No separation could be more cruel; its impact on me as strong today as on the first, seeming—if possible—even crueller, even bitterer. My mind now dwells longer on every circumstance connected with my loss, and it seems to me that I am racked by pain even sharper than before. A loss so irreparable allows for no hope of solace save in tears and regrets. I have not as yet had the strength to lift my eyes high enough to seek more solid conso- lation; here, below, they search in vain for the person who lavished love and benefactions on me . . .

The letter to Pomponne is a repetition, to some extent, of the pat phrases addressed to Moulceau on April 28. What strikes the reader of the correspondence is that the Countess de Grignan's letters to those two close family friends are far more impersonal, far more abstract than those of the Count de Grignan. It is the Count who speaks feelingly and touchingly of Mme de Sévigné's last days. Mme de Grignan skirts the subject. The Count speaks as a man who stood beside his mother-in-law's deathbed, within sound of her voice, within range of her glance, within reach of her arms. The Countess speaks as if by rote, as if at a far remove from the scene, confining herself to generalities, banalities, platitudes about mourning and bereavement.

The letters cited above—to Moulceau and Pomponne—constitute a major portion of the evidence which has led a number of eminent Sévign- istes—including Gérard-Gailly, one of the most renowned of twentieth- century Sévigné scholars—to conclude that Mme de Grignan's failure to reveal the last words exchanged with her mother on April 17 was not due to any reluctance on her part but to the fact that there was nothing to reveal, no such last words having been exchanged, no final interview between them having taken place; Mme de Grignan could not write movingly about her mother's last days for the reason that she had not been present in her mother's tower room when she breathed her last. Whether or not she was present in the Gallery of the Church of the Holy Savior on the day of the funeral is a much-debated question.

If not, why not? Theories abound; hypothesis is piled upon hypothesis, conjecture upon conjecture. Philippe de Dangeau may have touched it off with these few lines in his *Journal* under the date of April 26, 1696:

> *I learned of the death of Mme de Sévigné, who was at Grignan with her daughter, herself so very ill that word of her mother's death was kept from her.*

The most obvious, the only acceptable explanation for a daughter's absence from her mother's deathbed, from her mother's funeral—especially a mother as devoted as Mme de Sévigné—would be that the daughter herself lay critically ill at that hour.

One asks oneself, however, whether it would have been possible—even in a château as large as Grignan—to keep secret the news of a mortal illness and a death transpiring within the walls of the château itself, to hide or to hush the coming and going of physicians, priests and prelates, friends and family, casket-makers and coiffeurs, purveyors of the baked funeral meats. Would Mme de Grignan not have sent to ask for whom the bells tolled? Or would orders have gone out to still the bells?

But it would seem that precautions such as these were inordinate in view of the fact that Mme de Grignan was no longer critically ill—still anaemic, perhaps, still languid, but definitely on the mend, as is evidenced by the fact that none of Mme de Sévigné's letters to the Coulanges in the late winter or early spring of 1696—and none of theirs to her—even make mention of Mme de Grignan's health, proof in itself that she was out of danger, convalescent. In view of the fact that Mme de Sévigné took alarm if Mme de Grignan even cleared her throat, no news—in this instance—can only be construed as good news. That is how Gérard-Gailly, editor of the 1953 Pléiade edition of the Sévigné *Letters*, interprets it.

Only a month after her mother's death, as early as mid-May, 1696, the Countess appeared to one visitor, at least, to be well on the road to recovery. The Archives of the Ministry of Marine yield up a holograph letter from the Count d'Estrées to his superior, the Count de Pontchartrain, dated May 15, reporting a visit to Grignan en route to Toulon:

> *I stopped at Grignan [d'Estrées wrote] where I found everyone still in deep mourning for Mme de Sévigné. Mme de Grignan appeared grief-*

stricken, but although she shows the effect of her ordeal and of the protracted illness she has undergone, I did not find her as greatly changed as I had been led to expect, and I am convinced that she will regain her health in a better climate . . . better air . . .

"Better air" could be taken to mean the air of Paris—of which, in view of the improvement in the Countess's health, there was already talk at Grignan in early June of 1696, as is to be deduced from letters from the Coulanges in which they speak of their joy at word of the Countess's recovery and at her hint of an imminent visit to Paris. (Mme de Coulanges does admit dismay "at the thought that the one person in all the world most concerned about that [the Countess de Grignan's health] should not have been allowed to share this joy.")

Still, the rumor of Mme de Grignan's critical illness could not have spread to Paris, to Dangeau's ear, in April of 1696, had it not been widespread in Provence and, if it was widespread in Provence, it must be assumed that Mme de Grignan—as befitted an invalid—took to her bed, and thus put in an appearance at neither her mother's death chamber nor her mother's funeral.

And if Mme de Grignan was not gravely ill in April of 1696, how to account for her thus absenting herself? One theory is that she was away from Grignan, at the time.

A rumor was current in the mid-nineteenth century to the effect that she had been visiting the Marquis de La Garde at his Château La Garde-Adhémar where she sometimes repaired for a change of scene and air. The rumor originated with the Abbé Nadal who, in 1858, published a pamphlet entitled *Essai historique sur les Adhémars et sur Mme de Sévigné* (*An Historical Essay Dealing with the Adhémars and Mme de Sévigné*), in which he claimed that the Count de Grignan had taken his wife to his cousin's nearby estate to spare her the anguish of seeing her mother *in extremis*: "Her husband did not want her to witness the devastating scene," according to the Abbé, "and had taken her to La Garde where she was kept in ignorance for several days of the misfortune which had befallen her." The Abbé Nadal even produced a witness: an old man who remembered that, in his youth, another old man had told him that during Mme de Sévigné's illness, the Countess had been removed from Grignan, and that the bells had not rung out for the funeral.*

---

* The Abbé Nadal properly identified the Countess de Grignan's letter to Pomponne as having been datelined "At La Garde." So it was, but—as we have seen on page 498, it was dated July 15, three months after her mother's death.

Fuel was added to the fire of conjecture in 1860 when a letter came to light written in 1737 by a Baron de Guillibert,* a resident of Orange, and addressed by him to a friend in Brittany—a letter in which was drawn a shocking picture of a mother and daughter at loggerheads, irreconcilably alienated, a letter occasioned by the publication, that year, of the last two volumes of the Sévigné *Letters* edited by Perrin. "No one in this region," the Provençal nobleman claimed in his letter, "could be ignorant of the fact that these two women made up to one another for the bitterness of their arguments by the honeyed words they strewed, at random, across the pages of their letters." According to this poison pen, the discord between them was notorious, and not even death could reconcile their differences:

Mme de Sévigné fell mortally ill at Grignan, but even though they found themselves under the same roof, it proved impossible to bring them together; the mother—with her last breath—insisting that she would receive her daughter only if the latter asked to see her, and the daughter insisting that she would go to her mother only if the latter asked for her to come.

The Baron disqualifies himself as a trustworthy witness by the venom of his attack; writing forty years after the fact, he has never forgiven the Count de Grignan for storming the citadel of Orange, at the head of the King's troops; and he sees Mme de Sévigné as a supercilious Parisienne, and resents her witticisms at the expense of Bretons and Provençals.

It is the contention of the late Jean Cordelier, one of the most brilliant of all the generations of Sévigné scholars—whose *Madame de Sévigné par elle-même* (*Madame de Sévigné in Her Own Words*) defies categorization literarily, transcending as it does the genres both of essay and of biography—that it was Mme de Sévigné herself who forbade the door of her death chamber to her beloved—her too-well-beloved—daughter. Aware that she was facing death, she made the supreme sacrifice, denying herself the thing most dear to her in all the world—her daughter's presence—as a requisite to entering the presence of her Maker. Careful reading of the *Letters* provides ample support for this theory of Cordelier's. Mme de Sévigné, by her own account, was twice denied absolution because, in the opinion of the priests, her excessive love for her daughter left too little room in her heart for love of her Lord and Savior. Augustinian theory—in which Mme de Sévigné was

---

*Baron Guillibert, "Lettre inédite d'un gentilhomme provençal à une dame de Rennes en 1737 au sujet de Mme de Sévigné et du Chevalier de Perrin." *Bulletin historique et philologique,* 1909.

well versed—insists that love of the creature must not be allowed to interfere with love of the Creator. The first sacrifice Mme de Sévigné felt compelled
to make in contemplation of death was that of her "idol." (The saintly
Arnauld d'Andilly had called her, by her own admission, "an outright pagan"
on account of her "idolatry" of her daughter. Saint-Simon's obituary notice,
quoted earlier in this chapter, uses the same word—"idolatry"—in reference
to Mme de Sévigné's excessive love for her daughter.)

> *You laugh, my* bonne, *about that poor love of mine [she had written
> her daughter in 1675]. You think that it is to do it too much honor to
> consider it an obstacle to devotion. It could hardly be seen as a road-
> block to salvation, but I think it qualifies as a sin if it wholly occupies
> the heart, and whatever it may be that possesses us, it is more than
> enough to make us unfit to receive communion.*

In the light of this theory of Cordelier's, the Count de Grignan's letters
to the Marquis de Pomponne and to Moulceau—both devoutly religious
men—are clarified and bear rereading: the Count is describing what was
seen as an exemplary death: "That woman who was so weak and tender
when it came to those she loved," he had written Moulceau, "found herself
possessed of great courage and faith when she had reached the point where
she felt she should concentrate on herself and on her own salvation." (Almost
the very words Mme de Sévigné, herself, had used in 1671 when Arnauld
d'Andilly, Pomponne's father, had warned her that her "idolatry" of her
daughter was "pagan" and "sinful," and that she "had best," as she quoted
him, "begin to think of my immortal soul.")

She had found such courage and such resignation, at the end, because
she believed that it was by the grace of God that she had seen her daughter
come out of the valley of the shadow, by the grace of God that her own
death was to precede that of her daughter. Having been spared by the grace
of God from the horror of facing a life without her daughter, Mme de
Sévigné could face death without her. The Chevalier Perrin, who is the
mouthpiece of Grignan family tradition, states it categorically in the Preface
to his edition of her *Letters*:

> *Those strong religious convictions of hers which led her to ask for and
> to receive the last sacraments on the fifth day of her illness, prove
> beyond the shadow of a doubt that, in surrendering her life to God,
> she had also surrendered the great love of her life.*

She had turned to God, Perrin implies, and away from her earthly attachments. She had been long torn, as she had phrased it, between "love of the Creator" and "love of the creature." At the last, her immortal soul took precedence over even her daughter.*

An edifying death according to the criteria of the times, but inevitably traumatic for Mme de Grignan—possibly even humiliating, to be excluded from the death chamber, denied her mother's last embrace, her mother's blessing.

LIX

The keening over, legal and business matters confronted the heirs.

Jean Le Camus, a *Lieutenant-Civil* (an officer of the Civil Court in Paris) addressed a letter to the Countess de Grignan on July 2, 1696:

> *I do not know, Madame [he wrote], whether you are aware that Mme de Sévigné—on the eve of her departure—left with me a box sealed with her coat of arms. She did not write me about it, but I readily understood that it was to serve the same purpose and under the same conditions as when she confided the box to me on the eve of her previous voyage. The main reason was that she wanted you to make proper use of the enclosed papers in the event Monsieur your brother brought any claims against you ... One of Mme de Sévigné's maids having told Monsieur your brother that I had such a box, I explained to him Mme your Mother's intentions in the matter and, at the same time, at my request, he signed a paper of which I am sending you a copy ...*

Mme de Sévigné had left no will, made no bequests for the reason that she had earlier disposed of all she possessed, dividing it between her chil-

---

* There was precedence, in that century, for such gestures of renunciation, as is reflected in the deathbed scene of *The Princess of Cleves*—the remarkable novel by Mme de La Fayette—in which the Princess "turned away her face" and dismissed her daughter from her room two days before her death.

dren, giving to her son at the time of his marriage, as to her daughter, at the time of hers—reserving for herself for her lifetime only the usufruct of several of her properties. Le Camus's letter suggests that there was fear in her mind that if Charles came to consider any of these divisions inequitable, he might contest them.

If so, she did not truly know her son, and did him a grave injustice, as the following letter written by him to his sister—one of only two full-length letters in Charles's hand to survive—offers proof:

Now that I am back in my own part of the country [his letter begins], I need only know from you what disposition you want made of the money due you: whether you want it sent to you or held for you in Paris or paid to someone you designate. Your instructions will be promptly followed.

With his sister in Provence at the time of their mother's death, and unable—or unwilling—to go to Paris herself, it had devolved upon Charles de Sévigné to settle their mother's affairs in the capital, to dispose of the remaining furnishings, to pay off the skeleton staff retained at the Carnavalet, and turn over that Hôtel to its owners.

I found, among my Mother's papers [Charles's letter to his sister continued], one addressed to you and to Monsieur de Grignan, as yet unsigned ... My Mother had always made a secret of what had transpired between you two at the time she so generously made over certain properties to me, just prior to my marriage. She was never really open with me on that subject. She sometimes suspected me of being resentful and jealous of you because of all the tokens of love she had given you. I now have the pleasure of giving you proof of how I really feel about you. Monsieur the Lieutenant-Civil [Le Camus] was a witness to my first reactions which are always the most natural. I am very well content with what my Mother did for me during the time I was in the Gendarmes [Regiment] and at Court. I have not lost sight of what she did for me at the time of my marriage, to which I owe all the happiness of my life. I am well aware of how much she did for us both over so many years, to repeat the words of your letter. Nothing else mattered to me. Were it true that she always loved you better than she loved me, do you really believe, my dear sister, that I could have resented her finding you more loveable than me? ... You can peacefully enjoy all you possess through the generosity and kindness of my

Mother . . . Even if it were within my power to contest your share—the very thought of which is horrifying to me—I would consider myself a monster even to think of such a thing . . . The course of my life is three-fourths over. I have no children of my own, but you have given me some whom I love tenderly . . . I have no desire for more than I have . . . If I had any wish for greater wealth, it would only be for your sake and that of your children . . . Adieu, my very dear and charming sister . . . Is it not a consolation for us to know that in loving one another as tenderly and as naturally as we do, we are fulfilling the wish of the best and dearest of Mothers?

Charles de Sévigné, in 1703—finding the solitude of Les Rochers no longer solitude enough—gave up his post of King's Lieutenant in Brittany and all other worldly connections to go, accompanied by a wife as devout as he, to Paris, and there to take up residence in the Faubourg Saint-Jacques, close beside the Church of St.-Jacques-du-Haut-Pas and the Saint-Magloire Seminary, long a community of the devout. His mother would not have been too surprised; she had long ago discerned and remarked on his "anchoritic tendencies." His death occurred in 1713, in an odor of sanctity, his last years having been spent in a seminarian's cell at Saint-Magloire.

A man of his word, Charles bequeathed his estate to a child of his sister, as he had said he would. It was Pauline de Simiane who inherited her uncle's worldly goods; Charles's nephew, the Marquis de Grignan, had met his death in 1704, at age thirty-three, of smallpox, in the arms of his wife, the Marquise de Grignan, who had sped from Paris to Thionville (in Alsace) to nurse him. The Duke de Saint-Simon, who was usually stingy with praise for his contemporaries, lavished it on the Marquis de Grignan, writing in his *Mémoires* for the year 1704:

I lost a friend with whom I had been brought up, a very gallant man and one of great promise. He was the only son of the Count de Grignan and of that Mme de Grignan who was the object of such adoration in the Letters *of Mme de Sévigné, her mother—the eternal repetition of that admiration constituting their [the* Letters'*] only defect . . . [the Marquis] having greatly distinguished himself at the battle of Hochstedt, died at the beginning of October at Thionville, with smallpox said to be the cause. He had a regiment, he was a brigadier, and on the point of advancement.* His widow, who had no children, was a saint,*

---

*Michel Chamillart wrote the Chevalier de Grignan to tell him that "the King being well pleased" with the Marquis's valor at Hochstedt intended naming him a *Maréchal de Camp.*

but the saddest and most silent I have ever seen. She shut herself away in her house, where she spent the rest of her life—some twenty-five years, perhaps—without ever stepping out the door, except to go to church, and seeing no one whomsoever.

She may, from time to time—Saint-Simon notwithstanding—have seen her sister-in-law Pauline de Simiane, the only member of the Grignan household to smile upon her during those unhappy months she had spent at the Château de Grignan after her husband's departure for the front in early 1695, shortly after their wedding. In any event, it was to Pauline that she bequeathed the magnificent library she had collected throughout the years of her widowhood—years devoted to prayer and to reading. The sisters-in-law may have seen one another during the years Pauline spent in Paris with her husband, the Marquis de Simiane, who served—until 1715—as First Gentleman of the Bedchamber to the Duke d'Orléans in his Court at the Palais Royal.

The Countess de Grignan, the Marquis de Grignan's mother, could not—did not—long survive her son. He had died, after nine years of marriage, without issue and with him died the Grignan name; with his death, the Grignan line was doomed to extinction; that ancient and illustrious House, fated to vanish from the face of the earth.* This only son had been the family's pride and joy; all their hopes had been pinned on him; for him, they had ruined themselves. Infinite sacrifice had been made to forward his career, to buy him his regiment and to make it the best in the service. He, if not his father—it was to be hoped—would attain to the monarch's favor, and rebuild the Grignan fortunes. His wife's dowry was to have restored the family to solvency. With his death, that dowry had to be refunded. Mme de Grignan had dedicated her life to the perpetuation of the Grignan name and line; to that end—in pregnancy after pregnancy, in miscarriage after miscarriage—she had sacrificed her health, her youth, her beauty.

She dragged on a few months—ten, to be exact—after the death of the Marquis, and even managed to appear at the side of her husband in her role of Governor's Lady, to join in the official welcome tendered the Count of Toulouse,† who had come to Provence on a tour of inspection of the Mediterranean ports and harbors.

---

*In one last, desperate effort to perpetuate the family name, the Chevalier de Grignan—at the age of sixty-three—was persuaded to marry a Mlle d'Oraison in the hope that they could produce an heir to replace the one lost at Thionville, but the effort proved fruitless.

†The Count of Toulouse was Louis XIV's son by Mme de Montespan, legitimized—like so many of the royal bastards—by his father.

At the conclusion of that tour, the Countess de Grignan fell prey to smallpox, the same disease that had taken the life of her son and, like him, succumbed to it, expiring on August 13, 1705, at the age of fifty-nine, in the city of Marseille where she and the Count had been living since the end of 1696.

No longer able to afford the seigneurial way of life in either their château or their capital city of Aix-en-Provence, the Grignans had faced up to the final humiliation of giving up their château, and had taken cover in Marseille in a nondescript town house, on a street which today bears their name.

The eagle's nest at Grignan lay empty, deserted, echoing with silence; the orchestra of which the Count de Grignan had been so proud, disbanded— along with the half-hundred liveried servitors: what was ringing in the ears of the Count and Countess de Grignan as their carriage wound its way down the steep grade from the summit of the rock to the village and the valley floor was a requiem for the House of Grignan. The loss of a limb could not have been more acutely painful to a Grignan than to know himself cut off from the edifice erected by his ancestors, back in the mists of time. In abandoning that ancient pile to wind and dust and desuetude, the Grignans were abandoning their lares and penates, the sanctuary of their tutelary gods and spirits, abandoning countless generations of their forefathers slumbering in the crypt below the Church of the Holy Savior.

Though they had come precipitately down in the world from the heights of Grignan, the Count and Countess indulged themselves in one last burst of glory, prepared to empty their purse—or, if it was already empty, to borrow against their last unencumbered property, if one remained—in order to finance a final fling in honor of the Duke de Berry and the Duke de Bourgogne, the Sons of France (sons of the Dauphin, grandsons of the *Grand Monarque*) who were expected at the border of Provence on March 3, 1701. The Count de Grignan, with a retinue of two hundred Provençal noblemen, awaited the royal visitors at Beaucaire, wined and dined them, entertained them at grandiose balls, receptions and operatic galas at Aix, Toulon, Marseille and Lambesc, almost totally at his own expense.

To the end of his days, the Count de Grignan served King and country selflessly, indifferent to the fact that an indifferent monarch allowed him to bankrupt himself in the process. In 1707, two years after the death of his wife, he played a major role in the defeat of the Austro-Piedmontese army, forty thousand strong, which threatened to occupy all Provence. The Maréchal de Tessé had advised the King that all was lost, short of a miracle. The miracle was wrought, courtesy of seventy-five-year-old Grignan, who raised a motley force of noblemen, bourgeois, workmen and villagers to swell the Maréchal's cadres—the Count himself on horseback, in the thick of battle, for eight hours without dismounting.

Destitute of purse if not of honor, he lived to devote another seven years of his life to his monarch and his province, using himself up physically as well as financially in their service, nobly fulfilling his functions as Governor and Lieutenant-General. In late December of 1714, aged eighty-two and failing fast, he went to Lambesc to open the Assembly of the Communities of Provence, as had been his custom for almost half a century. The Assembly over, the Governor set out for Marseille on December 30. Halfway home, he became so ill that he had to be carried into a peasant's hut in the village of Saint-Pons, on the River Arc, where he expired during the night. He had not lived to see the dawn of the year 1715, the year of the death of his monarch (at age seventy-seven, in the seventy-second year of his reign).

The Duke de Saint-Simon in his *Mémoires* for the year 1714 did justice to the last of the Grignans, writing,

The Count de Grignan, serving alone in the post of Lieutenant-Governor and Commander of Provence, died at eighty-three years of age, in an inn, en route from Lambesc to Marseille. He was tall, a fine figure of a man although homely, fully aware of his rank and prestige, a very fine gentleman, very polished, very aristocratic, very obliging, and universally esteemed, loved and respected in Provence where, obliged to tremendous expenditure without adequate reimbursement, he ruined himself. Of his children, only two daughters survived him: Mme de Vibraye, daughter of the sister of the Duchess de Montausier, who had been forced—through mistreatment at the hands of the last Mme de Grignan (Sévigné)—to enter into a most unsuitable marriage, and who remained on bad terms with them [with her father and stepmother]— and Mme de Simiane, daughter of La Sévigné, adored by her mother as the latter had been by her own. Her marriage to Simiane was a love match. His duties were few, but he held the post of First Gentleman of the Bedchamber to the Duke d'Orléans, not a time-consuming post but one which earned him the appointment of Lieutenant-General of Provence, a post of which the King had not disposed at the time of his death.*

*The Duke d'Orléans, upon becoming Regent for young Louis XV in 1715, named the Marquis de Simiane to succeed his father-in-law as Lieutenant-General of Provence.

The death of the Countess de Grignan, in 1705, had not gone unnoticed by the Duke de Saint-Simon, although it would have been better for her reputation with posterity had he completely passed her by:

Madame de Grignan [as his Mémoires *relate], that old beauty and précieuse, of whom I have talked enough, died at Marseille . . . and, despite all Mme de Sévigné had to say in her* Letters, *she was little regretted by her husband, by her family or by the people of Provence.*

Saint-Simon, it must be remembered, however, is not infallible, and it is difficult to believe that Mme de Grignan was "little regretted" by her daughter Pauline, her mother's darling no less surely than Mme de Grignan had been that of her mother, Mme de Sévigné.

The Marquis de Simiane, Pauline's husband, who succeeded her father as Lieutenant-General of Provence in 1715, survived him by only three years, dying at the age of forty-seven, in 1718.

By 1720, a widowed Pauline had given up Paris to take up residence in Aix-en-Provence, and remained there until her death in 1737, leaving issue of three daughters: the eldest, a nun; the next, married to the Marquis de Vence; the youngest, to the Marquis de Castellane-Esparron. With the death of Pauline de Simiane, in 1737, finis was written to the saga of the immediate family circle immortalized by Mme de Sévigné in her *Letters.**

Little Coulanges, who was a member of the intimate—if not the immediate—family circle, had predeceased Pauline de Simiane by twenty-one years. Not only was Coulanges not overlooked by Saint-Simon, his death—in 1716—inspired the little Duke to one of his most delightful character sketches (much abbreviated here). "The world has also lost Coulanges," the *Mémoires* take note at the end of a long list of deaths. Saint-Simon hailed him as the

perfect dinner guest, with never a trace of inebriety or debauch, the life of the party, the ideal travelling companion. Above all, an unfailingly delightful conversationalist, and so kindly a soul as to be incapable of malice, he was sought after all his life, and made for himself a greater place in the world than might have been expected of a man of so futile an existence. He went more than once to Brittany, and even to Rome, with the Duke de Chaulnes, and made other voyages with other friends,

---

*The issue of the two Simiane girls—their children and their children's children—are the only ones who can lay claim today to being lineal descendants of the renowned epistolarian.

never spoke evil of anyone nor did anyone any harm, and enjoyed the esteem and friendship of the elite of his time to whom he was a constant joy and delight until his eighty-second year. In perfect health and with all his faculties until then, he died after a rather brief illness. His wife, who had greater wit than he and a keener intellect, had likewise made many friends in the Capital and at the Court, where she no longer set foot. They lived together in harmony, save for occasional dissonances which spiced their relations and titillated all their various circles of friends. She survived him by many years.* She had been very pretty, but always discreet and respected . . .

In 1737, with the House of Grignan extinct, the Château de Grignan was sold. Sometime in the mid-eighteenth century, Nicholas du Muy, son of the purchaser—in recognition of the by then growing fame of Mme de Sévigné, who lay buried in the Church beneath his château—laid down a marble slab, ornamented with asphodels and fleur-de-lys, to denote her final resting place.

She was not to rest in peace. In 1793, four years after the Fall of the Bastille—in a not atypical revolutionary excess—a mob from the village of Grignan, led by a Justice of the Peace and a notary, burst into the Grignan crypt and broke open the caskets, including that of Mme de Sévigné, ostensibly to reclaim the lead and other metals for much needed cannon balls for the Armies of the Republic. There could be no excuse, however, for the desecration of the bodies, the bones from the various caskets tossed unceremoniously into a common grave.

Scraps of the blue brocade gown in which Mme de Sévigné's body had been clad almost a hundred years earlier were grabbed as souvenirs; two are still to be seen: one, under glass, at the Musée Carnavalet; the other, at the Library of the Sorbonne. A lock of Mme de Sévigné's hair was snatched by the stonemason who had pried open the marble slab bearing her name and leading to the crypt below the floor of the Church. The notary was awarded a bit of rib which he exhibited in a medallion. The Justice of the Peace appropriated a tooth which he mounted in a gold ring, and was said to have sawed off a section of skull to send to a celebrated phrenologist named Gall for analysis.

Thus ends the grim story of Mme de Sévigné's mortal remains. The story of her literary remains is a happier one.†

---

*Mme de Coulanges enjoyed ill health into a ripe old age, her demise coming in 1723.

†The Château de Grignan, as well as the Church, was vandalized in 1793: windows and mirrors smashed, roof and terrace tiles ripped off, portraits of the hated Grignan aristocrats defaced—all save that of Mme de Sévigné. In the late nineteenth century, a restoration of that historic pile was undertaken by another purchaser, a not entirely authentic version of the original which is open to public view today.

LX

In 1696, within months of her death, Mme de Sévigné came to birth in the world of literature: five of her letters appeared in print, included in the *Mémoires* of the late Count de Bussy-Rabutin, which had been edited by his son, Amé-Nicolas. In 1697, *The Letters of Messire Roger de Rabutin, Comte de Bussy* were edited and published, likewise by his son: two of the four volumes of that edition were devoted to the correspondence between the Count and his favorite cousin, the Marquise de Sévigné. The hundred letters by the Marquise proved to be the ones to arouse the enthusiasm of the reading public—enthusiasm and critical acclaim enough to suggest publication of other letters from that gifted pen.

It may have been in 1715, after the death of her father, the Count de Grignan, that Pauline de Simiane began to give thought to publication of the thousands of letters exchanged between Mme de Sévigné and Mme de Grignan throughout the twenty-five years of their separations—letters which lay moldering and yellowing, tied in packets and stacked in coffers or boxes stored away at either the Château de Grignan or at Pauline's house at Aix-en-Provence or at Mazargues, a Grignan estate near Marseille.

It may have been—for, here, too, there are no incontrovertibly established facts to go by; here, too, we are back in the realm of conjecture—it may have been, and probably was, Pauline's friend and cousin l'Abbé Celse* de Bussy—rather than his brother, Amé-Nicolas de Rabutin—who induced her to send him either autographs or copies of the letters composing that huge mass of correspondence. It is established that some letters were sent—the first lot including 137 letters and a commitment that if her cousin found them interesting, as she said she felt sure he would, she would "search out others," even if it meant "burning the midnight oil" to do so.

The Abbé Celse de Bussy assured her of his delight in the samples she had sent him, and importuned for more. She followed up with another fifty

---

*Pléiade editor Gérard-Gailly is convinced that the Abbé Celse was the cousin with whom Pauline collaborated on publication of her grandmother's letters; Pléiade editor Roger Duchêne leans toward Amé-Nicolas as the cousin to whom she sent the letters.

letters. When they met in Paris, the next year, Pauline and her cousin decided to put off preparation of the edition; Mme de Sévigné's oeuvre, they agreed, deserved better than so limited a selection. More letters were to be sent to Burgundy when Pauline returned to Provence.

When she moved to Aix in 1720, she engaged a scribe to make copies of still more of Mme de Sévigné's letters to her daughter, which ran into the hundreds (all undated, bearing the day of the week or the month, but not the year, all in a handwriting difficult to decipher). Amé-Nicolas died in 1719, thus it must have been his brother, the Abbé Celse, with whom she shared that batch of letters.

If so, then it must have been he who turned them over to a publisher or allowed them to fall into the hands of literary friends who did so. Whoever the guilty parties were—and young Voltaire's name is on the list of suspects—the year 1725 saw the publication of the first volume dedicated entirely to the letters of Mme de Sévigné; it was entitled *Lettres choisies de Mme la marquise de Sévigné à Mme de Grignan sa fille qui contiennent beaucoup de particularités de l'histoire de Louis XIV* (*A Selection of Letters from the Marquise de Sévigné to Mme de Grignan Her Daughter, Containing Many Events of Interest in the History of the Reign of Louis XIV*). This slim, seventy-five-page, octavo volume bore the name of neither editor nor publisher nor place of publication. The twenty-eight letters it contained had apparently been selected for their anecdotal value vis-à-vis the Sun King's Court—letters, for example, describing the suicide of Vatel, the death of Turenne, the declaration of war against the Dutch, and the crossing of the Rhine, among others.

The first edition proved so successful that a two-volume edition followed shortly thereafter, in 1726, containing more examples of the mother-daughter correspondence and Mme de Sévigné's art. Entitled *Lettres de Marie de Rabutin-Chantal, Marquise de Sévigné, à Mme la Comtesse de Grignan, sa fille* (*Letters from Marie de Rabutin-Chantal, Marquise de Sévigné, to Mme the Countess de Grignan, Her Daughter*), the two volumes contained a total of 138 letters, and went into a second and then a third printing before the year was out. Pauline did her best to cast doubt upon the authenticity of this unauthorized version of her grandmother's work, and demanded that the authorities ban further distribution. Her demand was denied on the ground that no violation had occurred to justify such intervention, and the surreptitious *Letters* continued to enjoy the brisk sale which had gone on in secret during the controversy, if one is to believe the Paris rumor mills. The reading public had discerned a new genius, and was not to be put off.

An article in the *Journal de Trévoux* indicates that the reading public had long been on the track of the Sévigné letters. "Public curiosity is finally satisfied," the *Journal* reported in 1726: "What has happened to those long hidden letters is what usually happens to precious documents of that kind about which public curiosity has been aroused. They finally come to light."

If the public responded enthusiastically to those surreptitious publications of the Sévigné *Letters,* Pauline de Simiane was so infuriated by the products of the clandestine press that she decided to sponsor her own authorized edition of the letters, and selected a personal friend, the Chevalier Denis-Marius Perrin, a fellow citizen of Aix with excellent literary credentials, to serve as editor.

But, as it developed, the great mass of fascinating, engrossing, titillating material Pauline turned over to Perrin was tied up in a string of caveats. He was enjoined, first of all, to print nothing that might embarrass or humiliate the living, nothing derogatory nor derisive about the dead—especially none of those with descendants living in Provence, who might confront Pauline angrily on publication.

Pauline next made clear to Perrin that she would suffer no mention to be made of the mother-daughter quarrels, no invasion of her parents' privacy. Nor were the heart-to-heart mother-daughter talks to be allowed to become public property. (Strike out all reference to Mme de Grignan's menstrual periods! Strike out all reference to Mme de Sévigné's exhortations to sexual continence—or, if not continence, then precautions such as separate beds or, better still, separate bedrooms!)

Above all, the collapse of the Grignan family fortunes was to be kept secret: no mention was to be made of the sordid stratagems, the ignoble expedients to which that noble family had to resort to dodge dunning tradesmen, to stave off lawsuits, bankruptcy, public disgrace, dishonor—the embarrassments, the humiliations of the year 1690, to which Mme de Sévigné referred as "the Year of Ignominy."

These were the major injunctions laid upon Perrin, but not the only ones: Pauline's grandmother had been given to sallies of humor sometimes broad, sometimes bold; to stories sometimes risqué, sometimes daring, a bit off-color—stories at which Pauline might have laughed, in earlier years; at which she frowned in later years of intensifying religiosity and prudery. (Strike out all reference to Charles de Sévigné's erotic extravaganzas, to his bout with a venereal disease no less virulent for having been transmitted by a Duchess!) Pauline wanted to see her grandmother's genius as a letter-writer acknowledged, but not if it set skeletons rattling in the family closet.

There was one last taboo: all reference to Mme de Sévigné's aberrant religious tendencies was to be avoided.*

In the face of all these prohibitions, Perrin was left with little leeway. He even agreed to Pauline's proviso that the huge collection of autograph letters she had entrusted to him was to be returned to her upon completion of his task. It was her intention to destroy the originals of her grandmother's letters along with those of her mother; she would run no risk, in later years, of their falling into the wrong hands, no risk of exposure of the final ignominy. The Grignan ship had sunk, but Pauline would make sure that it was pictured as going down with all banners flying.

The first four volumes of the authorized Perrin edition, containing 402 letters, and entitled *Recueil des lettres de Mme la marquise de Sévigné à Mme la comtesse de Grignan, sa fille (A Collection of the Letters of the Marquise de Sévigné to Mme the Countess de Grignan, Her Daughter)*, were published in Paris in 1734. His good intentions to the contrary, Perrin had failed to eliminate all the material Pauline considered objectionable, and she made her displeasure felt. In the wake of the publication, she was swamped with mail—"thousands of letters," she wailed, showered upon her; more than she "could cope with," much of the comment resentful or censorious.

Pauline decided to eliminate the danger of any further exposé of family secrets. Mme de Grignan's letters to Mme de Sévigné were lifted from the coffers in which they had reposed for thirty or more years, and put to the torch.

Could it have been that concern over the keeping of family secrets was not Pauline's only reason for destruction of her mother's letters? Is it possible that what she did was done to spare her mother the censure of posterity? This could have been the case had Mme de Grignan's letters given evidence of that dark moodiness, that caustic tongue, that hauteur, that chill reserve—all those unpleasant qualities for which her mother and Saint-Simon—and ensuing generations of Sévignistes—have reproached her. Even so, one cannot but regret the loss. The Countess de Grignan lacked her mother's verve, her mother's flair, her mother's genius, but she wrote extremely well, as her few surviving letters attest. (Mme de Sévigné's extravagant praise of

---

*Mme de Sévigné gave every indication of leaning toward Jansenism, a mystical Roman Catholic movement which took its name from Cornelis Jansen, a seventeenth-century Dutch theologian, who based his doctrine on that of St. Augustine—the doctrine that the soul must be converted to God through divine grace. The fundamental purpose of Jansenism was a return to greater personal holiness; it fell afoul of the Church for its predestinarianism, its discouragement of frequent communion, its attacks on the Jesuits.

her daughter's epistolary talents must be discounted, for reason of her known bias.) One regrets, above all, that the dialogue was lost, because the correspondence was actually a "conversation," as Mme de Sévigné repeatedly referred to it—to lose a letter, in her words, was "to lose the thread of our conversation." With only Mme de Sévigné's letters extant, it is a monologue to which the world fell heir, not the dialogue the correspondence intended. The solo in which Mme de Sévigné's voice is raised throughout these many volumes is clear, compelling, exquisite—hers assuredly the superior of the two voices. Even so, one finds oneself forever turning pages, forever straining to catch even the echo of Mme de Grignan's words.

Having consigned her mother's letters to the flames, Pauline de Simiane demanded that Perrin return the letters of her grandmother which she had entrusted to him, and abandon the idea of any further publication.

Perrin, who was committed to his publishers to furnish the final two volumes of an announced set of six, withstood his patroness's onslaughts, and politely but firmly refused to comply with her demands. He could not— or would not—leave his "work unfinished," although he "wished," he admitted in a letter to Pauline, that he "had never undertaken the preparation of the correspondence for publication."

Three years later, in April of 1737, the final two volumes of *A Collection of the Letters of the Marquise de Sévigné* (212 letters, this time) came off the press. Whether it was ethical or unethical on Perrin's part—a not infrequently debated question in academic circles—he defied Pauline de Simiane by whom he had been commissioned, and thereby saved a masterpiece from oblivion.

It is doubtful that Pauline de Simiane, whose death occurred on July 3, 1737, had time to receive and read those last two volumes of her grandmother's ever more famous letters. She did not live to destroy the originals of those letters but, *in extremis,* she extracted from her son-in-law, the Marquis de Castellane-Esparron, a pledge that he—before his death—would ensure their destruction.

Year by year, other letters of Mme de Sévigné's to others than her daughter—to the Coulanges, to the Cardinal de Retz, to Mme de La Fayette, and to the Duke de La Rochefoucauld—came into Perrin's hands, some hitherto unpublished; these were published by him in 1751, in a volume of five hundred pages.

In 1754, seventeen years after Pauline de Simiane's death, Perrin produced still another edition of *The Letters of Mme de Sévigné,* this one running to 770 letters, in eight volumes. With Mme de Sévigné's granddaughter in her grave, the Chevalier Perrin had enjoyed far greater freedom of action and had restored some of the material earlier condemned by his patroness's prudishness. Not that this edition did not reflect a scrupulosity and a sense of propriety of Perrin's own (the kisses, for example, bestowed by Mme de Sévigné on Mme de Grignan's "fair cheeks and beautiful throat" were struck out by the Chevalier as overly fervent). Thus, Perrin imposed a censorship all his own, omitting some passages, abbreviating or "refining" others to suit his taste, tampering with vocabulary, orthography and syntax to suit his personal literary standards. (Finding the form of address "my *bonne*" inelegant and archaic, Perrin arbitrarily changed it to read—in nine cases out of ten—"my child" or "my daughter.")

Not until the late nineteenth century, when there was some basis for comparison with the few remaining originals and with exact copies of originals, would it become clear to what extent Perrin had expurgated, distorted and bowdlerized the letters of Mme de Sévigné. His excuse was weak: that she herself, had she foreseen that her letters would one day be published, "would have gone to greater pains" in their composition, would have "composed them more artfully." Perrin would seem to remind us that Mme de Sévigné had specifically requested the Count de Bussy to apply whatever finishing touches he considered necessary to those letters of hers that were to be included in the *Mémoires* he was at that time preparing to send to the King. Perrin should have remembered that Bussy had declined, pointing out that Le Brun would never have agreed to touch up a Titian.

Perrin did not live to reap the rewards of his long endeavor, dying—at age seventy-one—in February of 1754, a few weeks after having given final approval of the manuscript to the printer.

From 1754 on, editions of the Sévigné letters proliferated. The popularity enjoyed by the numerous volumes of the Marquise's correspondence spurred people to rummage through their desks, their archives and muniments rooms for other jewels from her pen.

In 1756, the Marquise's letters to President Moulceau came to light, in pristine condition, and were published with no alteration in the text.

In 1784, almost half a century after the death of Pauline de Simiane, her son-in-law, the Marquis de Castellane-Esparron, on his deathbed, remembered the pledge made her—on hers—to destroy the autograph letters of her grandmother. Somehow reluctant to perform the act himself, the old man called in a young cousin, the Count de Castellane-Saint Maurice, delivered the precious packets into his hands, and instructed him to burn them in his presence. The young man exclaimed in horror at the thought of such an act of vandalism. With the writer of the letters dead for almost a century, a fifth-generation member of her family found it difficult to understand a scrupulosity which would require destruction of an acknowledged masterpiece.

The Marquis insisted that as long as the originals remained, there remained a danger of exposure of family secrets thus far preserved. The Grignan line was extinct, but its name was glorious; he would not see it sullied by indiscreet revelations from the letters. "I gave my word of honor," the dying man said, "that this correspondence would perish with me." The pyre was lit; the auto-da-fé took place at the old man's bedside.

The deed was done; the promise kept. Sévigné scholar Gérard-Gailly, in describing that scene, felt that it was Mme de Sévigné's heart of hearts—not the organ buried with her body in 1696—which then, and only then, stopped beating.

In 1790, at Rouen; in 1801, at Paris, ten-volume editions of the Sévigné correspondence were published, including all the letters known to exist at that date.

The edition of 1806 was notable for the reason that the letters were, for the first time, arranged in chronological order. Until then, they had been grouped under the name of the correspondent to whom they had been addressed: all the letters to the Countess de Grignan, in one section; all those to Bussy, in another, and so on.

In 1814, a veritable treasure trove of letters was discovered, and promptly published: sixty-seven letters addressed by Mme de Sévigné to the Count and Countess de Guitaut, all sixty-seven holographs preserved in the Archives of the Guitauts' Château d'Époisses, in Burgundy.

The last edition to be based totally on Perrin was published by Nicolas Monmerqué in 1818-9. It has been called the first "modern" edition of the Sévigné letters in view of its critical approach to the material included. Monmerqué attempted to evaluate the authenticity of the various Perrin texts at his disposal.

The next year, 1820, Monmerqué experienced a bliss seldom vouch-safed a scholar. From the Château de Grosbois, in Burgundy, came a bulky manuscript addressed to the editor of the latest Sévigné edition. It was a leather-bound volume entitled *Letters of Mme de Sévigné,* and dated indubitably from the mid-eighteenth century. The Marquis de Grosbois had found it in the library of his château, amid other eighteenth-century documents and papers. To a Sévigniste like Monmerqué, it was soon clear that the Grosbois folio contained copies of originals, free of the taint of Perrin censorship or Perrin editing.

It was on this manuscript which Monmerqué based the monumental work of his which would appear, in 1862, under the title of *Letters of Mme de Sévigné, Her Family and Friends,* published by Hachette as the inaugural issue of its *Grands écrivains de la France (Great Writers of France)* series—a rare compliment, indeed, from the French literary establishment for a woman who was not even a professional writer, who could lay claim—properly speaking—to no works, no *oeuvre*. This great edition was composed of fourteen large volumes, and included not only all the letters which had turned up by then, but also a biographical section by Paul Mesnard, bibliographical and lexicographical notices, as well as all the requisite appendices.

In 1873, the Grosbois folio and the *Grands écrivains de la France* edition of the Sévigné *Letters* stood suddenly invalidated.

The true story of the Capmas manuscript and how it came to light in 1872 is stranger than any fiction. In January of 1872, at Sémur-en-Auxois, in Burgundy, the library of a once prosperous local family went up at auction, and an antique dealer from Dijon purchased, along with many other items, six calf-bound, folio manuscript volumes, with the words *Letters of the Marquise de Sévigné* embossed in gold on the spine. On display in a shop window in Dijon, these volumes caught the eye of Charles Capmas, a member of the law faculty of the university of Dijon. Out of his field, beyond his depth, Capmas consulted Sévigné scholars—to learn that he had made the find of the century, literarily speaking!

What the discovery of Pompeii and Herculaneum meant to archaeologists in the eighteenth century, the discovery of the Capmas manuscript meant to Sévignistes in the nineteenth. Research by Sévigné scholars indicates that the Capmas manuscript was a copy of autograph letters sent by Pauline de Simiane to her cousin in Burgundy, probably between the years 1715-20, at the time they were planning to prepare and publish their edition of Pauline's grandmother's letters. (What the Grosbois manuscript proved to be was a hasty, faulty copy of the Capmas.)

In 1876, Charles Capmas published fragments from the manuscript in two volumes entitled *Unpublished Letters of Mme de Sévigné*, but it was not until 1953—in the three-volume Pléiade edition of *The Letters of Mme de Sévigné*, edited by Gérard-Gailly—that full use was made of the Capmas manuscript.

For the first time, thanks to the Capmas, Mme de Sévigné appears in print in her true colors, speaks in her own voice, own words, speaks her mind with all her distinctive, original verve and vigor. Not only had Perrin omitted all the passages he and Pauline de Simiane deemed unseemly, indelicate or even inelegant; he, and Monmerqué after him, had taken liberties with her style and her syntax—the excisions, the truncations often resulting in garbled sentences, in lacunae in the text. The letters from the Capmas manuscript are uncut, uncensored, unadulterated, and in them finally, the Marquise comes through to us, with all her robust, salty sense of humor, her deceptively simple but highly sophisticated air. Not that she is everywhere herself in the new editions; she cannot be fully restored to life; the Capmas covers only 319 letters, less than half the correspondence with her daughter. For the other half, one must put up with Perrin, and a distortion of Mme de Sévigné's features.

Sévigné scholar Roger Duchêne makes a valiant effort to rescue her from Perrin's fatal embrace: Duchêne's three-volume, fully annotated edition of the *Correspondence,* published by Pléiade in the 1970's, very skillfully puts together—as if they were the pieces of a jigsaw puzzle—the various texts available, offering the reader a choice of several versions.

Fortunately, Mme de Sévigné's personality is so vivid, so vibrant that neither Perrin's mutilations nor Monmerqué's "refinements" can wholly blur or dim it, and wherever she is allowed to speak for herself, she dazzles and enchants the reader as she did her contemporaries. In print as in the flesh, she is ebullient, effervescent, irresistible, irrepressible. She involves us in her life: her "character grows and changes," in the words of Virginia Woolf: "she seems like a living person, inexhaustible." The world she has preserved for us in her letters remains as lively, as picturesque and as exciting as the day she signed and sealed them. Her dukes and duchesses, dressmakers and dramatists, maîtres d'hôtel and maréchals, muleteers and gardeners—handfuls of dust though they have long been—live on forever in her glowing prose, as real, as near and dear to us as the characters in our favorite novels. For the most part, the names of noblemen and courtiers of the Sun King's reign are forgotten—all save those evoked by Mme de Sévigné's magic pen! Versailles stands as a monument to the Splendid Century, but it is the Sévigné letters which people it, bring it back to teeming life.

She has created—or, rather, recorded—a world which the reader leaves regretfully. To arrive at the last letter in the correspondence is a shock ("All else aside, I weep and cry aloud at news of the death of Blanchefort, that charming boy"). Happily, with time on one's hands—and the best available edition, to date, within reach—one can settle back in one's armchair or one's hammock, and start all over again, begin at the beginning ("It seemed to me that my heart and soul were being ripped out of me—indeed, what a cruel separation!")

André Gide, in 1917, expressed his deep resentment at learning that he was not reading a trustworthy edition of Mme de Sévigné's *Letters.* There may never be one—unless the other half of the Capmas, containing copies of the other three hundred letters of the correspondence, turns up somewhere, sometime, which—although unlikely—is not beyond the realm of possibility. Meanwhile, we take Mme de Sévigné as we find her—if not always the scintillating original, then, at least, a reasonably good facsimile.

And even the facsimile retains an extraordinary measure of charm and fascination. Never has anyone attained to literary eminence by so tortuous a route or at longer odds than Marie de Rabutin-Chantal, the Marquise de Sévigné.

Pen-Portrait of Mme de Sévigné by the Countess de La Fayette

All those who undertake the portrayal of fair ladies usually break their necks to please them with flattery, without ever daring to mention their defects. As for me,* Madame, thanks to the privilege of being unknown to you, I am going to depict you very boldly, and feel free to tell you the truth about yourself without fear of calling down your wrath upon my head. I am in despair at having only agreeable things to say, for it would give me great pleasure, if having reproached you with a thousand faults, I found myself, this winter, as well received by you as a thousand others who have spent their lives in adulation. I positively refuse to smother you with praise or inundate you with encomiums or indulge myself by reporting that your figure is superb, that your complexion has a radiance and bloom typical of a twenty-year-old; that your mouth, your teeth and your hair are incomparable. I need not tell you all these things; you already know them from your mirror. But, since you probably do not converse with your reflection, what your mirror cannot tell you is how utterly entrancing you are when you are engaged in conversation, and it is that which I have to tell you. Be advised, Madame, if by chance you are unaware of it, that your wit so greatly adorns and embellishes your person that there is none other on earth so delightful as you when you are carried away in animated conversation from which restraint has been banished. Everything you say has such charm, and so well becomes you that your words invoke spontaneous laughter, bring smiles to the lips of those who surround you, and the brilliance of your mind brings such a glow to your face and such a sparkle to your eyes that— although it would seem that wit should strike only the ear—it is certain that yours dazzles the eye as well, and that when one listens to you talk, one is oblivious to your imperfections; one loses sight of the fact that your features

---

*This pen-portrait of Mme de Sévigné by Mme de La Fayette, under the nom-de-plume of "An Unknown," appeared first in early 1659 in a collection by a minor literary figure of the time and would be reprinted in the Chevalier de Perrin's 1734 edition of the Sévigné *Letters*. The word "unknown"—*"inconnu"*—is given in the masculine, purposely misleading in its implication that the writer was a man.

are not entirely regular; one credits you with a flawless beauty. You can see that if I am unknown to you, you are not unknown to me, and that I must have had more than once the honor of seeing and listening to you in order to have discerned what gives you such attractions as to startle all those about you. But I want also to show you, Madame, that I am no less familiar with those solid virtues of yours which strike me as the most outstanding, most impressive. You have a great and noble soul, capable of dispensing treasure, but incapable of stooping to acquire it. You are responsive to glory and ambition, but no less so to pleasure, and pleasure would seem to have been devised expressly for your benefit. Your presence enhances every occasion, and every occasion enhances your beauty. In sum, joy is the true state of your soul, and sorrow more alien to your spirit than to that of anyone else. You are, by nature, tender and passionate but, to the shame of our sex, that tenderness has availed you naught, and you have confined it to your own [sex]—with Mme de La Fayette as the only beneficiary. Ah, Madame, if there had been some man fortunate enough not to have been found unworthy of the treasure which she [Mme de La Fayette] enjoys, and had he not made every effort to possess it, he would deserve to suffer all the distress to which love subjects those who fall beneath its sway. What great good fortune to be the master of a heart like yours, the sentiments of which are expressed in the gallant wit with which the Gods have endowed you! Your heart, Madame, is doubtlessly a treasure of which no man is deserving; there has never been a heart so generous, so ardent, so faithful. There are people who suspect that you do not always allow it to be seen in its true colors, although on the contrary, you are so used to harboring in it no sentiment which is not honorable that you sometimes allow a glimpse of that which it would be more prudent to conceal. You are the most polite and obliging person in the world and, thanks to that sweet and easy way of yours, the simplest hail or farewell prescribed by social custom sounds—coming from you—like a protestation of friendship, and all the people who leave your presence leave convinced that they have won your esteem and consideration although they cannot recall, even to themselves, precisely what token you gave them of the one or the other. All in all, you have been blessed by Heaven with graces bestowed on none but you, and the world is grateful to you for having manifested a thousand delightful qualities hitherto unknown. I do not want to embark upon a description of them all because I would be breaking my resolve not to lavish praise upon you. Furthermore, Madame, to give you praise worthy of you and worthy of appearing in print, it would be necessary to be your lover, and that honor is not mine.

Appendix

It is regrettable that no English translation of the letters of Mme de Sévigné merits recommendation. None is complete, and the few that are available are literal, stilted, awkward, and totally devoid of style—a grave injustice to the author. A translation of a major portion of those letters (based on the large Paris edition of 1806) was made in England in 1811 (nine volumes published by J. Walker, London). Several rather grandiose editions of the Sévigné *Letters* appeared in England in the 1920's in celebration of the three hundredth anniversary of the Marquise's birth: the seven-volume Carnavalet Edition was copyrighted in England in 1927 and printed in the United States in 1928, with an Introduction by A. Edward Newton (the bibliophile and author of *The Amenities of Book-Collecting and Kindred Affections*). A ten-volume edition, entitled *Letters from the Marchioness de Sévigné to the Countess de Grignan, Her Daughter*, was published by Spurr and Swift in London in 1927. The third English edition of the Sévigné letters was a two-volume publication entitled *Letters of Mme de Sévigné to Her Daughter and Her Friends*, with an introductory essay by Richard Aldington. The text is identified as "a selection of the nine volumes printed for J. Walker, London, 1811." Curiously enough, all three of these editions of the 1920's are based on the 1811 translation. Curious, too, is Aldington's comment that "a reprint of the bulk of Mme de Sévigné's letters in an early-nineteenth-century translation needs no apology." Some twenty years later, in 1946, came Arthur Stanley's translation of a smattering of the Sévigné letters (246 out of a thousand and more) in his *Mme de Sévigné: Her Letters and Her World*. The next selection of Sévigné letters (272 this time) to come into print appeared in the mid-1950's (in the United States in 1955), under the title *Letters from Madame la Marquise de Sévigné*. The Introduction is by Somerset Maugham, and the translation bears the name of Violet Hammersley, more valorous than discreet in not clinging to anonymity, like all the other English translators save Stanley.

Bibliography

The potentially vast Sévigné bibliography is here confined to a list of the landmark editions of the *Letters*, along with a list of those relatively few books or articles to which reference is made in the text of this biography, and of those works that, although not cited specifically, have proved to be of especial interest to me in my research.

Earliest Editions of the Letters
of Mme de Sévigné to Mme de Grignan

Lettres choisies de Mme la marquise de Sévigné à Mme de Grignan sa fille qui contiennent beaucoup de particularités de l'histoire de Louis XIV. No publisher or place of publication given, 1725.

Lettres de Marie Rabutin-Chantal, Marquise de Sévigné, à Mme la comtesse de Grignan, sa fille. No publisher or place of publication given, 1726.

Lettres de Marie Rabutin-Chantal, marquise de Sévigné, à Mme la comtesse de Grignan, sa fille. The Hague, 1726.

Recueil des lettres de Mme la marquise de Sévigné à Mme la comtesse de Grignan, sa fille (ed. Chevalier de Perrin). Paris: Vols. I–IV, 1734; Vols. V and VI, 1737.

Earliest Editions of the Correspondence
Between Mme de Sévigné and the
Count de Bussy-Rabutin

Mémoires de Messire Roger de Rabutin, Comte de Bussy. Paris, 1696.

Les Lettres de Messire Roger de Rabutin, Comte de Bussy. Paris, 1697.

Lettres de Mme de Sévigné au comte de Bussy-Rabutin. Amsterdam and Paris, 1775.

Correspondence with Others

Recueil de lettres choisies pour servir de suite aux lettres de Mme de Sévigné à Mme de Grignan, sa fille. Paris, 1751.

Lettres de Mme de Sévigné à Monsieur de Pomponne. Amsterdam, 1756.

Bibliography

Lettres nouvelles ou nouvellement recouvrées de la marquise de Sévigné et de la marquise de Simiane, sa petite-fille. Paris, 1773.
Lettres inédités de Mme de Sévigné. Paris, 1814.

Modern Editions of the Sévigné Letters

Lettres de Mme de Sévigné, de sa famille et de ses amis (Les Grands écrivains de la France). Paris, 1862–8.
Lettres inédités de Mme de Sévigné à Mme de Grignan, sa fille, extraites d'un ancien manuscrit, publiées pour la première fois, annotées et précedées d'une introduction par Charles Capmas. Paris, 1876.
Lettres. Edition nouvelle, comportant de nombreux fragments inédits et restitutions de textes, établie avec une introduction, des notes et un index, par Gérard-Gailly. Paris, 1953–7.
Correspondance de Mme de Sévigné (ed. Roger Duchêne). Paris, 1972–8.

Letters, Memoirs, Journals, Poetry, Novels and Other Contemporary Works

Bussy, Roger de Rabutin, Comte de. *L'Histoire amoureuse des Gaules.* Liege, 1665.
Coulanges, P. E. de. *Recueil de chansons choisies.* Paris, 1694.
———. *Mémoires.* Paris, 1820.
La Fayette, Marie Madeleine Pioche de la Vergne, Comtesse de. *Correspondance.* Paris, 1942.
———. *La Princesse de Clèves.* Paris, 1678.
La Guette, Mme de. *Mémoires.* Paris, 1856.
Loret, Jean. *La Muse historique, ou recueil des lettres en vers contenant les nouvelles du temps, écrites à Son Altesse Mademoiselle de Longueville, depuis duchesse de Nemours (1650–1665).* Paris, 1857–91.
Ormesson, Olivier Lefèvre de. *Journal.* Paris, 1861.
Pomponne, Arnauld de. *Mémoires dans la collection Petitot des mémoires relatifs à l'histoire de France.* Paris, 1824.
Retz, P., Cardinal de. *Mémoires.* Paris, 1956.
Rochefoucauld, F., duc de La. *Oeuvres complètes.* Paris, 1964.
Rouvroy, Louis de, duc de Saint-Simon. *Mémoires de Saint-Simon.* Paris, 1879–1928.
Tallemant des Réaux, Gédéon. *Les historiettes de Tallemant des Réaux.* Paris, 1932–4.
Visconti, Primi. *Mémoires sur la cour de Louis XIV.* Paris, 1906.
Voltaire, François-Marie Arouet de. *Siècle de Louis XIV (1751).* Paris, 1914.

Books

Adam, Antoine. *Histoire de la littérature française au XVIIᵉ siècle.* Paris, 1948–56.

Bibliography

Aldis, Janet. *The Queen of Letter-Writers*. London and New York, 1907.

Allentuch, Harriet R. *Madame de Sévigné: A Portrait in Letters*. Baltimore, 1963.

Aubenas, J. *Histoire de Mme de Sévigné, de sa famille et de ses amis*. Paris, 1842.

Babou, Hippolyte. *Les Amoureux de Mme de Sévigné; les femmes vertueuses du grand siècle*. Paris, 1862.

Bailly, Auguste. *Madame de Sévigné*. Paris, 1955.

Benichou, Paul. *Morales du grand siècle*. Paris, 1948.

Celarié, Henriette. *Madame de Sévigné, sa famille, et ses amis*. Paris, 1925.

Cordelier, Jean. *Mme de Sévigné par elle-même*. Paris, 1967.

Duchêne, Roger. *Mme de Sévigné (collection Les Écrivains devant Dieu)*. Paris, 1968.

_____ . *Madame de Sévigné et la lettre d'amour*. Paris, 1970.

Faguet, Émile. *Dix-septième siècle: études littéraires*. Paris, 1903.

_____ . *Madame de Sévigné*. Paris, 1910.

FitzGerald, Edward. *Dictionary of Madame de Sévigné*. London, 1914.

Gazier, Augustin. *Jeanne de Chantal*. Paris, 1915.

Gérard-Gailly, Émile. *L'enfance et la jeunesse heureuses de Mme de Sévigné (réfutation d'une légende)*. Paris, 1926.

_____ . *Les sept couches de Mme de Grignan; Les sept fiancées de Charles de Sévigné*. Paris, 1936.

Janet, Paul. *Les lettres de Mme de Grignan*. Paris, 1895.

Lemoine, Jean and H. Bourde de la Rogerie. *Madame de Sévigné aux Rochers; Le livre de comptes de l'abbé Rahuel*. Rennes, 1930.

Lewis, W. H. *The Splendid Century: Life in the France of Louis XIV*. New York, 1954.

Masson, Frédéric. *Le Marquis de Grignan*. Paris, 1882.

Mongrédien, Georges. *La vie quotidienne sous Louis XIV*. Paris, 1948.

Montigny, Maurice. *En voyageant avec Mme de Sévigné*. Paris, no date.

Murbach, Janet M. *Le vrai visage de la comtesse de Grignan*. Toulouse, 1939.

Nicholich, R. "Madame de Sévigné and the Problem of Reality and Appearances." Microfilm, Michigan State University, 1965.

Orieux, Jean. *Bussy-Rabutin*. Paris, 1958.

Proust, Marcel. *À la recherche du temps perdu*. Paris, 1954.

Richard, A. *Les défauts de la comtesse de Grignan*. Paris, 1895.

Saporta, Gaston, Marquis de. *La famille de Madame de Sévigné en Provence*. Paris, 1889.

Sainte-Beuve, Charles Augustin. *Causeries du Lundi*. Paris, 1850.

_____ . *Portraits de femmes*. Paris, 1869.

Saint-René, Taillandier, Mme. *Mme de Sévigné et sa fille*. Paris, 1938.

Tilley, Arthur. *Madame de Sévigné: Some Aspects of Her Life and Character*. Cambridge, 1936.

Voltaire, Françoise-Marie Arouet de. *Siècle de Louis XIV*. Paris, 1914.

Walckenaer, Charles A., Baron de. *Mémoires touchant la vie et les écrits de Marie*

Bibliography

de Rabutin-Chantal, dame de Bourbilly, marquise de Sévigné. Paris, 1845–
52.

Wilder, Thornton. *The Bridge of San Luis Rey.* New York, 1928.

Wilhelm, Jacques. *La Vie quotidienne au Marais au XVII⁵ siècle.* Paris, 1966.

Woolf, Virginia. *The Death of the Moth.* New York, 1942.

Article, Pamphlets, Magazines.

Cordelier, Jean. *Madame de Sévigné seule devant la mort.* 3ᵉ Colloque de Marseille, *Revue Marseille,* no. 95, 4ᵉ Trimestre, 1973.

Duchêne, R. *Les Provençaux de Mme de Sévigné.* 3ᵉ Colloque de Marseille.

Gerard, M. *Les médecins dans la correspondence de Mme de Sévigné.* 3ᵉ Colloque de Marseille.

Magne, B. *Humanisme et culture féminine au XVII⁵ siècle.* 3ᵉ Colloque de Marseille, no. 95.

Montgolfier, B. de and M. Gallet. "L'Hôtel Carnavalet, ses bâtiments, sa decoration sculptée, ses hôtes." *Bulletin du musée Carnavalet,* nos. 1 et 2, 1974.

Rat, Maurice. "N'est on pas sévère pour Madame de Grignan?" *Figaro littéraire,* May 22, 1954.

Wilhelm, J. "Les portraits de Mme de Sévigné." *Bulletin du museé Carnavalet,* 1967.

Index

Index

Coudray, Monsieur de, 460

Coulanges, Abbé de (uncle), 8, 16, 20, 35, 60, 63, 98 and n., 118, 180, 185, 186, 243, 272, 289 and n., 330, 361, 365n., 371; death of, 362, 364

Coulanges, Angélique de, 69, 157–8, 286

Coulanges, Marie de (mother), 4–6; death of, 9; marriage of, 5–6

Coulanges, Philippe de (grandfather), 5, 11; death of, 9–10; influence on Mme de Sévigné, 8, 9

Coulanges, Philippe-Emmanuel de (cousin), 9, 69–70, 120, 356 and n., 357, 379, 407, 418, 419 and n., 445 and n., 449, 465, 468, 474–6, 491 and n., 495; death of, 509

Coulanges, Philippe II de (uncle), 8, 9, 16; as Mme de Sévigné's guardian, 10–11

Coulanges family, 5–6, 468

Cousin, Louis, 243n.

Crapodo, Monsieur de, 303

criminal procedures, 116

Cromwell, Oliver, 8, 53n.

Crusades, 3, 59

d'Acigné, Madame de, 422 and n.

dais, 308 and n.

d'Albret, Chevalier, 22

d'Alerac, Mademoiselle, 245, 269, 309 and n., 333 and n., 337, 339 and n., 391

Dalet, 452n.

Dalet, Countess de, 452 and n.; see also Coligny, Marquise de

dance, 52–4, 424 and n.

d'Andilly, Arnauld, 99, 502

Dangeau, Philippe de Courcillon, 224 and n., 226, 459n., 499

d'Angennes, Angélique-Clarice, 61, 309n.

Dauphin, Monsieur le, 82 and n., 294 and n., 322, 369 and n.; baptism of, 376

Dauphine, Madame la, 284 and n., 284–7, 322

d'Escars, Madame, 223 and n.

Descartes, René, 52, 331 and n.

d'Estrées, Maréchal, 410

d'Étauges, Count, 58

d'Hacqueville, Abbé, 81 and n., 109, 129, 180, 247, 257

d'Harcourt, Prince, 19

d'Haroüys, Monsieur, 188 and n., 196, 290

d'Herigoyen, Jean, 360

d'Huxelles, Madame, 129

Dictionary of Mme de Sévigné (FitzGerald), 116n.

Dio, Madame, 351 and n.

Discours de la Méthode (Descartes), 52

divorce, 182 and n.

d'Oraison, Mademoiselle de, 506n.

d'Orléans, Duchess, 130 and n.

d'Orléans, Duke de, 508 and n.

d'Ormesson, Olivier, 13, 15, 16, 44, 45

drawing and quartering, 198n.

du Bois, Seigneur, 430 and n.

Duchêne, Roger, 141n., 367, 420n., 511n., 519

duelling, 6

Dumesnil, 411 and n.

du Muy, Nicholas, 510

du Plessis, Mademoiselle, 116 and n., 296 and n.

du Plessis, Monsieur, 351 and n., 375

Durance River, 289

dusk, 200 and n.

Dutch War, 134, 141 and n., 149, 151, 159, 161, 171, 176, 188n., 206, 212, 227–8, 257, 432–3

dysentery, 489n.

Easter, 460 and n.

economy, 296 and n.

England, 7–8, 376, 384 and n., 394 and n., 433

Époisses, 164, 244, 318, 462

equipage, as status symbol, 357–8

erysipelas, 355

Essai historique sur les Adhémars and Mme de Sévigné (Nadal), 500

Essays on Morality (Nicole), 67n., 118

Estates General of Brittany, 351, 357

Esther (Racine), 380–1

Étampes, 334

Eugene, Prince, 435

Évreux, Bishop of, 253n., 282

executions, 198 and n., 223

Fagon, Guy, 252 and n., 255

Fall of the Bastille, 510

fashion, 104, 106, 351, 378 and n.

feminism, 17

feudal lords, 164n., 362

feudal tax, 422 and n.; see also taxation

fish, 424 and n.

FitzGerald, Edward, 116n.

Flamarens, Chevalier de, 245 and n.

Flanders, 432, 478

Fleurus, battle of, 432, 433

Fontainebleau, 213, 294

Fontanges, Marie-Angélique de, 284–5, 302 and n., 302, 319

Fougères, 188 and n.

Fountain of Vaucluse, 424n.

Fouquet, Nicolas, 32–4, 260 and n.; death of, 281 and n.; scandal and trial of, 40–8

French language, 27–8

Index

Montataire, Madame de, 450 and *n*.
Montausier, Duke de, 183, 245, 391
Monteil, Lambert Adhémar de, 59 and *n*.
Montélimar, 162, 163, 444 and *n*.
Montespan, Athénaïs de, 36*n*., 53, 55 and *n*., 172, 182, 183*n*., 211 and *n*., 224–7, 235, 285
Montespan, Marquis de, 55*n*.
Montgobert, Mademoiselle, 104 and *n*., 240
Montmor, Jean-Louis de, 470 and *n*.
Montpellier, 443 and *n*., 488*n*.
Montpensier, Mademoiselle de, 27
Montreuil, Michel, 24
Mont Ventoux, 399 and *n*.
More Conversations (Scudéry), 334
mortality rate, 9*n*.
Mortemart-Rochechuart, Athénaïs de, *see* Montespan, Athénaïs de
Moulceau, Philippe, 318, 358 and *n*., 443 and *n*., 477, 497
Mousteyret, 184
Murbach, Janet, 144

Nadal, Abbé, 500 and *n*.
Namur, 478
Nantes, 194, 290, 292, 398 and *n*., 461 and *n*.
Napoleon Bonaparte, 47
Neerwinden, battle of, 456
Netherlands, 134, 141, 149, 161, 166, 171, 257, 260, 432–3
Nice, siege of, 446
Nicole, Pierre, 67*n*., 113, 117
Nicolich, Robert, 471*n*.
Nîmes, Bishop of, 365
Noailles, Maréchal de, 465*n*.
noblesse d'épée, 467
noblesse de robe, 467
Normandy, 390 and *n*.
Nôtre Dame, 223 and *n*.
novena, 369 and *n*.

Old Régime France, 5, 49
opera, 279, and *n*., 411 and *n*.
Orange, 151, 166–8, 171
Order of the Garter, 376
Order of the Holy Ghost, 377 and *n*., 450*n*.
Ottoboni, Cardinal Pietro, 410 and *n*.
Ottoman Empire, 433

painting, 184 and *n*., 224 and *n*., 342 and *n*.; see also *specific painters*
Palatinate, 393*n*.
Paris, 74, 451, 458*n*., 462*n*.
Parlement of Brittany, 401 and *n*.
Pastor fido (Guarini), 166

peasant uprisings, 188 and *n*., 191 and *n*., 196–8
Pellisson, Paul, 242*n*.
pen-portraits, 24–7, 36, 37; of Mme de Sévigné by Mme de La Fayette, 521–2
Perrin, Denis-Marius, 494, 502–3; death of, 516; and publication of Mme de Sévigné's letters, 513–16, 517, 518–19
Peyrolles, 184
pharmacopoeia, 307, 326, 341, 344, 489 and *n*.
Philippsburg, siege of, 369, 370, 372 and *n*., 373
phlebitis, 355*n*.
Piedmont, 435
Pignatelli, Cardinal, 477*n*.
Pignerol, 260 and *n*., 281*n*.
Place Coulanges, 397 and *n*.
Place Royale (Place des Vosges), 5, 9
Polignac, Viscount Scipion-Sidoine de, 333 and *n*.
Pommier, 232 and *n*.
Pomponne, Marquis de, 43–6, 47, 99, 130, 136, 160, 166, 232*n*., 483; dismissed from office, 270, 271 and *n*.; restored to office, 449
Pontchartrain, Count de, 420, 448, 499
Port Louis, 403
postal service, 119–20, 133 and *n*., 202 and *n*., 444 and *n*.; surveillance of, 82 and *n*., 93 and *n*., 196, 285*n*.
posthumous publication of Sévigné letters, 511–20
Poussin, Nicolas, 184
Précieuses ridicules, Les (Molière), 28
pregnancy, 141 and *n*.
Prévalaie butter, La, 392 and *n*., 424
Prévost, Abbé, 257
Princesse de Clèves, La (La Fayette), 84 and *n*., 257, 503*n*.
Prisonnière, La (Proust), 78*n*.
Proserpine (opera), 279 and *n*.
Proust, Marcel, 78*n*., 82, 257; on love, 82–3; on Mme de Sévigné, 83–4, 99, 298
Provence, 63 and *n*., 102, 134–6, 166–8, 220*n*., 230–1, 251, 267, 296 and *n*., 420–1, 445, 472*n*., 506
Puy du Fou, Angélique de, 61, 105 and *n*., 142

Quimperlé, Abbé of, 414
Quinault, Philippe, 450*n*.

Rabelais, François, 408*n*.
Rabutin, Amé de, 3
Rabutin, Amé-Nicholas de, 511 and *n*., 512
Rabutin, Lénor de, 10
Rabutin, Roger de (cousin), *see* Bussy-Rabutin, Count de

rabutinage, 3 and *n.*

Rabutin-Chantal, Baron Celse-Bénigne de (father), 4, 5–6; death of, 7–8; duelling scandal, 6–7; marriage of, 5–7

Rabutin family, 3–4, 5, 15, 468

Racine, Jean Baptiste, 94 and *n.*, 100, 380–1

Rahuel, Abbé, 118

Rambouillet, Marquise de, 27–8, 61

Raphael Sanzio, 224*n.*

recession, 296 and *n.*

Recueil des lettres de Mme la marquise de Sévigné à Mme la comtesse de Grignan, sa fille (Perrin edition), 514

Reflections on the Métier of King (Louis XIV), 271*n.*

Regiment of Provençal Infantry, 254 and *n.*

Reinié, Madame, 411

Remembrance of Things Past (Proust), 82, 83

Remiremont, Canoness of, 258

Rennes, 196–8, 302, 340, 341, 349, 385, 390 and *n.*, 410, 411, 425–6

Rennes, Monsieur de, 303

Retz, Cardinal de, 60, 129, 176, 265–6

reversis, 224

Rhine River, 228

Rhône River, 80 and *n.*, 82, 87–8, 395, 424*n.*, 473

Rhône Valley, 156

rhubarb, 489 and *n.*, 490

Richelieu, Cardinal, 6, 7, 12, 17

Richelieu, Madame de, 286*n.*

Rivier, François, *see* La Rivière, Henri-François de

Robinet, 152 and *n.*, 441, 442

Rochebonne, Madame de, 122

Rochefort, Madame de, 286*n.*

Rohan-Chabot, Duke de, 29, 54

Rome, 403, 409, 418, 419 and *n.*, 447

Rouen, 389

Royal Ballet des Arts, 53–4

Royal Louis (ship), 142 and *n.*

Rubens, Peter Paul, 184, 224*n.*

Saint-Amans, Anne-Marguerite de, *see* Grignan, Anne-Marguerite de

Saint-Amans, Monsieur de, 468, 469, 479, 480, 481

Saint-Andiol, 272 and *n.*

Saint Augustine, 430 and *n.*, 501, 514*n.*

Saint-Bonnet, Henri de, 485 and *n.*

Saint-Cyr, 380

Saint-Denis, Abbey of, 490 and *n.*

Sainte-Beuve, Charles Augustin, 48

Saint Geneviève procession, 186–7

Saint-Geran, Monsieur de, 490, 491

St. John's Day, 438 and *n.*

Saint-Laurent, 386 and *n.*

Saint Martin's Day, 323 and *n.*

Saint-Simon, Duke de, 69, 74, 91*n.*, 144, 183, 227, 252*n.*, 481, 495 and *n.*, 502, 505–6, 508

salons, 27–8

Sanguin, 284 and *n.*

Sanzei, Madame de, 165, 166*n.*

Saumur, 336

Sauvignon, 453

Savoy, Duke de, 435

Scarron, Madame, *see* Maintenon, Marquise de

Scarron, Paul, 23

Schomberg, Madame de, 313 and *n.*

Schomberg, Maréchal, 227–8

script, 73

Scudéry, Madeleine de, 12, 24–5, 27 and *n.*, 256, 258, 325, 334

Segrais, Jean, 24

Seignelay, Marquis de, 442 and *n.*

Seilleraye, La, 290

Seine River, 389

Sémur-en-Auxois, 518

Senef, battle of, 176

Sévigné, Charles de (son), 20, 113, 117, 204–6, 273, 292, 294 and *n.*, 391, 474; birth of, 16; childhood and education of, 51–2; Court career of, 304, 402 and *n.*; death of, 505; and death of mother, 494, 504; impotence of, 95–8, 159–60; as King's Lieutenant for Nantes, 461 and *n.*; marriage of, 328–33, 338, 436; military career of, 63 and *n.*, 134, 159, 171, 176, 212, 227–8, 229, 242 and *n.*, 257, 283, 304, 324, 400; relationship with mother, 16, 51, 83, 94–8, 171, 203, 257, 304–5, 328, 330, 385, 504–5; relationship with Ninon d'Enclos, 94–5, 97; religion of, 343, 505; venereal disease of, 306–8, 312 and *n.*, 313, 360

Sévigné, Françoise-Marguerite de (daughter), *see* Grignan, Françoise-Marguerite de

Sévigné, Henri de (husband), 14; death of, 20–2; infidelity of, 16–22; marriage of, 14–20

Sévigné, Marie de Rabutin-Chantal de: as absentee landlord, 164*n.*, 362, 454, 456, 457, 458, 464; aging of, 171, 204–10, 236–7, 361, 417, 488; beauty of, 13–14, 23–6, 27 and *n.*, 171; birth of, 6; and Bussy scandal, 35–9; childhood of, 8–13; class prejudice of, 196 and *n.*; on Court life, 286, 295, 296 and *n.*, 352, 381 and *n.*; as cult figure, 23–4, 144–5; death of, 492–503; and deaths of parents, 8–10; education of, 12–13; on fantasy vs. reality, 470, 471 and *n.*; financial difficulties of, 347,

A NOTE ON THE TYPE

This book was set via computer-driven cathode-ray tube in Fournier, a
typeface named for Pierre Simon Fournier, a celebrated type designer
in eighteenth-century France. Fournier's type is considered transitional
in that it drew its inspiration from the old style yet was ingeniously
innovational in its narrow elegance and angling of the serifs. For some
time after his death in 1768, Fournier was remembered primarily as the
author of a famous manual of typography and as a pioneer of the point
system. Significant modern appreciation of his typeface began with
D. B. Updike's *Printing Types* in 1922, followed soon after by the
Monotype Corporation's revival of Fournier's roman and italic types.

Composed by Centennial Graphics, Inc.,
Ephrata, Pennsylvania
Printed and bound by The Murray Printing Co.,
Westford, Massachusetts

Typography by Virginia Tan